BEER
Packaging

Second Edition

Ray Klimovitz, Senior Editor
President, Klimovitz Brewing Consultants, Inc.
MBAA Technical Director Emeritus (1999–2010)

Karl Ockert, Coeditor
MBAA Technical Director

Master Brewers Association
of the Americas

Front cover:

Beer glass: copyright Nitr, used under license from Shutterstock.com
Kegging line **(bottom left):** Courtesy BridgePort Brewing Company
Robotic palletizer **(bottom middle):** Courtesy Intelligrated
Bottle rinse tray **(bottom right):** Courtesy Meheen Manufacturing Inc.

Reference in this publication to a trademark, proprietary product, or company name is intended for explicit description only and does not imply approval or recommendation to the exclusion of others that may be suitable.

Library of Congress Control Number: 2014933225
International Standard Book Number: 978-0-9787726-7-3

© 1982, 2014 by Master Brewers Association of the Americas
First edition published 1982
Second edition published 2014

All rights reserved.
No portion of this book may be reproduced in any form, including photocopy, microfilm, information storage and retrieval system, computer database, or software, or by any means, including electronic or mechanical, without written permission from the publisher.

Printed in the United States of America on acid-free paper

Master Brewers Association of the Americas
3340 Pilot Knob Road
St. Paul, Minnesota 55121, U.S.A.

PREFACE

This book is significant and timely for many reasons. Foremost is the fact that the first edition of *Beer Packaging* was published in 1982 and is out of print. Second is the fact that there has been a proliferation of small breweries established since the early 1980s and most are now making significant changes in the way they are packaging their beers—packaging their beers in cans and becoming acutely aware of total package oxygen control and of how packaging efficiency affects the bottom line. This book will help them, and all those working in other packaging operations, to be aware of the principles behind their operations.

The book covers beer packaging from start to finish—from the bright beer tank to the warehouse and all the stages in between. The chapters on beer containers—covering manufacturing, inspection, and quality control—are especially useful to anyone involved in beer packaging.

The very informative first chapter deals with the importance of beer packaging, packaging line systems, and personnel management.

Chapter 27, Packaging Quality Assurance, is a must-read for craft brewers and covers quality testing (and the reasons behind each test) throughout the packaging process.

The dynamics of innovation in beer packaging are slow moving but mostly creative and include the following.

- Light-weighting containers to save on shipping costs
- High-efficiency fillers with very low oxygen pickup
- Easier drinking-from-the-can pull tabs
- Big strides in container inspection, both empty and full
- Robotic warehouses
- Total package oxygen replacing the shake-out air
- Creative private-mold bottles replacing standard bottles
- Embellished can designs for sales advantage purposes
- Aseptic fillers and filling techniques for flavor preservation
- Improved pasteurization unit control for flavor preservation
- High-efficiency packaging lines
- Simplified keg filling systems

The chapter authors deserve thanks from all of us who deal with beer packaging. They comprise a collection of some of the most knowledgeable people in the industry and work for companies involved in beer packaging every day. They have contributed their time to make this book happen and we collectively thank them for that.

Many of the authors also volunteer their time teaching at the MBAA Brewery Packaging Technology course held every spring at the University of Wisconsin in Madison. We have worked with them in Madison and can vouch for their credibility.

The authors, and the two of us, hope that this book becomes a valuable "go-to" manual for those working with beer packaging.

Ray Klimovitz, Senior Editor
President, Klimovitz Brewing Consultants, Inc.
MBAA Technical Director Emeritus (1999–2010)

Karl Ockert, Coeditor
MBAA Technical Director

CONTENTS

CHAPTER 1 The Importance of Beer Packaging, Packaging Line Systems, and Personnel Management 1
Stephen Bates
Jaime Jurado

CHAPTER 2 Packaging Line Project Management 23
Beth Partleton

CHAPTER 3 Environmental Management of Brewery Operations 35
Becky Francisco

CHAPTER 4 Packaging Line Design, Control, and Instrumentation 41
Robert Seaman

CHAPTER 5 Canning Operations 71
William J. Forsythe

CHAPTER 6 Can Filling in the Brewery 87
Randy Dillman

CHAPTER 7 Double-Seam Technology 101
William J. Forsythe

CHAPTER 8 Glass Bottle Manufacturing 117
Dave Wendt

CHAPTER 9 Basic Principles and Operation of a Bottle Washer 129
Carlos Alarcon

CHAPTER 10 PET Bottles for Beer Packaging 147
Frank W. Embs

CHAPTER 11 Small Bottling Lines 161
Dave Meheen

CHAPTER 12 Small-Scale Canning Lines 173
James Gordon

CHAPTER 13 Bottle Filling and Crowning 189
Barry Fenske
W. G. Spargo

CHAPTER 14 Crowns and Crowning 209
James F. Everett
Daniel Malo
Juan Carlos Gomez

CHAPTER 15 Flash Pasteurization: Theory and Practice 225
Jeff Gunn

CHAPTER 16 Tunnel Pasteurization 235
C. Alarcon
J. R. Wilson

CHAPTER 17 Pasteurizer Water Treatment 251
Jack L. Bland
Thomas J. Soukup
Rick Brundage

CHAPTER 18 Labels 263
Mark Glendenning

CHAPTER 19 Labeler Operations 277
Frank Kaczmarski

CHAPTER 20 Modern Package Coding Technologies 297
Brian Burke

CHAPTER 21 Paperboard Manufacturing and Multipack Production 309
Graham Hand

CHAPTER 22 Container and Product Movement 317
Chuck McGrady

CHAPTER 23 Brewery Case Palletizing 333
Frank Pelligrino
Earl Wohlrab

CHAPTER 24 Keg Line Operations 343
Andy Brewer

CHAPTER 25 Brewery and Packaging Hall Cleaning and Sanitizing 365
George Agius

CHAPTER 26 Final Beer Filtration for Microbiological Stability 385
Ron Johnson
David Schleef

CHAPTER 27 Packaging Quality Assurance 393
Peter Takacs
Jeff Edgerton

CHAPTER 28 Inspection Equipment in the Brewing Industry 423
Jeff DeVoy

CHAPTER 29 Packaging Materials and Beer Quality 457
Phillip D. Israel

CHAPTER 1

The Importance of Beer Packaging, Packaging Line Systems, and Personnel Management

STEPHEN BATES
BridgePort Brewing Company

JAIME JURADO
Abita Brewing Company

The usage of beverage packages increases at a global rate of 4% annually. In 2007, beverage packages comprised 15% of the world's use of packages.

Brewery customers are visually oriented drinkers. If the packaging is pleasing, the customer considers purchasing the beer. Getting packaging right is a challenge and an opportunity for a brewery to broadcast excellence. New opportunities lie with the recent complexities of novel multipacks and different bottles, cans, and configurations from the packaging line. The Coca-Cola Company has driven the development of cans and of glass and polyethylene terephthalate (PET) packaging and serves as an example of product driving packaging development.

Beer packaging has six essential functions: containment, protection, apportionment, unitization, convenience, and communication. The different levels of packaging are identified as primary (cans, bottles), secondary (cartons, trays), and tertiary (pallets, stretchwrap, shrinkwrap). Taken together, packaging is the means of safe, efficient delivery of beer to the consumer, followed by the efficient recovery or disposal of material at a minimal cost.

● HISTORICAL INTRODUCTION

The Past

The packaging of beer is an idea almost as old as brewing itself. Preserving and holding beer, for later consumption, has been discussed in print for centuries. One 1609 reference addresses earthenware bottles of ale.

The True Bottling of Beer

When your Beer is 10 or 12 dayes olde, whereby it is growne reasonable cleare, then bottle it, making your corkes very fit for the bottle, and stoppe them close: but drink not of this beer, till they begin to work againe, and mantle, and then you shall find the same most excellent and spritely drinke: and this is the reason why bottle ale is both so windy and muddy, thundering and smoking upon the opening of the bottle, because it is commonly bottled the same day that it is laid into the cellar; whereby his yeast, being an exceeding windy substance, being also drawn with the Ale not yet fined, doth incorporate with the drinke, and maketh it also very windy.

(Sir Hugh Plat, *Delightes for Ladies*, 1609)

Until the twentieth century, most beer was still consumed at local establishments by the glass, from barrels, and on draft. In the latter part of the twentieth century, as packaging technology rapidly improved, there was a major shift in the way consumers preferred to purchase beer and ales. Draft beer from a keg or cask became a shrinking component of overall beer sales in North America. The share of sales of beer in small, shelf-stable containers that could be sold in grocery stores and other retail outlets increased dramatically. As this trend developed, the cost of packaging beer became, by far, the most significant cost in producing packaged beer products. With the quality of the beer at stake, packaging became an area of focus in the quest to preserve freshness. Since the 1980s, vast improvements have been made in the exclusion of oxygen from packaged beer. Fill-height measurement, improved pasteurization control, and other developments have made beer packaging a repeatable, efficient operation. The need to fill a diverse array of packages has yielded sophisticated changeover systems so that package changeovers take place rapidly. In a large brewery, the most sophisticated labelers can go from the application of paper labels to roll-fed polypropylene pressure-sensitive labels (PSLs) in turnaround times never before imagined through the use of engineered changeover carts with connectors ready for all services. But even with this great technical advantage, there are adjustments made at the line. For example, the rate at which paper labels can be applied probably exceeds the rate at which PSLs can be applied on the same machine. The benchmark of increasing packaging rates, specified in thousands of containers per minute, has been augmented by rapid changeover requirements to accommodate the need for greatest flexibility—and with that flexibility, new challenges need to be overcome.

The word "logistics" comes from Greek *logisticke*, which means applied mathematics. Packaging is part of the brewery puzzle of logistics in that it is the coordinated system of preparing beer for transportation, distribution, storage, retailing, and enjoyment by consumers.

The Present

Today's technical packaging professionals are tasked with supplying beer in packages that maintain the stability and fresh flavor of the product better than ever before while making the smallest possible impact on the environment. At the same time, competition among breweries and financial considerations demand that packaging departments maintain the lowest production costs and offer the least possible number of defective finished packages. Continuously refining the effectiveness of tools and perpetuating a desire for improvement on the work floor enhance packaging line operations.

In the current competitive market, packaging departments go to great lengths to streamline costs and maximize labor productivity. The effect of this is fewer line employees who bear greater levels of responsibility for higher product quality and line efficiency. At the same time, production employees are protected by the strongest labor regulations in history. This means that packaging management must consider many aspects in the design and management of modern packaging lines. Management must design the lines for speed, quality, and efficiency, as well as for safety, maintenance access, and ergonomics. Breweries, as do many companies, pride themselves on excellent safety records.

Quality is emphasized, more now than ever before, as the responsibility of each employee involved in the production and packaging of beer. An attitude of commitment toward zero defects is predominant, driven by the availability of advancing technology in the hands of a skilled packaging professional as well as by the trend of educated consumers demanding the highest quality in all purchases. The use of statistical techniques has greatly improved the quality of sampling plans. With these techniques, sampling plans can be designed to achieve defect rates of 1 in 10,000. Quality checks with these sampling plans are in place to ensure that the packaging process is under control. Since low levels of defects can escape detection, individual package testing must be state of the art.

Artisan-Scale Breweries

Innovative beers are increasingly available and craft brewers have introduced alternative packages, such as the 22-oz. or 750-mL single-serve bottle, possibly sealed with a cork and wire cage, and filled undecorated cans with a plastic-sleeve body label. There are also plastic kegs, small-pack one-use metal minikegs, and growlers from brewpubs and brewery taps.

A manually loaded and manually packed-out line shares many objectives with faster lines. Many examples exist of breweries running up to 100 bottles per minute (bpm) using manual labor to depalletize bottles at the start of the line and manual labor to pack and seal cartons at the end of the line.

The technical overlap of packaged beer from the smallest brewery and from the largest brewery lies in the integrity of the packaged beer. A beer packaged with 0.2 mL of headspace air is going to stay fresher than a beer packaged with 0.75 mL, regardless of the producer, the beer's style, or the specific package it is in. The ease of maintenance, robust operation, and effective use of labor are equally important parameters for packaging lines of any size. The role of automation is clearly recognized in today's breweries, where the fastest packaging lines in a large brewery may be manned by as many personnel as there are at the slowest packaging line in a craft brewery. And the spectrum of skilled personnel to safely and prudently operate a packaging line has no lower limit in production rate.

Breweries have sometimes struggled and have been challenged with maintaining appropriate skilled professionals for packaging. The only retort to the question Why do we painstakingly and carefully train staff who may leave us? might be this: Is it better to not train carefully and have personnel stay?

Technological Advances

The culmination of the knowledge gained and the technological advances made since the very first efforts to package beer is that beer can now be produced in convenient packages that keep it shelf stable and tasting fresh. Additionally, key performance indicator (KPI) metrics can improve the performance of the packaging operation. There is always room for improvement, and equipment suppliers are continually improving packaging materials and techniques to ship beer further, reduce the effects of age, and make the beer more appealing to customers. An example of these advances is the range of options now available in polymeric packaging with barrier properties that protect beer against the loss of carbon dioxide and the ingress of oxygen. These technologies are developing rapidly and represent the newest challenges facing today's beer packaging management.

The goal of a brewery packaging department is to do the best job possible of minimizing any negative effects that its processes may have on the beer while maximizing productivity of all packaging operations. Knowledge gained from real-time plant floor KPIs yield the forces of change that improve operations.

Engineering, maintenance, quality assurance, and microbiology of packaging play key roles in achieving consistently well-packaged beer. Packaging line management and maintenance, as well as packaging personnel (operators), complete the picture of successful world-class packaging. Accounting tools define and track direct labor (e.g., operators having specific assignments on the line) and indirect labor (e.g., maintenance staff assigned to multiple lines and cleaning and trash removal personnel).

Modern Risk Avoidance Equipment

While not universally accepted as necessary components of bottling lines, electronic bottle inspection (EBI) equipment is an efficient means of performing high-speed evaluations of empty bottles (an EBI typically includes a chipped neck and neck finish inspection, a complete bottle wall inspection, and residual rinse water detection, as well as the essential foreign particle detection and glass fragment intercept) (Fig. 1.1). In North America, every beer bottle produced has already undergone the scrutiny of EBI hardware at the manufacturer's plants. Yet the industry standard of "no more than 1 defect bottle per 10,000" cannot be challenged unless the brewery has its own EBI at the line. Since the advent of the narrow-neck press-and-blow process over the former blow-and-blow process, bottles are being made at lighter weights and featuring thinner walls; superior performance along with lightweighting is now expected. Unfortunately, EBIs can reject some acceptable ware. So if there is a rejection rate greater than 1 per 10,000, false positives from the EBI may be the cause. There are rejection modes, such as small "light streaks" at the base of the bottle (small, localized variations in the color of amber ware), that offer no physical integrity concerns but can nevertheless cause ejection at the EBI soft-push ram.

Small bottling lines face substantial challenges in justifying the cost of investing in an EBI.

Sophisticated full-bottle inspectors at the back end of the packaging operation and ultrasonic crown-integrity tests, as well as full-case inspectors, ensure the highest integrity in the modern bottling line. A best-of-class full-bottle inspector prevents beer bottles containing glass shards from getting to the case.

Beer canning is very different, and the emergence of can line solutions for the artisan brewery offers an attractive and often compelling alternative to bottles and a bottling line. In canning operations, double seaming is a method by which the flange of the can body and the curl of the end are folded over together such that the final joint is

FIGURE 1.1. An electronic bottle inspector on a brewery bottling line performing base and neck finish inspection; the soft-push ram and chute are at the right. (Courtesy Industrial Dynamics Company)

composed of five metal thicknesses. The beer can must withstand in excess of 90 pounds per square inch gauge (psig), and the fastest operations run 3,000 cans per minute on an 18-station seamer.

Can parameters are increasingly measured on-line; for example, curl diameter and depth and countersink depth are measured automatically in high-speed installations. While a standard manual seam inspection can take one operator as long as 1 hour to complete, recent automated stations require less than 1 minute of total labor for a complete inspection. Characterization of each seamer head in a sampling round is now possible in a very short time.

Breweries often deploy full-package at-line instruments, concentrating on measuring fill-height compliance, date coding, label orientation, etc. before the package is sent to the final packaging stages.

● PACKAGING LINE PLANNING

The process of specifically designing a packaging line starts with asking questions. What types of packages and sizes are to be filled and what combinations of materials, e.g., regular slotted cartons (RSCs) (prepacked or flat), wrap-around 12 packs, six-pack baskets, and 24-loose multipacks, will be used? Will cartons be manually packed and sealed by tape or hot glue? What label materials will be used and where are their locations on the packages? Will incoming glass be shipped in bulk or in cases? What is the full-pallet configuration (e.g., size of board, case pattern and number of layers, and maximum height)? What speed is appropriate for the line? Will there be a pasteurizer (flash or tunnel)? Is traditional water-based conveyor lubrication anticipated and how will spillout be controlled? Will the line be configured with silicone-based dry lubes? Or will it be lubeless, as found on many lines of 120 bpm or less?

As with anything worthwhile, answers lead to more questions. For example, if a high-speed bulk glass line is desired, what is the footprint and production speed for one or more case erectors and carrier inserter systems to ensure that adequate cartons are supplied at the target output? Is a partition inserter required for loose-pack configuration?

Once the goals are established, it is good to review options and for a packaging system integrator to prepare a scope of works. The hardware can be arranged so that a single operator might watch over more machines with ease. Ready access to all machines reduces maintenance labor hours. Specifications should integrate capability to readily derive those KPIs that can be used to expose and quantify waste—all activities that do not add value for the customer.

The team can then determine objectives, such as executing sterile filling, minimizing packaging labor, maximizing maintenance access for efficiency and safety, integrating automation, establishing critical data logging and management, and incorporating cleaning-in-place (CIP) methods. The optimal location for equipment can be determined early in the planning stage; the best place for depalletizing, palletizing, and shrinkwrap equipment may be at locations in a warehouse where materials are conveyed to and from the packaging hall. There are, of course, factors that affect the flow of materials, such as a new glass inventory and finished goods staging. A kegging line located near a working inventory of empty kegs or serviced by a conveyor and output to a refrigerated room (for unpasteurized kegs) is the norm. Integration of full-keg handling and automated stretchwrapping can be planned. Ease of service of the keg cleaning detergent sets, sterile filters, and the racker itself are figured into the installation geometry and design/layout.

Packaging system suppliers have great expertise and immeasurable experience in laying out a line for their customers. Because packaging line layout is a compromise of many factors, there is almost always something about each layout that is imperfect. For this reason, criticism can probably be found in every layout. In reality there are three key requirements, and a fourth opportunity, which is obvious.

1. Appoint an individual or a group to lead all aspects of the layout project.
2. Plan for the future so that the proposed layout will still be viable in 10 years.
3. Approve the layout.
4. Build morale with the new layout.

With priorities established, the number of operators needed can be determined in consultation with the equipment vendors. This number should be framed around the time interval between operator interventions for each system on the line, e.g., a labeler operator must refill a label magazine at some frequency and a filler operator must pull quality assurance samples at some frequency. It is important that experience and vendor input help determine the maintenance requirements. If a production line goes down, the reaction and response must be immediate.

Packaging Line Theory

The first concept that must be understood before a new beer packaging line can be designed is the function of each machine in relation to the rest of the machines on the line. The following is a simple illustration of the concept. With the simplest possible packaging line, e.g., a separate machine for each job on the line, all machine speeds must be designed relative to the speed of the slowest machine, the filler. A graphical representation of this concept can be found in Figure 1.2.

Of course, actual beer packaging lines are very complex and differ greatly in type and capacity. The differences between bottling and canning lines are significant, and many variations exist for each of these. A few are explored briefly below.

Examples of Packaging Lines

There are, of course, many variations and alternatives to packaging line configurations. The physical geometry available for a proposed line or for changes to an existing line often constrain the number of suitable options (Fig. 1.3). Overhead views of various bottling and canning lines are illustrated, and the location and number of operators are found in Figures 1.4–1.6.

In designing glass bottling lines, some breweries find that prepacked "shipper" cases can be used effectively, especially for small footprint areas. Figure 1.4 shows the layout of a compact bottling line with one filler and labeler using prepacked cases with bottles. Other breweries find that bulk glass systems can provide production and economic advantages but require

FIGURE 1.3. The location and orientation of packaging machinery is often specified to accommodate constraints in existing building space. (Courtesy Trumer Brauerei-Berkeley)

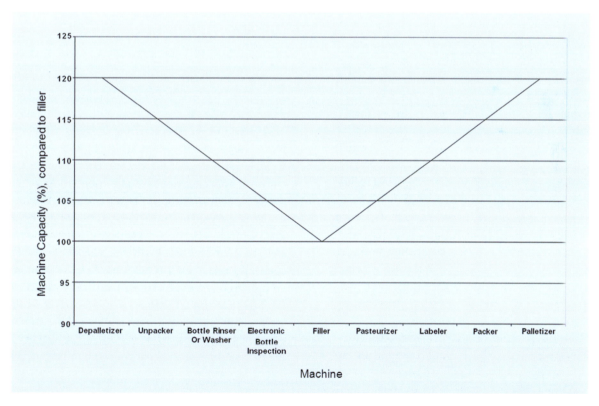

FIGURE 1.2. Line rating, or throughput capacity, for package line design is based on the filler speed specification, set at 100%. The need for higher ratings is to allow for removal of transient accumulations caused by short-term stoppages of parts of the line. This is a starting point for a line design, but if used absolutely, it can result in oversized lines at higher-than-needed costs. (Courtesy J. Jurado)

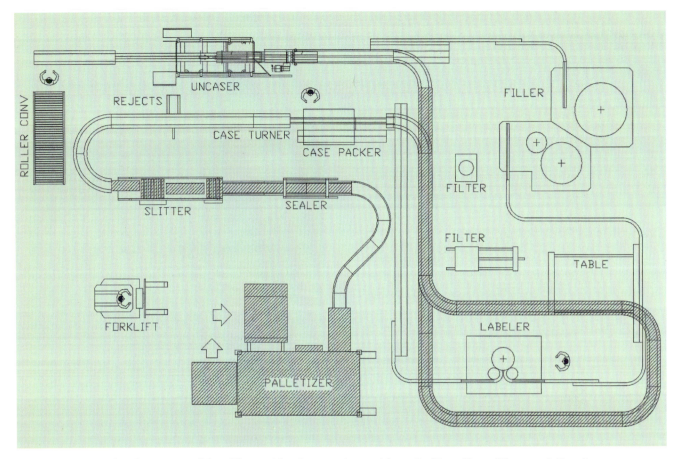

FIGURE 1.4. Bottling line 1: A small line filling 250 bottles per minute with sterile-filtered beer. (Courtesy S. Bates)

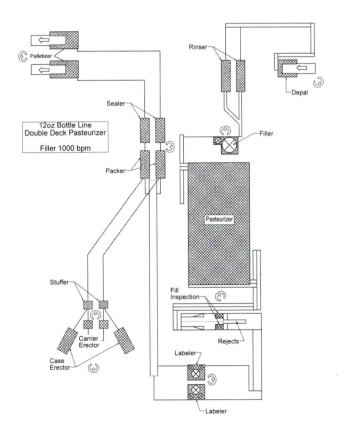

ancillary equipment, such as carton erecting and stuffing equipment (Fig. 1.5). The bottles are closely packed on pallets in layers (as are cans when delivered in bulk), with cardboard tier sheets between each layer. Some breweries have sweeper depalletizers, in which the pallet is elevated on a platform to meet the elevation of the outfeed conveyor and a layer of bottles is swept off onto the outfeed conveyor; the layer of ware below is then raised to the same point in advance of the next sweep. There also are lift-off depalletizers, which use grippers that lift ware, elevate, and swing to a discharge table. Alternatively, some breweries find that space concerns or economic considerations make buying glass already packed in cases the best situation for them.

Most can lines have filling and pasteurization equipment similar to those of bottle lines but they have many variations of final packing equipment, such as

FIGURE 1.5. Bottling line 2: A larger bulk glass line filling 1,000 bottles per minute (bpm) with pasteurized beer. (Courtesy S. Bates)

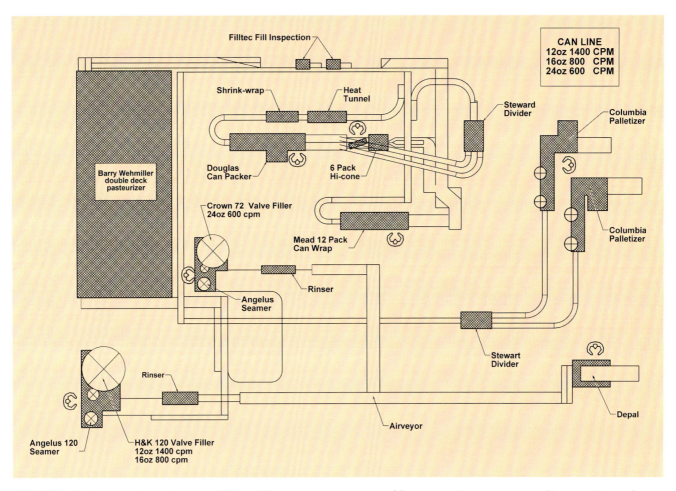

FIGURE 1.6. Canning line: A large line filling different can sizes using two fillers. cpm = Cans per minute. (Courtesy S. Bates)

high-cone machines for six packs coupled with tray-making machines, machines that package cans in wrap-around–style cartons, and machines that are adjustable for running many styles of final packing, e.g., traymakers and shrinkwrappers (Fig. 1.6). Flexibility is a key aspect for many packaging lines with today's demand for variety.

Planning for Keg Operations

Some breweries have their brewing operations production department manage and plan kegging operations, and some make this the responsibility of the packaging department. No matter which department owns this key area, accurate communication is required so that the correct volume of beer is ready in-spec and efficiently kegged.

The predominant keg package is the single-walled keg with U.S. Sankey fittings. This package is used for 15.5-gallon (one-half U.S. brewer's barrel [bbl]) containers, 7.75-gallon (one-quarter U.S. bbl) containers (mostly with containers that are the same height as the 15.5-gallon keg; hence it is slimmer), "sixtels" (one-sixth U.S. bbl containers, also the same height as the 15.5-gallon keg), and 50-L (13.2 U.S. gallons) containers. Common metrics in regards to keg operations are unique: kegs per hour.

A contemporary kegging line features robust automation and the use of robots or forklift clamp trucks, which are used to squeeze and hold kegs. These are increasingly used in breweries to handle empty kegs and palletize full kegs to eliminate manual offloading and palletizing. A keg line requires fewer personnel than does a canning or bottling facility, and suppliers can recommend a realistic manning level for an appropriate crew. A comprehensive chapter in this volume covers this important topic, but a brief summary of the stations follows.

An option not frequently exploited in the United States is flash pasteurization of the beer just prior to kegging.

Small breweries often clean keg exteriors manually with soap, a brush, and a hose. However, the first common process stage in the keg line is the external wash tunnel, which cleans the outside of the kegs. Some breweries install a keg precleaner station to put a preclean detergent solution in the keg before it progresses through the external wash tunnel. Some breweries follow the external keg wash with a torquer that tightens the keg valve.

Internal cleaning of the keg follows with distinct ullage beer drainage; cleaning, rinsing, and sterilizing phases; and repressurization; followed by filling of the keg with beer (Fig. 1.7). A checkweigher is often used as a go/no-go step, followed by capping the valve, inkjet labeling, and transferring to pallets. Contemporary kegging lines usually have easy-to-read screens along with easily readable gauges (Fig. 1.8).

● PACKAGING LINE ENGINEERING

Large brewing groups maintain their own engineering staff who are capable of designing new lines, while small companies may find it necessary to hire professional engineers as consultants. Many equipment vendors also provide design consultation services. The engineering technology of today uses the latest in computer graphics, such as 3-D layout software, to assist in the visualization of a proposed line. A key element in the design of a new line is to provide adequate accumulation space to allow for variations in line speed arising from short stops. The decision to move from static accumulation tables to new dynamic approaches using conveyors or new designs offers the advantage of "first-in, first-out" movement of the packages held in accumulation. Traditional accumulation tables offer "first-in, last-out" movement.

Computer-aided design can optimize line speed and accumulation spaces by simulating actual packaging lines directly on the computer screen. Effective use of this tool can help avoid costly mistakes in the initial design. Because a new packaging line is a major capital expenditure, modifying and upgrading existing lines is very common in many breweries. Relocating or retrofitting existing equipment might make more financial sense than do other options. Packaging line design and selection of equipment are decisions that are best made by engineering and key personnel in the packaging department.

Components must be easily accessible for maintenance (Fig. 1.9) and lines must be designed so that an acceptable "pressure" is on the packaged product (Fig. 1.10). The depalletizing or bulk glass-unloading hardware and the palletizers should be located in a place that requires the least transport distance, such as in the warehouse (Fig. 1.11). Having the equipment adequately sized to avoid pinch points is a key element in the line engineering process. Refurbished equipment (Fig. 1.12) or new equipment (Fig. 1.13) must satisfy the target throughput rate for that machine (see also Fig. 1.2). Ancillary equipment, such as crown feed hoppers and conveyors (Fig. 1.14), should be adequately sized to avoid any possibility of accidental runouts if the time interval between operator interventions has not been anticipated and planned.

FIGURE 1.7. Contemporary rackers fill metered volumes into kegs to ensure accurate fills and feature easy-to-read screens. (Courtesy BridgePort Brewing Company)

FIGURE 1.8. Easily read gauges indicate utility status of the keg line. (Courtesy BridgePort Brewing Company)

Unitized rinsers/fillers/crowners, so-called monoblocs (called alternatively, triblocs), bring three crucial operations into one integrated piece of equipment. Figure 1.15 shows a rotary rinser infeed, where bottles are inverted, rinsed, and drained before being reverted to normal standing orientation. Figure 1.16 highlights starwheels that gently offer mechanical transfer of bottles from one monobloc station to the next. The complexity of rinsing, filling, and closing operations is matched by the work accomplished at the labeler (Fig. 1.17).

Increasing Line Complexity

Changes in beer marketing strategies, such as revised bottle styles or new label shapes, add greater complexity to beer packaging lines. Equipment changes may be necessary

FIGURE 1.9. While reasonably accessible from the service aisle, the conveyor's side closest to the wall is hard to access for maintenance. (Courtesy Spoetzl Brewing Company)

FIGURE 1.11. Automatic palletizers, with an automatic pallet feed, and a stretchwrapping station may be optimally located in the finished goods warehouse. (Courtesy Trumer Brauerei-Berkeley)

FIGURE 1.10. There is often a concern regarding excessive pressure on bottles en route to case packing because of the potential for label scuffing, especially from sideguides (siderails). (Courtesy Spoetzl Brewing Company)

FIGURE 1.12. Refurbished uncasers sustain many smaller bottling lines. (Courtesy Trumer Brauerei-Berkeley)

FIGURE 1.13. A case packer that packs 20 cases per minute is suitable for a small line. (Courtesy Trumer Brauerei-Berkeley)

FIGURE 1.15. An integral rinser in a monobloc filler system fed by a worm infeed. (Courtesy Trumer Brauerei-Berkeley)

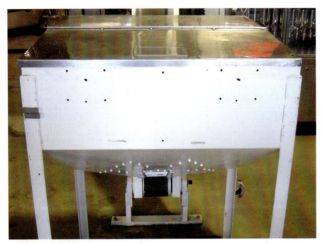

FIGURE 1.14. **Top,** Small crown hoppers might be simple floor-set units holding several crown boxes in volume. **Bottom,** The internal bin surface (crown contact). The outlet feeds to an enclosed magnetic conveyor to transfer crowns to the crown bin at the top of the crowner. (Courtesy B. Malloy from Trumer Brauerei-Berkeley)

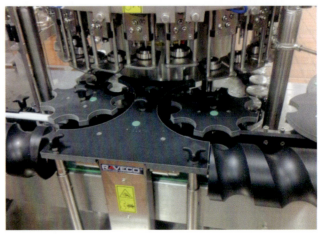

FIGURE 1.16. **Top,** Collection of starwheels, guides, and wormgears properly stored for easy access for machine changeovers. **Bottom,** Starwheels transfer filled bottles to the crowner. (Courtesy Susquehanna Brewing Company LLC)

FIGURE 1.17. A labeler set up for body and neck labels. The label magazines are not fully loaded. Wet glue labelers using casein-based glue have the broadest application, but the success of pressure-sensitive labels has led to the use of modular labelers capable of applying both types of labels. (Courtesy Trumer Brauerei-Berkeley)

to accommodate new packaging or to switch between various packaging configurations. Solutions evolve rapidly to accommodate the need for change. An example would be computer-controlled palletizing robots that distribute various packaged beer wraps/boxes on several styles of pallets after a simple button selection for the required configuration. A proven innovation is an electronic-controlled filler that offers rapid changeovers by adjusting fill levels at the touch of a button. Another example would be bottle washers (soakers) that wash bottles efficiently (e.g., as in Speers et al., 2002) yet maintain a brewery's goals of conserving utilities by keeping overall water consumption below 130 mL per bottle.

Returnable Bottles

Before the turn of the century, brewing companies utilized machinery to wash and reuse bottles. Although the U.S. brewing industry has all but eliminated reusable bottles, except for a few craft-scale breweries, they are still used almost exclusively in most other parts of the world. The Canadian bottling industry has a comprehensive bottle reuse program that is referred to as a closed-loop container system. It is a brewer to consumer and back to brewer approach that ensures a steady stream of returnable ware. Canada's method of rewashing and reusing is recognized as leading the world in environmentally friendly practices. In 2005, Canada boasted a 97% return on all bottles for rewash and reuse. Each bottle returned is cleaned through a process of chemical immersion and high-pressure jetting. Within the soaker, old labels are removed and flushed out of the machine; the sluice delivers broken glass to the collection bins.

Canadian brewers note that bottle reuse has advantages. Rewashing saves energy over remanufacturing, makes sense environmentally, and benefits consumers economically by keeping retail prices lower. Controlled management of returnable ware is possible in the strictly defined and managed retail outlets in Canada. Mexican brewers have also found success with returnables within the Mexican supply chain. It also is common in Germany, where a combination of regulatory tools and voluntary agreements are used. A returnable bottle can be used more than 30 times. If a brewery is local or regional, its cost of distribution is modest. The use of returnables clearly offers advantages where it is in practice. Bayern Brewing Company in Montana has the soaker most recently installed in the United States and is reusing industry-standard long-neck bottles. Years after the common practice disappeared, it is being renewed for economic and sustainability reasons.

Denmark has a metal container ban, requires permits for other containers, and has compulsory deposit-refund systems, resulting in very high reuse rates on beer containers. According to the Danish Environmental Protection Agency, the restriction on cans alone prevents 20% of the domestic waste in Denmark (Danish Environ. Prot. Agency, 1999).

While the rewash system has advantages, it is not without challenges. Bottle soakers take additional floor space, maintenance, cleaning, and monitoring (Speers et al., 2002) and use caustic chemicals for cleaning. Stringent safety precautions must be in place when working on or operating these machines. Soakers contain tanks with up to 4% sodium hydroxide solution for bottle washing. Disposal of these strong caustic chemicals requires that they must be treated prior to discarding. A survey at a Swedish brewery that opened in 1970 and runs 50% returnables quantified that 1% of the beers' original contents left in the bottle after consumption, 20% of the labels, and all glue leave with brewery wastewater. The citation stated that, in 1974, 0.25 L of water was consumed for every 33-cL bottle washed and 0.16-g chemical oxygen demand (COD) is formed (Meyer, 1973).

To exploit returnables, there is often dedicated uncasing equipment and special inspection equipment (e.g., EBIs) to monitor for residual liquid carryover in the bottle from the soaker and for bottle neck damage. The wet strength of the label stock used for returnables must be sufficiently strong to ensure label removal in the soaker without pulping.

The U.S. bottling industry, a long-time user of the closed-loop container system, has moved away from this approach to the use of lightweight nonreusable bottles. Using this method, the one-trip bottles are returned for deposit or recycled at curbside and then sent to the glass company to be remanufactured as new bottles.

The Emergence of Sterile/Near-Sterile Filling

The traditional larger brewery uses tunnel pasteurizers, which represent the biggest machine in the packaging line and the biggest consumer of energy in the line. To satisfy 1,000 bpm, a footprint of 200 square meters is required. It is always safer to package first and treat afterward to avoid reinfection, but very-high-integrity engineering proves that newer approaches are valid.

A flash pasteurizer requires a much smaller physical space for installation and maintenance, is much cheaper, and operates at less than 20% of the operating costs of a tunnel pasteurizer. Many large breweries also integrated sterile-fill operations and sterile filtration of beer years before the advent of craft brewing in North America.

Small North American breweries almost universally do not use tunnel pasteurization or flash pasteurization for microbiological assurance. A class of aseptic fillers are the norm in many craft breweries. Originally, special rooms or enclosures were built to accommodate fillers and crowners for draft (nonpasteurized) beer. However, shrouded enclosures are now typically accepted over rinser/filler/crowner monoblocs (Fig. 1.18). In shrouded enclosures, air filtration units are sized to provide 40+ air changes per hour to the filler housing (soft drink lines often specify five air changes per hour on water lines). The 40 air volumes per hour provides sufficient positive pressure to prevent any outside air from entering the filler housing through gaps in the guarding.

Engineers generally design for three main filtration stages.

1. Roughing filtration (prefilters): MERV* 1 to MERV 4; to stop visible parts (more than 10 μm)
2. High-efficiency filtration: MERV 5 to MERV 16; to stop small particles (1–10 μm)
3. High-efficiency particulate air (HEPA)/Ultra-low penetration air (ULPA) filtration (absolute filtration): MERV 17 to MERV 20; to stop particles as small as a virus (0.3 μm)

*The minimum efficiency reporting value (MERV) is a number from 1 to 16 that is relative to an air filter's efficiency. The higher the MERV, the more efficient the air filter is at removing particles. At the lower end of the efficiency spectrum, a fiberglass panel filter may have a MERV of 4 or 5. At the higher end, a MERV 14 filter is typically the filter of choice for critical areas of hospitals. Higher MERV filters are also capable of removing higher quantities of extremely small contaminants (particles as small as $1/300$ the diameter of a human hair).

Can Fillers: Sophistication—Not Complexity

Vintage beer can fillers require adjustment of the fill at each valve by manually turning the ball valve. This is a challenge because the much larger surface area of the can's cylinder geometry means the fill-height variance has a much greater effect on the filled volume in the can than does a similar variation in a beer bottle. The electronic filler uses a capacitance probe to determine when can filling should stop. With the capacitance probe, it senses the approaching level and throttles the fill to end to meet the target volume. The volumetric filler delivers a volume of beer specified by a magnetic flow meter or a mass flow meter to a dosing cylinder above the fill head and then to the can once purging is completed. There are other volumetric control systems available, such as measurement from the base of the chamber (cylinder) against a back pressure (Dunn, 2006; p. 587). Servo technology is now the standard for synchronizing the can filler and its seamer.

FIGURE 1.18. A shrouded enclosure above a filler monobloc ensures near-sterile filling if minimum efficiency reporting value (MERV) 14–16 filters are used; sterile filling requires MERV 17–20 filters. (Courtesy Trumer Brauerei-Berkeley)

Automation

Automation and control is normally provided by original equipment manufacturer (OEM) vendors who supply either individual packaging machines or completely integrated packaging lines. Packaging lines have a long lifetime, and it is common for the machinery to outlast the interface supplied with it. Control architecture and panels are often selected for their role in satisfying the packaging requirement within which specific machines will be running, and a view toward future upgrades may not be part of the package. Redundant operations coverage also would not be part of the package since each packaging machine is supplied with an individual panel that controls only that machine. The result of this is that the failure of any panel could bring the packaging line to a halt; there also may not be uniformity in operator interfaces from one machine to the next.

Problems may occur when machines from different manufacturers, sometimes built according to different standards, are integrated into a single packaging line. SABMiller and Anheuser-Busch are showing leadership to the U.S. industry by actively participating in the Packaging Workgroup (PWG) of Organization for Machine Automation and Control (OMAC), the roadmap to standardize packaging machine architectures and networks. The objectives of the OMAC PWG PackSoft Committee are to define software modules (based on appropriate standards) that describe basic packaging machinery control elements and to develop a programming convention and a set of functional software elements (Used with permission of OMAC Packaging Workgroup; www.omac.org).

Avoiding Waste and the Need to Define KPIs

Waiting time (idle time) in the packaging line represents an obvious waste. Other less obvious forms of waste are defects and overproduction. More subtle yet are waste actors such as unnecessary transport, unnecessary motion, and overprocessing. Excessive energy, water, and compressed air consumption are other related overhead wastes.

Waste in an existing line can be identified as changeovers, small stops, quality holds/production rejects, and breakdowns. These elements can be the basis of KPIs (or key performance indicator ratios), which quantify waste and improve processes.

The factor that can be controlled most by the line staff and support team is changeover time, but it requires effort to make changeovers happen faster. Installing new technologies may significantly reduce changeover time, and metrics should be in place to track any tangible reductions.

A challenging area of waste time is breakdowns. A good maintenance-oriented KPI should involve the entire team: top management, intermediate management, and people on the shop floor and in maintenance. Contemporary asset management (e.g., computerized maintenance management systems [CMMSs]) or manufacturing execution systems (MESs) can readily output KPI dashboards so everyone can visualize the metrics and agree on areas of concern while also understanding how well the line's maintenance needs are addressed. Manual tracking analyses are not difficult—just time-consuming.

Real-time feedback to the production team is by far the best information to share, since manual analyses are often compiled after a shift has ended. Manually managed data is important and useful when there is no means to allow operators to see how the line is performing minute-by-minute or to update often during the shift. Data from a real line, captured manually at each station and then compiled at the end of a shift, allows the team to see where the greatest loss of time has occurred.

A CMMS can assist in analyzing and quantifying the downtime of each element of the packaging line and in identifying clearly the major concerns. A major concern is a system that is receiving maintenance attention more often than others. Perhaps a cross-functional group that includes operators and maintenance staff can identify whether an overhaul is needed or can help prioritize an older system for replacement based upon the justification of reducing downtime and emergency maintenance.

An intuitive KPI allows visualization of performance. It can incorporate multiple factors and influences, and it must be able to be altered by the team on the line.

To improve productivity, the palletizer run rate or the number of packages packed per labor hour can be defined as a KPI. To quantify downtime impacts, the team could define the elapsed downtime, changeover times, downtime event tracking, and maintenance response/resolution time as a KPI.

A simple KPI is target, actual, and piece variance. Target specifies how much should have been produced, actual is how much was produced, and piece variance is the difference between the two. It is an efficiency number that operators can appreciate and can be the basis of discussion. A piece or time variance of zero represents ideality.

Another KPI that is useful is overall equipment effectiveness (OEE). An OEE score of 100% represents perfect production with no downtime. Its three components account for all losses: availability accounts for changeover and breakdowns, quality captures startup rejects and production rejects, and performance accounts for slow cycles and small stops (speed loss).

Many breweries have found that defining effective equipment and line efficiencies is useful.

● PACKAGING LINE EFFICIENCIES

One of the most common ways to measure how well a line runs is to calculate production efficiencies, reported as barrels (or cases) per man-hour of production realized. These calculations provide a baseline position with which to interpret current line productivity.

For example, if a small bottle line filler has a standard operating speed of 250 bpm and the line must run 300 barrels of beer, it would take 397 minutes to run at a calculated efficiency of 100%. If, in actuality, it took 450 minutes to run, the line efficiency would be 88%. If eight people were deployed, i.e., six line workers, one supervisor, and one maintenance worker, for a total of 64 hours to package 300 barrels of beer; the barrels per man-hour would be 4.69.

Manual compilation of waste on standard forms can be useful, if the reports are studied (Fig. 1.19). It is important to educate operators so they understand the metrics.

Compiling histories of line efficiencies and barrels per man-hour is one methodology for forecasting a realistic rate for production runs, setting production goals, and evaluating the overall production capacity of a packaging line. It can be used as another early warning system.

Analysis Tools

A packaging line can be analyzed from a personnel utilization standpoint to make sure that the best use of resources is being realized. Absolute minimization of personnel is not necessarily the most productive operation for a given line.

Evaluation of the machinery is important. Simulation software has been applied successfully in many

Bottling Downtime Report

Filler start time: 7:30am **Filler Stop time:** 2:15pm **11-Jul-07**

Run Hour:	7:30	8:30	9:30	10:30	11:30	12:30	1:30	2:30	3:30	4:30	5:30	6:30	Total	Explanation
Beer Supply													0	
Uncaser				3									3	down bottle jams from uncaser to rinser
Rinser			10										10	replaced bad bottle clip
Filler					2								2	exploded bottle
Jetter													0	
Crowner													0	
Labeler	5					3							8	label magazine adjustment
Peco													0	
Packer													0	
Slitter / Sealer													0	
Palletizer							3						3	pallet dispenser out of time
Conveyor													0	
Case Dater													0	
Electrical													0	
Materials													0	
Air													0	
Water													0	
CIP													0	
CO_2													0	
Personnel													0	
Other													0	

Total Minutes Down: 26

BBLS. Available: 276
Scheduled Run Minutes: 365
Actual Minutes Run: 391
Efficiency: 93%

COMMENTS:
Ran: IPA 24/12s
14 minutes down for crowner auto flush cycle

FIGURE 1.19. Bottling downtime report for one shift. (Courtesy S. Bates)

installations to improve line performance. Simulation requires real parameters from experience. Packaging lines rarely suffer long-duration breakdowns. They typically have short-timeframe disruptions. From recorded data on the history of breakdowns on each machine, assumptions can be made regarding short-term breakdown characteristics of each component of the line. The biggest element of "noise" probably comes from packaging variations from optimal conditions and quality. High humidity causes cartons to swell and labels to curl. Debris fouls up glue application and might prompt label flagging. The essential profile needed for any machine is the percentage of its operating time spent in a nonworking breakdown state and the duration of the average nonworking breakdown.

Real-time KPIs represent the most significant means to monitor performance, an ongoing analysis tool useful for everyone.

Near Real-Time Communication

In many installations, there is disparity between packaging line machine controllers, making it challenging to implement a real-time performance management system that operators can use proactively to manage the performance of their packaging lines. When an alarm occurs, operators may not have the means of knowing the cause and location of the problem without going to the controller where the alarm has been logged.

Success has been found when computers are attached to each of the packaging line stations and data entered about machinery operations. Information is sent to a server, which transforms the information into easy-to-understand displays. The displays are posted immediately on an intranet, where they can be read quickly on computer monitors by line operators. A standardized approach allows for alarms to be displayed on all panels. One such site also posts messages between operators and supervisors and tells operators where there is a line problem. In areas where such a system is installed, one brewery's rate of defects, such as broken bottles, fell from 5% to one-tenth of 1% (Palmer, 2000).

Heineken initiated a program to increase efficiency of packaging by 20% and found that the most effective improvements arose from the operators. The strategy was that it would give people at all levels in the plant access to reliable, accurate, and up-to-date management information. By focusing on the results of their work rather than on just performing a job, they would have the means and motivation to keep benchmarking their performance against the agreed targets. Where necessary, this would enable them to take immediate action to get back on track (Deaves, 2002).

Manual Tracking and Analysis

When starting analysis, charting breakdowns allows managers to graphically evaluate the frequency of failure incidents and the consequences of these incidents. The chart in Figure 1.20 was created from the lost time study data recorded in Table 1.1. Chart lost time studies are often easier to evaluate than are tabular lost time studies, although some information may not be seen, such as elapsed time between repeated breakdowns of the same type. Such information allows the packaging department to recognize which areas need further exploration. We can see from Figure 1.20 that the average time to repair the drop packer studied is roughly 7 minutes overall and, from Table 1.1, that the average time between faults is roughly 38 minutes.

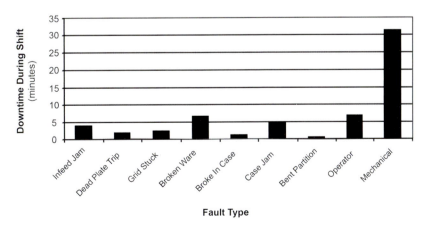

FIGURE 1.20. Frequency distribution of downtime for a drop packer (data from a drop packer lost time study; Manning, 1999; p. 346). (Courtesy J. Jurado)

Tracking and profiling breakdowns is the initial step of an approach to reduce downtime. There are many reasons for downtime, and unanticipated machine problems are just one component. Changeovers in packaging are a fact of life on many packaging lines, and time lost in changeover is normally recorded in the department.

Total productive management (TPM) is used in an attempt to obtain maximum productivity from both people and machinery. Zero losses in material and full utilization of people and resources are the objectives of TPM. Its methodology is strict, e.g., every wrench in the workshop should have its own standardized place. Its origins are in the manufacture of automobiles, but Heineken has been trailblazing this approach for its packaging lines.

A useful element of TPM is the availability analysis of different machines in the packaging line; this is based on the number of breakdowns and the total downtime of every machine. The mean time between two breakdowns and the mean time it takes to repair each machine are calculated. If the team plots the numbers calculated, conclusions are made regarding which machine to update first. The machine with the longest total downtime is not necessarily the one to focus on; the one that affects the rest of the process the most receives the focus.

Figure 1.19 illustrates that the labeler required 4 minutes on average to adjust and that it stopped twice during the shift. The average time between faults was 5 hours. The rinser had only one fault, which lasted 10 minutes. A TPM approach might dictate that the labeler gets attention as the priority.

Analyzing efficiency is an important task for packaging management. Manning presents a discussion of the effective rate of packaging equipment, packaging labor productivity, and efficiency considerations of production (Manning, 1999; pp. 344-345).

Simulation

Because of the complexity of larger packaging lines, software tools can supplement manual analytical tools effectively. Particularly in unusual cases in which a high-volume facility is striving to achieve maximized line output against a requirement of a multiplicity of labels applied to the filled bottles of differing sizes or in various secondary packaging configurations. Breweries involved in export quite often have to face such unique challenges. Simulation is a good tool to explore and design options, including very radical departures from traditional line design. Inputs to simulation include conveyor dimensions and speeds and equipment speed assumptions (based on individual and effective rates).

A good simulation can yield outcomes that reflect reality. For example, when a packaging line must output beer with different labels (having, for example, different languages and country-specific information), a simulation solution may suggest that the intermediate storage of unlabeled beer bottles via accumulation might allow the filling line to work with maximum utilization while allowing 3–4 minutes for label changeovers. Such a system disconnects the changing final packaging requirements from the performance of the filling and pasteurizing operations.

TABLE 1.1. Lost Time Study Data on a Drop Packer[a]

Fault	Duration of Faults (sec)	Time Between Faults (sec)	Elapsed Downtime (sec)
Infeed jam	123	150	
	20	956	
	86	3,720	229
Dead plate trip	45	4,500	
	76	900	121
Grid stuck	12	660	
	54	630	
	62	1,500	
	34	900	162
Broken ware	145	540	
	196	2,100	
	55	1,500	396
Broke in case	15	900	
	60	1,380	75
Case jam	256	1,845	
	45	745	301
Bent partition	26	14,400	26
Operator	120	930	
	75	1,500	
	85	720	
	120	2,700	400
Mechanical	600	7,200	
	1,320	1,380	1,920

[a]Data from a drop packer lost time study (Manning, 1999; p. 346).

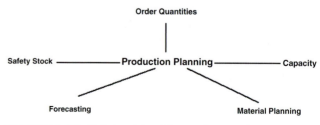

FIGURE 1.21. Relationship of the production planning function components. (Courtesy J. Jurado)

The production planning function might prompt the use of simulation. Production planning integrates material planning, forecasting, order quantities, safety stock, and capacity. Figure 1.21 maps the relation between the parameters that compose production planning.

Standard Cost Structure

Every brewery's financial picture is framed around standard costs. The standard labor cost can be added to container and material costs; costs of indirect workers (such as electricians and machinists); general overheads; and depreciation, insurance, and travel/training. The sum total represents the standard cost.

An example is a typical canning line that has five operators, one each stationed at the infeed/outfeed, the filler/seamer/fill-height detector, the packer/sealer, the palletizer/depalletizer, and relief. If the start-and-stop loss value is incorrect, then it skews the calculation of the canning line labor standards.

The example above, with the following parameters, can be calculated for an 8-hour shift.

- *Speed:* 1,400 cans per minute into 24-cans-per-case packs
- *Speed per 8-hour shift:* (1,400 cans × 60 minutes × 8 hours)/24 = 28,000 cases
- *Start-and-stop loss:* 10 minutes per shift (or 583 cases per shift)
- *Standard run for 8 hours:* 28,000 − 583 = 27,417 cases
- *Labor equivalent:* 5 operators × 60 minutes × 8 hours = 2,400 man-minutes
- *Man-minutes per case:* 2,400/27,417 = 0.09 man-minutes per case
- *Labor standard cost per case:* $40 per hour ($0.66 per minute) = $0.059 per case

Labor in Packaging

Labor requirements can be determined by many factors. These include the type of line, flexibility of the line, age of the equipment, etc. A modern packaging line is designed with an optimization of manning, and good line design incorporates functionality and ergonomic considerations so that one operator may safely and efficiently oversee more than one machine operation.

Yet it is the management of the packaging area that is the mission-critical element. Management establishes and communicates clear objectives and creates the environment for continued training of personnel.

Packaging Management Objectives

To ensure optimum utilization of a packaging line, overall objectives must be recognized. These objectives are to maximize line efficiency in a safe environment, to minimize breakdown and emergency maintenance, and to minimize labor while operating and maintaining the line in a hygienic operation. Secondary objectives include minimizing waste and effluents and reducing breakage of ware on the line, as well as maintaining inventories of all packaging-related materials—a diverse assortment of materials.

Where does a packaging line start? In many breweries, it is at the package release tanks, the final brewery tanks holding beer that has been approved by brewery or quality assurance personnel and that contain beer meeting the specification acceptable for release to packaging. Because of the dynamics of emptying tanks to a packaging line, and the fact that tanks are emptied, refilled, and cleaned repeatedly, a system of interaction between the brewing and packaging departments must be in place.

On the other side of packaging, there is finished goods dispatch and incoming materials delivery to the line, at the palletizers and depalletizers, respectively. For efficiency, these systems are often a considerable physical distance from the actual packaging line; yet, these areas are normally under the authority of the packaging department.

Just as an effective liaison is required between the packaging and brewing departments, a similar professional effectiveness must occur with the shipping and warehouse department to ensure a smooth flow of materials into and out of the packaging area.

A typical organizational chart for a packaging department in a larger brewery was created by Spire and remains valid (Spire, 1982; p. 18) (Fig. 1.22).

Management Structure

As a component of the brewery, packaging must be integrated into operating philosophies. Keeping beer inventories as low as practical in the warehouse may lead to higher product changeover frequencies. Optimizing one area of the plant, such as warehousing, can impact packaging performance. Managers must be in place to identify and review such effects.

The senior manager is the packaging manager, who often reports to the general manager/plant manager. The packaging manager is responsible for the efficient running of the department and is the key stakeholder for explorations into new packaging lines and packaging line modifications in the future. No matter the size of

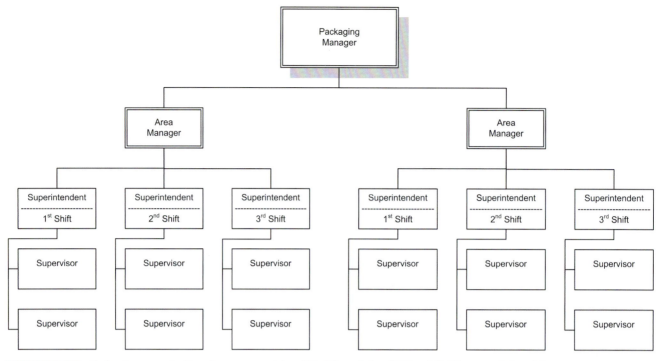

FIGURE 1.22. Packaging organizational management (modified from Spire, 1982; p. 18). (Courtesy J. Jurado)

the packaging line, it is prudent to designate an assistant packaging manager who maintains responsibility for the operation of the packaging department during inevitable periods when the packaging manager is away. Responsibilities may include warehouse operations and shipping. The assistant packaging manager is often the most experienced of the next tier of managers.

Efficiently utilizing personnel and equipment and maintaining operating costs at a minimum are the main responsibilities of the packaging manager, followed closely by effective safety and housekeeping in the work space. In conjunction with the brewery management, an inventory level of packaged beer must be ready at the specified time for distributor customers. However, there are constraints. Product age control standards define maximum inventory age before packaged product cannot be released for sale to distributors.

The packaging manager must administer established policies in regards to personnel. A key responsibility sometimes not expressed formally is to recommend to the plant manager and corporate operation staff any changes in policies or protocols that may enhance the efficiency of the packaging operation. The packaging manager also must monitor the performance of the maintenance professionals. There are manual tools, as well as formal reporting tools and dashboards, that can be built from modern asset management (e.g., CMMS) packages. An example is in Figure 1.23.

The area manager (or other equivalent position, e.g., bottling superintendent) is responsible for canning or for bottling or for a geographical assignment, such as all packaging in a designated area. The area manager has responsibility for the line around the clock, 7 days a week in many operations. Reporting to the area manager are the shift superintendents.

The shift superintendent is generally responsible for multiple lines for the duration of a shift. The line supervisor, responsible for the line or a portion of the line during a shift, reports to the shift superintendent. The can line supervisor is responsible for the portion of the line conveying the cans to the rinser all the way to palletizing packed cases or trays onto pallets. The bottle line supervisor typically is responsible for depalletizing bulk glass or conveying cases of empty bottles to the uncaser all the way to palletizing packed cases onto pallets.

The line supervisor is the first level of management on the line, often referred to as a foreman. Individuals employed as operators look after the "care and feeding" of specific machines on the line. There are also dedicated packaging machine maintenance personnel who assist with adjustments when required and who perform planned maintenance operations and emergency maintenance when systems fail.

The operator on a packaging line has defined responsibilities. Obvious ones include "staying safe" by following all safety requirements, monitoring the line to

Work Order Statistics
Data displayed for 2007-07-01 through 2007-07-31.

BOTTLESHOP

WO Type	Beginning Backlog	Received in Period	Total for Period	Beginning Backlog Completed	Received in Period Completed	Total Completed	Completion %	Ending Backlog
Breakdown	14	56	70	12	51	63	90	7
Multiple Equipment Child	115	2	117	6	2	8	7	109
Preventive maintenance	14	12	26	5	7	12	46	14
Minor project, no EPR required, booked to Maintenance.	3	2	5	1	1	2	40	3
Non-Emergency Repair, no immediate action required, can be scheduled.	19	21	40	14	20	34	85	6

FIGURE 1.23. Top-level maintenance work order fulfillment report. (Courtesy Spoetzl Brewing Company)

report signal lights or other malfunction indices, removing jams or fallen packages, and emergency stop (E-stop) responsibility.

Typical locations where operators may be stationed on various line configurations were indicated in Figures 1.4–1.6. An operator may supply labels and maintain online assurance that glue is evenly applied at a labeling station, ensure that crowns are fed properly to the feed chute and bottles are properly filled, or monitor reject rates from the EBI. Operators perform machine-specific tasks at defined areas of the line, which might cover several machines, and some of those tasks are just prudent observation. It is important to have written position descriptions that capture as many of these details as possible. Examples that may or may not describe all the activities, but which serve to illustrate, are as follows.

Depalletizer and Palletizer

The operator removes damaged pallets; removes broken wood or glass from rollers; observes vacuum/pressure gauges; keeps "magic eye" optical reflectors clean and properly aligned; monitors automatic stretchwrapper performance and adds new rolls of shrinkwrap as needed; monitors hydraulic oil level and pressure; keeps infeed rollers and case-stops clean; monitors overhang of units on pallets; and sweeps floors as time permits. A nonunion line might have the operator be responsible for oiling/greasing, troubleshooting, and additional maintenance types of activities.

Electronic Bottle Inspector

The operator runs go/no-go bottles at startup through the EBI; observes real-time analyses and elapsed run-to-current-moment display; inspects rejected ware; ascertains that inspection systems are operating correctly; and maintains proper lubrication.

Rinser/Filler/Crowner/Fill-Height Detector

The operator removes broken ware and follows specified full-flush (burst-bottle rinseout) protocols; monitors proper rinse water drainage; observes carbon dioxide pressure gauge and counterpressure gauge; monitors bowl level; measures crown crimps via go/no-go gauge and records the results; monitors crown feed supply to ensure a steady supply; and observes bottle rinse and rejects on fill-height detector. The operator also disinfects the floor around the monobloc daily, selects the assigned brands, changes brands, and queries the availability of releasable brands.

Labeler

The operator maintains a steady supply of cut labels in magazines (i.e., body and neck labels in station 1 and back labels in station 2) and of glue in reservoirs; monitors the quality of label adherence; observes air pressure; monitors performance and clarity of the coding device and the accuracy of the coding date applied; cleans glue pallets and machine when required; and checks focus of the ink date coder printer or laser if ware is etched with a date code.

Packer Stations

The operator maintains a supply of cartons, wraps, or multipacks; maintains glue levels in reservoirs; observes vacuum/pressure gauges; observes the quality of materials; removes cases with cosmetic damage; fixes hangups; observes fingers to alert when broken or bent; loads cartons into the hopper; inspects slitter/sealer applications; observes hot-melt glue application and temperature; maintains glue levels; cleans debris from rollers; and removes damaged cases. The operator also monitors the lubrication of packages and line pressure up to the packer.

Altogether, packaging management must maintain a productive environment where workers maintain safe protocols and contribute to maximizing line efficiencies.

Union and Nonunion Shops

The intended purpose of labor unions is to represent workers as a collective bargaining unit for the negotiation of wages, benefits, and working conditions. Unions can provide a stable, trained work force, and at the same time, a case could be made that unions have the effect of reducing flexibility and garnering greater workplace complexity. An example could be when there is more than one union present, such as in some large companies where work territorial issues reduce line efficiencies and can support a non-team atmosphere. Issues of whether an operator can do, or help with, a line changeover or whether a manager/supervisor can operate a machine is a matter of contract—not what may be most efficient for the line. It should be noted that many companies have experienced good labor union relations with multiple unions all working together. Whether a shop is union or nonunion, having good labor management relations fosters an environment that helps make it possible for a company to compete in this complex marketplace.

Training

The most important component of the packaging department is training staff to ensure the safe and efficient operation of the plant. Training should be a continuous process. The department should not stop when an operator is satisfactorily performing the assigned task on the packaging line. Cross-training on other components of the line allows flexibility for the future and maintains the interest of the operator in the overall success of the packaging line. Careful, comprehensive training allows each operator to become a future trainer of new employees. Vendors offer specialized courses for managers and maintenance personnel that can be exploited to offer useful information for operators learning about machines under their responsibility.

All staff must be hygiene educated and the training should be proactively reinforced at their work areas. They also need to understand and value the KPIs that management staff are using.

Maintenance personnel require special attention since they serve ultimately as the last guarantor that a machine is operating as specified. Great knowledge resides in experienced onsite maintenance staff. Opportunities to learn from other packaging lines and, if possible, in other breweries broaden the experience of maintenance personnel.

Strategic packaging planning offers employees insights into their own future operations. Situations will arise when capacity adjustments must be undertaken. Management can apply either the leading or the following strategy (Fig. 1.24).

The leading strategy is proactive, when the capacity is higher before the demand increases. When demand is increasing, this approach brings flexibility to grow the business. The following strategy is reactive, when new investment is planned only when increased demand has been realized and sustained. It offers low volume flexibility when demand is increasing, and a higher consequential stock level of finished beer in the warehouse is mandated during heavier seasonal shipping periods.

Sharing which approach is deployed serves as a trust-building tool in staff training.

The Master Brewers Association of the Americas offers an annual course in the United States on packaging, which is appropriate for all persons involved in any aspect of packaging beer. The Institute and Guild of Brewing also offer United Kingdom-based packaging modules. Besides this book, there are other high-quality reference books and technical journals that add to the body of growing information regarding beer packaging.

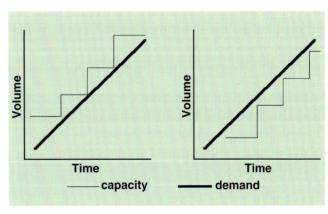

FIGURE 1.24. Leading (left) and following (right) packaging planning strategies. (Courtesy J. Jurado)

Safety and Ergonomics

Ergonomics is the study of human characteristics, abilities, and limitations that are relevant to design. Ergonomic design applies this knowledge to the design of machines, tools, jobs, and systems. Done properly, ergonomics integrate these designs into a safe, effective, and comfortable working environment.

The purpose of ergonomics in the brewery is to

- reduce occupational injury and illness,
- improve work quality and productivity,
- decrease absenteeism,
- comply with government regulations, and
- minimize the cost of workers' compensation insurance.

The procedures by which these goals are achieved are to

- identify, evaluate, and modify the work site to minimize risk factors;
- provide recommendations to reduce the identified risk conditions; and
- educate both management and workers regarding risk conditions.

Management's responsibility is to oversee and verify that proper work techniques are followed. Because of the repetitive nature of packaging department assignments, some brewery packaging departments have found it important to rotate and cross-train employees on the line. This provides employees with workplace variety and fosters a more interesting work environment, thereby promoting less absenteeism. Continued safety training with operators, maintenance staff, and managers at regularly scheduled intervals maximizes awareness of safety as a high priority for the organization. As with all other departments in the brewery, it cannot be stressed enough that packaging workers are required to understand and apply safety information. Personal protective equipment must be issued to all staff, its appropriate use and maintenance must be detailed carefully, and it should be constantly monitored. Safety education and prevention programs are an important part of keeping employees healthy and productive. An example of this would be providing a mandatory yearly hearing audit performed by trained occupational hearing specialists. This helps ensure that on-the-job hearing loss is minimized and the use of hearing protection is reinforced. Using appropriate safety equipment on packaging lines is vital and having a common plantwide understanding of an organization's approach to safety is paramount.

A packaging line inevitably features conveyors, and personnel might have to duck under conveyors if free access to stations is not available; this represents a risk. Safe cross-over stairs and platforms with handrails going over the conveyor should be available on the line. Slippery floors are also a threat to packaging line personnel. The capture of overspill lube, proper drainage, and nonslip floor treatments suffice to improve conditions on many workspaces.

CONCLUSION

Beer packaging encompasses a variety of materials and operations. Cans, kegs, bottles, PET, and polyethylene naphthalate (PEN) are available (Giles, 1999). Eighty percent of the PET output is in Eastern Europe, where the package weighs 10% that of comparable glassware.

Packaging is the most complex and sophisticated area of any brewery. Having a high-efficiency packaging operation requires good management, well-maintained equipment, enlightened employees, and work schedules focused on optimizing productivity. Good systems of communication with the brewing and warehouse/shipping departments are required to support efficient packaging.

High efficiency means nothing if the beer is not preserved in the package. Maintenance and quality assurance departments play their significant roles in maintaining the quality of the packaged product. Vendors make their contribution by consistently delivering high-quality materials.

Packaging operations today routinely use the minimum quantity of packaging materials and recycle unusable materials, resulting in increased proportions of recycled material in wraps, trays, and cartons. PET will probably be the next closed-loop recycling system, in which postconsumer PET will be reused to the extent found with glass and aluminum, once its collection is not collated with that of high-density polyethylene (HDPE), polyvinyl chloride (PVC), polypropylene, and other plastics. Sorting PET from PVC is difficult.

Some nations have mandated by regulation that packaging lines carry out analyses of and report on and update hazard analysis and critical control points (HACCP) on the packaging line. HACCP discipline requires supplier audits and regular quality reviews with improvement outcome plans. As of the printing of this book, it is not a regulatory requirement in the United States. Organizations such as the Master Brewers Association of the Americas are increasingly striving to increase awareness of HACCP for beverage professionals.

A definition of environmentally responsible packaging is not clear, but it is a new area capturing the world's attention. Packaging waste management in the future might follow principles seen in European Union environmental policy, such as the polluter-pays principle in which economic instruments are deployed. Besides municipal waste charges, packaging operations may have to finance government product charges. Poland has proposed a schedule of charges, converted from Polish zloty (PLN) to U.S. dollars (Fig. 1.25). The proposed rate of packaging charges is approximately 50% the level in Germany. A one-time increase in consumer prices would probably be the result.

Needs have emerged to quantify and audit greenhouse gas contributions from the packaging area (as well as from the broader brewery). The inevitable results will be new environmental KPIs not previously imagined.

Technical knowledge of packaging operations is the most important knowledge anyone involved in packaging management must possess. Subsequent chapters of this volume serve to inform and elucidate about specific components of packaging.

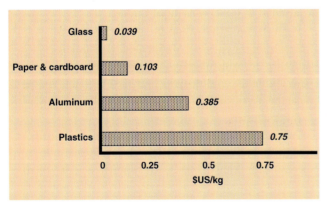

FIGURE 1.25. Packaging charges proposed for Poland (MOSZNiL, 1999); 1 U.S. dollar = 3.9 Polish zloty. (Courtesy J. Jurado)

ACKNOWLEDGMENTS

S. Anwar converted drawings used in Figures 1.2, 1.4, 1.5, and 1.6 to their final versions. B. Malloy kindly provided photographs for Figure 1.14.

The authors wish to thank Carlos Alvarez, chair of The Gambrinus Company, for permission to prepare this chapter, and former MBAA Technical Director Ray Klimovitz for the invitation to author it. Additionally, the current technical director of MBAA, Karl Ockert, and the retired MBAA executive vice president, Steve Nelson, are acknowledged for their efforts, support, and dedication to the realization of this project.

REFERENCES

Danish Environmental Protection Agency. (1999). Packaging for soft drinks, beer, wine and spirits. The Agency, Copenhagen.

Deaves, M. (2002). Bottoms up! Manuf. Eng. 81(6):267-269.

Dunn, A. R. (2006). Packaging technology. In: Handbook of Brewing, 2nd ed. pp. 563-606. F. G. Priest and G. G. Stewart, eds. CRC Press, Boca Raton, FL.

Giles, G. A., ed. (1999). Handbook of Beverage Packaging. Sheffield Food Technology, Volume 5. Sheffield Academic Press, Sheffield, England/CRC Press, Boca Raton, FL.

Manning, H. (1999). Packaging - Bottling operations. In: The Practical Brewer, 3rd ed. pp. 327-359. J. T. McCabe, ed. Master Brewers Association of the Americas, St. Paul, MN.

Meyer, H. (1973). Pollution problems in brewing. Proc. Congr. Eur. Brew. Conv. 14:429-443.

Ministry of Environmental Protection, Natural Resources and Forestry (MOSZNiL) (1999). Projekt ustawy o opłacie produktowej I opłacie depozytowej. MOSZNiL, Warsaw, Poland.

Palmer, A. T. (2000). Beer with a good head on its shoulders. Businessweek Online. September 18, 2000 Issue. www.businessweek.com/2000/00_38/b3699069.htm

Speers, R. A., Cameron, R. C., Paulson, A. T., Hamdullahpur, F., and Caley, W. F. (2002). Effects of metal ions and gluconate on surface residues on returnable bottles. Tech. Q. Master Brew. Assoc. Am. 39:7-12.

Spire, C. L. (1982). Packaging management organization. In: Beer Packaging. pp. 11-26. H. M. Broderick, ed. Master Brewers Association of the Americas, St. Paul, MN.

CHAPTER 2

Packaging Line Project Management

BETH PARTLETON
Miller Brewing Company (retired)

The discipline of project management has existed for many decades. Formalized in the mid-1960s, NASA, the aerospace industry, and the military founded the discipline to manage the complex projects for the space program. They developed many of the tools, techniques, and principles that are still in use today. Since then, other industries have come to understand the importance of project management. As reduced time-to-market has become more important, the companies that can react more quickly and reduce cycle time on product development have been the companies that have survived and grown. Project management has been an important part of that success. A culture of good project management can be a competitive advantage for any company.

In 1969, the Project Management Institute (PMI) was formed as a professional society for project managers. PMI has compiled and organized an extensive amount of the information about project management. The American National Standards Institute has accepted PMI's publication, *A Guide to the Project Management Body of Knowledge* (*PMBOK Guide*) (PMI, 2013), as the standard on project management principles. The *PMBOK Guide* outlines the principles of project management and is a reference for the practice of project management. These principles can be applied to any project in any industry and can be applied to any project in a company, whether it is a marketing project or a packaging project. When a company uses the same processes for all projects, it creates a repeatable process that promotes better project execution, especially when cross-functional teams are involved.

This chapter will do the following.

- Review what is a project and what is project management

- Review the nine knowledge areas of the *PMBOK Guide*
- Apply these concepts to a new packaging line project
- Present how to develop a project plan for a packaging project
- Describe how to monitor and control a project using the project plan

● WHAT IS A PROJECT?

In most organizations, construction projects or information system projects are recognized as projects. However, there are many other areas of an organization that do projects but they do not recognize their work as projects. All types of projects can benefit from the discipline of project management. A project is generally defined as any planned series of activities that

- has a specific objective;
- has been allocated resources, including time, money, people, equipment, and materials;
- involves a temporary organization; and
- has a defined start and end date.

The *PMBOK Guide* defines a project as "a temporary endeavor undertaken to create a unique product, service or result" (PMI, 2013; p. 3). This definition can include many activities, from planning a capital project to planning a business conference.

It has been said that a person is managing either a project or a process and everything falls into one of those two categories. If a person is in the quality lab analyzing samples consistently one after another, he or she is managing or involved in a process. The objective of analyzing samples is continuous; it doesn't have a defined start and end date.

If a person is preparing a departmental budget, feasibility study, or major organization change, he or she is managing or involved in a project. Developing a budget, feasibility study, or major organizational change has a specific objective, has a defined start and end, and usually has a team of people to accomplish the objective. That team disbands after the objective is completed, i.e., the team is a temporary organization.

Having good project management skills and processes within an organization benefits that organization in many ways. Project management can help an organization achieve its strategic goals. When an organization develops a strategic plan, that strategic plan is made up of specific objectives to be accomplished in a specific time period. Each of these objectives should be linked to one or more projects. The success of the strategic plan is often dependent on an organization's ability to plan and execute the projects supporting that plan.

Applying the principles of project management to the activities of a task force can greatly increase an organization's effectiveness. By definition, a task force is formed for the completion of a specific task or objective, which means the task force is working on a project. By applying the rigor and discipline of project management, the team should be able to complete its assignment effectively and disband. The work of a task force is not meant to be an ongoing effort. If it begins to work on routine functions, it should be called a standing committee or council.

Project management is a good training ground for general management in that the skills, knowledge, and experience developed in project management also help prepare a person for other managerial duties. It can be a career path to senior management.

● WHAT IS PROJECT MANAGEMENT?

The *PMBOK Guide* defines project management. "Project management is the application of knowledge, skills, tools and techniques to project activities to meet project requirements. Project management is accomplished through the appropriate application and integration of . . . the project management processes" (PMI, 2013; p. 5) of initiating, planning, executing, monitoring and controlling, and closing. The project manager is the person responsible for accomplishing the project objectives. Successful project management results in the project objectives being achieved on schedule and within the budget and resources allocated and at the desired level of technology or performance.

A key misconception is that project management is simply scheduling. Attending a class on how to use scheduling software is not a class in project management; it is only an introduction to one of the many tools of scheduling, which is only one of the knowledge areas of project management. Project management is a much broader discipline. A project manager is the person who leads the process. As presented by Harold Kerzner, the project manager "is responsible for coordinating and integrating activities across multiple, functional lines" (Kerzner, 1989; p. 10).

● PROJECT MANAGEMENT FUNDAMENTALS

According to PMI's *The Principles of Project Management*, any project can be broken down into four basic phases, known as the project life cycle (Adams et al., 1997; p. 188). The project life cycle phases consist of initiation, planning, implementation, and closeout, as shown in Figure 2.1.

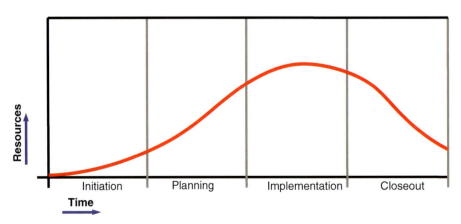

FIGURE 2.1. A project life cycle.

The key activities of the initiation phase are gathering data, identifying needs, establishing measurable goals and objectives, studying the feasibility of a concept, identifying how the project supports the company strategic goals, and designating the project manager. Alternatives should be identified and analyzed before selecting the final solution. Typically, project managers would present the plan to management for its review and approval before proceeding to the next phase.

In the first phase, stakeholders should also be identified. In the *PMBOK Guide*, a stakeholder is defined as "an individual, group or organization who may affect, be affected by, or perceive itself to be affected by a decision, activity or outcome of a project" (PMI, 2013; p. 563). Identification of all stakeholders is essential before moving into phase two.

The second phase, planning, includes development of a project plan; identification of a team; definition of the role of each team member; and development of a work breakdown structure, a budget, a schedule, and any policies and procedures required to execute the project. This is the time to assess risks and verify the justification for the project. Once the planning of the project is completed, project managers often seek another management review to obtain final approval to proceed.

The third phase, implementation, includes the procurement of goods and services, installation, and startup of the project. It includes monitoring the work being completed; controlling the scope, budget, and schedule; and adjusting the plan when the situation requires it. Problems may come up during this phase that will need to be resolved by the team. It is this phase that illustrates for project managers the importance of doing the planning phase well. Many problems during implementation could have been avoided by doing thorough planning and risk analysis.

The fourth phase, closeout, is the completion of the project and verification that the project objectives were met. Typically, customer or sponsor review and acceptance, settlement of all budget accounts, transfer of ownership or responsibility of the project to the end user, a review of the project to determine lessons learned, documentation of the results, and a closeout of the project using the company's specific closeout procedures all occur at this phase.

In Figure 2.1, the curve that extends across the four phases depicts the amount of effort (shown on the vertical, or y, axis) and time (shown on the horizontal, or x, axis) required. In the planning phase, the amount of effort required starts small and gradually increases. During the planning phase, effort continues to increase, usually because more team members are involved. During implementation, the amount of effort peaks as more resources are expended to install and start up the project. Effort then declines through the final phase until the project is completed.

It is important to note that, although planning requires less total effort, it is at this time that the future success of the project is determined. Without proper planning, much of the effort and resources that peak during implementation will not be used effectively because there was not a well-defined plan. Project managers often say they do not have time to do the detailed planning. In actuality, they do not have the time *not* to do detailed planning. When a crisis occurs during the implementation phase, the project manager will have to make time to solve the problems created by poor planning. At that time, more resources will be wasted than would have been used to do it right earlier in the project.

● PROGRAM VERSUS PROJECT

Sometimes a company strategy requires more than one project to accomplish a goal. In that case, a program may be required. In the *PMBOK Guide*, a program is defined as "a group of projects, subprograms, and program activities managed in a coordinated way to obtain benefits not available from managing them individually" (PMI, 2013; p. 553). A program might be the effort to reduce brewery waste, and individual projects within that program might include those for developing a better monitoring and tracking system or specific projects to target individual areas of waste. Typically, a program manager oversees the entire scope of the program, and project managers are assigned to manage their specific projects and report back to the program manager. The program manager may review all projects and justifications and eliminate the ones that do not support the overall program objectives. Figure 2.2 contains a diagram showing the relationship between a program, projects, and tasks.

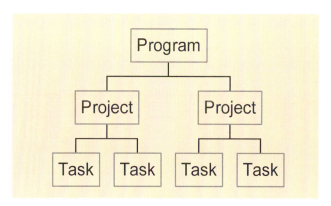

FIGURE 2.2. Program versus project.

THE PROJECT

To elucidate project management fundamentals, this chapter shows how they can be applied to a typical project in a brewery packaging operation. For the purpose of this example, the project will be the installation of a new bottling line. A brewery has determined it will need additional capacity in the line producing 12-oz., long-neck, nonreturnable bottles before the next peak season. The plant has adequate space in the packaging department to install a new line, so a building addition is not needed. Management has requested the project be completed in 12 months. The project will be structured using the 10 project management knowledge areas defined in the *PMBOK Guide* (PMI, 2013; p. 60).

- Scope management
- Time management
- Cost management
- Quality management
- Human resource management
- Communication management
- Risk management
- Procurement management
- Stakeholder management
- Integration management

Scope Management

As the *PMBOK Guide* defines it, project scope management includes "the processes required to ensure that the project includes all the work required, and only the work required to complete the project successfully" (PMI, 2013; p. 555). A project's scope is what is to be included in the project and more importantly what is not in the project. It sets the fence or boundaries for the project. Anything outside the boundaries is out of the scope of the project, and project team members must follow the established scope change procedure before adding new scope to the project.

The first step is to develop a scope statement, which is a brief description of the project that explains what, where, and why a project is being done. Although brief, it should be specific and define the location, number of lines, packages to be produced, sizes of containers, brands to be included on the line, etc. The scope statement for the project might be:

Design and construct a long-neck, nonreturnable bottle packaging line that produces 12-oz. bottles in twelve-count fiber packages with two packages in a corrugated tray at the West Coast Brewery. Overall operating efficiency of the line shall be 94%. Project is to be completed in 12 months.

Once the scope statement has been completed, the next step is to further define the scope by developing a work breakdown structure (WBS). As defined in the *PMBOK Guide*, a WBS is "hierarchical decomposition of the total scope of work to be carried out by the project team to accomplish the project objectives and create the required deliverables" (PMI, 2013; p. 567). It comprises descending levels of tasks that represent the detailed definition of the project's scope. It shows how the various elements of the work relate to each other and to the overall project. In the WBS in Figure 2.3, the first level is the project level. The next level identifies the various tasks or project phases; in this case, project initiation, project planning design and development, project implementation, and project closeout. The next level is the subtask level, which provides a further breakdown, or decomposition, of each task into smaller actions.

As an example, let's examine project implementation. It is a large, complex task that is best understood by breaking it down into subtasks, such as, in this case, the awarding of contracts, delivery and installation of equipment, verification that all contracted work has been completed in accordance with the drawings and specifications, and finally, startup of the line. Obviously, each of these subtasks can be broken down into further components. A WBS can be continuously broken down into smaller increments until the project manager feels there is enough detail to adequately define and manage the project.

Once developed, the WBS becomes the foundation for all subsequent elements of the project plan. It determines team assignments, team member roles and responsibilities, the budget, and scheduling. It can help define procurement planning by indicating the number of construction packages or equipment packages that may be required to execute the project.

Time Management

Time management or scheduling is composed of defining and sequencing the activities, estimating the resources needed and the duration of each activity, and developing and controlling the schedule (PMI, 2013; p. 141). To begin developing a schedule, project managers should take each box on the WBS and divide it into five parts (Fig. 2.4). The first part is the task name, which was already defined in the WBS. The second part is the estimated duration or time required to complete the activity. Skill in estimating the duration of tasks is learned through experience or by reviewing the records of other projects. The more project managers practice estimating a task's duration, the better their skill in this area becomes. Project managers should apply their best judgment or seek assistance from a subject matter expert. After estimating the duration of each activity, project managers determine the sequence of activities by defining which must be complete before another activity can start. These prior activities are called predecessors. Scheduling software

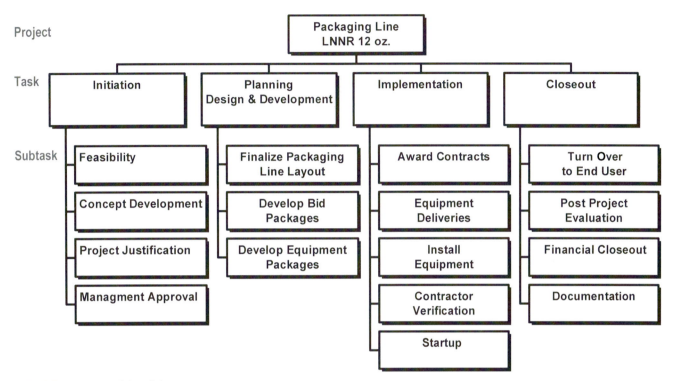

FIGURE 2.3. A work breakdown structure.

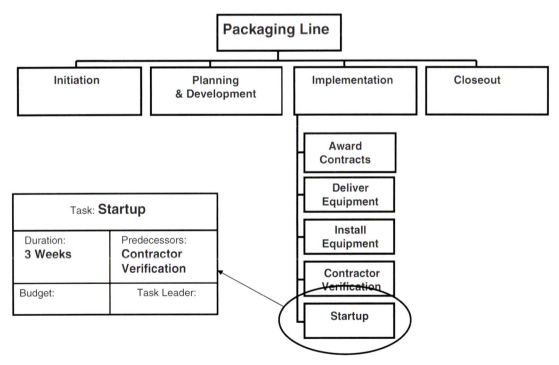

FIGURE 2.4. Adding scheduling to a task.

can automatically link tasks by defining predecessors. For instance, in the bottling line example, it will take an estimated 3 weeks to complete the debug, startup, and fine tuning of the line. The task of contractor verification has to be completed before startup can begin, so it is a predecessor to startup.

Once durations and predecessors are determined for each element of the WBS, the schedule can be developed. Several different types of schedule formats can be used, including bar charts, milestone charts, or network diagrams. The most common is the bar chart, also known as a Gantt chart (Fig. 2.5). Although the schedule in Figure 2.5 has been completed using a software scheduling tool, a Gantt chart can be as simple as bars drawn on graph paper. In Figure 2.5, tasks in the left-hand column are taken directly from the WBS. On a Gantt chart, the length of the bar indicates the length of the activity duration in specific units of time. Once the schedule is developed, a project manager can monitor against the planned dates to determine whether a project is staying on schedule and, if not, what needs to be done to get back on schedule. A project manager needs to understand which items in the schedule can float and which ones cannot change. "Float" means the schedule for that task can change without impacting the overall schedule. Items that, if their schedule is changed, will impact the final completion of the project are on the critical path. The critical path is "the sequence of activities that represents the longest path through a project, which determines the shortest possible duration" of the project (PMI, 2013; p. 536).

Cost Management

Project cost management or project budgeting is one area familiar to most people involved with projects. Cost management includes resource planning (both human and monetary), cost estimating, budgeting, and cost controlling the project during implementation. The best way to develop a budget is to assign an estimated cost to each of the boxes on the WBS, a method similar to adding schedule information to the WBS. The total project budget is determined by adding all the costs of all the tasks. Using the WBS helps the project manager develop a complete budget and not leave out an important cost element. In the example, the cost of the startup task is estimated to be $100,000, which covers startup resources and training (Fig. 2.6). It is prudent for the project manager to discuss each task with the appropriate team members. Such

Task: **Startup**	
Duration: 3 Weeks	Predecessor: Contractor Verification
Budget: $100,000	Task Leader:

FIGURE 2.6. Budgeting a task in a work breakdown structure.

Task Name	Start	Finish	Duration	Prede	Resource Names
Packaging Line - LIIIR 12 oz Bottle	Tue 1/2/07	Mon 12/10/07	245 days		
Initiation	Tue 1/2/07	Mon 3/5/07	45 days		
Feasibility	Tue 1/2/07	Mon 1/15/07	2 wks		Project Manager
Concept Development	Tue 1/16/07	Mon 2/12/07	4 wks	3	Project Engineer
Project Justification	Tue 2/13/07	Mon 2/26/07	2 wks	4	Project Manager
Management Review & Approval	Tue 2/27/07	Mon 3/5/07	1 wk	5	Project Manager
Planning & Development	Tue 3/6/07	Mon 5/21/07	55 days		
Finalize Packaging Line Layout	Tue 3/6/07	Mon 4/30/07	8 wks	6	Project Engineer
Develop Bid Packages	Tue 5/1/07	Mon 5/21/07	3 wks	8	Project Engineer
Develop Equipment Packages	Tue 5/1/07	Mon 5/21/07	3 wks	8	Project Engineer
Implementation	Tue 5/22/07	Mon 11/19/07	130 days		
Award Contracts	Tue 5/22/07	Mon 6/25/07	5 wks	9	Procurement Specialist
Equipment Deliveries	Tue 5/22/07	Mon 9/10/07	16 wks	9	Project Manager
Install Equipment	Tue 9/11/07	Mon 10/22/07	6 wks	13	Contractor
Contractor Verification	Tue 10/23/07	Mon 10/29/07	1 wk	14	Project Engineer
Startup	Tue 10/30/07	Mon 11/19/07	3 wks	15	Startup Leader
Closeout/Termination	Tue 11/20/07	Mon 12/10/07	15 days		
Turnover to End User	Tue 11/20/07	Mon 11/26/07	1 wk	16	Project Manager
Post Project Evaluation	Tue 11/20/07	Tue 11/20/07	1 day	16	Project Manager
Financial Closeout	Tue 11/27/07	Mon 12/3/07	1 wk	18	Project Manager
Documentation	Tue 12/4/07	Mon 12/10/07	1 wk	20	Project Manager

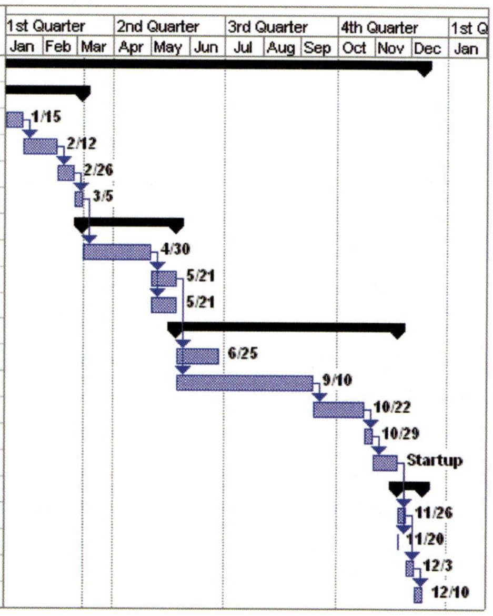

FIGURE 2.5. A Gantt chart.

brainstorming helps identify all costs, such as permits, taxes, and freight costs. Once costs are assigned to the individual tasks, account codes are developed. Most companies have predetermined account codes for such items. If not, the project manager needs to develop his or her own.

As the budget is determined for each of the tasks and subtasks on the WBS, the team should identify whether the costs are capital or operating expense items. Capital typically includes funds used to upgrade, replace, or add value to fixed assets of the company. Operating expenses typically include maintenance, repair, removal, and demolition, items that do not directly add value. Having a member on the team from the finance or accounting department is helpful at this point in the project.

If the team determines that it is developing a capital project, it will need to request capital funds through the company's normal procedure. In requesting capital funds, the team needs to prepare a business case for the project that explains why the company should invest in this project rather than in another project or even another business venture, such as an acquisition. Besides including the project's scope, schedule, and cost, the business case must describe the benefits, both quantitative and qualitative, as well as the risks involved if the project is to successfully deliver the results claimed.

Projects can improve a brewery in many ways. Sometimes a piece of equipment needs to be replaced just to maintain the current level of production or to reduce the risk of unplanned downtime. Other times, a project is needed to increase capacity, reduce operating costs, resolve a safety concern, or comply with a governmental regulation.

To allow for an analysis of the project's value to the company and to allow comparisons with other projects, the business case should provide a projection of the project's return on investment (ROI). Other methods used to determine the investment value are internal rate of return (IRR) and economic value added (EVA®; Stern Stewart & Co., New York, NY; www.sternstuart.com). A detailed analysis of any of these measurements requires a model that includes the cost of capital, depreciation implications, project life, cash flows, property taxes, income taxes, and many other considerations. The team member from the finance department can assist with the actual calculations. Before spending time on a precise determination, the project manager should do a rough estimate. That can be done by taking the annual savings provided by the project and dividing it by the project cost. For example, if a project costs $100,000 and yields annual savings of $20,000, the simple ROI is 20%. After applying a true ROI, IRR, or EVA model that includes the impact of taxes, depreciation, and inflation, the simple ROI is generally reduced by approximately one-third, so a simple ROI of 20% is closer to 13% true IRR.

Quality Management

Most project managers know the basic three constraints to every project: scope, schedule, and cost. These are three important knowledge areas in project management. However, there are seven other areas that a good project manager should understand. The first is quality management.

Quality management is composed of three areas: quality planning, quality assurance, and quality control. For a project, quality refers to the quality of the project and the project process itself, as opposed to the product quality of the beer produced. Quality planning can include determining ways to assure that the project process is done in a thorough and complete manner every time. Quality assurance is having the measurements in place to verify that the processes are following the plan. Quality control is taking action when deviations are discovered. ISO 9000 requirements are a key example of building quality into a process.

A common approach to quality assurance for projects is to use a Stage-Gate (Stage-Gate International, Ancaster, ON, Canada) or phase-gate process. In the process description, each gate is defined by the required deliverables and approvals needed for the project to pass to the next gate. If a preliminary description of operation (DOO) is required at gate three along with other preliminary design documents, the project manager will not be allowed to continue to gate four unless the preliminary DOO is acceptable to the gatekeepers. Certain defined deliverables are required at the end of each gate. If the deliverables are not approved, the project does not pass to the next gate.

Human Resource Management

Human resource management may well be one of the most challenging areas in project management. No project team can accomplish its objectives and complete the project on time and within budget if the team is not working together and performing as required. Human resource management includes planning the composition of the team, acquiring team members, and developing the team to be a successful part of the project. It also includes proper recognition of team members and dissolution of the team at the end of the project.

Developing the team organization for the project is based on the WBS. For instance, in the project WBS for a long-neck, nonreturnable bottle packaging line, the leader for each of the main tasks and subtasks needs to be identified (Fig. 2.7). The project manager can also be a task leader. Besides getting the necessary task leaders, the project manager also needs other team members who represent the various areas involved with the project. In a brewery, there is probably a separate project manager and a line manager for the new bottle line, as well as representatives from maintenance, safety, quality, engineering, and perhaps production planning. If the company has multiple facilities, there may be a central engineering group that executes projects. Their project teams may include representatives from finance, legal, procurement, marketing, or brand management. Getting the right people on a project team is critical to the project's success. Figure 2.8 shows the organization chart that represents the team structure for the long-neck bottle packaging line.

Once the right people are on a team, the next most challenging task is ensuring that all team members understand their roles and responsibilities. Roles and responsibilities can be communicated in a number of ways. One approach is simply providing each team member a written page or paragraph outlining what each is responsible for. Another way to more clearly delineate project responsibilities is by using a responsibility matrix. A responsibility matrix lists the WBS-defined tasks on the left-hand side and the key team members or stakeholders along the top of the matrix. The work or responsibility for each phase can be defined by a 1, 2, or 3. The number 1 means that the person does the work, 2 means that the person approves the work, and 3 means that the person has input to the work. Figure 2.9 presents a typical responsibility matrix.

Communication Management

Included in project communication management are areas such as communication planning, distribution of information, performance reporting, and administrative closure. For every project, the project manager should develop a communication plan. This plan may be as simple as defining when the team will meet, where it will meet, and what type of meetings it will have. Every team should have periodic regular meetings, whether it is once a day, once a week, or once a month, whatever is appropriate for the particular project. Regular team meetings keep everyone informed and everyone focused on fulfilling the project plan and meeting the schedule.

Part of a communication plan is also defining what information will be reported inside or outside the team. Items such as meeting minutes would be distributed within the team. Minutes are not always appropriate for distribution outside the team because they may include too much detail and often do not explain the entire situation. The team should consider sending all stakeholders or interested parties a monthly status report highlighting what has been accomplished during the past month and what will be accomplished during the next month. The frequency of stakeholder communication may change as the project moves to installation. Daily communication may be required during commissioning. If any part of the project begins to have problems, project leaders should

Task: **Startup**	
Duration: 3 Weeks	Predecessor: Contractor Verification
Budget: $100,000	Task Leader: **Joe Brewer**

FIGURE 2.7. Assigning a task leader in a work breakdown structure.

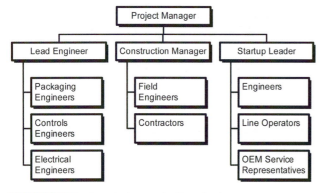

FIGURE 2.8. A project organization chart.

	Project Sponsor	Project Manager	Functional Manager	Design Engineer
Project Plan	2	1	3	3
Design		3	2	1
Team Development		1	2	3

1=Does the work
2=Approves it
3=Contributes to it

FIGURE 2.9. A responsibility matrix.

quickly communicate the issues and what is being done to correct them. It is always better to deal with problems openly than to deal with misinformation that gets out of control. The communication plan should also define the distribution of information, such as whether it should be sent via hard copy, e-mail, project website, or bulletin board.

Good communication includes having good meetings. Good meetings are well planned and have an agenda and a leader or facilitator. The meeting leader should keep an issues log that shows the outstanding issues on the project and possible resolution of those issues. Dates and accountabilities should also be assigned and tracked. At the meetings, other elements of the project plan should be reviewed to determine whether the team is still on track. Meeting minutes can be as simple as providing a list of agreements made during that meeting and a list of follow-up items.

Risk Management

Risk management is one of the most neglected areas in project management. Risk management includes risk identification, risk quantification, risk-response development, and risk-response control. As part of any project plan, the team should identify the major risks that may affect the project. Each risk should then be analyzed, and it should be determined whether the team should accept, mitigate, avoid, or transfer that risk (Fig. 2.10). For each identified risk, a plan should be developed describing what the team will do to accomplish its intended response. In the case of a mitigated response, the team should develop a contingency plan detailing what can be done to prevent or minimize the risk from occurring. If the team prefers to avoid the risk, it must determine how it is going to avoid it. Risk can be transferred to another by contractual means or perhaps by insuring against a risk. Contingency plans should be defined at the beginning of a project, and the elements that need to occur during the course of the project in order for the risk plan to succeed should all be worked into the schedule and the WBS. Throughout the project when the team meets, it should continue to review the risk-response plan and verify that the team is following the agreed-upon prescribed steps.

Procurement Management

Procurement management considers all items that need to be purchased or contracted throughout the project. Phases of procurement management include procurement planning, solicitation planning, solicitation, source selection, contract administration, and contract closeout. In procurement planning, the team should determine which items need to be purchased and how the items will be procured, e.g., by bid, negotiation, rent, or lease. When determining what is to be procured, project teams and project leaders have to decide whether to buy or lease or make a particular item that is needed. Once the team determines which items need to be procured, the next step of procurement management is solicitation planning. For the items that need to be competitively bid, the team should develop documents that specify the scope of the work to be purchased. After the scope documents and solicitation documents are completed, the items or services are issued for bid or pricing during the solicitation phase. After prices are received, source selection takes place. After the source is determined, a contract or purchase order is issued to purchase the service or equipment. Contract administration is the act of following up on the purchase order or contract to be sure that all terms and conditions are met, that deliveries are made on time, and that payments are done accordingly. The last phase of procurement management is contract closeout.

Another key area to consider during contracting and procurement is standardization. Standardization provides a number of benefits. Standardization across breweries or across packaging lines within a brewery helps to limit the number of vendors or suppliers involved in the project. It allows the purchaser to buy fewer items in larger quantities and, normally, at a lower unit price. Standardization allows for lower inventory and therefore better control of inventory. Standardization lowers the cost of procurement and receiving because there are fewer numbers of items to be handled at each stage. Standardization normally allows for quicker delivery because there are fewer items and fewer vendors to manage, reducing inventory stocking levels. Standardization also allows for a simplified design of systems and projects because there are fewer variables and those in the organization are more knowledgeable about each of the standardized items. The disadvantage

	Risk	Action	Plan
1	Equipment deliveries may be late	Mitigate risk	• Lead engineer to visit key vendors routinely to observe progress • Add penalty clauses to purchase order

FIGURE 2.10. A risk chart.

of standardization is that it may inhibit innovation by discouraging the option of trying a product or technology that is not a "standard". A balance should be struck between standardization and innovation. Every project manager needs to understand this and should review the impact of standardization with the project team and executive management.

Generally, purchased goods to be delivered at the site are procured using a purchase order. Services, such as construction, and goods that are purchased and assembled on site and work that occurs on the owner's property are usually procured using a contract.

There are three main types of contracts, with many variations of each. One is the fixed-price or lump-sum contract, the second is a cost-reimbursable contract, and the third is a time-and-material contract.

Lump-sum contracts involve a total price for a well-defined product or scope of services. In this case, the cost risk is on the contractor. The scope risk is on the owner. Simply put, the contractor has bid according to the scope documents, and if a mistake is made, the contractor bears the gain or loss of that pricing error. The owner, however, has specifically defined in the scope documents what product or services or end result he or she wants, and if the product or service does not turn out as the owner had desired, it is the owner who takes the risk. The contractor is responsible only to build or provide what is described in the scope documents. Incentives may be included in a fixed-price contract if the contractor or vendor is able to meet or exceed certain project objectives, such as a shortened schedule.

A cost-reimbursable contract involves payment or reimbursement to the contractor for the actual cost plus a markup for the contractor's overhead and profit. Costs are usually defined as direct costs, such as project labor and materials and salaries of project staff, and also as indirect costs, such as salaries of employees at the home office, the home office information system, or project controls. Indirect costs are usually calculated as a percentage of the direct costs.

The third type of contract is the time-and-material contract. In this case, the contractor is reimbursed for all his or her costs. Usually, the scope is not well defined and can be clarified during the course of the contract. The total value of the contract is not specified and increases as the work progresses. This works well for professional services, consultants, engineers, or often highway projects. Fees for professional service are usually based on hours expended for design services, etc. For highway construction projects, the unit price may be set per mile of concrete or asphalt paving. Time-and-material contracts have the most cost risk to the owner and the least risk to the contractor, since the contractor is paid for every cost incurred. Likewise, the lump-sum contracts have the most cost risk to the contractor because they have a fixed price. If the contractor forgets to price something shown in the bid documents, the contractor still has to provide it.

Stakeholder Management

Project stakeholder management "focuses on continuous communication with stakeholders to understand their needs and expectations, addressing issues as they occur, managing conflicting interest and fostering appropriate stakeholder engagement" (PMI, 2013; p. 391). Early in the project, the team should identify all stakeholders and the interests of each individual or group. A written plan should be developed on how the project team will engage and communicate with each stakeholder. Some stakeholders may need to be very involved and may be part of the decision-making process, while others may only need to be kept informed of the progress of the project.

Integration Management

Integration management is the overall planning and execution of a project and incorporates the nine other areas of project management already covered. Integration management includes development of the project plan, overall plan execution, and overall change control. Most areas of integration management are the responsibility of the project manager.

A key responsibility is developing and maintaining the project plan. The project plan is a complete overview of the project. The plan should be developed before funding is requested and it should be updated at each phase or gate of the project. The project plan is made up of several specific items.

- Scope statement
- Work breakdown structure
- Schedule
- Budget
- Definition of roles and responsibilities
- Communication plan
- Implementation strategy
- Key risk factors

Most of these items have already been covered. The one item that has not been discussed is the implementation strategy. The project plan should include a brief explanation of how the project will be carried out; what the critical constraints, such as time and budget, are; and how the project will be completed, that is, will it be sole sourced, competitively bid, done during a plant shutdown, or done during the first quarter and why. The implementation strategy should answer all of the following questions. What are the team's thoughts on getting the project done? What additional resources will be needed other than what has already been planned? What will be the sequence of testing and conversion to a new product? How will that impact inventories and distributors? Will other line downtimes be required while a new line is being built? Will there be any diversions between plants?

Once the project plan is completed, the project manager uses it for all team meetings and updates it throughout the course of the project. Few project plans remain unchanged through the life of a project. Events and situations will arise that cause the plan to change. Good project managers should be judged not on whether there are changes during the course of a project but on how they handle the changes that occur. Updates to the project plan should be distributed to all the team members as part of the communication plan. The project plan can be used throughout the life of the project to monitor the project execution. It is also a good way to quickly update new team members.

PROJECT CLOSEOUTS

As a project is completed, several things need to be done to close the project. Team members should be acknowledged, and the project's success should be celebrated. Team leaders should get feedback and develop lessons learned to pass on to future project managers and to educate team members about what activities worked well and which ones needed improvement. Feedback can be obtained by several means. A questionnaire or survey can be developed and sent to all team members, stakeholders, and other participants to get their view of how the project went. Another method is to hold a team meeting and facilitate a discussion on the project. All comments should be captured, and a lessons-learned summary should be developed. All lessons learned should be distributed to team members as well as to others in the organization. Lessons learned should not focus on what went wrong on the project but should focus on what the team would do differently on the next project and what worked well that the team would continue doing on the next project.

During the closeout phase, the actual cost, schedule, and performance should be verified and compared with the plan. Did the project accomplish its objectives? Did the project finish within budget and on schedule? Did the equipment pass the required performance tests? All contracts and purchase orders should be closed and payment to contractors verified. Final as-built drawings and descriptions of operations should be checked and filed in the appropriate document management system. Lastly, the project should be officially closed.

SUMMARY

This chapter provided an overview of project management and presented some ideas on how project managers can get started with packaging projects. To become a good project manager, one must learn the tools, techniques, and discipline of project management and then apply them in many projects. Project managers should not expect to have all the answers on their first project. Excellence in project management is a journey, and the destination will never quite be reached.

REFERENCES

Adams, J. R., Kirchof, N. S., Martin, M. D., Teagarden, C. C., Lambreth, C. F., Cavendish, P., Bilbro, C. R., Stockert, T. C., Cable, D., Dinsmore, P. C., Huettel, G. T., Campbell, B. W., Stuckenbruck, L. C., and Marshall, D. (1997). The Principles of Project Management: Collected Handbooks from the Project Management Institute. Project Management Institute, Publications Division, Sylvan, NC.

Kerzner, H. (1989). Project Management: A Systems Approach to Planning, Scheduling, and Controlling, 3rd ed. Van Nostrand Reinhold, New York.

Project Management Institute (PMI). (2013). A Guide to the Project Management Body of Knowledge, 5th ed. The Institute, Newtown Square, PA.

CHAPTER 3

Environmental Management of Brewery Operations

BECKY FRANCISCO
Miller Brewing Company (retired)

Kyoto Protocol. Global warming. Sustainable development. Regardless of the term used or whether there is total agreement on its definition, there is recognition worldwide that Earth's resources are not infinite and must be managed to sustain not only current generations but also future ones. This realization has led to the regulation of these resources by governmental agencies. Many businesses also recognize that the management of these resources, which are utilized both in manufacturing and the surrounding community, is an important consideration for business success. In addition to adhering to governmental regulations, many businesses have implemented their own programs to limit the environmental impacts of their operations. Traditionally, these resources are segregated into three broad categories: air, water, and land. The brewing industry is not without opportunities to manage operations to conserve and reduce its manufacturing impact on these resources.

● GOVERNMENTAL REGULATION

Whether it is the United States Environmental Protection Agency, Environment Canada, the Japan Ministry of Environment, or the Department of Environmental Affairs in South Africa, most countries in the world have regulatory agencies that protect the environment. These agencies regulate the quality of incoming water and determine any treatment required. They monitor wastewater discharges, air emissions, and in most instances, hazardous and nonhazardous waste disposal. Brewery operations can potentially have an impact on all of these aspects of the environment.

Incoming Water

Brewers obtain water from either municipal or public water supplies, groundwater, or surface-water sources, such as lakes or rivers. The chemical and microbiological quality of the water determines what, if any, treatment a brewery must implement to produce good brewing-quality water. Treatment processes can include filtration, softening, chlorination, reverse osmosis, and ozonation. The treatment depends on the location of the brewery and the technology available to it.

If the brewer is taking its water supply from either a municipal/public water utility or brewery-owned on-site wells, there may be regulations restricting the amount of water it can withdraw, and a permit may be required to use the water. In the regulatory world, this ensures that a water supply is available for all. To ensure that the water remains contaminant free, the municipal/public water utility is issued a permit that sets standards limiting the amount of biological, organic, and inorganic materials that can be in the treated water. Generally, brewers who purchase water from a public utility will not be required to obtain a permit to comply with these regulations.

Many brewers do not purchase water from a public utility and, instead, build their own water systems to supply water to their breweries. In addition to being used for brewing water, this water is also utilized as drinking water by brewery employees. In the event of natural disasters, breweries have also been known to bottle and provide drinking water to communities where the supply has been disrupted. Breweries that have their own water systems are required to obtain a water permit. In the United States, the permit requires the water to be treated for the following contaminants (although the list below is not inclusive).

- Microorganisms: *Cryptosporidium*, *Giardia lamblia*, *Legionella*, total coliforms (including fecal), enteric viruses
- Disinfection by-products: bromate, chlorite, haloacetic acids, total trihalomethanes
- Disinfectants: chloramines, chlorine, chlorine dioxide
- Inorganics: antimony, arsenic, asbestos, barium, cadmium, chromium, copper, cyanide, lead, mercury, nitrate, nitrite

If the brewery's water source is underground wells, additional concerns must be addressed to ensure a continuous supply of clean water. These concerns are addressed through a well-head protection plan. This plan determines

- the contaminants in the groundwater from off-site sources, such as cemeteries, petroleum facilities, and other chemical sources in the area;
- the time of travel for the contaminants to reach the brewery wells;
- the baseline withdrawal rates from the underground water source being used to determine what the impact will be if additional water withdrawers tap into the aquifer; and
- the potential future treatment that may be required because of contamination.

Wastewater Discharges

Wastewater is produced from three different areas of the brewery. Process wastewater is produced from beer production, cleaning, and support operations. Sanitary wastewater is produced from restrooms, cafeterias, and laboratories. A seldom thought about source of wastewater is storm-water discharges generated as rain or snow melt runs off the exterior surfaces of the brewery's roofs, paved and unpaved surfaces, and items stored outside the brewery, such as kegs and pallets. In some breweries, water used in cooling towers and pasteurizers is utilized once and discharged into the environment. These clear-water discharges, as well as process, sanitary, and storm-water discharges, have the potential to be regulated depending on the location of the brewery.

Similar to the handling of the water supply, breweries can discharge process and sanitary wastewater, either alone or in combination, to a municipal/public utility, or they can build their own wastewater treatment systems and discharge directly to a waterway. Municipal/public utilities are known as publicly owned treatment works (POTWs). POTWs are regulated under a permit issued by the government. These permits regulate where the wastewater can be discharged and determine the quality requirements for the wastewater and the quantity that can be discharged. Unlike using public utilities that supply water, a brewer that discharges to a POTW is generally required to have a permit issued by that entity before it can discharge to the public system. The POTW generally restricts the amount of organic material, flow, and metals that can be discharged to its wastewater treatment facilities. This ensures that the POTW, in turn, can meet the discharge requirements of its discharge permit.

Air Emissions

All breweries need vast quantities of energy for brewing beer, heating water for cleaning and pasteurization, and running equipment. Many larger breweries own their own boilers to produce steam, which is used to produce brews, clean the facility, and sometimes generate electricity through a steam-driven turbine. The fuel burned in the boilers can be fuel oil, coal, or natural gas. Air pollutants are produced when these fuels are burned. The amount of pollutants that can be discharged is regulated through government-issued air permits. Regulated air pollutants are shown in Table 3.1.

TABLE 3.1. Regulated Air Pollutants

Sulfur dioxide (SO_x)	Beryllium
Nitrogen oxides (NO_x)	Arsenic
Carbon monoxide	Reduced sulfur compounds
Volatile organic compounds	Mercury
Lead	Radionuclides
Dioxin/furan	Vinyl chloride
Fluorides	Carbon tetrachloride
Hydrogen chloride	Chlorofluorocarbons; var.[a]
Hydrogen sulfide	Hydrochlorofluorocarbons; var.
Sulfuric acid mist	Halons; var.
Total reduced sulfur	Methyl chloroform
Benzene	

[a]var. = variety of subchemical species.

Not all regulated air pollutants in a brewery are generated by burning fuel. Many brewers are not aware that volatile organic carbons (VOCs) emitted from brewing and packaging operations are also regulated. The inks used to code packages emit VOCs because of the methanol found in their formulations. Additionally, ethanol is emitted in container-filling operations. Another category often not considered is the particulate matter produced in malt-milling operations. All of the above have the potential to be regulated.

Solid and Hazardous Waste Disposal

Many wastes produced from brewing operations are also regulated. In some areas of the world, packaging wastes in the form of cans, bottles, can lids, and cardboard are banned from landfills and must be recycled. The most regulated brewery waste is hazardous waste. Hazardous wastes are either listed as hazardous, as determined by a regulatory agency, or they are categorized into four groups, each with a different characteristic, as shown in Table 3.2.

In breweries, hazardous waste can include waste ink from coding operations, laboratory wastes, batteries, and fluorescent bulbs. It is illegal to dispose of these wastes into the general trash or down a drain. They must be disposed of in regulated treatment, storage, and disposal facilities. Generally, a permit is not required to collect and outsource the proper disposal of hazardous wastes. However, a brewery may be required to register as a hazardous waste generator with a regulatory agency. Depending on the classification of the wastes, there can also be quantity restrictions and storage and labeling requirements that must be met. For example, regulatory agencies require that waste coding inks are stored in a flammable-rated, grounded drum. The drum must be labeled with the waste present, the hazardous waste category, and the date the drum was put into service. When the drum reaches 100 gallons, it must be shipped off-site within a specified period of time.

When the treatment of hazardous waste is regulated, its proper handling and disposal can be very complex. It is always recommended to investigate any requirements by contacting local, state, regional, and nationwide agencies.

● ENVIRONMENTAL MANAGEMENT

The need to protect the environment has not only resulted in the creation of government-enforced regulations but also in brewer-implemented environmental management systems. These systems seek to protect and conserve resources needed to maintain operations as well as to secure the resources for use by all members of the community in which the breweries operate. From microbreweries to large breweries, most all brewers have implemented some program to conserve resources and measure the program's success against specific goals. These programs and processes and the goals they are to meet are published in annual reports, which are becoming more accessible through the Internet.

Environmental Management Systems in Breweries

Numerous environmental management systems have been developed and prepackaged for use in breweries. One standardized system is ISO 14001. It sets very specific processes and standards for record keeping that must be maintained. Upon successful completion of implementation, breweries can become ISO 14001

TABLE 3.2. Hazardous Wastes

Characteristic	Description	Areas of Concern in the Brewery
Reactivity	Wastes that readily explode or undergo violent reactions (i.e., munitions)	Not normally found in a brewery
Toxicity	Wastes that are likely to leach chemicals into underground drinking water supplies	Wastewater treatment sludges, ash from coal, mercury and mercury-contaminated containers, batteries, lubricants, fluorescent bulbs
Ignitability	Wastes that readily catch fire and sustain combustion	Coding inks and ink-cleanup solutions, laboratory wastes containing methanol or ethanol
Corrosives	Acidic or alkaline wastes that can easily corrode or dissolve flesh, metal, or other materials	Batteries (including lift trucks), waste sulfuric acid, sodium hydroxide, hydrochloric acid (usually generated when contaminated and cannot be utilized for original use in the brewery)

certified. Since this certification is recognized worldwide, some breweries choose this system to demonstrate their commitment to their local and international consumers. Many environmental consultant businesses have also developed software to assist in developing management systems. However, developing and implementing an environmental management system does not have to be as detailed as the ISO standard or require investment in consulting services. An effective plan can be developed in-house using the brewery's existing resources.

Planning and Executing

When planning an environmental management system, brewers must determine why they are implementing a management system. Usually, brewers implement one as a means of ensuring compliance with regulations and preventing pollution from operations. Once brewers determine "why" they need a system, appropriate resources can be identified and a team formed to create an action plan to determine the targets and objectives, procedures and corrective actions, and method to audit the program. The best results are obtained when there is vigorous employee participation.

To establish targets and objectives, the team must determine a baseline that identifies brewery processes that contribute to environmental impacts and to what extent. In the environmental regulatory world, this is called identifying your environmental aspects and determining which are significant. This analysis is performed by considering the inputs and outputs of each brewery operation as a balance of materials, and the analysis should include both brewing and packaging operations as well as support functions, such as utilities operations and laboratory processes. Table 3.3 shows elements to be considered in determining a baseline for a typical brewery.

After obtaining the baseline data, goals can then be determined for the higher impact operations in the

TABLE 3.3. Operations Environmental Aspects Examples

Activity	Environmental Aspect	Reduction Strategy	Key Performance Indicator
Grain handling	Air pollution from particulate matter generated by malt milling Storm water contamination from grain spillage Waste grain disposal	Inspect and maintain malt-milling systems, especially bag houses Malt mill maintenance Contaminant areas or berms around unloading area Sell for use as animal feed	Numbers per barrel brewed or numbers generated per week Income per ton
Water management	Water usage	Inspection and maintenance of steam and condensate lines Optimize cleaning-in-place system cycles	Barrels used per barrels produced
Yeast and wort handling and transfer	High-strength wastewater—possible permit violation or contamination of receiving water body if direct discharge	Standard operating procedures developed and followed Inspection and maintenance of equipment	Wort loss to fermentation
DE, kieselguhr, or other filter aid management	Spent filter aid: wastes Particulate matter	Dispose of waste per regulations Discharge to brewery-owned wastewater treatment plant, if using an aerobic system, and dispose with sludge Use bag houses to capture particulate matter	Numbers per barrel produced
Filling operations	Beer spillage: wastewater	Bowl level control	Percent loss
Pasteurization	Increased water usage	Maintain water balance Repair and maintain steam system	Barrels of water per barrel of beer

brewery. Many breweries measure impacts based on barrels produced. For example, a brewery's baseline data may indicate that it is using 5.0 barrels of water, 15.0 kWh of energy, and 2 tons of waste for every barrel of beer produced. The brewery would then set reduction goals based on these metrics. These metrics are known as the key performance indicators (KPIs).

Once the goals are determined, the environmental team then needs to establish how to reach the goals. One means of achieving these goals is always employee education. Training programs can train employees on how their jobs impact the environmental performance of the brewery and how that performance impacts the community.

From an operations aspect, another approach is to implement or maintain an asset management program. This is an under-considered means for improving environmental performance. When air systems are not maintained and leak, more energy is expended in obtaining the same performance as a well-maintained system. When the filler-bowl level is not maintained, waste beer is produced that becomes part of the wastewater discharge. When production lines start and stop due to jams, when line flow is impacted by worn conveyors and sprockets, or when machinery is not set up correctly, not only is more energy expended in taking more time to produce beer but also more waste is created from rejected packaging materials. Water usage becomes excessive when pasteurizers are not maintained and water flows are not kept in balance. Usage is further increased by failing to maintain steam and condensate systems that supply brewing steam and hot water for cleaning-in-place systems. It is not enough to operate machinery according to the manufacturer's directions. Machinery must be maintained in order to obtain the best operating efficiencies, which in turn minimize energy and water usage and waste generated.

Measuring

KPIs are used to create a baseline that shows what a brewery's environmental impacts are and allows brewers to measure results against goals. However, another important use of the KPI is for short-interval control. By reviewing the KPIs on a weekly or daily basis, a brewery can determine whether any systems are becoming less efficient and causing increasing environmental impacts. A brewery that measures water usage on a weekly basis can quickly discover changes in usage. For example, if a brewery sees an increase in water usage from 4.0 to 5.0 brewer's barrels (bbl)/bbl, this information would prompt the brewery to investigate the cause and correct the problem to bring water usage back in line.

A properly executed environmental management system will continuously check and react to trends that impact the brewery's ability to manage environmental impacts. While there are several approaches, a short-interval control system can be very effective.

● REDUCING ENVIRONMENTAL IMPACTS: CAPITAL INVESTMENT

Many technologies reduce usage of water, electricity, and fossil fuels from brewing operations, as well as treat wastewater so that it is of an acceptable quality to discharge into waterways. These technologies usually require a substantial capital investment. Whether privately owned or publicly traded, breweries must carefully evaluate the investment in these technologies to determine whether they will realize a good return. If the investment is required to meet regulatory requirements, the return is the continued operations of the brewery. However, if the investment is to reduce an environmental impact, the return can be harder to justify financially.

One technology that has gained increasing acceptance in breweries is anaerobic wastewater treatment. Anaerobic wastewater treatment plants cost less to operate and maintain than do aerobic wastewater treatment plants. They also produce a by-product—methane biogas—that can be utilized in either natural gas- or coal-fired boilers or can be burned in biogas engines to generate electricity.

Anaerobic wastewater treatment is the biological treatment of wastewater without utilizing air or oxygen. In this process, anaerobic microorganisms convert the organic constituents of the wastewater to produce treated wastewater, methane gas, and carbon dioxide:

$$\text{organic pollution} + \text{anaerobic microorganisms} = CO_2 + CH_4 \text{ (biogas)}$$

For breweries with limited real estate in which to install wastewater treatment systems, the smaller footprint of the anaerobic wastewater treatment plant provides an advantage over an aerobic-activated sludge wastewater plant.

With the installation of an anaerobic plant, breweries are able to treat wastewater to meet the standards required and to use the energy produced to offset either electrical or fossil fuel usage. As the costs for fossil fuels and electricity increase, a return on this capital investment is easier to justify. Additional savings can also be realized from decreased sewage charges if the brewery is paying a municipal wastewater treatment plant to treat its discharges. If a brewery currently operates an aerobic wastewater treatment plant and replaces it with an anaerobic plant, additional savings can also be realized from decreased staffing, decreased electrical usage (since blowers are not required), decreased chemical costs (since sludge no longer needs to be conditioned for pressing), and decreased sludge disposal costs. These savings may further justify the capital investment.

Although not commonly found in breweries, solar panels are a technology that has just started to grow. Solar panels collect sunlight and convert it to either electricity or heat. Advances in the technology have created lighter-weight panels that can be installed on roofs without penetrating them. Since many panels are required to generate the electricity required by breweries, the lighter weight and ease of maintenance that the new technologies provide ensure that roofs are not damaged and their life expectancy is not diminished.

Unfortunately, the capital cost for solar panels is very high and difficult to justify with just the cost savings realized from reduced electrical usage. In the United States, there are government regulations requiring electric companies to use a certain percentage of green energy within their distribution systems. For the utility company, one way to meet the regulatory requirement is to offer incentives to its commercial and industrial customers to install the panels themselves. These types of incentives can be in the form of rebates or tax relief.

These incentives are offered not only by utility companies but also by various states and the federal government. And they are not restricted to just the installation of solar technologies. Incentives are also offered for the installation of biogas projects (anaerobic treatment described above), fuel cells, and wind and geothermal technologies. A concise list of incentives available from the states, utilities, and federal government can be found at the Database of State Incentives for Renewables & Efficiency website.

● SUMMARY

Regardless of where a brewery operates in the world, natural resources to support the operation are becoming less available or more expensive because of the demands placed on the breweries by the communities and regions in which they operate. These natural resources include clean water, fossil fuels, and the land to support them.

In order to conserve resources and reduce the environmental impact of brewery facilities, breweries can implement an environmental management system. The key steps to implementation are identifying the processes that impact the environment, measuring them, and then establishing KPIs that allow measurement of the impact of improved system operations and tracking of the processes that are getting out of control.

Further reduction of environmental impacts can be achieved through capital investments. Some investments are easily justifiable in terms of their return on investment, while justifying other investments can be more challenging. To reduce the capital costs of installing environmental management systems, federal, state, and local governments as well as utility companies may offer incentives in the way of rebates or tax relief. All possible funding avenues should be explored to determine whether capital offsets can be found.

REFERENCES FOR FURTHER READING

Field, J., and Sierra, R. (2005). Anaerobic granular sludge bed technology pages. www.uasb.org

Kawasaki, Y., and Kondo, H. (2005). Challenges in the brewing business in Japan toward an environmentally friendly company. Tech. Q. Master Brew. Assoc. Am. 42:107-112.

Kinton, K. (1999). Environmental issues affecting brewery operations. In: The Practical Brewer, 3rd ed. pp. 611-646. J. T. McCabe, ed. Master Brewers Association of the Americas, St. Paul, MN.

National Association of EHS Management. (2007). NAEM Network News. Fall 2007. The Association, Washington, DC.

North Carolina State University. (2013). Database of State Incentives for Renewables & Efficiency. www.dsireusa.org

Perron, P. (2003). Future challenges and opportunities for the brewing industry: European Brewery Convention/The Brewers of Europe joint session. May 2003. Vol. 61, No. 7.

U.S. Environmental Protection Agency. (2011). RCRA Orientation Manual. EPA530-F-11-003. www.epa.gov/wastes/inforesources/pubs/orientat

U.S. Environmental Protection Agency. Environmental Management Systems. www.epa.gov/ems

Vorne, R. A. (2007). KPIs from a lean perspective: Achieve goals, reduce waste. Plant Eng. 2007(7):49-59.

CHAPTER 4

Packaging Line Design, Control, and Instrumentation

ROBERT SEAMAN
D.G. Yuengling and Son Inc.

In modern breweries, instrumentation and controls are essential to ensuring the highest levels of productivity, operator safety, and product quality. Competition has forced new and innovative methods of keeping costs down, including techniques that allow brewing in larger quantities and packaging at higher speeds while using fewer personnel. Government regulations have promoted the use of automation to remove personnel from potentially dangerous operations, and new safety rules continually challenge the creativeness of equipment manufacturers and packaging engineers to meet these new requirements. An added emphasis on consumer satisfaction has raised the industry's awareness of product quality as well as its concern with the consumer appeal of the finished package.

The electronics revolution that has taken place since the late 1970s has had a significant impact on industry, and breweries have been no exception. Traditional mechanical-electrical instruments and controls no longer meet the expectations of results in milliseconds. Management has come to expect data to be presented in charts, graphs, and reports, all of which require modern techniques to gather and process production data. Solid state has become a way of life.

At the end of the day, however, the goal is to run packaging lines as efficiently as possible while meeting safety, product quality, and fiscal objectives. This is the challenge of the new packaging department employee. The competition to be the low-cost producer is fierce internationally, nationally, and within companies. Anyone considering working in a packaging department job must be prepared for the challenge, since packaging is typically the area where profitability can be lost very quickly.

Instrumentation and controls are key to the performance of a packaging line or department. While used extensively throughout breweries, instrumentation and controls in packaging departments help ensure that a quality product is produced at the lowest possible cost. When specified correctly, installed as recommended, and set up appropriately, these value-added pieces of equipment and software can positively affect quality in most any process.

The packaging department in most breweries is where the major labor, material, and utility costs are, and therefore, this is generally the area of the greatest financial focus from upper management. Also, the ability to meet customer demands for product is typically dependent on the packaging department's ability to meet production schedules.

This chapter provides an overview of packaging line control and design in the hopes of introducing it to new packaging employees and helping to further develop the skills of experienced employees. The chapter covers topics universal to large, national breweries as well as to small brewpubs. Where there are exceptions pertaining to breweries of different scales, options that may make it more practical and affordable, either alone or in combination, to accomplish the process control goals are presented.

When designing a line, the important process parameters to control, indicate, and record must be communicated to the packaging and controls engineers designing the line's instrumentation and controls and the packaging systems. It is extremely important to have this information up front. This data must be considered carefully in the design stages to ensure that the systems do not include useless functions or lack critical capabilities. In the end, the quality of communications dictates how well the control and packaging systems will be designed and implemented.

Regardless of the size of the brewery, brewers must know their business to the point that they can talk intelligently about their needs and expectations. Will the brewery need to expand and add additional equipment, controls, or both to the packaging line in the future? How much will it need to expand? What method will be used to add additional equipment or controls? If an outside engineering firm makes these decisions without input, the brewer may end up paying an excessive amount for something that does not accomplish what is needed. The brewery may also end up being constrained by a system that is not easily expandable or flexible enough to meet future needs.

So, what are the packaging line options available for brewpubs, microbrewers, and regional and national brewers? This chapter addresses this question and others, including considerations of packaging line design, line flow control, and packaging line process control.

● PACKAGING LINE DESIGN

To fully understand the control of packaging line flow, brewery operators must first appreciate what the line and its components are intended to accomplish. They must also understand the thought process informing packaging line design in order to appreciate the full scope of the challenges and opportunities in this area.

A packaging line is a series of machines connected by way of a network of case, bottle, or can conveyors with the objective of producing a quality product at the highest level of productivity and safety. Obviously, when building a packaging line, certain pieces of equipment, such as uncasers, fillers, and labelers, are required. How different machines are connected with conveyors and controls chiefly determines how well the line performs. The assembly of these machines to meet packaging line objectives is the challenge of the packaging engineer.

Concepts Behind Line Design and Control

Line design and how different machines are interconnected with conveyors and controls is a prime factor in determining how well the line performs. Line design generally varies from company to company, that is, individual brewers may have differing views or experiences that dictate how they approach the line design and the equipment that is selected. The real world issues that each brewer faces around the physical space available for a packaging line and the budget that goes along with it will have a direct impact on the design and the final production results of the line. Since theories on machine speed, accumulation, and conveyor speeds are as varied as the brewers themselves, no attempt is made in this chapter to discuss any particular design. Rather, some basic steps and general rules of thumb for line design are presented.

Equipment Selection

The filler is generally the critical machine on brewery packaging lines, and within the chapter, this will be the case. Line speed is based on filler speed, and the primary goal is to keep the filler running. This means that to meet quality specifications and achieve maximum throughput on the packaging line, it is essential to keep the filler running within reasonable costs.

On brewery packaging lines, the filler is generally the focal point and should be the slowest piece of equipment on the line. The nominal filler speed, which, as mentioned, also becomes the line speed, should be based on the speed guaranteed by the manufacturer and one at which the filler operates efficiently.

After the desired filler line speed has been determined, the selection of equipment upstream and downstream can begin. One of the major factors in selecting equipment is how fast each piece of equipment before and after the filler should be capable of running. As you move upstream of the filler, the rinser should be capable of running 10–15% faster than the filler. In turn, the uncaser or depalletizer that feeds the rinser should be capable of running 10–15% faster than the rinser, etc., etc. Likewise, the labeler that the filler feeds should be capable of running 10–15% faster than the filler. The packer that the labeler in turn feeds should be capable of running 10–15% faster than the labeler and so on. Obviously, it is assumed that the machine availability or operating efficiencies of each piece of equipment is very similar to that of the filler. If the efficiency is significantly lower than that of the filler, then an even higher speed capability beyond 10–15% may be desired.

Accumulation

Accumulation on a packaging line is expressed in time. The time (or accumulation) provided between each machine is critical to packaging line flow and efficiency. To compensate for the fact that each machine has a less-than-100% availability and that many of the faults or stops are microstops, accumulation is necessary between most machines on the packaging line. Because conveyors transport containers between each machine, some accumulation is inherent to the line. However, to ensure good line flow and efficient line operation, a precalculated amount of accumulation is required.

There are two basic techniques for inserting accumulation into a packaging line. The first technique is to use an accumulation table. An accumulation table is simply a wide conveyor that is connected and placed perpendicular to another conveyor. When containers back up on the conveyor, the accumulation table takes containers away from the conveyor and stores them on the table. When the conveyor is no longer backed up, the table begins to convey containers onto the conveyor and empty itself. One downside of using an accumulation table is that the first containers onto the table are the last containers off. Accumulation tables are also notorious for causing down containers on a packaging line, necessitating more maintenance on dead plates.

Dynamic accumulation is another method for managing line flow. In dynamic accumulation, very wide conveyors that allow more containers to be accumulated on the line between machines are installed. This is the modern, preferred method to install accumulation because it allows containers to move constantly toward the next downstream machine and causes many fewer down containers and less maintenance.

Why is accumulation needed? Imagine that all machines on the line are directly connected to each other with no conveyors between each machine. This means that, any time any one machine on the packaging line stops, the rest of the packaging line also stops. If it is considered that the availability of any machine on the line is less than 100%, then the potential maximum line production can be calculated by multiplying each machine's availability by each other. So, for example, each machine's availability might be as follows:

machine 1's availability = 98%
machine 2's availability = 97%
machine 3's availability = 98% (filler)
machine 4's availability = 92%
machine 5's availability = 99%
machine 6's availability = 90%
machine 7's availability = 98%

The potential maximum line production is calculated as

$0.98 \times 0.97 \times 0.98 \times 0.92 \times 0.99 \times 0.90 \times 0.98 = 74.8\%$

This demonstrates that, with the availabilities of each machine being what they are and with no accumulation between machines, the best that the line can possibly run from an efficiency point of view is 74.8%. However, it is conceivable that, by adding enough accumulation between each of the above pieces of equipment, a brewer could compensate for all these less-than-perfect availabilities, except for the filler contribution. From a practical point of view, the cost of accumulation and packaging line layout space limits the amount of accumulation that can be installed on a packaging line. This is a real-world fact influencing a packaging line's final design, and it ultimately affects the line's production capability. With enough accumulation added, a production line could produce at an efficiency of 98%, which is the availability of the filler in this scenario. This large amount of accumulation would make this type of efficiency possible.

This observation relates directly to the importance of machine availability. By ensuring that all machines on the line maintain a high state of availability, line operators can eliminate the need for a large amount of accumulation. The higher each machine's availability, the less accumulation is needed to account for that machine's faults.

Any properly designed packaging line incorporates the manufacturer-given machine availabilities of the equipment installed on the line. It is critical to maintain those specified machine availabilities as a minimum; otherwise, the originally calculated accumulation will not be sufficient to support the originally specified line performance.

Determining the amount of accumulation or container storage space to build in between various pieces of equipment is not quite as simple as following the rules for machine speed. For instance, imagine a very short packaging line with pieces of equipment placed end to end without accumulation in between. Basically, this is a one-for-one line flow, that is, one bottle is uncased and gets passed to the rinser. Then the rinser feeds the bottle directly to the filler, etc. The line would have the advantage of being very compact and relatively inexpensive but the disadvantage of being very inefficient since, when any machine stops, the entire line stops. To eliminate the delays experienced on one-for-one lines, accumulation, or the ability to store product between workstations, is essential to controlling the line flow and necessary for the efficient operation of the line. Rules for how much accumulation to place between pieces of equipment can be calculated based on previous equipment reliability through experience or on manufacturer-specified machine availability acquired prior to the purchase of the equipment. This information should be considered along with line layout, the actual physical room, and the amount of capital available to purchase and install accumulation. Generally speaking, the more accumulation the better, but in each situation, there is an economically ideal amount of accumulation.

Machine Speeds

Machine speed set points and their proper functioning are an absolute critical parameter of the packaging line. The machine speed set points need to be set correctly, maintained, and verified to be functioning properly on a regular basis. The speeds of packaging line machines can be set in several different ways, depending on whether they are a on-demand machine or a modulating machine.

On-Demand Machines

On-demand machines have only two speeds. They either run at their maximum speed or are stopped. Good examples of these types of machines are depalletizers, drop packers, and palletizers. These machines come with a speed-capability rating. For example, a depalletizer on a can line may run at a rate of 1,500 cans per minute (cpm). The depalletizer is rated at 2,200 cpm. This means that the depalletizer runs only 68% of the time under normal conditions and is stopped the remainder of the time. This time percentage can be calculated as follows.

(1,500 cpm/2,200 cpm) × 100 = 68% run time

Running on an on-and-off basis is not harmful to the depalletizer since it generally just means that the sweep arm sits and waits for the machine's discharge conveyor to be cleared of cans before it sweeps again. The same holds true for a palletizer and the drop packers. It is not harmful to these machines to sit and wait for packages to run.

Modulating Machines

Modulating machines vary considerably from on-demand machines. These types of machines typically are programmed to run on three speeds. The first is low speed, the second is called run speed, and the third is high speed. Several requirements must be met before the machine will run at any of these particular speeds.

In a typical machine speed control design, several sensors are placed upstream of the machine to sense the population of containers on the conveyor (Fig. 4.1). The sensor setup consists of a prime sensor, which is used to ensure that there are a minimum number of containers upstream or on the infeed of the machine, allowing it to keep running. Once the prime sensor becomes uncovered and there are no containers in front of it, the machine stops. Once the machine stops, the infeed conveyor continues to run. When the prime sensor becomes covered again, the machine still does not start up immediately. First, the containers must back up to the next sensor upstream of the prime sensor, which is the low-speed sensor. Once the prime sensor and the low-speed sensor are covered, the machine runs in low speed. Low speed is set to the slowest speed at which the machine can still produce a quality product. If, with the machine running in low speed, containers continue to back up farther upstream, the containers eventually back up to the run-speed sensor, which is upstream of the low-speed sensor. If containers back up to the run-speed sensor, the machine then functions in run speed. The run-speed set point is usually set at about 5% greater than the filler speed set point. By setting the machine run speed to a rate that is slightly faster than the filler speed, the machine then cycles between run speed and low speed. This keeps the machine at speeds that do not push its limits from a quality or maintenance point of view. If containers continue to back up when the machine is in run speed, then the containers will back up to the high-speed sensor, which places the machine into high speed. This would typically happen when the machine shuts down momentarily for a problem or another machine shuts off downstream because of some type of a problem. High speed is typically set to the highest speed that the machine can run and still produce a quality product.

Some machines have a fourth speed called surge speed. Surge speed is used on machines that run in parallel and

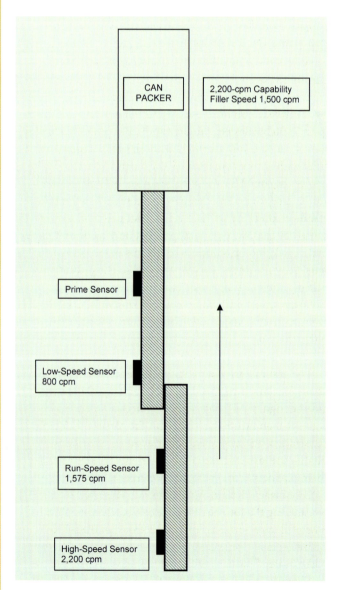

FIGURE 4.1. Infeed control sensors on a can line's variable-speed packer. cpm = cans per minute. (Courtesy R. Seaman)

are typically not capable of running at the filler speed by themselves. Labelers are excellent examples of these kinds of machines. With two labelers running in parallel, each labeler has a low, run, and high speed. Each of these speeds is set so that the labelers each handle 50% of the total throughput. However, if one of the labelers stops running, the other labeler is programmed to run on surge speed. This is typically not the full filler speed but is faster than high speed and helps to reduce filler stops and increases the accumulation time between the filler and the labeler.

Conveyor Speeds

Conveyor speeds are no less critical to the packaging line than are the machine speeds themselves. An inappropriate speed setting on one conveyor can affect the efficiency of the complete line's operation. Conveyors operating at proper speeds not only ensure that containers are taken away from one machine and delivered to the next but they also keep all machines running steadily.

The speed at which conveyors should run can be partially based on machine speeds. For example, if a filler runs 1,000 bottles per minute (bpm), the conveyors feeding it must run a minimum of 1,000 bpm just to supply the filler with empty containers. How much faster should the conveyors run? This question has no one single answer since, in setting conveyor speed, factors such as container stability, container friction coefficient, potential damage caused by the conveyor (e.g., product denting or breakage, and noise), and up-sloping and down-sloping conveyors must be considered. However, a good starting point and rule of thumb is that, in the case of a filler running at 1,000 bpm, accumulation conveyors should be capable of running from 1,400 to 1,600 bpm. As mentioned, this is only a starting point. Methods for optimizing these speeds are discussed later in this chapter.

The vast majority of packaging lines incorporate the above four machine speed control elements. Computer-aided design (CAD) engineers lay out equipment and conveyors on prints that fit within the physical building constraints, and engineers and executives review and modify the layouts based on equipment characteristics, their experience, and personal preference.

Often when designing new lines, in addition to considering the four elements discussed, designers find it helpful to review existing installations to determine optimum machine speeds and accumulation. Engineers make in-depth studies of a machine or series of machines to determine the causes of line delays. Delays are classified as upstream, internal, or downstream delays and are used to calculate an overall machine efficiency or reliability.

With this information, engineers can make adjustments in machine speeds and accumulation to minimize these delays in new designs. One main drawback to this method is that it is impossible to look at the entire line at one time because of the complexity of the machines interfacing with each other. An entire line cannot be manually simulated at one time. This approach to improving line design is also extremely time-consuming.

PACKAGING LINE FLOW CONTROL

Packaging line flow control is central to ensuring the desired line efficiency, quality parameters, and safe operation of packaging lines. A great deal of the theory of line control focuses on motor controls via start/stop circuitry and speed control. A typical high-level list of modern line control components would consist of programmable logic controllers (PLCs), variable frequency drives (VFDs), motor starters, proximity sensors, solenoid valves, temperature controllers, pressure switches, and flow meters. All of these components should be affordable for even the smallest brewery.

Packaging line control systems are intended to ensure that the filler runs the maximum amount of time possible while the upstream and downstream machines react appropriately so that the filler continues to run. Good line flow is critical to the efficient operation of the packaging line, as a result reducing the oxygen content in packages, maintaining consistent minimum pasteurization units, and ensuring precise fills.

Line Flow

The interaction between the machines, the conveyors, and the packages they handle is referred to as line flow. The term "flow" in this sense does not simply mean getting the container from machine to machine and eventually into a case and off the line. Rather, flow is the interaction of machine speeds, accumulation, conveyor speeds, and control that permits the line and its machines to operate in a smooth and continuous fashion.

As mentioned, the filler is the focal point of the line, and the purpose of the line controls is to keep the filler running. To achieve this, all equipment before, or upstream of, the filler must provide a continuous line of containers, and all equipment downstream must continually take them away from the filler. This is where machine speeds, accumulation, and conveyor speeds become critical. Consider a simple situation in which a rinser immediately upstream of the filler feeds directly to the filler, as pictured in Figure 4.2. If the filler speed is 1,000 bpm and the accumulation between the two holds 3,000 bottles, based on the rule of thumb for equipment speeds, the rinser should be capable of running 10–15% faster than the filler or approximately 1,100 bpm minimum. Imagine now that the two machines run independently of the rest of the machines on the line. The rinser has all the bottles needed to run, and the filler has no downstream delays. As the two machines begin to run, the rinser produces bottles 100-bpm faster than the filler is taking them away. The excess is stored, or accumulated, in the area between the two machines. If this condition exists for 10 minutes and then the rinser experiences a fault, what would happen? Since the rinser has been running at a 100-bpm advantage for 10 minutes, there must be 1,000 bottles stored in the accumulation area or queue. When the rinser stops, the filler continues to run by using the bottles stored in the accumulation area. With 1,000 bottles stored and the filler running at 1,000 bpm, the accumulation could absorb a delay of up to 1 minute at the rinser before the filler would run out of bottles. When the rinser starts, it would again begin filling the accumulation at a rate of 100 bpm. These bottles would continue to be stored until the accumulation area is filled or until the next instance of rinser delay, at which time the filler must again call on the accumulation area to supply it with bottles.

This basic example illustrates how accumulation and overspeed prior to the filler work to maximize filler efficiency. It is important to note that conveyors upstream of the filler are typically designed to remain 100% populated whenever possible. With the rinser capable of running at 1,100 bpm once all of its associated accumulation is full, the rinser would ideally then run at the same speed as the filler until another need to run faster exists.

Obviously, this example illustrates that more overspeed and more accumulation are advantageous. Theoretically, a rinser running infinitely fast with infinite accumulation between it and the filler would never cause filler downtime because of its delays. However, in reality, there are practical limits to how fast equipment can run and how much accumulation can be provided. Generally speaking, the faster a piece of equipment runs, the more subject it is to faults and loss of performance. Eventually, a break-even point is reached between overspeed and reliability, and beyond this point, any increase in speed is offset by additional machine downtime.

A similar situation exists in accumulation. Accumulation costs money in the addition of conveyors or accumulation tables and requires the physical space to house this equipment. Again, with accumulation, there is a break-even point, that is, there is a point at which the cost of adding accumulation is not justified by a greater savings in decreased downtime for the filler. It is also important to note that it is desirable to keep all conveyors upstream of the filler as full as possible at all times. This ensures maximum accumulation for the filler to draw from if needed.

Consider now a situation after the filler, as shown in Figure 4.3. If the same filler running at 1,000 bpm feeds a labeler, which by rule of thumb is capable of running at 1,100 bpm, there will be 3,000 bottles of accumulation between the two units. (For the purposes of this example, the pasteurizer between the two machines will be omitted, since this is actually a slow-moving, nonaccumulating conveyor.) As the machines run with all of the designed accumulation available, bottles are being fed from the filler to the labeler at a rate of 1,000 bpm, and the labeler, with a speed-capability advantage of 1,100 bpm, also is running at 1,000 bpm. Now imagine that the labeler experiences a 2-minute delay. What would happen? The filler would continue to run and the bottles would be stored in the accumulation area upstream of the labeler. After the 2-minute delay, the labeler would resume running, and the filler would experience no downtime. Also, the labeler would now run at 1,100 bpm, eliminating the 2 minutes of accumulation created by the labeler being down. This overspeed would eventually empty out the bottles accumulated during the downtime and make room for accumulation during future delays. It is essential to note

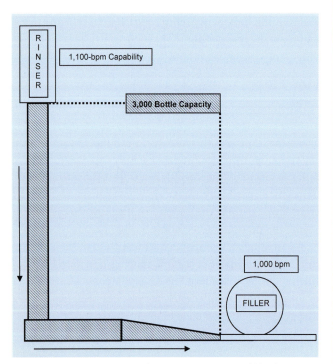

FIGURE 4.2. Rinser supplying containers to a filler. bpm = bottles per minute. (Courtesy R. Seaman)

that the general rule of thumb and design theory is to keep all conveyors downstream of the filler 50% empty under normal line flow conditions.

These very simple examples present the two opposite applications of overspeed and accumulation on the same packaging line. For equipment upstream of the filler, the objective is to keep the accumulation area full, whereas the use of overspeed downstream of the filler is intended to keep the accumulation area empty. Both are essential to keeping the filler running at maximum efficiency.

Maintaining optimum conveyor speeds is also necessary to maximizing line performance. Conveyors that run too slowly extend line downtime, while conveyors that run too fast actually create line downtime. The rule of thumb for conveyor speeds is that they should be capable of running 40–60% faster than the machine they are feeding. This is referred to as "catch-up speed" and serves to reduce the effect of machine downtime on the downstream machine. In the case of the rinser–filler discussed previously, the shorter the travel time along the conveyors between the two machines, the longer the rinser can be down and still catch up to the filler without interrupting production. However, increasing conveyor speed to the point of causing tipped containers, broken glass, excessive noise, and excessive maintenance results in more downtime and serves only to reduce filler efficiency. Generally speaking, the 40–60% capability rule of thumb is a good place to start but often the optimum conveyor speeds can be attained only by adjusting speeds in the field.

There are two schools of thought on line control, and most line operators follow one or a combination of both to maximize line performance. The first method divides the line into control units, or domains. Pieces of equipment are grouped together based on their interaction with each other. Consider the section of line in Figure 4.4. The labeler and its immediate infeed and discharge conveyors are considered to be part of one control unit, that is, since to function properly, the labeler must control these conveyors, they are in the same domain. The next control unit is the section of the bottle conveyor from the labeler discharge to the packer infeed. In this section, the conveyors are allowed to control themselves. Based on the number of containers on the conveyor, sensors determine whether containers are full or if there is demand for product at the packer and cycle the conveyors accordingly. The packer, along with its immediate infeed and discharge conveyors, is the next unit. Again, the packer

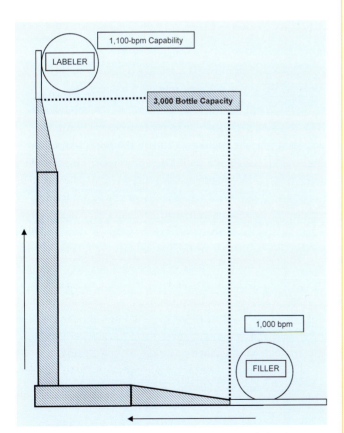

FIGURE 4.3. Filler supplying containers to a labeler. bpm = bottles per minute. (Courtesy R. Seaman)

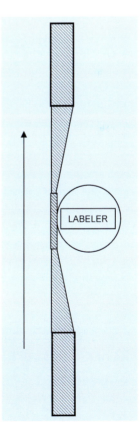

FIGURE 4.4. Labeler divided into a domain with its infeed and discharge conveyors. (Courtesy R. Seaman)

must control these conveyors to function properly. Some control unit's sensors may extend beyond their domain for the purpose of controlling the unit. In this example, the labeler no doubt has sensors downstream of the conveyor's domain to warn it of a backup or a jam. Also, the packer has sensors located upstream of the conveyor's domain relaying information on speed, e.g., how many containers have accumulated and therefore how fast the packer should run. In each case, sensors cross boundaries; however, the actual control ability of each unit is still limited to that unit's domain.

The "control unit" approach has the advantage of being quite simple to understand and, therefore, easy to troubleshoot when problems occur. Set rules can be established as to how machinery and conveyors will operate, and these rules can reduce the confusion that may result from complicated controls. The disadvantage of this system is that it only works on lines where domains are easily defined. On shorter, more-compact lines, domains often are not clear-cut, and the control scheme becomes more complicated.

The second approach to line control utilizes control overlap. Often referred to as "anticipate and command", this approach uses direct signals to and from pieces of equipment, often in lieu of line sensors, to achieve flow and maximize production. Most often found on shorter lines, this type of control generally is used to compensate for a lack of accumulation between pieces of equipment. Anticipate and command is often employed to eliminate machine cycling after a line restart. In these instances, after a backup between two machines, the downstream unit signals the upstream unit that is has restarted. The upstream unit then neglects its downstream sensors and begin production. This early start reduces or eliminates the usual gap that occurs in restart and allows the downstream machine to run continuously.

The disadvantage of this type of control is that circuits often are extremely complicated, difficult to understand, and time-consuming to troubleshoot. However, anticipate and command control permits engineers to compensate for physical problems, such as conveyor layouts, lack of accumulation, and speed limitations, and lets them achieve acceptable line performance.

Building Blocks of Good Line Flow

Good line flow starts with the proper design of the packaging line. To understand packaging line controls, it is critical to understand what they need to accomplish. Some of the considerations that go into designing packaging lines are the space available to install the line, the types of packages to be run, the speeds to be run, machine availability, and the number of operators to be employed, just to name a few.

Machine Availability

In the perfect world, each machine would be 100% reliable, and each component on the packaging line would never fail and would never stop during normal production, except for changeovers. Realistically, however, all machines have less than 100% availability, and each component of each machine has a limited lifespan and reliability.

Machine availability is defined as how well a particular machine is performing in a given period of time. It is the ratio of the total machine fault time to the total machine operating time that it should have been in service. This can essentially be expressed as percent availability.

percent availability = (fault time/run time) × 100

A machine fault or, more specifically, an internal machine fault would be anything that shuts down the machine that was not caused by an upstream or downstream fault source, such as a lack of containers on the infeed or containers backed up on the discharge. For instance, an internal machine fault could be a carrier misfeed on the machine, an operator pressing the stop button, a down container in the machine, or a machine motor overload.

Machine availability is a critical issue in packaging line control and good line flow. As a machine's availability upstream or downstream of the filler declines, that machine eventually degrades the accumulation designed into the packaging line to the point that it shuts down the filler. Obviously, the closer to the filler a machine is, the sooner its poor performance begins to affect the filler's run time because it is not supplying containers to the filler or it is causing containers to back up to the filler.

Another important point that should not be overlooked is that many conveyors on the packaging line are not typically considered part of a machine. However, conveyor performance can affect machine availability. Therefore, it is critical that the availability of all conveyors on the line is considered and that all conveyors are well maintained.

The official formula for machine availability is as follows.

machine availability = [MTBF/(MTTR + MTBF)] × 100

MTBF and MTTR will be explained in depth below.

Mean Time Between Failures

How can machine availability be improved? Two components make up machine availability. The first is mean time between failures (MTBF). MTBF speaks to what the average time is between internal faults on a machine. It essentially indicates how long the machine runs on average before it experiences an internal fault. The longer that a machine can be kept running before it faults again, the better. In the case of the filler, MTBF is not only a measurement of how well the machine performs but it also directly correlates to the output of the packaging line. The MTBF on packaging line machinery is also a good measure of how often a machine operator needs to intervene in the process. A low MTBF number indicates that the machine is not running well and that the operator is getting involved frequently. An MTBF of 3 minutes indicates that the operator has to get involved with some type of machine problem on an average of once every 3 minutes. Conversely, an MTBF of 180 minutes indicates that there are very few machine issues and that the operator rarely has to intervene in the machine operation. Depending on the machine and its function and location on the packaging line, various MTBF numbers can be acceptable. For instance, it would be expected that the MTBF of a pasteurizer be very large, such as 1,080 minutes. On the other hand, a packer MTBF may be acceptable at 30 minutes. In any case, increasing the MTBF on any machine ultimately improves the chances for better packaging line performance and reduces operator and maintenance frustrations.

To increase the MTBF, the quantity of faults and what is causing them must first be understood. By concentrating on preventing machine faults, the MTBF for each machine on the line can systematically be increased and the MTBF continually improved to an acceptable level for each machine.

Mean Time to Repair

Mean time to repair (MTTR) is the second component of machine availability. This is the average time it takes to return the machine to an available or run-ready condition after a fault. The longer the MTTR, the lower the machine availability. To maximize machine availability, line operators need to minimize the MTTR. The issues surrounding the MTTR could be lack of operator awareness that a fault occurred, inability to access the fault to repair it, difficulty in diagnosing the fault, and slow response to the fault. If possible, operators should concentrate on reducing the time it takes to get the machine back in service by solving the issues that drive the MTTR up. For instance, if it is difficult to access the spot on the machine where the fault is caused, operators and maintenance should address the accessibility problem.

Microstops and Macrostops

The faults that a machine experiences can be divided into microstops and macrostops.

Microstops are machine faults that generally last less than 4 minutes. Most of these stops are caused by minor incidents occurring on the packaging line, such as down containers in the machine, carrier misfeeds, flagging labels, or operators pressing the stop button. For these issues, generally the time to restore the machine to a ready-to-run state takes less than 4 minutes. In most situations, these are the events that are most frequent on a packaging line. Also, because of the shear number of these types of events on a machine and throughout the line, they are typically responsible for the majority of machine availability problems and, in turn, for poor packaging line efficiency. Some people describe microstops in a packaging line as "being pecked to death by sparrows". That really is an accurate description of how it feels for packaging personnel who experience an inordinate amount of microstops.

Macrostops consist of machine faults that last more than 4 minutes. They can be as short as 4 minutes and as long as several hours. These types of stops generally are not the nagging occurrences that consistently and frequently make operators get involved. They are more likely to be major equipment failures, such as a broken valve on a filler, a broken air line on a packer, or a main bearing failure on a filler. When macrostops occur, they typically start to affect line performance because of the amount of time the machines are down.

Time to Go Back to Normal State

Time to go back to normal state (TGNS) refers to the time that it takes for the packaging line to return to a desired state of line flow. More specifically, it refers to the state at which all machines are running at the filler speed and the amount of accumulation designed into the line is again available at all locations. TGNS is affected by machine MTBFs, MTTRs, total accumulation available, proper conveyor-speed set points, and proper machine set points. If the MTBF for the cell of a packaging line is less than the TGNS, it means that the accumulation will not be restored before the next fault on that machine is seen. This eventually depletes all accumulation, and at that point, any machine stop on the line shuts down the filler, creating a situation similar to having no accumulation between machines.

Regardless of the size of a brewery's packaging department, the concerns and items listed above are relevant. The question that each brewer needs to answer is what kind of budget is available for considering and designing solutions to these issues in the packaging line or company. For the brewpub with a single filler head supplying bottles for takeout, the answer may be that very few of these items are critical concerns. For a microbrewery with a volume that is relatively larger and that operates a packaging line running at 200 bpm, the challenges and concerns are much greater. Regional and national brewers certainly want to counter the potential negative effects of poor line efficiency, particularly its effect on labor costs and customer-order fulfillment. In any scenario, safety and quality issues cannot be discounted. The importance of all of these issues should not be underestimated. The competitive market that today's brewers face does not allow a lapse in any of these very important areas of the business.

Machine Control Components Affecting Line Flow

To this point, the coverage has been fairly general in regards to how machines are controlled and the components used to control them. To provide a deeper understanding of machine controls and the details of their operation, this section covers in greater detail those things useful in identifying and eliminating packaging line problems.

Generally speaking, for purposes of this discussion, machine controls refer to solid-state circuits that are confined to an individual machine and regulate the operation of the machine. These circuits are commonly 110 volts AC or 24 volts DC and employ PLC ladder logic to achieve the desired response in the machine.

In an age of ever increasing concern for safety, machine controls are designed to reduce the possibility of operator injury. Engineers employ a series of electromechanical interlocks that ensures the access doors are closed and machine guards are in place. Machine manufactures often resort to exotic and redundant interlocks to ensure that the safety system is not bypassed. However, for any interlock system designed, there is always some way to mechanically or electrically bypass it. Unfortunately, if this is the goal of the operator or maintenance personnel, it most certainly will be accomplished. It is the responsibility of management to ensure that employees are trained on the importance of machine safety devices. It is only through education and awareness at the operator and maintenance level that the integrity of the machine's safety controls can be maintained and improved.

A second function of machine controls is to protect the machines on the line, preventing situations that cause damage to the machine. As packaging line speeds increase, so do the speeds of the individual machines on the line. To avoid machine damage when faults occur at high speeds, manufacturers have developed electromechanical sensing devices that sense a problem at its earliest possible state and initiate a reaction, usually shutting off the machine, to avoid serious damage to the equipment. Such controls are especially valuable since they protect the user's investment in the equipment and ensure operator safety. Qualified personnel should therefore scrutinize modifications to machine-protection circuits prior to their implementation. Manufacturers build in these circuits to overcome problems that have arisen in the past. Again, if changes are made, it is recommended that engineers keep good documentation and obtain the manufacturer's consent.

The third purpose of machine controls is to assist in the smooth operation of the machine itself. Generally, all major pieces of equipment on a packaging line are purchased prewired, meaning that the control logic has been determined and the electrical, mechanical, and pneumatic devices have been assembled to implement this logic. This setup has several advantages. First, the equipment manufacturer, who should have the best knowledge of the machinery, decides on the method of control. This also helps protect the warranty and service agreements, since manufacture's service personnel use machine or control modifications as an excuse for their machines' poor performance. If the machines have been modified, they will no longer service them or honor the warranty. To avoid warranty and service problems, it is best to rely on controls furnished by the equipment suppliers. Modifications to machine control circuits should be made sparingly and always with safety in mind. As stated earlier, control modifications should always be well documented and the manufacturer consulted. Also, operators should always be alerted to changes in the controls, since the controls interface directly with the machine, and they should be aware of how their machine will react in any situation.

The fourth function of machine controls is to help the machine interface with the line. Generally, each machine has a domain on a packaging line. This includes its immediate infeed, the machine itself, and its immediate discharge. The ability of the machine to control or sense the condition at its immediate infeed and discharge conveyor is critical to its operation. One common infeed control determines whether there is material available to be processed by the machine, and another common control determines how much. The first control often determines whether the machine runs or waits for materials and is referred to as prime. In packaging terms, prime is the accumulation of containers (e.g., bottles, cans, or cases) prior to a machine that requires a minimum supply be maintained to ensure proper machine function. The remainder of the infeed controls tells the machine how fast to run. Often, high-speed equipment can run at multiple speeds. Its speed is based on the queue (or waiting line) in front of the machine. If there is an adequate supply, the machine runs at normal line speed. If there is an excessive supply, the machine goes into high speed, or surge, to reduce the excess of containers at its infeed.

In general, two important discharge controls are fed back to the machine. The first is the normal backup condition, which is caused by equipment downstream not taking the product away. In this case, the machine generally goes into low speed, and if the backup is severe enough, it goes into cycle stop, in which a machine stops in an orderly manner, usually clearing the machine of product.

The second discharge control is the downstream emergency backup, which indicates a malfunction or jam at the machine's discharge area. This is a serious condition and, to avoid damage to the machine, usually results in an emergency shutdown of the equipment. Emergency stops generally do not clear a machine of product.

Machine control logic relies on information input to determine the machine's activities. Basically, the information must be automatically or operator initiated and must come from one of three sources. The first relies on switches or sensors to provide information regarding an internal physical condition or one upstream or downstream from the machine. These switches are automatically triggered by physical conditions and are usually electronic, metal proximity, or limit switches that sense the presence of product. This presence is relayed to the machine control by completing a circuit that is part of the overall machine logic. The logic determines what action, if any, is to be taken. Starting in the mid-1990s, the use of communications networks have made it possible for machine PLCs to communicate with each other and provide information that allows the controls to have even finer oversight of the process. Switches, push buttons, human–machine interface (HMI) screens, and other devices allow operators to relay their intentions to the controls' scheme, which acts according to a preplanned scheme.

In these three applications of machine controls, the inputs give notice of a condition, and the logic acts accordingly. The logic referred to is actually a well-thought-out game plan for machine operation. Developed by a controls engineer, the logic is actually a series of electromechanical devices arranged by means of a control circuit that reacts in a predetermined manner. The machine control logic processes inputs according to a preplanned control scheme and initiates outputs that direct both the machine and operator. Signals may be given to automatically start or stop, speed up or slow down, or open or close bottles or can stops, among other things. Controls aid operators by providing indicator lights to help in troubleshooting. Warnings, such as open machine guards, low on materials, and product jams, can all be indicated to speed operator knowledge and reaction and improve machine performance.

Another form of machine control inputs and outputs are customer contacts. These are simply sent between the machine control and the line control to aid in the coordination of the machine with the line. These signals generally indicate conditions or events that are happening outside the machine's domain and allow the machine to perform as part of the line.

As previously discussed, machines have a domain, that is, each machine has its own logic and acts accordingly. Individual machines are also tied together to form a coordinated packaging line.

Packaging lines do not function at their best if each machine is a stand-alone unit. Each piece of equipment on the line, including the conveyor, benefits from being able to respond to the status and speed of the other pieces of equipment. By integrating packaging line equipment and allowing these machines to communicate with each other, packaging line designers have endless possibilities for creating sophisticated solutions for waste reduction, process control, and communication. Automation is a powerful tool and can accomplish much if it is used correctly and with a practical approach in mind.

To address the need for automation, packaging department managers need technically savvy people to assist them. For instance, a local controls engineering firm can help. Never underestimate the amount of help that local automation suppliers can provide and how much they are willing to do. Remember, too, system suppliers know that brewers will need someone who understands how to employ these systems effectively if they are going to make a purchase. If the suppliers are unable or unwilling to help with the controls project directly, they should be able to recommend a good local controls engineer who is familiar with their products and capable of helping with the process.

Interestingly, much like developments in the personal computer market, the cost of automation hardware and software has come down tremendously over the years, and its sophistication has increased dramatically. In fact, the costs of the systems themselves may not be the true limiting factor for brewers but rather the technical expertise needed to support these automation platforms. Make no mistake about it, as incredibly reliable as these systems are, brewers will eventually need talented, well-trained personnel to troubleshoot, modify, and program this equipment. Brewers must keep the technology and the support personnel issue in mind as they upgrade to new technologies.

Controllers

Some of the equipment directed with process controls are modulating control valves, solenoid valves, air cylinders, VFDs, pumps, control valves, and current to pressure (I/P) converters.

Programmable Logic Controller

The PLC has proven itself to be a versatile, powerful, and affordable automation tool that can be used in relatively harsh environments. For those not familiar with it, a PLC is an industrial computer used to control machines through the sending and receiving of electric signals. A basic PLC consists of a microprocessor and electrical inputs and outputs (Fig. 4.5). The microprocessor monitors the inputs into the PLC and uses these inputs to monitor the process and control the outputs of the PLC, based on the instructions programmed into its microprocessor. Even smaller PLCs have combinations of inputs and outputs that can consist of digital and analog inputs and outputs as well as resistance temperature detector (RTD) inputs.

There are now small PLCs that cost only a couple hundred dollars, but the cost of PLCs can range as high as several thousand dollars, depending on their speed, size, and memory. The smaller PLCs are certainly within the reach of the small brewer, and brewers should consider them whenever an electrical controls project is necessary.

Variable Frequency Drive

A variable frequency drive (VFD) is used in place of a conventional across-the-line motor starter (Fig. 4.6). Compared with a conventional motor starter, a VFD is much more sophisticated and provides many options. An electrical input tells it to start the motor that it is connected to. In the case of packaging, a VFD is generally used to operate the motor on a machine or conveyor. Unlike a conventional motor starter, a VFD is able to change the speed of the motor that it is connected to by varying the frequency that it supplies to the motor. In doing so, the VFD is able to change the speed of the machine or conveyor that the motor drives, letting the machines and conveyors change speed based on the need of the line flow. Beyond that, a VFD can accelerate and decelerate to the desired speed as programmed. It can run forward or in reverse, has thermal-overload protection, can accept multiple styles of speed references, and can trigger an alarm. A VFD can have 200–300 parameters, each of which can be adjusted to handle very advanced applications. Finally, because a VFD can vary the speed of the motors it drives, it in turn requires less power to run the motor than an across-the-line starter does and, therefore, should save energy.

This is another industrial automation component whose price and size have dropped considerably since its inception. VFDs provide capabilities far beyond most

FIGURE 4.5. Typical example of a programmable logic controller (PLC). (Courtesy D.G. Yuengling and Son Inc.)

FIGURE 4.6. Variable frequency drive (VFD). (Courtesy D.G. Yuengling and Son Inc.)

needs in a brewery and are well within reach of most any brewery. The cost of VFDs starts at a couple hundred dollars and runs up to several thousand dollars, depending on the size of the motor operators are trying to control.

Human–Machine Interface

A human–machine interface (HMI) is a display typically used on packaging machines in the areas where people work. The HMI is programmable to display the desired information on the process it monitors, and its display can vary in size. HMI displays come in both color and grayscale, each available with touch-screen and push-button controls. An example of an HMI is shown in Figure 4.7.

HMIs are powerful tools that allow operators to view and have input into the process being monitored. They can be used throughout the packaging department and they communicate with process controllers, such as PLCs, to act—just as the name implies—as an interface between the process and the human reviewing it. The human may be an operator, electrician, mechanic, engineer, supervisor, or any other person who needs to retrieve or provide information or to control a process.

HMIs communicate with a process controller or controllers typically by way of a communication protocol, such as DH+, Mod bus +, ControlNet, etc. They can look at registers or individual bits of data and display that information as programmed. For instance, data provided to the HMI may be displayed on the screen as a message, such as an alarm message. The HMI data display may provide the operator with number values or equipment status (Fig. 4.8). The data can also show machine status through a display that uses automated moving objects, such as an image of a filler turning. So, with an HMI display, an operator can view a screen that displays a picture of a filler running as well as information on the speed of the filler, the number of containers that have been run, the step in the run sequence, the product name on the line, and the time and date. These are just a few examples of the valuable information HMIs can supply. Basically, if the information is in the process controller, it can be presented on the HMI. Because the HMI is typically on the communications network that is used across the line, lines, or plant, it is possible with an HMI to display or have input into any other machine or area of the plant as long as that machine is on the network. Considering the number of different lights, readouts, push buttons, switches, and data displays there are, it can be seen that HMIs, if used properly, can save a large amount of time, money, and space along with the savings gained through the elimination of components in maintenance parts storage and on packaging lines.

However, a word of caution on using HMIs: critical machine inputs, such as start and stop buttons, should not be limited to being just on the HMI. If the HMI fails, operators will not be able to run the packaging machine. Instead, critical inputs should be installed on both the HMI and the operator panel.

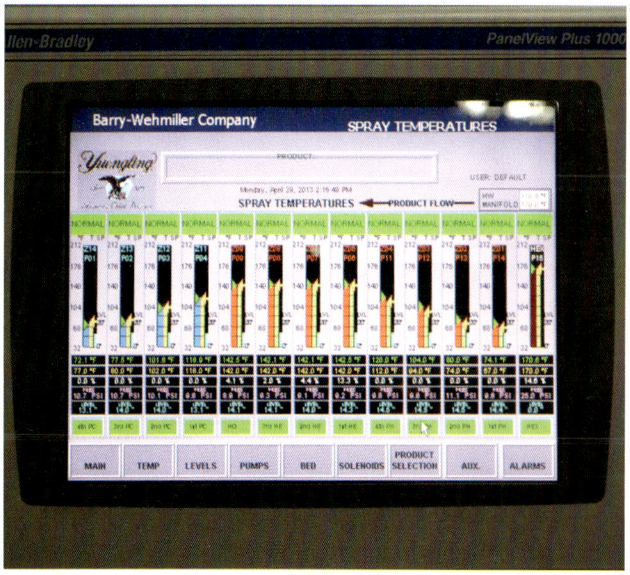

FIGURE 4.7. A typical example of a human–machine interface, which can use either touch-screen or push-button controls. (Courtesy D.G. Yuengling and Son Inc.)

FIGURE 4.8. An example of a filler application on a touch-screen human–machine interface. (Courtesy D.G. Yuengling and Son Inc.)

Proximity Sensor

The most common type of sensor used on packaging lines is the proximity sensor (Fig. 4.9). These devices use electrical inductance to sense the presence of metal without physically touching the object monitored. Operators mount the proximity sensor to a swing arm bracket. The swing arm swings underneath the conveyor side rail, and when containers are present, the arm is forced back, which moves a metal tab in front of the proximity sensor mounted to it. One advantage of proximity switches is that there are no moving parts. The sealed, watertight sensing unit only needs to be within 0.5–1 inch of the object being sensed to give a good, consistent result. The sensors are generally available with built-in delay timers, which delay the signal on or off. Packaging line operators should avoid sensors that come equipped with adjustable timers. This adjustment adds a variable into the process and allows timers to be changed by anyone with a screwdriver. It is best to use a timer that is programmed into the PLC. This limits access to the timer and eliminates a variable in the process.

Photoelectric Eye

Another popular sensing device is the photoelectric eye, also known as the photo eye (Fig. 4.10). Like limit switches, the photoelectric eye is commonly used in all breweries. Consisting basically of a transmitter and receiver, a photoelectric eye emits and receives a beam of visible or invisible light. When this beam is broken—that is, when the presence of the product has been detected—a signal is sent to the control circuit. Some photoelectric eyes do not require separate transmitters and receiving devices but instead use a plastic reflector to return the beam to a combination transmitter and receiver unit. These are referred to as retroreflective photoelectric eyes. Still, more advanced photoelectric eyes do not require reflectors but instead rely on the object being sensed to reflect the infrared light back to the receiver and thus allow the receiver to sense the presence of the product. Photoelectric eyes also are generally available with built-in timing devices and are comparable in price to proximity switches. Large breweries that have multiple shifts and more than a couple people involved in equipment maintenance and troubleshooting should avoid using built-in timing devices and instead should use a timer programmed into the PLC.

Control Logic

Today's modern packaging lines consist of complete PLC control for any machine involved directly with production. PLC hardware and the developed programming logic collaborate to monitor inputs to the PLC and control outputs from the PLC to supply the desired operational results for individual and total packaging line machinery. Although there may be a few auxiliary machine functions that are exceptions, almost any piece of equipment has a PLC that can communicate via networking with all other PLCs.

FIGURE 4.9. A proximity sensor. (Courtesy D.G. Yuengling and Son Inc.)

FIGURE 4.10. A photoelectric eye sensor. (Courtesy D.G. Yuengling and Son Inc.)

Operator inputs provide a second method for putting information into the control system. These consist mainly of push buttons, selector switches, and HMIs that, when activated by operating personnel, send a signal to the control circuit. Consisting mainly of off/on- or start/stop-type signals, operator inputs transmit the operator's order to stop conveyors and machines to the line control unit.

Machine interfaces, or the machine vendor electrical contacts discussed in the Machine Control Components Affecting Line Flow section above, are the third type of input to control systems. These signals from the machine indicate the machine's status to the line. Commonly operating by the opening or closing of an electrical contact, these signals allow the machine to function as part of the line in a smooth, continuous fashion. Today's machine PLCs also have the ability to use networks such as Ethernet to communicate to other machines as well. Information transmitted to the line logic may indicate that the machine is ready to accept product and, therefore, the infeed conveyor may be started. Or it may indicate that the machine is shut down and therefore does not need product. These signals automatically generated by the machine are important to its proper function as a coordinated member of the line.

Components of Control Logic

As noted, there are three methods of putting information into the line logic: through networked PLCs, operator inputs, or machine interfaces. How this information is used, or the basis for decision-making, is called line control logic. The equipment that physically receives these inputs and processes decisions is called line logic hardware.

Again, as in individual machine controls, the logic employed in packaging line control is generally PLC ladder logic. Inputs enter the PLC via proximity sensors, photoelectric eyes, or operator inputs. These are physically connected to an input card that converts the 110-volt or 24-volt DC signal to a low-voltage signal input and sends it to the processor. The processor, or brains of the control, has been preprogrammed with relay logic, allowing it to make decisions based on these inputs. The output from the PLC output cards is the signal that directs the events that take place on the line. Usually at 110 volts, these signals can activate motors, conveyors, indicator lights, alarms, and air solenoids as directed by the control logic to make the line run smoothly.

By using a computer and monitor that displays the program's ladder logic, operators can replace all of the relay logic components consisting of moving parts that consume critical control-cabinet real estate with software. The PLC then interprets the ladder logic and determines when action is required. A low-voltage signal is sent to an output card, which then converts this signal to 110 volts and operates the appropriate control device.

PLCs have several advantages over traditional electromechanical relays. They have proven to be extremely reliable and have no moving parts. If problems occur, their own diagnostics can quickly locate and display certain faults. They are easily programmed and require no special training for experienced electricians, since the symbols PLCs use are familiar to relay users. If the number of external devices is changed, changes or additions to the circuits—which in the past in a conventional relay system would have required additional relays and rewiring—can be done in minutes using a computer, a monitor, and the appropriate development software. Certain control devices or logic can be added online with a minimum of line downtime. Documentation, or ladder diagrams, are easily obtained by means of a printer that lists the logic contained in the controller. With this documentation, an updated program is available at any time.

Motion Control/Position Measurement

With the increased use of motion control on packaging lines, position-sensing and feedback instrumentation have become critical to some machine operations and changeovers. The critical settings that can be achieved and maintained by these motion controllers have provided quicker hands-off changeovers, and they can be incredibly accurate and consistent. Encoders are used extensively on modern packaging equipment as a way to communicate the position of a machine component at all times. Encoders output a pulse for a specified measurable amount of movement. For instance, an encoder may output 1,000 pulses for each revolution of a 100-station filler. This provides extremely exact information as to the location of any filling valve on the filler at any time, thus allowing valve performance to be tracked and providing cues as to when processes should start and stop, for instance. Generally, PLC processors are used with these motion control encoders to enable the storage of data and communication with other machines and processes.

Packaging Line Performance-Monitoring Software

Performance-monitoring software provides an excellent means of monitoring, troubleshooting, and collecting data for short or long periods of time in order to increase line production efficiency. When configured correctly, performance-monitoring software can provide data on machine efficiency, causes for downtimes, and length of that downtime. Figure 4.11 presents a typical line-status chart that shows the state of all of the machines on the packaging line. By having the information on each machine and conveyor on the packaging line, packaging personnel can quickly focus on troublesome areas in order to eliminate problems and increase line throughput.

When set up, understood, and used correctly, these software packages are extremely valuable to all levels of the organization and should be leveraged to the maximum. The advantages of this software become increasingly valuable as the complexity and physical layouts of the packaging lines in a facility become greater and the number of people become fewer. In any case, the ability to look at data coupled with the input from packaging personnel is invaluable. The ability to steer maintenance personnel, vendors, and capital to the areas on the packaging line that need it the most to improve output easily justifies the investment needed to install this type of software.

Computer Simulation

A fairly recent advance in this area has been the use of computer simulations to help create line design and justify packaging line modifications and improvements to line flow. In this process, rule-of-thumb equations are combined with the machine-delay information gathered to produce simulations of the line running over long periods of time, and all using only a few minutes of actual computer time.

Basically, the major equipment, or workstations as they are called in some simulation programs, are laid out in a series or in parallel arrangement, either alone or in combination, to form a flow chart representing the actual line. The workstations are connected by lines, which represent the bottle or can conveyors but which have no reference to their length or configuration. In front of each workstation is the accumulation (or queue) that is possible between that workstation and the one directly upstream of it. When completed, the information on the flow chart is coded and entered in the simulation program, where it serves as the framework for the simulation. As previously mentioned, this information gives no indication of the physical distances or configuration of the line; it only provides the computer the information on the machines and queues in the system.

Information on the physical qualities of each component of the line layout is then compiled. For workstations, this includes information on machine speeds (e.g., low, medium, and high) and what upstream-queue population or level of accumulation will activate the specific speeds. Machine-delay information is also entered. Compiled in the course of engineering studies, this information is basically a profile of that workstation's internally generated downtime, e.g., the average length of delay and the average time between delays. (As previously mentioned, queues represent the accumulation available prior to a workstation. This is usually measured in cases, bottles, or cans of product and represents the total number of containers that can be stored in front of a machine on

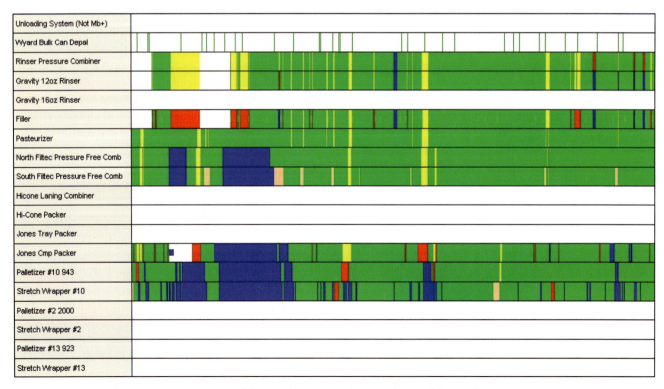

FIGURE 4.11. An efficiency-improvement tool display. (Courtesy D.G. Yuengling and Son Inc.)

the actual conveyor.) The final information needed is the conveyor speed or travel time, that is, the minimum time it takes a container to travel from one workstation to another. When all of this data has been fed into the program, the actual simulation can begin.

In simulation, the line operates within the parameters entered. Bottles, cans, or cases ("transactions" in simulation terminology) travel from machine to machine and are processed or delayed just as they would be on an operating line. Work centers operate at specified speeds and experience delays that conform to the pattern identified in the engineering studies. Queues, or areas of accumulation, empty or swell accordingly to line conditions. In fact, the simulated line is basically identical to an operating line, except that the simulation runs a production shift in a matter of minutes.

The true value of line simulation is in the areas of data analysis and experimental changes on packaging lines. Information regarding queue sizes, average machine speeds, conveyor speeds, machine control, etc., can be reviewed to determine the limiting factors on the line's performance. Then a change or changes can be made in the model and the simulation rerun. This trial-and-error approach is invaluable since it allows brewers to optimize line performance before the first piece of equipment is purchased and before costly line modifications need to be made.

● PACKAGING PROCESS CONTROL

Line flow control has been discussed and now the discussion focuses on controls that deal with temperature, liquid flow, liquid level, and pressure. This section explores how these controls are used chiefly in the capacity of product-quality control, not in line flow control. Some of the examples of process control on a packaging line might be steam flow to a pasteurizer heat exchanger, filler-bowl counterpressure control, filler-bowl level control, and pasteurizer zone temperature control.

In the discussion of process control in this section, some basic terms need to be understood. These terms include controlled variable, measured variable, manipulated variable, and set point. A controlled variable is a quantity that should remain constant and must be observed as carefully as are dependent variables. A measured variable is a quantity, property, or condition being measured. It is sometimes referred to as the measurand. A manipulated variable is a quantity or condition that is altered as a result of an actuating error signal so as to change the value of the directly controlled variable. A set point is the target value an automatic control system is to reach.

There are two basic types of automated process control: open loop and closed loop, in which loop refers to information traveling continuously from one component to another in a closed circuit. Open-loop control indicates that the system being controlled provides no feedback to the controller, that is, when a signal is given, a preprogrammed change is made within the system and the effects of this change are not fed back to the controller for evaluation or adjustment. An example of this type of system is an automatic washing machine, in which the cycle is initiated, follows a preprogrammed routine, and provides no feedback as to whether the clothes are being cleaned. The machine follows its cycle, regardless of its results, and can make no corrections to get a cleaner wash. This off/on logic is not used to control critical processes and is generally found in controls for water softener regeneration equipment, cleaning-in-place (CIP) systems, etc., where the cycle length is designed to achieve and ensure the desired results.

In closed-loop control, the system being controlled provides feedback as input to the controller. This feedback is used to further control the process and, ultimately, achieve the desired results. Figure 4.12 is a schematic of a

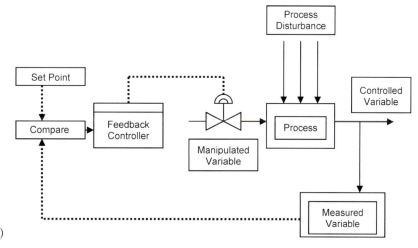

FIGURE 4.12. Typical closed-loop process control system. (Courtesy R. Seaman)

typical closed-loop system. In this system, the three key elements of a closed-loop system exchange information to achieve a preselected set point. Basically, the measurement device, or sensor, monitors the process and sends information regarding its status to the controller. The controller, which is the brains of the system, compares this status with the set point and decides what corrective action, if any, is needed to achieve the set point. This action signal is sent to the actuator, which directs the controlled variable (e.g., steam) and changes the manipulated variable (e.g., temperature) in the process. The sensor device detects this response in the process and relays the information to the controller, and the closed loop is completed.

A closed-loop process control system, like the one diagrammed in Figure 4.12, is applicable regardless of the process parameter being controlled. What differs are the components used in each application, the process disturbances, etc. Each type of process has its own special circumstances that need to be understood if it is to be controlled properly. There are typically only a few people in a brewery who truly understand the application and design of instrumentation and controls systems and their talent is extremely valuable. Most processes are designed to control either temperature, pressure, level, flow, position, analytical parameters, or a combination of several of these factors at the same time.

Much like controls for packaging line flow, process controls compensate for process disturbances. They provide a means to return the process to its desired state, or its set point. Some examples of process disturbances are a change in pressure, flow, temperature, or level.

Components of a Closed-Loop System

The components of a closed-loop system include the process, measurement devices, controller, and final control element.

Process

Process is the characteristic being measured and controlled. Some common processes that are controlled in packaging include systems that monitor pressure, temperature, flow, and level.

Measurement Devices

The function of measurement devices is identical to that of indicator devices, except that a measurement device can also transmit its findings by means of a mechanical, pneumatic, or electronic signal and inform the controller about the status of the process. Such devices include temperature transmitters, pressure transmitters, and level transmitters, among others.

Controller

The brain or decision center for the control loop, the controller has a preset goal, or set point, to meet, and it compares the measurement received from the transmitter with this set point. The difference between these two values is measured, and based on its magnitude, a correcting signal is sent to the control element to achieve a set point. Controllers are categorized as electronic, pneumatic, or mechanical and are usually some combination of two or more of these systems. It is not uncommon, for instance, for an electronic signal to enter a pneumatic controller and by means of a mechanical linkage send a pneumatic signal to the control element.

The basis for the control decision process is called the method of control. Simply stated, this is the logic the controller has been given to use when the process measurement varies from the set point.

Final Control Element

The final control element controls the variable, changing the characteristic being measured. This is usually a valve, but it could be a heating element, motor-speed control, or mechanical actuator. In the packaging department, the most common control element is the pneumatically operated control valve (Fig. 4.13). This valve consists basically of a body or a valve assembly that, when operated, changes the flow rate of the variable in the process. The valve is mechanically connected to an actuator, which moves, or "operates", the valve according to the magnitude of the output signal it receives from the loop controller. These valves, which change the variable in the process, are referred to as modulating, or control, valves.

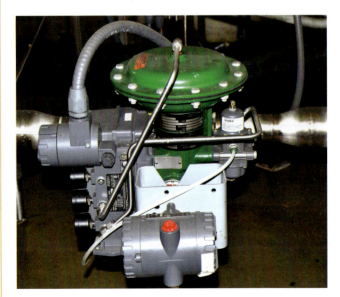

FIGURE 4.13. A modulating control valve, a typical final control element. (Courtesy D.G. Yuengling and Son Inc.)

Types of Control

As previously mentioned, the controller is the brain of the closed-loop system. In the packaging area, its decisions are generally based on what is called proportional control. This means that the signal sent to the final control element is proportional to the difference between the measurement and the set point. The ratio of proportional control is expressed in terms of proportional band, which, stated simply, indicates how far the measured value will be away from the set point before the final control element is activated 100%. For example, in a controller with a scale of 0–100, a 50% proportional band, and a set point of 50, the final control element will be fully closed at a measurement of 25 and fully opened at a measurement of 75, since the difference between these two points on the scale is 50, and 50 is 50% of the 100 scale.

The proportional band is always centered about the set point. For instance, in the previous example, the valve would be half open when the measurement matched the set point of 50. For any process control loop, only one value of proportional band is best, and this can only be determined by proportionally tuning the loop, that is, by adjusting the bandwidth until an optimum performance is achieved. If the band is too small, the controller overreacts to small measurement changes, and there is a constant oscillation around the set point. If the band is too wide, the controller does not resend enough, and the process control is not as close to the set point as possible.

One drawback to pure proportional control is that the controller rarely maintains the set point; it is always above or below it. This variance is called offset and is acceptable in instances in which the process need not exactly follow the set point. If offset cannot be tolerated, a second control factor can be added to more closely achieve the set point. This is called reset. Simply stated, reset is a corrective action taken by the controller to achieve the set point and is based on how far the measurement is from set point and how much time has elapsed since the last reset signal.

Perhaps a simple example provides the best way to visualize how the proportional band and reset function. Imagine a tank filled 10 feet deep with water. It can be drained by opening a bottom valve and can be refilled by opening the water-inlet valve. Assume that the goal is to keep the tank's level at 5 feet deep, or half full, and that the controller has a 100% proportional band. When the bottom valve is opened, the tank begins to drain, and the level drops. With a 100% proportional band, the level must drop 100% of the scale for the inlet valve to be opened 100%. Therefore, with a 10% drop in level, the operator adjusts by opening the inlet valve 10%. With a 20% drop, the operator opens the valve 20% and so on. Imagine the same situation with a 50% proportional band. This means that the level must move only 50% of the scale for the valve to need to be opened fully. Since the proportional band is always centered around the set point, the operator just begins to open the valve when the level drops to 7.5 feet, and the valve is wide open at 2.5 feet. This can be expressed as 7.5 feet minus 2.5 feet equals 5.0 feet, and this is 50% of the total band of 10 feet. Therefore, this control is a 50% proportional band in the system.

The operator can continue to tighten the proportional band to attempt to achieve the desired level; however, the band will eventually become too narrow a range, and the operator will overreact to changes in level and continually overshoot the set point. To help achieve the set point, another action can be taken after proportional control. This is reset. With reset, the valve will still be opened according to the proportional band; however, the operator now has the ability to compare the tank level with the 5-foot set point and initiate action to achieve set point. The operator can then open or close the valve and wait to see what effect these actions have on the system. Having seen the effect, the operator can again adjust the valve and again wait to see how close the level gets to the set point. The operator will continue this routine until the set point is achieved. It is important for the operator to wait to see the effect of the change before making another change. The time required for a change in a system is referred to as lag, or dead time. In a controller, reset is measured as minutes per repeat, or repeats per minute. If the reset time is less than the lag or dead time, the controller goes into what is called reset wind-up, in which it overcorrects, and the process continually oscillates around the set point.

Control Loop Applications

The types of instrumentation loops common in packaging include both pneumatic and electronic installations. In pneumatic control systems, low-pressure air is the signal used to communicate between various loop components. These signals are usually 3–15 pounds per square inch gauge (psig), with 3 pounds being 0% and 15 pounds being 100% of a full-scale reading. Electronic instruments use a 4- to 20-milliamp (mA), 5-volt signal to communicate. In these instruments, 4 mA usually represents 0% and 20 mA represents a full-scale reading. Each system has its advantages and disadvantages, and for this reason, many combination installations, in which both pneumatic and electronic devices interact in the same loop, have been installed.

Many breweries control the beer level in their filler bowls by means of a control valve at the filler inlet. Two types of systems are most popular. The first uses a float

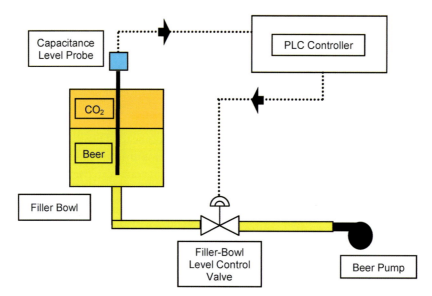

FIGURE 4.14. Filler-bowl level control. (Courtesy R. Seaman)

or capacitance probe as a measurement device to signal what the level is directly to the controller. The controller compares this measurement with the set point and adjusts the beer level by sending a pneumatic output signal, which operates a control valve and adjusts the flow of the beer into the filler. The system is accurate, and there is never any question as to what the beer level is in the bowl. The disadvantage, however, is that the signal from the sensor on the filler bowl must go through a rotating connection to communicate with the controller. This connection point can often require a high level of maintenance or result in lost production if not properly attended to.

A simplified diagram of a control system for filler-bowl level is shown in Figure 4.14. This control system operates in a fairly straightforward manner. The capacitance probe monitors the level of beer in the bowl and sends a signal back to the PLC that is linear to the bowl level. An example would be if the bowl has a total internal depth of 30 inches and the probe is calibrated so that, at 0 inches of beer, the level probe outputs a 4-mA signal to the PLC and, at 30 inches of beer, the probe sends an output signal of 20 mA. The probe's signal is linear from 0 to 30 inches. Therefore, when the beer level is 15 inches deep, the output signal would be halfway between 4 and 20 mA, or 12 mA. In this manner, the PLC tracks the beer level in the filler bowl at all times. By tracking the beer level in the bowl at all times, the PLC can signal to either open or close the filler-bowl level control valve and maintain the set point level by speeding up or slowing down the rate of beer flowing into the bowl. The PLC's control instruction, called a proportional–integral–derivative (PID) instruction, has several parameters that can be tuned to allow the valve to react in an optimized manner to maintain the level within a tight range.

Some process disturbances that require the use of closed-loop control are stopping or starting the filler, a change in filler speed, a change in the beer-pump discharge pressure, a change in the counterpressure, and a bottle breaking while filling. All of these process changes require that the filler-bowl level control valve react to maintain the level set point in the bowl.

Figure 4.15 shows a single zone of a pasteurizer and how it can be controlled to maintain a constant temperature at the spray header. The first thing to note in this system is that two pumps supply water flow through two separate circuits. The first pump is the spray header pump. Its function is to constantly spray water over the top of the beer cans or bottles as the containers pass underneath on their way through the pasteurizer. The spray header pump runs constantly during normal operation, and water continuously recirculates from the zone water sump and back to the spray header. The second water pump is the heat-exchanger water pump. Its function is to constantly circulate water from the zone water sump through the heat exchanger and back to the zone water sump. The RTD installed in the spray header circuit measures the temperature of the spray header water and sends the temperature signal to the PLC. The PLC compares the measured temperature with the temperature set point and adjusts the steam control valve to increase or decrease the temperature of the water discharged from the heat exchanger, keeping the spray header water at the appropriate constant temperature required for proper pasteurization.

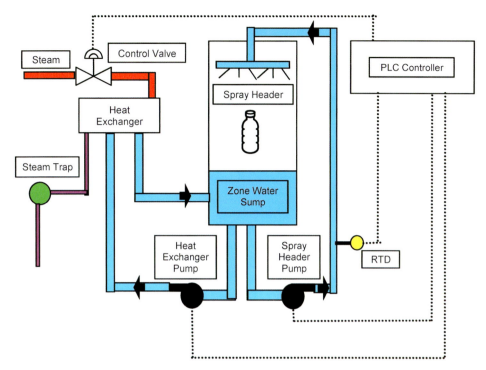

FIGURE 4.15. A simplified temperature control system in a single zone of a pasteurizer. PLC = programmable logic controller. RTD = resistance temperature detector. (Courtesy R. Seaman)

Some process disturbances that necessitate the use of a closed-loop temperature control system are a pasteurizer zone filling with containers (which provides a greater load to the heat exchanger) or emptying of them (which provides a decreasing load to the pasteurizer zone). Other disturbances are a pasteurizer zone registering a temperature change in the products entering the zone or a drop in pressure to the steam control valve on the heat exchanger.

A similar but slightly more complicated pasteurizer application is the single-set-point, dual-actuator controller. This control is very common in regenerative-type pasteurizers in which the front zones are used to heat containers and the back zones are used to cool them. This type of controller has two methods of controlling the sump temperatures. If the temperature is too low, steam is added, and if the temperature is too high, chilled water is added. Using a dead band located directly at the set point, operators ensure that both steam and water are not added at the same time.

Controllers

Single Controller

Stand-alone, single-input controllers are capable of providing very good local indication and excellent process control, particularly for pressure, level, temperature, flow conductivity, and position. In most instances, these controllers accept a 4- to 20-mA, 0- to 10-VDC (voltage direct current), or RTD input and provide a 4- to 20-mA or 0- to 10-VDC signal for their outputs. Users must decide what is appropriate for their systems. Typically, these controllers are offered in a wide price range, depending on their capabilities. These controllers are relatively inexpensive to install, require no software to program, and can be ordered with auxiliary capabilities as needed. However, the range of processes they can control is fairly limited, and they are very difficult to expand.

Programmable Logic Controller

As previously mentioned, a basic PLC consists of a microprocessor and electrical inputs and outputs. In the process control areas of packaging, this still holds true, but the inputs and outputs have tended to become more diverse as temperature, flow, level, and pressure are being monitored and controlled by means of both analog and digital inputs and outputs. As discussed in the Packaging Line Flow Control section above, the PLC microprocessor is used to monitor inputs and to use these inputs to monitor the process and control the PLC's outputs, based on the programmed instructions it contains. Again, PLCs are well within the price range of any size brewery. The key for brewers will be knowing what is needed and how to set up the systems so that they perform their desired functions.

PACKAGING LINE INSTRUMENTATION

Measurement Components

When a change in a process is noted, there usually must be a means to measure it. This has been true since sundials were first used to tell time by the movement of a shadow, and it is equally true today when laser beams are used to measure long distances with precision and accuracy. Over the years, the concept of measuring a process has not changed; only the methods used and the increased accuracy of the results have changed. Instruments are the most basic and traditional measurement tools.

Packaging technology, as in all other industries, has made great advances in speed, productivity, and quality achieved, but instrumentation engineering of the process still remains fairly straightforward. There is a need for accurate measurements of the processes affecting brewery operations; however, these can often be obtained using traditional equipment and do not necessarily require state-of-the art instrumentation. The size of the operation, the impact of labor costs, and the skill sets of the employees probably determine the instrumentation and controls required. A review of some of the most common types of measuring and indicating instruments in the packaging area can assist in their selection. These instruments can have a positive impact on a packaging department. It is essential, however, that brewers have well-thought-out, long-term objectives when designing and purchasing instrumentation and controls.

Instrumentation commonly found in the packaging area generally achieves one or two purposes. It can be used to measure and indicate or to measure, indicate, and control a physical process. Both of these applications are reviewed in the following discussion.

Temperature Measurement Devices

In several areas of packaging it is necessary to measure and control temperature. For example, the temperature of glue pots for carton sealing must be maintained, and line operators must track product temperatures, pasteurizer zone temperatures, bottle-wash zone temperatures, and machine bearing temperatures, as well as the temperature of water/chemical solutions used in cleaning. When it is necessary to provide temperature information for control or remote readout, it has become fairly common to use RTDs to measure temperature in packaging processes, although thermocouples are still used in some cases. If only local temperature readout is desired, then a dial thermometer can be installed.

Resistance Temperature Detectors

RTDs are relatively inexpensive, accurate, and linear. They can be installed in a sanitary manner, are waterproof, and can be connected to a variety of control system and readout components to accomplish their tasks. A typical RTD is shown in Figure 4.16.

One of the most linear, stable, and reproducible temperature sensors is the platinum RTD. The RTD's resistance versus temperature characteristics are stable, reproducible, and have a near-linear, positive temperature coefficient from –200 to 800°F (–129 to 427°C). These attributes establish RTDs as the industry standard.

Temperature is determined by measuring resistance and then using the RTD's resistance versus temperature characteristics to extrapolate temperature. RTDs have linearity over a wide operating range, a wide temperature operating range, a high temperature operating range, interchangeability over a wide range, and good stability at high temperatures.

RTD Operational Theory

The resistance method of measuring temperature relies on a sensing element that changes temperature along with the process, and in doing so, changes its electrical resistance in a predictable and repeatable manner. Commonly referred to as RTDs, resistance temperature detectors use a sensing element, a small wire or coil sealed in a probe and put into contact with the process. The coil could be one of several metals but is usually made of copper, nickel, or platinum, with platinum having the most desirable properties. Platinum's resistive change is most linear with temperature change.

FIGURE 4.16. A typical stainless-steel resistance temperature detector with a watertight wiring connection box. (Courtesy D.G. Yuengling and Son Inc.)

There are two methods for the RTD to communicate the temperature it is sensing. It can be connected directly to a recorder/local readout/controller or it can use a temperature transmitter whereby the temperature is transmitted to the recorder/local readout/controller via a transmitted 4- to 20-mA or 0- to 10-VDC signal that is linear and covers the range of the RTD. For instance, if an RTD is capable of measuring from –200 to 800°F (–129 to 427°C), 4 mA would indicate –200°F (–129°C) and 20 mA would indicate 800°F (427°C).

The RTD is connected directly to an electronic circuit, which is basically an automated Wheatstone bridge. This is true whether it is using a temperature transmitter or a direct connection of the RTD to some type of controller/indicator. Very simply, the controller/indicator compares the RTD's resistance with a reference resistance and adjusts it to match the reference. An RTD can achieve an accuracy of ±0.5% of full scale and allow for remote installation, that is, the sensor and recorder may be separated by long distances without taking on special equipment and extra costs.

Thermocouples

Thermocouples, another popular form of electronic devices used to measure temperature, were discovered by Seebeck in 1821. He observed that an electromotive force (EMF) was generated in a closed circuit between two different metals when their junctions were at two different temperatures. The sensing junction, or thermocouple, is formed by simply connecting the ends of two dissimilar metal wires, such as iron and constantan (a 55% copper + 45% nickel alloy) or copper and constantan, to form a measuring, or hot, junction. The hot junction is then inserted into the process where the temperature is to be measured. The reference, or cold, junction (at the opposite end of the wires that make up the hot junction) is generally connected to the measuring instrument's terminals. As the temperature of the process increases, so does the difference in temperatures between the hot and cold junctions. With this difference in temperatures, an EMF is generated, and when connected to a sensitive instrument, the EMF can be measured and the instrument calibrated to read temperature directly. Key advantages of thermocouples include very rapid response to temperature changes and very high accuracy in the ranges of ±0.3% of full scale.

Dial Thermometers

Dial thermometers are used quite frequently to allow individuals to monitor temperature in specific locations. For instance, they may be installed at eye level on pipes to provide a temperature readout of water exiting a heat exchanger or the product temperature of beer entering the filler. The dial thermometer is relatively inexpensive, can be installed in a sanitary manner, and can be calibrated to ensure reasonable accuracy.

Measurement Recorders

Many times it is advantageous to record measurements as a function of time. All of the previously mentioned devices have this capacity, recording measurements usually in the form of either a circular chart or a continuous strip. Each has its advantages and disadvantages, and the format chosen is usually determined by the nature of the operation. The charts or strips are preprinted, scaled to the process being measured, and usually can be read directly.

Rotating charts, or circular charts, are widely used in the packaging area and represent predetermined time periods, that is, one revolution represents, for example, one shift, 24 hours, or 1 week (Fig. 4.17). Charts of this type are very easy to install and are especially convenient when recording for a constant unit of time. For example, it is often convenient to file the daily pasteurizer temperature charts with the production reports for that day.

Continuous strip charts, or strip charts, are often used when the process being measured is long term and not interrupted by the changing of a shift or day. They tend to

FIGURE 4.17. A circular chart recorder. (Courtesy D.G. Yuengling and Son Inc.)

be more common in the utilities area where continuous services are measured. Strip charts have an advantage over circular charts in that their scales are a consistent width across the chart, while on a circular chart, the size of the time scales vary, being narrower at the center and wider at the outside edge. This variation may hamper readability of the lower ranges in the circular scale.

Multiple-Pen Recorders

When two or more properties of the same system are measured, such as pressure and temperature, it is often convenient to record all measurements on the same chart at the same time. To do this, multiple pens with different colored inks are used. The measurements are recorded side by side in the same timeframe, making comparison and visual correlation much simpler. Multiple-pen recorders are available in both circular and strip configurations. A multiple-pen, paperless strip chart recorder is shown in Figure 4.18.

Pressure Measurements

Pressure needs to be monitored in many places throughout a packaging facility. It should be monitored at pump discharges, filler bowls, product piping, pressure regulators, air supplies, steam supplies, water supplies, CIP lines, and filter pressure and vacuum pressure to name a few sites. Several instruments can be used to measure pressure and in several different ways. Most instruments measure pressure by comparing the atmospheric pressure with the pressure in the process being measured. This is called pounds per square inch gauge (psig). Our atmosphere generally has a pressure of 14.7 pounds per square inch absolute (psia) or 0 psig. The practice is to measure in absolute pressure, which is the comparison between 0 psia, or no atmospheric pressure, and the pressure of the process being measured.

Bourdon Tube Pressure Gauge

Many of the pressure gauges used on process lines are Bourdon tube types of gauges (Fig. 4.19). Essentially, the gauge is made up of a Bourdon tube, an indicator needle, and a lever connection. The Bourdon tube appears as a flattened-out, sealed tube that is then coiled. As pressure is applied to the Bourdon tube, it tends to straighten and come out of the coiled position. However, because of the strength of the coil, the tube responds only in a relatively small manner to the pressure. The Bourdon tube's movement is a known, repeatable value that is linear to the pressure applied to it. When the Bourdon tube is coupled to the indicator needle, the needle visible on the front of most gauges moves to the value on the gauge that corresponds to the pressure applied to the Bourdon tube.

Pressure Transmitters

Another type of pressure-measuring device is a pressure transmitter. Most of the popular pressure transmitters use the pressure measurement to vary capacitance in an electronic circuit and convert that change in capacitance to an output signal from the transmitter. Pressure transmitters send an analog signal. It can be a 4- to 20-mA, 0- to 10-VDC, or 1- to 5-VDC signal that is input to a PLC, a stand-alone controller, or a readout.

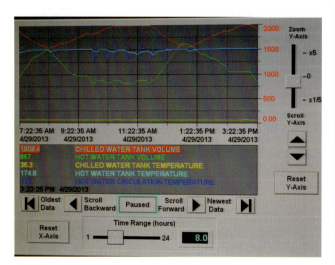

FIGURE 4.18. A paperless, multiple-pen recorder. (Courtesy D.G. Yuengling and Son Inc.)

FIGURE 4.19. A Bourdon tube dial pressure gauge. (Courtesy D.G. Yuengling and Son Inc.)

Usually when money has been invested in a pressure transmitter to monitor pressure, the process tends to be more critical and one that must be controlled and monitored very closely either locally or at a distance. A good example of the use of a pressure transmitter in a packaging line is on the filler-bowl counterpressure control. Here, a pressure signal is used to control a valve that controls the feed pressure to the filler bowl. By tracking the pressure at all times and by using a PID loop, the pressure control valve is modulated to drop the correct amount of pressure across it to supply the filler bowl with the correct counterpressure. This type of system is constantly updating the pressure applied or supplied through a closed-loop control system so that the filler counterpressure is held very steady.

This technology is also used to measure differential pressure (DP), which is used to determine the flow through pipes and the levels in tanks. The capacitance DP cell operates on a force-balance principle. A flexible diaphragm, which separates the two different areas under pressure, moves back and forth as the two pressures vary. This movement is transmitted to a capacitance circuit by the movement of the two pressure cells that are independently connected to the process at two different points and that counteract each other until a differential equilibrium is reached and the capacitance dictates the transmitter's signal. DP transmitters are discussed in more detail in the upcoming Level Control section of this chapter.

Pressure Switches

Pressure switches are generally pressure-sensing devices containing actuators that change the state of an electrical microswitch that is mounted in the pressure-sensing device. A pressure switch has a dead band. A dead band is a range of pressure within which the switch trips and resets so that the switch does not change states. An inherent part of the pressure switch, the dead band is a positive attribute. For instance, in a process that normally operates at 50 psig, it is possible that, without the dead band, a 0.1-psig change in pressure could make the pressure switch set and reset a large number of times in a short timespan. This would wear out the switch and make the process monitor react for no good reason. It is important to note that, typically, the pressure switch feeds a timer via a PLC or timing relay, which ensures that, before its action triggers a reaction, the switch stays in the predefined state for a certain amount of time. Again, this ensures that the process monitoring the pressure switch does not react prematurely.

The switch's change of state indicates that a significant event has happened in the process (e.g., an area is under either a low or high pressure) and that the event is unacceptable to a specified degree. The switch's action can set off an alarm, shut down a piece of equipment, or energize a beacon. A pressure switch is used, for instance, on pasteurizer pumps in the packaging department. The pressure switch protects the pasteurizer pumps from running dry and ruining pump components.

Level Control

Several areas in a packaging line use level control. One critical parameter for this control is filler-bowl level, as discussed earlier in the chapter. For the filler to fill containers properly, it is essential to maintain the filler-bowl level under many different operating conditions. The bowl level on a filler can have a subtle or severe impact on the filling process if it is not maintained properly. Each product, along with the filler it is running on, has its own optimum operating range.

There are several means to measure level, but the most common types found in packaging include the following: floats, capacitance level probes, and DP transmitters. For the most part, capacitance level probes have taken over the filler-bowl level control market. Capacitance level probes are discussed below.

Point Level Control

Point level control instruments can only sense and react to a process based on one point in the process. For instance, if the goal is for a solenoid to turn on when the water level in a pasteurizer drops to 15 inches, a point level control float could be used so that, when the water level drops to that depth, the float on the rod would trip a switch on the probe, which in turn energizes a solenoid that allows water to pass through the solenoid. When the water rises above 15 inches, the ball releases, and the switch de-energizes the solenoid, stopping the water flow.

Analog Level Control

An analog level instrument typically uses a 4- to 20-mA signal that corresponds to a range of level. For instance, if a filler bowl has a depth of 18 inches, the probe is set up so that, at 0 inches, the probe output reads 4 mA, and at 18 inches, it reads 20 mA. This tells the PLC, or stand-alone controller, receiving the 4- to 20-mA signal what depth of beer is in the bowl.

Capacitance Level Control

Capacitance level probes have no moving parts, are sanitary, and are easy to calibrate. They can be produced to ignore foam from beer so as to eliminate errant measurements, and they can be ordered with several types of output signal options. The capacitance level probe is inserted into the process to be monitored or controlled. Generally, it is inserted into the filler bowl from the top, and a seal is formed around the probe to prevent carbon dioxide from leaking from the bowl. As the level rises in the bowl, the output signal also changes proportionally with the level of beer in the filler bowl. A 4- to 20-mA signal is typically used as the output for this type of instrument.

Differential Pressure Level Control

DP transmitters are another means by which to measure level, although how they are employed depends on the process being measured. DP transmitters have two process connections. To measure level in a vessel that is open to the atmosphere, the high side of the pressure transmitter must be connected to the bottom of that vessel. The low-side process connection is left open to the atmosphere. In this manner, the transmitter compares the pressure registered at the high side against atmospheric pressure. (In instrumentation, this would be a psig reading.) These transmitters also typically use a 4- to 20-mA output that corresponds to the level that it is recording. For instance, if the transmitter were connected to a straight-sided, 30-foot-tall vessel, 4 mA would refer to 0 feet and 20 mA would refer to liquid that reaches the 30 foot height, the vessel's maximum fill line. Therefore, 12 mA would refer to the halfway point in the vessel, or 15 feet of liquid.

Flow Control

Flow monitoring and controls have several applications in packaging. Flow is monitored in evaluating product flow to the filler, steam flow to pasteurizers and bottle washers, flow of carbon dioxide to fillers, water flow to pasteurizers, CIP flow rates, and flow in conveyor lube and chemical treatment dosing.

Rotameters

Rotameters measure the flow rate of liquid or gas in a closed tube. It is occasionally misspelled as "rotometer". In the packaging department, rotameters are typically used to measure the flow rate of carbon dioxide. The device has a calibrated scale on the outside with a hollow tube running though its center. A float sits in the bottom of the hollow tube when there is no gas flow. When gas flow is present, the float rises, and the distance it rises correlates with the scale on the front. By aligning the front scale with the float, operators can find the flow rate measured in whatever units the scale is designed in.

Magnetic Flow Meters

Magnetic flow meters (Fig. 4.20) can be utilized in many flow measurement applications. They can measure flow rate and the total flow of a process. In the packaging department, some common applications include measuring product flow to the fillers and pasteurizer makeup water. Magnetic flow meters are accurate and

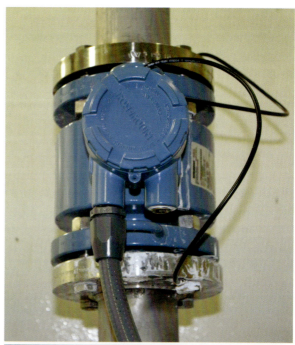

FIGURE 4.20. A magnetic flow meter measurement tube (top) and a magnetic flow meter transmitter and display (bottom). (Courtesy D.G. Yuengling and Son Inc.)

affordable and have no wear parts. Magnetic flow meters come in a variety of sizes to fit most any application. It is critical that they are sized and installed properly.

Mass Flow Meters

Mass flow meters are used to measure the gas flow rate and the total gas used in packaging. The flow rate of carbon dioxide, for instance, is of concern when monitoring the amount of carbon dioxide being used and when ensuring that the filler is being replenished with pure carbon dioxide. Mass flow meters are also used to measure the flow of product, steam, and water. These meters are typically more sensitive than are magnetic flow meters, which makes them an excellent choice in critical process control areas.

Differential Pressure Flow Transmitters

DP flow transmitters are typically used to measure pressure drop across a flow element mounted in a pipe. Measuring the steam flow rate and the total steam sent to the pasteurizer is an excellent application for this type of instrument. It can also be used to measure compressed airflow throughout the plant.

Flow Switches

Flow switches are used in applications in which it is important to verify that there is a minimum flow but it is not necessary to know the exact value. Flow switches are used to assess lubrication flow at a labeler station and water flow at the vacuum pump seal.

Analytical Measurements

In the packaging area, it is not uncommon to require the use of electrochemical measurements, which are generally referred to as measurements of conductivity. These measurements are based on the current-carrying properties of solutions containing ions and are used to determine the concentration of a specific solution.

The most common use of conductivity measurements in packaging is in determining the concentration of sodium hydroxide (NaOH), commonly referred to as caustic soda, in a solution. Used extensively in keg washing, bottle washing, and process sanitation, sodium hydroxide is purchased in a concentrated liquid form, usually 50% concentration, and diluted for use, generally to 2–4%. In some plants, creating the solution is an entirely manual process, that is, a predetermined amount of caustic soda is added to a certain amount of water and mixed thoroughly. Samples are then taken, titrated, and the concentrations determined. Any adjustments are made by adding more caustic soda or water.

While the caustic soda is in use in the keg or bottle washer, periodic checks must be made to determine whether the solutions' concentration is correct to ensure proper cleaning. In manual systems, this means that samples must be taken and titrated and the caustic soda levels adjusted accordingly. Automatic conductivity-measuring devices and controllers that adjust the concentrations according to a predetermined set point are commonly used and are an alternative to the manual monitoring of caustic soda concentrations.

All electrochemical measurements rely on the current-carrying properties of solutions containing ions. The system used for measuring concentrations of sodium hydroxide measures all ions in the solution, determining its electrolytic conductivity. A liquid that conducts electricity is referred to as an electrolyte. The unit of electrical conductance is mho, the reciprocal of electrical resistance, which is measured in ohms. The material's conductance, or its ability to pass an electrical current, varies with the shape of the conducting path. Conductance increases directly with the cross-sectional area and indirectly with the length of the sample.

In taking actual measurements, a conductivity cell is placed directly into the caustic system to be measured. By using two electrodes and passing a current between them, evaluators measure conductivity and a signal is sent to an indicator, a controller, or both. Generally calibrated in terms of percent concentration or parts per million, the indicator is read directly. If an indicating controller is being used, a set point is entered, and the unit activates a signal to add caustic soda, water, or both to the system to achieve the desired concentrations. Often, when measuring conductivity, the solution being measured may not be compatible with the electrodes, that is, the probes may be subject to polarization, fouling, or chemical action. In these cases, electrodeless conductivity systems are used. Two toroidally wound coils are encapsulated within close proximity in the sensor, which is placed in the solution. An AC signal is applied to one coil, and a current is generated in the second, which varies directly with the conductance of the solution. Accurate to within ±2% of the upper scale, conductivity controllers reduce the time required to mix cleaning solutions and ensure the concentrations are maintained to provide proper cleaning.

A second type of electrochemical instrument that can be found in the packaging area is a pH monitor, a controller, or both. Most commonly used to control pH levels in process water, it is also used to monitor and control pasteurizer water systems where pasteurizer cooling water is reclaimed and recirculated to the pasteurizers for reuse. Proper pH is essential in maximizing the performance of the chlorine in the water and in protecting the pasteurizer from corrosion. Similar in operation to the previously mentioned conductivity probe, the pH system measures only the acidity or alkalinity of the solution. Made of a special type of glass that is sensitive to hydrogen ions, the probe is immersed in the fluid being monitored. The glass probe contains a chamber filled with a reference fluid that maintains a constant pH. An internal electrode is submerged in this liquid and connected by means of a shielded cable to the pH indicator, the controller, or both. If the hydrogen ion concentration is greater in the process than it is in the reference fluid inside the tube, a positive electrical potential exists across the glass tip of the probe. If the process has a lower hydrogen concentration than that of the reference fluid, a negative potential exists. The relationship between the potential difference and the hydrogen ion concentration follows the Nernst equation. An electronic controller processes the signal received from the probe, according to the equation. As with the conductivity controller, the pH controller can also be set up to record and control to a preset set point.

Sanitary Requirements of Sensors

This chapter provides a quick review of some of the various instruments commonly found in the packaging area. Steam, air, carbon dioxide, beer, and water (whether hot, ambient, or refrigerated) are among the factors measured by these devices. Each instrument selected to measure a process should be suited to the application. Operating conditions—such as temperature, pressure, speed, and accuracy required—should be considered, and the instruments should be matched to the parameters of the process. The instrument should be selected to function in its optimum range during normal system operations and be capable of withstanding the maximums of the system without damage.

The demand of working within sanitary conditions is an important consideration often overlooked when selecting instrumentation. In the packaging area of a brewery, several systems require sanitary conditions and are frequently cleaned and regularly monitored for microbiological growth by quality control personnel. These include the water (process), carbon dioxide, and beer supply systems. These systems all come in contact with the final product, and for this reason, they must be maintained at a high state of cleanliness. To ensure that instrumentation complies with the sanitation requirements, the terms "sanitary" or "food grade" have been applied to installations and equipment that meet these criteria. In terms of instrumentation, the label "sanitary" refers to the physical characteristics of the sensor's surfaces that come in contact with the process being measured. Surfaces that permit the collection or entrapment of material supporting microbiological growth and that are not removed during normal equipment cleaning are not acceptable for use with food. Sanitary installations are noncorrosive, have smooth surfaces and no pockets for the stagnant collection of material, and are cleaned as the system is cleaned.

Compromises to save cost or time and employees' lack of sanitation knowledge are probably the most common causes for the use of nonsanitary instrumentation. To cut costs or to save time, a nonsanitary sensor might end up being used. This is an extremely easy pitfall to be caught in because, generally speaking, sanitary instruments are significantly more expensive and require additional time and expertise to install. Often, inherently nonsanitary instruments, fittings, or piping arrangements are installed on systems that come in contact with food because the personnel doing the work have not been exposed to sanitary concepts and are not aware of the systems' special requirements. To prevent this problem, training hourly personnel, equipment designers, and supervisors on food-grade installations is most helpful. Hazard analysis and critical control point (HACCP) standards are increasingly being applied in world-class manufacturing, and HACCP training is almost becoming mandatory.

For an installation to be sanitary, it has to be cleanable during normal system cleaning. This cleaning can happen in two ways. First, and least advantageous, is cleaning that requires a large amount of operator involvement. This includes dismantling equipment, hose connections, and special tools and relies heavily on the operator to ensure that the proper procedures are followed. This approach is often referred to as cleaning out of place (COP). Often in this approach, when time is short, tools are misplaced, untrained operators perform the cleaning, or steps are missed in the cleaning procedure, and the system's sanitation is compromised. The second, and most popular, cleaning technique is cleaning in place, or what is commonly called CIP. With CIP, instrumentation is left intact and is cleaned automatically as the system is cleaned. Modern CIP systems generally require little operator input since they are automatically cycled though a programmed series of wash–rinse cycles.

To eliminate the sanitation problems in instruments, special sanitary or food-grade sensors and adaptors have been developed. When installed properly (to eliminate cracks, crevices, dead legs, etc.), these devices permit accurate monitoring of the process without fear of inadvertently causing microbiological growth.

Sanitary Temperature Measurement

The temperature measurement devices discussed previously in this chapter all require a probe to be placed in contact with the medium being measured. To facilitate this measurement and maintain a sanitary installation, thermowells are used. Basically, a thermowell is a hollow metal tube, open at one end and sealed at the other. A sensor is inserted into the tube and allowed to make contact or bottom out with the end of the sidewalls of the well. It is important that a good contact between the sensor and the well is achieved to ensure each sensor reaches the same temperature as the medium it is measuring.

Thermowells offer several advantages. First, the well is usually made of stainless steel, and when installed properly, it is sanitary and can be cleaned during normal CIP. Second, the well acts as a positioner, or holder, for the sensor. By varying the thermowell length, the sensor can be exactly positioned in the system being measured. Third, since the well penetrates the system and provides a seal between the system and the probe, the probe may be removed from the well without disturbing the medium, that is, the system does not need to be emptied or depressurized to remove the sensor.

Sanitary Pressure Measurement

As stated previously, the Bourdon tube is the most popular pressure measurement device. However, from a sanitation point of view, it is obvious the device cannot be used in contact with food since the material will travel up and collect in the tube itself. This buildup cannot be removed during normal CIP and would soon become a source of contamination. However, liquid-filled systems using the Bourdon tube are available for sanitary pressure measurement. They consist basically of a diaphragm and a reservoir that is connected to a Bourdon tube. The entire system is filled with a noncompressible liquid and sealed. It should be noted, however, that this liquid must always be nontoxic, should not have an adverse effect on the process if a leak were to occur, and must be FDA approved for use with food products. A common liquid used in breweries for this purpose is propylene glycol. In these pressure measurement devices, the diaphragm is made of stainless steel and is mounted in a special gasketed socket assembly. The entire assembly usually fits flush with the wall of the system and lends itself well to normal CIP. As the pressure of the system changes, the diaphragm flexes in and out. This movement attempts to compress the fluid within; however, since the system is filled and sealed, the Bourdon tube is distorted just as it is when measuring the system pressure directly.

Another system of sanitary pressure measurement commonly used to determine the levels in tanks is the sanitary DP cell. With this device, a stainless-steel diaphragm is mounted in a gasketed socket and attached flush to the bottom or lower side of the tank. The pneumatic-force balance system is used to generate an air signal proportionate to the tank level, and the signal may be displayed directly or used as an input to other controls. The diaphragm, if installed properly, does not collect contaminants and can be cleaned during normal CIP of the tank.

Sanitary Flow Measurement

Sanitary flow instruments do not have any stagnant areas of flow or any areas that can harbor bacteria. Both the magnetic flow meter and the mass flow meter typically do not have any of these areas since they have no moving parts and their internal parts are very smooth. These instruments are easily cleaned in place, which reduces downtime and minimizes the effort to maintain the system in a sanitary manner. Figure 4.21 presents an example of a sanitary mass flow meter using flange connections.

Pasteurization Unit Measurement

Since pasteurization is a critical packaging process in almost all major breweries, the instruments used to verify the performance of pasteurization systems merit more extensive discussion. Usually operated by a quality control department, these instruments measure and record the temperature–time relationship that is the key to the pasteurizer process.

The most common type of pasteurization unit (PU) survey is the solid-state PU computer. This device is the most widely used, is relatively new, and combines

FIGURE 4.21. A sanitary mass flow meter. (Courtesy D.G. Yuengling and Son Inc.)

the advantages of all of the older instruments. It has the convenience of a traveling clock, the accuracy of electronic sensors, and the added feature of automatic PU calculation. Basically, it consists of a microprocessor contained in a waterproof enclosure with two RTDs as temperature sensors. The sensors are placed in the container and, along with the enclosure, ride through the pasteurizer. Temperature and time changes are recorded within the processor's memory, where they are stored for future reference. At the end of the survey, the computer displays the total PUs achieved, along with the maximum temperature reached by the container. Also, with the proper software, the unit can be connected to a computer and then the data can be displayed on a computer monitor, stored in computer memory, and printed. This allows for analysis of the external spray temperature and internal beer temperature.

The unit's one shortfall is that it only measures temperatures in the pasteurizer within a narrow band. The units cannot indicate clogged nozzles or pans except in the area the instrument passes through. This speaks to the importance of good pasteurizer maintenance.

Instrument Calibration

The importance of a good instrumentation calibration program cannot be overstated. The instruments gathering information, which is then collected and monitored by personnel to be used for controlling processes, are only as good as the calibration they receive and the frequency in which they are calibrated. Manufacturers supply general rules of thumb for calibrating their instruments. However, plant personnel must be able to determine what works best for their process, the environment in which the instruments are located, and the criticality of the process being measured. A nuclear power plant has redundant instruments measuring reactor water level at multiple points and with several types of instruments. Its instruments are calibrated more frequently than perhaps are those in a brewery that measure the caustic soda concentration in a tank. It is the brewery plant personnel, however, who make the decisions that ultimately affect cost, accuracy, and processes.

DEDICATION

This chapter is dedicated to the memory of Lee Holland. He was a friend and a true champion of the brewing industry who always delivered with passion, boundless energy, and a smile.

REFERENCES FOR FURTHER READING

Anderson, N. A. (1980). Instrumentation for Process Measurement and Control, 3rd ed. Chilton Company, Radnor, PA.

Broderick, H. M., ed. (1982). Beer Packaging. Master Brewers Association of the Americas, St. Paul, MN.

Dataforth Corporation. RTD, Resistance Temperature Detector. Application Note 105. The Corporation, Tucson, AZ. www.dataforth.com/catalog/pdf/an105.pdf

Murrill, P. W. (2000). Fundamentals of Process Control Theory, 3rd ed. ISA Publishing, Research Triangle Park, NC.

Omega Engineering. (1998). Glossary. In: Transactions in Measurement and Control, Vol. 3: Force-Related Measurements, pp. 74-80. Omega Engineering, Stamford, CT. www.omega.com/literature/transactions/volume3/glossary.html

CHAPTER 5

Canning Operations

WILLIAM J. FORSYTHE
Canning Technology

● CAN AND END MANUFACTURE SPECIFICATIONS

Canned beer was first sold in the United States on January 24, 1935, when the G. Krueger Brewing Company opened a test market of the new package in Richmond, VA. That test market led to a successful package introduction. In the ensuing years, the can has become the primary single-serve package for beer in the U.S. market. More than 50% of all packaged beer sold in the United States is in cans.

Since the early 1980s, the United States brewing industry has converted entirely to using the drawn and wall-ironed, two-piece aluminum can and a 202-diameter, stay-on-tab (SOT) type end. For that reason, this chapter concentrates on modern, two-piece aluminum beer cans and ends. This chapter covers how the can and end are formed from a flat sheet of metal, how and why can and end specifications have changed, and what modifications to brewery filling lines have been required by these new specifications. Because two-piece steel cans are still used outside the United States, this chapter highlights the differences in manufacturing processes and specifications between two-piece aluminum and steel cans.

Prior to the move to two-piece aluminum cans, several different types of three-piece cans incorporating different metal substrates were developed and used successfully for packaging beer. So as not to lose this history, Appendix I provides a chronology of major developments in commercial beer can manufacture in the United States.

Can Manufacture

A typical two-piece aluminum can manufacturing line (Fig. 5.1) starts with the placement of a coil of aluminum on the coil car/upender, which orients the coil, allowing it

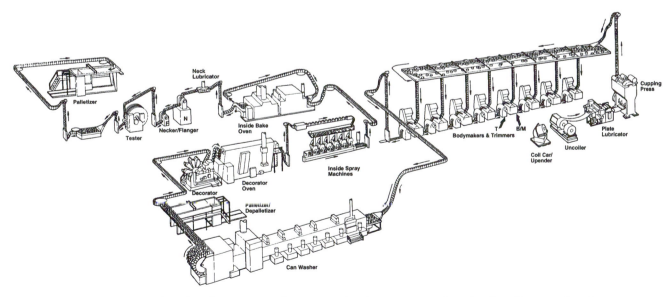

FIGURE 5.1. Equipment and product flow in a typical two-piece aluminum can manufacturing line. (Courtesy Canning Technology)

to be moved to the uncoiler (Fig. 5.2). The uncoiler unrolls the strip of aluminum, feeding it to the plate lubricator.

The plate lubricator deposits a thin film of water-soluble lubricant on both sides of the aluminum sheet. The metal must be lubricated so that it flows smoothly over the tool surfaces in the cupping press. Can forming begins in the cupping press (Fig. 5.3).

Cupping presses typically contain 12–14 multiple-action dies, meaning each press stroke produces 12–14 cups and each die performs more than one operation. In the first die action, the cut-edge die blanks, or cuts, a disc. The scrap, or skeleton, is discharged from the press and recycled.

The dimensions of the disc are important. There must be a sufficient amount of aluminum to form a complete can. The dimensions of the cut-edge die precisely set the diameter of the disc, and its thickness is the metal starting gauge.

The second die action forms a cup. The draw punch (Fig. 5.4) forces the disc through the cupping die, and

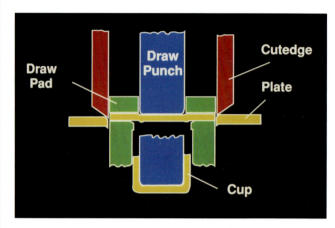

FIGURE 5.4. Cupping press schematic drawing showing cup formation from a disc. (Courtesy Canning Technology)

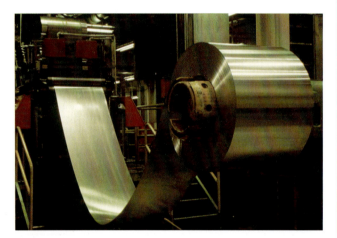

FIGURE 5.2. Uncoiler feeding the plate lubricator. (Courtesy Canning Technology)

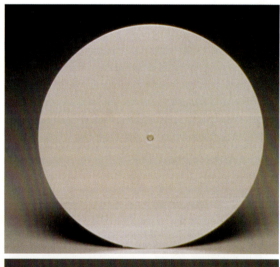

FIGURE 5.5. Blank (top) and cup (bottom). (Courtesy Canning Technology)

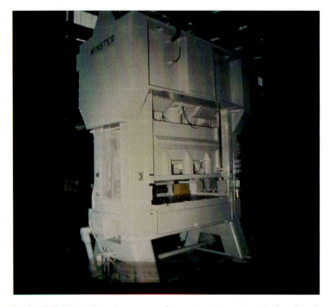

FIGURE 5.3. Cupping press. (Courtesy Canning Technology)

the cup drops through the die onto the cup conveyor. The starting blank and the finished cup are shown in Figure 5.5.

From the cupping press, the cup is conveyed to one of a series of bodymakers or wall-ironing machines (Fig. 5.6). A trimmer is located at the discharge of each bodymaker.

Each bodymaker contains a punch that forms the can through a series of ring-shaped dies. The punch is shaped so that metal is placed in the can body at the points required to maximize its strength (Fig. 5.7).

The thickness of the bottom of the can remains very close to the original metal's starting gauge. This has a direct bearing on the can's buckle resistance—its ability to withstand the increased internal pressure generated during pasteurization without permanent deflection. The side wall thins as the can is formed. The thick wall provides increased strength where the neck profile and double seam are formed.

In operation, the cup is centered in front of the punch. The punch moves horizontally, forcing the cup through the redraw die, then through three wall-ironing dies, and finally, into the doming die (Fig. 5.8).

FIGURE 5.6. Bodymaker or wall-ironing machine. (Courtesy Canning Technology)

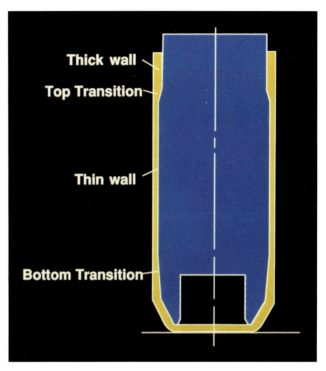

FIGURE 5.7. Punch shape and resulting wall thickness variation. (Courtesy Canning Technology)

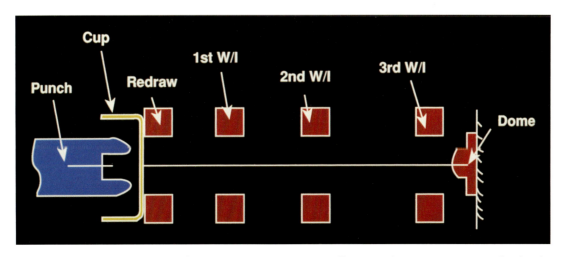

FIGURE 5.8. Bodymaker metal-forming components. W/I = wall ironing. (Courtesy Canning Technology)

In this first step, the punch enters the cup and begins to stroke through the redraw ring (Fig. 5.9). The redraw reduces the cup's diameter and shapes the cup so that it conforms to the punch (Fig. 5.10). The punch forces the can through three progressively smaller-diameter wall-ironing rings, thinning (ironing) the wall and increasing the can's height (Fig. 5.11). At this point, the walls are not of uniform height (Fig. 5.12). At the end of the punch stroke, the bottom of the can contacts the extractor and doming die, forming the bottom profile (Fig. 5.13).

While these operations have been discussed as though each were separate, they are part of a continuous process.

Each cupping press stroke blanks a disc and draws a cup through each individual die pocket. Likewise, each wall-ironing punch makes one continuous stroke through the redraw die, through the wall-ironing rings, and into the doming station, producing a can.

As the punch retracts, the can is stripped and discharged through the trimmer, which corrects the can wall's nonuniform height by removing a band of metal from the top of the can (Fig. 5.14).

At this point, the cupper and bodymaker have produced a full-sized can from the original flat sheet of aluminum (Fig. 5.15).

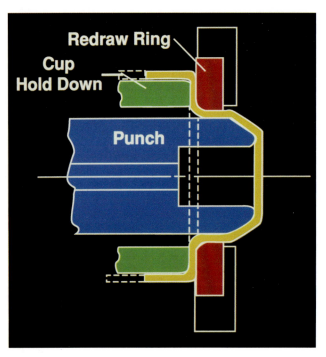

FIGURE 5.9. Punch entering the cup and beginning to stroke through the redraw ring. (Courtesy Canning Technology)

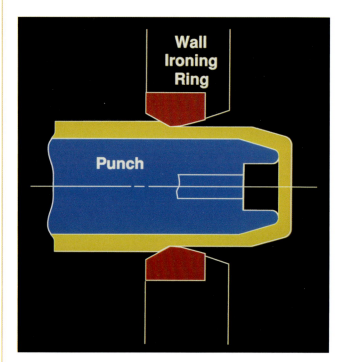

FIGURE 5.11. Punch forcing a can through a wall-ironing ring. (Courtesy Canning Technology)

FIGURE 5.10. Redraw progression. (Courtesy Canning Technology)

Canning Operations • 75

FIGURE 5.12. Third-stage wall-ironed can. Note that the height is not uniform. (Courtesy Canning Technology)

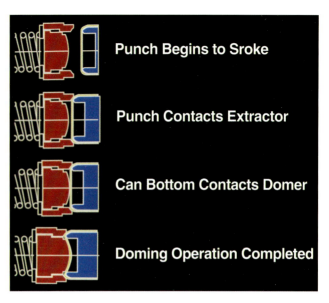

FIGURE 5.13. Doming progression. (Courtesy Canning Technology)

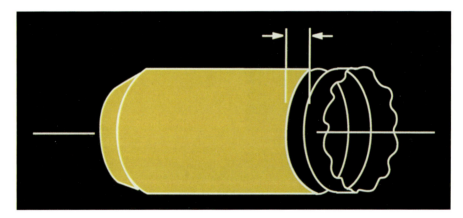

FIGURE 5.14. The trimmer removes the rough band of metal from the top of the can per the specified dimension. (Courtesy Canning Technology)

FIGURE 5.15. The complete two-piece can manufacturing progression from disc to can. (Courtesy Canning Technology)

The metal forming in the bodymaker is an intense process. During the operation, the punch, redraw die, wall-ironing rings, doming station, and can are bathed with a water-soluble lubricant to both provide the necessary surface lubrication and dissipate the frictional heat generated between the aluminum and the dies.

The lubricant, or coolant, is reused after having been recirculated through a filter to remove aluminum fines. The coolant must be removed from the can before applying the outside decoration and the inside protective coatings. This is accomplished in a can washer. Can washers resemble tunnel pasteurizers (Fig. 5.16).

The cans are inverted and conveyed through the washer on a moving wide-mesh mat. They are sprayed, inside and out, with chemical solutions that perform the cleaning. Prior to discharge from the washer, the can is rinsed clean of all washer chemicals, including a final rinse with deionized water. The cans are then dried with heated, forced air. Figure 5.17 contrasts the brightness of a washed can with an unwashed can.

The clean, dry can is then conveyed to a decorator, which applies the exterior lithography, or label, and the bottom chime varnish. Depending on the design, decorators can apply four to eight colors.

The decorator infeed places the can on a mandrel, which supports and rotates the can while the lithography is applied. Each color, or print, has a separate ink fountain that meters the appropriate amount and color of ink onto

FIGURE 5.16. Typical can washer. (Courtesy Canning Technology)

FIGURE 5.17. Comparison of an unwashed, untrimmed can body (left) to a washed, trimmed can body (right). (Courtesy Canning Technology)

FIGURE 5.18. Lithography progression in which prints are applied to the blanket on a commercial beer label. The separation sequence is to illustrate the process—cans are not decorated in steps. (Courtesy Canning Technology)

an engraved cylinder. The cylinders transfer the ink to a blanket, which applies the complete label to the can in one pass. Figure 5.18 shows how prints are applied to the blanket on a commercial beer label.

The can, now coated with wet ink, next contacts a rotating varnish application roll, which overvarnishes the entire sidewall with a clear, protective coating. The can is transferred from the mandrel onto a pin, which contacts only the can's inside surface, and is conveyed through the decorator oven, or "pin" oven. This oven hardens the exterior lithography with forced hot air.

At the infeed to the pin oven, the bottom of the can contacts a roll coater that coats the bottom chime, the surface on which the can is conveyed, with varnish. This is the first major difference between the manufacturing processes for two-piece aluminum and steel cans. With aluminum cans, only the actual bottom chime riding surface is coated. On steel cans, the entire bottom surface must be spray coated to prevent rusting.

If the label requires a base coat, it is applied in a separate base-coating unit before the decorator. In the base-coating unit, the can is also supported on a mandrel, but the printing cylinders apply a solid color to the blanket and then to the can. Base-coated cans are dried in a separate base-coat pin oven and then fed to the decorator for lithography application.

Following lithography application and drying, the can is conveyed to an inside spray machine, where the inside of the can is coated. This coating prevents the product from contacting or reacting with the metal in the can body.

The inside spray coating is cured by forced-air heat in the inside bake oven. This oven also provides the final cure for the exterior lithography and overvarnish.

The amount of inside spray coating used is the other area of major difference between two-piece aluminum can and steel can manufacture for beer. Aluminum cans receive one inside spray coat. Because dissolved iron has a much more deleterious effect on beer flavor than aluminum does, two-piece steel cans receive a double coat of inside spray.

After discharge from the inside bake oven, the can passes through a neck lubricator that applies a thin film of lubricant to the exterior of the top of the can. The can is then conveyed to the necker/flanger, where the neck and flange are formed.

U.S. brewers have adopted a 202/211-diameter can body. This means the top of the can is reduced, or "necked in", to $2\text{-}2/16$ inches (5.3975 cm) in diameter while the body remains $2\text{-}11/16$ inches (6.8263 cm) in diameter. There are a number of manufacturing methods for necking in and flanging a can. The steps in forming a $202/211 \times 413$ beer can using the smooth die neck process are shown in Figure 5.19. Flanging is the final metal forming step. The can is now complete.

All finished cans are evaluated for leakage with a light tester. The can flange is clamped against a sealing surface while the outside is exposed to a bright light source. A photocell inside the can detects any entering light, which, if found, triggers a reject mechanism. The photocell detects and rejects leaks as small as 0.001 inches (0.0254 mm) in diameter.

FIGURE 5.19. Three of the fourteen necking steps and one flanging operation required to form a $202/211 \times 413$ beer can from a straight wall can (far left) using the smooth die neck process, the most common method. (Courtesy Canning Technology)

On some lines, the light tester discharge has been retrofitted with a high-speed video camera that "looks" inside each can. The camera detects and rejects foreign contamination, such as grease, or defects, such as missing or incomplete inside spray. Following testing, the cans are placed on pallets for shipment to the customer's plant.

Can End Manufacture

As in the manufacture of cans, modern manufacture of can ends starts with the placement of a coil of aluminum on an uncoiler. Unlike the aluminum used for cans, the aluminum used for end manufacture is precoated on both sides with organic protective coatings that contain internal lubricants. There are no plate-coating, baking, lubrication, or washing operations in a modern end manufacturing plant.

The uncoiler feeds the strip directly into the shell press, which, similar to the cupping press in the can plant, contains several multiple-acting dies. Most shell presses have 22 dies, producing 22 shells per press stroke.

The first die action blanks a disc (Fig. 5.20). As the stroke continues, the second die action forms the countersink and center panel (Fig. 5.21).

The shell is then discharged into a curler, which forms the upright edge, or lip, of the curl into the precisely rounded shape necessary for good double-seam formation. The latest-design shell presses die form the curl, eliminating the separate curling operation.

From the curler, the ends move to the compound liner where a nozzle applies a liquid sealing compound. The shell is rotated rapidly while the compound is applied so that centrifugal force moves the liner into the correct position, which is termed "placement". Shells treated with solvent-based compounds air cure. End lines using water-based compounds are equipped with drying towers.

From the compound liner, the shells are fed to a conversion press where several operations are performed simultaneously. Seven forming operations convert the compound-lined shell into an SOT end (Fig. 5.22).

Integral within the shell press is a 10-station tab die, which forms a narrow strip of aluminum into a finished tab (Fig. 5.23).

Coining strengthens the end. Flattening the panel radius increases its resistance to unfolding, which, in turn, increases the end's buckle resistance. A newer design replaces the coin bead with a Stolle Step®, which further increases buckle resistance (Fig. 5.24).

The conversion press completes the end manufacturing process. The finished ends are conveyed to the packing station, where they are placed in paper sleeves and the sleeves are stacked on pallets for shipment to the customer.

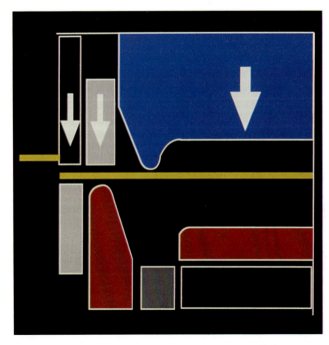

FIGURE 5.20. First action of a double action shell die: blanking. (Courtesy Canning Technology)

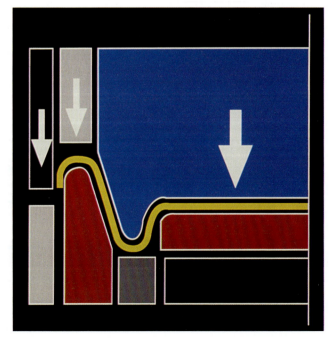

FIGURE 5.21. Second action of a double action shell die: countersink and center panel formation. (Courtesy Canning Technology)

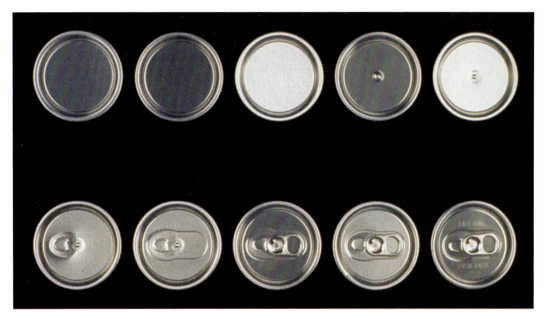

FIGURE 5.22. Progression of converting a compound-lined shell into a stay-on-tab end. (Courtesy Canning Technology)

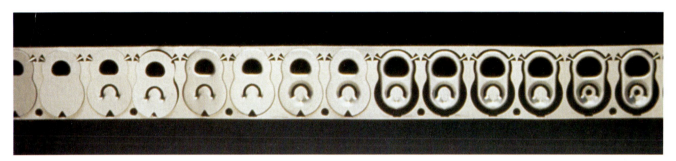

FIGURE 5.23. Progression of forming a tab. (Courtesy Canning Technology)

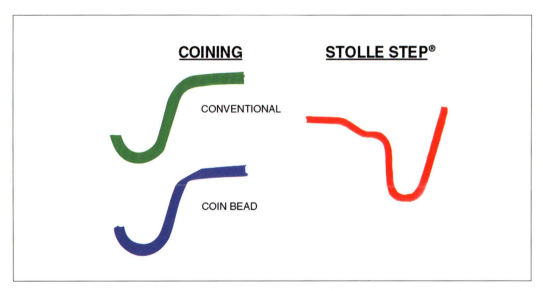

FIGURE 5.24. The coining process to strengthen the can end. (Courtesy Canning Technology)

Can End Specifications and Their Impact on Performance

Cans and ends must meet the following basic performance parameters.

Capacity

The can must hold the stated contents (Table 5.1). Since a can filler fills a can to a vertical height, can capacity is specified in inches of headspace at nominal fill.

The accepted industry interchangeability specification is 0.470 inch ± 0.020 inch (1.1938 cm ± 0.0508 cm), meaning a can filled to 0.470-inch (1.1938 cm) headspace, using 68°F (20°C) water as the standard, contains the stated contents.

Axial Load

The can must withstand the vertical load applied during filling and double seaming, normally a minimum load of 175 pounds (79 kg).

Buckle Resistance

Both the can bottom and the end must withstand the internal pressure developed during pasteurization without permanent deformation, called buckling. Buckle resistance is commonly specified at a minimum of 90 pounds per square inch gauge (psig) (6.2 bar).

Metal Exposure

The inside spray coating on the can and the coil-applied protective coating on the end must provide a nearly continuous film coating to prevent aluminum or iron from dissolving into the product. The enamel rater provides a standardized test for measuring the amount of coating. Usually the brewer and the can supplier agree on mutually acceptable limits.

TABLE 5.1. Typical Commercial Two-Piece Aluminum Can Sizes and Their Nominal Capacities

Can Size	Designation	Nominal Capacity
204/207.5 × 413	10 oz.	10.0 fluid oz. (U.S.)
204/211 × 413	12 oz.	12.0 fluid oz. (U.S.)
204/209 × 504	Tall 12 oz.	12.0 fluid oz. (U.S.)
204/211 × 603	16 oz.	16.0 fluid oz. (U.S.)
202/211 × 413	12 oz.	12.0 fluid oz. (U.S.)
202/211 × 603	16 oz.	16.0 fluid oz. (U.S.)
206/209 × 710	24 oz.	24.0 fluid oz. (U.S.)
209/300 × 710	24 oz.	24.0 fluid oz. (U.S.)
300/307 × 603	0.75 L	750 mL
300/307 × 710	32 oz.	32.0 fluid oz. (U.S.)

End Opening Forces

The SOT end must open with reasonable consumer effort. Standardized tests are available for measuring both the force required to initially score break, vent or "pop", the can and the force needed to complete the opening tear, or "push". Ordinarily the brewer and the end supplier develop mutually acceptable limits.

Flavor

Neither the can nor the end can contribute any undesirable tastes or odors to the product or change the product flavor, aroma, or foam characteristics in any way.

This is a complex standard involving the washer's effectiveness in cleaning the can; the coatings, lubricants, and other materials used in can and end manufacture; coating bake schedules; and the conditions under which empty cans and ends are stored. These standards are usually jointly developed by the brewer and the can manufacturer as new materials and processes are qualified.

Dimensions

Cans and ends must be manufactured within certain consistent dimensional tolerances so that cans and ends perform on-line and run interchangeably between different suppliers. The industry-recommended interchangeability dimensions for 12- and 16-oz. cans are summarized in Table 5.2.

Since approximately 1980, when the U.S. brewers fully converted to using two-piece aluminum cans and SOT ends, the industry has focused on reducing both the amount of aluminum in the can and the cost of the packaging to the brewer.

This effort has focused on three major areas.

- Reducing the can's starting gauge, a process known as lightweighting or down-gauging
- Using ultra-lightweight ends, an effort that has produced several end designs
- Reducing the diameter of the can end, also known as necking-in the can

When the gauge of the can or the end is reduced, the buckle resistance decreases. Since the pasteurization process still generates the same amount of pressure, the package must be strengthened or it will fail on-line.

With reduced-gauge cans, the bottom profile is redesigned to increase its strength. This usually includes reducing the diameter of the bottom chime, a change that, as a side effect, makes the can tip over more easily when conveyed. Brewers and can makers have jointly developed better ways to convey lightweight cans to resolve this concern.

TABLE 5.2. Industry-Recommended Interchangeability Dimensions for Beer Cans and Ends

Cans

		202/211 × 413 (12 oz.)	202/211 × 603 (16 oz.)
A	Body outside diameter	2.600 in. ± 0.008 in.	2.604 in. ± 0.008 in.
B	Flange width	0.082 in. ± 0.010 in.	0.082 in. ± 0.010 in.
C	Flanged can height	4.812 in. ± 0.015 in.	6.190 in. ± 0.015 in.
D	Neck-plug diameter	2.063 in. ± 0.007 in.	2.063 in. ± 0.007 in.
E	Flange angle	12° maximum	12° maximum
	Headspace	0.470 in. ± 0.020 in.	0.470 in. ± 0.020 in.

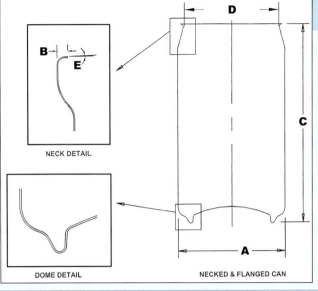

202-Diameter Conventional End

		English	Metric
A	Curl diameter	2.340 in. ± 0.010 in.	59.44 mm ± 0.25 mm
B	Curl height	0.080 in. ± 0.005 in.	2.03 mm ± 0.13 mm
C	Countersink depth	0.270 in. ± 0.005 in.	6.86 mm ± 0.13 mm
	Ends per 2 in.	24 ± 2	24 ± 2
	Buckle pressure	90 psi minimum	620.5 kPa
	Material	Aluminum	Aluminum

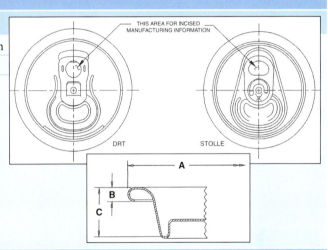

202-Diameter Reformable End

		English
A	Curl diameter	Consult end supplier
B	Curl height	Consult end supplier
C	Countersink depth	Consult end supplier
D	Panel height	Consult end supplier
	Ends per 2 in.	Consult end supplier
	Material	Aluminum

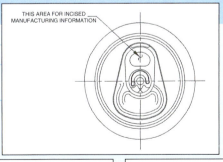

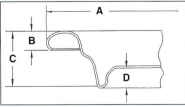
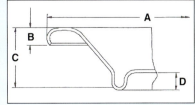

The combination of ultra-lightweight ends and further necking-in the cans allows manufacturers to further reduce the amount of aluminum needed for the end.

Ultra-lightweight ends and the latest innovation—ends that are reformed in double seaming—incorporate design changes that require changes to a brewery's closing-machine tooling (chucks, rolls, and cover feeds) so that the tooling fits the revised end dimensions.

Further necking-in the can saves metal not only by reducing the diameter of the end but also by permitting further gauge reductions, since the product pressure will be exerted on a smaller area and the total force on the end will be less.

To fill, close, and package these reduced-diameter cans, the brewery must acquire new filler valves plus closing machine and secondary packaging machine change parts.

These design changes are important and ongoing. Industry members need to understand how these changes affect brewery operations in order to commercialize them efficiently. Brewers and can makers, however, have a good track record of jointly accomplishing these changes.

Since the two-piece aluminum can was introduced in 1965, the starting gauge has been reduced approximately 0.0060 inch (0.1524 mm), saving about 16 pounds (7.26 kg) of aluminum per thousand cans. Between the ultra-lightweight end profiles and the diameter reduction from 211 to 202, the gauge of the SOT end has been reduced more than 0.0050 inch (0.127 mm), saving more than 4 pounds (1.8144 kg) of aluminum per thousand ends. The brewing and can manufacturing industries have worked together to "reduce, reuse, and recycle".

● SHIPPING AND STORAGE OF EMPTY CANS AND ENDS

Modern Shipping Methods

Since the introduction of the beer can, can manufacturers and their brewery customers have used several methods for shipping empty cans. These have progressed from using reshipper cartons through employing various bulk delivery systems. Today, all cans are delivered on compression-pack pallets (Fig. 5.25). The change to the standard pallet was driven by the increase in both can-making and filling line speeds plus the need to protect the lightweight, two-piece aluminum can from shipping and handling damage.

For interchangeability, the industry has developed standards on pallet size, number of cans per layer, and number of layers per pallet. Those used for the different commercial can and end sizes are detailed in Tables 5.3 and 5.4.

Cans are loaded onto pallets automatically by a palletizer. The first step is placing a separator sheet on a pallet. A quantity of empty cans is placed on this base, patterned to cover the area without any overhang. In the case of 12-oz. cans, there are 389 cans per layer. Additional

TABLE 5.3. Typical Can Pallet Packs

Can Size	Pallet Size (inches)	Cans per Layer	Layers per Pallet	Cans per Pallet
10 fluid oz.	44 × 56	472	20	9,944
12 fluid oz.	44 × 56	389	21	8,169
16 fluid oz.	44 × 56	389	16	6,224
24 fluid oz.	44 × 56	314	13	4,082
0.75 L	44 × 56	240	15	3,600
32 fluid oz.	44 × 56	240	13	3,120

TABLE 5.4. Typical End Pallet Packs

End Diameter	Pallet Size (inches)	Ends per Sleeve	Sleeves per Pallet	Ends per Pallet
202	44 × 56	552	630	347,760
206	44 × 56	552	574	316,848
204	44 × 56	560	538	301,280
209	35 × 37	408	253	103,224
300	35 × 37	384	181	69,504

FIGURE 5.25. Palletized cans with plastic dividing sheets and strapping. Note the pallet tag containing production information. (Courtesy K. Ockert)

layers of cans are stacked on the pallet with a separator sheet, or slip sheet, placed between each layer until the pallet is complete. Again, in the case of 12-oz. cans, there are 21 layers per pallet.

A separator sheet is placed over the top layer of cans. A top frame is placed over the last separator sheet to prevent the strapping from damaging the can flanges. The loaded pallet is conveyed to a strapping station where a compression unit applies a vertical load while the pallet is secured with plastic strapping in both directions. The completed pallet is either moved to a warehouse for storage or shipped directly to the brewery for filling.

The can manufacturing industry in the United States has converted to using plastic pallets, separator sheets, and top frames, replacing wood and paper. Plastic separator sheets must be cleaned periodically prior to their reuse.

At the brewery, the cans are unloaded by an automatic depalletizer, which reverses the action of the can plant's palletizer, sweeping off one layer of cans at a time, feeding them into the empty-can conveying system, which supplies the filler. The depalletizer has gripper fingers that hold each separator sheet to prevent its being swept forward with the cans. The can pattern must not allow the grip fingers to damage adjacent cans. Most can depalletizers automatically remove and stack top frames, separator sheets, and pallets for return to the can manufacturing plant for reuse.

Like cans, end packaging has evolved into a standardized system. Ends are packed in paper sleeves approximately 4–5 feet long. The sleeves are stacked on pallets and secured by an interlocking strip of plastic called a "snake wrap", named for the way it snakes through the pallet and around the sleeves (Fig. 5.26). The load is stabilized with a plastic stretch wrap.

Code Identification in Can and End Manufacturing

Both can and end pallets must identify, at minimum, the plant that produced the cans or ends and the date, shift, and line on which they were manufactured. Ideally, pallet coding will also include the time the pallet was loaded and the order in which it was packed. Normally, this information is printed on tags affixed to two sides of each can or end pallet. It should also be printed on the individual end sleeves.

The brewery must retain this information, further identified by the dates the cans and ends were filled, until the brewery is certain there are no problems with the product in its distribution system. This information also helps the brewery comply with product traceability and hazard analysis and critical control point (HACCP) requirements. In the event of a quality problem requiring a product hold or recall, this data will be valuable in identifying and minimizing the size of the held lot.

Each individual can's lithography must identify the plant, line, date, and shift of manufacture in a readily legible format. The inscription on each end must identify the plant and conversion press lane on which the end was produced and as much information on the date of manufacture as will fit in the limited space available.

Standards for Shipping and Storage

There are three main areas of concern in shipping and warehousing cans and ends prior to their use.

- Preventing contamination
- Preventing damage
- Preventing loss

Packagers and shippers want to prevent two major types of contamination: contamination caused by dirt or foreign material and that caused by odors.

Since cans are shipped open end up on pallets, various kinds of debris can contaminate the inside of them. This is particularly the case if cans project beyond the pallet's separator sheet so that the insides of the cans are exposed to the environment or if the cans are stored under unsanitary conditions or handled improperly so that they shift from beneath the separator sheet.

FIGURE 5.26. Pallet of packaged ends in sleeves. (Courtesy Canning Technology)

Cans and ends can also absorb odors from the storage environment. These can be transferred to the product, causing off-odors, off-flavors, or both.

Trailers employed for delivering unfilled cans and ends are usually reserved exclusively for this purpose. Trailers should be cleaned prior to reuse. Prior to loading, they should be inspected for

- unsanitary conditions, such as dirt or other debris, including glass particles, which can come from the return of packaging materials that have been exposed to a brewery environment;
- holes in the roof or walls of the trailer, which allow water or vehicle exhaust to enter the trailer;
- damaged interior walls, especially those with protruding objects that can damage cans or ends; and
- odors—especially diesel exhaust.

Warehouses used for storing empty cans or ends should always be inspected prior to use, and periodically thereafter, for the same conditions as the trailers used to ship them.

In addition, warehouses must be monitored to ensure that there are

- adequate rodent, insect, and bird controls to prevent contamination from these sources;
- adequate ventilation to prevent water damage from condensation;
- adequate training of warehouse personnel, especially forklift operators, so that they handle pallets correctly to prevent damage, contamination, or loss of either cans or ends;
- protection from direct sunlight, which can fade lithography; and
- no source of odors. Warehouses used to store unused cans or ends must not have been used for storing things such as tires, soaps or laundry detergents, or disposable diapers since odors from these products can be absorbed by can or end coatings or compounds and transmitted to the product.

When it is likely that the cans or ends being produced will be stored for a period of time before filling, the brewer and can manufacturer should develop a program in which a portion of this production is filled and monitored on-line. This practice will minimize the chance of storing cans or ends with unrecognized defects.

Typically, the can manufacturer segregates every tenth pallet produced until a truckload is accumulated. This truckload is then shipped for immediate filling and evaluation.

APPENDIX I

Major Developments in the Manufacture of Commercial Beer Cans

1935	G. Krueger Brewing Company test markets the first canned beer in Richmond, VA, using flat-top, three-piece tinplate, soldered side-seam cans supplied by American Can Company.
1958	Hawaiian Brewing Company sells beer in an impact-extruded, two-piece aluminum can.
1963	Iron City Brewing introduces Alcoa's lift-tab, easy-open aluminum end.
1964	Reynolds Metals Company commercializes drawn and wall-ironed, two-piece aluminum cans.
1965	Continental Can Company introduces ring pull-style, easy-open ends.
1968	Tin-free steel replaces soldered tinplate with Continental Can Company's Conoweld welded-side seam and American Can Company's Miraseam cemented-side seam containers.
1972	Two-piece, drawn and wall-ironed tinplate cans are produced.
1975	Reynolds Metals Company introduces the SOT, easy-open aluminum end.
1979–1980	U.S. brewers convert from 209- to 207.5-diameter ends.
1985–1986	U.S. brewers convert from 207.5- to 206-diameter ends.
1992–1996	U.S. brewers convert from 206- to 204-diameter ends.
2003–2007	U.S. brewers convert to 202-diameter ends.

APPENDIX II
Glossary

Cans

axial load—a can's vertical crush resistance, measured in pounds. The can's axial load resistance must be greater than the load applied during filling and seaming. When the axial load is measured, the test can must be undamaged and the load must be applied vertically. A filled can has a significantly higher axial load since the can is supported by the product's carbonation.

bearing surface—the bottom surface on which a can "rides" when conveyed upright; also called rest diameter or chime diameter

bottom profile—the can's integral bottom. The design, or shape, which includes the rest diameter, has a direct bearing on the can's buckle and growth resistance.

buckle resistance—the resistance of the can's integral bottom to permanent deformation by internal pressure, expressed in psig. This is important to a can's ability to withstand the pressures generated during pasteurization. Buckle resistance is controlled by a combination of the starting gauge and bottom profile design.

capacity—Brimful capacity is the maximum amount of liquid a can will hold, measured with water at 68°F (20°C) and stated in fluid ounces. Nominal capacity is the headspace, measured in inches, when a can is filled to its label-declared fill.

dome—*see* bottom profile

finished can height—the height of an empty can, measured in inches from the bearing surface to the top of the flange; also called factory-finished can height, or flanged can height, and abbreviated FFCH

flange—the flared projection at the top of the can, which becomes the body hook in the double seam

flange width—the width of the flange, measured in inches from the inside body wall to the flange cut edge. This measurement is indicative of the amount of metal available to form the body hook, which is a critical double-seam component.

gauge—the thickness of the metal from which the can is formed, measured in inches; also known as the starting gauge

growth—the amount a filled, pressurized can increases in height (measured in inches) when the pressure within the can increases, as during pasteurization. Some permanent height increase is normal. If the growth is excessive, the can may buckle or jam in the filled-can conveying system.

headspace—the height, measured in inches, between the liquid surface and the plane of the flange in a filled, unseamed can. The industry-accepted dimension for specifying capacity on 12- and 16-fluid oz. cans is 0.470 inch ± 0.020 inch (1.1938 cm ± 0.0508 cm), measured when the can is filled with 68°F (20°C) water.

inside spray—the organic protective coating sprayed on the inside of the can and subsequently heat cured, which prevents the product from contacting or reacting with the aluminum or iron

lithography—the label, consisting of a pattern of colored inks printed on the can's outside surface, overcoated with a clear varnish, and subsequently heat cured; frequently abbreviated as litho or deco

neck-plug diameter—the inside diameter of the neck of the can, measured in inches

neck profile—the shape of the top portion of the can where the diameter is reduced from the major body diameter

overvarnish—the clear, organic protective coating applied over the lithography inks and heat cured. Varnish adds gloss, minimizes label scuffing, and contains lubricants that assist can mobility on the manufacturing can filling lines.

rest diameter—the diameter of the can's bearing surface. This dimension may be reduced to increase the can's resistance to buckling. Reducing the bearing surface diameter, however, may affect the can's stability when conveyed.

thick wall—the portion at the top of the can where the wall is left thicker to add strength. This is the section where the neck profile, flange, and double seam are formed.

thin wall—the major section of the body wall, which is wall ironed during can manufacture

transition—the two tapered portions of the body wall, one at the top of the can between the thick wall and thin wall and one at the bottom of the can between the thin wall and the bottom profile

Ends

buckle resistance—the end's resistance to permanent deformation by internal pressure, expressed in psig

bulge resistance—the internal pressure, measured in psig, at which the tab of a double-seamed end protrudes above the plane of the double seam. The end's bulge resistance must be greater than the content's internal pressure to prevent the tab from snagging on conveyors when the inverted can is conveyed after pasteurization.

coatings—an organic protective coating applied to both sides of the aluminum sheet and heat cured by the aluminum manufacturer. This coating is referred to as coil coating or coil-coated end stock. The end's internal coating prevents interaction between the product and the aluminum; the external coating protects the end from scuffing and water spotting.

coining—flattening or beading the panel radius of the end to increase buckle resistance

compound—a solvent- or water-based synthetic rubber material placed in the curl of the end to act as a sealing gasket in the double seam

converted unit depth—the depth, measured in inches, from the top of the seaming panel to the bottom of the countersink radius of the unseamed end. After seaming, this becomes the countersink of the double seam.

curl—the outer portion of the end that forms under the can flange and becomes the end hook in the double seam. Curl dimensions and curl shape are critical to good double-seam formation.

curl diameter—Outside curl diameter is the overall diameter of the end, measured in inches. This dimension is important for feeding ends through the cover feed of the closing machine. Inside curl diameter is the diameter, measured in inches, between the cut edges of the curled end. This dimension must be larger than the maximum can flange diameter to permit assembly of the end on the can prior to double seaming.

curl height—the height, measured in inches, of the curled portion of the end. This dimension is critical to feeding the end into the closing machine.

LOE—an abbreviation for large opening end, that is, an end with a significantly larger opening than a standard SOT end provides. An LOE provides for improved pouring—less "glug"—and makes it easier to drink from the can.

opening disc—the portion of a nondetach end that is pushed inward when the end is opened; sometimes called scored opening

opening force—the force, measured in pounds, required to open the end. Two separate forces are involved in opening a nondetach end: the initial and the completing force. The pop, or vent, is the initial force required to break the score and vent the headspace gas. The second component of opening is the force needed to push the opening disc down and fully open the can.

reformable end—an ultra-light end profile designed to be reshaped during double-seam formation. The seamed end has higher buckle resistance than does a conventional end, permitting the use of thinner aluminum end stock in the end's manufacture.

score—the thinned area of the end designed to break when the end is opened

score residual—the amount of metal remaining in the thinned area. This specification is critically controlled to prevent the manufacture of ends that either open prematurely, are hard to open, or both.

SOT—an abbreviation for stay on tab, an end design in which the tab and opening disc remain attached to the end after opening. SOT ends have been the standard end for beer cans manufactured in the United States for several years since they satisfy environmental protection requirements.

Stolle Step®—a design that forms a step in the panel radius, giving the end additional strength and providing an improvement in buckle resistance over coining

tab—the lever that, when raised, fractures the score and opens the end. The tab is attached to the end by an integral rivet, formed from the end metal.

Customer Operations

closing machine—a machine that closes a filled can by double seaming an end onto the can body; also known as a double seamer or seamer

double seam—the structure that attaches an end to a can. It is formed by interlocking the end curl with the can flange and compressing the folds of metal.

CHAPTER 6

Can Filling in the Brewery

RANDY DILLMAN
KHS USA, Inc.

There are two main types of filling equipment in the brewing industry. There is high technology equipment, which are the higher-end electronic-type controlled volumetric fillers. And then there is what is called the legacy equipment, which uses mechanical cams and valves for filling. Most breweries with a can filler have legacy equipment in their plants; so this chapter focuses on legacy can fillers, the can filling process, can handling, can filler setup, and troubleshooting suggestions. No matter what type of equipment the plant may operate, the fundamentals of can filling apply in some form or fashion. There may be some subtle differences between makes and types of fillers, but the fundamentals are going to be similar because filling is a process just like making beer is a process. There are certain steps that must be completed properly in the brewing process to make sure the beer comes out as desired and the same theory follows for quality container filling, be it cans or bottles. Proper filling is just as important as the manufacturing of the beer because if it is not done correctly it will quickly ruin the product.

First, basic fundamentals that affect the filling processes need to be reviewed; these essentials will help build the foundation that can be used for understanding the high speed filling process and will be a guide through the troubleshooting sections of this chapter.

What Types of Fillers Are These? Pressure or Gravity?

All fillers, for cans or bottles, are gravity fillers. The pressure of the container is equalized to the pressure in the supply bowl at the start of the filling process; so the only force that is working on the product is the weight or gravity of the beer that drops into the container. Both legacy and volumetric fillers are gravity fillers.

What Is CO_2 Pressure Used For on the Fillers?

Carbon dioxide (CO_2) gas pressure is used to keep the CO_2 level or carbonation of the product (volumes of gas) in solution. In other words, the goal is to try to control the processing of the beer from the beer supply tank into the filler and into the container while maintaining control of the CO_2 content. Along with maintaining carbonation, CO_2 is used to flush, purge, and pressure equalize the cans before filling occurs. If the cans are not flushed, purged, and pressure equalized, the CO_2 gas will come out of solution during the filling process. This can cause the beer to have foaming problems and bad fills. By maintaining the CO_2 pressure at the proper level, the CO_2 will stay in solution and this part of the filling process will be controlled.

What Is a Volume of CO_2 Gas?

One volume/volume of CO_2 gas means that for every volume of liquid there is an equivalent volume of CO_2 gas dissolved in that liquid, where the CO_2 gas density is based on 1 atmosphere (14.5 pounds per square inch gauge [psig] or 1 bar) of CO_2 total pressure at 32°F (0°C). (This is the defined standard temperature and pressure for carbonation.) Basically, 1 volume/volume of CO_2 is equivalent to 1.98 g of CO_2 per liter of beer.

What Is the Volume of CO_2 Gas in the Product?

The volume of CO_2 gas in the product depends on what product is being run and its carbonation specification. Specifications from the lab may say that there must be anywhere from 2.5 to 3 volumes of CO_2 in the beer. A volume of gas is the CO_2 content that is dissolved in the product. The process uses CO_2 pressure to control that volume and keep it in the product.

One volume of atmospheric pressure is basically 1 bar of pressure or 14.5 psig. So, 2.5–3 volumes of gas are really about 2.5–3 bars of pressure (36–44 psig), and this is the pressure that must be maintained. The filling process does not usually add carbonation volumes to the product. The product usually loses carbonation during the filling process, and that is why proper CO_2 pressure, whether filling cans or bottles, is so critical to successful filling.

What Is the Gas Tube Used For in the Filling Valve?

Whether it is a long-tube filler or a short-tube filler, the filling valve has a gas tube, also called a vent or air tube. Most of the fillers built now are short-tube-style fillers. The gas tube serves three functions in the filling process and, whether it is a can or a bottle filler, its functions are basically the same.

First, it is used to flush, purge, and pressurize the can with CO_2 gas. Most of the time, on a mechanical filler, the gas tube is used to bring CO_2 into the container.

Second, the gas tube allows the CO_2 gas in the container to move out; the fill valve opens up when pressure equalization is achieved with the bowl. At that point, the beer falls into the container and pushes the CO_2 gas out of the container, back up the gas tube, and into the filler bowl headspace or wherever it is designed to go.

The gas tube serves a third purpose. What happens when the liquid covers the end of it? Why doesn't the container fill all the way to the top? As soon as the product covers the end of the gas tube, it stops the filling process because there is no place for the residual or leftover CO_2 gas content to go and a bubble is created. So, in effect, it is the device that sets the fill height within the container. The fill height is related to the container's fill volume.

In some makes of can fillers, a check ball gas tube is used. The check ball performs the same functions as the gas tube. As soon as the liquid rises, it pushes the ball up against the bottom of a seat so there is no place for the gas to go, the fill stops, and gas creates a bubble. This is how it sets the fill height.

What Is the Fluid Director Used For?

A can filler uses a device called a fluid director or fluid nozzle, which functions the same way as a gas tube spreader does on a bottle filler.

The spreader on the gas tube directs the flow of product down the sides of a bottle in a smooth flow or laminar flow. It is very important that the flow be laminar and not turbulent, because the flow during the fill exposes a large surface area inside the can, which will absorb any residual oxygen in the gas. The less turbulence and the smoother the flow, the less absorption there is of any residual oxygen present. Also, the less chance there is for foam formation. The fluid director performs the same operation in the can and similarly creates a smooth laminar flow of beer along the inside wall of the can.

What Is the Purge Used For in Can Fillers?

Most modern bottle fillers use a vacuum to suck out and reduce the air (oxygen) content of the bottle prior to counterpressuring and filling. Can fillers used to use a vacuum, which was problematic since the cans became more lightweight and flimsy. Instead, can fillers now use a purge step with CO_2 gas; however, the idea is the same: reduce the amount of oxygen in the can prior to filling.

The original reason for using a vacuum pump and removing air from the container was not to increase shelf life but to reduce the foaming that occurs during the filling process. Total package oxygen (TPO) was not measured at the time; only headspace air was measured. But when running beer with 2.5–3 volumes of CO_2 gas saturation in an air environment, the gas wants to separate from the beer and tends to create foam. The reason to reduce air content was mostly for runability, not because of shelf life.

When beer is running down the inside of the container, it increases the exposed surface area of the product to its immediate atmosphere. In an air environment, the gases want to come to equilibrium with their surrounding atmosphere, so the oxygen in the air wants to get into the beer and the CO_2 in the beer wants to get out to the atmosphere, which is why beer foams. The more the air content in this atmosphere is reduced and turned into CO_2, the less CO_2 breakout and foaming occurs.

However, of course, the other important advantage of reducing air content is to reduce beer oxidation and increase the shelf life of the product. Especially as beer is shipped to far away markets, a longer shelf life has become very important and the TPO of the package is used as a benchmark to indicate how stable the beer flavor will be. Whether it is a vacuum system used for bottles or a purging system used for cans, air reduction in the package is essential for an increased and stable shelf life of the beer.

What Is the Difference Between the Headspace Air, Dissolved Oxygen, and Total Package Oxygen?

It is important to understand what the measurements are for determining oxygen pickup during filling and where those measurements come from.

Total package oxygen (TPO) is the total amount of oxygen in the filled and sealed container, and it is a valuable tool to predict overall shelf life. TPO is expressed in parts per million (ppm), which is milligrams of oxygen per liter, or parts per billion (ppb), which is micrograms of oxygen per liter. It is essentially the total oxygen pickup of the beer from the time it enters the filler to the time it is sealed in the can, including the oxygen dissolved in the beer and the oxygen present in the headspace.

Dissolved oxygen (DO) is the amount of oxygen dissolved in the beer at any point during the process. As with TPO, DO is expressed in parts per million or parts per billion.

Headspace air is the atmosphere in the headspace of the container, and it is expressed in milliliters of air. The headspace air test involves dissolving any CO_2 in the headspace with sodium hydroxide, leaving only the nitrogen, which is essentially inert, and oxygen gas fraction behind. Obviously, the lower the milliliters of headspace air, the less oxygen there is to react with the beer.

Problems with high TPO can be addressed by investigating where the oxygen is being dissolved. The filler directly influences DO in the beer during the filling process, whether it is a bottle or a can. If purged correctly, the container will have a reduced air content, but even with proper purging, there is always some very small amount of residual air left in the container. The actual fill is the only place during the filling process where there is an interaction between the air and the CO_2 that can increase the DO. To diagnose filler issues, the DO of the beer coming into the filler must be determined and then compared with a fresh, unshaken sample from a sealed container. This provides an indication of oxygen pickup across the filler. High levels of DO indicate a fill problem that may have to do with improper purging or filling valve performance.

Headspace air comes from the beer's exposure to the atmosphere once the container leaves the filler prior to sealing. It is the amount of air trapped in the container headspace after it is sealed. High levels of headspace air can be a result of poor undercover gassing during the double-seaming operation (Chapter 7).

When the process has high levels of DO, there may be problems with the beer coming into the filler and in the filling process itself. But if there is a headspace air problem, there may be issues downstream of the filler, e.g., undercover gassing issues or, in the case of bottles, jetter performance issues. Understanding where the TPO comes from in the process is very important to success, whether it is a big or small operation, a single-head or multiple-head filler, a can or bottle, or whatever it may be.

What Is a Screen Used For in a Valve?

Many people think the filler valve screen is there to catch debris and keep it out of the beer. Although that may indeed be a secondary function, the screen's primary functional design is to create surface tension. Surface tension is how a bubble is created to stop the flow of beer and produce a fill height. Once the beer covers the bottom of the gas tube, it stops filling all the way to the top because of the screen and bubble formation. There are multiple devices used to create that surface tension, e.g., screens, kidney rings, stacked discs, and comb valves. They are all used to create the bubble on the top of the container, whether it is can or bottle filler, and they, along with the gas tube, create the fill height.

Without that surface tension device in there, the beer would fill all the way to the top of the container, even though it hit the bottom of the vent tube, because it is at equal pressure to the bowl. The surface tension device is there to stop the flow and create a bubble so that the gas bubble has no place to go and the fill stops.

How Does the Screen Create Surface Tension?

Essentially, surface tension is caused by the cohesive forces of liquid molecules. At the surface of the liquid, the molecules tend to loosely bond with each other, forming surface tension. In a small area, the cohesive forces are more powerful. The wire mesh, comb, or other surface tension device designs take advantage of and accentuate this property by using very small areas for the liquid to collect and form stable cohesion.

What Is the First Step in the Filling Process?

The first part of the filling process, and in many ways the most critical, especially with cans, is the handling or delivery and presentation of the container to the filling valve. If poor presentation of the can to the filling valve is made, the chances of sealing and filling correctly are diminished significantly.

This has changed from the days when 209 or 206 cans were run; the cans were heavier and more forgiving, and correct presentation was easier. Since the industry converted to lightweight 202 cans, there is no longer forgiveness in can handling and presentation. In the 1970s, when can manufacturers started lightweighting aluminum cans at the request of the breweries, they made the 100 cans from the particular weight that they are now making 200 cans from. As the can lid opening has been reduced, in steps, from 209 to the smaller 202 opening, the can body diameter has stayed the same at 211, or 2.6875 inches (68.26 mm). The change from 204 to 202 has only decreased the can opening diameter by 0.125 inch (3.175 mm), but it makes all the difference in the world to the physical properties of the can and how to get the filling process to work. Brewers must ensure that the can is presented correctly, i.e., it is centered and in the center of the valve and the valve seal is correct.

● CAN HANDLING

Can handling is the first step in the can filling process. It includes an infeed can stop that stops and starts the cans into the infeed screw and is controlled by sensors feeding information into the filler's programmable logic controller (PLC) (Fig. 6.1).

The infeed worm or screw (Fig. 6.2) separates the cans and positions them into the infeed star pockets and back guide (Fig. 6.3), which is timed to the filler can pads and backrest assemblies.

The infeed star is a placeholder and the cans are moved forward by the star, but the cans are free to move in the pocket of the star. At high speed, the cans follow the outside guide because of centrifugal force and let the star push them forward. But when it gets to the transfer point (tangent), the cans must move on their own onto and into the can pad and backrest with centrifugal force. When the cans get to this point just before the deflector guide (Fig. 6.4), the transfer plate stops and the can pad on the filler starts. Once transferred into the back of the pocket, the only thing that is holding the can in place is the deflector guide. If set up correctly, the cans move all the way into the backrests and are centered and held in place until captured by the tulip can seal assembly.

It is very important on 202 cans that the trailing end of the back guide at tangent is in the correct location. This is probably the item that most commonly gets damaged on

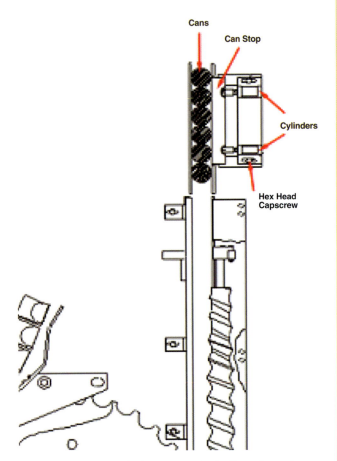

FIGURE 6.1. Can infeed stop controls the flow of cans into the filler. (Courtesy KHS USA)

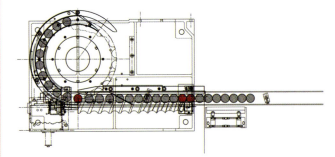

FIGURE 6.2. The can indexing worm spaces the incoming cans for positioning into the infeed star pockets and back guide. (Courtesy of KHS USA)

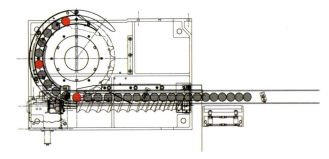

FIGURE 6.3. The cans are fed onto the infeed star and sit into the pockets and back guide. As the cans transfer to the can pads and backrests, the deflector guide holds them in position in the backrests. (Courtesy KHS USA)

the filler handling equipment. If something is left on top of one of the backrests and the machine is turned on, it runs right into the back guide assembly, bending it. If this guide is damaged, it pushes the cans out of the backrests and the deflector guide cannot be set up correctly to hold the cans centered under the valve sealing assembly. It lets the cans "float" around out of control, and it can cause can damage, e.g., rolled flanges, damaged flanges, cut can seals, and creases in the can body.

This problem changes the presentation of the can at the point where the flow is changing direction of motion. The cans are traveling from one rotational direction feeding in and then changing to the opposite direction feeding out. The cans are separating from the infeed star and the guide is designed to ensure that, once the can is in the backrest, it stays in the backrest. It is not pushed into the backrest, it is allowed to move into the backrest and then held in the backrest. There is a difference. The can is in the backrest just before it enters the deflector guide. That guide is designed to keep it in the pocket, that is all. Once the can is in the pocket, it is now waiting for the tulip and seal to come down and capture it at the right point.

The centerline of the pocket, the centerline of the can pad, and the centerline of the center column is what is called tangent. The tulip captures the can at 1 to 1.5 stations, or pitches, past tangent, depending on the size of the machine. The goal of proper presentation of the can is to control the can during the transfer before the tulip comes down on top of it, ensuring that its placement is centered underneath the tulip.

For can pad drop-off from the transfer plate, the filler pads with 211, 209, or 206 can handling used to require only ±0.025 inch (0.635 mm) tolerances. Tolerances for 204 and 202 cans have tightened down to ±0.005 inch (0.127 mm) or even less. Figure 6.5 shows the setup and tolerances of the infeed can pads. These tighter tolerances provide better consistency for 202 can handling. Can handling is part of the process. It is the first part of the process. The can pad height tolerances must be brought down to minimize the effects to the process.

• OVERVIEW OF THE CAN FILLER

Figure 6.6 shows the typical setup for a legacy high-speed rotary filler having from 30 to 165 filling valves. The can fillers are all basically set up the same way. The setup includes the can infeed star and guiding system, the transfer, the can filling process, and then the discharge transfer onto the seamer, the seamer transfer, and finally, the seaming step.

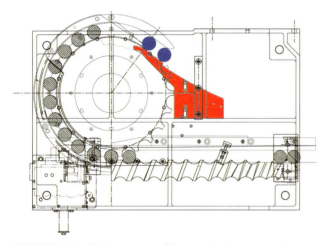

FIGURE 6.4. Timing setup of the cans to be captured. (Courtesy KHS USA)

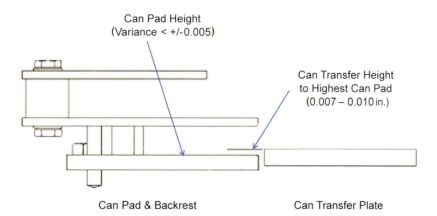

FIGURE 6.5. In setting up the infeed, the can pads and backrests are the foundation. The can pads must be set up to be within ±0.005 inch of each other. (Courtesy KHS USA)

The filler layout starts at the infeed can conveyor can control stop. As the cans are released, the infeed screw separates the cans to time them to the infeed star for timing to the filler can pad backrests (Fig. 6.7).

The cans are captured by the valve tulip and the filling process is started. The valve controls are on the outside control ring of the machine. The valve can sealing tulips are actuated by the long cam between the discharge and the infeed can transfers supported on the filler bowl outside control ring. After the cans are filled, the valves are closed and the pressure is released, cans are then released from the tulips and transferred to the seamer, where an end is applied and sealed.

Figure 6.8 shows the filler profile and the relationship between the can pads, backrests, and filling valves. It also shows the product inlet piping and CO_2 supply

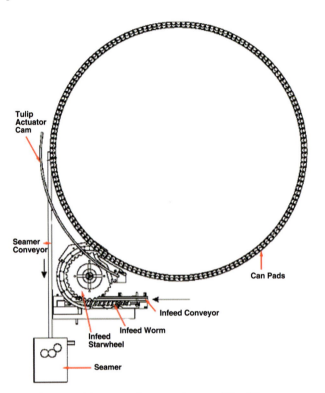

FIGURE 6.6. Top view of a 165-valve can filler. (Courtesy KHS USA)

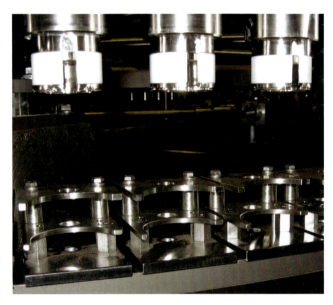

FIGURE 6.7. Filler can pads and backrests with filling valves. (Courtesy KHS USA)

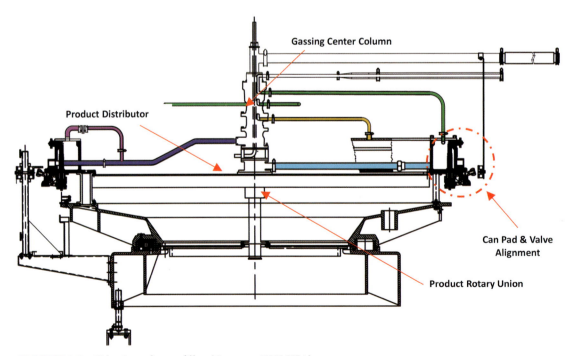

FIGURE 6.8. Side view of a can filler. (Courtesy KHS USA)

and the return gas and cleaning-in-place (CIP) center column assembly.

The center column is a rotary union with separated channels and pathways to provide CO_2 to the filler bowl for counterpressure during the filling process. It also has a CO_2 bowl exhaust pathway to control the oxygen content and help control bowl pressure. The third gas pathway is used for can depressurization and is also the main CIP return pathway.

The product comes through the bottom rotary union and is distributed through eight pipes to the filler bowl. The incoming product line uses a product control valve to allow the product to flow at the required amount to maintain product level in the bowl, which is normally dictated by electronic level controls at about one-half to three-quarters bowl height.

Figure 6.9 shows the bowl piping to and from the filler bowl for the CO_2 supply, CO_2 exhaust, snift exhaust, CIP return, and product supply. The four valve assemblies on the snift exhaust/CIP return lines are open during CIP to ensure that the bowl is completely flooded so all surfaces come in contact with the chemical solutions and rinse water. These remain open for full water contact during the hot sanitizing CIP cycle, which is critical for even and faster heating of the bowl and associated piping and for holding the required temperature over the cycle time.

The center column is a vital component for keeping consistent operation control of the filling process. Failure to maintain the center column and beverage inlet causes loss of CO_2, product, and CIP solutions and allows air into the filler bowl, reducing can cleaning performance and efficiencies with elevated DO and TPO levels.

Progressing to can handling and the infeed area of the filler, the infeed is the heart of any high-speed can filler. The infeed must be properly set up to prevent can damage and beer loss. Figure 6.10 is a typical can filler infeed. The cans come into the infeed screw (on the right) and they

FIGURE 6.10. Can handling infeed of a 120-valve can filler. (Courtesy KHS USA)

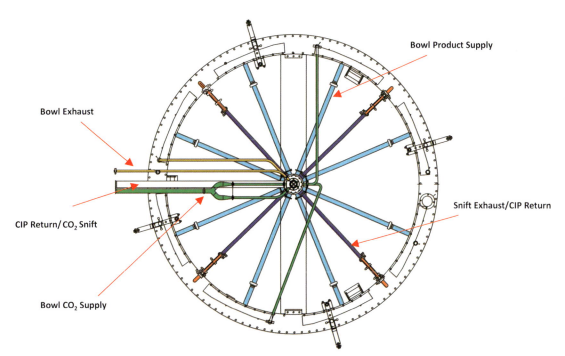

FIGURE 6.9. Top view of the filler bowl supply piping: CO_2 supply (green), CO_2 exhaust (yellow), snift exhaust (purple/white), CIP return (white/orange), product supply (blue), and valve assemblies (orange). (Courtesy KHS USA)

are separated and timed to the infeed star (lower center), traveling along the star back guide past the can sensor (bottom center). The star transfer is timed to the individual can pads and backrests aligned to the filling valves (center back of the star). Once on the can pads, the cans are controlled until they are captured and sealed.

The can filler tulips and tulip actuators (Fig. 6.11) are used to capture and release the cans at specific times during the can handling and filling processes. On most machines, the tulip actuator raises and lowers the tulip onto the cans, although some fillers raise the can up to the tulip. Most can filling valves use a gas tube (center of the tulip) (Fig. 6.12) to control the fill heights in the cans by cutting them to a length required by the type and size of cans and the speed being run.

Figure 6.13 is a typical can valve assembly showing the internal and external parts and the gas pathways through the valve.

● THE FILLING PROCESS

Timing and setup of the high-speed filler infeed is the first necessary step in the can filling process. The can must be timed, presented, centered, and captured by the tulip seal to successfully start the can filling process. Poorly done, improper, or damaged setup of the infeed can cause more filling issues on high-speed can fillers than just about anything else.

Operating levers (Fig. 6.14) open and close the filling valves for different phases of the purging, pressurization, filling, shutoff, and snifting process. There are different

FIGURE 6.11. Tulip actuator for raising and lowering the tulips. (Courtesy KHS USA)

FIGURE 6.12. Can filling valve tulips, seals, and gas tube. (Courtesy KHS USA)

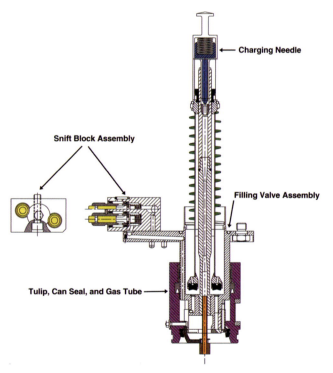

FIGURE 6.13. Typical can filling valve assembly. For the snift block assembly, the top left button is for purging and CIP flow and the lower right button is for controlling the snifting of the can after filling. The tulip, can seal, and gas tube seal the can to the valve body for purging and pressurization and provide the exchange of gasses during the filling process. The charging needle controls the CO_2 gassing and the vent gas return between the can and the bowl. The filling valve assembly controls the flow of product into the can, the gas flow rate, and the fill level. (Courtesy KHS USA)

types or configurations of the levers that are used on high-speed fillers, but all of them perform similar functions for the filling process.

Step One: Can Capture

As soon as the can comes from the infeed star, it is transferred onto the can pad and into the horseshoe-shaped can backrest that fits a 202 can. The can sits in the backrest and, when the can goes underneath the tulip, the tulip comes down on top of it and seals it. There is little pressure from the tulip onto the can at this point, but it is mechanically secure. Force is applied to the seal as the can is purged and pressurized.

Step Two: Purging

Purging the can of air is the second step of the high-speed can filling process (Fig. 6.15). Once again, the goal of the purge is to reduce the amount of air in the container, making it easier to fill and reducing the interaction between the oxygen in the container atmosphere and the laminar flow of beer as the container is filling. This is critical to avoid high DO pickup. Note however, if the container is not clean, then the DO will be elevated no matter how good the purge step is done. In the past, most high-speed can fillers used a vacuum pump, but purging is now done with CO_2 or other inert gas, depending on the product. When bringing in CO_2 gas, most beer fillers run somewhere between 28 and 35 psig.

FIGURE 6.14. Valve actuating levers on the filler bowl. (Courtesy KHS USA)

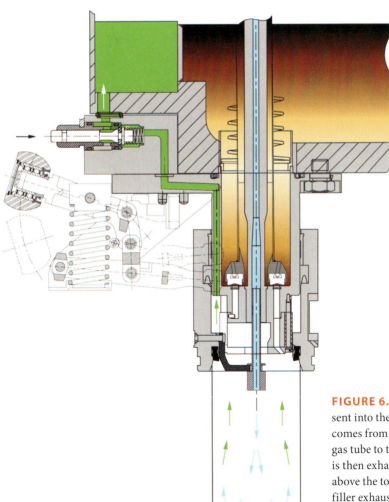

FIGURE 6.15. Purge step. CO_2 gas is sent into the can to flush out air. Gas comes from the filler bowl through the gas tube to the bottom of the can and is then exhausted out through a port above the top of the can within the filler exhaust system to the atmosphere. (Courtesy KHS USA)

Both the CIP and snift ports are opened during purging to get maximum gas flowing into and out of the container; however, the system can push more gas into the can than it can release out during the purge, allowing the can to start prepressurizing.

CO_2 from the bowl is used to purge the container. The gas comes from the top of the bowl into the container, coming back up, through, and out a channel of piping to the outside atmosphere. The open and direct pathway from the bowl at a higher pressure causes prepressurization in the lower pressure can. Prepressurization affects what is occurring inside the container.

First, the flimsy 202 can becomes stronger when it is under pressure, which is very important to the filling process. The can is presented to the tulip and the tulip is brought back down on top of the can and mechanically seals the container. As it begins to pressurize during the purging process, the can begins to become more rigid. Because there is a difference in the surface area, when the tulip starts to pressurize, a downward force is created because the tulip is larger in diameter internally than the opening of the container. The tulip drops down about 0.0625 inch (1.6 mm) as it is forced onto the can. The initial container seal is done mechanically, but the actual seal is completed by the entire purge and pressurization process until pressure equalization is achieved.

Purging the container is the most critical step in reducing the DO pickup and TPO of the package. Basically, most packaging operations are trying to reduce the amount of air in the container to a very low ppb/ppm number, and they do that by extending the purge. There is only so much time on the filler rotation for the purging process to occur until the can has reached full pressure equalization. How much the plant wants to reduce the TPO depends on how much it wants to spend on CO_2 during this step.

Step Three: Pressurization

After purging, the can continues to be pressurized until it is equalized to the pressure in the bowl (Fig. 6.16). This is done for the purposes mentioned previously, keeping the CO_2 in the product and providing a quiet fill without foaming. When full pressure equalization is completed, between 28 and 35 psig depending on the bowl pressure set point, there is about 100 psig of downward force on the internal surface area difference between the tulip and the opening of the can. That is when the container is actually sealed fully prior to filling. That is why the presentation is very important, especially on 202 cans, because they are unforgiving. If positioning is off, it is not going pressurize correctly to create the downward force and it is going to crush the flange on the can.

Step Four: Filling

The filling process starts once pressure equalization is essentially reached. The system can overcome the weight of the beer to start the fill by pulling up the internal valve seat tube by a spring and opening the fill valve. It is very important how this is set up. Overcoming the weight of the product, the spring diameter and tension, and other details must be correct for proper function. The filling valve on legacy machines is a mechanical valve. The valve spring is an essential part of the filling process. If it breaks or weakens, chances are it is probably not going to fill correctly. Whether it is a bottle filler or a can filler, the valve spring function is similar.

The valve spring is designed to work within a range to overcome the weight of the product at pressure equalization. Even if the bowl product level is all the way to the top, the spring would still work. However, the product level, whether more or less, affects the operation of the spring opening the valve. There is an operational range within which the spring operates best with the product level maintained in the bowl. Over time, springs get weaker because they get heated and cooled during CIP and production, so the springs need to be changed periodically or they will not function correctly, if at all.

The bowl product height has an impact on the fill rate of the can. The more beer in the bowl, the more weight in the gravity fill process and the faster the fill rate. However, it is critical to keep a consistent product level in the bowl between one-half to three-quarters within the sight glass to obtain the best results. Electronic level sensors have made bowl level consistency much more reliable and easier to maintain, and they can be changed during operation for different product types for best filling.

When the can reaches pressure equalization, the valve spring overcomes the weight of the product and opens the can valve and starts the filling process. The flow of beer is being directed inside the cans with a laminar flow. This is done by the fluid director, which performs the same kind of function that a gas tube spreader does for filling bottles. The fluid director deflects the flow down the sides of the can in a laminar flow. Each can valve has a fluid director. Figure 6.17 shows a can during the filling phase, but the depiction is not exactly accurate since the liquid would actually be at an angle in the can because of the centrifugal force caused by the rotating filler machine.

A straight-down fill from a static flowing valve might exist for inline can fillers but not with filling on rotary machines. In a rotary filler, the rotating bowl has centrifugal forces that work on the product in the bowl, in the container, and in the fluid director. Inside the can, the centrifugal angle formed is the same as that in the bowl.

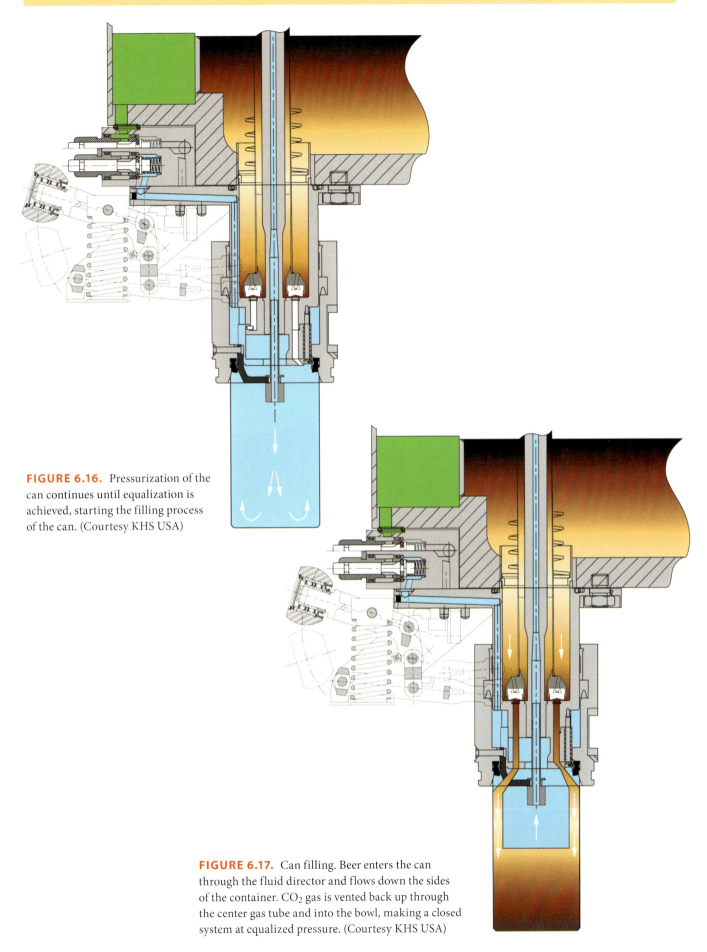

FIGURE 6.16. Pressurization of the can continues until equalization is achieved, starting the filling process of the can. (Courtesy KHS USA)

FIGURE 6.17. Can filling. Beer enters the can through the fluid director and flows down the sides of the container. CO_2 gas is vented back up through the center gas tube and into the bowl, making a closed system at equalized pressure. (Courtesy KHS USA)

Typically on a high-speed filler, the angle is somewhere between 22° and 25° at top speed. Looking at a can during its filling process, the laminar flow is thicker or more directed toward the front of the can on the outside of the filler.

As the beer flows into the can through the fluid director, it creates a fluid umbrella. Due to the centrifugal force of the rotating bowl on the system, the fluid umbrella is not directed straight down; it is going to be shifted outward. What is going to happen when the beer, now filling at an angle, comes in contact with the gas tube? It is going to change the dynamics of what is occurring inside this container and how it reacts. It is going to change how it fills.

When the filler speeds up and slows down, the angle of the product changes in the can, bowl, and fluid umbrella. These changes have effects on the filling process. At slower speeds, the angle is lower, and as the can fills, the product comes into contact with the gas tube later, causing a slightly higher fill and less turbulence. Running at top speed, the angle and turbulence increases and the product comes in contact sooner, causing slightly lower fills.

Step Five: Fill Stop and Snift

The fill stops and leaves a headspace. In most call filling applications, the headspace is 0.472 inch (12 mm). The proper headspace is very important, especially for the pasteurizer process, since it cushions the pressure of the expanding beer. Figure 6.18 shows the filled can. Note that the liquid that is in the gas tube (shown in brown) is the same distance from the bottom of the can to the height in the gas tube when compared with the distance from the valve screen to the top of the liquid in the bowl. There is always some residual beer, whether it is a bottle filler or a can filler, in the gas tube. This is affected by the bowl level. Most fillers use electronic level control so it is easier to control and maintain a consistent level and make this residual more consistent.

As the beer in the can rises, meets, and covers the gas tube, it stops the gas from venting out and creates the headspace. It also helps create the bubble between the screen and the open area in the tulip between the can and the tulip. Some valves, depending on what style it is,

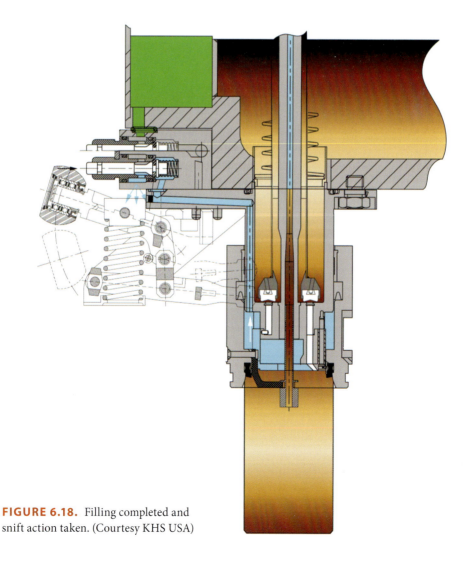

FIGURE 6.18. Filling completed and snift action taken. (Courtesy KHS USA)

have a high screen valve. When beer covers the bottom of the gas tube, there is already liquid that is spilling through the high screen valve before it creates surface tension. This liquid, as the surface tension is created, "drops" into the can. That is called the drop. So this residual liquid, as it creates surface tension, is released and is the final part that fills part of the headspace. The vent tube length allows for this drop amount for the correct fill height.

The internal valve screen device creates surface tension that keeps the bubble from escaping, which helps maintain the fill height. At this point, the filling process is stopped because the bubble is formed, stopping product flow, and the gas cannot leave the can. Once the filling valve is mechanically closed, the process is stopped, and the can must be brought back to atmospheric pressure and disengaged from the tulip, breaking the valve can seal from the can. If this is done in an uncontrolled manner, CO_2 would instantly come out of solution and cause foaming. If that happens, there will be overfoaming and a "popping" noise.

Snifting is the process of bringing the can back to atmospheric pressure in a controlled manner prior to breaking the can seal. When bringing it back to atmospheric pressure, two things are occurring. One is a reduction in pressure, but at the same time that the container is filled, it creates surface tension. The filling process is stopped because the bubble is formed, which stops the product flow and shuts off the fill valve, so the gas cannot leave the can by the gas tube. Because of the residual liquid, there is an expansion chamber in the gas tube. The expansion chamber is designed to push the residual liquid out of the vent tube and back into the container while the valve and can are brought back to atmospheric pressure.

Once the can disengages from the tulip, it is exposed to the outside air that fills the headspace. "Bubble breakers" were once used to break up big fisheye-type bubbles formed after the can seal was broken, but with today's TPO concerns, the bubble breakers are now bubble makers. This step is meant to fill the headspace back up with tight foam, like jetters do on bottle fillers, before the can goes into the seamer. Whether it is a small or large machine, the bubble breaker can be set too high or too low. A happy medium is best, because if it is too high, it will blow away and waste too much beer from the container, and if it is too low, it will allow too much headspace air. Plant management must decide on a filling level and determine the amount of beer loss on the transfer that is acceptable. Plant management has to decide how much they are willing to blow out so that the TPO levels are in an acceptable range.

The open can travels to the seamer, which has an undercover gasser. An undercover gasser basically blows CO_2 gas across the top of the container as the lid comes down, playing an integral part in the final headspace air. Setting the undercover gas level too high can actually pull air in because of the velocity, so a balance must be determined.

● MACHINE SETUP

Pre-setup of the machine can be made at ambient temperature when maintenance is performed, but it must always be checked again after it reaches operational temperature at startup and adjustments must be made as necessary. This is important because, as the bowl temperature chills from ambient to 32°F (0°C), it shrinks in diameter. A bowl that is 18 feet in diameter can change about 1 inch (24 mm) in diameter between CIP temperature and operational temperature. Even in small fillers, the change will be 0.08–0.12 inch (2–3 mm).

Figure 6.19 shows how to set up the cams to make sure that they are pressing in the poppets enough. Once adjusted to press in the poppets 0.08 inch (2 mm) or two-thirds of the way in, pushing in another one-third of the way is not going to let any more gas out during the purging process.

Figure 6.20 shows the closing cams. There are two closing cams, the primary and the secondary. The primary gently closes the butterflies that close the fluid seal internally in the filling valve. The secondary cam is designed to control one butterfly at one time. When only

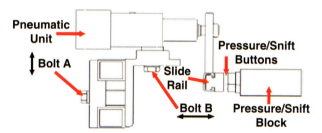

FIGURE 6.19. Purge and snift cam setup. The pressure/snift buttons should go no more than two-thirds of the way in. (Courtesy KHS USA)

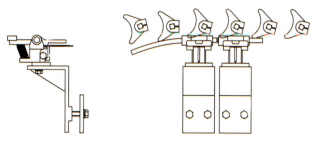

FIGURE 6.20. Closing cams. (Courtesy KHS USA)

one butterfly, for the associated valve, is in the middle of secondary cam, it starts to depress the snift button to bring the can back to atmospheric pressure. This is to make sure that one valve is closed and it is under control, so the snifting process can start.

TROUBLESHOOTING THE FILLING PROCESS

Can- and bottle-filling processes are similar and troubleshooting is also very similar. Most issues or problems in the filling process generally fall into two categories: individual valves or global/process control issues. Observation, following a methodical analysis process, and using the troubleshooting guide for the equipment helps determine the issue and the repairs that are required. First, it must be determined which troubleshooting path should be followed: individual or global/process.

If observation does not indicate which troubleshooting path to follow, there is a test that can be performed to help determine this. With the filler at the normal operational speed and temperature, running for approximately 20 minutes, one full round of sample cans should be taken in consecutive order to be tested, with no gaps. It does not matter which valve is pulled first as long as the cans are taken consecutively. From that information, the performance of each valve can be evaluated for fill height, DO, etc. and it can be determined whether each valve is operating within its operational limits. The evaluation can also indicate whether there are individual valve issues or process issues.

The analytical information can be plotted on a histogram showing the performance of all the valves for each parameter and their variations, which can then be compared with a bell curve for specified performance. A typical bell curve shows the specified operational parameter in the center and the stand deviations or sigma values away from those parameters on each side. Commonly, the machine supplier can supply the optimal parameter and the first, second, and third sigma values. At that point, the actual valve performance can be compared to determine whether it is working correctly.

If there are two or three valves out of specification in a sample set, but most are in the middle of the bell curve, then the implication is a valve-specific issue. The problem valves will need to be serviced. If most or all the valves are operating outside of the bell curve, then this implies a process issue, e.g., pressures, temperatures, carbonation level, and bowl height. In that case, there must be an investigation into the setup and operations of the machine as a whole.

GENERAL TROUBLE ISSUES AND POSSIBLE CAUSES

Overfills:
- Bad screen in valve
- Vent tube too short
- Slightly stuck snift or vacuum poppet
- Liquid level in bowl too high
- Infeed setup and seal problem

Underfills:
- Speed too fast
- Bad seamer transfer
- Vent tube too long (a height change of 1 mm = approximately 0.1 fluid oz. (3 mL)
- Liquid level in bowl too low
- All foaming

No Fills:
- Can has not sealed on tulip properly
- Incorrect setup on infeed
- Stuck snift poppet
- Valve trip not operational
- No product

Heavy Foaming:
- Product too warm, above 38°F (3.3°C)
- Closing cam—snift not set correctly
- Bad screen in valve
- CIP cam engaged

High DOs/TPOs:
- Inconsistent fills
- Leaks in piping from beer supply tank to filler
- Center column seals leaking
- Purge cam worn or not set
- Seamer bubble breakers/undercover gasser set too low

CHAPTER 7

Double-Seam Technology

WILLIAM J. FORSYTHE
Canning Technology

Good double-seam formation, or "can closing", is critical to ensuring that a high-quality, finished package reaches the consumer. All the time, effort, and money expended to brew, advertise, and distribute a high-quality canned beer are lost if the can leaks in distribution.

Preservation of canned products requires a hermetic—gas proof—seal. In the case of canned foods, this means keeping spoilage-causing microorganisms outside the can. With a pressurized beverage such as beer, it means retaining both the product and the pressurizing gas inside the can, since if either component is lost, the product cannot be sold.

A can is "closed" in a machine, appropriately called a closing machine, that attaches an end unit to a can body. Modern brewery closing machines have 12–18 seaming stations and produce from 1,200 to more than 2,400 finished cans per minute. The structure used to attach the end to the can is called a double seam. Properly formed, it makes a hermetic seal.

This chapter provides a basic understanding of

- the can and end components critical to double seaming,
- the major closing machine parts that form the seam,
- the formation of the double seam, and
- the key factors affecting double-seam quality and how to evaluate them.

The chapter also emphasizes recognizing and correcting potential problems before they cause can leakage, especially in modern, lightweight, two-piece cans and ends.

● DOUBLE-SEAM TERMINOLOGY

It is important to recognize the components that make up a double seam—or to "speak the language" of double seaming. The external components of a double seam are illustrated in Figure 7.1. Countersink, seam thickness, and

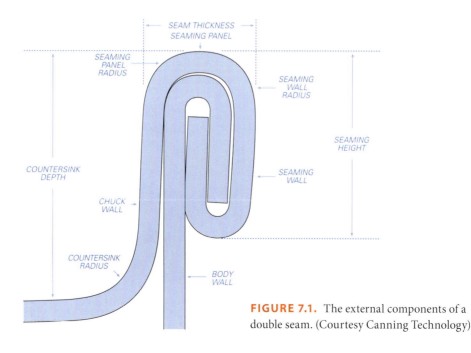

FIGURE 7.1. The external components of a double seam. (Courtesy Canning Technology)

seam height are important elements affecting double-seam quality and must be maintained within specification. Seam thickness is a direct indication of seam tightness with ultra-lightweight ends.

The internal components of a double seam are illustrated in Figure 7.2. The body hook and overlap are critical to good double-seam performance and must be controlled within specified limits.

● CRITICAL CAN AND END COMPONENTS

Regardless of the neck diameter, bottom profile, or input gauge of the can, certain can dimensions must be maintained within specific tolerances to ensure a quality double seam (Fig. 7.3).

Factory-finished can height is important to undercover gassing. This dimension affects the flange-to-gassing turret relationship. The can flange becomes the body hook in the double seam. Flange width and, to a lesser degree, neck-plug diameter affects body hook length. Excessive flange diameter may cause can and/or end assembly problems.

Can ends must also be kept within close tolerance of specifications to ensure a quality double seam (Fig. 7.4). Curl diameter and curl height are critical to ensuring that ends separate and feed properly into the closing machine. The outside curl diameter is the overall diameter of the end, whereas the inside curl diameter is measured between the cut edges of the curled end. To allow high-speed assembly of the end and can, the minimum inside curl diameter of the end must be greater than the maximum flange diameter of the can. (The flange

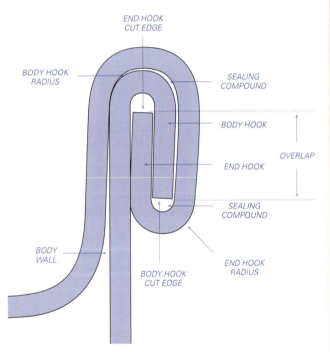

FIGURE 7.2. The internal components of a double seam. (Courtesy Canning Technology)

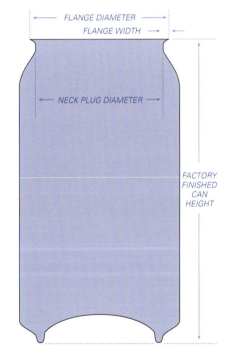

FIGURE 7.3. The can dimensions flange width, flange diameter, and neck-plug diameter are important for a quality double seam. (Courtesy Canning Technology)

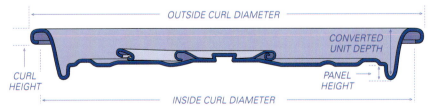

FIGURE 7.4. The end dimensions curl diameter and curl height are important to double seaming. (Courtesy Canning Technology)

diameter is the diameter across the outside edges of the can flange.)

The converted unit depth of the end must match the dimension of the double-seaming chuck lip (Fig. 7.5). This is the lower portion of the double-seaming chuck, the tooling that supports the end during double seaming. Curl shape is critical to good first-operation seam formation. The curl must be round and free of flat or straight areas. Panel height and converted unit depth of the end directly affect the end's buckle resistance as well as the "fit" of the end on the double-seaming chuck.

● KEY CLOSING MACHINE COMPONENTS

During seam formation, the can rests on the lower lifter, which clamps it against the double-seaming chuck (Fig. 7.6). The lower lifter is cammed up and down and spring loaded to provide the necessary clamping force. The double-seaming chuck is fixed on a vertical plane. It must not move, or "float". Both the lower lifter and the double-seaming chuck are gear driven and rotate, turning the can and end. The seam is formed by the interdependent actions of a first-operation seaming roll and a second-operation seaming roll. The double-seaming chuck lip must be fully seated into the countersink radius of the end prior to the start of double-seam formation (Fig. 7.7).

During double seaming, the knockout pad fits into a recess in the seaming chuck so that it clears the tab of the end. The pad is umbrella shaped to avoid contacting and turning the tab, which can cause opening failures.

A note on the dimensions and fit of the end and chuck: currently, the brewing industry is converting to a new design of an ultra-lightweight end (Fig. 7.8). Breweries converting to this type of end must consult with their end supplier for double-seam tooling and seam specifications. While the basic double-seam structure is unchanged with the new technology end, the chuck fit characteristics are different from those of a conventional end. Depending on the end manufacturer, the new end requires different double-seaming chucks and seaming rolls.

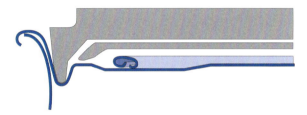

FIGURE 7.5. The dimensions of the end and the double-seaming chuck must match. (Courtesy Canning Technology)

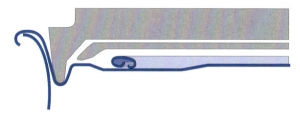

FIGURE 7.7. The end countersink radius must match up with the chuck lip. (Courtesy Canning Technology)

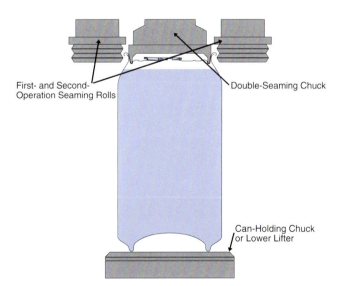

FIGURE 7.6. Key closing machine components—lower lifter and double-seaming chuck. (Courtesy Canning Technology)

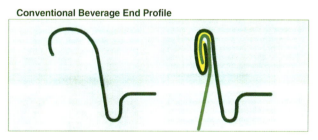

FIGURE 7.8. Comparison of conventional and new technology ends. (Courtesy Canning Technology)

CLOSING MACHINE OPERATION

Prior to the start of double-seam formation, as the can and end are being positioned beneath the double-seaming chuck, the closing machine's undercover gassing turret flushes the can's headspace with carbon dioxide to remove air (Fig. 7.9). The infeed chain positions the can on the lower lifter, which is centered under the double-seaming chuck. The end is still in the cover guide track, which conveys the ends from the cover feed where each was separated. The pusher centers the end under the double-seaming chuck directly over the can. The knockout pad is lowered, controlling the end as the lower lifter raises the can so the flange of the can enters the curl opening of the end (Fig. 7.10).

As the knockout pad retracts, the lower lifter continues to raise the can until the can and end are assembled and seated on the double-seaming chuck. At this point, the lower lifter and the double-seaming chuck rotate the can and end, and the first-operation seaming roll cams in to start forming the double seam.

FORMATION OF THE DOUBLE SEAM

A double seam consists of five interlocking thicknesses of metal—three from the end and two from the can—joined together and compressed tightly to form a hermetic seal. The groove in the first-operation seaming roll performs the interlocking. The groove profile is shaped for the end gauge being seamed. Figure 7.11 is a cross section of a well-formed double seam. All double seams should look like the one in this figure.

At the start of the process, as the can and end rotate, the first-operation seaming roll is cammed in, forming

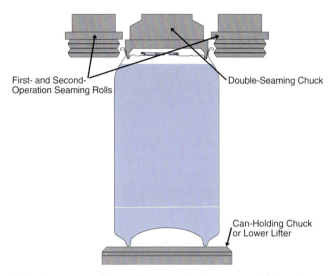

FIGURE 7.10. The can flange and end are assembled and ready for the double-seaming operation. (Courtesy Canning Technology)

FIGURE 7.11. A cross section of a well-formed double seam. (Courtesy Canning Technology)

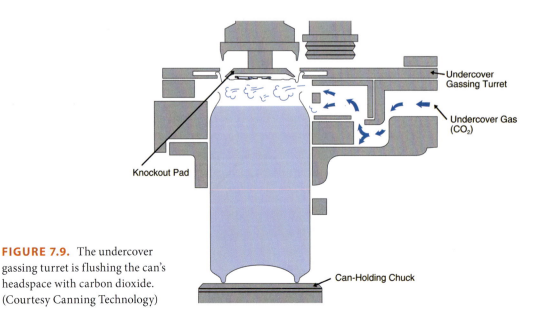

FIGURE 7.9. The undercover gassing turret is flushing the can's headspace with carbon dioxide. (Courtesy Canning Technology)

the curl of the end under the flange of the can. The steps of this process, from the start of the first-operation seam through its completion, are presented in Figures 7.12–7.14. The first-operation seam formation is critical to good double seaming. Figure 7.15 shows a normal seam formed in the first-operation seaming roll. Ninety percent of the seam structure is created by the first-operation roll.

When troubleshooting seaming issues, keep in mind:

- The seam structure is formed during the first-operation seaming cycle.
- Any time there is a seam defect, other than a simple loose seam, the first-operation seam should be checked before making any adjustment.

The double seam is completed when the second-operation seaming roll groove "irons out" the interlocked folds of metal, compressing, or tightening, the seam and creating the hermetic seal (Fig. 7.16).

The primary seal of the double seam is formed by embedding the cut edge of the body hook into the sealing compound and placing the compound in this area under compression. The primary seal is shown in Figure 7.17.

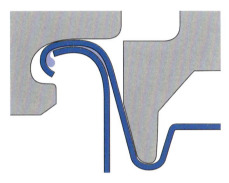

FIGURE 7.12. Start of first-operation seam formation. (Courtesy Canning Technology)

FIGURE 7.15. Normal "classic" first-operation seam. (Courtesy Canning Technology)

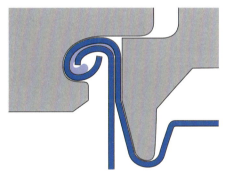

FIGURE 7.13. Partially formed first-operation seam, forming the end curl under the can flange. (Courtesy Canning Technology)

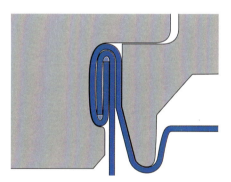

FIGURE 7.16. The second operation "ironing out" the interlocked metal folds. (Courtesy Canning Technology)

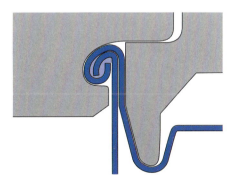

FIGURE 7.14. Finished first-operation seam. (Courtesy Canning Technology)

FIGURE 7.17. The primary seal of the double seam. The hook is embedded in the sealing compound. (Courtesy Canning Technology)

Laboratory research, confirmed by commercial experience with billions of cans, has proven that the end hook serves as a trough that keeps the sealing compound in contact with the body hook cut edge. As long as there is an adequate overlap of the body and the end hooks, the length of the end hook is not a direct indication of seam quality. For this reason, most commercial double-seam specifications do not contain an operating specification for the end hook. To summarize, the primary attributes controlling double-seam integrity are body hook, overlap, and tightness.

It is beyond the scope of this chapter to define a double-seam control program that would apply to different brewery operations. It does, however, list the critical items that should be controlled and the method by which they should be evaluated. These recommendations are based on commercial experience with ultra-lightweight cans and ends in which traditional methods may not provide adequate control.

● DOUBLE-SEAM EVALUATION

The first-operation seam structure is critical to producing good-quality double seams. It must be evaluated on a set frequency as a normal part of the double-seam control process. Typically, this is done once per week of closing machine production or *before* making any closing machine adjustments. The evaluation samples should be taken while the machine is "hot", normally, at the end of a shift, before the machine is cleaned.

Evaluating First-Operation Double Seams
External First-Operation Seam Measurements

The first-operation countersink depth and seam thickness (Fig. 7.18) should be measured on each seaming station on the closing machine. Seam specifications normally state that these two dimensions and the lower lifter spring force are guides, not firm specifications. This means they can vary, as required, to produce body hooks and overlaps within required guidelines.

Operators should not raise or lower the head of the closing machine to adjust the body hook. This changes the pin gauge height of the machine, altering the relationship of the can flange to the undercover gassing turret, which may adversely affect the removal of air from the can.

Internal First-Operation Seam Evaluation

With modern cans and ends, in addition to making external measurements, operators should take cross sections of the first-operation seams and evaluate the structure for potential problems that may occur even when the external dimensions are within the guidelines. With conventional seamer tooling, the first-operation seam should look like the first-operation seam shown in Figure 7.19. In this "classic" first-operation seam,

- the end hook and body hook are parallel to each other and to the body wall and chuck wall,
- the end hook cut edge does not contact the body wall,
- the body hook is formed into the primary seal area, and
- the overlap is well established.

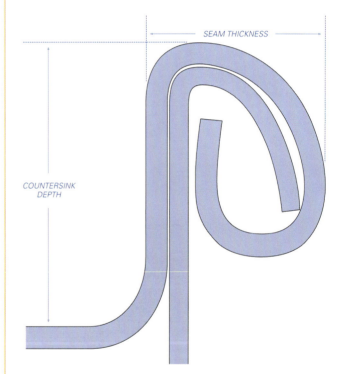

FIGURE 7.18. Countersink depth and seam thickness. (Courtesy Canning Technology)

FIGURE 7.19. Normal "classic" first-operation seam. (Courtesy Canning Technology)

Figure 7.20 shows a loose first-operation seam. The end hook and body hook are parallel to each other but not to the body wall and chuck wall. As a result, the second-operation roll may force the end hook into the body wall. A loose first-operation seam can cause punctures in the body wall and/or short end hooks—sometimes called dips—at this location.

Figure 7.21 shows a first-operation seam that is too tight. The end hook is overformed into the body hook radius. This forces the body hook into the end hook radius.

First-operation seams that are too tight (Fig. 7.21) may cause unpredictable finished seams. The second-operation roll may push the end hook down, causing short end hooks and low overlap. In other cases, the long end hook may cause short body hooks and low overlaps. The overformed end hook may also produce Vees, a defect discussed in the second-operation double-seam evaluation section below.

Any time a first-operation seam looks as though it has produced a potential body wall fracture like the one in Figure 7.22, operators should immediately shut down the closing machine for a recheck and corrective action. If corrective action is not taken in these instances, the second operation will cause the end hook to fracture the body wall, producing a leaking can.

Recently, the brewing industry has converted to using a new design of a first-operation seaming roll groove, which forms end hooks very rapidly. The new design is intended to prevent the end hook from contacting the body wall and to minimize the formation of Vees in ultra-lightweight ends. This first-operation seaming roll groove produces excellent quality double seams, but the cross section of the first-operation seam looks different from the cross sections produced by conventional tooling.

In spite of the loose appearance of the seam (Fig. 7.23), the following is true.

- The end hook and body hook are parallel to each other and to the body wall and chuck wall.
- The end hook cut edge does not contact the body wall.
- The body hook is formed into the primary seal area.
- The overlap is well established.

Again, operators should remember that any time there is a seam defect, other than a simple loose seam, the first-operation seam structure should be checked before making any adjustments.

FIGURE 7.20. A loose first-operation seam. (Courtesy Canning Technology)

FIGURE 7.22. A potential body wall fracture. (Courtesy Canning Technology)

FIGURE 7.21. A tight first-operation seam. (Courtesy Canning Technology)

FIGURE 7.23. A normal first-operation seam formed with new design tooling. (Courtesy Canning Technology)

Evaluating Second-Operation Double Seams

When checking double seams, the brewery control program must evaluate at least one can, both externally and internally, per seaming station within a set frequency. Typically, this is done once every 4 hours of closing machine run time.

External Second-Operation Seam Measurements

The external evaluation should include measurement of countersink depth, seam height, and seam thickness (Fig. 7.24). Countersink depth and seam height provide information on both the tooling setup and the wear life. As mentioned earlier, with modern ultra-lightweight ends, seam thickness is a direct indication of seam tightness. Seam thickness should not exceed the maximum specification.

Internal Second-Operation Seam Measurements

Once the external measurements are complete, the seam should be cross-sectioned and the body hook and overlap should be measured in one of several commercially available seam projectors. To take these measurements of lightweight ends, evaluators should cut the seam at two points, one parallel and one perpendicular to the grain of the end unit. Figure 7.25 illustrates the body hook and overlap.

In addition to permitting measurement of the body hook and overlap, the cross section of the double seam provides other indications of seam quality, such as seam tightness or looseness, compression or thinning of the body wall, and body hook and/or end hook distortion. Seam tightness will be apparent in the cross section. The seam shown on the left in Figure 7.26 is 100% tight, while the one on the right is 50% tight. The cross section will also show whether body wall compression is excessive, as shown in Figure 7.27. Figure 7.28 shows how seam distortion will be visible in the cross section. The end on the left has a normal seam, while the one on the right shows an unbalanced seam.

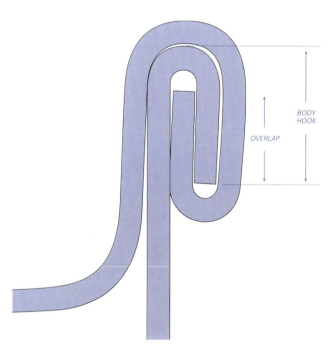

FIGURE 7.25. Body hook and overlap. (Courtesy Canning Technology)

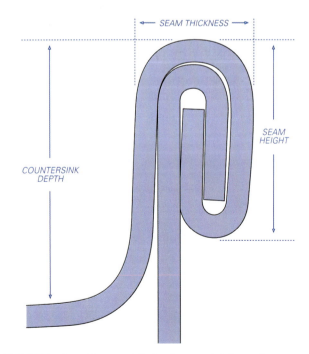

FIGURE 7.24. Countersink depth, seam height, and seam thickness. (Courtesy Canning Technology)

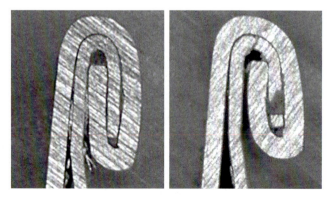

FIGURE 7.26. Tightness differences visible in the cross section. The seam on the left is 100% tight; the one on the right is 50% tight. (Courtesy Canning Technology)

Tightness Rating

Because a loose seam is the most common cause of double-seam leakage, seam tightness is a critical seam specification. The tightness rating of a seam is a visual evaluation of how well looseness wrinkles are removed or "ironed out" from a seam. To rate seam tightness, the double seam must be torn down, or "stripped", so that the face (or B view) of the end hook can be subjectively evaluated. This rating is expressed as a percent, rounded to the nearest 10%. In judging the severity of a wrinkle, evaluators must be sure to also look at the cut edge of the end hook, or A view. If there are no wrinkles, the seam is rated 100% tight (Fig. 7.29). If the wrinkles extend 30% of the way down the face of the end hook, the seam is 70% ironed out, or 70% tight (Fig. 7.30). Wrinkles that cover 50% of the end hook result in a 50% tightness rating (Fig. 7.31). The absolute minimum acceptable tightness rating for a two-piece aluminum or steel can is 90%.

Tightness rating remains the standard specification for seam tightness. However, with the narrow end hook of the modern double seam and the ease with which the reduced-gauge ends now in use can be formed, wrinkles are not

FIGURE 7.29. A 100% tight seam, shown from cut edge (top) and face (bottom) views of the end hook. (Courtesy Canning Technology)

FIGURE 7.30. A 70% tight seam, shown from cut edge (top) and face (bottom) views of the end hook. (Courtesy Canning Technology)

FIGURE 7.31. A 50% tight seam, shown from cut edge (top) and face (bottom) views of the end hook. (Courtesy Canning Technology)

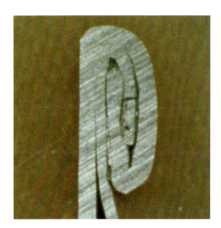

FIGURE 7.27. A cross section showing excessive body wall compression. The seam is too tight. (Courtesy Canning Technology)

FIGURE 7.28. Seam distortion visible in the cross section. The seam on the left is normal, the middle seam is R-ing, and the one on the right is an unbalanced seam. (Courtesy Canning Technology)

as apparent, and their magnitude is much more difficult to rate. In addition, other factors must be considered to determine whether seam tightness is correct. These factors include seam thickness; the appearance of the body hook, end hook, and body wall in the cross section; and the development of a pressure ridge.

Seam thickness (Fig. 7.32) must be maintained within recommended guidelines. If it exceeds the maximum specification or if average readings are consistently on the high side of the specification range, evaluators should carefully re-evaluate those stations to ensure correct seam tightness.

The cross section provides a good indication of seam tightness. When the seam is tight, compression of the body hook, end hook, and body wall is apparent (Fig. 7.33 left). The radii are sharply defined. If the seam is loose, the end hook appears "soft" or rounded (Fig. 7.33 right). The radii are not distinctly formed.

The pressure ridge (Figs. 7.34 and 7.35) is formed by the pinching action of the second-operation roll groove in the primary seal area. The pressure ridge in the body wall will be easily visible if the seam is tight. It should be continuous around the entire circumference of the can. If it is not readily apparent or if it varies in depth around the can, that station should be carefully evaluated to ensure correct tightness.

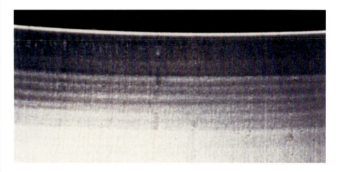

FIGURE 7.34. Internal view of the pressure ridge. (Courtesy Canning Technology)

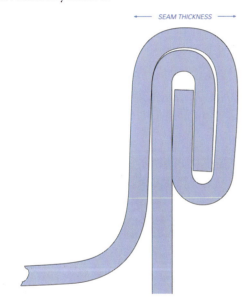

FIGURE 7.32. Seam thickness. (Courtesy Canning Technology)

FIGURE 7.35. The pressure ridge. (Courtesy Canning Technology)

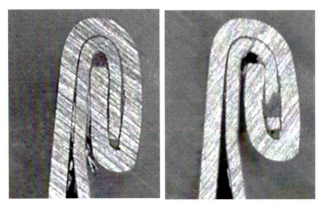

FIGURE 7.33. The seam on the left is 100% tight; the one on the right is 50% tight. (Courtesy Canning Technology)

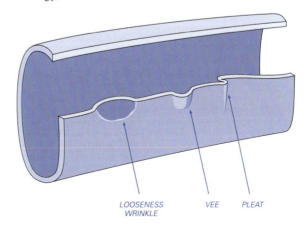

FIGURE 7.36. A looseness wrinkle, a Vee, and a pleat. (Courtesy Canning Technology)

During tightness rating, the end hook should also be evaluated for wrinkles that are not caused by seam looseness. These types of wrinkles are commonly called Vees or pleats, which are very severe Vees (Fig. 7.36).

It is important to recognize the difference between a looseness wrinkle and a Vee since the corrective actions for each are very different. Looseness wrinkles result from a loose second-operation seaming roll. The problem is corrected by tightening the second-operation roll.

Vees are formed during first-operation seaming. Adjustments to the second-operation roll will not correct this problem. When Vees appear, the first-operation cross section should be evaluated and adjustments made to the first-operation roll as required. If a Vee is mistaken for a looseness wrinkle and the second-operation roll is tightened to correct it, the Vee may penetrate the body wall, causing metal exposure and leakage.

FIGURE 7.37. Short body hook. (Courtesy Canning Technology)

FIGURE 7.38. Long body hook. (Courtesy Canning Technology)

FIGURE 7.39. Short end hook. (Courtesy Canning Technology)

APPENDIX I

Double-Seam Defects and Their Causes

The following are common two-piece aluminum double-seam defects along with their probable causes and actions needed to correct the defects. The list is by no means all inclusive, but it includes problems most frequently encountered.

Defects and Their Causes and Areas for Corrective Action

1. Defect: Short Body Hook (Fig. 7.37).
   Possible causes:
   - Pin gauge height set too high
   - Lower lifter spring force set too low
   - First-operation roll set too tight
   - Second-operation roll set too loose

2. Defect: Long Body Hook (Fig. 7.38).
   Possible causes:
   - Pin gauge height set too low
   - Lower lifter spring force set too high

3. Defect: Short End Hook (Fig. 7.39).
   Possible causes:
   - Lower lifter spring force set too high
   - First-operation roll set too loose
   - Worn first-operation roll
   - Countersink depth set too deep (first and/or second operation)

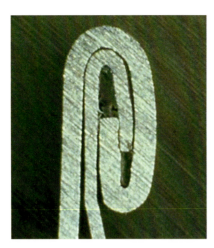

FIGURE 7.40. Excessive seam height. (Courtesy Canning Technology)

FIGURE 7.41. Excessive seam gap. (Courtesy Canning Technology)

4. Defect: Excessive Seam Height (Fig. 7.40). Possible causes:
   - First-operation roll set too loose
   - Second-operation roll set too tight
   - Excessively worn second-operation roll

5. Defect: Excessive Seam Gap (Fig. 7.41). Possible causes:
   - Excessive first-operation seaming roll float
   - Incorrect seaming chuck—lip height is too high for the end unit converted unit depth

6. Defect: Fractured Seaming Panel/Clam Shell (Fig. 7.42A). Possible causes:
   - Overformed first-operation seam (Fig. 7.42B)
   - Second-operation roll too tight
   - Excessive body hook length
   - Incorrect roll groove-to-chuck lip relationship in the first or second operation
   - Gross excess compound in the end curl

7. Defect: Body Wall Fracture/Penetration by End Hook (Fig. 7.43A–D). Possible causes:
   - First-operation roll set too loose
   - Excessive end hook length
   - Wrong first-operation roll groove
   - Worn first-operation roll groove
   - Poor shape of the end curl—it is not round

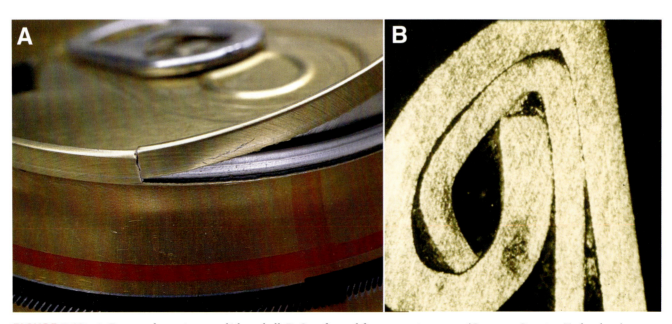

FIGURE 7.42. **A,** Fractured seaming panel/clam shell. **B,** Overformed first-operation seam. (Courtesy Canning Technology)

8. Defect: Body Hook R-ing/Hairpinning (Fig. 7.44). Possible causes:
   - Unbalanced seam—a long body hook with a short end hook (see defects 2 and 3)
   - Excessively tight seam

9. Defect: Body Wall Thinning (Fig. 7.45A and B). Possible causes:
   - Second-operation roll set too tight
   - Excessively long body hook

10. Defect: Broken (Chipped or Pitted) Seaming Chuck (Fig. 7.46). Possible causes:
    - Severe wear on chuck
    - Rolls dragging on the chuck, causing excessive wear
    - Corrosion, especially at chuck marking dimples
    - Damage from a closing machine jam

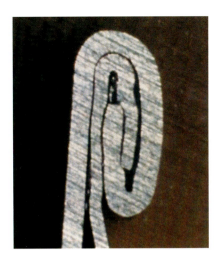

FIGURE 7.44. Body hook R-ing/hairpinning. (Courtesy Canning Technology)

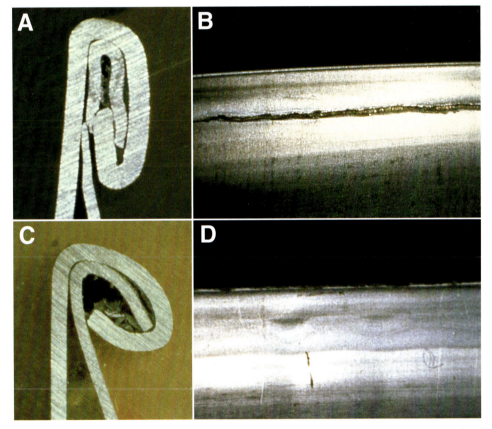

FIGURE 7.43. A, Cross section of a body wall fracture by the end hook. B, Internal view of a body wall fracture. C, Cross section of a first-operation seam that produced a body wall fracture. D, End hook Vees puncturing the body wall. Note the difference in appearance between the end hook fracture (B) and the puncture caused by V-ing. (Courtesy Canning Technology)

11. Defect: Misassembly (Fig. 7.47). Possible causes:
    - Damaged can flange (flange bent inward)
    - Incomplete assembly of can and end
    - Improper closing machine timing or clearances
    - Improper cover feed timing
    - Improper drop off from transfer table wear strip into closing machine
    - Worn or damaged lower lifter wears plate surface

12. Defect: False Seam/Knocked-Down Flange (Fig. 7.48A and B). Possible causes:
    - Damaged can flange (flange bent outward)
    - Damaged or bent end
    - Mushroomed can flange
    - Closing machine not properly timed

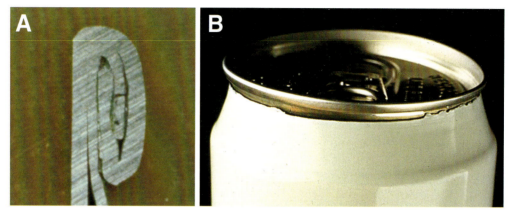

FIGURE 7.45. A, Cross section showing body wall thinning. B, Body wall thinning to the point of fracture. (Courtesy Canning Technology)

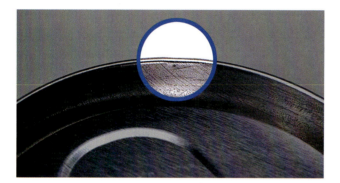

FIGURE 7.46. Broken seaming chuck. (Courtesy Canning Technology)

FIGURE 7.47. Misassembly of the body and end. (Courtesy Canning Technology)

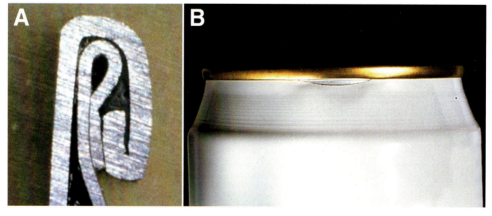

FIGURE 7.48. A, Cross section of a false seam. B, External view of a knocked-down flange. (Courtesy Canning Technology)

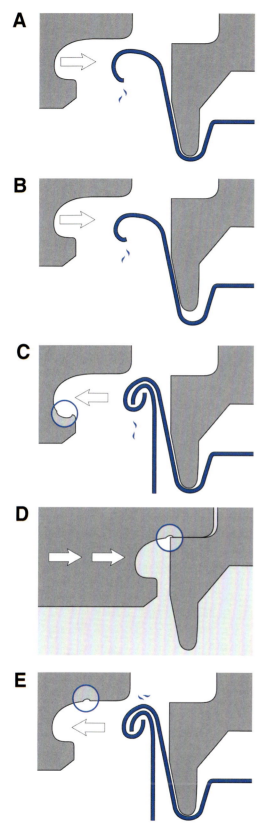

FIGURE 7.49. A, First-operation roll set too high. B, End not fully seated on the seaming chuck. C, Normal wear of the first-operation groove causes slivering. D, Damage to the top of the first-operation roll groove. E, Slivering on the top of the first-operation seam. (Courtesy Canning Technology)

13. Defect: Hairing, or Wooling. Possible causes: The location of the wooling is often a good indication of the cause. If the illustrated conditions are not present, the machine should be evaluated for damaged, worn, or dirty cover guide rails or separator disc.
    - First-operation roll set too high, causing a sliver to be shaved off the end unit cut edge as the roll moves in (Fig. 7.49A)
    - End not fully seated on the seaming chuck, causing the first-operation seaming roll to sliver the end unit cut edge (Fig. 7.49B)
    - Normal wear of the first-operation groove causes slivering as the roll moves out after completing the first operation (Fig. 7.49C)
    - First-operation roll set too low, causing damage to the top of the first-operation roll groove, resulting in slivering on the top of the first-operation seam (Fig. 7.49D and E)

APPENDIX II

Glossary of Double-Seaming Terminology

Can- and End-Related Terms

can body—the can

curl diameter—the outside curl diameter is the overall diameter of the end. This dimension is important for high-speed cover feeding. The inside curl diameter is the diameter of the area between the cut edges of a curled end. To permit assembly of the end on the can, the minimum diameter of the inside curl must be greater than the maximum diameter of the can flange.

curl height—the height of an individual end curl. This is important for high-speed cover feeding.

end unit—a can end, also known as a lid or cover

flange—the flared projection at the top of the can, which is formed into the body hook in the double seam

flange diameter—the diameter across the outside edges of the can flange. The maximum diameter of the can flange must be smaller than the minimum inside curl diameter of the end to allow the end to be assembled on the can.

flange width—the amount of metal available to form the body hook

headspace—the height above the liquid level and the plane of the flange in a filled can prior to seaming

neck-plug diameter—the inside diameter of the neck of the can

sealing compound—a water- or solvent-based synthetic rubber gasket material placed in the end curl. Embedding the cut edge of the body hook into the compound and compressing the compound produces the primary seal of the double seam.

Closing Machine-Related Terms

assembly—the bringing together, prior to the start of seam formation, of the end on the can followed by the end on the double-seaming chuck

closing machine—a machine that double seams a can end onto a can body, also known as a double seamer or seamer

cover feed—the part of a closing machine that separates the stack of ends, delivering them individually into the cover guide track

cover guide track—the track that conveys the ends from the cover feed, centering them under the double-seaming chuck

cover pusher—the part that moves the end through the cover guide track

double-seaming chuck—the closing machine tooling that supports the end during double-seam formation

double-seaming chuck lip—the lower portion of the double-seaming chuck that serves as the anvil against which the double seam is formed

double-seaming roll—the closing machine tooling that forms the double seam. There are two rolls. The first-operation roll forms the double-seam structure by interlocking the end curl with the can flange. The second-operation roll tightens the seam, providing a hermetic seal.

double-seaming roll groove—the portion of the seaming roll that actually contacts the end forming the double seam. The first- and second-operation roll grooves have different shapes specifically designed for their different functions as well as for the end gauge being seamed.

infeed chain—the carrier chain that pushes the can across the transfer table located between the filler and the closing machine and delivers it onto the lower lifter

knockout pad—an umbrella-shaped tool that fits in a recess in the double-seaming chuck. It is cammed down at the assembly of the can and end to hold the end in place on the can until the end is seated on the double-seaming chuck.

lower lifter—the part of a closing machine on which the can rests during double-seam formation. The lower lifter rotates in conjunction with the double-seaming chuck and has an adjustable spring that provides clamping force. It is also known as a base plate or can-holding chuck.

lower lifter spring force—the force, measured in pounds, exerted by the lower lifter against the double-seaming chuck during seam formation, also known as base plate or can-holding chuck force or "pressure". (The term pressure is a misnomer; force is correct.) This is the primary factor controlling body hook length.

undercover gassing turret—the device in the closing machine that purges air from the headspace of the can just prior to assembly of the end and can

Double-Seam–Related Terms

body hook—the portion of the can flange that is turned downward during double-seam formation, this is a critical double-seam dimension

dip—a localized area where the end hook length decreases

double seam—the structure that attaches a can end to a can body

droop—a localized area where the seam height increases and the end hook radius projects downward below the balance of the double seam

end hook—the portion of the end curl that is formed between the can body and the body hook during double-seam formation, also known as the cover hook

end hook wrinkle—the degree of waviness remaining in the end hook after second-operation seam formation, also called looseness wrinkle or tightness wrinkle. The amount of wrinkle is indicative of seam tightness.

overlap—the amount, measured in inches, that the body hook and end hook extend over one another

pressure ridge—the impression on the inside of the can body resulting from the pressure applied by the seaming rolls. It should be visible and uniform around the entire circumference of the can.

seam gap—the space between the top of the body hook radius and the underside of the seaming panel. It may or may not be devoid of sealing compound. Excessive seam gap reduces the seam's capacity to withstand abuse, allowing hooks to partially disengage and causing cans to leak during distribution.

seam height—the maximum external dimension of a seam when measured parallel to the body and end hooks, also called seam length or seam width

seam thickness—the maximum external dimension of a seam when measured perpendicular to the body and end hooks. In lightweight aluminum ends, seam thickness is an important indication of seam tightness.

unbalanced seam—a seam in which either the body or end hook is significantly larger than the other

uneven hook—a body hook or end hook that is not uniform in length around the can

Vee—a localized V-shaped deformation of the end hook extending from the cut edge down to the end hook radius. Vees are also called reverse wrinkles, pin wrinkles, puckers, or pleats.

wooling—slivering of the end resulting in a thin string of aluminum projecting from the seam or the buildup of aluminum shavings in the closing machine. Wooling is usually caused by abrasion to the end during feeding or seaming. This slivering is also known as hairing or angel hair.

CHAPTER 8

Glass Bottle Manufacturing

DAVE WENDT
O-I

● WHY IS BEER BETTER IN GLASS?

Glass protects the quality of its contents. Unlike other materials, with glass there is no chemical or flavor transfer. Beer that is packaged in glass tastes just like the brewer intends, with no flavors added or taken away.

In addition to its unique ability to preserve taste, glass is also the best packaging choice for the environment because it is 100% recyclable and can be recycled endlessly with no loss of purity or quality. Using recycled glass requires less energy to melt than does using raw materials, thus making it even more appealing.

● GLASS FACTORY OVERVIEW

A typical glass factory (Fig. 8.1) starts with the batch house. Raw materials are delivered to the batch house via rail or truck. In the batch house, the raw materials are measured before being delivered to the furnace, where they are then melted together with recycled glass. From the furnace, the molten glass travels to the forehearth and into the forming area, where it drops into forming machines.

In the forming area, gobs of hot glass drop into molds to make bottles. Newly formed bottles travel from the forming machines to the lehr, where they are heat stabilized and surface treatment is applied. The section of

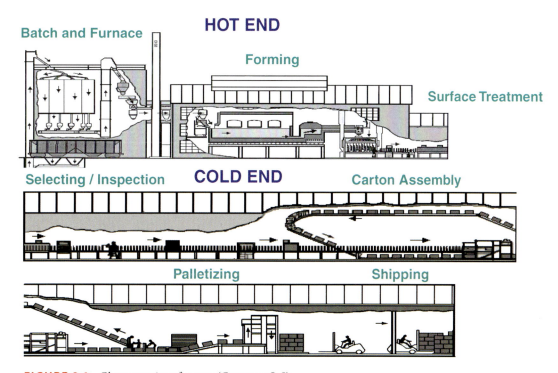

FIGURE 8.1. Glass container factory. (Courtesy O-I)

the glass plant that extends from the furnace to the lehr is called the hot end. After exiting the lehr, the bottles are then inspected and packaged in the area of the plant called the cold end.

GLASS MANUFACTURING PROCESS—STEP BY STEP THROUGH THE FACTORY

The Batch House

Raw materials are stored in silos in the batch house (Fig. 8.2). For each "batch" of glass, materials are weighed, mixed, and transported to the furnace in the appropriate quantities.

Primary Raw Materials

The primary ingredients used to make glass are sand, soda ash, and limestone. In addition, colorants and oxidizers are added for some products. For example, iron is added to make amber glass, while cobalt is added to make blue glass. In cases in which subtle variations in color are desired, such as in the production of green wine bottles, coloring agents, called minors, are added.

Recycled Glass

Recycled glass, known as cullet, is added to the raw materials as well. While the amount of recycled glass used in the manufacturing process varies greatly, some glass furnaces routinely use up to 80% recycled glass. Using cullet aids in fuel efficiency because it melts at a lower temperature than raw materials. Every 10% increase in cullet used results in a 3% decrease in energy use.

The recycled glass used to make new bottles undergoes a process of crushing, cleaning, and color sorting to remove contaminants. First, the recycled glass is crushed to a size of 0.75 inch (19 mm) or smaller. The crushed cullet is then screened and vacuumed for contaminants, such as labels and plastic caps. Magnetic separation is then used to remove metallic contaminants, such as crowns.

The commonly used techniques for cleaning and sorting recycled glass often are not able to remove ceramics or ovenware that may be mixed in. These items melt at different temperatures than the glass used for producing bottles and can result in "stones" in the finished glass, which in turn can weaken the bottle.

The Furnace
Sideport Furnace

When raw materials leave the batch house, they are fed continuously into the furnace (also called the tank), where they are melted to make glass. The depth of the molten glass in the furnace must be controlled to within ±0.01 inch (±0.25 mm) for proper forming machine operation.

The glass furnace consists of three main parts: the melter, the refiner, and the regenerators (also known as checkers). The melter is a rectangular basin in which the actual melting and fining (seed removal) takes place. In a sideport furnace (Fig. 8.3), the batch is charged into the

FIGURE 8.2. Batch house. (Courtesy O-I)

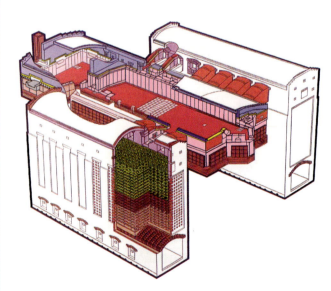

FIGURE 8.3. Sideport furnace. (Courtesy O-I)

furnace through the doghouse, which is an extension of the melter, protruding from the back wall.

Along each side of the melter, above glass level, are three to seven ports that contain the natural gas burners and direct the combustion air and exhaust gases. Most furnaces are designed to use natural gas but are capable of using alternate fuels, such as oil, propane, and electricity, if necessary.

Furnaces range in size from about 450 square feet to more than 1,400 square feet of melter surface. A properly operated and well-maintained furnace will last for approximately 10 years with just one partial repair and will produce more than 1,000 tons of glass per square foot of melter surface over the life of the furnace.

The melter basin is separated from the refiner by the bridge wall (also known as the throat end wall). Glass passes from the melter to the refiner through the throat, a water-cooled tunnel that extends through the bridge wall.

The refiner acts as a holding basin where the glass is allowed to cool to a uniform temperature before entering the forehearth. The melter and refiner are covered by crowns to contain the heat.

Oxygen-Fueled Furnace

Figure 8.4 shows an oxygen-fueled furnace. With an oxygen-fueled furnace, normal combustion air is replaced with a supply of pure oxygen, which enters the furnace directly through the burners, along with the fuel being burned.

In the case of a 100% oxygen-fueled furnace, normal combustion air (containing 21% oxygen and 78% nitrogen) is totally eliminated and replaced with oxygen. This results in a total reduction of approximately 80% of the waste gases being discharged from the furnace. As a result, the regenerators are also eliminated.

The molten glass comes out at the forehearth of the machine. The forehearth is the area where the glass is refined and checked for any "seeds" or blisters that may have formed.

Figures 8.5 and 8.6 show the inside of a furnace. The furnace itself is about two to three stories tall, and the melter area is typically 6–10 feet deep. Figure 8.5 shows the melter area, where the raw materials enter. Figure 8.6 shows a man standing in the furnace, indicating how deep a furnace is typically filled with molten glass.

FIGURE 8.5. Melter area. (Courtesy O-I)

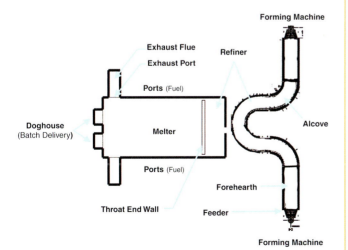

FIGURE 8.4. Oxygen-fueled furnace. (Courtesy O-I)

FIGURE 8.6. Entry to the refiner/alcove; glass flow is to the small opening at the back. (Courtesy O-I)

Glass Temperature During Formation

Approximate temperatures inside the furnace range from 2,600 to 2,900°F (1,427 to 1,593°C). In the forehearth, temperatures range from 2,000 to 2,200°F (1,093 to 1,204°C). At gob formation, the temperature of the glass gob ranges from 1,500 to 1,750°F (816 to 954°C).

When bottles come out of the machine and onto the conveyor, they are about 1,200–1,400°F (649–760°C). At the entrance to the lehr, the bottles are about 850–1,000°F (454–538°C).

As soon as a bottle comes out of the mold, it is already developing a hard skin on the outside but is still very hot and requires tongs for handling.

Forehearth

After melting in the furnace, the glass flows into a forehearth, where further conditioning takes place to prepare the glass for the forming process. The molten glass flows from the refiner through the forehearth with the help of gravity. From there, the glass is carefully cooled to a uniform temperature and viscosity prior to reaching the feeder. Using the pull of gravity, the hot glass flows through the orifice at the bottom of the feeder. Glass flow is controlled by the height of a ceramic tube in the feeder—a raised tube creates a heavy flow, while a lowered tube results in a reduced flow. The glass flow then undergoes a "mixing action" created by the rotation of the ceramic tube. This helps to make the temperature consistent while the downward motion of the plunger accelerates the glass flow.

This action is timed with the shearing of the glass flow as it falls beneath the feeder to shape the gobs. After the gob has been sheared from the feeder, it falls into a series of chutes, where it is delivered to the blank mold on the individual section (I.S.) machine.

The furnaces, once fired, operate 24 hours per day, 365 days per year, and are never shut off. They can be reduced in volume, called a "low", in which smaller batches are added, but the furnaces themselves are not shut off. Once a furnace is shut off, there can be 6–8 inches of residual glass left on the inside, which must be removed with jackhammers.

The feeder is shown in Figure 8.7. Glass is formed into gobs as it is pushed through openings at the bottom of the feeder via a ceramic tube. Because the temperature of all the glass must be the same, the tube rotates and mixes continuously throughout the entire process in order to achieve a uniform temperature. As the tube forces the glass out, it is cut underneath by shears. This is a timed operation: the tube pushes down and the shears come up, resulting in a repeated action of push, cut, push, cut.

Figure 8.8 shows a gob of glass sheared from the feeder. The gob is 0.375–4.0 inches in diameter and 0.5–6.0 inches long. The gob must contain the exact amount of glass needed to make a particular size or shape of bottle. There cannot be any more or any less, since such a discrepancy would result in bottle capacity issues.

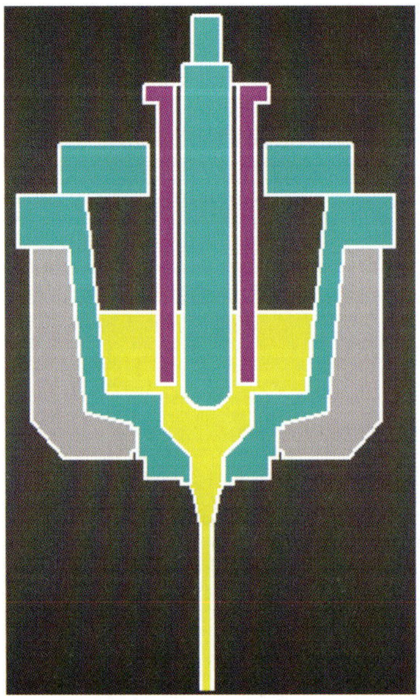

FIGURE 8.7. Glass (yellow) is formed into "gobs" by a ceramic tube pushing the glass through orifices or openings at the base of the feeder. Glass is cut into by a timed shearing mechanism located under the feeder orifice. (Courtesy O-I)

FIGURE 8.8. A gob is a specific amount of molten glass that will be formed into a glass container. Diameters are 0.375–4.0 inches and lengths are 0.5–6.0 inches. (Courtesy O-I)

There are three parts of machinery the gob needs to travel through once it leaves the feeder prior to it becoming a bottle.

- The delivery equipment
- The blank side, or backside, of the forming machine
- The mold side of the machine

The delivery equipment is shown in Figure 8.9. The gob comes out of the feeder and goes into a scoop, which routes the gobs through a section. The machine typically has eight to twelve sections. The scoop rotates quickly back and forth and the gob is then sent into a trough that delivers it to the proper deflector. At that time, the deflector drops the gob into the blank mold.

The troughs on a large 12-section machine have what is called an air ride, with holes drilled in and air pushing the gob. The air ride acts to shorten the amount of time it takes for the gob to get out to the deflector, a process that takes longer with larger-sectioned machines. This operation is all timed to keep the machines functioning uniformly.

Each mold station is called a section. A quad has four bottles produced on each section at a time, one each from four cavities. A 12-section quad is 12 individual sections producing four bottles at each section. Each cavity has a unique number on it and serves as the actual bottle mold. The numbers allow identification of where the bottle was made, on what section and in what cavity on that particular machine. Sections come in 10-triple sections, 10-double sections, 8-triple sections, 8-double sections, and even 6-single section machines to make 3-L bottles.

Since the sections are individually run, one section can be turned off when it requires service or maintenance work while the rest continue to operate.

Any bottles pulled from the line or with defects are sent to a basement area, where they are crushed into cullet and later transferred back to the furnace to be remelted.

The gob is delivered into the blank side of the machine and formed into a parison, or blank (Fig. 8.10). The parison is formed either by a press-and-blow or a blow-and-blow process. During the formation cycle, lubrication is manually applied to the blank molds and blow molds. This lubrication process is called swabbing. The lubricant is a carbon- and oil-based material that must be applied to the back of the machines to prevent the glass from sticking to the metal mold cavity.

A parison is specifically shaped and blows up like a balloon in the mold to form the bottle. This happens on the blank side of the machine, where the finish is made. The finish got its name because traditionally, when bottles were blown by hand, the finish at the top was the last thing that was made on the bottle. In modern glass bottle making, the finish is the first thing made. The parison is hollow on the inside. The cooler skin or enamel is on the outside surface and is about 1,300°F (704°C). The cooler skin contains the exact amount of glass that the container needs.

Once it leaves the furnace, gets cut, and drops into the mold, the gob has lost 100°F (38°C) in about 2 or 3 seconds. The temperatures of the blank molds are controlled. Once it is taken out of the mold, the new bottle goes onto a cooling pad to start cooling the outside surface.

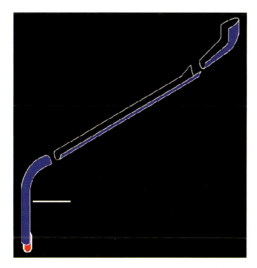

FIGURE 8.9. The gob exits the feeder into the delivery equipment, where a scoop then routes it to a ready section. The trough subsequently routes the gob to the proper deflector, and the deflector provides a controlled path for the falling gob to gain exact alignment in the center of the blank. Upon delivery into the blank, the gob can now form a parison. (Courtesy O-I)

FIGURE 8.10. A parison is a specifically shaped formation of glass that is blown up like a balloon in the blow mold to form the bottle. (Courtesy O-I)

Narrow-Neck Press and Blow

The full narrow-neck press-and-blow process is shown in Figure 8.11.

The gob enters the blank side of the machine, and then the press starts where the plunger is pushed up (Fig. 8.12).

When the plunger is pushing up, it is driving the glass down to form the finish of the bottle. How the parison is loaded or dropped into the blank affects where the glass goes when it is formed in the mold. Different shapes of blanks are used to ensure there is more glass at the contact points on a bottle, less in the sidewalls, and more in the bottom.

Once the parison is formed, it is inverted or transferred into the mold side (Fig. 8.13). Once the outside surface is a certain temperature, gas begins to vent out and then the glass is blown to the sides of the mold. As it is blown, a vacuum is applied, which helps pull the glass out to the sides of the mold.

Once the bottle is formed, "takeouts" then pick up the bottle (Fig. 8.14) and send it over a cooling plate, where cool air is applied. The bottles sit on the bed of air and then are swept onto a conveyor (Fig. 8.15) and the cooling process is started. The bottles are held above the cooling plate while air is forced up. The bottom of the bottle is cooled first, because that is the surface it will rest on while traveling on the conveyor.

Once the bottle has been set onto the cooling plate, it is then swept out to the machine conveyor. The machine conveyor cools from the bottom and then the bottles move to the tin hood (Fig. 8.16). The bottles travel through the tin hood to the cross conveyor that leads into the lehr for the annealing process.

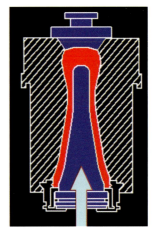

FIGURE 8.12. Parison formation: gob entry, start press, and full press. (Courtesy O-I)

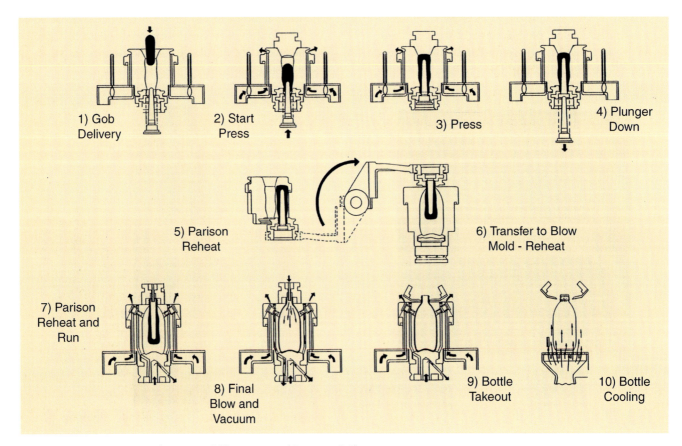

FIGURE 8.11. Narrow-neck press-and-blow process. (Courtesy O-I)

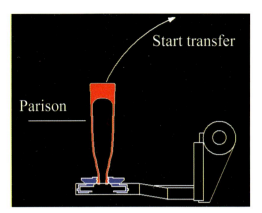

FIGURE 8.13. The parison is formed and transfer is started. (Courtesy O-I)

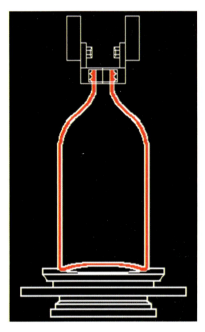

FIGURE 8.14. Formed bottle is taken to a cooling plate. (Courtesy O-I)

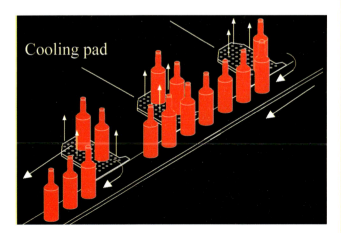

FIGURE 8.15. Containers are transferred to a conveyor cooling pad. (Courtesy O-I)

Annealing Process

The annealing process is started between the discharge from the forming machine and the entry into the lehr. Annealing is the controlled removal of heat from the glass container. Without annealing, a bottle taken fresh off the machine and set onto a table would crack and cave in on itself in about 15 minutes. This is because the outside is cooling faster than the inside. The annealing process prevents this internal pressure from forming.

Surface treatment protection is applying as a slick surface onto the outside of the container in two stages. The first part of the surface treatment is applied to the container in the tin hood. This hot end treatment is vaporized onto and actually into the glass upon leaving the machine.

The Lehr

The lehr basically works the same as a pasteurizer. The bottles, now below 800°F (427°C), head into the lehr and are heated to almost 1,200°F (649°C). Figure 8.17 shows the heating and cooling curve.

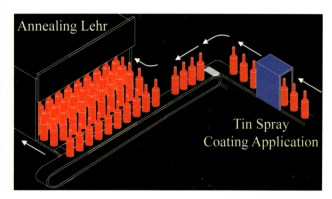

FIGURE 8.16. Containers are transferred into the annealing lehr. (Courtesy O-I)

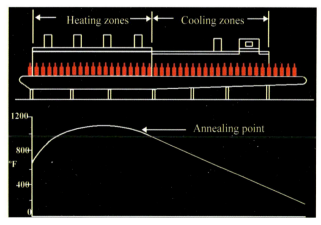

FIGURE 8.17. Annealing lehr cross sectional view (top) and typical annealing temperature curve (bottom). (Courtesy O-I)

The lehr reheats the bottle and holds it to equalize the temperatures inside and out, and then it slowly returns the bottle to room temperature. Depending on the size and shape of the container, this process takes approximately 20–90 minutes. At the lehr discharge (Fig. 8.18), the bottles are still very hot but can be picked up with bare hands.

There can be serious issues with annealing if not done correctly. The process is checked using a polariscope (Fig. 8.19). The polariscope uses one to five calibration discs to compare colors and find heat stress issues.

Stress can be seen in a bottle through a polariscope, because the polariscope refracts the light to give different colors depending on the tempering. There is always a certain amount of annealing stress. To determine the amount of stress, the discs are held up and compared against standards (Fig. 8.20). If stress areas are found, the glass-making process is altered to correct the stresses.

The Cold End

Polyethylene is sprayed onto the bottles within the cold end after they have left the lehr (Fig. 8.21). The polyethylene coat sticks to the tin applied previously and keeps the bottles from scuffing. The spray heads apply the polyethylene with a top spray and a backup spray below the bottle finish, ensuring nothing gets into the bottle.

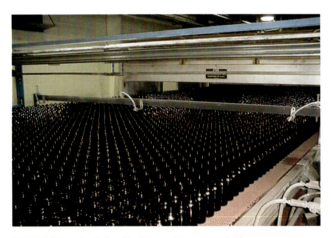

FIGURE 8.18. Lehr discharge. (Courtesy O-I)

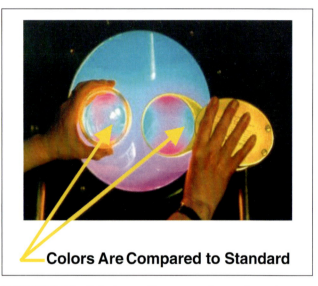

FIGURE 8.20. Polariscope discs are used to evaluate the annealing process. (Courtesy O-I)

FIGURE 8.19. Samples are obtained immediately prior to the overhead sprays to check the annealing using a polariscope. (Courtesy O-I)

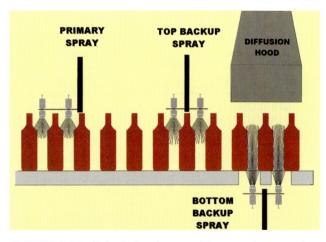

FIGURE 8.21. Polyethylene is sprayed between the rows of bottles. Backup sprays are also used to ensure proper coverage of the bottle. A diffusion hood is used to keep the bottom backup spray from reaching the finish of the bottle. (Courtesy O-I)

The bottles then travel through the diffusion hood and are sprayed from the bottom with a bottom backup spray; the hood uses a cushion of air so the spray does not get onto the finish. The backup sprays make sure a coating is applied evenly.

Bottle Inspection

Automatic inspection is designed to catch and eliminate problem bottles. This process effectively removes defects and alerts operator personnel of problems on the machine.

The inspection units use light-reflecting technology to find defects that may not be visible to the human eye. Lighting and cameras are set up in the inspection equipment in order to easily detect defects. The bottle spins in the inspection machine and a light shines into it. If the machine detects what is referred to as a shine or a flash, a defect has been found and the bottle will be discarded to the cullet bin.

All glass defects happen in the hot end. Figures 8.22 through 8.26 show various bottle defects.

Defects such as stones, scabby bottoms, birdswings, blisters, fused glass, and checks are detectable with the light reflection equipment. The inspection starts in the hot end, as the bottles run through the tin tunnel, where cameras and infrared sensors are located.

The inspection and quality control decisions are based on percentages of loss. A pick system in the hot end keeps

FIGURE 8.24. Scabby bottom that was not rejected after swabbing. (Courtesy O-I)

FIGURE 8.22. Split finish caused by a cold plunger. A split is caused by a difference of only 5°F (2.8°C) between the temperature of the plunger and that of the glass. (Courtesy O-I)

FIGURE 8.25. Birdswing caused by a parison collapsing on an inversion. (Courtesy O-I)

FIGURE 8.23. Dipped finish caused by too little glass or too light of a press during formation. (Courtesy O-I)

FIGURE 8.26. Stone caused by contaminated cullet. (Courtesy O-I)

track of what is being rejected in the cold end and what defects are being found in the cold end that should have been found in the hot end. If there is a serious issue, then a cavity identification (CID) is issued and all bottles from that cavity will be rejected in the cold end. The inspection equipment can be instructed to identify every bottle with the particular dot code and reject it. This is done until the problem is fixed in the hot end. Once fixed, the cavity can be released and used again.

Inspection also occurs regularly for every cavity on the section in what is called a "set out." In a 10-triple machine, one set out is 30 bottles, one bottle from every single cavity. Each bottle from each cavity is inspected individually. A full set out is inspected once or twice a shift. Additionally, a five-bottle random sample is pulled from the hot end about every 20 minutes and analyzed for measurements.

These measurements include the bearing surface, the bottom of the bottle, and the thickness of the glass. Other inspections are conducted to test the degree of leaning, sidewall thickness, any other issues seen with this particular container, and issues that the customer has reported should be watched for. Completing a five-bottle random sample inspection every 20 minutes over the course of a shift ensures that bottles coming from every part of the machine are checked thoroughly.

Dimensions, including height, diameter, roundness, thin spots, lean, and glass thickness, are automatically measured in the cold end with various pieces of inspection equipment. Challenge samples are run every one-half hour on the cold end with a series of five or six defect samples placed onto the line to make sure the machine rejects them properly. If the machine does not recognize and reject the defects, then a mechanic will make adjustments until the equipment functions correctly.

Glass is a noncrystalline solid or a super-cooled liquid, meaning it never truly hardens 100%, which is why fracture analysis can be conducted in a lab. When there is a check or a little crack in the glass, it continues to grow.

Table 8.1 shows the five forces that will affect a glass container.

Impact

The first force factor is impact, which is when a bottle hits another glass container, falls over, drops, etc. The most important question regarding impact issues pertains to whether it was hit hard or there was a defect that caused the glass to fail.

Thermal Shock

Thermal shock involves rapid thermal changes and is seen when the inside of a cold container is heated rapidly, while the outside is cooled rapidly. With beer, there is a

TABLE 8.1. Forces that Affect a Glass Container

Force	Description
Impact	Created when a container is contacted by another container or object
Thermal shock	Created by rapid thermal changes: the inside surface of a cold container is heated rapidly or the outside surface is cooled rapidly
Internal pressure	Created by the product or its expansion
Vertical load	Created when a compressive vertical force or weight is applied to the top of a container
Hydrodynamic load	Created when the product is set in motion and the container stops

shock on the inside and outside of the bottle once it is filled with cold liquid and then sent through a pasteurizer. The rule of thumb is to have the glass and the product within 70°F (21°C) of each other to avoid thermal shock, whether it is during filling or cooling. In a pasteurizer, the whole bottle is experiencing thermal shock because the stress is on the cold surface. The cold surface is the location of the highest amount of stress, and the bottle is filled at 38°F (3°C), making it cold on the inside. The bottle is then run through a pasteurizer and heated to 140°F (60°C), making it cold on the inside and hot on the outside. Then at the end, it is hot on the inside and cold on the outside. So if there is anything wrong with the bottle, the pasteurizing process is going to find it.

Internal Pressure

Internal pressure finds any defect in the glass and forces a failure. One of the best pieces of bottle inspection equipment is the beer filler, during the vacuum and pressurizing phase of deaerating the bottle, and the pasteurizer. The rapid vacuum and pressurization during the pre-evacuation steps in the filler, coupled with the rapid expansion of pressure from heating the beer in the pasteurizer, will cause internal pressure forces and any defect present to blow up the bottle.

Vertical Load

Vertical load is a compressive force on the top of the bottle, but it runs in different ranges. The pressure at the crowner is about 70 pounds per square inch gauge (psig) for a split second, but in a warehouse, the bottles are stacked in pallets, many layers high, for a relatively long period. Glass only fails in tension when it is getting pulled apart, and a properly designed bottle can handle a large amount of vertical load.

Hydrodynamic Force

Hydrodynamic force occurs when the bottle is filled with beer. Force on the filled bottle will cause a water hammer. When the bottle is hit, the water hammer drives the headspace pocket down, and the product slams into the glass, causing the water hammer to tear the surface off the glass. The other hydraulic force is called surge. An example of surge would be putting tension on the outside of the bottle, such as that seen in a drop packer. When the filled bottle is dropped, the fluid goes up into the neck and then it slams down, putting stress on the outside of the container.

The design of the bottle is critical to ensure it withstands each of these forces. In designing any new container, bottle designers must fully understand how the bottle will be handled, filled, packed, etc.

Palletizing

Finally, the bottles are packed either into cartons or onto bulk pallets with tier sheers (Fig. 8.27). According to customer request, some bottles are packaged in cartons as six packs or with partitions (Fig. 8.28). Whether packed into individual cartons or onto bulk pallets, the bottles are palletized and then wrapped in plastic stretch film with a pallet tag containing production information, including manufacturing date and time. The pallets are stored at the glass plant until shipped to the brewery.

FIGURE 8.27. Bottles are placed onto tier sheets and stretch-wrapped with plastic. (Courtesy O-I)

FIGURE 8.28. Bottles are also packed into various types of corrugated packages. (Courtesy O-I)

CHAPTER 9

Basic Principles and Operation of a Bottle Washer

CARLOS ALARCON
Barry-Wehmiller Companies

Bottle washers clean and remove labels from soiled returnable bottles. This task is achieved when physically and biologically clean bottles are discharged from the rinser. Unlike returnables, nonreturnable bottles do not need to be processed through the bottle washer. A simple rinsing device is sufficient to prepare nonreturnable bottles for the filling operations.

Several factors determine the effectiveness of bottle washers:

- The design of the bottle washer
- The condition of the returnable bottles
- The composition of the bottle-washing solution
- The temperature of the solution
- The submersion or contact time
- The quality of the water

● TYPICAL BOTTLE-WASHER OPERATION

Basically, bottle washers are designed to facilitate the following sequence of operations.

1. In order to remove loose soil and foreign material, bottles are subjected to internal and external prerinse sprays or subjected to soaking in water in the first compartment.
2. The bottles are alternately immersed in washing solution and drained by passing them through a series of isolated tanks, each containing large quantities of solution. High-volume, low-pressure flows directed across the bottles create a shearing action, which aids in separating soil and labels from the bottles and dispersing both in the solution.
3. The soiled washing solution is drained from the bottles as they pass from one tank to another.
4. The bottles are rinsed of the washing solution.

Types of Returnable Bottles

Soiled returnable bottles fall into one of four categories (Duncan, 1982): normal trade returns, storage bottles, ditch bottles, and uncleanable bottles.

Normal trade returns (Fig. 9.1) make up the bulk of the bottles coming to the brewery. These are bottles that make the round trip from the brewery to the trade and back again in less than 3 months time.

FIGURE 9.1. A dirty normal trade return bottle. (Courtesy Barry-Wehmiller Companies)

129

Storage bottles (Fig. 9.2) are those kept in warehouses, basements, garages, etc., for longer periods. These bottles are more difficult to clean than are normal trade returns.

Ditch bottles (Fig. 9.3) are characterized by a heavy accumulation of soil along the interior of one sidewall as a result of their lying on the side of the road or other outdoor location for extended periods of time. The soil may be dried mud, sand, mold, and algae or any combination thereof. Ditch bottles are normally collected by salvage operators and can arrive at the plant in single or multiple deliveries of significant quantities. Under these circumstances, the bottles should be segregated and washed separately at the end of a production run when special attention can be given to the washing operation.

Uncleanable bottles (Fig. 9.4) have substances such as tar, paint, plaster, or weld splatter adhering to the glass surface. These soils are insoluble in normal bottle-washing solutions, and the bottles, therefore, cannot be cleaned. These bottles should be discarded before they are loaded into the bottle washer.

Composition of the Washing Solution

Bottle-washing solutions are made up of caustic soda (sodium hydroxide [NaOH]) and additives, which are mixed thoroughly with water to prescribed solution strengths. The chemical effect of the washing solution is to disperse soil adhered to the bottle surface and to avoid its redeposition onto the cleaned bottle. Good washing-solution wetting and rinsing properties are essential in order to obtain the desired cleaning effect. Cleaning power varies with the concentration of the solution and the operating temperature. As a rule of thumb, the same germicidal effect can be obtained either by raising the temperature 10°F (5.5°C) or by increasing the strength of the solution by 50%. However, it should be cautioned that the application of this rule might only be valid within a narrow range.

FIGURE 9.2. A storage bottle. (Courtesy Barry-Wehmiller Companies)

FIGURE 9.3. A ditch bottle. (Courtesy Barry-Wehmiller Companies)

FIGURE 9.4. An uncleanable bottle. (Courtesy Barry-Wehmiller Companies)

Selecting solutions with high concentrations of caustic soda ensures the desired germicidal effect but these solutions also produce excessive pulp and fibers from paper labels and etch bottles. It may also require the installation of neutralizing units to meet local effluent specifications, and in concentrations over 5%, may lead to waste due to carryover.

Temperature of the Solution

Higher washing-solution temperatures accelerate the cleaning process of the bottles. High temperatures are also necessary to sterilize bottles, so correct temperature adjustment is quite important. If bottles are subjected to an excessive temperature change, breakage can occur due to thermal shock, which produces a characteristic crack extending completely around the base and often up the sidewall of a bottle. The temperature differential between compartments should not exceed 100°F (56°C) when heating the bottles (on the up-leg of the temperature–time curve) and 40°F (23°C) when cooling the bottles (on the down-leg of the temperature–time curve). Even at these limits, some breakage may occur due to thermal shock.

Hot soak temperatures make the vapor zone very hot, and this can cause contaminates to bake on if the bottle washer is stopped for a long period. High temperatures also tend to cause fast drying of the bottles in the vapor zone, which in the absence of a wetting agent may result in an alkaline dry-on, also known as blush or caustic bloom.

Submersion or Contact Time

Submersion time (also called soaking time) constitutes the time a bottle is submerged in the caustic solution and does not include the time used for rinsing or for bottle transfer from one compartment to the next. On the other hand, contact time refers to the time that a bottle is subjected to the action of the caustic solution, which is equal to the submersion time plus the time spent in transfer from one solution compartment to another. It should be noted that the Canadian standard of accepted practice is a minimum of 20 minutes of submersion time. Total time refers to the number of minutes required for a bottle to complete its passage through the washer from loading to unloading.

The longer the contact time, the greater the cleaning effect. However, prolonged contact time should be avoided because of the corrosive effect of caustic soda solutions on glass. Under those conditions, beer bottles may acquire a cloudy appearance.

As a bottle travels in and out of hot caustic soak compartments, its soiled surface is subjected to two separate and distinct cleaning mechanisms. One—the soaking sequence—is time dependent, and the second—the filling and emptying sequence—is time independent. The first refers solely to the time the bottles are submerged in hot caustic. The second, time-independent process relates to the number of times the bottles are filled and emptied. The phenomenon has been described by Jennings (1965) as Dupre's effect, which in turn depends upon the number of times an air–liquid interface sweeps across a soiled surface. For example, in a single-compartment washer, a bottle has two interfaces, i.e., one filling and one emptying, whereas in a three-compartment washer, it has six interfaces. When Barry-Wehmiller Companies conducted lab tests designed to simulate bottle-cleaning processes, the results indicated that when soaking times were equal (in the 6- to 9-minute range), a three-compartment washer could remove twice as much soil as a single-compartment machine. From this finding, it becomes clear that the effectiveness of bottle-washing machines cannot be judged solely by their soak times.

The Quality of the Water

In bottle washing, the degree of water hardness plays a crucial role. In North America, water hardness is expressed as milligrams of calcium carbonate ($CaCO_3$) per liter, despite the fact that a variety of cations (Ca^{++} and Mg^{++}) and anions (SO_4^{--}, Cl^-, and NO_3^-) may be present.

Temporary hardness is due to the presence of a bicarbonate, such as calcium bicarbonate ($Ca(HCO_3)_2$) or magnesium bicarbonate ($Mg(HCO_3)_2$), and can be partly removed by boiling. In contrast, what is known as permanent hardness results from the presence of sulfates of calcium and magnesium, and boiling has no substantial effect on their concentration. Hard water causes scaling in the bottle washer and reduces the efficiency of the washing solution. In the rinser section, hard water can plug spray nozzles and lead to undesirable spotting on cleaned bottles. Temporary hardness in the rinser is also of concern, since the sodium hydroxide carryover reacts with calcium bicarbonate to form the precipitating calcium carbonate. Good results have been obtained by adding polyphosphates to the rinse water. These compounds combine (sequester) with calcium and magnesium ions and stay in suspension.

Bottle-washer operators very often seek to remove scale-producing ions from the rinse water. The most commonly used water softener is a bed of sodium zeolite resins, which exchanges sodium ions for scale-forming ions of calcium and magnesium ions for scale-forming ions of magnesium.

Regeneration is achieved by treating the exhausted resin with 10% brine solution. During this process, the calcium and magnesium ions are replaced by sodium ions.

BASIC FUNCTIONS OF A BOTTLE WASHER

Soiled bottles are mechanically loaded into carrier pockets from which they are discharged after completion of the cleaning cycle. When loading and discharge take place at the same end, the washer is called a single-ended machine. More common, however, are double-ended machines, where loading and discharge take place on separate ends of the machine. Single-ended machines need only one operator, whereas double-ended machines require two operators but allow for a more hygienic operation. In double-ended machines, machine arrangements are also available that allow loading and unloading to take place at different floor elevations.

Pretreatment Prerinse

Before the bottles are subjected to the main cleaning process, they are pretreated with warm water or mild caustic. This is done to flush out liquid residues, to remove excessive soil, and to temper the bottles for the following soak in hot caustic. Good pretreatment also reduces contamination of the next compartment.

There are two variations of this process: presoaking and prejetting. Presoaking reduces breakage due to thermal shock, allows heat recovery, helps labels come off earlier in the process, and does not require the installation of additional pumps. In presoaking, the first compartment is filled with warm water, a wetting agent (surfactant), and no caustic. A continuous water supply comes from the rinse compartment or the second postsoak compartment. In contrast, prejetting removes excessive soil more effectively and makes it easier to control the undesired development of microorganisms in the pretreatment stage. The cleaning pretreatment is accomplished with pumps and spray nozzles that direct spray into the neck opening and onto the bottle heel. Water for these sprays comes from the rinse compartment.

Main Cleaning

After pretreatment, the bottles travel automatically into the section of the washer where the main cleaning process takes place. Hot alkaline solutions soften and dissolve label adhesives and disperse soil resides and microbial contaminants. Soaking and jetting the bottles with washing solutions in several compartments accomplishes the main cleaning process. Although the makeup of aluminum foil labels differs substantially from that of paper labels, it takes a very similar amount of time to remove either label type, although metallized paper labels appear to take longer to remove. It is desirable to separate the labels as quickly as possible from the washing solution to avoid disintegration of the label into minute pulp fibers that plug jets and filters. High-volume label removal systems are employed to aid in removing labels.

High-volume label removal systems form an integral part of bottle washers. They are designed to continuously remove labels while the machine is in production. Without high-volume label removal, the life cycle of the washing solution would be greatly reduced.

Final Rinse

All machines have a final rinse stage that removes alkaline bottle-washing compounds from the glass surface and tempers bottles prior to the filler. This section of the washer consists of undershot jets and overhead sprays, which first apply diluted caustic and then fresh water to the bottles to remove the last traces of soil and residual detergent. At the end of the washing process, the bottles are drained of rinse water and automatically discharged from the carrier pockets to a conveyor.

BOTTLE-WASHING SOLUTIONS

In bottle washing, the detersive system consists of three major elements: the bottles, the soil or dirt attached to the bottles, and the washing solution. This section deals only with the last element, the washing solution.

Properties of Bottle-Washing Solutions

As a basic requirement, bottle-washing solutions must lessen the adhesiveness of soil to the glass surface and keep unwanted foreign matter in suspension for easy rinsing. Close inspection of these basic requirements reveals that the washing solution must consist of the following attributes.

Germicidal Properties

A solution's ability to destroy harmful microorganisms depends upon its composition, the temperature during the cleaning process, and the submersion time. Many countries and states have enacted laws governing the strength of bottle-washing solutions, and it is to the brewer's advantage to be aware of these regulations. The minimum requirements for sterilizing bottles, as recommended by the American Beverage Association, originally called the American Bottlers of Carbonated Beverages and then the National Soft Drink Association, are that unclean bottles shall be exposed to a 3% solution of which not less than 60% is caustic (NaOH) for a period of not less than 5 minutes at a temperature of not less than 130°F (55°C) or to an equivalent cleansing and sterilizing process.

Solutions that are germicidal equivalents to the above recommended solution may be obtained through various combinations of time, caustic concentration, and temperature. Table 9.1 presents equivalent caustic concentrations for achieving 99.9% germicidal efficiency.

Wetting or Penetrating Properties

The ease with which a solution allows the bottle surface to be wetted is an important property of the washing solution. This property permits the solution to contact the entire soiled surface and to penetrate deposits of dirt, residue, and foreign material. It does so by reducing both the surface tension of the liquid and its interfacial tension with the glass. Surfactant is a commonly used word to describe these surface-active agents.

Good wetting properties are important for the rapid removal of both paper and foil labels in large pieces. Speedy label removal reduces label breakdown into pulp and fibers, which are more difficult to remove from the washing solutions.

Rinsing Properties

During the rinsing process, all soil and detergent residues must be removed from the bottles. A detergent with good rinsing properties facilitates this operation. One should not expect the rinser to remove materials that remain strongly adhered to bottles. It is the major function of the soaking compartments and the jet-rinse sections to break the soil–glass bond. Good rising properties promote drainage and reduce the quantity of caustic carryover from compartment to compartment, resulting in savings in caustic consumption.

Sequestering Properties

A sequestering, or chelating, agent is a chemical compound that combines with metal ions in solutions to form water-soluble complex ions. In bottle washing, it is primarily the calcium (Ca), iron, aluminum, and magnesium (Mg) ions that require sequestration.

The formation of Ca^{++} and Mg^{++} chelates in the washing solution is necessary to prevent the deposition of insoluble calcium and magnesium salts, which form an unsightly film on bottles and produce a heavy scale on carrier chains, carriers, and tanks. Scale interferes with heat transfer, plugs nozzles, and increases the physical load on the machine. Also, scale on the carrier chains and carriers acts as a porous sponge, increasing the alkali carryover from compartment to compartment.

Deflocculating or Dispersing Properties

Washing solutions with deflocculating properties aid in dispersing soils by keeping colloidal particles in suspension.

Emulsifying Properties

Emulsification is the suspension of particles within a second liquid phase. In bottle washing, this property aids in removing oil films from surfaces.

Anticorrosion Properties

A good washing solution protects the soaker/rinser against corrosion, which can result from high alkalinity levels in the washing process.

Antifoaming Properties

Excessive foaming reduces the effectiveness of the cleaning process. Adhesive soils are primarily responsible for foam formation in the soaker because they combine

TABLE 9.1. Germicidal-Equivalent Required Concentrations in Percent Sodium Hydroxide at Various Temperatures and Soak Times[a]

Time (min.)	Temperature					
	110°F (43°C)	120°F (49°C)	130°F (54°C)	140°F (60°C)	150°F (66°C)	160°F (71°C)
1	11.8	7.9	5.3	3.5	2.4	1.6
3	6.4	4.3	2.9	1.9	1.3	0.9
5	4.8	3.2	2.2	1.4	1.0	0.6
7	4.0	2.7	1.8	1.2	0.8	0.5
9	3.5	2.3	1.6	1.0	0.7	0.5
11	3.1	2.1	1.4	0.9	0.6	0.4
13	2.8	1.9	1.3	0.8	0.6	0.4
15	2.6	1.7	1.2	0.8	0.5	0.3

[a] According to a Barry-Wehmiller Companies internal study.

with caustic to form "soaps". Foam depressants are frequently added to the soaker solution to make it a more effective cleaner.

Lubricating Properties

A properly designed washing solution should also lubricate the exposed drive components, carrier chain, and parts in the interior of the soaker.

Dissolving and Neutralizing Properties

Washing solutions must also make some soils soluble and neutralize acid residues.

Solubility

Maintaining the optimum concentration of the washing compounds is important. A completely soluble washing solution is a prerequisite for this undertaking.

Cost Economy

The operating costs for bottle cleaning should be kept as low as possible without jeopardizing quality. Although it is indeed a technical challenge to design a quality, cost-effective bottle-washing solution, washing compounds should balance these two basic requirements.

Makeup of Bottle-Washing Solutions

Unfortunately, no single compound available today possesses all of the above properties. It is therefore necessary to combine several chemicals to obtain a washing solution that meets most of the mentioned requirements. The main bottle-washing compounds and ingredients are described below.

Caustic Soda

Sodium hydroxide, as it is called chemically, is a strong alkali and it is the principal ingredient of almost all bottle-washing solutions. It is usually shipped as a liquid in 50% concentration, and when diluted with water, an evolution of heat takes place.

Caustic soda is relatively economical to use and has excellent germicidal qualities. In solution, it is a powerful solvent that readily peptizes soil and saponifies oils and fats. However, it does have several drawbacks and limitations.

- It contributes to scale formation.
- It has poor rinsability, and if caustic is used alone, carryover between tanks would be excessive.
- It foams under high pressure.
- It promotes scuffing and etching of bottles if used in high concentrations.
- It also reduces labels to pulp when used in high concentration on low-wet-strength labels.

Because of these drawbacks, caustic additives or improvers are needed to obtain an effective washing solution. Brewers either add the necessary ingredients to the caustic or purchase already-blended bottle-washing compounds.

Sequestrants

To prevent scale formation, sequestrants are added to the caustic solution. The most frequently used sequestrants are gluconates, glucoheptonates, polyphosphates, and organophosphonates. Ethylenediaminetetraacetic acid (EDTA) is also used, although primarily in conjunction with phosphates.

The properties of various sequestering agents determine their effectiveness in bottle-washing formulations. The sugar acids (gluconic and glucoheptonic) are added to the soaker compartments at sequestration levels to control Ca^{++}, Mg^{++}, and other metals. However, when diluted to threshold levels during alkaline and fresh-water rinse stages, they fail to prevent scale formation.

Inorganic polyphosphates are effective scale inhibitors when used in the fresh-water rinse. They are, however, ineffective as scale inhibitors in the alkaline rinse stage, and they also hydrolyze in hot caustic solutions and convert to orthophosphates, forming insoluble Ca^{++} and Mg^{++} salts, which precipitate.

Like inorganic polyphosphates, phosphonates are effective sequestrants and soil deflocculants. But unlike polyphosphates, they are hydrolytically stable in hot caustic solutions and thus prevent precipitate formation at all washing stages. In addition, they are effective threshold agents in the alkaline as well as in the fresh-water rinse.

Surfactants

Surface-active (wetting) agents may be employed in small quantities of 1–3% caustic. They are complex chemical molecules with a hydrophilic or hydrophobic component. Most commonly used as surface-acting agents are nonionic defoaming surfactants, which are characterized as having good dispersing, emulsifying, wetting, and rinsing properties.

Foam Depressants

Silicones are not used very often as foam depressants in bottle-washing solutions. Modern surfactants are designed to include defoaming qualities.

Formulated Premixes

The key to a correctly formulated premix is obtaining the correct blend of detergent ingredients in order to achieve all the necessary cleaning steps without overuse of any ingredient. This is not an easy task since the conditions for bottle washing differ widely from one operation to another and even within the same soaker operation. Conditions change as the soil load within the soaker increases until it is finally dumped or until the washer solution is recycled.

The individual components required in a soaker detergent have all been mentioned: alkali, sequestrants, wetting agents, soil-suspending agents, defoamers, etc. The correct ratio of ingredients for any particular soaker requires expertise that can best be provided by specialized chemical supply companies. Obtaining this correct balance of ingredients is important, for if the amount of one ingredient is too low, the quality of the washed product might suffer, the machine might form scale, the washing solution might foam, or the bottles might be improperly cleaned. Overuse of any of the ingredients not only leads to unnecessary costs but also has more subtle effects. Excessive use of caustic or sequestrants can lead to bottle etching, and excessive use of defoamers can result in residual films.

On a direct weight basis, formulated bottle-washing compounds are always more expensive than the individual components. However, the costs of using site-prepared washing formulations that are not carefully balanced can very often exceed the apparent cost advantage of purchasing each ingredient separately. Such costs include extra labor and overhead to blend materials as well as the raw material and finished-product storage costs. In addition, blending individual detergent components in a bottle shop can be a time-consuming and potentially hazardous practice.

Custom-blended formulations supplied by chemical specialty companies can be used in the full range of bottle-washing equipment and for all conditions of water quality, temperatures, etc. Representatives of these companies are able to provide use/cost effectiveness analyses that can help identify the most efficient product and concentration for any particular situation.

Aluminum Foil Label Removal

Aluminum foil labels differ considerably from paper labels, so the process of their removal warrants special attention. Foil labels are manufactured from aluminum foil, approximately 0.003 inch (0.08 mm), laminated to paper. The paper is bonded to the aluminum foil either with paraffin wax or with an adhesive. Paraffin wax-bonded labels are preferred for returnable bottles because they separate easily in hot caustic and thus require less washing solution to remove them.

Label removal is an important aspect in bottle washing, and its effectiveness depends primarily on the following factors: detergent temperature and concentration, soaking time, and type of label and glue.

Different types of labels respond differently to these factors. The caustic soda solution simultaneously disintegrates inks and dissolves aluminum, the bonding agent, and the glue that attaches the label to the bottle.

Specially designed inks are used in conjunction with foil labels to visually indicate the distinctive feature of the product, such inks contain titanium oxide (TiO_2) and carbon blacks as coloring media. The ink pigments are usually insoluble, and a large portion will settle to the bottom of the compartments; occasionally, however, the suspended ink particles will float to the surface of the washing solution and become lodged on the inner surface of the bottles. Such bottles exhibit unsightly "ink spots".

When aluminum reacts with sodium hydroxide, free hydrogen gas is produce. Assuming the lot includes 100% foil-labeled bottles, approximately 17–27 cubic feet/minute of hydrogen gas is generated in a bottle washer that processes 1,400 bottles per minute. When hydrogen is combined with dry air in certain proportions, it will explode if ignited by a spark or flame. Since hydrogen is lighter than air, the danger area is above the level of the washing solution. To prevent accidents, the best rule to follow when removing aluminum labels is to vent all bottle washers on top and keep open flames and open electrical switches below the level of the solution.

The other reaction product, sodium aluminate, is formed at the expense of sodium hydroxide. This depletion occurs in addition to the caustic consumed for cleaning and sterilizing. In the presence of water, sodium aluminate undergoes hydrolysis to produce aluminum hydroxide ($Al(OH)_3$) and sodium hydroxide. The equation represents an equilibrium, with the reaction proceeding in both directions. Initially, the main force of the reaction is to the right, but as the concentration of aluminum hydroxide and sodium hydroxide increases, the reaction slows down.

Sodium aluminate and soluble silicates (from bottles and from fillers in paper labels) form a sodium–aluminum–silicate compound, which is insoluble and believed to be the main constituent of the hard, siliceous scale found on heater coils. It is important that washing solutions contain ingredients that prevent the settling of these silica-producing compounds.

EQUIPMENT AND OPERATIONS PRIOR TO THE BOTTLE WASHER

Bottle Handling Prior to the Soaker

Ideally, a bottling facility processing empty bottle returns would operate with the returns matching production requirements on a first-in/first-out basis, with a minimum time lag between the customer and the bottle-cleaning process. However, because of seasonal or other imbalances in returns, on-site or remote empty bottle storage may be required, which will, in effect, age the returns and render them ultimately harder to clean.

Uncasing

In most new bottling lines, the uncasing system is designed with enough capacity to provide between 115 and 125% of the filler capacity. The type(s) of cases used and the amount of in-line inspection equipment or manual labor employed determine the type and size of the uncasing system. Each facility has to determine the equipment required for its situation.

Empty Carton Handling

Empty cartons are either single trip or retrippers. Single-trip cartons are the easiest to contend with. These cases are baled and sold to recyclers after they have been emptied and debris removed. Some breweries have built their own saw-cutters to cut off the tops of the single-trip cartons to allow for easy removal of the bottles. Retrippers, whether they are cardboard or plastic, must be inspected and cleaned prior to reuse. Carton partitions also have to be dealt with. These can be totally scrapped or culled and reused. Again, each facility needs to determine the carton-handling process that is best for its situation.

Bottle Conveying System—Uncaser to Soaker Load

This system plays an important role in maintaining continuous bottle-washer operations. It must be designed to prevent bottles from falling and to provide a continuous supply of bottles to the soaker infeed. Sufficient surge capacity should be built into the system to accommodate short uncaser stops. Generally, a 2-minute accumulation at maximum soaker speed is considered an absolute minimum for providing the necessary flow of uninterrupted bottles.

From the standpoint of appearance and customer acceptance, scuffing of returnable bottles has become a major concern to most companies utilizing this type of container. Scuffed bottle tests have revealed that a major portion of damage to bottles occurs on the uncaser-to-soaker load section of the conveying system, where bottles are dry, dirty, and subject to significant bottle-to-bottle abrasion. Therefore, considerable thought must be given to the design of this bottle transport/accumulation system to minimize the conditions that cause bottle scuffing.

Prewetting

To assist the conventional bottle-washing operation, it may be possible to provide additional prewetting time by spraying or cascading rinse water from either the pasteurizer or the soaker (water that would otherwise be destined for the sewer) over the bottles after they leave the uncasing station. This operation effectively adds prewetting time equivalent to the conveyor system accumulation time and enhances the effectiveness of the bottle-washing process.

Bottle-Washer Loader

Located at the unscrambler portion of the load table, the washer-loader operator ensures that all bottles exiting the bottle conveying system are upright and devoid of crown or other defects that would adversely affect the cleaning operation. Most companies use an automatic control for maintaining bottle "prime", otherwise it can be left to the operator to run the start/stop table operation. Currently, all bottle-cleaner control systems automatically control load-table speed, which when combined with the control for the supplying conveyor, should keep the load table primed with bottles without creating excessive pressure on the load table. Adding bottles to the load table faster than the rotary loader can place them into the carriers causes this pressure. The design of the bottle deflector system is important to the operation of the table, since excessive pressure can cause bottles to break and/or overturn in the lanes. Alternately, excessive pressure can cause the bottle supply to the washer infeed to be reduced, causing starvation of the infeed lanes supplying the rotary loader and/or fallen bottles.

Variable-speed table chains greatly assist in optimizing bottle handling and bottle pressure. The load-table mechanism takes the bottles from the individual lanes and moves each into the row and then gently and securely into each carrier pocket across the width of the bottle washer.

If for any reason a bottle or a row of bottles does not index properly into the carrier pocket and causes a jam, a safety device stops both the pusher mechanism and the bottle washer. In these instances, the device indicates a washer-load safety trip. This type of fault normally requires the washer infeed operator to manually correct the fault and remove the obstruction. Following this corrective action, the operator must reset the bottle-pusher mechanism, which then clears the safety trip and allows the bottle washer to be restarted. From a control standpoint, this operational area can play an important role in the monitoring of bottle-line performance. By utilizing a computer-assisted monitoring system or simple on/off clocks or by filling in a simple operating form located by the washer infeed operator, operating management can create pertinent downtime records that allow them to administer the entire bottle infeed/uncasing operation. For reference, a typical manual control form for the washer load area is shown in Figure 9.5.

● DESCRIPTION AND DESIGN OF A TYPICAL BOTTLE WASHER

Bottle-Washer Types

Although various bottle washers are manufactured in a number of countries throughout the world, their basic design and operation follow the same general guiding principles as described earlier. The differences among the machines usually relate to the degree of emphasis given one aspect of the cleaning process rather than to some radical departure from the recognized principles of bottle washing.

Because a number of the mechanical functions performed by bottle washers are reasonably complex—e.g., loading and unloading bottles, synchronizing spray with bottle movement, protecting machinery, removing labels, etc.—there is a tremendous range of design approaches for bottle washers. The evaluation and selection of one machine over another depends on the user's acceptance of a particular design approach and machine configuration as being most suitable for the company's particular needs and operational conditions. In North and South America, Australia, Japan, and Africa, the modular-designed multitank machines seem to find general acceptance. In Europe and some other parts of the world, the compact and very efficient single-tank machines are often used.

One difference in machine design is the location of the bottle infeed and discharge. On single-ended machines, the bottle infeed is usually arranged below the bottle discharge. On double-ended machines, the infeed and discharge are located on opposite ends of the washer. In a further variation on double-ended machines, the infeed and discharge of the machine are located at different floor elevations.

In single-tank machines, the lower portion of the machine contains the bottle infeed, the prerinse and presoak section, and the main soaking tank. The soaking tank is arranged in a horizontal configuration and provides for several submerged horizontal passes of the carriers through the tank before the solution is drained from the bottles. The upper portion of the machine contains the postsoak drainage section, followed by a series of independent spray-rinse sections providing both internal and external caustic rinsing. The last spray-rinse section operates with fresh water followed by a drain

SOAKER LOADING REPORT				DATE:			
SHIFT		MACHINE		START		FINISH	
MACHINE STOPS (MIN,)	1/4	1/2	3/4	1	2	MAJOR STOPS	TOTAL
MECHANICAL							
POCKET STOPS							
BROKEN GLASS							
FLIPPING BOTTLES							
MISC. BOTTLE SUPPLY							
BOTTLE SHOP							
CLOCK START				CLOCK FINISH			

FIGURE 9.5. Sample of a soaker loading position report form. (Courtesy Barry-Wehmiller Companies)

section. Bottles exit the drain section and are discharged from the machine directly above the bottle infeed. The single-tank design allows for a very compact and highly energy- and water-efficient bottle washer.

In the modular-designed, multitank, double-ended machines popular in the United States (Fig. 9.6), the bottom of the machine is an open channel that accommodates the bottle carriers and chain returning empty from the bottle discharge to the bottle infeed. The upper or main body of the machine contains the various soaking, caustic-jetting, and spray-rinse compartments. The carrier chain passes through the various compartments in a serpentine configuration, with the bottles draining back into each compartment prior to moving on into the succeeding compartment. With the modular-designed washer, a user may select the number of compartments, as well as the height of compartments, in order to provide the required amount of submerged soaking time and the number of fill–empty cycles desired in the soaking process.

The overall process sequence can vary considerably in the modular-designed bottle washer. A typical sequence might be as follows: bottle infeed, prerinse sprays, warm presoak compartments, several soaking compartments with the compartment temperatures and caustic concentrations of each increasing until the required maximums are reached, a pulsating caustic internal-jetting compartment, postsoak compartments, a recirculated water section with internal and external sprays, a final fresh-water-rinse spray section, and a drain section followed by bottle discharge.

A typical machine currently in service might be 68 pockets wide and have five to seven compartments, including one caustic jetting compartment and one rinse section, all of which would provide an output of 2,200 bottles per minute and total soak time of 20–30 minutes.

Bottle-Washer Components

The following information relates primarily to U.S. bottle-washer construction and is given mainly to highlight some of the design and operational considerations that must be taken into account in the manufacture of a bottle washer.

Tank

The tank essentially forms the main frame, or body, of the machine, to which all other components and operating systems are attached. The tank is a fabricated steel structure divided into sections according to the compartment requirements for a particular machine. The tank is supported clear of the floor, and the empty carriers and the carrier chain return from the discharge to the infeed positions in a channel provided at the bottom of the tank structure.

Bottle Transport

Each bottle is supported in a pocket that carries the bottle through the entire washer sequence of operations. Pockets can be made of plastic or steel, with plastic now being the preferred material throughout the world. The

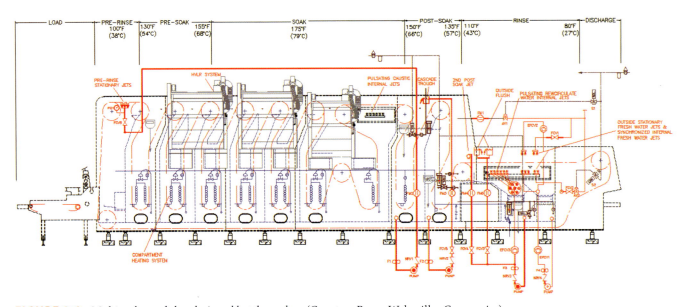

FIGURE 9.6. Multitank, modular-designed bottle washer. (Courtesy Barry-Wehmiller Companies)

pockets are constructed in rows, generally 68 pockets wide on current standard machines. The total row assembly of pockets is referred to as a carrier. The individual carriers are supported at each end by the carrier chain, which follows the serpentine path through the machine. The carrier chain in effect supports a continuous series of carriers throughout its length, and the whole assembly of carriers on the carrier chain, as installed in the machine, is often referred to as the carrier blanket.

In spite of its length and rugged service, the carrier chain is a precision item, and it must be installed and operated with great care. The empty return carriers and carrier chain run in a special support track located in the channel at the bottom of the tank structure. To reduce the required force and the wear associated with moving this massive assembly, the return tracks are provided with a built-in lubrication system.

The carrier chain hangs loose in each compartment and is guided by brackets attached to the tank sidewalls. The loose suspension is accomplished by driving both the infeed and discharge ends of the chain in each compartment at the top. Bottles are kept in the carriers through the use of solid-sheet deflectors, which are also supported from the compartment sidewalls. This solid-sheet deflector also creates an interior tank that is used in the high-volume label removal system.

Bottles are fed into the carriers at the washer infeed position by means of a rotary loading mechanism, which in turn is supplied with bottles by the load table (Fig. 9.7). The load table serves to guide a bottle from each loading lane into curved bottle guides arranged to correspond with each pocket in the carrier. The rotary loader picks up the bottles in their upright position and propels them up the curved bottle guides, where they gradually assume a horizontal position ready to enter the carrier pockets at the appropriate instant. Pusher cams synchronized with the travel of the carrier chain propel the bottles into the carrier pockets.

Bottles are unloaded from the carriers at the washer discharge position by means of a cam arrangement that accepts them from the carriers and lowers them gently onto the discharge table (Fig. 9.8). To make this possible, the carrier chain is routed to the discharge position with the carriers positioned so that the bottles are in an upright position. As the carrier approaches the discharge, a deflector is provided to support the bottles. The deflector is arranged so that the bottles gradually drop away from the pockets until finally they are supported on the lobe of the discharge cam. After the bottles are lowered onto the discharge table, the cam continues to rotate, and its profile moves the bottles away to provide clearance for the next row of bottles to come down onto the discharge table.

Synchronized Sprays

Synchronized spraying is used in bottle washers where internal jetting is to be provided in addition to submerged compartment soaking. In the hot sections of the machine, synchronized sprays consist of pulsating jets of hot caustic. In the rinse section, the sprays utilize hot, recirculated water for prerinse and warm, fresh water for the final rinse.

The carriers move continuously throughout the entire machine, and any system for internal spraying must take this into account. One way that internal, hydraulic spraying can be accomplished is by synchronizing the movement of the spray heads so that they are in exact registration with the open necks of the moving bottles while the pulsating spray action is in progress. To register

FIGURE 9.7. Bottle-washer loading position. (Courtesy Barry-Wehmiller Companies)

FIGURE 9.8. Bottle-washer discharge position. (Courtesy Barry-Wehmiller Companies)

the jet sprays with the open bottlenecks, the sprays are mounted on a moving rack. A cam controls the rack's vertical and horizontal movement. The rack moves vertically to engage the bottle and then moves horizontally, synchronizing with the bottle carrier's movement for the greater part of the cam's forward stroke. The cam then lowers the rack and makes a rapid horizontal return so that the next row of bottles will be contacted as the rack reaches its maximum height. Many of the faster machines now contact every second row.

Some machines use oscillating spray nozzles instead of pulsating sprays. This is a different approach to dislodging all of the material at the bottom of the bottle. Sent through rubber hoses, hot caustic under pulsating pressure is applied to the spray racks. The bottle mouths are aligned with the spray nozzles by means of centering cups clamped onto the spray pipes on the rack assembly.

Heating System

Each compartment is provided with a multiple-pass heating coil. Control is through a programmable logic controller (PLC), a computer, or direct-acting temperature controllers. The normal heating medium is saturated steam, but high-temperature hot water systems are also used. A steam header is mounted on the machine for its full length, with an isolating valve on the connection to each compartment. When the washer is operating normally, the heaviest heating demand occurs on the load end compartments, which must bring the bottles, carriers, and carrier chain to the maximum operating temperature. In the remaining compartments, heating is required only to compensate for heat losses and maintain the required operating temperatures.

Main Drive Assembly

The design of the drive system must take into consideration the large machine size and the high inertia associated with the carrier blanket, as well as the various mechanical subsystems powered from the main drive, e.g., load and discharge assemblies and spray racks. The traditional main drive consists of a constant-speed induction motor, a variable-speed drive, a special controlled-action clutch and brake assembly, and the main speed-reducer unit moving the chain drive system. Today, a cardanic system is available. The difference between the typically used chain drive and the cardanic transmission is that the latter offers a cleaner design with less need for lubrication, ease of maintenance, reduced noise, and fewer moving parts. Many of the current machines are driven by a series of individual variable frequency drives (VFDs) that are controlled through a sophisticated computer program. VFDs provide low maintenance costs, simplified chain-slack adjustment, and simplified timing in the machine infeed, discharge, and hot hydro and rinser rack. Whether shafts are driven by a traditional main drive system or the new VFDs, it is essential that they be controlled so that they all move as one.

In the traditional main drive system, the motor is coupled to the variable-speed drive unit, which permits adjustment of the washer speed in relation to the speed of the overall bottling-line operation. The variable-speed drive in turn is coupled to the clutch–brake input shaft. The clutch–brake assembly is controlled by a special power supply, which regulates the torque transmitted to the main gear reducer unit, in accordance with a predetermined operating sequence. In a typical starting sequence, the drive motor starts and comes up to full speed at no load. At this point, the clutch gradually increases the torque applied to the washer mechanical drive system. This procedure eliminates starting shocks both on the machine and on the electrical supply. After a time delay to allow the washer to come up to speed, the clutch controller sets the output torque to a much lower level, providing the mechanical drive system with an additional measure of protection. On stopping, the clutch instantly disconnects from the motor and variable-speed drive, and at the same time, the brake is energized on a progressive basis, bringing the washer to a smooth, controlled stop. On reaching full stop, the brake locks the mechanical drive, preventing any further motion until a new start is initiated.

Label Removal

Currently, labels are removed using a high-volume, low-pressure label removal system. This system removes the labels from the detergent solution before the label has a chance to become pulp. In a multitank machine, the majority of the labels become free of the bottles in the first two or three compartments, and the remaining hard-to-remove labels are distributed through the succeeding compartments. The objective is to remove the labels as early in the process as possible so that the labels remain intact. It is important to remove the label before it has a chance to disintegrate and cause problems by coating the internal parts of the compartment.

A high-volume label removal (HVLR) system passes a high volume of detergent solution through a deflector window. The solution goes from the outer tank to the inner tank, forcing the labels onto a moving screen and trapping them and taking them out of the solution. A blower and brushes remove the labels from the moving screen onto a conveyor and then to a label press or a floor hopper. The solution goes back to the inner tank and is suctioned up by a high-volume pump and starts the cycle over again.

For this reason, when a machine has an HVLR system, the detergent solution will be cleaner for a longer period of time compared with solutions in a machine not having an HVLR system.

● OPERATION AND MAINTENANCE

Operating Procedures

Well-written and detailed formal operating procedures are a prerequisite to any successful bottle-washer operation. They provide continuity of operation, operational control, and basic data for supervisory and operational training. The operations and maintenance departments should collaborate on the preparation of these operating procedures for all of the operating and maintenance systems. These written procedures will ensure proper bottle-washer operation and allow for the production of acceptable bottles at minimum labor, material, utility, and maintenance costs.

To produce these documents, all relevant technical design criteria, including any peculiarities of the bottle washer, should be noted. This information usually provides the basis for determining cleaning efficiency and levels of water consumption and of solution consumption and reclaim. Having this information in one document centralizes all the basic data needed to crosscheck the operational data collected from the various control reports. The manufacturer's published operating and maintenance manual can be used as the basis for this document, adapting sections pertinent to the actual operation. An operating procedure document should include the following information.

Bottle-Washer Equipment Data
- Design details, including bottle type and dimension limits
- Equipment number (plant)
- Manufacturer and model number
- Operating speed (design and maximum)
- Submerged soak time (product type and soaking minutes and machine design)
- Travel time through soaker and rinser in minutes

Compartment Details for Each Compartment
- Compartment name and number
- Capacity (volume)
- Control temperature
- Solution concentration, including upper and lower control limits

Spray Details for Each Location
- Identification
- Location and number of spray heads
- Capacity (volume)
- Pressure

Label Removal Equipment Details and Location

Bottle-Washer Solutions
- Solution components
- Solution percentages
- Other special considerations with regard to solution makeup

In addition to containing basic machine data, the operating procedure manual should fully describe all details pertaining to operation, cleaning, and maintenance of the bottle washer. While exact details will vary from one machine to another and from one bottle shop to another, all manuals should include the following basic categories of information.

- Machine startup and shutdown procedures
- Daily and weekly cleaning procedures
- Solution management procedures, including daily operational checks
- Solution testing
- Maintenance
- Performance and safety evaluations

The following sections provide general guidance on what information should be documented in each of these areas of the operating procedure manual.

Machine Startup/Shutdown Procedures

Startup

Any formal procedures developed for the bottle-washer operation usually focus on utilities (e.g., steam, water, and air) and on ensuring that various components are operational in advance of the shift startup time. Because of the nature of temperature control equipment, steam demands can be excessive at startup and some manual intervention may possibly be required until temperatures come under control. To ensure proper operation, all pumps and conveyors should be turned on well in advance of startup, approximately 1 hour before operations. All compartment temperatures should be checked to ensure that they are in control and at the proper settings. General monitoring of the temperatures should continue until the bottle washer has been completely filled with bottles. At this time, the heating demands should stabilize. The levels in all tanks should be checked along with the operation of any sprays and HVLR units.

Shutdown of the bottle washer involves making sure that basic components are turned off. Operators should check that the following are shut down: all soaker and rinser controls, main steam supply, any associated conveyors, and air and water as necessary. All bottles should be cleared from the rinser discharge.

Cleaning Procedures

Proper cleaning includes both daily and weekly routines. The following list of action items should form the basis for a daily bottle-washer cleaning procedure.

- Use a low-pressure hose to wash down the load table, infeed conveyor, and rotary infeed.
- Clean screens in the prerinse area.
- While bottle cleaners are operating, visually check all sprays and hoses in the recirculating, reclaim, and fresh-water sections to locate plugged nozzles and defective hoses. Replace or correct as required.
- Clean spray racks nightly. Plugged nozzles usually lead to an increased reject rate.
- Clean any compartment screens.
- Open and clean any drip pans over the bottle discharge.
- Hose down and clean the entire discharge assembly, including the discharge conveyors. Some cleaning agents may be incorporated into the cleaning and wash-down procedure to sanitize or improve cleaning. Utilization of high-pressure, low-volume cleaning units is recommended.
- Avoid direct hosing of electrical motors and electrical components.
- Dump the final postsoak tank water daily to avoid detergent solution carryover. This is normally the procedure; however, the need to dump or partially dump the first postsoak tank will depend on the tank and the amount of solution carryover to that tank. Again, experience and operating hours will dictate the requirements.
- Add sanitizer to the reclaimed rinse water prior to startup. This action will depend on the prevailing biological norms for the plant.
- Make efforts to remove any caustic from the outside walls or top of the bottle washer by rinsing them with water. Remove excess grease by wiping it off or using solvent cleaning.

The weekly cleaning regime includes the following procedures.

- Complete the recommended daily cleaning cycle.
- Drain, clean, and refill any compartment scheduled on the checklist.
- Remove spray heads and clean and/or replace them. From an operational and maintenance standpoint, it is usually more desirable to have spare spray heads available for replacing the ones in use. This permits proper maintenance and cleaning of the used spray heads on a controlled basis, allowing standardization of the spray head maintenance replacement service.
- Dump any compartment listed on the cleaning schedule.
- Remove scale from equipment. Consult the soaker manufacturer for the proper procedure.

Solution Management Procedures

All efforts made to produce high-quality beer can be negated if the product is put into unclean bottles. It is therefore crucial that completely clean and commercially sterile bottles are discharged from the bottle washer. Constant control of the temperature and the composition of the washing solution must be carried out to ensure that the desired cleaning effect is achieved.

Bottles exposed to the hot caustic solution in the soaker compartments become sterile; however, recontamination of bottles in the rinse water compartment or passing through the rinsing station is common. Routine examination of the caustic concentration and tests for biological contamination of the rinse water is therefore an essential part of the total quality control program in beer packaging.

There are three aspects to the effective management of the washing solution and the contents of the rinse section compartments.

- Prepare fresh solution.
- Maintain solution strengths in the various compartments of the washer. This includes checking for buildup of organics and aluminates.
- Remove solution for processing outside the washer or for dumping to the sewer as necessary.

Most bottle shops use washing compounds received in the liquid form, prepared usually at a concentration of 50% by weight. Very little use has been made of solid or flake compounds. Details on the preparation of solution from these forms can be obtained from the compound supplier or from a book by D. G. Ruff and K. Becker (1955).

Liquid caustic soda is stored in tanks that are normally kept inside to avoid the necessity for heating, since 50% caustic solidifies at temperatures below 59°F (15°C). The caustic soda is then transferred by gravity or pump through a batch-type totalizing meter to a mixing pit or tank in order to make up batches of intermediate strength solution, typically 20–25% by weight. The exact quantities required for dilution can be determined with the assistance of the compound supplier.

When charging a compartment in the bottle washer, water is first used to partially fill the compartment, then the correct volume of intermediate-strength solution is added, and finally water or reclaimed solution is added if necessary to bring the level up to the working level.

Because of wide variations in machine design across Europe and North and South America, as well as differing bottle return conditions and label removal systems, it is almost impossible to specify an ideal solution concentration for the compartments. Traditionally, European machines are run at lower solution levels, in the area of 1.5–2.5% concentration, whereas the North American norm is on the higher side, ranging up to 2.5–3.0% alkalinity. The highest level of alkalinity recommended is 4.0%. Very few machines are operating at this level today. Most are between 2 and 4%, depending on their cleaning requirements. In-plant testing and the analysis of cleaning results usually dictate the concentrations and limits needed for any particular bottle shop.

Maintaining the effectiveness of the solution in the washer usually involves adding fresh intermediate-strength solution. Although the compartment concentration may have to be checked a number of times each day, the addition of fresh solution is not normally required more than once per shift. The addition of fresh intermediate-strength solution will also be required if the compartment has been partially refilled with reclaimed solution after being cleaned out.

In both cases, a nomograph should be used to determine the required volume of intermediate-strength solution. Adding solution is best done when steam is being supplied to the compartment or some other form of agitation is present so as to minimize stratification and encourage good mixing.

Methods for Testing Soaker Solutions

Two approaches are used to test washing solutions: one is based on a differential titration, while the other is based on the measurement of electrical conductivity. A brief summary of the two methods is outlined below. More details about these methods are available in a *Brewer's Digest* article by W. Leipner (1975).

Differential Titration

Differential titration is most useful since it allows operators to test for levels of free causticity, sodium aluminate, and total alkalinity side by side. This is achieved by titrating the soaker solution with sulfuric acid to the phenolphthalein endpoint to determine the free caustic after the carbonates have been precipitated with barium chloride. After this determination, the remaining aluminate is hydrolyzed by the addition of sodium fluoride, and further titration yields the amount of sodium aluminate. Total alkalinity is determined by the quantity of acid consumed without the addition of barium chloride.

Electrical Conductivity

Solution conductivity controllers are frequently used to monitor caustic concentration. Some models are designed to transfer liquid caustic automatically from the storage tank into the soaker compartment. These units use a temperature-compensated probe to sense the caustic concentration.

The conductivity instrument, however, has certain limitations that must be recognized. While sodium hydroxide has a specific conductance, so do other electrolytes that may be present in the solution. For instance, sodium aluminate has about one-tenth the conductivity of sodium hydroxide. The conductivity of the solution reflects, therefore, the conductance of all ingredients, and results have to be interpreted with some caution. However, the conductivity instrument provides a very rapid method for determining solution concentration.

Inspecting Performance of the Rinse Section

Regular inspection of the contents of the rinse section is also important to determining whether carryover of washing solution is occurring or whether biological contamination is present in the rinse water. Below are examples of tests for the rinse section.

Testing Residual Alkali in Bottles

Alkaline reaction in bottles indicates excessive caustic carryover and/or inadequate rinsing. Tests for determining the presence of residual alkali are very simple and involve the addition of a small amount of water and an indicator, such as phenolphthalein.

Biological Examination of Empty Bottles

Bottles can become contaminated with microorganisms in the rinse section of the bottle washer. The recommended method for testing for such contamination is based on the plating technique. A measured quantity of sterile water is added to a bottle exiting the rinser, and the bottle is closed with a stopper previously soaked in alcohol. An aliquot portion of the water is then transferred onto a solid medium in a petri dish. After incubating the inoculated medium under standardized conditions, visible colonies will develop from single cells. By counting the colonies, researchers can derive an indication of the number of organisms that were originally present.

To keep the number of microorganisms in the rinse section at a minimum, a level of 1–5 mg of chlorine per liter of water is maintained. The desired chlorine level is obtained by the addition of a hypochlorite compound to the water. The concentration of chlorine in the rinse water can be determined by means of an orthotolidine comparator kit, which is available from chemical supply houses.

Draining Soak and Rinse Compartments

There is no universally accepted standard that governs how often the soaking compartments should be cleaned. Each plant must establish criteria that suit its particular mode of operation and conditions. The type of maintenance and the condition of the water, bottles, and label removal system, etc., greatly influences whether solutions need to be changed and/or compartments dumped. In the interests of material and manpower savings, the frequency of this cleaning process should be kept to a minimum and should be based on quantifiable measures or observations of

- the effectiveness of the cleaning process, which can be measured either biologically or by percentage of rejects;
- the presence of label particles and solid contamination, which can be identified visually or, again, by tracking the percentage of empty bottle rejects; and
- an adverse effect on mechanical components, which can be measured in downtime or recurring mechanical problems.

If the label removal system operation and sequence is satisfactory and bottle breakage due to thermal shock is not a problem, the frequency with which soak compartments should be drained becomes a function only of the buildup of fine, suspended paper fibers or of insoluble organics from glues and dirt and aluminates, the latter from aluminum foil labels if present.

Provided the strength of the bottle-washing solution is maintained by the addition of concentrated solution from time to time, the compartment contents need only be emptied when the buildup of aluminates and solids is such that severe precipitation is starting to occur in the compartment and operations are affected.

For relatively clean bottles with exclusively paper labels, the number of bottles that can be washed before the first or second compartments have to be drained can be as high as 250,000 bottles per cubic meter (1,000 bottles per gallon) of total soak volume. However, in batches of bottles where aluminum foil labels are used almost exclusively and where a proportion of ditch or "basement" bottles appear, the solution may have to be changed after only 25,000 bottles per cubic meter (100 bottles per gallon) throughput. These figures are based on performance results of a washer operation that featured an old label removal system that allowed the label to pulp before it was removed. This system allowed many more label fines to become part of the solution. With the advent of high-volume label removal in which the label does not pulp, the solution lasts much longer. Today, the level of aluminates in the solution determine when the soak compartments should be cleaned.

Obviously, owing to varying conditions, there is a wide range of cleaning intervals, and practical experimentation is encouraged. An example of such experimentation has been performed and reported by Leipner (1975). Where large quantities of bottles with aluminum foil labels are to be washed, some plant operators have decided to drain compartments based on a predetermined acceptable percentage of sodium aluminate, often 2–3%. However, some evidence suggests that concentrations in excess of this figure will not affect washing since the aluminates can precipitate with other solids to the bottom of the compartment. In summary, as long as the bottle washer discharges clean and sterile bottles and there is no interference with the mechanical or heat transfer components, there is generally no need to clean the soaker solution or discharge it to the sewer.

In any case, a schedule for changing the solution in soak compartments must be drawn up. It should be based on time but should reflect, if possible, a consideration of the numbers of bottles that have been washed. For the purposes of manpower scheduling and cleaning control, bottle shops with multiple lines and bottle washers may be required to set up formal, planned cleaning schedules that identify the specific work to be carried out on a daily basis. Whatever the interval chosen for cleaning soak compartments, it is desirable that the spent solution be transferred to a caustic reclaim system so that even premature draining will not result in unnecessary losses. Unless rinse section water compartments contain usable concentrations of solution, they are normally drained to the sewer daily, immediately after bottling operations have ceased.

Maintenance

Performing maintenance on a bottle washer normally involves lubricating the moving parts, such as drive chains, bearings, gearboxes, and the main carrier chain. The maintenance department is usually charged with this responsibility, and it must be carried out on a regular, predetermined basis. The manufacturer's operating and maintenance manuals present most of the recommended lubrication requirements. Costs and individual plant practices will determine whether an automatic, mechanical lubrication system will perform this task or whether it is to be done manually.

The caustic detergent solution is the primary lubricant for the main chain. As long as the main chain is submerged in the caustic solution, it is well lubricated. As the main chain returns to the infeed from the machine discharge, it will dry out and experience excessive wear. Using a soap lubrication system supplied by the plant's main soap system that also supplies the bottle conveyors will ensure that the main chain is lubricated when it is out of the caustic solution. Because of the cost of replacing main carrier chains, it is recommended that the carrier chain's lubrication system is checked on a daily basis and that this check be included in the operational log.

From a preventative maintenance standpoint, it should be standard procedure to check the chain's slack in any compartment that has been emptied and cleaned prior to recharging.

No attempt is made in this chapter to define preventative maintenance requirements or regularly scheduled overhaul programs. Any unusual behavior of the bottle-washer machinery should be investigated and corrected immediately to avoid future damage and downtime. Continuous stops initiated by the machinery safety devices are an early warning signal indicating the need for adjustments and maintenance.

Bottle-Washer Performance

The relative success of these procedures in producing clean bottles should be measured. The commonly accepted method of measurement is to monitor the reject ratio at the empty bottle inspection (EBI) device. It is generally agreed that this ratio should not exceed one bottle per thousand, or 0.1%. This figure represents cleanable bottles that fail to be cleaned, and it should not include other classes of bottles, such as false rejects or broken, uncleanable, or liquid-filled bottles, in the calculation. Any reject rate in excess of this figure indicates a malfunction of the cleaning process, which will require troubleshooting and remedial actions.

Health and Safety

As noted previously, the aluminum portion of the foil labels reacts with the bottle-cleaning solution to produce hydrogen gas. This gas can collect at the top of the bottle washer or escape into the bottle shop and collect at high points of the ceiling. Since accumulated hydrogen can be explosive, it is usually advisable to provide a positive venting system to remove the generated gases. This system should also be designed to remove other vapors and fumes emanating from the hot bottle-washing solution. This is especially true in bottle shops that have low overhead clearance and minimal plant air changes.

Bottle-washing solutions must be handled with great care, and it is therefore mandatory that proper procedures and safety gear be provided to anyone assigned to solution makeup and bottle-washer cleaning or to those who may come in contact with the soaker solution. Proper safety eyewash and overhead shower facilities should be provided at strategic locations adjacent to the bottle washer.

In the most modern machines, the fresh water used in the final rinse is reused in the postsoaking compartments to maintain causticity. It is also used in the prerinse sprays and then goes into the sewer.

● SUMMARY

The returnable bottle is well established in the majority of domestic beer markets worldwide, especially outside the United States. In spite of the market appeal and convenience of many nonreturnable containers available today, the basic economics of the returnable bottle in established markets ensures that it will remain a dominant container in the brewing and soft drink industries for years to come. Bottle washing, the key element in the returnable bottle cycle, will therefore continue to be a subject of central importance to the brewing industry.

While the fundamental principles of bottle washing have remained unchanged, great strides have been made in developing high-speed, efficient bottle washers.

Many different machine arrangements are available to accommodate operating conditions encountered in different parts of the world. Concerted industry efforts have improved the performance of bottle-washing solutions, and custom formulations suited to various conditions are now available from qualified chemical companies.

ACKNOWLEDGMENTS

Contributors to this chapter include J. L. Kappele, L. M. Laishley, M. J. W. Hancock, E. A. Pfisterer, and L. Terrill.

REFERENCES

Duncan, D. G. (1982). Basic principles of bottle washing. Brew. Dig. 57(2):29-33.

Jennings, W. G. (1965). Hard-surface cleaning. Tech. Q. Master Brew. Assoc. Am. 2:160-164.

Leipner, W. (1975). Soaker solutions…Extending the service life of caustic solutions in bottle washing machines. Brew. Dig. 50(10):48-54.

Ruff, D. G., and Becker, K. (1955). Chapter 3: Bottle cleaning; Chapter 4: Bottle washer compound and characteristics; and Chapter 12: Quality control in beer packaging. In: Bottling and Canning of Beer. Siebel Publishing Co., Chicago, IL.

CHAPTER 10

PET Bottles for Beer Packaging

FRANK W. EMBS
Indorama Ventures PCL

The lighter weight, clarity, unbreakability, and recloseability of polyethylene terephthalate (PET) bottles and containers have made them a preferred packaging choice for many beverages. Consumers and manufacturers value the convenience and safety PET packaging offers. Brand owners and packagers value PET bottles' dimensional stability as well as the ease of processing and handling and the safety they offer.

PET packaging offers environmental benefits as well. In a life cycle inventory study conducted by the PET Resin Association (PETRA), the total energy requirements from raw material extraction through container disposal for PET packaging were 35% lower than those for aluminum packaging and 59% lower than those for glass containers. In addition, PET bottles can be processed into postconsumer recycled (PCR) PET flakes, which can be refined into recycled PET resin and used for beverage packaging (bottle-to-bottle) or extruded directly for use in fiberfill and strapping tape.

In large-volume beverage markets, such as those for carbonated soft drinks, bottled water, and ready-to-drink beverages and teas, PET containers are used extensively in an effort to appeal to the consumer's desire for convenience. Aluminum cans, particularly 12-oz. (350-mL) cans, are the preferred packaging for beverages in higher-volume, lower-margin market segments and have reached a substantial share of packaging for carbonated soft drinks and beer in the United States. Glass packaging has been relegated to packaging high-end niche products and beer (Table 10.1).

Glass bottles hold a significant portion of the market in beer, wine, liquor, and low-volume specialty drinks packaging. In fact, beer packaging represents more than 80% of the entirety of glass bottle production and is the last market sector of any significant volume for glass bottle manufacturers. This is particularly the case in the United States, one of the few countries where beer is sold nearly exclusively in one-way, nonreturnable, glass bottles and 12-oz. (350-mL) aluminum cans.

In contrast, the rest of the world packs beer predominantly in returnable, refillable glass bottles. Besides historical reasons for this packaging choice and the capital already invested in extensive systems of bottle collection and cleaning, returnable, refillable glass bottles provide proven reliability and cost-effectiveness, an added benefit for brand owners. In particular, in countries that

TABLE 10.1. 2012 Global Beverage Packaging in Billion Containers[a]

Beverage	Aluminum Cans	PET Bottles	Glass Bottles	Other Packages	Total
Carbonated soft drinks	115	105	50	<1	270
Juice	15	30	15	50	110
Water	<1	215	25	15	255
Beer	120	10	240	<1	370
Wine	<1	<1	30	3	33
Total	250	360	360	68	1,038

[a] Indorama Ventures PCL internal estimates (*unpublished data*).

have a large volume of beer consumption, such as China, Germany, and Brazil, returnable, refillable glass bottles extend to an 80% unit share of packaged products.

However, because PET bottles are shatterproof, lightweight, and recloseable, they can be safer and easier to handle than glass bottles and more sanitary and convenient than aluminum cans. For example, a typical PET bottle is 5 to 10 times lighter than the equivalent glass container, and the drinking surface on a PET bottle is protected by the closure until the bottle is opened, in contrast to an aluminum can.

PET containers can be produced in sizes ranging from packages of a few ounces (or several milliliters) to 1-gallon (4-L) bottles to up to 15.5-gallon (58-L) kegs. With their clarity, PET containers are perfect for beer packaging. They have a low absorption of flavor components and make minimal flavor contributions to beer. The addition of barrier technologies provides PET containers with excellent protection against oxygen ingress and with the carbonation retention characteristic required for beer.

Barrier PET containers are the preferred solution for beer packaging when packaging performance, consumer convenience, and cost-effectiveness are the main considerations. In particular, PET offers benefits for making larger containers, from 1-quart (or approximate 1-L) bottles to full-size (60-L) kegs. One exception may be the already established, cost-effective, returnable, refillable glass bottle systems.

With PET barrier technologies widely in use in beer packaging and proven to be successful in numerous commercial applications since 2005, brewers now have the data to evaluate the benefits of PET packaging in their own operations and can calculate the risk and return of converting to PET containers. They can decide whether to take the leap forward to establish consumer acceptance.

● BEER IN PET CONTAINERS TODAY

In 2012, beer was packed and sold in an estimated 10 billion PET containers, the packaging accounting for approximately 3% of the 340 billion beer containers sold. With double-digit growth rates in recent years, PET containers have been established as a viable packaging solution for beer, with its market share expected to continue growing in the years to come.

By region, market penetration looks to be even more extensive. Beer packaged in PET has gained 7% of the market in Germany, one of the most traditional beer-making countries that feature high-quality production and sophisticated beer consumers. In Eastern European countries, such as Russia and Romania, PET bottles have become a popular packaging choice for premium and high-quality beer and hold at least 50% of the packaging share in the beer segment.

In developed beer markets, a primary driver for the adoption of PET bottles for beer is legislation on a regional or country level, such as that addressing safety concerns in venues in the United States or the recycling mandates in Germany. However, in fast-growing beer markets, such as Russia and Romania, the driver for choosing PET over glass is the significantly lower capital required for investment into greenfield filling plants. In addition, PET allows for the production of cost-effective and safe containers larger than 1 quart (1 L). These are sold as single-serve containers in Russia and as multiserve containers in Latin America.

Approximately half (or 5 billion) of all PET beer bottles sold in 2010 employed a variety of active oxygen-scavenging and passive gas-barrier technologies to protect beer from oxygen ingress and to retain carbonation levels throughout the product's shelf life. (The remaining bottles used standard PET because of their shorter shelf life requirements. This was particularly the case in Eastern Europe.) Three barrier PET technologies—internal coatings, multilayer injection, and monolayer barrier blend—are used equally for beer packaging in the market today.

Internal coating technology, namely Actis™ from Sidel (Octeville-sur-Mer, France), has been applied exclusively by Brouwerij Martens in Belgium and its related breweries, such as Frankfurter Brauhaus in Germany. The five-layer technology proprietary to Graham Packaging Company (York, PA) has been used to make PET beer bottles in the United States, whereas converters in Europe, South Korea, and China have employed commercially available multilayer machines from Kortec (Rowley, MA) to make PET bottles for beer.

In recent years, PET bottles using monolayer barrier blends have demonstrated the highest rate of adoption, since they allow for more flexibility in production with reduced complexity and easier handling. Barrier materials, such as blends of INVISTA's PolyShield® resin (Wichita, KS) with up to 5% nylon-MXD6 (Mitsubishi Gas Chemical Co., Tokyo), provide the required long-term shelf life for beer in virtually haze-free, tinted containers, and PET containers with these materials have successfully penetrated the market worldwide. With minor equipment changes, monolayer barrier blends run on existing, standard injection machines. Because adding monolayer barrier blends requires at most an additional feeder and a separate dryer, manufacturers risk less capital in moving to this PET barrier technology, which could account for its relatively rapid adoption. Figure 10.1 shows a variety of shapes, sizes, and colors for PET containers.

PET CONTAINERS

Polyesters

Polyesters are a group of plastics produced via polycondensation by reacting an acid group with an alcohol group and then removing a water molecule under vacuum at a higher temperature with a catalyst present. Typically, monomers carrying two acid groups are reacted with monomers carrying two alcohol groups to make a linear molecule with alternating polyester functions.

Polyethylene Terephthalate

Polyester can be made from paraterephthalic acid (PTA), an aromatic ring with two acid groups attached in opposite positions, and ethylene glycol (MEG), which consists of two carbon atoms with an alcohol group attached to each carbon. Such polyesters are called polyethylene terephthalate (PET) and can be made cost effectively (Fig. 10.2). PET is widely used in technical applications and in packaging, including beverage and food containers and bottles for carbonated soft drinks, bottled water, juices, isotonic drinks, peanut butter, ketchup, and many other products.

Polyethylene Naphthalate

Polyethylene naphthalate (PEN), a different polyester, can be made by using naphthalate diacid (NDA), which consists of two aromatic rings attached to each other, each carrying an acid group. Reacting NDA with MEG forms PEN, a polymer that exhibits better physical properties, such as higher heat resistance and an improved gas barrier. PEN has seen limited use in returnable, refillable beer bottles in Europe but has never made any inroads into the production of nonreturnable, nonrefillable, one-way bottles because of its high cost.

Glass Transition Temperature

PET is a semicrystalline polymer that melts around 460°F (238°C) and exhibits a softening point, called the glass transition temperature (T_g), between 167 and 185°F (75 and 85°C), depending on the degree of crystallinity. Semicrystalline means that part of the polymer is crystallized and does not change or melt below the melting point. The remaining amorphous part of the polymer, however, is not crystalline and starts to melt at a much lower temperature, namely at T_g.

Crystallinity

A higher degree of crystallinity improves the physical and thermal properties of the polymer and provides better performance in application. In particular, higher crystallinity results in higher material density, less bottle expansion under pressure, and reduced shrinkage under heat. In addition, the polymer crystals have a much lower rate of gas permeation than the polymer at the amorphous phase so that higher crystallinity results in an improved gas barrier.

FIGURE 10.1. Typical polyethylene terephthalate (PET) beer containers in different sizes and shapes. (Courtesy Indorama Ventures PCL)

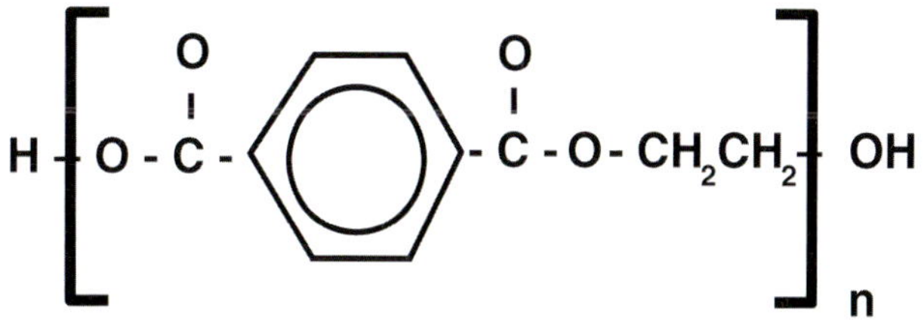

FIGURE 10.2. Chemical repeat unit of the polyethylene terephthalate (PET) polymer. (Courtesy Indorama Ventures PCL)

Oriented PET

Crystallinity can be increased during the bottle-blowing process. At temperatures above the softening point (T_g), shearing and stretching of the container material orients the amorphous polymer chains and allows them to crystallize. Crystallinity can be further increased by slower cooling or by maintaining the temperature of the polymer just above the T_g for a longer period to allow the amorphous polymer chains to rearrange and form more crystals.

PET Container Design

Beverage containers today range in size from several-milliliter containers weighing less than 10 g to 20-L kegs. The shape, weight, and form of containers are determined by packaging requirements such as portion size, dimension and type of closure, and rigidity and dimensional stability of the package and by its ability to withstand and retain carbonation, protect against oxygen ingress, and withstand filling and processing under certain conditions such as hot-fill, aseptic, and tunnel pasteurization. PET allows for great design flexibility in terms of container size, weight, and shape.

The beauty of PET for the packaging designer, however, is its versatility. It can be formed into containers of a wide variety of shapes that provide the required packaging functionality while allowing for easy differentiation of products on the shelf and other points of sale (Fig. 10.3). Today, manufacturers can make virtually any reasonable container shape by injection-molding a preform and subsequently blowing it into a vessel. Even containers with handles can be effectively manufactured on slower one-step machines using a process called extrusion blow-molding.

PET container shapes can vary from perfect balls, such as the 5-L party kegs used by some European breweries, to straight cylinders, such as the 20-L beer kegs for commercial use, to contoured and embossed bottles, such as those commonly used for carbonated soft drinks. Closure threads range from 28- to 68-mm twist closures over crown finishes to threads that receive fittings suitable for today's draft-dispensing systems. The most common base finishes are multifooted bases, such as the pentaloid or petaloid ones used for most soft drinks, while champagne-style bases are in limited use.

The wall thickness of containers in use today ranges from 200 to 800 micrometers (μm), the size varying according to each container's requirements for dimensional stability when under carbonation pressure and when opened and without liquid support.

Manufacture of PET Containers

A two-stage process involving two separate machines is the most common method of manufacturing PET containers. During the first stage, PET is extruded and injected into a mold to form "preforms" that are subsequently cooled and ejected into bins. During the second stage, the preforms are reheated with infrared light to a temperature just above the preforms' T_g. They are then clamped into a bottle mold and subsequently blown into the mold to form the final container.

Injection-Molding Preforms

During the injection-molding process, PET resin is extruded at temperatures of approximately 527°F (275°C) by melting the resin with heat and shear. It is subsequently injected into molds to form preforms. These PET preforms are the precursors for PET containers and look like small test tubes with a bottle thread. They, however, are much shorter and have thicker walls than the final bottles.

Standard, commercial injection machines contain molds having 48–194 cavities, which can make the same number of preforms at each injection cycle. Cycle times depend on the weight of the preforms. They can vary between several seconds for a preform of 10 g to up to a minute for preforms of several hundred grams. In a typical

FIGURE 10.3. Polyethylene terephthalate (PET) resin as extruded amorphous chips and molded into a preform, bottle, and jar. (Courtesy Indorama Ventures PCL)

setup, a 144-cavity injection machine can run 17-second cycles and produce about 30,000 26-g preforms per hour, resulting in about 200 million preforms per year.

Blowing Containers

During the second stage of the two-stage process, the preforms are picked up at the thread and run on a conveyer past infrared lamps that heat the tube section to a temperature of approximately 212°F (100°C)—just above the T_g. The hot and soft preforms are then clamped into a mold of the final bottle. After the mold is closed, a metal rod pushes the bottom down to extend the preform to its full length. Subsequently, high-pressure air blown into the preform expands and presses the preform's walls into the bottle mold.

The stretching and blowing process exerts physical stress on the PET container and increases the degree of orientation and crystallinity of the material, resulting in improved physical stability of the final PET bottle. Process parameters, such as stretch speed, blow pressure, and temperature setting, are critical in determining the final material distribution and crystallinity, thus affecting mechanical container properties, such as dimensional stability, top load, and container expansion under filling pressure.

Commercial blow molders have a wide range of capacities and speeds. Typically, a blow molder can make between 8,000 to about 48,000 bottles per hour (each bottle sized at 500 mL and 24 g). Blow molders can operate separately from injection and filling lines; however, it is more common to combine blow-molding with filling in one line to reduce bottle transportation, storage, and handling costs.

Filling Containers

PET containers today contain virtually any beverage type, from carbonated to noncarbonated soft drinks to beer, wine, and hard liquor, and they can be filled at a wide range of filling speeds. Typically, PET filling lines match the filling speeds of glass filling lines, and the lines can include semimanual individual bottle fillers to filling lines in the range of 48,000 bottles per hour.

PET bottles may require cleaning and disinfection before filling if the bottles have been blown and stored before use. However, such steps can be eliminated if the bottles are blown in-line and immediately filled. Attaching the blow molder directly to the filler in a single blowing–filling block can further optimize processing by eliminating the bottle conveyor and buffer storage between the machines.

● BEER PACKAGING IN PET

Freshness and Taste

If effective brand marketing and management of distribution channels allows a preferred beer to reach its consumers in a given region, then reliably delivering a beer with fresh and consistent taste is a prerequisite to success. Maintaining freshness and a constant flavor profile for the entirety of the beer's shelf life is therefore an essential performance requirement of any beer package.

The flavor and freshness of beer can be affected by various environmental influences. In particular, oxygen can create a strong off-taste in beer, carbonation loss can affect freshness, and visible and ultraviolet (UV) light can change the flavor of the beer and accelerate the oxidation process (Fig. 10.4). In addition, microbial growth can create turbidity and an off-taste even in optimally designed packaging; therefore, tunnel pasteurization of the container maybe be required to ensure the best product performance throughout its shelf life.

Flavor Consistency

Standard PET has received regulatory clearance for food packaging in the United States for most food and beverage applications. In addition, PET has been utilized in food and beverage packaging throughout the world since the 1970s. PET has received clearance for use in packaging beer and is considered safe with respect to potential flavor contaminants and their migration into beverages, including beer. With PET containers, only acetaldehyde (AA) can potentially migrate into the beer.

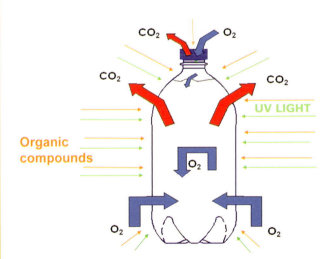

FIGURE 10.4. Potential influence on beer taste and freshness over the shelf life of a polyethylene terephthalate (PET) container. (Courtesy Indorama Ventures PCL)

AA is a volatile molecule and can be generated when PET is reheated in applications, such as during the injection-molding process. AA also forms during the first oxidative metabolic step of the degradation of ethyl alcohol. AA has a characteristic fruity taste and is part of the inherent flavor components of beer, wine, juice, and many other beverages.

The extremely low concentrations of AA that might potentially migrate from the container into the beverage are at levels well below the AA concentrations already present in beer and wine. In three-way blind taste tests with live consumer panels, because of the presence of AA, consumers detected a slight off-taste in nonflavored, pure water packed in PET but not in any flavored beverages, such as beer.

Protection from Oxygen

Oxygen is the most detrimental contaminant of beer. Depending on the type of beer, even minimal amounts of 1 part per million (ppm) of oxygen (defined as 1 mg of oxygen per 1 L of beer) can noticeably affect taste. That amount is equivalent to about 0.001 g of oxygen in 1,000 g of beer, assuming a density for beer of 1 kg per liter.

Oxygen can enter beer in different ways and from various sources. The presence of oxygen in the headspace of the container and dissolved in the beer are common to all packaging containers. PET containers, however, exhibit two additional sources of oxygen ingress, namely oxygen already dissolved in the PET and oxygen permeating the wall of the PET container and into the beer.

Minimizing the amount of oxygen entering beer from the brewing process is beyond the control of packaging. Minimizing the oxygen levels in the container's headspace can be achieved by optimizing the filling process. However, reducing or avoiding oxygen ingress through the PET container wall requires a significant improvement in PET's oxygen barrier so that it meets requirements for beer packaging.

A standard 500-mL, 26-g PET container can allow as much as 1 ppm of oxygen ingress within 2 weeks of its being filled. To reach a 4- to 12-month shelf life, the barrier needs to be improved by at least a factor of 10 to 25. To achieve such a high oxygen barrier with a barrier improvement factor over that of PET of about 25, a good passive barrier, such as a diamond-like carbon or silica-oxide barrier coatings, is required.

Alternatively, active oxygen-scavenging materials can be built into the bottles in the form of additional barrier layers between the layers of PET or as blends with the PET material. Such scavengers effectively react with the oxygen present in the PET matrix and prevent oxygen from permeating the bottle to the beer packaged inside. Good oxygen scavengers tend to provide the best oxygen barrier and can keep the oxygen ingress below 1 ppm for more than a year in a standard 16-oz. (500-mL) container.

Carbonation Retention

The carbonation level affects the perceived freshness of beer and can alter its taste. Carbonation levels can range between 4 and 6 g (two to three volumes) of carbon dioxide (CO_2) in 1 L of beer. The majority of brewers agree that up to 15% loss in carbonation during shelf life is tolerable for most beers, since consumers will have difficulty noticing any difference in products having this minimal amount of carbonation loss. At higher levels of carbonation loss, consumers notice a flat taste and an alteration in the overall taste of the beer.

In PET containers, there are three sources of carbonation loss: bottle expansion during filling, absorption of CO_2 into the PET, and permeation of CO_2 through the PET wall. Bottle expansion results in a lower overall partial pressure of CO_2 in the container and, consequently, in a lower carbonation of the beer. Absorption and permeation of CO_2 actually results in a net loss of carbonation in the container and therefore in the beer.

By slightly overcarbonating the beer, brewers can easily address the issue of carbonation loss due to container volume expansion during and directly proceeding filling and before distribution. Overcarbonation can also compensate for carbonation loss due to the absorption of CO_2 in the PET wall that occurs at the same time. To reduce the amount of CO_2 permeating PET walls during the remainder of the product's shelf life, an improved passive gas barrier that functions beyond that of standard PET is required.

The initial expansion of PET bottles takes place during and directly following filling when the container is pressurized up to 3 bar with up to 6 g (three volumes) of CO_2 per liter. This expansion can result in a volume increase equivalent to 3–10% carbonation loss. Bottle expansion is due to the intrinsic material properties of PET. It can be minimized by optimizing the container's dimensional stability through adjustments to the container design and to the preform weight and design. It can also be minimized by optimizing weight distribution in the container during blow-molding and by increasing the crystallinity of the material.

Under pressure generated by carbonated beer, PET bottles expand during and directly before filling. This bottle expansion should be taken into account when designing a container to ensure the proper filling height at the accurate nominal volume.

Absorption of carbonation into PET starts right after product carbonization and reaches a saturation point after a few days. After saturating the PET, CO_2 starts desorbing on the outside of the container, and a process of CO_2 permeation is established, driven by the approximate gradient between the partial CO_2 pressure inside and outside the container. To meet the product's required shelf life with a carbonation loss of less than 15%, a passive barrier that functions above that of standard PET is required.

Protection from Visible and UV Light

PET can be made into transparent, glasslike, crystal-clear containers that show less than 1% haze and allow for an attractive presentation. The transparency of PET allows consumers to see both the product and the amount of product in the container. Most beers, however, require protection from visible and UV light at certain wavelengths to prevent photooxidation and light degradation of the product.

Various UV blockers and a variety of color pigments and dye colorants have been developed, tested, and demonstrated to work well for PET packages containing beer. When compared with glass containers, PET containers offer many more colorant and UV barrier choices and much more flexibility in protecting beer from undesired wavelengths of light. In particular, it is an easy process to change bottle colors and the colorants used during the manufacture of PET preforms.

Pasteurization

Potential microbial contamination of beer during the brewing, handling, and filling process can cause microbial growth in the package, resulting in taste degradation and the formation of product turbidity during its shelf life. To ensure that the growth of microbes introduced during the brewing and filling process is minimized and controlled, tunnel pasteurization of beer-filled containers may be required. Today, the vast majority of beers throughout the world are tunnel pasteurized to mitigate any contamination risks during brewing and filling.

In general, PET containers can be designed so that they withstand tunnel pasteurization conditions, that is, internal temperatures up to 146°F (63°C) for up to 45 minutes. However, the higher internal temperature and pressure resulting from tunnel pasteurization increase the strain on PET containers. This further increases bottle expansion, and during the pasteurization process, it increases the absorption and permeation of CO_2, which results in further carbonation loss in the range of 3 to 6%. Such loss of carbonation, however, can be compensated for by overcarbonating the beer prior to the filling process.

Brewers should note that some barrier technologies lend themselves to the tunnel pasteurization process better than others. In particular, coatings may lose their capacity to act as a barrier against passive oxygen ingress owing to an increase of microcracks formed as a result of bottle expansion. Depending on the type of barrier material used, some multilayer compositions may delaminate, and some active scavengers may lose their oxygen-absorbing capability as a result of exposure to heat, humidity, or pressure from CO_2.

Monolayer PET barrier blends, such as PolyShield® resin/nylon-MXD6 blends, which retain their oxygen-scavenging activity during tunnel pasteurization and do not delaminate, seem to be the best solution if tunnel pasteurization is required. It should be noted that such PET containers can be pasteurized using much less energy than the pasteurization of glass containers require, since the much lower-weight plastic containers can be heated to pasteurization temperature faster and cooled down more quickly.

Alternatively, flash pasteurization or cold filtration before filling can minimize any growth of microbes introduced during the brewing process. Such sterilization techniques usually require a clean and nearly microbe-free filling operation to avoid the reintroduction of microbes during the filling process.

Safety

In terms of safety, PET bottles hold a significant advantage over glass. Container breakage and loss of product during handling, filling, distribution, and retailing is minimal for PET bottles. Additionally, with PET containers, bodily injuries resulting from damaged packages in the supply chain and with consumer handling are significantly lower. In particular, in the United States, most sports venues and beaches prohibit glass containers because of the potential for injuries.

Sustainability

PET bottles can protect product flavor, freshness, and taste throughout a product's shelf life. They serve as attractive, transparent, glasslike containers that weigh significantly less than glass bottles. A typical 500-mL PET beer bottle used in Germany weighs around 23–28 g, whereas a 330-mL glass bottle used in the United States weighs between 250 and 350 g.

The lower weight allows for less energy consumption during transportation and handling.

Recycled PET is in demand not only in the United States but also around the world. Clear PET containers can be collected and recycled into various applications, including full-circle or closed-loop recycling back into beverage containers. Most tinted PET bottles, such as colored beer bottles, can be recycled into secondary applications, such as strapping tape and fiberfill products.

● BARRIER MATERIALS

To provide beer with the required protection from oxygen and to retain carbonation levels throughout its shelf life, PET containers need to incorporate additional gas-permeation barriers to oxygen and CO_2. Various barrier materials can be employed in three principal barrier technologies: coatings, multilayer bottles, and monolayer blends.

Such barrier materials can be divided into passive-barrier materials, which prevent gas permeation through a plain physical barrier, and active scavengers, which react with and bind to the oxygen. As of today, active oxygen-scavenging materials can be used only in multilayer bottles and containers made from monolayer blends.

Passive Permeation Barriers

Using materials having lower gas permeation than the semicrystalline PET in the container wall can improve carbonation retention and reduce oxygen ingress. The degree of gas permeation through permeable materials such as polymers is defined as gas solubility in the polymer multiplied by gas diffusion through the polymer. Solubility is defined as the amount of gas in the material, whereas diffusion is defined as the rate at which gas can move through the material.

Therefore, using materials with lower CO_2 solubility and a lower rate of CO_2 diffusion than semicrystalline PET reduces the permeation of CO_2. Modified polyesters, such as the above-mentioned PEN, polyglycolic acid (PGA), and certain aromatic nylons such as MXD6, work well when added in small amounts to PET in monolayer blend and multilayer containers. These materials also provide a passive barrier to oxygen that is not sufficient in most cases to meet the stringent limits for oxygen ingress into beer.

Barrier coatings applied to the outside of containers, such as diamond-like carbon and silicate coatings, provide an even better permeation barrier and are effective at retaining carbonation at the high levels present in beer. Such coatings are not as effective in protecting against the small amounts of oxygen ingress that can alter beer flavor, since they tend to form cracks during bottle expansion and under carbonation pressure.

Active Oxygen Scavengers

Passive-barrier materials can provide an excellent barrier for retaining large volumes of gas, such as carbonation in the container; however, these barriers are much less effective in preventing very small amounts of oxygen from permeating the container. Active oxygen-scavenger materials built into the sidewall of the PET container are much more effective in providing an oxygen barrier and in protecting beer against flavor deterioration caused by exposure to oxygen.

Oxygen scavengers are materials that react with and bind to oxygen molecules when in the presence of an oxidation catalyst. Provided that such oxygen scavengers are evenly distributed in the form of small material domains in the sidewall of a PET container, they can react with incoming oxygen molecules and effectively prevent them from permeating the bottle. Essential for an effective oxygen barrier, each oxygen molecule must have a high chance of meeting one of the scavenger domains and reacting before it permeates the sidewall.

At room temperature, most oxygen scavengers require activation by way of an oxidation catalyst. The most commonly used catalysts are cobalt salts in various forms that can be easily added into the PET or the scavenger material. By adding the catalyst separate from the scavenger master batch and directly to the PET resin, as is the case with PolyShield® resins, the risk of early oxidation of the scavenger during handling and processing before preform injection can be significantly reduced.

Oxygen scavengers have a defined oxygen-binding capacity, which determines the oxygen-barrier shelf life of a container. The concentration of the oxygen-scavenger material in the bottle wall and the wall thickness determine the effectiveness of the scavenger material as a barrier between the environment and the beverage. These factors directly impact the overall oxygen-barrier shelf life. The greater the oxygen-binding capacity, wall thickness, and concentration of scavenger material, the longer the product shelf life will be.

Oxygen scavengers can provide from a few months up to a few years of oxygen-barrier shelf life. Oxygen scavengers are available in a wide range of scavenging capacities, defined as cubic centimeters (cc) of oxygen absorbed per weight of scavenger material in grams. A typical scavenger with the theoretical capacity of 150 cc/g can provide a shelf life of about 1 year to a 500-mL bottle with an average wall thickness of 250 μm, when added at 5%/weight.

In most cases, oxygen scavenging is already active in the preform, and the countdown for product shelf life starts when the bottles are blown. Storing empty bottles can significantly shorten the effective shelf life of the packaged product, since the oxygen capacity is eaten up nearly twice as fast with double the amount of oxygen passing through the PET sidewall from inside and outside the bottle during the storage of bottles to be filled. In particular, low-capacity oxygen scavengers in empty bottles can lose their scavenging capability and therefore their effectiveness as an oxygen barrier relatively fast.

Because of the much thicker wall and the much smaller surface of the preform as compared with those of a bottle, preforms have a significantly lower exposure to oxygen and a much longer product shelf life than bottles. Therefore, when some of the better-performing oxygen scavengers are used under typical operating conditions, preform storage does not affect the effective shelf life of the final container.

In conclusion, oxygen-scavenging materials are the most effective way of providing a sufficient oxygen barrier to protect the taste of packaged beer throughout its shelf life, particularly if light-weight bottles and a shelf life beyond a few months are desired.

● BARRIER TECHNOLOGIES

Currently, there are the three principal technologies providing PET containers with an improved barrier against oxygen ingress and carbonation loss. They are internal and external coatings, barrier bottles produced via multilayer extrusion, and monolayer barrier blends. All three technologies can improve the passive gas barrier of a PET container; however, only multilayer extrusion and monolayer blends can employ active oxygen-scavenging technologies.

Coatings

Coatings that reduce the gas permeability of PET containers can be applied to a container's internal or external surface. Coating technologies can use either organic or inorganic materials and range from low-tech dip coating to high-tech plasma deposition and sputtering. Coatings can provide an excellent barrier against carbonation and oxygen permeation, but they cannot employ the active oxygen-scavenging technologies required to ensure low levels of oxygen ingress and to meet longer shelf life requirements.

Internal coatings, which are applied to the inside surface of bottles, come in contact with the beverage. Examples of commercially available, vapor- and plasma-deposited carbonlike coatings include Actis™ and DLC from Kirin (Tokyo) as well as silicon oxide coatings, such as Plasmax® from KHS GmbH (Hamburg, Germany).

External coatings are applied to the outside surface of either the preform or the bottle via spray or dip coating. These include Bairocade™ from PPG Industries (Pittsburgh, PA) or plasma-deposited coatings, such as BestPET™ from Krones AG (Neutraubling, Germany).

Internal Barrier Coatings

Internal barrier coating technologies are currently used for packaged beverages, including beer, to retain carbonation and provide a passive barrier against oxygen ingress. Such coatings are applied in separate coating machines under vacuum via vapor or plasma deposition and, therefore, cannot incorporate active oxygen-scavenging technologies or materials. Coated bottles require oxygen-scavenging barrier closures to address the oxygen present in the headspace and to meet the oxygen ingress limits and provide the shelf life required for beer.

Installing the required separate coating machines not only means more upfront capital investment but also requires additional floor space for the machines. In addition, the machines for the high-tech chemical process are not easily installed in-line between the blow-molding and the filling lines at the brewery. Microcrack formation during bottle expansion can be controlled under standard filling conditions; however, it limits light-weighting to the current 26 g for a 16-oz. (500-mL) bottle and prohibits tunnel pasteurization because of the additional expansion that occurs to bottles under higher pressure and temperature.

Strengths and Weaknesses

Internal barrier coatings provide several advantages and disadvantages. Their strengths include the following.

+ Internal barrier coatings offer a high passive barrier that provides excellent carbonation retention and a good oxygen barrier.
+ Inert coatings come in contact with beer without introducing potential contaminants.
+ PET bottles with internal barrier coatings offer good clarity, and silicon oxide does not show any color.
+ The coatings are inert and can potentially be removed during the recycling process.
+ Some coatings are cleared for PCR PET recycling into clear recycled PET.

Internal barrier coatings also have some weaknesses.

- They cannot employ active oxygen-scavenging materials required for longer shelf life. As a result, oxygen dissolved in the PET bottle wall will react with the beer and oxygen dissolved in the headspace is not absorbed or scavenged by the container.
- The coatings can form microcracks during a bottle's expansion while filled under pressure. As a result, internal barrier coatings can only be applied to fully blown bottles.
- They limit the effective shelf life of beer because of the presence of oxygen in the bottle and of later possible ingress of oxygen via microcracks.
- Use of internal barrier coatings requires a separate coating machine and floor space for that machine.
- The high-tech chemical process can restrict the use of in-line blowing, coating, and filling.
- Coatings can potentially flake off during bottle filling and when handled by consumers.
- Cracks in the coatings and loss of the oxygen barrier can occur as a result of bottle expansion during tunnel pasteurization.
- It limits potential light-weighting because of crack formation produced during bottle expansion.

Critical Factors and Issues to Consider

- To obtain bottles with glasslike clarity, the coatings must be transparent and match the refractive index of PET.
- The coatings must have good adhesion to PET to withstand abuse during handling and use.
- The coatings need to be cleared for contact with food, and they cannot change the flavor profile of the beer.
- The technology requires an effective filling process after flash pasteurization or cold filter.

External Barrier Coatings

Manufacturers have not had much success in using external coatings in packaging beverages requiring a gas barrier. In particular, external coatings are not well suited for the use of active oxygen-scavenging technologies or materials, and they cannot protect the beverage from the oxygen present in the PET container wall. Currently, external coating technologies can provide a sufficient passive barrier for carbonation retention but they do not meet the stringent limits on oxygen ingress into beer.

Strengths and Weaknesses

External barrier coatings provide the following advantages.

- + The beer does not come into contact with the external barrier coating, only with the PET container. As a result, the PET wall forms a barrier between the beer and potential contaminants.
- + Coatings can potentially be removed during the recycling process.
- + Some coatings can potentially be applied onto preforms before the bottles are blown.

External barrier coatings pose the following disadvantages.

- External barrier coatings can provide a passive barrier but have only a limited capacity for active oxygen scavenging. As a result, oxygen dissolved in the PET bottle wall will react with the beer.
- The preliminary passive oxygen barrier may not provide a sufficient barrier against oxygen ingress for beer.
- They require capital investments in an additional and separate coating machine.
- They require additional floor space and may significantly slow in-line blowing and filling.
- The barrier's effectiveness can be lost because of bottle scuffing and exposure to humidity and other environmental conditions.
- The coating can flake off during the filling, handling, and transportation of bottles and during use by the consumer.

Critical Factors and Issues to Consider

- To obtain bottles with glasslike clarity, the coatings must be transparent and match the refractive index of PET.
- The coatings must have good adhesion to PET to withstand abuse during handling and use.
- To allow for the recycling of PCR PET, it must be possible to separate the coating from the PET.

Multilayer Containers

Multilayer preform injection technology allows the barrier material to be sandwiched between external PET layers. Such barrier layers can contain plain passive-barrier materials and active scavengers. Multilayer extrusion concentrates the barrier material in a single or double middle layer and may reduce the amount of material required.

Multilayer preform injection machines are significantly more complex than their monolayer counterparts and require additional extruders and much more complex molds. Those converting to this technology will put substantially higher capital at risk because of the significantly higher cost of multilayer machines. In addition, mold changes are significantly more expensive because of their more complex design.

Multilayer machines using a three-layer, sequential, preform injection process are available commercially. Many of these machines have been installed in Europe between 2000 and 2005 for the construction of beverage preforms. However, installations for such an application have somewhat slowed after the advent of less capital-intensive barrier solutions that can be employed on existing standard injection equipment.

Some European converters are using a three-layer technology to convert existing monolayer machines to multilayer machines in house. Typical passive- and active-barrier materials used by converters in multilayer structures include Amosorb™ from ColorMatrix Corporation (Berea, OH), Aegis® from Honeywell (Morristown, NJ), and MXD6, and they appear in varieties such as valOR® from Valspar Corporation (Minneapolis, MN), Oxbar® from Constar International (Trevose, PA) and Americhem Europe (Cuyahoga Falls, OH), and SolO2 from ColorMatrix Corporation.

Multilayer machines using a proprietary five-layer, simultaneous preform injection technology developed by Continental PET Technologies (owned by Graham Packaging Company) are currently used in house by Graham Packaging Company in the United States to make proprietary barrier containers using Graham's proprietary passive-barrier and active oxygen-scavenging materials.

Strengths and Weaknesses

Multilayer preform injection technology offers the following advantages.

+ These containers provide a good passive barrier for excellent carbonation retention and a good barrier against oxygen ingress.
+ Beer comes in contact only with the inner PET layer, which separates the barrier layer from the beverage.
+ Various and different barrier materials can be built into the middle layers.
+ The technology offers an improved oxygen barrier and shelf life when active oxygen scavengers are used in the barrier layer.
+ Because the barrier is built into the preform, no additional treatment of the final container is needed.

Its disadvantages include the following.

- The technology requires a much higher capital investment at the converter compared with what is required for standard injection machines.
- Oxygen dissolved in the inner PET bottle wall will partially react with the beer.
- Oxygen dissolved in the headspace will not be scavenged by the container and will react with the beer.
- Bottle expansion during tunnel pasteurization can result in delamination and barrier loss.
- There is a limited potential for light-weighting because of the minimum thickness required for the barrier layer.
- If the bottle base and thread are not covered by the barrier layer, the effectiveness of the gas barrier is reduced.

Critical Factors and Issues to Consider

- To obtain bottles with glasslike clarity, the coatings must be transparent and match the refractive index of PET.
- The coatings must have good adhesion to PET to withstand abuse during handling and use.
- Packagers will need to demonstrate that the barrier material or its by-products do not migrate into the beverage.
- The technology requires an effective filling process after flash pasteurization or cold filter.
- It must be possible for the barrier material to be effectively separated from the PET if the containers are to be recycled.
- A minimum amount of barrier material is needed to make a continuous layer and an effective barrier.
- To serve as an effective gas barrier, the barrier layer must cover the entire bottle, including the thread base and wall.

Monolayer Barrier Blends

Today, many barrier technologies based on PET resins or master batch additives can be processed or added during standard preform injection with only minimal equipment changes or additions and at a minimal additional investment and capital risk. Such monolayer barrier blends require at most a master batch feeder and a separate dryer for the barrier materials. For some active scavengers, a nitrogen blanket may be required during preform injection to prevent oxidation during the injection process.

Most of these monolayer barrier materials—such as Amosorb™, DiamondClear® from Constar International and Americhem Europe, MXD6, and their oxygen-scavenging variations—are available as master batches that can be added to most standard PET resins at the injection machines. In case active oxygen scavenging is required, the materials' compatibility with the PET base resin and all other additives, such as a colorant or UV barrier, needs to be tested before implementation.

Using active oxygen-scavenging monolayer barriers based on modified PET resins, such as PolyShield® resin/nylon-MXD6 blends, eliminates the risk of incompatibility with the base resin. These barrier technologies provide a more reliable process and oxygen barrier performance through more accurate and reliable dosing and better and more even distribution of the reactive components in the resin. They also offer significantly better haze reduction and control, in particular when MXD6 is used.

In recent years, monolayer barrier blends have made strong inroads into barrier packaging for beverages such as beer, wine, and juice. Because these blends can run on most existing injection machines with minor changes, they allow for flexible scheduling and, in particular, allow brewers to make smaller-volume runs and test trial projects on existing equipment before investing in new capacity. In addition, the variable-cost nature of such additives minimizes capital risk and mitigates any risk inherent in developing new commercial projects.

Strengths and Weaknesses

Monolayer barrier blends offer the following advantages.

+ Some barrier materials provide a good passive barrier for carbonation retention.
+ Some active scavengers can provide an excellent oxygen barrier over a long shelf life.
+ Some barrier materials provide excellent active and good passive barriers in one.
+ Monolayer barrier blends can run on most existing, standard preform injection machines with a master batch feeder.
+ The barrier is provided in the preform, and no additional treatment of the bottle is required.
+ The barrier is present throughout the entire bottle, including the thinner base and the unstretched thread.
+ Since only minimal capital is needed to use the technology, it allows for startup and small-volume projects.
+ Using monolayer barrier blends puts no additional capital at risk and requires no extra floor space.
+ The active scavenger reacts with any oxygen in the PET container's sidewall.
+ Some scavengers are active enough to compete with the beer for headspace oxygen.
+ It can serve as a very reliable barrier if the material is accurately dosed and mixed, as with resin-based blends.
+ Some excellent oxygen-barrier materials offer significant light-weighting potential.
+ Bottles with some barrier blends can be pasteurized above 140°F (60°C) and withstand up to 45 pasteurization units.

The disadvantages posed by monolayer barrier blends include the following.

− Most barrier materials are not cleared for PCR PET recycling into clear recycled PET.
− All barrier materials need to undergo migration testing to receive regulatory clearance.
− Some barriers materials add haze to the container when blended with plain PET.
− The effectiveness of the passive carbonation barrier is similar to that of multilayer but much less than what coating technologies offer.

Critical Factors and Issues to Consider

- To obtain bottles with glasslike clarity, the coatings must be transparent and match the refractive index of PET.
- To obtain containers with glasslike clarity requires the use of compatibilizers for the best distribution of very small barrier domains.
- Introducing additives via master batch requires accurate blending and mixing before injection.
- All barrier materials and their oxidation by-products need to receive regulatory clearance.

BARRIER TECHNOLOGIES IN COMMERCIAL APPLICATIONS

Several of the technologies discussed in this chapter have found their way into commercial use for various reasons, in part because of their ability to meet performance requirements, contain variable and fixed costs, and outperform competitive alternatives and as a result of brewers' ability to take on the capital investments for the technologies required. The following section provides some examples, although not an inclusive overview, of PET barrier technologies used today.

Actis™ coating employs a carbon vapor deposition process and is used commercially on more than 20 machines installed around the world. It is used predominantly for packaging ready-to-drink tea in Japan and beer packaging at Brouwerij Martens in Belgium and its related breweries Frankfurter Brauhaus in Germany and in China. Newer 48-cavity machines with the capacity to run up to 36,000 bottles per hour (bph) are now available, and they can reduce the fairly high cost of coating with the installed 12,000-bph-capacity equipment to a more competitive cost.

Plasmax® is a silicate coating that is applied in a single-bottle plasma deposition process. There are just a few of these machines installed for packaging ready-to-drink beverages in Japan and juice in Europe as well as one machine in the United States that runs at about 12,000 bph. Higher-output machines that can reduce the fairly high barrier cost premium have yet to reach the market.

Multilayer barrier bottles from Graham Packaging Company are used commercially predominantly in the United States for packaging various beverages, including a significant portion of the approximately 300 million PET beer bottles produced per year by American breweries.

Multilayer injection machines can employ a variety of barrier materials, such as ethylene vinyl alcohol (EVOH), MXD6, Aegis®, Amosorb™, DiamondClear®, and others. They are installed at converters throughout the world, with approximately half of them in Europe. Typical packaging applications for such three-layer barrier bottles include those for juice, milk, beer, carbonated and flavored water, and ready-to-drink beverages.

Nylon-MXD6 is used in monolayer barrier blends via a variety of passive- and active-barrier master batch products, such as MonOxbar® from Constar International and Americhem Europe, valOR®, and SolO2. Such nylon-MXD6 monolayer barrier blends provide an improved passive gas barrier over that of plain PET, and in most cases, the oxygen-scavenging capacity of these nylon-MXD6 monolayer barrier blends activate by a catalyst. These blends have found niche applications in packaging a variety of oxygen-sensitive beverages, such as juice, wine, energy drinks, and in some cases beer.

Monolayer blends with Amosorb™ and DiamondClear® provide active oxygen scavenging to reduce oxygen ingress, but they offer no additional passive barrier for carbonation retention. Amosorb™ is widely used for packaging oxygen-sensitive products that do not need carbonation retention, such as juice, ready-to-drink teas, and a very few beer products.

Nylon-MXD6 is also used in combination with PolyShield® resin to create monolayer barrier blends. These blends result in virtually haze-free containers that offer good carbonation retention and an excellent oxygen-ingress barrier. The PolyShield® resin incorporates a catalyst that activates the oxygen-scavenging capability of the nylon-MXD6 and is modified to significantly reduce the haze usually apparent in other PET/nylon-MXD6 blends. Since their introduction in 2005, bottles made from PolyShield® resin/nylon-MXD6 blends have seen significant growth throughout the world and, in particular, in Europe, doubling sales every year and capturing a significant portion of the barrier-packaging market.

After the adoption of multilayer solutions became well established in the early 2000s, monolayer barrier blends seem to have captured the most growth in recent years, and they continue to provide barrier solutions for beer and various other oxygen-sensitive applications. Similarly, most coating machines have been in place for quite some time; recently, however, some coating capacity has been added in Germany and China.

CONCLUSION

PET packaging has made some significant inroads into beer packaging. In 2008, it represented more than 2% of all unit packaging worldwide, and it is expected to remain a viable option for beer packaging. In some regions, the adoption of PET containers has reached something of a tipping point. For instance, in Eastern Europe, more than one-third of all packaged beer sold is in PET containers.

PET packaging can be a cost-effective and sustainable solution, and when investments in greenfield solutions are considered, PET containers offer particularly strong advantages over the use of nonreturnable, one-way glass containers.

On the market, PET packaging that incorporates passive- and active-barrier technologies in combination with UV blockers and colorants as light absorbers has met or even exceeded the shelf life requirements for beer packaging. Such PET containers for beer range in size from containers of several fluid ounces or milliliters and a few grams in weight up to 50-L kegs. They provide a shelf life of a few weeks to several years, depending upon the requirements of size, container weight, and type and amount of barrier material employed.

Currently, three primary barrier technologies are employed to provide the required carbonation retention and barrier against oxygen ingress: internal plasma-deposited coatings, coextruded multilayer containers using various barrier materials in the middle layer, and monolayer blends that incorporate barrier additives directly in the PET resin or via master batches that are added at the preform injection machine. Of these technologies, monolayer barrier blends provide the barrier in the preform and can run on existing, standard preform injection machines without requiring any significant capital investment.

Assuming minimal unit volume production, the most cost-effective approach for brewers who seek to use PET containers would be to purchase preforms that already contain the required barrier material and blowing these preforms into bottles in-line right before filling. This requires investing in a blow molder and setting aside some floor space in the vicinity of the filling line, but it will significantly reduce the cost associated with shipping and cleaning bottles. Furthermore, backward integrating and injection-molding preforms can provide brewers additional cost savings, provided the scale of production justifies the investments, as has been the case with some European brewers.

The technology for packaging beer in PET containers is ready and available and appears to be gaining broad acceptance. Beer is the last large product category utilizing glass packaging, a packaging format that beer's target consumer group has not grown up with and may consider inconvenient and old fashioned. However, this group is familiar with PET bottles because of their use as soft drink containers. In fact, in Europe, glass continues to be used for beer packaging largely because of the existing infrastructure and because of the cost advantage of returnable, refillable glass bottles.

Considering recent trends, it might be concluded that, in 5–10 years, PET containers will be a major part of beer packaging throughout the world, taking its place beside cans and glass bottles. PET containers will allow brewers to use innovative packaging design to differentiate their brands and attract the core group of 21- to 35-year-old consumers who grew up with PET containers as the packaging used for virtually every beverage they consumed.

CHAPTER 11

Small Bottling Lines

DAVE MEHEEN
Meheen Manufacturing Inc.

Packaging is by far the most technically and financially demanding area of any brewery's operations. A missed step in financial planning, brewing, bottling, or marketing can spell disaster for the brewery. However, in most areas, bottled or canned beer accounts for more than 80% of the market and affords the largest access to customers. This chapter explores some of the aspects involved in developing a successful packaging operation, including pricing and cost analysis, selection of equipment, and brewery and filling operations for smaller breweries.

● MARKET

One of the first steps to complete before launching any packaging operation is evaluating the potential market and establishing realistic and achievable goals. What types of products appeal to the potential audience? What information and geographical statistics are available about the population and what percentage of that population might be interested in the product? What does a cost and pricing analysis reveal? After all, without this detailed information, brewers will not be able to evaluate the feasibility of their proposed operations.

The market is the audience, the demographic most drawn to the product. Evaluating the market includes considering population density in the area in which the product is to be distributed and the characteristics of this population, e.g., its age distribution; income levels; type of work pursued, whether white collar or blue collar; and recreational interests. The first step is to identify with the target audience. Brewers should consider whether they themselves are in the group. In creating a product, brewers may find that, chances are, the segment of the market that shares their interests in foods, beers, sports, and other activities is the population that would be attracted to their product.

To characterize and identify the target area, brewers can start by simply gathering information about the population and making notes about age distribution, income levels, job types, and interests. This information helps determine not only the number of potential customers but also the types of products to package and the kind of advertising and labeling materials that will attract this audience. Many of these decisions come from a "gut feel" about the buyer, but it is also a good idea to involve others whose opinions the product developer trusts to help with evaluating the market.

Ultimately, brewers want to make and market a product that has the most appeal and will establish brand loyalty. These days, a diverse group is attracted to craft-brewed, specialty, and distinctly flavored beers and will pay a premium price. This is fortunate especially for smaller brewers and should help in planning product types and styles that will be well received.

Once a product and its audience have been identified, brewers need to consider how to get the product to the consumer. Do they want to use distributors to place the product or are they going to remain a small operation and distribute the product themselves or maybe simply package for a pub? This decision allows them to begin to estimate the size of the equipment needed to support their business plan. Brewers should always plan for a bottling or canning capacity that is adequate for the original, planned run and yet also allows some room for expansion. These estimates also affect the size and type of equipment needed.

Let's say, for example, that a brewer has reviewed the marketing research and established that their operation will create a bottled or canned product for the local region and distribute it with the use of two to three distributors. Distributors often have a good feel for the amount of product they can move. But, again, to make the best estimate, brewers should anticipate growth and future expansion of their market.

Once the type of product and the production and distribution plan have been established, it is time to start looking at the costs associated with packaging and to begin to set a retail price for the product. The product's retail pricing should be competitive with the pricing of other products already on the market. It should also, of course, reflect what it is going to cost to get the product to market.

Let's say, for example, that the target "front line" retail price is $8.99 for a six pack ($35.96 per case) in the grocery store, where the store has a 30% margin (% profit to cost) and the distributor has a 30% margin. These figures help establish the price of the beer the brewer sells to the distributor. The cost of getting the beer to the distributor subtracted from the sale to the distributor gives the profit. In this example, the store would buy the case from the distributor for $25.17 and the distributor would buy the case from the brewery for $17.62. The difficult part for many brewers is getting an accurate estimate of all the brewery's costs in getting the beer to the distributor.

Brewery costs need to be complete and accurate, so a little legwork will be involved and some estimating as well. The cost of producing the beer is relatively easy to establish since the brewer's costs are known and brewers should be able to translate those costs directly to the bottled product. Packaging costs, however, can be surprising, especially if brewers are making minimum orders of six-pack carriers, bottles, crowns, labels, and boxes. These consumable items may also have die and printing charges and will take up floor space in the brewery. All of these costs need to be figured into the startup cost.

The following is an example of package costs. The figures are estimates only and probably inaccurate to the current market. To make accurate evaluations, brewers should determine their own actual costs.

Example: Packaging costs for 12,500 bottles

Bottles at $0.20 each, 2,500 per pallet, minimum order of five pallets:	$ 2,500
Labels at $0.05 each, minimum order of 100,000:	$ 5,000
Six-pack carriers at $0.35 each, minimum order of 50,000:	$17,500
Case boxes at $0.85 each, minimum order of 5,000:	$ 4,250
Crowns at $0.02 each, minimum order of 5,000:	$ 100
Total	$29,350

For this example, with the inclusion of artwork fees and shipping costs, the estimated initial packaging costs would be $33,000.

Once these costs are determined, the next step is to establish the equipment capacity needed to support the proposed product run. In this example, machinery producing 1,200 bottles per hour (bph) would be adequate to support the product run, but the labor cost involved in operating the equipment should also be consider a per-package cost. A larger machine producing 2,000 bph or more can be operated with the same amount of labor, but the cost of labor per package is reduced by 40%, which in a short period of time could make up the cost difference of acquiring and operating the faster, larger machine.

Many considerations come into play when choosing plant equipment, and they are discussed later in this chapter. For the purpose of estimating equipment-related costs, for this example, the bottling machines and labeling equipment of this scale will cost a total of $65,000. In estimating the cost per package, brewers need to not only establish the initial cost of the equipment but also set an anticipated lifespan of the equipment to try to account for interest costs and square-footage costs over time. For this example, equipment costs will be set at $0.01 per bottle. Assuming three people can run 2,000 bph, the labor cost of packaging the beer will be $0.02 per bottle and $0.11 per bottle for the beer.

Before proceeding with the plan, the brewer needs to find out whether the bottled beer will be profitable at the set price and with these estimated costs. This can be determined by simply calculating the costs versus the distributor's payment for the beer. Distributors take full cases, so again working backwards from the retail price of $8.99 per six pack or $35.96 per case (price to customer or PTC), the retailer buys this case from the distributor for $25.17 (price to retailer or PTR), and the distributor would pay $17.62 per case to the brewery (freight on board price or FOB). Now let's compare the costs.

Bottle, label, and crown at $0.27 × 24 bottles/case:	$ 6.48
Six-pack carriers at $0.35 each × four carriers/case:	$ 1.40
Case carton:	$ 0.85
Beer at $0.11 × 24 bottles/case:	$ 2.64
Equipment at $0.01 × 24 bottles/case:	$ 0.24
Packaging labor at $0.02 × 24 bottles/case:	$ 0.48
Total cost for brewery per case of 24 bottles:	$12.09

Taking the price the distributor pays per case minus the brewery's costs in producing the beer (i.e., $17.62 − $12.09), the brewery should make about $5.53 per case or a 31% profit. Once again, the brewer must verify their own actual costs and selling points from this example!

CHOOSING A FILLER

Once it is established that the packaged beer can be profitable at the set price, brewers should review the filling equipment that suits their needs and provides the quality of product that ensures success. After reviewing equipment, brewers may find that they need to adjust the cost estimate for the equipment and make changes accordingly. In the brewing industry, quality bottling means a bottling process that provides the best sanitation, gentle and nonturbulent filling, and little to no air pickup in the product during bottling. As with any sized filler, air pickup is by far the most critical issue affecting quality control and shelf life, and it is the main factor determining the freshness date of bottled beer.

Oxygen in beer causes it to go stale and develop an oxidized (cardboard) character. The less oxygen in the finished bottle, the longer the product's shelf life is and the longer the beer remains fresh. In many cases, process changes in the brewery are necessary to minimize the presence of oxygen in the beer before it ever gets to the bottling machine. In the brewery, valves, filters, pumps, and the simple action of just moving the beer are common sources and causes for oxygen intake into the beer. Keeping all brewing equipment in good condition and replacing seals and parts associated with filters and tank transfers can reduce this problem. On the bottling machines, air can enter the product at several points on the line, from the pressure bowl on top of the filler to the point where the beer is foamed just before crowning. Not all bottling machines use pressure bowls, but for those that do, brewers must make certain that the bowl's headspace is properly flushed and filled with carbon dioxide (CO_2) and that the seals and valves are all in good condition.

By far, the biggest pickup point for unwanted air is the crowning station. To produce finished bottles that contain little air, the machine must have some mechanism that causes the beer to foam just before applying the crown. This foaming releases CO_2 from the beer, which displaces air from the neck of the bottle. Just as the foam mushrooms over the top of the bottle, the bottle is crowned. Several mechanisms are used to cause the beer to foam, from pressure changes at the filling station to "knockers" that hit the side of the bottle with a small hammer to high-pressure jets that stream warm water into the beer just before bottles are crowned. Regardless of how the beer is foamed, this is an essential step for controlling the amount of air or oxygen in the finished package.

Basically, two types of filling heads are used on beer filling machines, a short tube or a long tube. The first kind of filling tube is very short and sticks into the bottle only a short distance. When this tube is used, the beer flows over a small hat-shaped piece that directs the flow onto the inner sides of the bottle so that the beer is delivered more gently than it would be by pouring the beer directly from the small tube. The deflected flow also prevents the beer from splashing. However, this type of filler spreads the beer into a thin moving layer, which allows maximum exposure of the product to any air present in the bottle. To avoid excessively high air pickup in the product, short-tube filling machines need to have at least one, if not two, pre-evacuation stages. During each evacuation stage, a vacuum is applied to draw out the air within the bottle, and then the vacuum is stopped and the air is replaced with CO_2. If the pre-evacuation process is repeated again before the bottle undergoes counterpressure and is filled with beer, the air content in the bottle will be low enough to produce acceptable levels of air in the finished bottle.

Long-tube fillers (Fig. 11.1) have tubes that extend nearly to the bottom of the bottle and fill from the bottom of the bottle up. This configuration exposes far less of the beer to the atmosphere in the bottle and causes less product turbulence and agitation, which in turn results in less air pickup during filling. Just as with short-tube filling machines, long-tube fillers are available with pre-evacuation capability. Regardless of filling type, it is critical to foam the beer after filling and just before crowning because, as with the short-tube fillers, this displaces any remaining air from the neck of the bottle at the time of sealing. Generally, a 12-oz. (355-mL) bottle

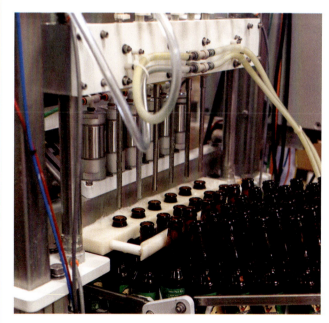

FIGURE 11.1. Long-tube filler valves that fill from the bottom of the bottle and produce little turbulence. (Courtesy Meheen Manufacturing Inc.)

of beer containing less than 0.5 mL of headspace air has adequate shelf life for most local distribution scenarios.

Bottle conditioning or retaining a small amount of yeast in the beer can help reduce oxygen content quickly and extend shelf life. Also available are crowns with oxygen-scavenging liners, which absorb oxygen in the beer headspace, and oxygen barrier crown liners, which can help keep oxygen from entering the crowned package. Brewers should be aware that some of these liners "scalp" or absorb hop aroma compounds.

Another issue, which is often forgotten but very important to beer quality and operating costs, are filler cleaning requirements. Like any other piece of equipment used in the brewery, the filler has its requirements for cleaning and sanitation. Due to its complexity and moving parts and valves, bottle-filling machines, regardless of size, require much more vigorous cleaning regimens than other pieces of packaging equipment. Machines with pressure bowls must have not only the contact surfaces of the bowl cleaned but also the valves and seals used for each filling station.

These machines require a good cleaning-in-place (CIP) system to remove beer residues and mineral stone buildup and to sanitize prior to use. Also, machines using pressure bowls require periodic maintenance of valves, seals, and conveyors. Some smaller machines with computer controls are able to manage bottling and bright tank pressures using a manifold, eliminating the need for the pressure bowl. The manifold (Fig. 11.2) has several advantages from a cleaning, maintenance, moving parts, and cost of operation standpoint. Regular maintenance, replacement of consumable parts, and repairs should be factored into any evaluation of overall machinery and operating costs.

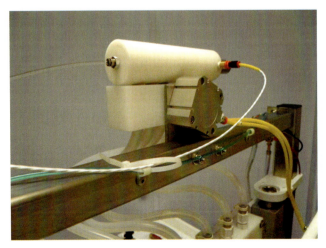

FIGURE 11.2. Manifold for a small filler collects beer from the supply hose and delivers it to six filling heads. (Courtesy Meheen Manufacturing Inc.)

● BREWERY BOTTLING OPERATIONS

In small or large packaging operations, whether bottling or canning, the beer needs to be in proper condition to be packaged. This means that the beer is essentially cold and carbonated to an appropriate level for the package that it will be going into. For most applications, the temperature is appropriate when it is near freezing or 32°F (0°C) and the beer is contained in a bright tank that has refrigeration and can maintain pressure. There are also factors of conditioning that come into play and will affect the way the beer is packaged. Factors such as how the beer is carbonated and how it is conditioned or stored can have an effect on the CO_2 staying in solution during the filling process and how it foams.

Several factors come into play for conditioning the beer and preparing it for the packaging process. Among these factors are how the beer is force carbonated, i.e., slow-step carbonation that produces smaller bubbles or rapid carbonation that tends to produce larger bubbles, flushing out and reducing hop aromas, head foam potential, and less-stable CO_2 in solution. Another factor is temperature. The glycol system chilling the bright beer tank and conditioning it for packaging should generally be set around 30°F (–1°C). A glycol temperature that is too cold (below 28°F [–2°C]) can cause freezing and thawing of the beer, which when dispensed to the filler can cause gushing and foam control problems. So for the best results, carbonation should take place with the glycol system set for just below freezing, the bright tank set at 32°F (0°C), and a good quality CO_2 stone. Using a slow-step process to achieve small bubbles and good absorption with minimum pass-through and venting of the CO_2 from the tank will achieve better CO_2 saturation and reduce the loss of beer aromas.

Brewery operations and beer handling can greatly affect the quality and presentation of bottled beer. In the brewery, the two critical factors affecting product quality are, again, air pickup and CO_2 levels. Air pickup in beer before it reaches the filler most often comes from transfer and filtering operations. One source of air pickup is the centrifugal pumps used to move and filter beer. Centrifugal pumps work by bringing the beer in through the center of the pump housing and then slinging it toward the outside of the pump housing. This creates a low-pressure area at the center of the pump, which can allow air to be drawn in through loose pump inlet connections or a faulty shaft seal and drive it into the beer.

Any time beer is moved, brewers run the risk of the product picking up air. To minimize air pickup in the brewery, good seals should always be maintained in all valves, pumps, and filters and beer should not be moved more than necessary. To help displace air that may have been picked up during transfer and filtering operations, brewers can perform final carbonation in the bright tank before sending it to the filler. Light CO_2 flushing helps to displace the air and ensures that CO_2 levels are where they should be; however, brewers should be aware that flushing also carries away hop aromas and reduces the head foam potential of the final beer.

Once a brewery has product on store shelves, customers expect that each bottle of that brewery's beer they purchase will be identical to the last. To achieve this consistency, CO_2 levels must be consistent at all times. CO_2 is a major component of mouthfeel and provides some bite to the beer, which affects its flavor. The importance of consistent CO_2 levels cannot be stressed enough. The importance of CO_2 to product flavor can be seen in cola. If the CO_2 was removed from one can of cola and it was compared with a can of carbonated cola served at the same temperature, the noncarbonated cola would taste excessively sweet compared with the carbonated cola. CO_2 in beer serves much the same function, and if the CO_2 levels in beer change from batch to batch, the product's taste will change accordingly. To maintain consistency in CO_2 levels, a strict procedure for carbonating should be adopted in the brewery and followed every time. Of course, part of the carbonation formula depends upon maintaining a consistent beer temperature. So for the brewery to be successful, the cooling system must work properly and hold a consistent temperature.

Dynamics of Tank Carbonation

While there are several methods of carbonating beer, one of the easiest to understand and use for the smaller brewer is tank carbonation that uses a stone to create small bubbles of CO_2, which are absorbed into the beer. This section provides a description of one method of this carbonation process using a refrigerated pressure tank.

Brewers should be aware of the tank's pressure rating and not exceed this pressure. A pressure regulating valve (PRV) set to below the tank's rated pressure capacity should always be used to avoid overpressure and possible tank rupture.

To understand the dynamics of CO_2 dissolved in beer, it helps to first understand the solubility of CO_2 in beer and the terms and measurements used to describe the presence of CO_2. CO_2 is very soluble in beer, and its solubility increases with pressure and decreases with temperature. The amount of CO_2 dissolved in beer is most often described in terms of volumes. Volumes of CO_2 are defined as the volume the CO_2 gas would occupy if it were removed from the beer at atmospheric pressure and 32°F (0°C) compared with the original volume of beer. Thus, if 1 quart of beer was carbonated to 2.5 volumes and all the CO_2 were removed from the beer, it would occupy 2.5 quarts, as illustrated in Figure 11.3. Most packaged beers are considered normally carbonated at 2.45 to 2.85 volumes of dissolved CO_2 per volume of beer. Generally speaking, during the bottling and kegging process, 0.1–0.15 volumes of CO_2 are lost, so this amount plus the desired packaged content should be added in the bright tank.

The volume of CO_2 in beer is easily determined by noting the temperature and pressure conditions of the beer at equilibrium conditions and reading the volumes directly from a chart, such as the one in Table 11.1. Equilibrium is the point at which the same amount of CO_2 diffuses from the beer as is dissolved back into solution. When determining CO_2 volume, it is critical that the readings are taken with accurate instruments when the product is under equilibrium conditions. The impact of false readings on determining the volumes of CO_2 can be dramatic, as illustrated in Table 11.1. For example, the largest errors often result from pressure readings taken from gauges that are often plus or minus as much as 1–7 pounds per square inch gauge (psig). If a reading of 10 psig is taken from a faulty gauge for a container of beer at 35°F (1.7°C), the CO_2

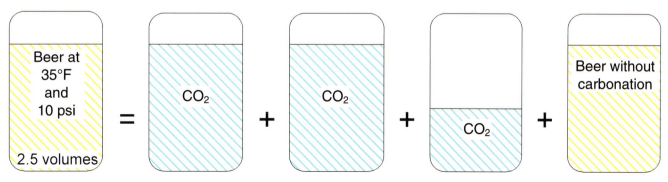

FIGURE 11.3. Carbon dioxide (CO_2) volume displacement, with CO_2 at atmospheric pressure and 35°F (1.7°C). (Courtesy Meheen Manufacturing Inc.)

reading obtained from the chart is 2.52 volumes. But if the actual pressure is 15 psig, in reality, there are 3.02 volumes of CO_2. Not only is the beer carbonation beyond normal gas levels, it is excessively high, and excessively high pressures can causing gushing when opened or even present a dangerous condition because the containers are overpressurized.

Other factors can often produce false volume readings from the chart even when accurate instruments are used. For example, a gas leak from a manway or pressure relief valve can produce a false result if brewers are using tank readings to determine volumes. If there is a gas leak, readings of CO_2 volumes will be incorrect because the tank is not under equilibrium conditions. To be certain of obtaining a correct reading of tank carbonation, a sample should be properly taken from the tank and tested with an appropriate tester. The basic tester is a device that makes a sealed attachment to the sample container and is equipped with a thermometer and pressure gauge for reading the equilibrium conditions in the sample container. The tester must be shaken vigorously several times before readings are taken. This is to ensure that as much CO_2 comes out of solution as is being dissolved back into solution and that equilibrium conditions are obtained. If brewers do not have a tester and tank conditions are used to determine CO_2 levels, they must always be certain that

TABLE 11.1. Beer Carbonation, Expressed as Volumes of CO_2, at Various Temperatures and Pressures[a]

Temp.		Pressure in Pounds per Square Inch Gauge (psig)																				
°C	°F	5	6	7	8	9	10	11	12	13	14	15	16	17	18	19	20	21	22	23	24	25
−1	30	2.25	2.37	2.48	2.60	2.71	2.83	2.94	3.05	3.17												
−1	31	2.20	2.31	2.43	2.54	2.65	2.76	2.87	2.98	3.10	3.21											
0	32	2.15	2.26	2.37	2.48	2.59	2.70	2.81	2.92	3.03	3.14	3.24										
1	33	2.10	2.21	2.32	2.43	2.53	2.64	2.75	2.85	2.96	3.07	3.17										
1	34	2.06	2.16	2.27	2.37	2.48	2.58	2.69	2.79	2.90	3.00	3.10	3.21									
2	35	2.02	2.12	2.22	2.32	2.43	2.53	2.63	2.73	2.83	2.94	3.04	3.14	3.24								
2	36	1.97	2.07	2.17	2.27	2.37	2.48	2.58	2.68	2.78	2.88	2.98	3.08	3.18								
3	37	1.93	2.03	2.13	2.23	2.33	2.43	2.52	2.62	2.72	2.82	2.92	3.01	3.11	3.21							
3	38	1.90	1.99	2.09	2.18	2.28	2.38	2.47	2.57	2.67	2.76	2.86	2.95	3.05	3.15	3.24						
4	39	1.86	1.95	2.05	2.14	2.24	2.33	2.43	2.52	2.61	2.71	2.80	2.90	2.99	3.09	3.18						
4	40	1.82	1.92	2.01	2.10	2.19	2.29	2.38	2.47	2.56	2.66	2.75	2.84	2.93	3.03	3.12	3.21					
5	41	1.79	1.88	1.97	2.06	2.15	2.24	2.33	2.43	2.52	2.61	2.70	2.79	2.88	2.97	3.06	3.15	3.24				
6	42	1.76	1.85	1.93	2.02	2.11	2.20	2.29	2.38	2.47	2.56	2.65	2.74	2.83	2.92	3.00	3.09	3.18				
6	43	1.72	1.81	1.90	1.99	2.07	2.16	2.25	2.34	2.43	2.51	2.60	2.69	2.78	2.86	2.95	3.04	3.13	3.21			
7	44	1.69	1.78	1.87	1.95	2.04	2.12	2.21	2.30	2.38	2.47	2.55	2.64	2.73	2.81	2.90	2.98	3.07	3.16	3.24		
7	45	1.66	1.75	1.83	1.92	2.00	2.09	2.17	2.26	2.34	2.43	2.51	2.59	2.68	2.76	2.85	2.93	3.02	3.10	3.19		
8	46	1.64	1.72	1.80	1.89	1.97	2.05	2.13	2.22	2.30	2.38	2.47	2.55	2.63	2.72	2.80	2.88	2.96	3.05	3.13	3.21	
8	47	1.61	1.69	1.77	1.85	1.94	2.02	2.10	2.18	2.26	2.34	2.43	2.51	2.59	2.67	2.75	2.83	2.91	3.00	3.08	3.16	3.24
9	48	1.58	1.66	1.74	1.82	1.90	1.98	2.06	2.14	2.22	2.30	2.38	2.47	2.55	2.63	2.71	2.79	2.87	2.95	3.03	3.11	3.19
9	49	1.56	1.64	1.71	1.79	1.87	1.95	2.03	2.11	2.19	2.27	2.35	2.43	2.50	2.58	2.66	2.74	2.82	2.90	2.98	3.06	3.14
10	50	1.53	1.61	1.69	1.76	1.84	1.92	2.00	2.08	2.15	2.23	2.31	2.39	2.46	2.54	2.62	2.70	2.77	2.85	2.93	3.01	3.09
11	51	1.51	1.58	1.66	1.74	1.81	1.89	1.97	2.04	2.12	2.20	2.27	2.35	2.43	2.50	2.58	2.65	2.73	2.81	2.88	2.96	3.04
11	52		1.56	1.63	1.71	1.78	1.86	1.94	2.01	2.09	2.16	2.24	2.31	2.39	2.46	2.54	2.61	2.69	2.76	2.84	2.91	2.99
12	53		1.54	1.61	1.68	1.76	1.83	1.91	1.98	2.05	2.13	2.20	2.28	2.35	2.43	2.50	2.57	2.65	2.72	2.80	2.87	2.94
12	54		1.51	1.59	1.66	1.73	1.80	1.88	1.95	2.02	2.10	2.17	2.24	2.32	2.39	2.46	2.53	2.61	2.68	2.75	2.83	2.90
13	55			1.56	1.63	1.71	1.78	1.85	1.92	1.99	2.07	2.14	2.21	2.28	2.35	2.43	2.50	2.57	2.64	2.71	2.78	2.86
13	56			1.54	1.61	1.68	1.75	1.82	1.89	1.96	2.04	2.11	2.18	2.25	2.32	2.39	2.46	2.53	2.60	2.67	2.74	2.81
14	57			1.52	1.59	1.66	1.73	1.80	1.87	1.94	2.01	2.08	2.15	2.22	2.29	2.36	2.43	2.49	2.56	2.63	2.70	2.77
14	58				1.56	1.63	1.70	1.77	1.84	1.91	1.98	2.05	2.11	2.18	2.25	2.32	2.39	2.46	2.53	2.60	2.67	2.74

[a] To find the volume of carbon dioxide (CO_2), locate the temperature reading in the left-hand column and then find the pressure reading across the top. Where the two intersect is the volume of CO_2.

the tank is under equilibrium conditions and that accurate instruments are used.

Some breweries still practice the more traditional method of natural carbonation through krausening and refermentation under pressure, but tank carbonation is most often accomplished by introducing CO_2 into the beer either in-line on the way to the bright beer tank or in the tank through a carbonating stone. At the end of normal fermentation, beer contains between 1 and 1.7 volumes of CO_2. Tank carbonation using a carbonating stone is used to introduce the remaining CO_2 into the beer and bring it to the desired carbonation level.

Carbonating stones are made of ceramic or sintered stainless steel and have very small openings, which produce very small bubbles when CO_2 is forced through them (Fig. 11.4). These small bubbles expose a large surface area to the beer and are thus more easily dissolved into the beer. The stones are placed off-center in the bottom of the tank to produce a rolling action of the beer. Since carbonating stones have minute pores, the capillary resistance of the stone must be overcome before any bubbles are produced in the beer. This capillary resistance is often referred to as wetting pressure, which can be between 1 and 8 psig. The amount of liquid head pressure above the stone also affects the total internal pressure required for the stone to produce bubbles. Every 28 inches depth of liquid is the equivalent of approximately 1 psig. Consequently, the higher the liquid level rises above the stone, the higher the internal pressure needs to be to overcome the wetting pressure of the stone.

Using a stone to carbonate beer in a tank can take anywhere from a few hours to several days. Generally, the best results are achieved using a relatively slow carbonation process. It is also highly desirable at the beginning of carbonation to maintain a relatively low differential pressure between the stone and the headspace in the tank while bleeding gas from the top of the tank. This scrubs out of the beer any unwanted dissolved air that was picked up during product transfer or the brewing process.

The following is an example of how to carbonate beer at 34°F (1°C) using a carbonating stone with a wetting pressure of 5 psig. First, brewers must determine the volume of CO_2 desired in the finished product. An example is 2.58 volumes. Using Table 11.1 and locating 34°F in the left column, follow the row to find the CO_2 volume of 2.58. As indicated at the top of the chart, the corresponding pressure is 10 psig. The next step is determining the appropriate head pressure of the beer above the stone. In this example, the beer level rises to 84 inches above the stone (Fig. 11.5). Since 28 inches of liquid is the equivalent of 1 psig, this 84 inches can be divided by 28 inches to obtain 3 psig of head pressure. It is important to mention at this point that 28 inches per psig is an approximation for water, and brewers may wish to obtain a more accurate figure, especially when working with higher-gravity beers. To obtain a more accurate estimate of pressure, brewers should multiply the total inches of liquid above the stone by the specific gravity of the finished beer and then divide by 27.684 inches per psig. Generally speaking, for a fully fermented beer, this level of accuracy is not warranted for most conditions.

FIGURE 11.4. Stainless-steel carbonating stone in a bright beer tank. (Courtesy K. Ockert)

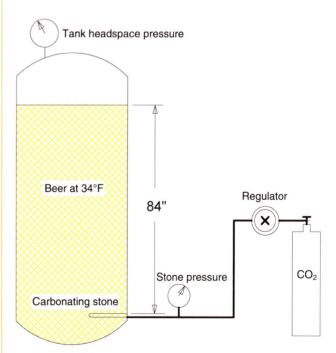

FIGURE 11.5. Tank containing beer with a carbonating stone and regulated carbon dioxide (CO_2). (Courtesy Meheen Manufacturing Inc.)

To obtain the total pressure needed for the carbonating stone to begin producing bubbles, brewers should add the wetting pressure of the stone to the liquid head pressure above the stone. For example, a wetting pressure of 5 psig plus a liquid head pressure of 3 psig indicates a required pressure of 8 psig. This means that, when the head pressure of the tank is at atmospheric pressure and 8 psig of pressure is applied to the carbonating stone, the stone will begin releasing CO_2 bubbles into the beer. To carbonate the product slowly, the differential pressure should be kept low. A pressure of 9 psig on the stone would give a differential pressure of 1 psig above the bubble break pressure needed to break both the capillary and head pressure constraints. As the pressure in the tank's headspace increases, it is necessary to increase the pressure on the carbonating stone. Since the target carbonation level in this example is 2.58 volumes at 34°F (1°C), the head pressure gauge on the tank should be 10 psig when the beer is carbonated. The pressure applied to the stone must be 18 psig to produce the desired carbonation level, i.e., the wetting pressure, plus the liquid head pressure, plus the final equilibrium pressure (5 + 3 + 10 = 18).

Carbonating in the tank in this manner requires accurate pressure gauges and a great deal of attention. To reduce the amount of labor required for tank carbonation, one option is to use a adjustable regulator that can be set to the desired final head pressure (Fig. 11.6). A more elaborate option is a commercial unit tank carbonator, which maintains a constant differential pressure during the carbonation process. Even if the beer is carefully carbonated with accurate pressure gauges, it is still a good idea to check the beer using a good carbonation tester.

Beer-Filling Operations

Before any filling can take place, the packaging equipment needs to be thoroughly cleaned and sanitized to avoid any nonbiological or microbial contamination of the finished package. Any surfaces that the product will be exposed to must be sanitized. This includes the machine itself and any components that come into contact with the beer. Machines that use a pressure bowl on top are significantly more involved to clean and sanitize than are those utilizing a simple manifold system with the beer supplied by a pressurized bright tank with direct hose connections. To this end, the beer only contacts the interior surfaces of the hoses between the bright tank and the bottle itself. Hoses delivering beer to the bottling machine need to be checked periodically for damage and foreign materials and should be replaced as a regular service item. Many different chemicals are available today that can perform these cleaning tasks well, although brewers need to choose which chemicals will work best for them. Bottling machine manufacturers may recommend specific chemicals and cleaning procedures that work best for their equipment. Recommendations from chemical suppliers and other brewers may also help in identifying the best chemicals and procedures for a particular application.

Some small filler machines feature cleaning- and sanitizing-in-place automated functions. To perform a cleaning or sanitizing function, a small submersible pump is connected directly to the beer hose leading to the bottling machine and the cycle is run. The cycle will automatically pulse cleaning or sanitizing solutions through all of the lines, valves, and fittings for a couple of minutes and then automatically stops with a message to let you know the machine is ready for the next cycle. Once this is completed, the beer hose can be connected directly to the bright tank using a sanitary fitting such as a tri-clamp. Pressure in the bright tank is used to dispense beer to the bottling machine. By using CO_2 head pressure to push the beer, no pumps are used since these can be a source of air pickup before the beer reaches the bottle. All the clamps connecting the hoses and the connection to the pump inlet should be checked to ensure they are tight. With tri-clamps, this can be achieved by tightening the clamp nut as the clamp hinge is tapped with the back of a channel lock plier or another clamp. All hoses should be packed with water (preferably deaerated) and the water should be pushed out with beer, this eliminates air from

FIGURE 11.6. Adjustable carbon dioxide (CO_2) regulator on a bright beer tank vent line. (Courtesy K. Ockert)

the hoses, and the pump if used, all the way to the filler. Starting procedures vary based on the type of machine used. They are different for machines using a pressure bowl than for those that do not. (Meheen Manufacturing machines, for instance, do not have a pressure bowl but rather use a dispensing tank using headspace pressure to push the beer through a filler manifold [Fig. 11.7]). One element of the starting process, however, is similar regardless of the type of machine used, and that is the need to cool the equipment after cleaning and sanitizing to establish constant flow conditions. Warm equipment warms the beer and causes the CO_2 to come out of suspension and foam, which causes bottle losses. This cooling can be accomplished by pumping cold sanitizing solution through the hoses and manifold and pushing it out with chilled beer. It is important that all the sanitizer is pushed out, and this can be checked by pH and taste.

Machines with pressure bowls take a little longer for the equipment to cool to beer temperature simply because they have more mass and more contact surfaces to cool and typically one or two "bowl dumps" are used. Typically, with smaller manifold-type machines, brewers lose only a few rounds of bottles before the equipment is cooled to the point needed for normal operations.

With counterpressure fillers, when the bottles are pressurized for filling, brewers need to make sure that the pressure is adequate to maintain the level of CO_2 in solution. Because the beer is warming on its way to the bottle, generally the counterpressure in the bottle should be as needed for the beer condition. This means that if the beer contains 2.59 volumes of CO_2 at 32°F (0°C) in the tank and the beer temperature has risen to 34°F (1°C) by the time it reaches the bottle, there should be slightly higher pressure at the bottle to compensate for the increased temperature of the beer. It is easy to estimate the increased pressures required by referring to Table 11.1.

The packaging process for bottling and canning lines should include rinsing of the containers prior to being loaded onto the filling machinery to ensure they are free of dust and foreign materials. Another reason for rinsing is that it provides a wetting film that will help reduce foam during the filling process. Bottle rinsing can be accomplished using several different types of rinsing machines. Twist rinsers are just as the name implies, a set of twisting rails that invert the bottles, rinsing them as they move, and then draining and returning them to the upright position to be placed on the filler. Another more manual type of bottle rinser commonly used by smaller operations involves bottle-handling plates that grab an array of bottles by the necks. The handling plate is placed with the bottles inverted into a rinse tray, where all the bottles are rinsed and drained at the same time (Fig. 11.8). From the rinser, the bottles are manually placed on the bottling machine to be filled.

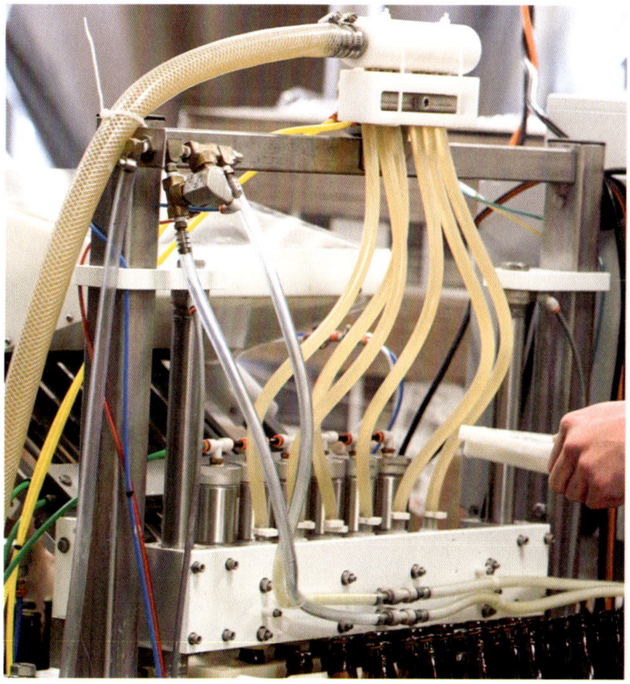

FIGURE 11.7. A filler manifold system supplying valves on a small filler. (Courtesy Meheen Manufacturing Inc.)

FIGURE 11.8. Bottle rinse tray to rinse bottles before manual placement on the filler inlet table. (Courtesy Meheen Manufacturing Inc.)

After bottle rinsing, bottles are moved into the filler and filling heads are sealed on the bottle. Prior to filling, most fillers have a pre-evacuation process where atmosphere in the bottle is drawn out by vacuum and then replaced with CO_2 to a pressure level appropriate for the conditions of the beer being poured. Once the pressure is correct in the bottle, the filling will start. Ideally, the pressure in the bottle will be sufficient enough to maintain all the carbonation in solution of the beer, providing a dark pour (no foam or bubbles during filling). On many smaller fillers, beer flow control is accomplished using a tubing pinch valve that effectively pinches a silicone beer hose to start and stop beer flow to the bottle.

Once bottles are full and the filling has stopped, the pressure inside needs to be released in a controlled manner to avoid excess gushing or foaming over. This process is different for different machines. Generally speaking, machines that have the crowning station some distance from the filling position will reduce the pressure from the bottle slowly in a process known as snifting. This is done to ensure the bottle is not foaming over as it travels to the crowner. Once the full bottle reaches the crowner, it is desirable to cause the beer to foam up to displace air from the neck of the bottle. There are several ways of doing this, one of the more common is sending a tiny stream of hot water into the bottle as it enters the crowner. The hot water acts to disturb the CO_2 from solution, causing it to foam. Fillers that have the filling and crowning stations right next to each other can actually have the controls for foaming the beer built into the filling head so that the beer is foaming as it moves to the crowner. Foaming in this case is a rapid release of pressure within the bottle or a pulse to agitate the beer, releasing CO_2 from solution. Crowning on foam is essential to ensure low air and long shelf life regardless of the type of filler.

Crowners on small machines must use some kind of sorter and positioner so that the crown is presented to the crowning head in the correct orientation. A rotary drum sorter with crown guides is shown in Figure 11.9. The crown fits into the crowning head and pneumatic pressure is applied to force the crown onto the bottle and crimp down. A crimp gauge can be used to measure over the crown and check the tightness of the closure (Fig. 11.10). After the bottle is crowned, beer residue is rinsed off the bottle (Fig. 11.11).

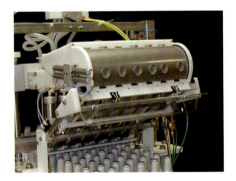

FIGURE 11.9. Crown sorter and guides in a small filler. (Courtesy Meheen Manufacturing Inc.)

FIGURE 11.10. Crown crimp gauge. (Courtesy K. Ockert)

FIGURE 11.11. Bottles are rinsed with water postcrowning. (Courtesy Meheen Manufacturing Inc.)

Once a steady flow has been established on the filling line, maintaining the smooth operation of the bottle filler becomes a process of fine-tuning and watching for trouble areas, such as excess foaming; bottle, crown, and label supply; and beer temperature. Tracking the filler's performance, ensuring proper filling and crowning, and making adjustments as needed keeps the process going. Effective operations also include maintaining a proper supply of bottles, crowns, labels, and case packing of finished products. Each brewery and brewing operation will be different, so when it comes to packaging operations, brewers should be flexible and adaptable (Fig. 11.12).

• SUMMARY

Packaging in general is the most technically challenging and difficult process any brewer, large or small, ever undertakes. To accomplish great results and ensure quality is maintained for the consumer, strict attention to many details come into play.

- Beer should be properly conditioned, carbonated, and cold. Generally speaking, beer at 30–32°F (–1 to 0°C) in the bright tank is desirable for packaging and helps to keep CO_2 in solution while filling.

- Carbonation stability can be affected by freeze/thaw cycles in the bright tank if the glycol cooling system is too cold, so the glycol temperatures should be kept between 28 and 30°F (–2 to –1°C) to avoid this possibility.

- Filtering prior to the bright tank using centrifugal pumps and hoses is one area that unwanted air can enter into the beer. The type and condition of the filter itself can also contribute to air pickup prior to the bright tank through loose clamps or faulty pump seals. Brewer should ensure that filters, pumps, hoses, and valves are all in good working order and well maintained and that lines are packed with water and pushed out with beer to ensure low air pickup.

- Sterile, clean equipment throughout the beer handling process, including the filler and crowner, is essential. One area that sometimes is overlooked when cleaning is the crowner heads. Because beer foam gets into the crowner during operations, each head needs to be washed and cleaned thoroughly after each use to keep mold and other contaminates off the swage, which could be transferred to the bottles being crowned.

- Only hoses suited for connection between the bright tank and the filler should be used. In some cases, using a standard brewers hose can cause beer dispensing issues at the filler. Minimizing the distance from the bright tank to the filler reduces temperature differences. Under warm weather conditions, it might be beneficial to insulate the beer hose feeding the filler to maintain chilled beer temperatures.

- Brewers should avoid trying to bottle from single-shell tanks in a cold room since it is very difficult to get the beer cold enough and to maintain consistent carbonation for packaging.

- Bottles should be rinsed with sterile water before filling. This helps to cool the bottle and provides a wetting film that helps reduce foam during the pouring of the beer.

- An adequate CO_2 supply system should always be available to supply the bottling machine as well as the bright tank. Inadequate CO_2 volumes or pressures can cause CO_2 to come out of solution and bottling machines to fail in filling bottles properly.

FIGURE 11.12. Typical arrangement for a small-scale bottle filler. Filler is placed in close proximity to the bright beer tank for better control of temperature and flow. (Courtesy Meheen Manufacturing Inc.)

CHAPTER 12

Small-Scale Canning Lines

JAMES GORDON
Cask Brewing Systems

This chapter covers three different canning systems, manual, semiautomatic, and fully automatic canning lines, some of the basic steps of their operations, and how to clean them.

From a quality point of view the aluminum can is a great container: it is lightweight, recyclable, completely protects the product from light contamination, and provides a tight seal that resists oxygen ingress and helps keep the product fresh. Larger brewers have used cans in one form or another since the 1930s, but only since the early 2000s has craft-brewed beer been put into cans and gained acceptance by customers. The advent of small-scale manual and automatic in-line canning lines has allowed a growing number of craft brewers to bring their beer to market in cans.

The benefits of using cans for smaller brewers include

- low capital cost to enter the packaging market,
- ease of operation,
- compact design and flexibility of orientation, and
- low levels of dissolved oxygen.

MANUAL TWO-HEAD LINES

There are very small, two-head, manually operated can fillers available for brewpub-size operations covering a 2 × 5-foot footprint (Fig. 12.1). These are very manual and can be run by a single operator, but most are typically run by two people to make about 10–15 cases per hour. To maximize production, three people can operate the line and produce as many at 23 cases per hour with one person filling, one person seaming, and the other person six-packing and stacking. These are very simple machines and require minimal upfront investment.

Commonly, a sink is installed next to the line to both prerinse empty cans and postrinse them after they are filled. The operator has about 5 or 6 seconds to prerinse the cans, drain them, and get them ready while the cans are filling on the two filler heads. The person operating the filler can easily prerinse and keep up with the person operating the seamer. Typically, there is a table mounted on wheels that can be wheeled directly to the dispense end and the six-pack rings can be applied there by the person operating the seamer.

Beer for the filler is dispensed straight from the bright beer tank using controlled head pressure. Temperature is also controlled. Temperature and pressure control are critical with this type of fill. These two parameters must be set at consistent levels to achieve proper fill levels and to achieve the filling rates desired.

FIGURE 12.1. Two-head manual can filler with a one-head seamer features an automatic shutoff and compact design and is capable of filling eight cans per minute. (Courtesy Cask Brewing Systems)

SEMIAUTOMATED THREE-HEAD LINES

Figure 12.2 shows a semiautomated can filler and seamer. This system uses three filling heads and one seamer. Instead of picking up cans from the filler, placing them onto the seamer, and then manually placing ends on top of the cans, the process is automated so the operator loads empty cans on the infeed side and takes full cans off the discharge side.

The footprint of the semiautomated line is still quite compact at 2 × 6 feet, and two operators can produce up to 15 cans per minute (cpm) (37 cases per hour). All that is needed to operate these machines is a 220-volt, 15-amp circuit and a small air compressor.

FULLY AUTOMATIC LINES

Figure 12.3 shows a five-head filler with a 2 × 10-foot footprint. This line uses the same seamer as the manual system and the same lid application system but it now fills with five heads and can produce 30–35 cpm (about 85 cases per hour).

At 35 cpm, the operator is no longer feeding cans into the machine manually. The system involves automatically loading the cans a layer at a time from the pallet load. The cans flow through to the filler heads, through the lid application, through the seamer, and then onto a collection table.

Mechanized six-pack ring application becomes necessary, especially if these machines are doubled up to run in parallel, effectively producing 70 cpm (175 cases per hour).

DEPALLETIZING

The can pallets come with strapping tape holding everything together. Cans are extremely unstable until they are filled, and once the tape is cut, it would be very easy to have the pallet fall apart completely without something to stabilize it. Typically, the simple solution is to construct a three-sided box to drive the pallet into and support it. In order to feed cans into the machine, there needs to be a way to get them off the pallet. Cans come in pallets that are 8 feet high. The pallets have several layers of cans, depending on the can size. For 12-oz. (355-mL) cans, there are 21 layers with 389 cans per layer and 8,169 cans per pallet. For 16-oz. (473-mL) cans, there are 16 layers with 389 cans per layer and 6,224 cans per pallet. Each layer has a plastic divider.

For manual canning lines, the operator can feed cans off the pallet directly without a depalletizer; however, a rudimentary semiautomated depalletizer is shown in Figures 12.4 through 12.6.

FIGURE 12.2. Semiautomated can filler features three filling heads and one seamer and is capable of filling 15 cans per minute. (Courtesy Cask Brewing Systems)

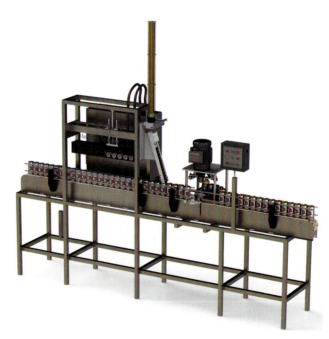

FIGURE 12.3. Five-head automatic can filler and seamer. It is capable of filling 35 cans per minute. (Courtesy Cask Brewing Systems)

In the semiautomated depalletizer, the operator will pause at each layer to raise the pallet up with either a forklift or a pallet lifter and then will go up a stair or ladder to pull one layer of cans onto the feed table at a time. It takes about 15 minutes at average speed to run through each layer. The infeed table has a height equal to the top layer of the incoming pallet. It should have a shaker motor on it to help move the cans down through the prerinser and then onto the filler/seamer and to avoid bridging.

The operator also has to keep up with feeding the ends or lids by stocking them into the can lid chute. Ends come in sleeves of 554 pieces. The operator loads the ends and makes sure there are always ends supplying the seamer. This system can be run as a two-man operation. One operator is there to ensure that the machine does not run out of cans and ends and to clear any can jams that occur. The other operator does the packoff, either assembling filled cans into six-packs or straight into cases if they are sold as singles or into cartons, six-pack cartons, 12-pack cartons, etc. There are a number of final package options discussed later in this chapter.

With the automatic five-head machines, the can layers must be fed in faster and, at these production speeds, an automatic depalletizer becomes more necessary (Fig. 12.7).

The pallet of cans is driven straight into a three-sided cage on the depalletizer, which raises the cans up automatically, one tier sheet at a time, and sweeps the

FIGURE 12.4. Loading the infeed shaker table. Position the cans as close as possible and parallel to the right side or rear of the shaker table. Slide the blue plastic divider to carefully transfer the can layer onto the tabletop. (Courtesy Cask Brewing Systems)

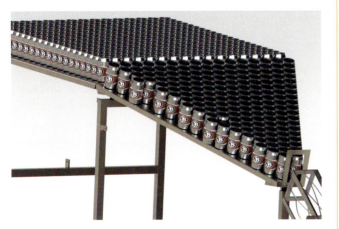

FIGURE 12.5. Cans are extremely unstable until packed together by vibration from the shaker motor. Raise the table to move the cans down to the filler/seamer by gravity. (Courtesy Cask Brewing Systems)

FIGURE 12.6. Fill the conveyer all the way to the gate below the filler tubes. (Courtesy Cask Brewing Systems)

FIGURE 12.7. Fully automated can depalletizer for 30–70 cans per minute. It features a three-sided pallet cage. The pallet of cans is placed in and the top sheet taken off. A lift moves the pallet up and slides the cans onto the infeed conveyor. The machine then removes and stacks the tier sheets. (Courtesy Cask Brewing Systems)

FIGURE 12.8. Five-head automatic filler with an automatic depalletizer. (Courtesy Cask Brewing Systems)

layers of cans off onto a conveyor, feeding them down to the rinser, which runs down the side of the depalletizer and into the filler. Figure 12.8 shows a five-head line with a fully automated depalletizer.

Craft brewers especially require flexibility in layout designs to accommodate their brewery premises. Figures 12.9–12.11 show various layouts for the five-head line. Figure 12.12 shows a doubled-up five-head line configuration.

FILLING

The filling technology on small canning lines is quite a contrast to the high-speed rotary systems. One method is to use flow control at each filler head. Basically, the filler is supplied directly from the bright beer tank and uses

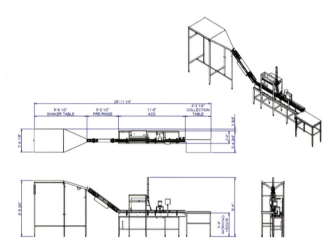

FIGURE 12.9. Five-head filler in-line layout with manual depalletizing. (Courtesy Cask Brewing Systems)

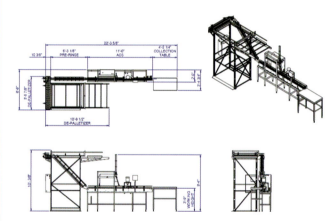

FIGURE 12.11. Five-head filler in-line layout with an automatic depalletizer. (Courtesy Cask Brewing Systems)

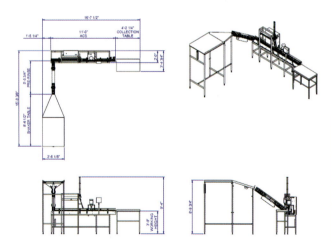

FIGURE 12.10. Five-head filler 90° layout with manual depalletizing. (Courtesy Cask Brewing Systems)

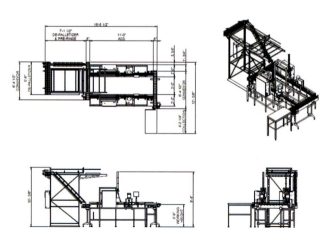

FIGURE 12.12. Two five-head fillers paired up with an automatic depalletizer. (Courtesy Cask Brewing Systems)

controlled head pressure and beer temperature. The closer to the tank that the filler is situated, the better control of the temperature, especially during warm seasons. The beer is run through a 0.1875-inch (5-mm) restriction hose so that the beer is flowing at a slow, calm rate and not foaming.

Unlike a high-speed fill line, these machines need to create foam for a quality fill. Since there is limited undercover gassing in the relatively slow system, there is the possibility of trapping air in the container. By seaming on foam, the machines can achieve very low air pickup with oxygen levels under 20–50 parts per billion.

Prior to filling, the cans are gassed with a small amount of carbon dioxide (CO_2). The CO_2 enters through a long tube dropping down into the bottom of the can. As it gasses the can with CO_2, it evacuates most of the air present. CO_2 is three times heavier than air. Air moves to the top and out of the can, but the key is gassing the can slowly. When gassing the can very slowly with CO_2, there is no turbulence and the CO_2 simply fills the entire container. To help achieve a quiet fill with low air pickup, the fill head drops down to the bottom of the can and fills the can with the head submerged. Five heads gas while the five heads are filling in this in-line system. Figure 12.13 shows a five-head filler manifold with the five-head pre-evacuation station.

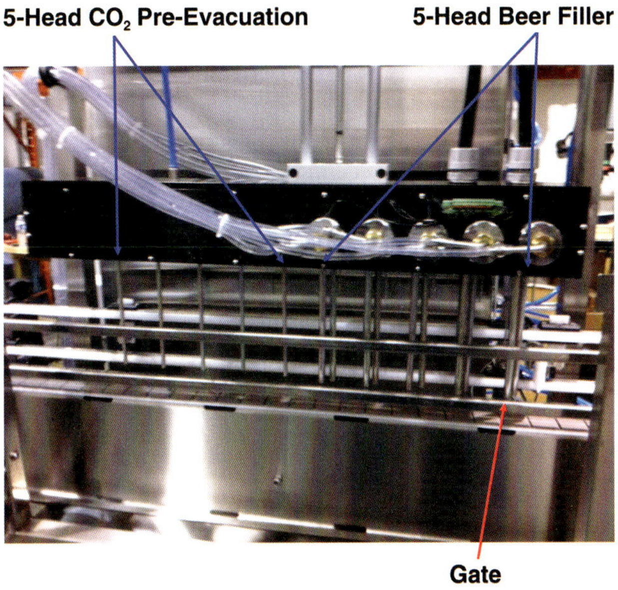

The five evacuated cans then move into the filler position. There is a fill tube and a foam tube for each container, 10 tubes in all for filling five cans at a time. The cans are filled from the bottom into a CO_2 environment. There is also a fill sensor in each can (Fig. 12.14). The fill sensor is adjustable and controls the actual height of the fill. The sensor can be raised or lowered to adjust the fill higher or lower. The sensor runs on low voltage and contact is made as foam touches the sensor tube, sending a signal to stop the beer flow and lift the heads out of the cans. By filling into a CO_2 environment, there is very little or no mixing of air at this point in the process. Figure 12.15 shows the heads involved with both the CO_2 pre-evacuation and the filling process.

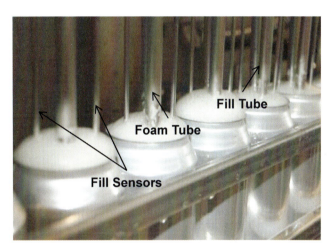

FIGURE 12.14. Fill tube, foam tube, and fill sensors. The fill sensors are adjustable and determine the height of the product in the can. (Courtesy Cask Brewing Systems)

FIGURE 12.13. Five-head filler with five-head carbon dioxide (CO_2) pre-evacuation. There are 10 cans under the fill heads. The first five are purged with CO_2 as the last five (already purged) are filled with beer. (Courtesy Cask Brewing Systems)

FIGURE 12.15. Filler tubes (left) and carbon dioxide (CO_2) pre-evacuation tube (right). (Courtesy Cask Brewing Systems)

As the can is leaving the fill area, it should be slightly foaming up over the top and actively foaming until the lid is applied to it. This is somewhat similar in concept to the bottle jetting and crowning process using the CO_2 coming out of the beer to flush air out of the headspace as the crown is applied on foam.

A top up valve and top up timer are used to create foam when necessary. These two work in conjunction. When foam hits the sensor and stops the fill, the heads then start to withdraw from the can. The top up valve and top up timer are set up to reopen the fill valves as they withdraw from the can. This replaces the displaced volume from the tubes in the can and also creates turbulence because now it is adding beer as it is coming up and thus creating foam. If the beer is very cold or has a very low carbonation level, the machine will use foam creation valves. The foam creation valves essentially work the same way as a draft beer faucet at a bar to create a little foam on top of a glass. By cracking the faucet valve open a little and very quickly, the beer comes through a restriction and creates foam. In this case, a shuttle opens and closes the beer valve. It forces the beer through a pinhole in the center of the front shuttle; so the beer comes out at high velocity and creates the desired foam.

Breweries using small canning lines are filling from 5- to 100-barrel tanks. These tanks normally have refrigeration jackets, and the beer at the start of the day will be at the temperature set by the controller—typically 34°F (1°C). Then as the contents of the tank drop during packaging, the beer that is sitting right next to the refrigeration jacket can often be one or two degrees colder than the starting beer temperature. This has an effect on the foam level in the cans. As the colder beer flows, suddenly the foam level drops and air pickup can increase. The machine allows the operator to anticipate this and very quickly compensate, increasing the amount of foam or increasing the top up.

● LID DISPENSER

After the can is filled, an end or lid is placed over it prior to seaming. The basic lid dispenser takes one lid at a time off a stack of lids (Fig. 12.16). However, the can lid is convex, and if dropped directly onto a filled can, it will trap air in the convex space, which will lead to high air pickup in the sealed container. To avoid this situation, CO_2 gas is run into holes inside the lid chute. The CO_2 comes up into that convex area underneath the lid and then also cascades down onto the top of the can and onto the top of the foam so that the lid is falling on

FIGURE 12.16. Lid dispenser holds one sleeve of 552 lids. The lid automatically drops when the can is seamed. The slide holds seven lids. (Courtesy Cask Brewing Systems)

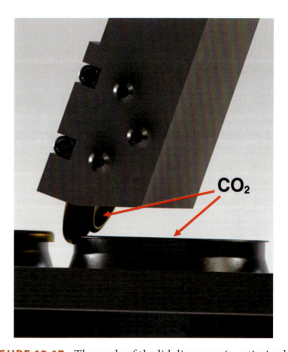

FIGURE 12.17. The angle of the lid dispenser is optimized for can contact. The leading edge of the can grabs and pulls the lid out. Carbon dioxide (CO_2) is dispensed through the bottom of the slide to make sure the top surface of the product is covered with a layer of CO_2. (Courtesy Cask Brewing Systems)

CO_2 rather than on foam (Fig. 12.17). CO_2 is running continuously and evacuating any air that might have been trapped.

● SEAMING

As described in Chapter 7, the seaming process starts by placing the lid or end onto the top of the can, which has a body flange. The seamers on small can lines are the same as those found on the large high-speed rotary 2,000-cpm machines. The seam is formed on these small machines essentially the same way as it is on higher-speed lines. The can enters the seamer with its two seaming rolls and a seaming chuck (Fig. 12.18). The can is lifted into the chuck, which spins the can at about 500 rpm (Fig. 12.19). The first-operation seaming roll comes in and causes the end hook to curl over the body flange's body hook. The second-operation seaming roll then comes in and squeezes the end hook and body hook together, forming the tightened double seam (Fig. 12.20). There is a gum material on the body hook to help completely seal the seam.

● DRY END PACKING

Filled cans must be rinsed after the fill to remove any beer present. In order to avoid corrosion weakening of the tab opening, it is advisable to warm the cans past their dew point using a can warmer or to at least allow for adequate ventilation in the final package so condensation can dissipate.

There are many different options for the final package. Cans may be packed loose into cases or trays or grouped into four- or six-packs and then packed into cases, half cases, or trays. Many craft brewers have adopted specially designed plastic rings to make four-packs or six-packs. The rings form caps that cover the entire top of the can and are relatively easy to apply by hand, although machines are available for automatic application. Standard plastic six-pack rings can be applied with small machines now available. Finally, paperboard wraps can be used for a package that adds more marketing space.

● MACHINE CIP

The fill heads are all fed by 0.1875-inch (5-mm) restriction hoses, and cleaning the machine is similar to cleaning a draft line. The cleaning-in-place (CIP) mode on

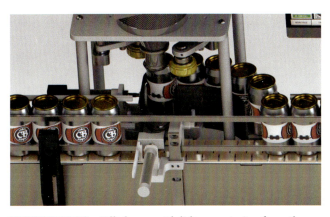

FIGURE 12.18. Filled cans with lids are entering from the left into the seamer. (Courtesy Cask Brewing Systems)

FIGURE 12.19. Seamer lift table. The lift table raises the can to the seaming chuck. The seaming chuck spins the can. (Courtesy Cask Brewing Systems)

FIGURE 12.20. Seaming roll A curls the lid end hook around and underneath the can body hook. Seaming roll B compresses the seam. A = Seaming roll #1; B = seaming roll #2; C = seaming chuck; D = seaming roll spindle; and E = pivot arm. (Courtesy Cask Brewing Systems)

the touch screen (Fig. 12.21) is basically there to shut off the sensors so that the machine will run continuously. It takes about 15–20 gallons of 1–2% caustic at a temperature between 140 and 158°F (60 and 70°C) to recirculate and clean. Some manual spraying down of the splash areas is done as well.

The fill valves are cleaned by leaving cans in place to clean the inside and outside of the fill valves. There is a cycle that the fill head goes through so that all of the insides of the valve, including the foaming apertures, are cleaned. It is critical not to exceed 158°F (70°C) so as not to damage the plastic fill hoses. Hot temperatures will have a negative effect on the polyvinyl chloride (PVC) hoses. Over time, they will stretch, and if the inside diameter of the hoses start to vary because of this stretching, there will be varying fill rates across the fill heads.

Once the caustic recirculation is finished, the system is flushed with water and tested for neutral pH. Many breweries follow the water rinse with a sanitizer flush and leave it packed for the next day. Peracetic acid is a common sanitizer for this purpose. Breweries can then chase the sanitizer out with beer and start right away without the necessity of going through another cleaning cycle.

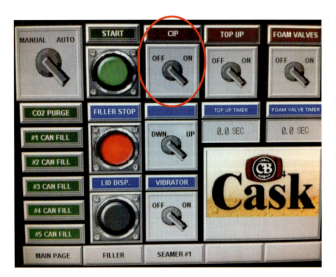

FIGURE 12.21. Cleaning-in-place (CIP) of the automated five-head line. A proper cleaning should focus on all the splash areas, including the seaming station, fill location, and under the lid dispense tray. The whole system should be sprayed down with a hose and then dried as much as possible using compressed air. What cannot be dried with air should be wiped down with a paper towel or a clean, dry cloth. (Courtesy Cask Brewing Systems)

● SEAM CHECKS

How are seams measured accurately to maintain seam integrity? High-technology seam-checking equipment is available to evaluate how well the seamer is operating. Figures 12.22 and 12.23 show a digital workstation and seam-cutting station, respectively. The seam evaluation equipment not only measures the seam dimensions and automatically compares them to specifications, it actually shows the seam visually and helps detect flaws.

Without that kind of equipment, the next best thing is to manually tear the seam apart and use manual instruments to measure it. This will provide basic measurements but will not allow a look at the actual seam

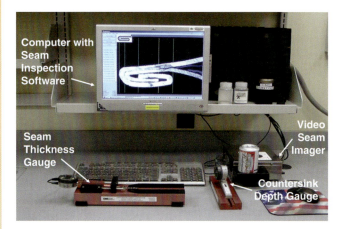

FIGURE 12.22. Digital seam inspection workstation. (Courtesy CMC-KUHNKE Inc.)

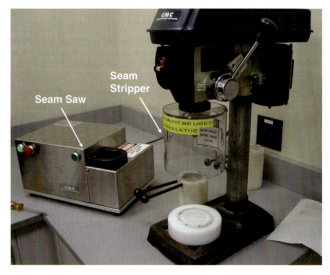

FIGURE 12.23. Seam saw and seam stripper equipment at a seam-cutting workstation. (Courtesy CMC-KUHNKE Inc.)

to check for flaws. Even with the best analysis equipment for seams on the market, it is still valuable to know how to perform a manual seam teardown because it is the only way to fully inspect the seam. The manual teardown relies on a relatively inexpensive can seam micrometer, a caliper micrometer, and a pair of side cutters for tearing the seam apart (Fig. 12.24).

A can seam micrometer is calibrated in thousandths of an inch. The can company will supply the specific target dimensions to be evaluated, but a typical seam representation is in Figure 12.25. There are four critical dimensions to measure when doing a can seam teardown:
seam height, seam width, body hook height, and cover hook height. When they all meet specifications, then the seams should be of adequate quality.

Before taking any measurements of the can, the evaluation process should start with an evaluator simply looking at and feeling the seam. It should look and feel like a nice, smooth, consistent rolled seam. There should be no damage to the body or cover of the can; this includes any warping or impact points or fractures of the seam itself.

When formed properly, there are measureable dimensions, including seam width and height. These give a very useful and quick evaluation. There are slightly more complicated measurements of seam thickness to see just how the cover and body hooks have come together.

The can seam micrometer fits on top of the can seam. It is easy to center at the correct height and then tighten the can seam dial until it is just tight. The scale will indicate the seam thickness (Fig. 12.26).

To measure the seam height, it is much quicker and easier to use a dial or digital caliper micrometer (Fig. 12.27).

Every can company is going to have a different set of seam specifications. Each will also have setup parameters and operating parameters. Sometimes the can seams are in specification ("in spec"), but they could be very close to the edge of the operating parameters, which tend to be wider than setup parameters. When setting up a seamer, try to be right in the middle of the seam specifications provided, not at the outer edge. This is because as a seamer loosens over

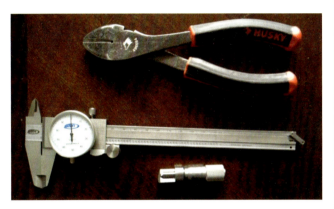

FIGURE 12.24. Side cutters, caliper micrometer, and can seam micrometer. (Courtesy Cask Brewing Systems)

FIGURE 12.26. Manually measuring the seam width with a can seam micrometer. Use proper pressure and orientation; take two or three measurements per seam and average them; and be wary of variations more than 0.003 inch (0.0762 mm) per seam. A special property of the can seam micrometer is its curved surface. (Courtesy Cask Brewing Systems)

FIGURE 12.25. Seam representation with typical dimensions. (Courtesy Cask Brewing Systems)

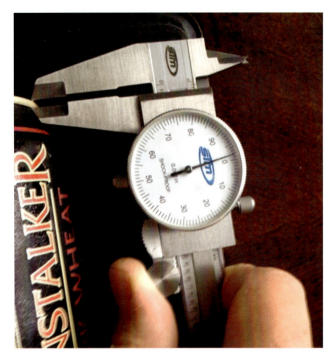

FIGURE 12.27. Manually measuring the can seam height with a dial caliper micrometer. Use proper pressure and orientation and measure the distance from the bottom to the top of the seam at various points around the can. The seam height should be relatively consistent, although some slight variances are to be expected, i.e., 0.001–0.002 inch (0.0254–0.0508 mm). An advantage of the dial caliper micrometer over the can seam micrometer for this measurement is speed. (Courtesy Cask Brewing Systems)

time it will stray from specifications, causing beer to be shipped with problematic seams.

The seamer goes through the repetition of the process, squeezing metal repetitively, over and over again, millions of times. It is never going to tighten on its own; in fact, over time, it is always going to loosen. Try to set up a little bit on the high end or on the low end of the seam thickness so that, when it expands, which it very often will on the first few thousand cases, it will stop in the middle of the range.

Can seam measurements must be done every production day. It is important to build these checks into the daily operation routine; this is not something that is checked periodically. Breweries starting up a new line will begin by checking their seams every day, every hour, or every 5 minutes and perhaps making some small adjustments. They then notice that nothing is significantly changing beyond the first few thousand or so cases, so they stop taking measurements and eventually run into major quality problems as the adjustments loosen up.

There are a number of ways in which a seamer can go out of adjustment. If a brewery is not on top of it and does not take the few minutes necessary to perform a can seam teardown and measurement, suddenly it can have a real problem.

After measuring the seam width and seam height, the end or cover hook and body hook dimensions are measured. This involves tearing the top of the can off without damaging the cover hook and the body. Figures 12.28 through 12.35 illustrate this process.

FIGURE 12.28. The first step of a manual seam teardown is to tear away most of the material on the cover using cutters. Use caution since the aluminum is sharp. (Courtesy Cask Brewing Systems)

FIGURE 12.29. With a manual seam teardown, once a little hole is carved, make a cut in the lid toward the seam. (Courtesy Cask Brewing Systems)

Small-Scale Canning Lines • **183**

FIGURE 12.30. With a manual seam teardown, once the cut is made, tear the cover until the top of the can body is exposed. (Courtesy Cask Brewing Systems)

FIGURE 12.31. With a manual seam teardown, remove the top of the cover from the can body, exposing the inside surface of the can body all the way around. (Courtesy Cask Brewing Systems)

FIGURE 12.32. With a manual seam teardown, make a little cut, just cutting through the seam. Push down and some of the gummy sealing residue is apparent. That residue is inside the end and is seen on a very tight seam. (Courtesy Cask Brewing Systems)

FIGURE 12.33. With a manual seam teardown, extract the finished end hook from the finished body hook. It must be undamaged for measuring. (Courtesy Cask Brewing Systems)

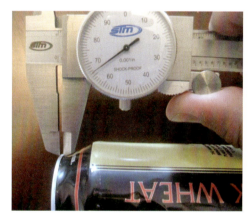

FIGURE 12.34. Measuring the body hook with a caliper. (Courtesy Cask Brewing Systems)

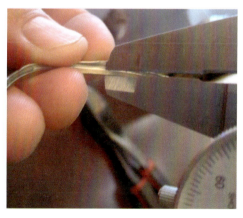

FIGURE 12.35. Measuring the end hook with a caliper. (Courtesy Cask Brewing Systems)

Many people make the mistake of putting too much pressure on the caliper when they are closing it. When taking the measurements, simply close it and then take your thumb off and see where it sits, with no added pressure. With a little pressure, it is possible to condense the measurement another 0.003 or 0.004 inch. That does not sound like a lot, but with such a tiny measurement, it can be the difference between an in-spec and out-of-spec condition.

Figure 12.36 shows two different end or cover hooks. Notice how flat and smooth the surface is on the inside of the top cover hook. Now look at the bad one at the bottom and see how it is bulged out and dimpled instead of being nice and flat. When measuring a cover hook, look for two things: measurements within the specifications that the can company has provided and visually see whether it is properly formed, flattened, and ironed out.

When performing a can seam teardown, be very careful to get the dimensions exactly right because there are other dimensions that are not taken. A manual can seam teardown, for instance, cannot measure the seam overlap because it has been effectively removed. Instead, there is an inference that if the seam height and seam thickness are good, the body hook and cover hook are good and the seam overlap should be good as well.

The teardown is a partial picture, so it is important that the measurements stay very close to the center of the specification so that everything else will be good as well.

● ROLL ADJUSTMENT

What affects the dimensions of the seams and whether they are formed properly has to do with the relative position of the seaming rolls as they come into contact with the can against the chuck. The difference between the small-scale seamer and high-speed seamers is that the small-scale seaming rolls are driven in contact with the can through air pressure (pneumatics), whereas higher-speed seamers are cam driven. Pneumatics is a little bit slower than high-speed cam-driven seamers, but this allows extra time to form the seam. When setting up the seamer, there is an order of adjustment:

1. Base plate pressure
2. First-operation seaming roll height
3. First-operation seaming roll proximity
4. Second-operation seaming roll height
5. Second-operation seaming roll proximity

The first adjustment made is the base plate pressure. In the case of high-speed machines, it is called pin height. It is basically how much pressure is in play on this can body as a function of how hard the base is pushing the can up against the chuck. Adjustment points are indicated in Figure 12.37. The pressure must be firm and the base plate must be able to continuously spin at about 800 rpm. Press on the side of the can, and if there is enough pressure, there is a little pinging sound when the can pops back. A sign of inadequate pressure is a very low body hook.

The next step is adjusting the position of the first-operation seaming roll. Figure 12.38 shows the adjustment set screws for setting the height for both the first- and second-operation seaming rolls. This is a function of how high the seaming roll is relative to the chuck and how close it gets to the chuck. The seam height is controlled by setting a gap. Figure 12.39 shows the first-operation seaming roll with its set screw, which holds it in place, for height adjustments. When the screw is loosened, the roll can either be raised or lowered.

FIGURE 12.36. Two cover hooks. The top is a normal flat and smooth example, the bottom has bumps and dimples. (Courtesy Cask Brewing Systems)

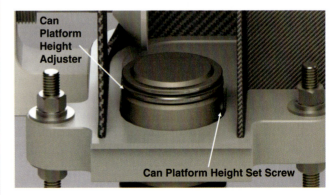

FIGURE 12.37. Base plate adjustment points. (Courtesy Cask Brewing Systems)

To adjust the seaming roll height, first set the machine controls into hand or manual mode.

- Loosen the set bolt, which is located on the arm directly above the seaming roll (Fig. 12.40 top).
- Grab the nut at the base of the seaming roll (or use an Allen key [Fig. 12.40 middle]) to turn the seaming roll. Clockwise moves the roll up. Counterclockwise moves it down.
- Observe the gap between the top surface of the chuck and the overhanging section of the seaming roll (Fig. 12.40 bottom). There should be approximately one paper width of gap apparent on the first-operation seaming roll (0.003–0.005 inch [0.0762–0.127 mm]). Approximately 1.5 times that for the second-operation seaming roll.

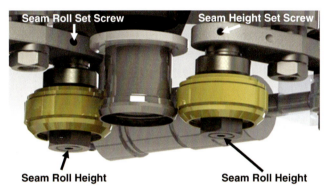

FIGURE 12.38. Adjustment points for setting the first- and second-operation seaming rolls. (Courtesy Cask Brewing Systems)

FIGURE 12.39. Loosening the height adjustment set screw. (Courtesy Cask Brewing Systems)

- Once the seaming roll height has been adjusted, retighten the set bolt.

The next adjustment is the proximity of the first-operation seaming roll to the chuck (Fig. 12.41).

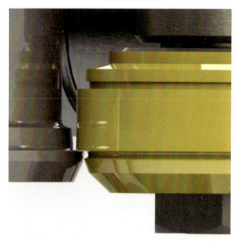

FIGURE 12.40. Seaming roll height adjustment. **Top**, The set bolt is located on the arm directly above the seaming roll. **Middle**, The nut is at the base of the seaming roll. An Allen key can be used in the hole in the middle of the nut. **Bottom**, There is a gap between the top surface of the chuck and the overhanging section of the seaming roll. (Courtesy Cask Brewing Systems)

Figure 12.42 shows the adjustment points for the first-operation seaming roll proximity.

To adjust the first-operation seaming roll proximity, first set the machine controls into manual mode.

- To adjust the proximity of die #1 (first-operation seaming roll), first move this die into the chuck by turning on the selector switch for die #1. (If the die does not move be sure that the emergency stop [E-stop] buttons are not engaged and that the air is on.)
- Locate the set bolt (or Allen key head) on the block that the piston, which controls the movement of die #1, is threaded into. This set screw must be loosened with two or three full turns.
- Once loosened, the piston can now be rotated with a 0.5-inch wrench.

Rotating the piston on the first-operation seaming roll in a clockwise direction will move the seaming roll CLOSER to the chuck. Watch the gap between the seaming roll and the chuck as the piston is turned.

- Reduce the gap between the seaming roll and the chuck until the roll actually contacts the chuck. You can verify that it is touching by spinning the seaming roll with your fingers as you tighten. You will feel (or see) the chuck begin to spin as you spin the seaming roll once it reaches the point of contact.
- Once this position is reached, perform a first-operation seaming roll test and measure the width of the roll. Look for a consistent 0.074–0.078 inch (1.88–1.98 mm) width. If the width is higher than this, continue moving in the seaming roll *past* the point of initial contact (seaming roll must be placed in the "out" position) to do this. One-half to two-thirds turn increments should be tried until the desired first-operation seam width is achieved.
- Once the position has been adjusted, retighten the set bolt.

Once the first-operation seaming roll is adjusted, adjust the second-operation seaming roll in the same way. Table 12.1 shows a troubleshooting guide to poor seaming performance.

FIGURE 12.41. First-operation seaming roll position relative to the chuck. (Courtesy Cask Brewing Systems)

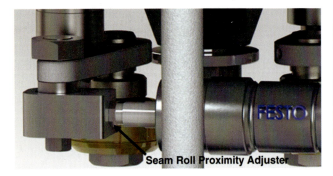

FIGURE 12.42. First-operation seaming roll proximity adjuster. (Courtesy Cask Brewing Systems)

TABLE 12.1. Seam Troubleshooting

Issue	Resolution
Body/cover damage	Dies impacting the can and moving into the chuck too fast
	Dies set too close to the chuck
Long seam height	Die #1 set too far from the chuck
	Die #2 set too close to the chuck
Short body hook	Lift table set too low
	Die #1 set too close to the chuck
	Die #2 set too far from the chuck
Long body hook	Lift table set too high
	Die #1 set too far from the chuck
Short cover hook	Lift table set too high
	Die #1 set too far from the chuck
Long cover hook	Die #1 set too close to the chuck

BEARINGS

There are several sets of bearings in the seamer. There is the base plate that is pushing the can up and spinning, the chuck that is spun by the motor, and then the seaming rolls coming into contact and spinning. Each of these bearing sets will wear over time. At startup at the beginning of the day, do the test seam and teardown and then do a bearing check. This is essentially spinning those rolls to make sure there is no motion or looseness. They have to be solid. The first symptom of worn bearings is typically a dimension on one side of the seam that is not the same as the dimension on the other. Most breweries will figure out a schedule of when the bearings should be changed. These are not expensive replacement parts, but there are factors that can be done to extend bearing life. Beer and cleaning chemicals can wear down bearing seals, so it is important that the bearings are rinsed off as part of the machine cleaning procedure.

Figure 12.43 shows a typical bearing set.

Figure 12.44 shows the inside of the spindle, this is the part that is spinning the chuck.

Figure 12.45 shows the base plate assembly.

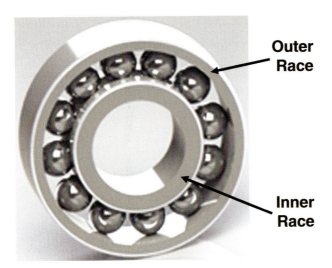

FIGURE 12.43. Typical bearing. When installing bearings on a shaft, always press on the inner race. When installing in a housing, always press on the outer race. (Courtesy Cask Brewing Systems)

FIGURE 12.44. Chuck spindle parts. 1 = Spindle; 2 = spindle housing, place over top of spindle; 3 = bearing, slide onto spindle and into spindle housing; 4 = spindle housing bearing spacer; 5 = spindle bearing spacer; 6 = bearing, slide onto spindle and into spindle housing; and 7 = bearing retainer ring and four bolts. A lock washer and spanner nut are used to install the chuck spindle. DO NOT overtighten the spanner nut since the bearings are NOT designed for preload and overtightening could result in premature failure. Only tighten until a very slight drag is felt and back the nut off one-eighth of a turn. This will ensure adequate tightening. (Courtesy Cask Brewing Systems)

FIGURE 12.45. Base plate parts. 1 = Can table top; 2 = slide bearing onto shaft; 3 = install snap ring retainer into groove; 4 = slide second bearing onto shaft; 5 = insert bearings and can table top into can table top housing (external threads); and 6 = screw table top housing into mate. (Courtesy Cask Brewing Systems)

Check the base that the can spins on. If there is any movement, it will result in a variation in the can seam height. It is going to be higher on one side than on the other. This is a classic example of when to replace those bearings. The bearings that need replacement the most are those on the can lift table.

Seam teardowns and measurements and bearing inspections should be part of a standard operation procedure. In addition, the following simple set of maintenance checks should also be incorporated into the operations of the canning line.

Daily
- Clean canning system with regular CIP procedure

Quarterly
- Check drive belt for wear and tear
- Inspect seam bearings
- Check nut and bolt torques

Annually
- Clean air regulator filter bowls
- Replace beer lines and beer valve O-rings

CHAPTER 13

Bottle Filling and Crowning

BARRY FENSKE
Krones USA

W. G. SPARGO
Anheuser-Busch Companies (retired)

The bottle filler is the key piece of equipment on the bottle line. Its significance cannot be overemphasized because the performance of the line and the quality of the finished package is directly dependent upon the filling operation.

All equipment preceding the filler on the manufacturing line operates, and is designed to operate, to provide a continuous supply of bottles to the filler. As long as the filler is running, it should receive a bottle for every filling station. Similarly, the design and operation of the bottle line following the filler is also based on filler output so as to enable the filler to discharge a filled and crowned bottle from each filling station without interruption. Thus, the entire line before the filler is designed to provide an abundant bottle supply, and the entire line after the filler is planned so that it takes bottles away at least as fast as they are filled and crowned.

Optimum line efficiency occurs when the filler is able to run and satisfactorily produce filled and crowned bottles every minute of the shift or other run-time period. The filler should be able to run at the maximum speed for which it and the entire line are designed and/or set. Needless to say, optimum line efficiency also requires the delivery of good bottles as well as no bottle breakage and no equipment malfunction or breakdown that would adversely affect the filling operation.

Another very important item that is absolutely essential to a satisfactory bottle-filling operation is a properly designed beer supply that not only supplies a sufficient quantity of beer but also delivers the beer to the filler at the proper rate of flow, a rate compatible with all conditions of the bottle-filling operation from start/stop to continuous operation for extended runs. The beer supply operation must also preserve the integrity of the beer by maintaining proper beer temperature and an acceptable equilibrium pressure of carbon dioxide (CO_2) (2.5 bar above saturation pressure). To prevent product punishment and possible damage, it must also maintain the instantaneous rates of flow without exceeding acceptable line speed and maintain a constant supply pressure.

To provide an overview of bottle-filling and -crowning operations, this chapter presents a general discussion of the filler itself followed by a discussion of various facets of the filling operation.

● BOTTLE FILLERS—GENERAL

Bottle fillers can be as small as a stationary, single-filling valve laboratory filler or as large as designers and manufacturers decide they should be (or what is limited by shipping constraints). There are now fillers on the market that have more than 200 filling valves with speed capabilities in excess of 1,400 bottles per minute (bpm).

Generally, bottle fillers are rotary machines. Fillers have been built to rotate either clockwise or counterclockwise. The majority of the bottle fillers in the United States move bottles clockwise, with the empty bottles entering the filler from the left when viewed from the operating position. Smaller and slower fillers, such as 40- and 50-valve machines, may or may not have a timing screw to index bottles into the infeed star. Usually 60-valve and larger fillers are provided with timing screws, also called infeed worms (Fig. 13.1), although with larger fillers, other devices, such as half-pocket chains, have been introduced. A device for stopping the flow of bottles is usually provided at the infeed of the timing screw and is referred to as a bottle stop star, or for higher-speed fillers, a pneumatic infeed gate (Fig. 13.2). The pneumatic infeed gate is only used on fillers running more than 400 bpm and is essentially a sliding stop star that absorbs some line pressure shock at a stop. Actuating this device stops the flow of bottles to the filler and permits operators to clear the filler of bottles for a backup and shut-down condition.

The filling process on modern glass bottle beer fillers using vent tubes can be broken down into the following steps.

- Pre-evacuation
- CO_2 flush
- Evacuation

FIGURE 13.1. Putting bottles on pitch at the filler infeed. (Courtesy Krones USA)

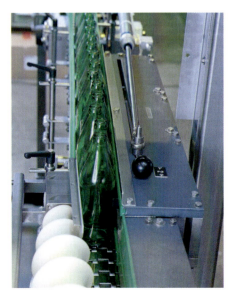

FIGURE 13.2. Pneumatic infeed gate for higher-speed applications. (Courtesy Krones USA)

- CO_2 flush/pressurize
- One-speed filling
- End of filling, and settling
- Snift

Bottle fillers perform the same basic functions, namely indexing empty bottles, transferring them to the filler carousel platforms, lifting them up to the filling valve, placing the bottles under counterpressure, and filling them with beer. Most modern fillers have an additional feature: they pre-evacuate the bottle before it goes under counterpressure. Some have double pre-evacuation.

After filling, bottles are transferred from the filler platforms to the crowner. During the transfer, a blast of hot water, known as jetting, causes the beer to foam slightly from the top of the bottle, which forces air out of the headspace just prior to the actual crowning of the bottles.

Pre-evacuation and jetting are part of the process to get the total package oxygen (TPO) pickup from the filling and crowning down to the lowest possible count it can be. This is critical to extend the shelf life of the packaged product.

While the basics of the bottle-filling operation are the same for all fillers, the equipment used differs with different manufacturers' designs. All fillers have a bowl or similar device to receive beer from the beer supply line and distribute it to the various valves. Filler bowls vary from relatively small center bowls to torus or doughnut-shaped ring bowls to separate bowls placed at a distance from the filler. Most bowls have level-detection devices that signal beer control valves and/or supply pumps. Filler bowls usually have pressurized gas in the bowl above the level of the beer, set about 1 bar above the CO_2 saturation pressure. At least one type of filler uses an annular ring-type chamber to distribute beer to the valves. This chamber is completely filled with product and does not have gas in the chamber. Some fillers require CO_2 to be above and in contact with the beer in the bowl while others claim to achieve similar performance using either CO_2 or compressed air.

Filling concepts, valves, and assemblies are also quite varied. There are, however, three basic approaches to filling.

Filling to a Level

Filling to a level can be achieved by using either long tubes that convey the beer to the lower part of the bottle, with the gas from the bottle being vented out a separate passage of the tube, or the vent tube concept in which beer enters along the inside of the bottle and the gas is vented out a vent tube in the center of the container until beer covers the tip of the tube. There are electronic probe fillers on the market as well that fill to level.

Displacement Filling

Filling by displacement is achieved by using a tube to completely fill the bottle, with the dimensions of the tube determined by the desired displacement.

Filling to Volume

Volumetric filling is a method using either a flow meter or a metering chamber to measure a specific volume of beer for the can. The inductive flow meter measures the required volume. Beer flows into the can, and once the flow meter senses the specified volume, a signal is sent to a programmable logic controller (PLC) to close the filling valve. The metering chamber also measures and fills by volume, but it requires no conductivity.

● BOTTLE-FILLING OPERATIONS

Scope of the Filling Operation

When designing a bottle-filling operation, the designer must pay attention to the conveyor system from and including the bottle rinser to the filler as well as the bottle conveyor system from the crowner to and including the pasteurizer or beer warmer. The designer must also include the beer supply system with the release tanks and their gas supply, tank outlets, and related items, as well as the actual beer line and fittings from the release tanks to the filler bowl and, optionally, the beer-measuring device. The release system is important because it is to supply consistent, quality-approved product to the filler. When the beer has been delivered to the filler intact, it must then be distributed throughout the bowl to the valves and into the bottles with minimum loss and without significant loss of its inherent properties.

Importance of the Filling Operation

The bottle-filling operation encompasses the following steps: handling the product and the clean, empty bottles, placing the product in the bottles, removing headspace air from the filled bottles, and crowning the bottles. And it must perform these steps at the required high speeds without adverse effect on the product, using bottles and crowns from various manufacturers and with minimum product loss. The bottle filler is often times referred to as the key piece of equipment on the line, and as noted, it often determines the design of the early side of the line, which feeds bottles to the filler, as well as the design of the late side of the line, which follows the filler. Filler speed therefore determines line speed, and line efficiency is based on this speed.

The quality and characteristics of the beer can be either preserved or partially lost depending upon the filling operation. The quality of the filling operation is determined primarily by oxygen (O_2) pickup and CO_2 loss during the filling and crowning operation.

Beer Supply

For the filler to produce satisfactorily filled bottles, it must first receive the beer in a satisfactory condition. The majority of modern bottle fillers fill beer at a temperature between 32 and 37°F (0 and 3°C). In Europe, the trend is 43–54°F (6–12°C). The pressure in the finished-beer release tank and release lines should not be allowed to fall below 12–13 pounds per square inch gauge (psig) (preferably using CO_2 counterpressure) or the CO_2 in the beer will be released from the solution. To prevent a drop in pressure at the tank outlet, the outlet fitting must be properly sized for the desired flow rate so that the velocity does not exceed 7.5 feet/second (2.3 m/second). A suitable vortex breaker at the drain outlet may also be used to prevent a vortex from forming and drawing CO_2 into the line with the beer.

The beer line and fittings should be selected to correspond to the expected flow rate of beer through the system. Beer should not be subjected to velocities of more than 7.5 feet/second, and it should not have to negotiate right-angle turns, e.g., as experienced in pipe tees. Large radius elbows should be used for all changes in direction. The only place beer should normally be allowed to flow in excess of 7.5 feet/second is in the beer control valve before the filler. Because of the special design of these valves, the high velocity at this one point does not damage the beer as long as the pressure drop across the valve is not excessive.

Measuring Beer Delivery

Measuring the quantity of beer delivered to the bottle filler is necessary not only for company and tax records but also for monitoring and controlling beer losses. Beer to the filler can be measured in basically two different ways, using release tanks or in-line meters.

Release Tanks

By knowing the capacity of the release tank and having the use of a graduated sight glass on the tank, operators can determine and record the volume of beer released to the filler.

In-Line Meters

A meter can be placed in the release line to the filler. A turbine meter can be used, but a magnetic meter is better suited for beer since it has no moving parts to wear and it offers the most cleanable design. Magnetic flow meters are very accurate when properly calibrated. One absolute requirement for accurate metering with a magnetic flow meter is ensuring that the supply line is packed with solid liquid. There must also be a sufficient length of straight pipe before and after the meter to ensure good laminar flow. Stringy beer—beer that has experienced CO_2 loss—cannot be accurately metered by a magnetic flow meter.

A magnetic flow meter can be calibrated by using a turbine meter in line with the magnetic flow meter. The use of turbine meters for normal operation at high speeds is not recommended.

Beer Supply to the Filler

There are several types of beer supply systems.

- Gravity systems with tank bunging pressure on beer and with a beer supply control valve
- Gravity systems with special release pressure on beer and with a beer supply control valve
- Centrifugal pump systems that use a beer supply control valve
- Positive-displacement pump systems
- Loop or manifold systems

The first gravity system, which uses tank bunging pressure on beer, is the simplest. In this system, CO_2 gas is supplied to the tank headspace above the beer at 12–15 psig. This prevents CO_2 from escaping from the beer without adding carbonation to the beer. With properly designed tank outlets and properly sized beer lines, the pressure at the low pressure point of the supply line should be at least 1 psig greater than the equilibrium pressure to maintain the carbonation in solution. With this system, sufficient pressure exists at the beer control (flow-modulating) valve to achieve the maximum flow required by the filler. This system is the simplest in design and the simplest to operate and control.

Systems that employ gravity with special release pressure are normally used on operations in which the hydrostatic pressure from the tank to the filler is not sufficient to provide proper operating pressure at the beer control valve during filler startup or normal running. This dual-pressure system uses normal bunging pressure of 12–15 psig when the tank is not supplying beer to the filler. A higher pressure is used when the system is ready for the filler to run. This higher pressure is set high enough to provide the necessary driving force for proper flow through the beer control valve to the bowl.

A centrifugal pump is used when the static head caused by tank bunging pressure is too low for proper beer control valve and filler operation and a dual-pressure system is not desired or cannot be used. If a centrifugal pump is sized properly to match the filler speed, the pump can run continuously while the filler is stopped for short periods of 1 minute or less without overheating or damaging the beer. If a positive-displacement pump is used, it must receive a signal from the filler level control telling it when to run and stop. It often runs on a variable frequency drive (VFD) controlled by the filler PLC.

With any of these release systems, except the positive-displacement system, operators must use a level control valve placed just prior to the filler in order to keep the beer inside the filler bowl at the correct level. Beer in the supply line must also always be kept at a point above the equilibrium pressure, even during startup and running.

The loop or manifold system is often used to deliver beer to several fillers in the packaging center and is used mostly in large breweries running a lot of one product. This manifold system consists of a stainless-steel pipe loop sized to meet the full supply requirements of the various fillers in the building plus a 10 or 15% return through a smaller pipeline. A large centrifugal pump with a fluid drive is used to transfer the beer through the manifold. As the demand for beer changes, the fluid clutch responds to a signal from a pressure control, which is set to maintain pressure at approximately 25–30 psig above the maximum counterpressure of the filler bowls. The small quantity of excess beer that returns passes through a cooler and then through a pressure control valve into the suction side of the main pump. A small jockey pump is also incorporated into the system. This pump is sized so as to circulate the beer at the manifold return rate when the manifold is not in use, such as on the weekends. This pump keeps the beer in the manifold packed and cold at a reduced energy level.

Each filler location has a drop-leg with a block valve and a control valve, which receives a signal from the filler liquid-level control. It also has appropriate fittings desired by the operating department, such as a sight glass, drain valves, sampling ports, and thermometer. It is very important that proper procedures be used to initially supply the beer to the filler. The drop-leg from the manifold should be supplied with a venting device at the highest point, and the entire line from the manifold to the filler should be filled with water prior to the opening of the beer block valve. Every effort should be made to keep the manifold free of air and gas. A bleeder should be installed at the highest point in the manifold and should be opened on a periodic basis. The beer control valve at the base of each filler closes automatically when it receives a signal, triggered by either an electrical or mechanical failure, from the manifold low-pressure system. The automatic closing of the valves maintains the manifold in a packed condition. All beer lines should be well insulated.

Bottle Supply to the Filler

As stated previously, the filler determines the efficiency of the line. A constant supply of bottles to the filler must be maintained. As fillers become larger and faster, the bottle feed system must supply bottles at greater speed. Because of this, most high-speed fillers have a multispeed drive, which allows for a slow start and smooth acceleration. The higher operating speeds can also cause bottle breakage and other problems if the filler gate is closed during line operation, forcing moving bottles to come to an abrupt stop.

Bottle-Indexing Devices

Once a proper bottle supply is established, bottles are then indexed and transferred to the filler platforms. Immediately prior to the filler, bottle flow is normally controlled by a start/stop device, such as a gate or metering star. The gate or other device does not regulate the speed of the bottle flow but only releases, or stops, the flow of bottles to the filler. An indexing device is located after the gate and receives bottles in a back-to-back manner. This device is normally a timing screw, or infeed worm (Fig. 13.1). The pitch, or bottle spacing, of the screw gradually changes to the pitch of the next downstream device, usually a transfer star, and the bottles are accurately transferred to this device at the pitch required by the filling valves. The star wheel then places the bottles onto the filler platforms. At this point, a guide strips the bottles from the star wheel and positions them against a bottle backrest and/or under a centering bell. As the bottle platform rises, the centering bell contacts and centers the bottle and allows the bell to slide up the fill tube.

Bottle-Filling Machines

Production-model bottle fillers are rotary machines. The number of valves in these fillers is determined by the manufacturer, according to the filling speed of the valves and the speed range planned for the particular model filler. Fillers are available from some manufacturers as clockwise-rotating machines only. Other manufacturers offer bottle fillers that operate either clockwise or counterclockwise. Different arrangements of feed conveyors with bottle combiners as well as various arrangements of the crowner discharge conveyor are also available. The conventional arrangement includes a clockwise-rotating filler with the bottle supply entering from the left and the filled and crowned bottles discharging either to the right (straight through) or to the rear of the crowner. However, counterclockwise machines are available as well (Fig. 13.3).

FIGURE 13.3. Transfer from the rinser to the filler. (Courtesy Krones USA)

The importance of proper handling of the beer to the filler bowl is very often underestimated. For all bottles to be properly filled, the beer level in the bowl and the bowl pressure must remain constant.

Filler Bowls

Filler bowls come in two basic types and are referred to as torus bowls and center bowls. Torus bowls, sometimes referred to as either ring or doughnut bowls, can be either square (Fig. 13.4 left) or tubular (Fig. 13.4 right) and usually have relatively small cross sections. This type of bowl usually has from four to eight radial pipes to distribute beer from the supply line manifold to the bowl. Distributor tubing from the bowl to the valves is not needed, since the valves are mounted either in the bottom of the bowl or attached to the outside of the bowl.

Torus or ring bowls produce a standing wave in the bowl when the filler is rotating and filling. Centrifugal force raises the beer level along the outside of the bowl and lowers it along the inside of the bowl. Because of the standing wave and the effect of centrifugal force, the level of the beer is difficult to control. If a float is used for measurement, it will pass through this standing wave. If multiple dip tubes or conductivity sensors are used, the system should be set up to measure the low point rather than the high point of the wave in order to maintain level when running and to prevent overfilling of the bowl when the filler is not filling bottles. Because of the large amount of surface area on top of the beer in a ring bowl, CO_2 should be used for counterpressure to prevent excess air pickup.

Center bowls (Fig. 13.5) have no standing wave. Centrifugal force exerted on the beer by rotation attempts to cause the level of the beer in the center of the bowl to lower and the beer level at the outside of the bowl to rise. Because of this, the beer level-detecting device should be placed at the intersection of the horizontal level when the filler is not running, and it should be placed along the sloping surface of the beer when the filler is running. At this intersection in the bowl, the beer level remains constant. When a center bowl design is used, the small amount of surface area in contact with the counterpressure gas can be further reduced by the use of a float, which reduces the contact surface to the peripheral space between the outside of the float and the inside of the bowl. This float serves no purpose during the filling process other than to minimize the surface area of the beer in contact with the gas in the bowl.

If the filler has a center bowl, the beer supply line to the bowl normally comes through a rotary joint in the center

FIGURE 13.5. Central filler bowl. (Courtesy Krones USA)

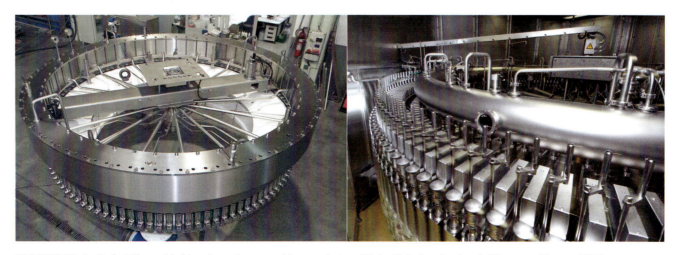

FIGURE 13.4. **Left,** Filler welded bowl nearing assembly completion. **Right,** Tubular ring bowl. (Courtesy Krones USA)

of the bottom of the bowl (Fig. 13.6). If the filler has a ring bowl design, the beer supply line is normally connected to a rotating manifold with a rotating joint and the beer is delivered by equally spaced distribution pipes to the bowl, as mentioned previously.

A gas pressure-regulating and/or -relieving valve maintains bowl pressure, and the beer level in the bowl is maintained by a float or by conductivity probes or differential pressure tubes. With the float method, the float usually opens and closes a port as it raises and lowers. The CO_2 or air flowing through this port is then restricted and causes an increase in pressure. This changing pressure controls either a beer flow control valve or starts and stops a pump.

With the conductivity probe method, when the beer level rises or lowers, an electric signal is either initiated or discontinued. The signal is used to regulate a beer flow control valve or pump.

When measuring differential pressure, one method runs two dip tubes, one short and one long, into the filler bowl. One tube ends in the headspace of the bowl. The other tube extends to a point near the bottom of the bowl. By forcing a small amount of CO_2 through the dip tubes, the pressure differential between the two tubes can be measured and a signal produced to control the beer control valve or pump.

Filler Tubes

Different filler manufacturers use different filling valve and tube designs. Primarily, filling tubes either operate by tube displacement or fill to a level. The latest innovation is volumetric filling using flow meters or metering chambers for polyethylene terephthalate (PET) bottles.

Tube Displacement

When using tube displacement, bottles are filled completely. When the bottles are lowered from the filling tubes, the amount of beer remaining in the bottle should be the stated volume for that size bottle. Variations in beer levels are primarily the result of variations in the bottles' volumes (or overflow capacities).

Filling to a Level

With a long vent tube system for filling to a level, there are two passages in the filling tube. Beer moves through the large passage in the tube to the bottom of the bottle. As the beer level rises in the bottles, the displaced gas escapes through the smaller passage in the tube. When the fill level covers the vent passage opening, gas can no longer escape through this vent, causing beer to stop flowing into the bottle.

With the short vent tube system of filling to a level, beer enters the bottle over spreaders along the surface of the bottle's inside wall. Gas escapes through a vent tube (Fig. 13.7), a small-diameter tube, the lower opening of which is placed at a specific elevation in the bottle. When the proper fill has been obtained, this specific placement

FIGURE 13.6. Product distributor. (Courtesy Krones USA)

FIGURE 13.7. **Top**, Vent tube testing in the lab. **Bottom**, Vent tubes. (Courtesy Krones USA)

prevents gas escape and beer entry. The vent short tube-style valve offers exceptional oxygen guarantees and is less costly.

Volumetric Filling (for PET)

Volumetric filling for beer uses a metering chamber filling valve. This valve has a cylindrical chamber, which houses a probe and float that measure a metered volume. The process begins with the inlet valve opening and beer flowing into the chamber. The float rises on the probe, and once the float gets to a point that coincides with the desired volume, it sends a signal to the PLC to close the inlet valve. Then the volume is ready to be displaced into a bottle. This filling valve is commonly used for placing beer in cans.

The filling valve assembly itself has multiple passages for controlling pre-evacuation (in some fillers), counterpressure, and vent gas escape from the bottles, which as a result controls filling and bottle headspace pressure. Some fillers control the passages by poppet valves. In other fillers, one multiposition valve is used, while in still other fillers, multiple single valves are used.

Filling Sequence of Modern Fillers

A modern beer-filling sequence is shown in Figure 13.8. Once the bottles are on the platforms and raised into position, the filling process begins. For some fillers, the first and second step in the process is pre-evacuation. With this process, a partial vacuum is drawn on each bottle.

The next step, whether or not pre-evacuation is used, is introducing counterpressure into the bottle. This step provides pressure inside the bottle sufficient to preserve product carbonation, that is, enough to keep the pressure of the gas in contact with the beer above the equilibrium point during filling so that CO_2 is not released from the beer. The counterpressure gas is CO_2.

After the counterpressure is established, the filler valve is repositioned to the filling mode, opening both the beer supply to the filling tube and the vent passages. As the beer enters the bottle through the tube, the counterpressure gas in the bottle is displaced through the vent passage to either the bowl, a vent chamber, or the atmosphere. During the filling operation, some beer enters the vent line or passage. After filling, the vent line

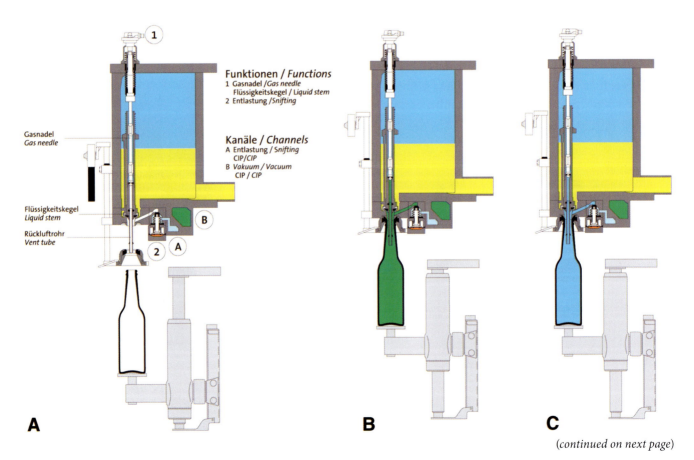

(continued on next page)

FIGURE 13.8. A modern beer-filling sequence. **A**, Basic position. **B**, First pre-evacuation. **C**, CO_2 flush. **D**, Second pre-evacuation. **E**, Pressurization. **F**, Filling. **G**, Filling complete, settling. **H**, Snifting. **I**, CIP. (Courtesy Krones USA)

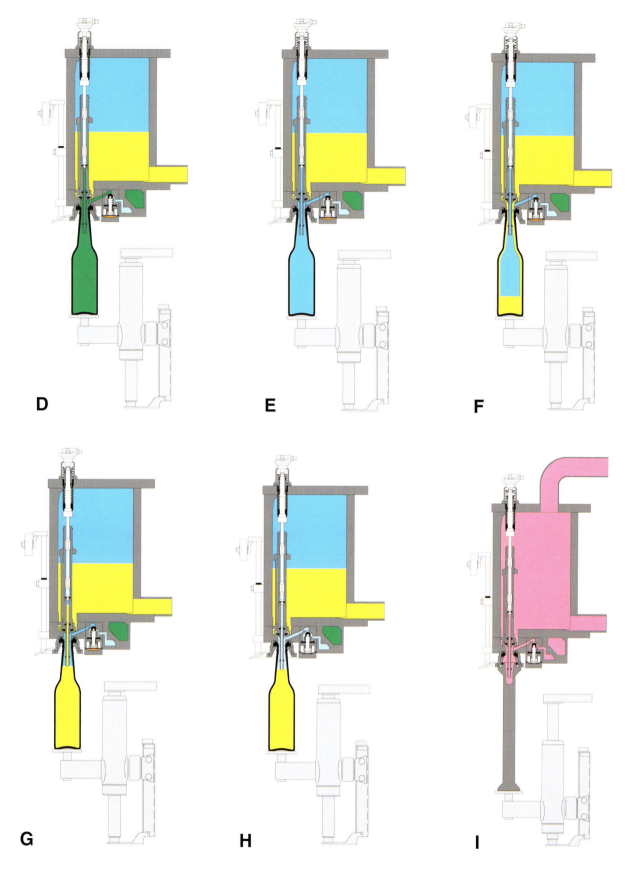

FIGURE 13.8. (continued from previous page)

must be purged to provide a clean passage for venting for the next bottle.

After filling, the beer flow is stopped by stopping the gas escaping from the bottles and repositioning the filler valve. If all of the adjustments are made properly, the bottle reaches the desired fill point immediately before the beer shut-off cam (or solenoid in today's electro-pneumatic filling valves). After closing all of the passages to the bottles, some fillers use bottle headspace pressure relief or snift. This is the release of pressure from the bottle before the seal is broken with the valve and centering bell. This release of pressure produces a calmer beer upon leaving the filler.

Filling Sequence of Older, Short-Tube Fillers

The filling sequence of a typical short-tube filler with mechanical valves is as follows.

- A bottle enters the filler and is lifted so that it is sealed tightly against the tulip assembly.
- The bottle is then subjected to a vacuum, which evacuates atmospheric air. This may be performed twice.
- The presence of the bottle sends a signal to an opening trip, which causes the charging valve to be lifted and allows CO_2 to flow down through the charging valve into the bottle.
- When the differential pressure between the bowl and the bottle becomes small enough, a spring lifts the fill valve and allows beer to flow down toward the bottle.
- The beer flows down the outside of the tube and is deflected onto the side of the bottle to reduce turbulence. As the beer flows downward, gas flows back up into the bowl through the vent tube.
- Filling stops when the liquid reaches the bottom of the vent tube. Further filling is prevented because the gas remaining in the bottle has nowhere to go and exerts an upward pressure that stops the flow of beer. Gas cannot escape up through the fill valve because of surface tension in that area.
- The filling valve is then closed by a cam.
- Another cam rail then opens a valve that contains a small hole to the atmosphere. This opening allows a gradual depressurization of the bottle, a process known as snifting.
- The bottle is transferred to a star wheel and goes toward the crowner.

Here are other important facts to note about short-tube fillers.

- Over time, air flowing up the tube from the incoming bottles will build up. To counteract this buildup of air, the bowl is continuously purged to the atmosphere, with new CO_2 flowing in to replace that lost by the purge.
- The level of beer in the bowl is usually controlled by a modulating valve on the incoming beer line at the base of the filler. The valve is, in turn, controlled either by a pressure sensor that, working in conjunction with a float in the bowl, senses the amount of beer in the bowl, or it is controlled by probes in the bowl.
- The lift cylinders that lift the bottles up to seal them against the tulip assembly operate under pneumatic pressure. Lift cylinder pressure must be higher than bowl pressure.
- Bowl pressure is controlled by a pressure-reducing valve, and it must be higher than the saturation pressure of the CO_2 in the liquid.

Air Evacuation from the Bottle Headspace

After filling, the bottle is removed from the filling tube and discharged from the filler to the crowner via a star wheel or a half-pocket transfer chain. At this point, it is necessary to eliminate air from the bottle headspace prior to crowning to prevent O_2 entrainment during the crowning process. (Any entrained air beneath the crown will quickly oxidize the beer.) Eliminating air from the bottle headspace is accomplished by using one of three devices: a bottle knocker, an ultrasonic foamer, or a water jetter.

Bottle knockers are used on relatively slow-speed bottle fillers. This device employs a metal rod with an adjustable spring. The knocker is cocked as each bottle passes and the knocker strikes the following bottle. This causes the beer to foam and expel the air from the headspace of the bottles.

The ultrasonic foamer utilizes an ultrasonic generator and a transducer with a stainless-steel shoe that contacts the bottles while they are still on the filler. The vibration of the transducer shoe causes the beer to foam and expel gas from the bottle's headspace. This method is an improvement over the bottle knocker because it can be used on higher-speed lines without causing bottle breakage. However, with this process, out-of-round bottles and variations in glass thickness can result in inconsistent levels of beer foaming in the bottles.

Another beer-foaming device especially suited for use on high-speed bottle fillers is a water jetter (Fig. 13.9). This is the industry standard. This system employs a high-pressure, sterilized source of water delivered through a fine solid-stream nozzle. With this system, only a few microliters of water enter each bottle, but the high pressure used creates an effective beer-foaming action. When the nozzle is attached to an adjustable arm, the distance from the point of the water jetter's spray to the crowner can be varied. This enables accurate control of the amount of foaming, permitting minimum beer loss while eliminating any entrained air during crowning. A newer, more reliable method is to automatically adjust the pressure of the jet of water based on filler speed.

Bottle-Filler Drives

Bottle fillers and crowners are driven by hydraulic or AC or DC electric drive motors or the newer synchronous and servo motors, which are becoming more popular. Each has its advantages and disadvantages, and each installation must be evaluated according to which features are most important to that particular installation.

Hydraulic Drives

Hydraulic drives present some of the following advantages.

- Simple, constant-speed electric motors can be used to drive the hydraulic pump.
- The pump drive can remain running even when the filler is idling or stopped.

- The pump and speed control assembly can be placed in a remote location relatively free from beer and water.
- Various speeds, accelerations, decelerations, torque limits, etc. can all be controlled with these drives.
- It is possible to obtain maximum torque at 0 rpm.

Hydraulic drives also pose some disadvantages.

- Personnel may not be familiar with hydraulics, and as a result, it may require greater time to diagnose and correct problems in an electro-hydraulic system.
- Oil leaks and/or oil spills can occur.
- Hydraulic drives may require water cooling.

Electric Drives

There are several types of electric drive systems, including those using AC with frequency inverter, single- or two-speed AC, AC with soft start, DC, eddy current clutch drives, or wound-rotor recovery drives. These drives can be furnished as totally enclosed fan-cooled units; however, the eddy current clutch drive must be water cooled when totally enclosed.

Of electric drives, those featuring AC with frequency inverters appear to have many advantages. These systems use a standard AC induction motor, which, when totally enclosed and fan cooled, can be placed in the filler base. The inverter can regulate speed, acceleration, deceleration, and torque limits. Nevertheless, although they have only one type of system (electrical), a qualified electrician is needed for proper adjustment and maintenance of these units.

The single- or two-speed electric drives, as well as AC electric drives with or without soft start, do not allow speed to be adjusted electrically. They can be adjusted mechanically, at least on slower-speed fillers.

DC electric drives provide the flexibility of an AC inverter drive, but they require more maintenance.

The eddy current clutch drive system provides the flexibility of a hydraulic system since the motor runs at a constant speed, while the eddy current clutch controls the drive output. This system's major disadvantage is that, if it is to be totally enclosed, it must be water cooled.

Synchronous Drives

In fillers with synchronous drives, the filler is driven by a homokinetic joint shaft from the main drive of the crowner (or vice versa). As a result, both machines operate synchronously.

FIGURE 13.9. **Left**, Jetter off. **Right**, Jetter running. (Courtesy Krones USA)

BOTTLE-CROWNING OPERATIONS

After filling, bottles must be crowned (Fig. 13.10). Because of the foaming action required to evacuate air from the headspace, the time from the point of jetting to the crown application must remain constant for a particular foamer setting. When the bottle reaches the crowner, it is on a platform directly below a crowner head. As the crowner rotates, the crowner head is lowered, and the crown is pressed down onto the crown ring or threaded finish of the bottle. At this point, a tapered throat is forced down over the crown, and the crown skirt is crimped to the proper crimp dimension. The standard crown ring diameter is 1.050 inches. The amount of crimp is controlled by adjusting the depth at which the tapered throat is forced down over the crown.

Bottle Crowners

The many manufacturers of bottle crowners provide a variety of crowner concepts and component arrangements. The following section provides an overview of the basic components of bottle crowners.

The crowner dial is a rotating device that feeds or supplies single lines of individual crowns to a rectifier chute or tube. The single-file device may be placed either vertically or horizontally. When it stands vertically, a large amount of crowns are placed in the hopper in contact with the dial. As the dial rotates, the crowns are supplied to a vertical chute. When the dial is placed horizontally, only two to three layers of crowns are required in the hopper.

The crowner dial feeds the rectifier chute or tube. The rectifier chute is designed to take the crowns received from the crown dial and orient them so that they are all in one plane and facing one direction (Fig. 13.11). Rectifier chutes come primarily in two designs: tube shaped or flat.

The crown chute extends from the rectifier chute or tube down to the crowner assembly platforms or plungers. In some cases, the crown chute delivers the crowns directly to the crowner platform. In other cases, the crowns are delivered via an intermediate transfer wheel to the underside of magnetic crown-plunger assemblies. Crowners can be equipped with either single- or dual-crown chutes. With single-crown chutes, a detection device on the crown chute usually sounds an alarm when there are no crowns. When necessary, it can also shut off the bottle flow to the filler. With a dual-chute system, when a jam occurs in the primary chute, an alarm can be sounded and the secondary chute activated.

Many crowners employ a crown platform to receive and position the crown of the bottle below the throat. The platform can either be solid or floating (also called

FIGURE 13.10. **Top**, Crowner discharge. **Bottom**, Crowning. (Courtesy Krones USA)

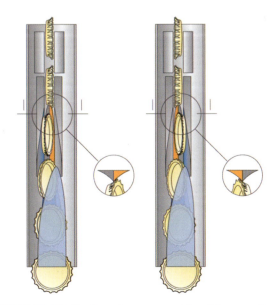

FIGURE 13.11. Backwards crown rectifier. (Courtesy Krones USA)

compensating). Long-neck bottles, such as the standard, returnable export-type bottle, permit the use of a solid platform. Short-neck bottles with a high shoulder require compensating platforms, which permit the crowner throat to lower and crimp the crown even though the high shoulder prevents further travel of the platform. This compensating type of platform is more costly and difficult to maintain but is necessary for many crowners.

After being delivered to the crowner via star wheel or tangential half-pocket transfer chain, the bottles must be centered under the crowner heads. This is accomplished by using half-pocket backrests or well-designed plastic stars. After the bottles are placed into the pockets, the crowner head starts to descend onto the bottles. With some crowners, a centering device centers the bottle to ensure proper crowning. After the bottle is centered, the crown contacts the crown ring of the bottle and the throat is forced down over the crown, crimping the skirt to the proper "crimp" as discussed previously.

● FILLER CLEANING AND SANITIZING

As a food product, beer must be handled and packaged in a sanitary manner. The parts of the filler that come in direct contact with the beer must be kept free of bacteria or any other foreign material, such as oils and lubricants. Filling operations for bottle lines without pasteurizers require that the filler be kept clean. This requires continuously spraying the filling tubes, valves, and bells with fresh water and/or taking other cleaning and sanitizing measures determined to be necessary.

On all fillers, the filler bowl, valves, tubes, and beer supply and distribution lines must be periodically cleaned. This is most easily done with a cleaning-in-place (CIP) system in which a suitable cleaning solution is circulated through the various passages, lines, valves, and in some cases, bottles through to the beer supply line. By properly sizing beer flow passages and the CIP system, operators can ensure that cleaning solutions are directed in velocities effective enough to clean the components without causing damage. After cleaning has been completed, the cleaning solution must be drained and the system thoroughly rinsed with a fresh-water flush. Modern fillers allow an external foam-cleaning system to be built onto the filler.

Ultrasonic cleaning of tubes is also an effective method. The tubes are removed from the adapters and put into stainless-steel mesh baskets and immersed into a 140°F (60°C) solution of biodegradable detergent and water in an ultrasonic bath machine and held for 20–30 minutes. They are then removed and rinsed in clear water for approximately 15 minutes. The tubes are then reassembled with the adapters and are ready for the bottle filler.

● PRECAUTIONS

When the beer-foaming device on a filler has been set to create foam sufficient enough to ensure proper evacuation of the headspace air with minimum beer loss, the device performs efficiently only at that particular filler speed. Consequently, the filler should not be stopped when bottles are in the filler or when they are between the filler and the crowner, as this will adversely affect the fill level and the air content in the bottle and cause beer loss. To ensure a proper fill of all bottles, it is essential that bottle backups and/or jams be detected far enough in advance so that the filler and crowner can be cleared at a normal running speed.

Beer Loss

On modern fillers without level correction, beer loss can be less than 1%. This does not include beer loss from bottle breakage or underfills or from missing or faulty closures. Beer loss can be controlled through proper design, maintenance, and adjustment of the filling equipment, such as the pull-down cams, etc. It is also achieved through proper adjustment of the foaming devices prior to bottle crowning. Generally, losses with bottle filling are higher than those with can filling because bottled beer must be caused to foam in order to expel air from the bottle headspace before crowning.

Contaminants

Contaminants—such as carton fibers, litho dust from crowns, and airborne or "drop in"-type foreign matter—can be reduced by placing protective shields over the open tops of bottles on the conveyer running from the bottle washer or rinser to the filler infeed. They can also be reduced by installing a vacuum dust-collecting device on the crowner dial and chute entrance. Proper adjustment of the bottle-centering devices on the filler and crowner and immediate replacement of bent or broken filler tubes can eliminate glass inclusion. Modern fillers have burst-bottle detection systems that automatically underfill several of the bottles that immediately proceed and follow a burst bottle to ensure their rejection. After a bottle breaks on the filler, it can either close the bottle infeed and stop, close the bottle infeed and run out the remaining bottles, slow down, or continue at speed. No matter what method is chosen, the filler will go into a high-power rinse cycle at the filling valve zone that had the exploded bottle. This rinse can be for one or multiple bowl revolutions.

MAINTENANCE AND TROUBLESHOOTING

As with all precision machinery, expert maintenance, lubrication, and repair of parts are absolutely necessary for the system's satisfactory performance. Manufacturer instruction manuals must be followed closely, and operators should question vendors' service engineers and technicians thoroughly on how to keep machinery in proper operation. Normal maintenance consists of sanitizing and lubricating parts and making minor adjustments and repairs, all of which can normally be accomplished during shift changes. Whether operating problems occur commonly or infrequently, troubleshooting is necessary to ensure the proper operation of the filling machine. When attempting to identify and eliminate a problem in machine operation, the following should be remembered.

Analyze Carefully

Do not jump to conclusions. No two problems or defects are identical; therefore, each one requires careful and persistent analysis. Do not solve symptoms; instead, identify and solve the problem.

Follow a Logical Sequence

Systematically test and confirm or eliminate possible causes of the problem. Haphazard adjustments waste time and can be injurious to the equipment.

Do One Step at a Time

If the adjustment does not correct the problem, restore the original condition before making a different adjustment.

Each brand of filling machine is different from its competitors, yet all fillers are sufficiently similar that the troubleshooting guide in Table 13.1 should be of value.

TABLE 13.1. Troubleshooting Guide: Bottle Filling and Crowning

Symptom	Cause	Solution
Incorrect Bottle Fill		
Overfilling	Damaged or incorrect gasket	Replace gasket
	Snift and/or shut-off incorrect	Tighten or replace gaskets and shut-off cams or valves
	Vacuum snift leads (if equipped)	Tighten or replace O-ring
	Bottle damage	Check infeed, tubes, and centering devices
	Screen damaged	Replace screen and check vent tube installation
	Valves leaks	Install O-ring or gasket correctly, tighten valve, and replace valve disc
	Vent tube not seated	Install properly
	Guide off center	Install properly
	Short vent tube	Replace
	Incorrect filling tube	Replace
Underfilling	Vent tube bent	Replace vent tube (be sure bottle infeed handling and positioning are correct)
	Spreader damaged	Replace spreader (be sure bottle positioning at infeed is correct)
	Nozzle damaged	Replace nozzle
	Screen damaged or dirty	Replace screen (be sure vent tube installation is correct)
	Bowl level low	Set bowl level correctly with float
		Be sure pressure valve setting is correct

(continued on next page)

TABLE 13.1. Troubleshooting Guide: Bottle Filling and Crowning (continued from previous page)

Symptom	Cause	Solution
Incorrect Bottle Fill (continued)		
	Valve lever too low	Loosen clamp screw and adjust lever
	Neutral cam too high	Lower neutral cam
	Vent tube too long	Replace with correct length vent tube
	Sealing rubber worn or cut	Replace sealing rubber
	Vacuum system not working	Be sure cam position is correct
		Be sure vacuum hole is not plugged
	Valve sticking	Replace valve
	Filling tube is wrong diameter or length	Replace
	Shut-off cam incorrect	Check cam and valve lever
	Filler speed too great	Adjust speed of filler
No fill	Bottle damaged	Replace bottle and check infeed timing and alignment
	Centering tulip rubber damaged	Replace rubber
	Vacuum valve stuck open	Be sure valve is clean
	Snift valve stuck open	Be sure snift valve is clean
		Check for broken spring
	Valve sticking	Remove bent top assembly (this indicates installation problem)
	Valve spring broken	Replace spring
	Tulip rubber not seated on nozzle	Align tulip correctly
		Be sure tulip spring pressure is correct
	Vent tube nipple loose	Replace valve
	Cam missing, broken valve	Check and replace as required
	No beer supply	Check sight glass and beer trip cam
	Malfunction of valve trip plunger	Check air connection
		Check plunger mounting
		Check piston
	Valve trip sensing	Not opening up valves (check sensor under filler or wand sensor mounted on the outside, whichever is used)
Excessive product foaming when bottle leaves filler	Vacuum pump not working	Be sure vacuum pump is operating correctly
	Three-way valve positioned incorrectly	Be sure to return valve to operating position after cleaning
	Vacuum too low	Look for vacuum system leaks and tighten connections
	Product too warm	After prolonged stoppage, it may be necessary to increase product pressure in filler
	Filler pressure too low (counterpressure)	Be sure pressure controller and pressure valve are set correctly
	Bottles not clean	Clean and remove foreign substance, which can react with product
	Bowl level too high	Check float orifice for damage and repair/replace if necessary
	Vacuum valves not operating	Be sure vacuum cam is correctly located
	Stirrup pressure too low	Check panel gauge and adjust
	Changing tanks in cellar	Air pockets; bleed product until it looks clear in the sight glass
	Foamer set too high	Adjust for less foaming

(continued on next page)

TABLE 13.1. Troubleshooting Guide: Bottle Filling and Crowning (continued from previous page)

Symptom	Cause	Solution
Incorrect Bottle Fill (continued)		
Excessive air in bottles	Excess air may be in product entering filler	Check air in product entering filler
	Vacuum too low	Be sure vacuum system is operating correctly
	Too little foam as bottle enters crowner	Be sure foam jetter is clean and positioned properly
		Increase jetter pressure
	Bottle underfilled	Too little liquid allows larger percentage of air reading; check length of vent tubes
	Bottle transfer is not smooth	Sloshing of liquid does not allow for good foaming (be sure bottle guide is properly positioned)
	Product too cold	Check temperature
	Snift cam worn or not properly adjusted	Replace or adjust cam
	Speed too fast, not allowing time for foam to rise	Reduce speed
	Jetter pump malfunction	Check for water leaks or bad diaphragm and tighten water connections and replace diaphragm
Incorrect Liquid Level in Bowl		
High level in bowl	Damaged orifice on float	Replace orifice insert
	Gas pressure too low	Adjust regulator to provide sufficient gas supply
	Exhaust float does not close orifice	Float may be stuck in down position; replace float
		Float may be leaking; repair/replace/tighten
	Excessive product pressure	Be sure pressure valve and controller are properly set
	Gas not entering bowl	Broken gas hose; repair/replace
		Plugged center column
	Float not adjusted	Remove float and readjust correctly
	Gasket and butterflies leaking	Replace gasket
	Cleaning valves open, causes CO_2 loss	Close valves (be sure beverage control valve, pressure controller, and pressure transmitter are properly set)
	Differential pressure cell not adjusted	Check air pressure, connections, etc.
Low level of liquid in bowl	Float not adjusted correctly	Remove float and readjust correctly
	Product valve not operating	Check air supply to instrument's controller; must operate correctly
	High CO_2 bowl pressure	Be sure float cap is open for venting during startup
	No beer from cellars	Check with line supervisor
	Differential pressure cell not adjusted	Check pressure, connections, etc.
Erratic levels of liquid in bowl	Pressure controller not adjusted	Be sure pressure system is operating properly
	Vent cap not clean	Wash vent cap
	Sporadic hanging up of product float in open or closed position	Clean or replace valve linkage
	Differential pressure cell	Inspect and adjust
Bottle Breakage		
Breakage at bottle stop	Bottle stop positioned incorrectly	Adjust bottle stop
	Rail positioned incorrectly	Be sure rail distance from bottle stop is correct
	Bottle stop pressure incorrect	Adjust pressure regulator

(continued on next page)

TABLE 13.1. Troubleshooting Guide: Bottle Filling and Crowning (*continued from previous page*)

Symptom	Cause	Solution
Bottle Breakage (*continued*)		
Breakage at infeed worm	Infeed worm not properly timed	Time worm with infeed star
	Infeed worm rail (back plate) is loose	Broken spring on rail; replace spring
		Rail too tight on swivel shafts; loosen rail
	Bottle not fed smoothly into infeed worm	Conveyor may have glass under belt; remove glass
		Wear strips may be worn; replace wear strips
	Conveyor speed too slow	Be sure infeed conveyor is properly adjusted
	Infeed worm damaged	Replace worm
	Tipped bottles	Check soap lines and check reason for tipping
	Bottles out of spec	Change bottle lot
	Wrong infeed worm	Replace worm
Breakage at infeed star	Star not timed with infeed worm	Time worm with infeed star
	Wear plates not at proper height	Replace plates periodically
		Watch for bent plate; replace bent plates
		Check for worn lift cylinder rollers
	Screw head protruding	Be sure screw heads are flush with wear pads
	Star pocket vs. bottle guide clearance is insufficient	Check for oversize bottles
		Bottle guide casing loose and shifted; adjust
		Be sure star and bottle guide are correct size for bottle being run on filler
	Star not timed with life cylinders	Be sure star is timed to cylinders
	Lift cylinders too high	Pull-down cam worn; contact factory representative
	Burrs on infeed worm	File off, cut off, or replace
Breakage at filler discharge	Filler not timed	Time pocket chain to bowl using in-motion timer
	Wear plates at incorrect height	Periodically replace wear plates
		Look for bent plate
	Chain pockets vs. guide clearance is insufficient	Check for oversize bottles; use correct size bottles
		Bottle guide loose and shifted; adjust
	Bad centering tulips (bottles hanging in tulips at discharge)	Check tulips; replace bad tulips
		Check for oversized bottles
	Bottles out of spec	Change bottle lot
	Take-off guide not correctly aligned	Align take-off guide
Breakage at crowner entry	Crowner too low	Adjust crowner height correctly
	Bottle guide clearance is insufficient	Check for oversize bottles; use correct size bottles
		Be sure bottle guide is correct for bottle being run on filler
	Dead plate is too high	Lower dead plate
Breakage in crowner	Crowner is too low	Adjust crowner height
	Crown throats are incorrect size	Install proper crown throats
	Crown platform bored too small	Be sure crown platform allows free entry of bottle and does not permit crown to fall through hole
	Worn or broken pressure foot	Periodically replace pressure feet
	Broken springs	Replace springs periodically
	Bottle size out of spec	Check bottle tolerances

(*continued on next page*)

TABLE 13.1. Troubleshooting Guide: Bottle Filling and Crowning (continued from previous page)

Symptom	Cause	Solution
Bottle Breakage (continued)		
	Crown pads worn	Replace pads periodically
	Crowner not timed	Time crowner with crowner chain sprocket
Breakage at crowner exit	Bottles lifted by crown platforms	Replace broken spring
	Insufficient clearance between pockets and bottle guides	Be sure bottle dimension is correct
	Worn crowner pads	Replace pads
	Wear plate too low	Raise wear plate
Crowns not holding in platform	Magnets not holding	Be sure magnets are properly located in platform
	Platform hole too large	Be sure platform hole allows bottle to fit through but does not allow crown to fall through
	Crown wiper not adjusted	Adjust wiper
		Be sure wiper spring tension is correct
Missing Crowns and Uncrowned Bottles		
Crown not feeding to chute	Incorrect clearance setting on crowner selector disc	Adjust selector disc to allow crowns to enter chute freely, yet not double up and cause blockage
	Bent crown enters chute	Clear the chute
	Pocket formed in crown hopper	Reduce weight of crowns in hopper
	Crowns hanging on rim at selector disc	Check for protrusions on crown rim
	No air on top ventway	Be sure crowner air supply is adequate
	Crowner dusty	Wash with water
Crowns not moving freely	Incorrect dimensions for chute shunt	Be sure opening of chute shunt is no more than one crown in width
	Crown disc worn	Replace disc periodically; disc must have free movement
	Crown chute worn	Plastic parts can become worn by sharp crown edges; replace crown chute
	No air on bottom ventway	Be sure air supply to crowner is adequate
	Bent crowns entering chute	Be sure there are no bolt protrusions in hopper
		Check for overloaded magnetic belt
	Crowner is dusty	Wash with water
Crown will not exit chute	Exit positioned too high or too low	Adjust crown chute exit properly
	Air connection plate is rough	Repair/replace
	Air connection plate bent incorrectly	Repair/replace
	Crown head twisted	Be sure crown heads are properly aligned
	Insufficient air pressure	Adjust
	Bent crown in bottom of chute	Check incoming crowns to filler; remove bent crowns
	Crowner element too low	Check head, roller, and locking bolt; adjust
Crowns not holding in platform	Magnets not holding	Be sure magnets are properly placed in platform
	Platform hole too large	Be sure platform hole allows bottle to fit through but does not allow crown to fall through
	Crown wiper not adjusted	Adjust wiper
		Be sure wiper spring tension is correct
	Chute too far from platform	Adjust to correct position

● SUMMARY

The troubleshooting guide presented in Table 13.1 applies to all types of bottle fillers, whether they are center bowl, ring bowl, or remote bowl fillers. It also applies to fill-to-level bottle-filling designs, including those using vent tube-type fillers, level-type long-tube fillers, or displacement filling. Volumetric filling using flow meters or metering chambers is the latest filler design. Note that the old-style, mechanically actuated fillers are giving way to the newer and much more flexible electro-pneumatically actuated fillers.

Low-velocity beer flow, well-designed passages, and minimum restrictions are all necessary to minimize turbulence and agitation of the product. In addition, the pressure on the product from the release tank as well as the counterpressure in the bottle must be sufficient to retain the CO_2 in solution in the beer. The rate of the release of the counterpressure gas from the bottle must be controlled. Its release controls the rate at which beer enters the bottle, thereby minimizing agitation and preventing CO_2 from being released from solution, which would result in excess foaming, low CO_2 contents, and low fills.

Different filler designs present their own advantages and disadvantages. Experience, personal preference, and the economics of a particular installation all help determine which design is best suited for a specific brewery. Needless to say, brewers should be certain to perform the necessary research before committing to purchase a filler.

CHAPTER 14

Crowns and Crowning

JAMES F. EVERETT
Kerr Glass Manufacturing (retired)

DANIEL MALO
Famosa Crowns (deceased)

JUAN CARLOS GOMEZ
Famosa Crowns

HISTORY

Closures for beer bottles have evolved from the natural cork stopper through several hundred patented closures to the present-day, plastic-lined crown. It is a fascinating account, and the following pages present highlights from that history. This chapter also provides an overview of the contemporary manufacture of bottle crowns, including standards and performance testings for crowns and concluding with a brief discussion of the aluminum roll-on pilfer-proof closure.

Cork, taken from the outer bark of the cork oak (*Quercus suber*), was for centuries the primary source of stoppers for many kinds of vessels, including those containing beer. To create stoppers, cork bark is stripped from mature trees. After the bark is boiled, cleaned, and dried, it is ready to be processed into dozens of useful products, including cork stoppers.

By the late nineteenth century, machines were being invented to produce all manner of commercial articles and replace much of the tedium of manual labor. Among these new machines were those designed to fill and cap bottles. While cork stoppers were effective closures, the need arose for a more uniform closure that could be applied more quickly, and this need spurred the development of a range of inventions.

The patented Codd bottle stopper (1873), the Hutchinson stopper (1879), the Lightning stopper (1875), and the loop seal closure (1885) were but a few of the myriad bottle stoppers in use during the late nineteenth and early twentieth centuries. All these stoppers sealed the bottle inside the neck, that is, they plugged the bottle opening. At that time, all glass bottles were handblown, and the bottles' openings were not particularly uniform. Hence, the stopper had to accommodate some of the dimensional deficiencies in handblown ware.

In 1903, Michael J. Owens succeeded in developing a fully automatic machine for making glass jars and bottles. This invention made it possible to produce low-cost containers of uniform size, capacity, and finish. It was now possible to consider other means of sealing the bottle opening.

When patent no. 468,226 was issued to William Painter on February 2, 1892, there were few contenders left who could compete with the simplicity and efficiency of what became known as the crown closure. Painter's crown closure had a corrugated skirt and was lined with a natural cork disk. Subsequently, paraffin-coated linoleum disks were used. Ultimately, cork-composition disks were developed that could withstand the rigors of pasteurization. Later, "spots" (disks) of varnished paper, vinylite, tinfoil, or aluminum foil were adhered to the surface of the cork-composition disks to prevent undesirable components of the cork-composition disk from leaching into the bottled product and affecting its taste.

Between 1906 and 1909, Samuel C. Bond designed and patented a closure akin to the familiar crown closure except that, at first, it had no corrugations in the skirt.

Early versions of the closure were lined with a natural cork disk. Later, a composition-cork disk replaced the natural cork disk. A machine applied the closure to the bottle finish and in the process formed corrugations in the closure.

With refinement of the crown closure, standardization of bottle finishes, and improvements in bottling equipment, the process of filling and sealing beer bottles became quite efficient. However, standard materials for closures were growing scarce.

During World War II, extensive stripping of cork bark—needed for life jackets, insulation, and other materials for the war effort—ravaged the cork forests along the shores of the western Mediterranean. As a result, the price of good-quality cork rose steadily as its availability declined. However, the plastics industry, spawned by the war and then in its infancy, took hold in the United States, and soon plastic materials were available that showed promise as cork substitutes. Polyethylene, elastomers, and vinyl polymers were among the materials investigated as substitutes for composition cork. Early in 1955, the Bond Crown Division of the Continental Can Company introduced the first commercial, solid, molded polyvinyl chloride (PVC)-lined crown.

With the introduction of plastic linings in crowns came changes in the dimensions of the crown shell. Cork-lined crowns were greater in overall height than the later plastic-lined crowns because the first cork-composition disks were almost 0.1 inch (2.54 mm) thick. Thinner cork-composition disks became commercially available in the mid-1950s, and these prompted dimensional changes in the crown shell that carried over to the plastic-lined crown. In the end, plastic-lined crowns all but eliminated the familiar cork-composition–lined crowns by the mid- to late 1960s.

In 1966, the Armstrong Cork Company introduced a crown closure that could be removed from the bottle finish without the aid of the familiar bottle opener. In its dimensions, this crown was identical to contemporary crowns, but it was made of thinner, softer metal. It was lined with a foamed PVC sealing ring that had lubricant incorporated within it to facilitate the crown's removal from the bottle finish. The crown was referred to as the "twist-off" crown. Along with the twist-off crown, a special four-lead threaded bottle finish was developed to which the crown was applied and from which it could be unscrewed by hand. Its development exemplified the then infant trend in convenience packaging.

Other so-called convenience closures came to be used in the brewery. Roll-on aluminum caps, pull-tab aluminum caps, and all-plastic closures are a few examples of these closures.

CROWN MANUFACTURE

Manufacture of the crown basically consists of coating and lithographing sheets of metal. Crown shells are punched from the decorated metal, and the shells are lined with plasticized PVC gaskets. The finished crowns are then inspected, counted, and packaged for shipment.

Crown Metal

The steel used in the manufacture of crowns is a low-metalloid steel, designated type MR. The metal is single reduced to gauge and then electrolytically coated with either tin or chromium/chromium oxide. Raw, uncoated steel (known as black plate) rusts rapidly without the presence of these metallic coatings.

The thickness of steel produced for tin mill products is expressed in pounds per base box (pounds/base box). This expression of gauge can be translated into inches. The usual gauges of metal used in crown manufacture are 75, 78, 80, 85, or 90 pounds/base box. Those weights of metal translate into 0.0083 to 0.0099 in. ± 10%, respectively (Table 14.1).

Besides the gauge of the metal, there is the matter of metal hardness. After the steel has been cold rolled to gauge, it is necessary to relieve the stresses in the steel as well as to heat treat it to the proper softness required for punching and forming the crown shells. The process is known as annealing. The results of annealing can be measured with an instrument called the Rockwell hardness tester.

Tin mill products used in the manufacture of crowns are annealed to one of two tempers: T-3 or T-4. The tempers of tin mill products can range from T-1 to T-6; the higher the number, the harder the metal. Each temper designation has a range of values. In the case of T-3, the desired range is 54 to 60; for T-4, the range

TABLE 14.1. Nominal Base Weight Expressed as Theoretical Thickness and Thickness Tolerance

Nominal Weight (pounds/base box)	Theoretical Thickness (inch)	Thickness Tolerance (inch)
75	0.0083	±0.0008
78	0.0086	±0.0009
80	0.0088	±0.0009
85	0.0094	±0.0009
90	0.0099	±0.0010

is 58 to 64 (Table 14.2). These numbers can be obtained from the dial gauge on the Rockwell hardness tester when the specimen is checked for hardness.

The gauge of metal used for pry-off crowns (e.g., those used on GPI 600 series finishes (Glass Packaging Institute, Alexandria, VA) is usually 75–90 pounds/base box, while its hardness range measures at tempers T-3 or T-4. Metal used for twist-off crowns is thinner and softer, usually around 75–80 pounds/base box. A metal temper of T-3 is generally specified for twist-off crowns.

Since uncoated steel (black plate) rusts quite rapidly, metallic coatings are applied to the steel to prevent this. Tin has been used in this capacity for many years. Initially, this was accomplished by dipping the sheets of steel into a bath of molten tin. The modern practice is to electrolytically deposit the coating of tin. The amount of tin deposited on the steel is also measured in pounds per base box. For crowns, the most widely used tin-coating weight is 0.25 pound/base box. This means that a 0.25-pound coating of tin is placed on both sides of the sheet over an area equivalent to 62,720 square inches (a base box is equivalent to 112 sheets, 14 × 20 inches each).

Tinplate is available in two forms: bright tinplate and matte tinplate. Bright tinplate has a bright, lustrous surface achieved by remelting the electrolytically deposited tin at carefully controlled temperatures and then allowing it to cool to form the mirrorlike surface. Matte tinplate has a satinlike appearance and is not as lustrous as bright plate. The surface characteristics of matte tinplate result from the electrolytic deposition of tin on steel.

The volatility of tin prices and the wide swings in its availability prompted a search for an alternative. The result of this worldwide search was the development of a tin-free steel (TFS) that could be used in coatings. In this coating process, very thin coatings of chromium and chromium oxide are electrolytically deposited on the steel to produce either a fairly shiny surface or a matte surface, according to the customer's preference. Chromium/chromium oxide coating thickness is expressed in milligrams per square foot (mg/square foot). Chromium is applied at a minimum weight of 5.0 mg/square foot, and the thickness of the chromium oxide coating ranges from 0.75 to 2.0 mg/square foot.

The finished, coated coils of tinplate (or TFS) are coated with a very thin film of lubricant to aid in the handling of the sheets in the manufacturing operations. Materials used for this purpose include butyl stearate, dioctyl sebacate, and acetyl tributyl citrate.

The metal is manufactured in coil form in the steel mill but must be cut into sheets to enable the crown manufacturer to use it. The sheets may be cut to an approximate size in the mill and then trimmed to close tolerances by the crown manufacturer. The mills can also cut sheets to close tolerances, thus eliminating this operation for the crown manufacturer. The sheets must not only be cut to very precise dimensions but also must be square at the corners. If the sheets are not cut within the allowable tolerances, it will have serious consequences in the decorating and punching operations of crown manufacture.

TABLE 14.2. Temper Designations of Single-Reduced Tin Mill Products

Temper Designation	Rockwell Hardness Range, HR30T[a]	Characteristic	Examples of Usage
Box annealed			
T-1	49 ± 3	Soft drawing	Drawn requirements, nozzles, spouts, and closures
T-2	53 ± 3	Moderate drawing	Rings and plugs, pie pans, closures, and shallow-drawn and specialized can parts
T-3	57 ± 3	Shallow drawing, general purpose with fair degree of stiffness to minimize flutings	Can ends and bodies, large-diameter closures, and crown caps
T-4	61 ± 3	General purpose when increased stiffness desired	Can ends and bodies and crown caps
T-5	65 ± 3	Stiffness, rephosphorized steel used for hardness to resist buckling	Can ends and bodies and moderately or noncorrosive packs
Continuously annealed			
T-4-CA	61 ± 3	Moderate forming; fair degree of stiffness	Closures, can ends, and bodies
T-5-CA	65 ± 3	Increased stiffness to resist buckling	Can ends and bodies

[a] These ranges are based on the use of the diamond anvil.

Crown Production

The crown manufacturing process begins with the application of coatings to the metal sheets. In the case of tinplate, a primer coating is roller coated to at least one side of the sheet—the side that is to be lithographed with the decoration. If this is not done, the decoration does not adhere well to the bare tinplate surface. The surface of chromium oxide film on TFS is such that lithographing inks and coatings adhere rather well without the benefit of size coatings.

Coatings are applied to the side of the metal that will become the inside of the crown. These coatings serve two purposes: they protect the metal and prevent direct contact of the product (beer) with the metal, contact that would give the product an iron pickup taste. Coatings inside the crown also provide a surface that lining materials adhere to quite tenaciously. The coatings used inside crowns are generally vinyls or they are epoxy formulated since these materials allow little flavor to be extracted from the crown materials or transferred to the beer, a process called scalping.

The coatings and inks used in the coating and lithography operations are "cured" by passing the coated (decorated) sheets through long, temperature-controlled ovens. To achieve optimum cure of the coating material or decorating inks used in the process, each coating or decorating operation has its own temperature specifications. The oven temperatures used in the decorating process vary for each material, but they are usually in the range of 300 to 400°F (150 to 205°C).

Decorations or brand designs are placed on crowns through a process known as offset lithography. The inks used in this printing process are described as conventional inks, that is, they are inks that require some heat to set or harden them. Recently, inks have become available that are set through the use of ultraviolet (UV) light. Besides the colorants in the ink, these inks contain photopolymers. Photopolymers, along with activators, form larger polymer chains, which when exposed to intense UV light sources result in film formation. The UV light sources used in this process are usually quartz lamps that employ mercury vapor as their UV light source. By using UV-curable inks, the crown manufacturer can eliminate at least one pass through the gas- or oil-fired ovens normally used to cure conventional inks.

Inks used in the crown metal decorating process employ pigments, dyes, or "lakes" to achieve the specified color. Some of these pigments, notably lead chromate and lead molybdate, have been used to prepare specific colors, e.g., red and yellow as well as some greens and blues. However, concern over the dust generated during hoppering of the crowns and the potential for lead-containing crown dust to contaminate the bottled product has prompted crown manufacturers to seek so-called lead-free inks to replace those formulated with lead-based pigments. While these inks are not literally lead free, they do not contain any lead-based pigments. Any lead found in these lead-free inks is minimal (generally less than 300 parts per million [ppm]) and is a result of unavoidable contamination of the ubiquitous metal.

When the coating and decorating operations are complete, the sheets of metal are ready for the punch press, where the crown shells will be produced. The punch presses are double acting, that is, in one stroke, the press performs two operations: blanking and forming. The punch press may have 16–27 complete sets of tools, so with each stroke of the press, a like number of crown shells are produced.

Briefly, the punch press operates in the following manner. A set of punch press tools contains a punch and die, inside of which is housed a ram and former. The ram is housed in the punch, while the former is in the die. As the press closes, the punch and die cut a disk of metal from the sheet. The disk is held between the punch and the former; the ram descends and pushes the disk of metal into the former to produce the familiar shape of the crown shell.

During this punching operation, the dimensions of the crown shells are checked regularly. This ensures that the crowns can be used in, and will retain their mobility within, high-speed crowning operations.

Sealing Compounds

After the punch press, the crown shells are conveyed to the assembly operation, where the sealing gasket is placed in the shell. The two most common materials used for lining crown shells are plasticized PVC and non-PVC, or PVC-free, formulations. Both are used in the form of a dry blend, or pellet, or as a plastisol (thick paste). Nowadays, in the crown caps industry, the pellet form is being used instead of the plastisol version. Other ingredients mixed with both PVC and PVC-free resins are plasticizers, antioxidants, stabilizers, and if required, foaming agents, lubricants, and colors. To make the plastisol (paste), very fine, powdered PVC resin is blended with the other ingredients in a low-intensity mixer. A much coarser, porous PVC powder is blended with the other ingredients in a high-intensity mixer to make the dry blend, which can be used as a powder or converted to pellets.

Both PVC and PVC-free formulations destined for use in producing pry-off crowns usually have little or no lubricant added to the liner formulation. Those destined for use in creating twist-off crowns must have some kind of lubricant system added to the formulation to allow the crimped crown to be removed from the bottle finish by hand.

Types of Lined Crowns

Pressurized nozzles or "guns" meter out the plastisol to make one of three types of lined crowns: spin-lined crowns, sealing rings, or molded lined crowns. To make a spin-lined crown, a drop of plastisol is placed in the center of the shell. The shell is spun at high speed to move the plastisol to the corner radius and sidewalls of the shell. The lined shell then enters an oven for liner polymerization and foaming. For crowns with a sealing ring, a sealing ring or bead of plastisol paste is put (at a certain diameter) in the shell by turning the shell one revolution. The lined shell enters an oven for liner polymerization and, if desired, foaming. To make a molded lined crown, a metered amount of hot plastisol is placed in the center of the shell. Then, with the materials under heat and pressure, a molding punch shapes the liner. Final polymerization can occur during the molding operation, or the crowns can enter a small oven for final polymerization and, if desired, foaming.

The dry-blend powder (or dry-blend powder converted to random-size pellets) is used to make molded lined crowns only. The dry-blend powder (or pellets) is fed into an electrically heated extruder. A screw conveys the material through the extruder, where it is melted, completely polymerized, and forced through an orifice in a continuous manner. A rapidly revolving knife in front of the extruder cuts off a very precise amount of extrudate and, after a 180° turn, places the pellet into a rapidly moving, induction-heated crown shell. Figure 14.1 shows examples of the liner patterns available from current major crown suppliers.

If the liner is to be a foamed liner, it will start puffing as soon as the plastic exits from the extruder orifice, and it will be completely foamed as the crown enters the molding station. The molding punches are warm and are kept from becoming too hot by cooling water that flows through the inside of the punches. When the crowns exit the molding turret, the liners are completely cured and no further curing is required.

The lined, cured crown is discharged onto a conveyor belt for cooling and inspection. From the inspection belt, the crowns enter counter bowls that feed them very rapidly, single file, past electronic eyes, or scanners, that count the crowns as they enter the crown cartons. Whether performed visually or mechanically, this inspection and the counting operation are common to all crown manufacturing.

All major crown manufacturers have their version of the special scavenger liner, which absorbs oxygen molecules trapped in the container headspace during bottling and prevents further oxygen ingress over time. This absorption/barrier process keeps product flavor fresher and extends shelf life and can well be worth the extra expense for packaging delicately flavored pale beers. This crown is available with both PVC and PVC-free liners, and it can be used for pry-off and twist-off finishes. To comply with European Union legislation, crowns have to be PVC free.

For shipping, crowns are usually packaged in 70-, 72-, and 1,757-gross (equivalence in thousands) containers. The container is a double-walled corrugated box or plastic container fitted with a polyethylene liner bag to protect the crowns from dust and dirt. Boxes or containers can be individually sealed with tape, water-based adhesives, or hot-melt adhesives. The individual boxes are palletized, strapped, shrink-wrapped. or stretch-wrapped, according to the crown manufacturer's choice or the customer's specification.

Types of Crown Caps

Contemporary pry-off and twist-off crown caps can accommodate a range of sealing compounds. Pry-off and twist-off crowns can employ PVC and PVC-free sealing compounds, and both versions can include an oxygen scavenger package. Oxygen barrier liners are only available for pry-off–type crowns. The type of sealing compound used is largely determined by product application and by regional preference or legislative requirement.

Both types of crowns are available with TFS and electrolytic tinplate (ETP), also known as bright steel. Steel thickness goes from 75 to 90 pounds/base box.

Pry-Off Crown Caps

Pry-off crown caps with PVC sealing compounds are used mainly on returnable bottles or on bottles containing specialized beverages, such as juice, sodas, spirits, and ciders, among others. Pry-off crown caps with PVC-free sealing compounds are used mainly in Europe on beer or soft drink bottles or in Latin America on soft drink

FIGURE 14.1. Crown liner patterns. (Courtesy Famosa Crowns)

containers. Pry-off crown caps employing PVC-free with oxygen-barrier sealing compounds are designed to extend product shelf life and preserve the freshness and flavor of beer by blocking oxygen ingress to the bottle. These types of crown caps are currently used by several craft brewers in the United States.

Twist-Off Crown Caps

The amount of force needed to remove a twist-off crown cap is measured in torque. It is also an indicator of the strength of the seal, and the amount of torque required in a twist-off crown cap can vary by packaged product. Twist-off crown caps can employ either low-torque or regular-torque PVC sealing compounds. Low-torque PVC sealing compounds are recommended for cap crowns used in bottling handcrafted specialty beers and draft beers. Regular-torque sealing compounds are recommended for use with light beers. Twist-off crown caps employing PVC-free with oxygen-scavenger sealing compounds are designed to extend product shelf life and preserve the flavor of beer by using oxygen-absorbing compounds. As mentioned previously, PVC-free sealing compounds that can be used with twist-off crown caps have not yet reached final development. These PVC-free sealing compounds are being designed mainly to comply with European legislations.

Crown Shell Dimensions

Crowns delivered to the customer's plant must perform in a way that contributes to production efficiency. The first sign of good-quality crowns is the efficiency with which they move through the crown hoppering and feeding system. The dimensions and profile of the crown shell must be within specification if this part of the filling/crowning operation is to proceed efficiently. Over the years, as crown liner materials changed from cork composition to plastic, the height of the crown shell changed to accommodate the thinner plastic liners. Otherwise, crown shell dimensions have remained quite constant. The pry-off and twist-off crown profiles shown in Figure 14.2 represent the current industry standard.

Crown Liner Specifications

Although crown shell dimensions have been standardized, each crown manufacturer establishes the dimensional parameters for the particular liner configuration produced. The Glass Packaging Institute's finish specifications serve as the guidelines used in determining sealing ring configuration and dimensions.

● TESTING AND PERFORMANCE STANDARDS

Crown Testing

How well a crown seals is measured through laboratory tests as well as by its performance on the bottling line. One test of sealing performance is described in Appendices 2A and 2C of the *Brewing Industry Recommended Closure Purchase Specifications* (United States Brewers Association, 1978). The test requires filled packages to be submerged for 24 hours in a hot-water bath at 120–140°F (49–60°C). The test bottles are checked from time to time during the course of the test for evidence of leakage—that is, bubbles

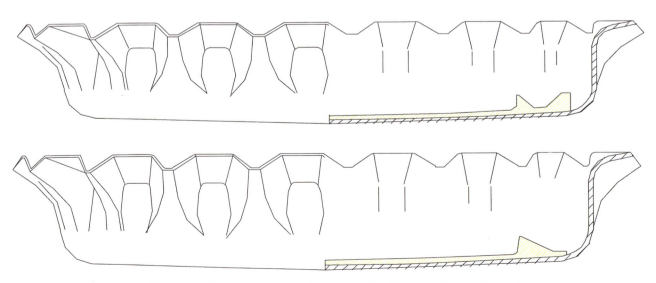

FIGURE 14.2. **Top,** Pry-off crown profile. **Bottom,** Twist-off crown profile. (Courtesy Famosa Crowns)

of carbon dioxide (CO_2) escaping from beneath the crown. At the conclusion of the test, the test packages are cooled and then checked for CO_2. This test can be used on bottles sealed with either pry-off or twist-off crowns. Since the test requires so much time to perform, some brewers use a modified version of this test. In this modified version, the bottles are submerged in a 140–160°F (60–71°C) hot-water bath for 1–2 hours. The bottles are observed periodically for signs of leakage. An occasional bubble coming from a bottle is normal and is no cause for concern. If, however, bubbles emanate in a steady stream from the crown skirt, the bottle and crown should then be examined for evidence of the cause of leakage. This investigation should also include an examination of the crowning operation.

In all of these tests, control packages, of course, must be used to establish baseline data. Control packages are held for the same amount of time but not subjected to the test conditions. For example, control packages can be checked for CO_2 fresh off the filling line (or pasteurizer discharge). Another group of filled bottles from the same part of the production run as the test bottles can be held at room temperature for the duration of the test period and then checked for CO_2 retention.

Crown Crimp

When the crown is applied to a bottle, the effectiveness of the application can be measured by using a crimp gauge (Fig. 14.3). This gauge simply measures the outside diameter of the crimped shell. In the course of applying a crown to a bottle finish, the crowner must accomplish a certain amount of mechanical deformation of the crown shell in order to properly attach it to the bottle finish and effect a seal. Crimp diameter is measured by using a stainless-steel gauge that has two or more accurately dimensioned holes machined into it.

Crimp gauges may take several forms. They may have only two holes, which identify the maximum and minimum specified crimp. More often, they are multiple-hole gauges, with the hole sizes ranging in 0.005-inch increments from 1.120 to 1.150 inches. Gauges of this type can be used in production, quality control, and maintenance.

FIGURE 14.3. Nine-hole ideal bottle crown crimp gauge. (Courtesy Famosa Crowns)

The range of acceptable crimp diameters for crowns is generally between 1.125-inch no-go to 1.135-inch go. This means that the gauge hole that is 1.125 inches in diameter will not fit over the skirt of the crimped crown, and the 1.135-inch-diameter hole will fit (or slide over) the skirt of the crimped crown. If a 1.135-inch ring gauge hole will not go over the crimped crown but a 1.140-inch ring gauge will, this is also satisfactory and will not cause leakage. However, as soon as convenient, the crowner should be brought into the recommended specifications.

When the crowner throat begins to act on the flutes (corrugated ridges) of a pry-off crown, the force is translated into leverage at the bend (turnover angle) in the crown skirt. This force pushes the turnover angle under the locking ring, using it as a fulcrum. The skirt of the crown is reduced in diameter in the process. This reduction in diameter is the crimp diameter measured by the gauges described above. Figure 14.4 shows the configuration of a pry-off crown before and after crimping.

During the application of a twist-off crown, however, the crown throat contacts the corrugations and literally straightens the panels (and the corrugations) as they are coined around the threads of the bottle finish. As a consequence of this reforming of the crown skirt, the crimp diameter of the twist-off crown will be smaller by about 0.005 inch than the crimp diameter of the pry-off crown. Figure 14.5 shows the configuration of a twist-off crown before and after crimping.

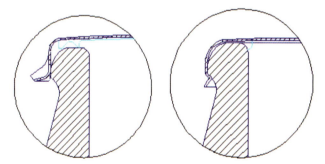

FIGURE 14.4. **Left,** Pry-off crown before crimping. **Right,** Pry-off crown after crimping. (Courtesy Famosa Crowns)

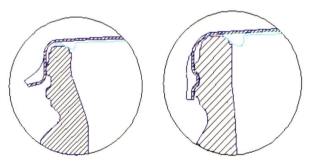

FIGURE 14.5. **Left,** Twist-off crown before crimping. **Right,** Twist-off crown after crimping. (Courtesy Famosa Crowns)

While crimp diameter is one measure of the correct application of the crown, it is by no means an ultimate measure of the sealing performance of the crown. For example, a crown may have a "correct" crimp diameter but be slightly cocked during application, which adversely affects the seal. If this is the case, then corrective action needs to be taken.

Removal Torque

Twist-off crowns must be readily removed by hand. To measure this capacity, a torque tester is employed. The most widely used are spring torque testers (Fig. 14.6). All torque testers read in newton meters and inch-pounds. The spring torque testers come in different ranges: 0–25 inch-pounds, which reads in increments of 1 inch-pound; 0–50 inch-pounds, which reads in 2-inch-pound increments; 0–100 inch-pounds, which reads in 5-inch-pound increments; and 0–150 inch-pounds, which reads in 10-inch-pound increments. Spring torque testers also comes in 0–2, 0–5, and 0–10 inch-pound ranges. Also available are digital torque tester models and models with computer interface. Both have a range of 0–100 inch-pounds and read in 0.1-inch-pound increments.

To assess removal torque, testers place the bottle inside the adjustable posts or a custom-made bracket on the meter table and tighten it in position by turning the knob on the side of the table. Testers can then grasp the twist-off crown (or spun-on cap) with their bare hands, or a suitable rubber grip can be used to assist in gripping the crown. The crown is rotated counterclockwise in a steady twisting motion until the crown starts to unscrew from the finish. This usually coincides with a maximum torque reading on the scale.

The spring torque tester is equipped with a follower, or indicator, for the pointer on the meter as an aid in reading the maximum torque registered. There are a few notes of caution. When measuring the removal torque, a smooth, steady turning motion must be employed, otherwise, the needle "bounces" and pushes the follower past the actual maximum value. Technique varies from operator to operator; one may turn the crown at a faster rate than another. To account for any variation across operators, all torque data should be initialed so that data gathered and compiled by more than one operator can be compared for such differences.

Motorized cap torque testers are also available (Fig. 14.7). A motorized torque testing system has the advantage of eliminating all variations across operators. The force applied to a cap is precisely the same in each testing cycle, regardless of who may be operating the machine or how strong they are. Some motorized torque testers offer programs for measuring removal torque and tamper-evident band (bridge break) torque on roll-on–type closures. The system can also drive in the closing direction to obtain strip torque. These measurements are to the 0.01 inch-pound, and live data and curves are shown on the system's touchscreen for each test.

Very high removal torques (i.e., those in excess of 10–11 inch-pounds) can be understood as a consequence of a number of circumstances, for instance, the bottle finish may be cracked. In this instance, the problem is easily identified as soon as the crown is twisted, and the test should be stopped immediately to prevent injury.

The bottle finish may have extrusions of glass at the vertical parting line (sealing surface of the bottle finish)

FIGURE 14.6. Example of a spring torque tester. (Courtesy SecurePak)

FIGURE 14.7. Example of an automated cap torque test system with brewery shield. (Courtesy Vibrac LLC)

that scrape against the inside of the crown shell as the crown is being removed. This causes the removal torque to be higher than usual.

If the horizontal parting line between the guide ring and the neck ring tools becomes worn, it too will produce glass extrusions (protrusions) at the site of the parting line. In this case, the initial removal torque of the crown will be normal (5–10 inch-pounds) and then increase quite suddenly as the crimped crown skirt encounters the protrusions.

When there are glass extrusions at the neck ring parting line or at the parting line of the guide ring and neck ring, evidence of the scraping action of the protrusions can be seen when the crown is removed. Bright, shiny metal will appear inside the crown skirt where the coating has been scraped away down to bare metal.

Still another factor that can affect removal torque is the hot-end coating applied to the glass containers. Hot-end coatings are applied to new bottles so that the contact areas of the bottle (i.e., where one bottle would contact the other) are covered. There should be minimal overspray of the coating at the neck and finish. This requires some rather careful control, and sometimes overspraying is almost unavoidable because of bottle dimensions. Excessive hot-end coating can be detected rather easily on amber glassware since the glass exhibits a gunmetal or bluish hue. Visual detection of excess hot-end coating on flint glass is not as easy. In any event, the amount of hot-end coating on or near the finish can be rather accurately measured with a special instrument designed and marketed by American Glass Research (Butler, PA). As a guide, hot-end coating applied in any amount over 20 coating thickness units (CTUs) is considered excess coating.

Excessive hot-end coating can increase the removal torque, from the original or initial value, by 1–2 inch-pounds on average. High removal torque resulting from hot-end coating can be a matter of degree. In that case, it may be best to conduct tests with one or two other sources of competitive ware to provide a data comparison. In addition to this comparison, the American Glass Research coating meter should be used to compare hot-end coating levels on the ware being tested.

Dried beer solids that become trapped between the crown skirt and the bottle finish can also affect removal torque. When bottles are filled and then transferred to the crowner, the bottled beer is made to foam with the use of a mechanical knocker, high-pressure water jet, or ultrasonic energy source. The foam displaces air in the headspace of the bottle. Since the crown is applied as the beer is foaming out of the bottle, there is a distinct possibility that foam will be trapped between the crown and the bottle finish. Some of the foam will drain from the crown. Some will be washed or diluted as the bottle travels through the pasteurizer. To ensure removal of the beer foam immediately after crowning, bottles can be sent through a spray system on the conveyor line that directs streams of water up and under the crown skirt. If this is not done, there is a possibility that some beer foam will remain. When it dries, it will form a strong bond between the crown skirt and the bottle. The adhesive power of dried beer solids is unbelievably strong. If present in sufficient quantity, it can make crown removal by hand virtually impossible without some mechanical assistance.

While hot-end coatings can cause higher-than-normal removal torques, cold-end coatings can cause another phenomenon called crown back-off. Cold-end coatings are sprayed on bottles shortly after they emerge from the annealing lehr. Their purpose is to provide a lubricated glass surface, which enhances the mobility of the bottles on the filling line. The temperature of the bottles as they emerge from the lehr and the amount of spray directed at the bottles—particularly when the spray is near the finish—can be factors that subsequently cause crown back-off. If, when the bottles emerge from the lehr, the surface temperature is high enough, i.e., it exceeds the softening point of the solid ingredients in the cold-end coating, the material will tend to spread and form a more or less continuous coating on the glass surface. When this ware is sent through the filling line, bottles coming from the crowner discharge will be sealed correctly, and the crimp will be within specification. But, when the bottles emerge from the pasteurizer, a percentage of them will exhibit what is known as a high foam collar, or they will actually have beer foam oozing from beneath the crown skirt. An examination of bottles exhibiting these characteristics reveals that the crown has apparently "backed off", and in fact, if the crown is turned clockwise, it is possible to turn it back or tighten it on the threaded finish and seal the bottle. Retightening the crown must be done immediately at the pasteurizer discharge before the leaked beer dries on the bottle.

The problem may come and go sporadically or persist for some period of time. On rare occasions, it may affect a small number of specific bottle cavity numbers. This could come about because of the mechanical setup of the spray device and its mode of operation.

There is no certain method of detecting the presence of cold-end coating that can be used to identify production dates of ware that may have caused the problem. Cold-end coating cannot be easily washed off the finish. The only way it can be removed effectively is to burn off the coating by passing the bottles through a series of burners that are directed at the finish. Alternatively, the ware can be sent through a lehr, with the temperature controlled to burn off the coating without reaching the softening point of the glass.

Testing Packages

The ninth edition of the *Methods of Analysis* (American Society of Brewing Chemists, 1999) has a section devoted entirely to testing methods for packages and packaging materials. The section on testing bottle closures includes a defects glossary and classification and a list of testing methods, which include the following.

- Internal pressure for crowns
- Internal pressure for 28-mm pilfer-proof closures
- Internal pressure for plastic-lined crowns applied to GPI 500 series finishes
- Gas retention capability of crowns
- Lithography resistance for crowns and 28-mm pilfer-proof closures
- Removal torque procedure for crowns and 28-mm pilfer-proof closures

Internal-pressure testing of finished packages certainly has merit as a means of measuring sealing performance, but by no means does it take into consideration the effects of shipping, warehousing, and handling encountered in the trade. Measuring the physical (mechanical) abuse packages must withstand and its effect on sealing performance is a more difficult task.

To this end, several methods have been employed. None of these methods are universally accepted, but they can provide useful guidance. One rather straightforward method for testing sealing performance involves packaging beer, including the wraps and carton, and then placing a number of cartons on a pallet, usually in amounts sufficient to constitute one or two layers on a pallet. One or two full pallets of finished packages are stacked on top of the test cartons. The test stack is left for some period of time—1 week, 1 month, or 2 months—after which the test packages are removed and the product is checked for presence of carbonation.

Another more direct, but time-consuming, method is a shipping test. Again, test packages are prepared in an amount sufficient to constitute the usual shipping unit (e.g., one pallet or more). These are placed on a common carrier (e.g., truck or rail) and sent to some prearranged destination. Upon arrival at the destination, the shipping units are examined for damage, and the general appearance of the packages is inspected. Finally a selected number of packages are checked for product carbonation.

Many home-grown tests have been devised in an effort to obtain some measurement of the crown's resistance to impact abuse. Impact to the crown can occur on the production line when filled, crowned bottles fall over or in the trade when cartons of filled packages are handled, stacked, unpacked, or stored as individual bottles in coolers. Tests of this nature have significance only if they relate to actual production experience or distribution factors. Nevertheless, impact tests can be useful in package development as a means of evaluating changes in crown liner design or bottle finish.

The most common commercially available equipment used to evaluate crown-sealing performance is a secure seal tester (Fig. 14.8). The secure seal tester is designed to test the integrity of carbonated-beverage containers sealed with aluminum roll-on closures, twist-off crowns, or plastic caps. By detecting gas—rather than liquid—leakage, the secure seal tester provides more sensitive, accurate readings. It operates at 175 pounds per square inch gauge (psig) minimum of compressed air, nitrogen, or carbon dioxide, and it is capable of handling up to 3,000 psig of inlet pressure.

The secure seal tester uses a hollow, self-threading steel needle (puncture tip assembly) to pierce the closure on glass bottles. The puncture tip assembly is connected to a hose that is attached to the secure seal tester, which has a controllable pressure source (either compressed air or CO_2). With the closure pierced and seated against the puncture tip assembly, the bottle is fully submerged in a water-filled tank. This protects against the hazards of the

FIGURE 14.8. Example of a secure seal tester. (Courtesy SecurePak)

bottle exploding during the testing and allows evaluators to observe the bottles for leakage.

CO_2 or air is introduced through the piercing needle at a predetermined rate and is increased steadily until the seal fails or the pressure reaches a predetermined maximum level. Bubbles of gas escaping from beneath the crown skirt indicates leakage or failure of the crown seal. When the test is completed, the pressure in the bottle is vented, and the package is removed from the tank.

Interpreting the results obtained from a secure seal tester must be done with an awareness of all the variables that can affect the test's outcome. Examples of such variables are crown application, bottle finish dimensions, amount of time elapsed between closure application and testing, and package processing. Individual breweries have adopted these procedures or variations on them and use them in daily bottle shop quality control procedures as well as for qualification protocols.

● ANALYSIS OF PACKAGING PROBLEMS

As in any production situation, problems arise that require analysis to determine their cause and the means to correct them. To analyze crown-related problems, a number of steps should be taken to collect evidence that can be brought to bear on the problem. If the problem has an obvious solution, e.g., a leak caused by an obvious defect in the glass finish or an obviously cocked crown, then the evidence is immediately at hand. However, when the solution to the problem is not so evident, the following steps will aid in an orderly collection of data.

When investigating a packaging problem, evaluators should first mark both the crown and the bottle with a number. They should do the same with all samples involved in the problem. Next, with a marker, they should draw a line down the skirt of the crown and onto the bottle. This line helps to relocate the original position of the crown with respect to the bottle later on. A data sheet should be prepared with the following as column headings.

- The number assigned each sample
- The cavity (mold) number of each bottle
- The crimp diameter of each crown
- In the case of twist-off crowns, the removal torque of the crown (as measured with a torque meter)

Before any crowns are removed, they should be examined for unusual or repeated marks that might provide a clue. For example, a worn plunger (presser foot) on a crowner leaves easily identifiable marks on the top of the crown. This could be an indication of bottle misalignment and subsequent cocked application of the crown.

Next, the crowns should be removed carefully. When removing pry-off crowns, testers should use an opener with some care so as not to distort the crown more than necessary. Once the crown is off, the sealing surface of the bottle can be examined for defects. The crown sealing ring can be examined for uniformity and completeness of impression. A note of caution: plastic-lined crowns must be exposed to heat in order for a permanent impression of their contact with the bottle sealing surface to be produced. Samples taken from the pasteurizer discharge exhibit such an impression. Samples taken from the crowner discharge exhibit the impression for only a short period of time since the "memory" of the thermoplastic PVC causes the sealing ring to recover almost all of its original shape. To obtain a more lasting impression, testers should place the bottles in a hot-water bath (at about 140–160°F [60–71°C]), or they should placed the bottles under hot tap water for 5–10 minutes and then let them cool. When the crowns are removed, the sealing ring impression is visible for quite some time.

It is best to examine a crown sealing ring impression with a hand lens or a low-power microscope. The bottle sealing surface should also be examined in this way. Details to look for in the sealing ring impression are

- completeness of the impression;
- uniformity of the depth of the impression;
- completeness of the ring seal (no part of the ring should be cut through); and
- centering of the ring seal. If the impression appears to be off-center with respect to the rest of the sealing rings, evaluators should check whether the crown skirt is "pulled down" more on one side than the other. If so, this is an indication that the crown was cocked during application.

With problems associated with glass finishes, specific flaws and other details also emerge. With twist-off glass finishes (GPI 500 series finishes), product testers should look for the following details.

- Fine fissures known as lines-over in the sealing surface
- Small checks in the edges of the threads on the finish
- A "rolled-in" sealing surface, i.e., one where the sealing surface slopes downward toward the bottle opening
- Dips or "saddles" in the sealing surface
- Unfilled threads or poorly formed threads (best observed with the use of an optical comparator)

When evaluating pry-off glass finishes (GPI 600 series finishes), testers should look for the following.

- A chipped sealing surface
- Excessive glass extrusion at the parting lines on the sealing surface
- Locking ring contour and height (best observed with the use of an optical comparator)

Table 14.3 lists many common crown and crowner issues along with possible causes.

ALUMINUM ROLL-ON CLOSURES

The aluminum roll-on closure has been used as a closure for beer bottles since 1966, and its emergence coincided with the growth of the trend toward convenience packaging. The 28- and 38-mm roll-on closures are the only sizes used in beer packaging (Fig. 14.9). At one time or another, the 28-mm closure has been used to seal 12-, 16-, 32-, and 40-oz. bottles. Its use in contemporary beer packaging is now largely confined to the 32- and 40-oz. bottles. The 38-mm closure is primarily used for 40-oz. bottles.

Although the American rights to produce the pilfer-proof closure under a British patent had been acquired earlier, the pilfer-proof version of the roll-on closure was first produced commercially in April 1933. The pilfer-proof feature minimized the possibility of tampering with product integrity. Repeal of Prohibition in the United States in December 1933 created a demand for the roll-on closure. The added pilfer-proof feature provided additional impetus for the sale of roll-on pilfer-proof (ROPP) closures in the wine and liquor market. In this application, there was no need to contain pressure or for the product to withstand exposure to elevated temperatures in the packaging process.

The use of roll-on closures in beer packaging, however, presented a different situation. A modification of existing roll-on bottle finishes was required to develop a seal that would withstand the internal package pressure generated while packaging beer. Different lining materials were needed to maintain a pressure seal as well as withstand pasteurizing temperatures. Both of these objectives were met in the development of the contemporary ROPP closure.

The contemporary ROPP closure is more familiarly designated the 28-mm top-seal, pilfer-proof (TSPP) closure. The "top seal" designation arises from the fact that, in the course of applying the cap, the dome (or top) of the cap is reformed by a pressure block in the capping head. This serves to shape the dome of the cap, and the liner immediately beneath it, into a configuration that forms a tight seal against the top and side of the bottle sealing surface.

There are two styles of pilfer-proof closures. The original style had a series of horizontal lances or cuts around the skirt about 0.125 inch up from the open end. The uncut metal between these cuts formed a series of what might be called "bridges" that held the pilfer-proof band to the top of the closure. When the applied closure was unscrewed, the bridges fractured, and a ring of metal stayed on the bottleneck.

TABLE 14.3. Troubleshooting Crowner Issues and Possible Causes

Issue	Possible Cause
High crimps	Worn crowner throats
	Turret head too high
	Worn or improperly set up crowner elements
	Broken or incorrect spring in element
	Incorrect crowner throat inside diameter
	Worn or misaligned ball control in element
	Worn crowner pads
High torques	Bottle finish incorrect
	Incorrect lubricant in crown liner
	Incorrect crowning force during crowning; broken or incorrect/weak spring
	Incorrect crown throat
	Rust under crown

FIGURE 14.9. The 38-mm (left) and 28-mm (right) aluminum roll-on pilfer-proof closures. (Courtesy Famosa Crowns)

The other version of the pilfer-proof cap has vertical scores, plus horizontal lances and bridges. When the applied closure was unscrewed or taken off the bottle, the scores cracked open, and the entire closure (including the pilfer-proof band) was removed from the bottle.

When either pilfer-proof-type closure is applied, the pilfer-proof band of the closure skirt is rolled, or formed, under a mating bead on the glass finish. The closure cannot be removed without cracking the scores or fracturing the bridges. To keep closures from blowing off because of the high CO_2 content in the packaged beverage, closures may include a series of cavities (usually on the upper knurling) that allow the gradual release of internal pressure and prevent any potential injuries to the costumers.

Closure Manufacture

Aluminum sheet stock is the raw material for the roll-on shell. The aluminum is an alloy, CH14, with a hardness of H-19 and a thickness of 0.009 ± 0.001 inch. For the 38-mm cap, a special, high-strength alloy is employed. The metal thickness for this size cap is 0.0095 ± 0.001 inch.

The materials and processes used to decorate the aluminum sheets are quite like those used to decorate metal in the manufacture of crowns. The decorated aluminum sheets are fed through a punching press to form cups. The punch press tooling consists of a mating punch and a die, which cuts a disk of metal as the punch descends and meets the die. Inside the die is a die plug. As the punch descends, it compresses the draw ring, and the aluminum disk is drawn around the die plug and pushed into the punch by the draw ring. This action forms a cup. At the bottom of the stroke, the clearance between the outside diameter of the die plug and the inside diameter of the punch is so close that it pinch trims the small ring of excess metal from the cup.

The finished cup and the pinch trim ring are ejected from the punch press. The pinch trim makes a cup of very uniform height. The clearance between the die plug's outside diameter and the inside diameter of the punch is such that the diameter of the cup is quite uniform.

The cups are conveyed to a hopper that feeds them into a beading machine. The beading machine changes the outside profile to form the knurling and roll groove and lance the skirt of the shell to form the bridges that become the pilfer-proof band. The vertical scores found in the pilfer-proof band of some roll-on caps are formed in the beading machine. Another method of accomplishing the same end is to have the tooling in the punch press form these scores.

There are two kinds of lining processes used in the manufacture of roll-on closures: the in-shell process and the inserted-liner process. The liners used in roll-on closures are generally made of plasticized PVC materials, foamed or unfoamed. For the in-shell process, the liner material is usually melted during the extrusion process and a drop of melted compound is applied in the shell and compressed by a punch to form the liner shape. For the liner-inserted process, the liner material is usually formulated and then extruded into tape form from which the individual liners are punched and inserted in the shells. The liner is inserted and bonded to the cap by heating the thermoplastic coating in the cap.

After the closures are lined, they are inspected, counted, and packed in paper bags. Usually, four paper bags filled with caps are placed in a corrugated shipping carton. The cartons are palletized and then strapped or shrink-wrapped for delivery to the customer. Palletized cartons of roll-on closures must be stacked properly to prevent loading excessive weight on the cartons of caps, which would bend some caps and subsequently cause cap-feeding problems on the closing machine. Caps should be stored in a clean, dry area, free from odors, insects, and rodents. Partially used cartons or bags of caps must be tightly reclosed to prevent contamination.

Closure Application

Proper application of the aluminum roll-on closure is essential to producing a finished package with a seal of ensured integrity. Proper and regular maintenance of the closing machine is imperative if uniform application is to result. Each closing machine manufacturer can supply detailed instructions on required maintenance, and the instructions should be followed scrupulously.

Operators should check the caps applied by each headset of the closing machine on a regular basis, noting the results of cap application. Keeping daily records on cap application is a necessary part of any quality control scheme, and these records also provide useful data related to machine maintenance.

The cap application process can be assessed through a visual examination of the caps. The basic elements of such an examination are as follows.

- A review of the cap contour
- An examination of cap threads
- A close inspection of the thread formation on the cap
- An examination of the tuck on the pilfer-proof band

The top of the cap should be reformed to a uniform contour. The radius at the circumference of the reformed dome should be well defined and of uniform depth all around the cap.

The threads should be fully formed from a full turn to a full-and-a-half turn of thread. The formed thread should extend down to the thread runout just above the pilfer-proof band.

Special attention should be given to the thread formation. The two extremes of thread formation are shallow, poorly formed threads and threads that are completely cut through as a result of improperly adjusted thread rollers.

Last, there should be a complete and uniform tuck of the pilfer-proof band. The formed band should be examined to determine whether any of the bridges or scores have been prematurely broken during application.

Since proper maintenance of the capping machine and a proper closure application are inseparable, it is necessary to maintain regular and accurate records about each headset and its daily performance. Records of this kind enable production personnel to anticipate problems before they get out of hand.

Besides making a visual inspection of the applied closure, operators can employ another method to ascertain the effectiveness of the closure application. Pressure-testing equipment, such as the secure seal tester described earlier, can be used to test the pressure retention capability of a roll-on closure applied to a bottle. This is a measure of the correct application of the cap. Using this equipment as a quality control tool, inspectors can collect sample bottles from each operating headset at some predetermined interval, for instance, twice per shift. In this process, the bottles are marked with the number of the headset that produced the sample. A visual examination of each cap (as described above) then follows. Evaluators should note any observed departures from acceptable cap application.

Evaluators should then test the packages on the secure seal tester, following the manufacturer's instructions on correct test procedures. Typically, properly applied 28- and 38-mm closures should exhibit pressure retention values in excess of 150 psig. If a sample fails to retain at least 150 psig, the sample should be tagged, the headset from which it came should be noted, and the cause of the failure should be investigated. Packages produced before the discovery of a sample with unacceptable pressure retention should be held for further sampling and investigation.

Cap Removal Torque

Cap removal torques are another indicator of cap performance and require attention. Although removal torque in and of itself is not a definitive indication of proper cap application, under certain circumstances, it can provide a clue to cap application problems as well as point to unexpected deficiencies in the bottle finish. For example, a chipped thread causes the need for an abnormally high removal torque. Poorly formed, or shallow, threads also exhibit the need for high removal torques; as the cap is loosened, the shallow threads tend to wedge between the bottle threads and produce that result.

There are two distinct torques evident when a cap is loosened. The first is the starting torque that breaks the seal between the liner and bottle sealing surface. The second torque occurs as the closure is further unscrewed and the vertical scores (or bridges) of the pilfer-proof band are broken. It is good practice to record both torques, although some laboratories record only the highest torque, that is, the one the consumer will first encounter. For the 28-mm cap, a range of 5 to 14 inch-pounds is usual. For the 38-mm cap, 10 to 20 inch-pounds is the normal range.

Again, for emphasis, cap removal torque is NOT a measure of proper cap application. A condition could exist in which the removal torque of the closure is within the normal range, yet the closure is poorly applied. Removal of the closure under these circumstances might result in premature release, that is, pressure in the bottle could blow the cap off, with potentially harmful results.

Certainly, the bottle finish is a significant factor in the effectiveness of a closure application. Specified dimensions for the bottle finish must be adhered to. Other attributes must also be present, or flaws absent, in order for the finish to function properly. Several of these are mentioned in the following paragraphs.

The sealing surface must be free of fissures (lines-over). The sealing surface should not be more than 0.020 inch out of parallel with the base of the bottle. These details affect the seal and cap application, respectively.

Caps must exhibit correct thread depth, profile, and thread length. These elements are essential to proper application and sealing integrity.

The diameter and profile of the locking ring, as well as the dimension, which controls the vertical location of the locking ring, are critical to correct application of the pilfer-proof band.

All bottle finish dimensions must be within specification to provide correct diameters for proper application, especially in reforming the cap and rolling the thread. Chipped, mismatched, or poorly formed thread profiles interfere with both application and removal of the cap.

Combination finish gauges are available that can be used to check these dimensional aspects of the finish. Their planned, regular use in an incoming quality control program can aid materially in the production of properly and safely sealed bottles.

RINGCROWN® CLOSURE

A ring pull-cap closure produced in Finland by Finn-Korkki Oy (Hämeenlinna, Finland), the RingCrown® convenience closure, is well established in the European beer, juice, water, and energy drink markets. This cap has the same diameter as the traditional crown cork and fits the same bottle mouths. It is a steel tear-off closure, produced in two sizes, the 26-mm size and the 42-mm size used in conjunction with the GPI 710 finish.

A principal feature of this closure is its readily accessible gripping ring, formed as an integral part of the closure. The ring is part of a scored tear-strip section of the cap, which allows the user to pull out and up on the ring, tearing out the scored section and removing the cap.

The RingCrown® closure is adapted for use with existing crowning equipment that has been modified. This modified equipment can accept special crimping heads for applying the closure as well as special cap-feeding hoppers and chutes for feeding the closures in correct orientation to the crimping heads.

The cap-feeding and orientation equipment is specially designed for high-speed applications. The hopper can be mounted either directly on the crowner column, or it can be free standing and adjacent to the crowner column. The closures are chute fed, oriented in a ring-trailing position from the centrifugal hopper to the cap release mechanism. As the bottles pass below the release mechanism, the cap is wiped onto the bottle finish and held in place by a hold-down device that keeps the cap in position until the crimping head completes the crimping action.

The crimping heads are adaptable to many other types of crowning equipment. In most instances, a special adaptor is supplied for each of the crowner slides so that the standard crowner mechanism can be interchanged with the RingCrown® crimping head for maximum bottling flexibility.

This convenience closure is completely tamper proof and provides a clean, reliable seal on returnable or nonreturnable glass, polyethylene terephthalate (PET), polyethylene naphthalate (PEN), and aluminum bottles requiring a hermetic seal. It is suitable for carbonated and noncarbonated pasteurized and nonpasteurized beverages.

REFERENCES

American Society of Brewing Chemists. (1999). Methods of Analysis, 9th ed. The Society, St. Paul, MN.

United States Brewers Association. (1978). Brewing Industry Recommended Closure Purchase Specifications. The Association, Washington, DC.

CHAPTER 15

Flash Pasteurization: Theory and Practice

JEFF GUNN
IDD Process & Packaging, Inc.

Fortunately for the brewer, beer does not support the growth of pathogens, the bacteria that make you sick (Bunker, 1955). Not considered a good medium for microbial growth, beer only supports the growth of yeasts and a few varieties of bacteria that unfortunately impair quality (Campbell, 2003). Brewers, therefore, use pasteurization to protect beer quality since it is not needed for consumer protection.

Since the 1880s, filtration and tunnel (immersion) pasteurization have been used to reduce the number of viable spoilage organisms in beer and other beverages to a level that renders them ineffective. Flash pasteurization, on the other hand, has been in use in the brewing industry only since the 1950s and has served as an efficient, low-cost, and effective alternative to traditional methods. To understand flash pasteurization and how it differs from tunnel pasteurization, it is worth reviewing a brief history of pasteurization as a method of controlling microbial growth.

HISTORY

What Is Pasteurization?

Pasteurization of beer can best be described as the use of heat to attain a 5 log (99.999%) or better reduction in live microbial organisms in the product without adversely affecting its flavor or character. Pasteurization is never described as achieving 100% reduction in microbial organisms because this level of reduction would be sterilization.

Louis Pasteur (1822–1895), the father of microbiology and pasteurization, found that heating wine in baths of hot water would kill microorganisms without damaging the wine. His findings were published in 1876 in his work *Études sur la Bière* (*Studies on Beer*) (Pasteur, 1876). Interestingly enough, he concluded at that time that it was impractical to pasteurize beer, a conclusion drawn probably because of his recognition of the high oxygen content in beer, the effects of which were not understood at the time. The politics of the day and a rivalry between the French and Germans over who could claim to be the technological leader in wine and beer production likely also affected his conclusion. As records suggest, Austrian winemakers were the first to coin the phrase "pasteurization" and were among the first, if not the first, to use the technology commercially.

The method of pasteurizing packaged products by placing them in hot-water baths and steaming cabinets continued virtually unchanged until the 1940s. Through the 1940s and into the early 1950s, new developments were underway, and in 1951, with the publication of a paper entitled "Thermal death time studies on beer spoilage organisms," Del Vecchio et al. (1951) presented data that suggested that the time needed to destroy a known quantity of organisms during pasteurization could be plotted along a thermal death time curve. The article further illustrated that this lethal rate data for the pasteurization cycle could be plotted, with a logarithmic curve for time and a linear scale for temperature.

As stated in an earlier unpublished article drawn from research at the American Can Company's laboratory, H. A. Benjamin suggested that the reference pasteurization temperature for beer is 140°F (60°C) and that 1 minute at 140°F (60°C) could be defined as one pasteurization unit (PU), or unit of lethality (*unpublished data*). The time–temperature curve can be described as an accumulation of PUs.

The Z value is the point at which the curve intersects 140°F (60°C) in passing through one log cycle. The Z value is equal to 12.5°F (7°C) and 5.6 PUs (Fig. 15.1).

The use of flash pasteurization for beer arose in the late 1950s and early 1960s with the shipment of beer over long distances in the then newly developed single-valve or Sankey-style keg, as we know it today.

Flash pasteurization has not been widely used in North or South America due in part to "indifferent" trials and experiences by a number of North American brewing companies in the late 1960s and early 1970s. According to some estimates, by 1981, fewer than 10 flash pasteurization systems were operating in the Americas. Europe and Asia by this time had hundreds of such systems in

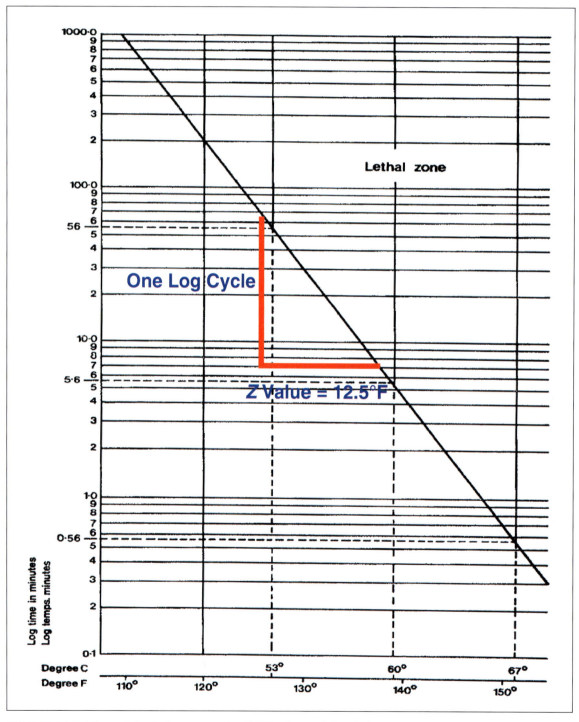

FIGURE 15.1. Thermal death time curve, after Del Vecchio et al. (1951). (Courtesy IDD Process & Packaging, Inc.)

operation for keg beer. Since the 1990s, the technology has increasingly been used as an economical and efficient means of pasteurizing keg and small-pack beers. The use of flash pasteurization for keg and bottled beers will continue to increase in North America, particularly for products to be packaged in barrier and oxygen-scavenging polyethylene terephthalate (PET) bottles currently used by the brewing industry.

DESCRIPTION

Flash pasteurization is a method of pasteurizing beer and other beverages prior to the product's placement into containers. The pasteurization process is used primarily to kill microorganisms that spoil beer quality. In this process, the product is handled in a controlled, continuous flow through a plate heat exchanger (PHE) and subjected to high temperatures, normally in the range of 160°F (71.5°C) to 165°F (74°C), for a period of 15–30 seconds. The amount of heat imparted to the product during the elevated temperature and time period is expressed in PUs. When used in combination with a Sankey-style keg and a suitably adapted keg, glass bottle, PET bottle, or can filling line, a flash pasteurization system provides an economical, sterile filling condition without affecting the beer's color and flavor profiles (IDD Process & Packaging, Inc., 2012).

Brewers should be aware of the key factors differentiating flash pasteurization from tunnel pasteurization. While tunnel pasteurization occurs while the product is in the container, flash pasteurization is carried out prior to filling. As a result, flash pasteurization does not have any effect on organisms introduced during filling. Therefore, to prevent the reintroduction of organisms, a controlled, sterile filling operation is essential.

Flash pasteurization systems used on beer typically employ a two- or three-stage PHE with initial regeneration (heat transfer between incoming and outgoing beer). Hot water serves as the final heat exchange medium. This allows a controlled, turbulent beer flow and thin film (or sheeting) to take place, which ensures that the beer is evenly and rapidly heated to temperatures 3.5–7°F (2–4°C) higher than the desired pasteurization temperature (ΔT). After the temperature-holding period, the beer is rapidly cooled by the second-stage regeneration section and the optional chilling section. All these steps together ensure that the beer receives the same PU input with a limited time at elevated temperatures.

At this point in the discussion, it is worth noting that any form of pasteurization accelerates the degradation of beer if the level of dissolved oxygen (DO) in the beer is high prior to pasteurization. To avoid this problem, brewers attempt to control the level of DO. Today, the most common and easily achievable target for DO is less than 0.05 parts per million (ppm), although many brewers attain levels much lower than this target level.

There are two basic approaches to process control in flash pasteurization systems: steady-state flow and variable flow.

Steady-State Flow

With systems using the steady-state flow approach, flow, pressure, and temperature stay constant at all times during beer pasteurization. Once the sterile beer tank (SBT) has been filled, the water used in pasteurization is recirculated within the system thus maintaining a constant, controlled operating state.

Variable Flow

With systems using the variable flow approach, flow, pressure, and temperature are varied to maintain a controlled level of beer within the SBT. As the SBT fills, the flow rate automatically slows down. The temperature and pressure within the system are automatically adjusted to maintain the balance between PU and carbon dioxide (CO_2) in solution. Conversely, as the SBT empties, the flow rate increases and the system parameters revert to the original settings.

As a method of system control, steady-state flow has proven over the years to be more reliable. When variable flow systems operate in conjunction with a packaging line that is, for whatever reason, in a stop-and-start mode, performance suffers. The control system variables brought into play with this changing rate of flow, pressure, temperature, and temperature hold time can cause system variability. The variable flow system relies heavily on precise instrumentation and reaction time (with minimal lag), as well as on the care and effort in setting up and maintaining the system.

Equipment

A flash pasteurization system generally includes the following components (Fig. 15.2): a high-head centrifugal beer pump, a triple-stage PHE with regeneration, and heating and cooling sections. The system has an external holding tube, a recirculating hot-water set that includes a pump and steam heating device, an SBT for the pasteurized beer, and a process valve manifold. A panel-mounted control system incorporating a printable and visual display of temperatures, plus all the necessary instruments and controls for automatic or semiautomatic operation, is also part of the system.

A fully automated system is typically skid mounted and includes an integral cleaning-in-place (CIP) system to ensure cleanliness and sterility of the flash pasteurization system and the filling line it serves. A skid-mounted design for system components ensures economy of space, energy efficiency, and automated operation of system components without compromising the pasteurization of the carbonated beer, regardless of internal or external process variations that might occur during operation.

Production-style flash pasteurization systems, including all auxiliary hardware, can typically handle flow requirements from 4 to 640 U.S. beer barrels per hour (5 to 750 hL/hour).

Essential factors to consider when designing a flash pasteurization system include the following: constant diameter of the holding tube; minimal recirculation of the beer in the system; controlled heating of the recirculated water; and controlled flow, pressure, pressure drop, and temperature.

Holding Tube

The holding tube should be of a constant diameter to maintain the ratio of mean to peak values in the velocity distribution across the tube diameter, as defined by Coulson and Richardson (1965). A constant Reynolds number (Re) helps maintain a PU constant for all product passing through the holding tube.

Minimum Recirculation of Beer

Brewers should always seek a method of control that prevents the overpasteurization of beer through beer recirculation and the "dumping" of beer to the drain.

Heating System

To maintain a minimum temperature differential between heated water and beer (ΔT), beer should be heated indirectly by recirculated water (typically heated with steam) running through the PHE plates. This is also the most accurate method of PU control.

Flow

The beer flow rate should not exceed 6 feet/second (1.8 m/second). To achieve optimal CIP in the PHE-adjacent product lines and temperature-holding

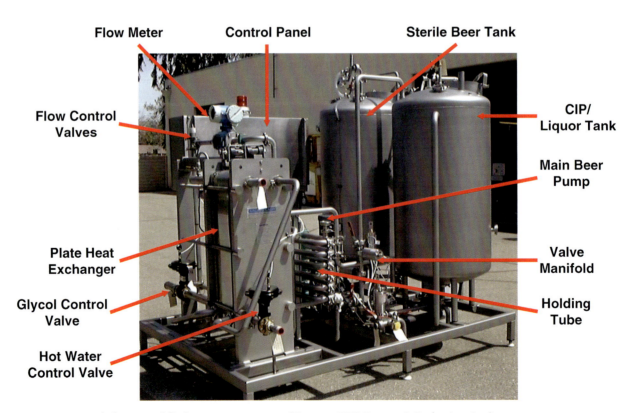

FIGURE 15.2. Skid-mounted flash pasteurizer system. (Courtesy IDD Process & Packaging, Inc.)

tube, the CIP flow rate should be at least 150% that of the beer flow rate but not less than 8 feet/second (2.4 m/second).

Pressure

To keep CO_2 in solution during the pasteurization process, the pressure within the "hot" section (holding tube) of the system must be at least 10% greater than the "vapor point" release pressure of the CO_2.

Pressure Drop (ΔP)

To retain CO_2 in solution throughout all sections, the PHE plate pack design must optimize the pressure drop without sacrificing the flow rate during CIP, when the higher flow rates are required. Any breakout of CO_2 in the PHE during the pasteurization process results in gas bubbles forming a thermal barrier, which will subsequently reduce the PU input to the beer.

Temperature

Using a three-stage PHE operating with heating and optional cooling loads maintained at 5–10% of the heat exchanged (regenerated heat), it is standard practice to achieve an economical heat-exchange efficiency (regeneration) of 92–96% during pasteurization.

Cleaning and Sterilizing/Sanitizing in Place

Equipment cleaning prior to a production run is accomplished with a normal 2% hot-caustic cleaning regime, and the system and lines are sterilized by circulating hot water heated to a minimum of 185°F (85°C) through the system for at least 30 minutes. After this period of time, the steam supply to the CIP/sterile liquor tank is closed off and the PHE temperature control point is lowered to the pasteurization temperature. Cold water is added to the CIP/sterile liquor tank, and the system is allowed to cool as much as possible prior to the introduction of glycol cooling to the PHE. At no time should the temperature in the heating section of the PHE and holding tube fall below the pasteurization temperature set point. After the system stabilizes at normal operating conditions, the water is chased out with beer.

As an alternative to sterilizing with hot water, an approved direct-food-contact chemical sanitizer can be used. When this regimen is adopted, the procedure after cleaning is to flush the system and lines with cold water and then dose in the sanitizer and circulate it for the period of time specified by the sanitizer manufacturer. While the sanitizer is circulating, the temperature of the sanitizing water in recirculation is progressively raised until the pasteurization temperature is achieved and maintained.

When setting up any cleaning regime, it is advisable to avoid cleaners containing sodium hypochlorite (household bleach). Sodium hypochlorite-bearing compounds in the form of free chlorides will damage 304- and 316-grade stainless-steel PHE plates at levels as low as 100 ppm of free chlorides. The plates will form stress corrosion fatigue cracks (normally in a "star burst" form) at the PHE plate pressure points, and these cracks will render the PHE plate pack useless. Reducing the risk of cracks caused by stress corrosion fatigue can be achieved by using titanium-grade stainless steels, such as 316Ti.

A boost pump in the holding tube section can serve as an add-on preventative system for the flash pasteurizer. It raises the pressure in the secondary side of the regeneration section of the PHE and ensures that pasteurized beer flows into the unpasteurized beer section of the PHE in the event of a plate or plates cracking. This system add-on is sometimes viewed as a cure to the cracked-plate problem. Although a useful addition (and in some applications a mandatory one), the boost pump tends to be a band-aid approach that often gives the operator a false sense of security. The best preventive action still is the use of a nonchlorinated cleaner, annual static pressure checks, and ultraviolet-dye penetrant testing of the PHE plate pack.

Operating Outline

Primary (DE) filtered beer at 32–34°F (0–1°C) is pushed from the cellar tank by counterpressure or a boost pump to the flash pasteurization system's high-head, main beer pump. From this pump, the beer enters the first-stage regeneration section of the PHE, where it is heated by the outgoing hot pasteurized beer on the other side of the heat exchanger plates. This regeneration section typically recovers 92% of the heat from the outgoing beer. The preheated beer then passes into the heating section, where hot water heats the beer to a typical pasteurizing temperature of 161°F (71.5°C). The beer leaves the PHE and enters the holding tube, where it is held at pasteurizing temperature for a predetermined time interval of 20–30 seconds (15–23 PUs). The required pasteurization temperature and hold time are determined by the individual beer, the live cell count, and a brewer's specifications provided to the system supplier.

Useful guidelines for determining PUs needed for primary filtered and/or centrifuged beers are as follows (IDD Process & Packaging, Inc., 2012).

Autolyzing residual yeast (i.e., in wheat beers): 5–8 PUs
Pasteurizing light lager beers: 8–15 PUs
Pasteurizing full lager beers: 12–20 PUs
Pasteurizing ales: 12–25 PUs

After pasteurization, the beer leaves the holding tube and returns to the second stage of the regeneration section of the PHE, where its heat warms the incoming cold beer. The second pass reduces the temperature by 92% to approximately 45°F (7°C). The beer then passes into the cooling section of the PHE, where it is cooled by a refrigerant to the required filling temperature, usually 32–35°F (0–2°C). The beer then leaves the PHE and passes to the SBT. The beer is then transferred to the filler by a boost pump.

Steady-state flow systems control alarm functions and ensure that only pasteurized beer goes to the SBT. If the SBT fills or any alarm sounds, beer is in some instances diverted back to the main beer pump suction for up to two passes through the PHE. After this point, it is normal practice to chase the beer out of the system to the SBT and revert to water recirculation. Water recirculation is maintained under the same controlled and stable pasteurization conditions until such time as the level in the SBT decreases (Fig. 15.3).

The control functions in variable flow systems attempt at all times to maintain the system in a forward-flow mode by constantly monitoring and adjusting the flow rate to keep the SBT level constant. At the same time, the temperatures and pressures within the system must also be monitored and compensated in order to maintain a constant PU input.

SYSTEM CONTROL REQUIREMENTS

Major system control requirements for a beer flash pasteurization system are as follows.

Temperature Control

It is essential to control both the pasteurization temperature of the beer in the holding tube and the temperature of the beer leaving the cooling section of the

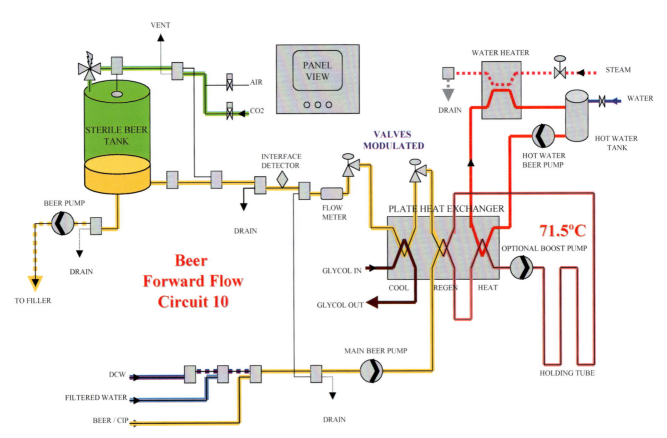

FIGURE 15.3. Schematic of a flash pasteurization system. (Courtesy IDD Process & Packaging, Inc.)

PHE. This can be accomplished through the use of a two-pen temperature recorder and controller unit or process logic controller (PLC)-generated software. A temperature probe at the discharge of the holding tube senses the pasteurization temperature. A proportional control valve in the steam line to the hot-water set controls the steam heating the hot water. The temperature recorder and controller also control the temperature of the beer leaving the PHE cooling section via a proportional control valve in the coolant line.

Back-Pressure Control

It is essential to sustain the CO_2 present in the beer in solution. To this end, a back-pressure control valve is incorporated into the system design to ensure that the system pressures at the holding tube discharge are constantly maintained at approximately 10% above the CO_2 equilibrium pressure at pasteurizing temperature (Fig. 15.4). The design of the PHE plate pack also allows the proper pressure drops to occur as the beer passes through the second-stage regeneration and chilling sections.

Flow Control

A constant flow control valve is provided as part of a flash pasteurization system. This ensures that a constant flow of beer is obtained. Some manufacturers provide a magnetic flow meter with a flow-sensing alarm and indicator for automatic monitoring.

Flow Diversion

An automatic valve system is required to prevent any unpasteurized beer from entering the SBT. The valves, in the form of double block and bleed arrangements, are normally controlled by temperature- and interface-sensing systems.

SBT Level Control

Once started in automatic mode, the system operates continuously at a constant flow rate. When the filler stops and the SBT fills, a level control probe or load cell on the SBT indicates to the control system to divert the beer, chase it out with water, or both.

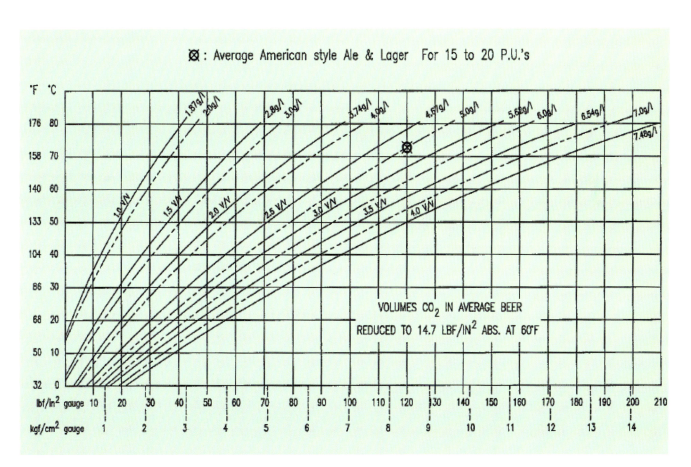

FIGURE 15.4. Flash pasteurization carbon dioxide (CO_2) equilibrium chart. (Reprinted, by permission, from IDD Process & Packaging, Inc., 2012)

Control Console

A complete array of switches, sensors, interlocks, and safeties are required. This control equipment gives visual readouts of temperatures, pressure levels, and rates of flow to ensure that only pasteurized beer reaches the SBT and the beer filler.

● OTHER USEFUL TECHNICAL INFORMATION

Two PUs ≈ 1 log reduction in cell count. Therefore, 10 PUs ≈ 5 log reduction, 12 PUs ≈ 6 log reduction, etc.

Figure 15.4 presents a pressure–temperature–CO_2 equilibrium chart designed to help brewers determine the operating parameters for flash pasteurization systems for beers with 1.0–4.0 volumes of CO_2 in solution (1.87–7.48 g/L).

Figure 15.5 presents a British thermal unit (BTU) load chart for a 92%-regeneration flash pasteurization system. This chart allows users to determine the heating and cooling loads for beer flow rates ranging from 10 to 500 hL/hour.

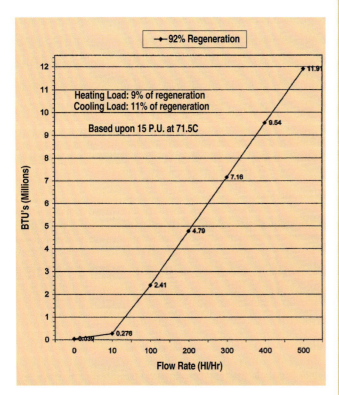

FIGURE 15.5. Flash pasteurization heating and cooling loads at 92% regeneration. (Reprinted, by permission, from IDD Process & Packaging, Inc., 2012)

The following presents the formulas commonly used for calculating PUs and pasteurization temperature and holding time when designing flash pasteurization systems.

In °C:

$$PUs/minute = 1.3932^{(T-60)}$$

$$t = (60 \times PUs) \div 1.3932^{(T-60)}$$

In °F:

$$PUs/minute = 1.2023^{(T-140)}$$

$$t = (140 \times PUs) \div 1.2023^{(T-140)}$$

Where PU = the number of pasteurization units to which the beer has been exposed at the end of the holding time, T = the pasteurizing temperature, and t = the holding time in seconds.

● DETERMINING WHETHER BEER IS PASTEURIZED

This section describes a procedure for determining whether beer has been pasteurized. The procedure was presented in the American Society of Brewing Chemists annual meeting proceedings (Owades et al., 1960).

Principle

Unpasteurized, or not fully pasteurized, beer contains active invertase. When sucrose is added to a beer containing invertase, the sucrose is hydrolyzed to fructose and glucose. The presence of glucose in beer after adding sucrose indicates that the beer has not been sufficiently pasteurized. The presence of glucose can be detected using glucose oxidase-sensitized paper strips.

Reagents

A: Test tape for glucose
B: Powdered sucrose

Procedure

Testers should add 1 g of powdered sucrose to 5 mL of beer and allow the solution to stand for 30 minutes at room temperature. After this period, testers should partially immerse a short strip of the test tape into the beer and then withdraw it, wait 2 minutes, and observe the color of the test tape. If the test tape turns green, the beer has not been sufficiently pasteurized. To allow a color comparison of test strips and ensure accuracy, the test should be run simultaneously on an unpasteurized beer sample.

A point to note: This American Society of Brewing Chemists method indicates only whether the beer is pasteurized—**NOT** how much it is pasteurized.

Unlike the laboratory method described above, the invertase test can now be carried out very rapidly using modern handheld instrumentation.

Typical Operational Results

With a 160°F (71.5°C) and 20-second flash pasteurization regime (15 PUs), production results for bottled beer taken from 154 samplings were averaging as follows: prior to flash pasteurization, <40 yeast cells per 100 mL, <20 *Lactobacillus* cells per 100 mL, and <20 *Pediococcus* cells per 100 mL; after flash pasteurization, <1 cell per 100 mL of each.

Trials with beer inoculated with 1.8 million *Lactobacillus* cells per milliliter prior to flash pasteurization yielded final cell counts of 6 aerobic cells per milliliter, <1 *Lactobacillus* cell per milliliter, and <1 anaerobic cell per milliliter after flash pasteurization at 163°F (73°C) with a 20-second hold time (25 PUs). The brewery typically uses 160–162°F (71.5–72°C) and 20 seconds for its bottle and keg beer production.

Trials with a temperature of 154°F (68°C) and a 20-second hold time (4.75 PUs) were used to immobilize yeast prior to reinoculating a new strain into bottled wheat beer. Prior to flash pasteurization, typical cell counts were 50,000 viable yeast cells per milliliter and 3 *Lactobacillus* cells per milliliter. After flash pasteurization, the viable cell count was <1 yeast cell per milliliter.

DISADVANTAGES AND ADVANTAGES OF FLASH PASTEURIZATION

Because flash pasteurization treats product before it is packaged, a sanitary and sterile filling operation following flash pasteurization is necessary. Without this sterile filling operation, it is possible that beer-spoilage organisms may be reintroduced during filling.

However, despite this concern, flash pasteurization presents many advantages. When combined with the PHE high-turbulence, thin-film concept, it is an easily controlled automated process that provides a repeatable, uniform treatment of beer passing through the system. Its other advantages include the following.

- Correctly designed and manufactured flash pasteurization systems do not affect product flavors, a problem usually associated with tunnel pasteurization.

- Flash pasteurization requires lower capital and operating costs as well as lower maintenance costs. Due to 92% or more regeneration, it consumes less energy. It is space saving, features mechanical simplicity, and offers permanent records for quality control historical product checks.

- Lightweight glass bottles and PET bottles can be used in flash pasteurization since they do not have to withstand the pressures and temperatures induced by tunnel pasteurization. As a result, flash pasteurization allows for equipment cross-utilization for glass and PET bottles, cans, and keg products.

- Carbonated and noncarbonated products can be handled on the same system.

- With flash pasteurization, the PU input is finite and under closer control than it is in tunnel pasteurization.

- Under flash pasteurization, the product is evenly pasteurized, resulting in an undetectable flavor change (with DO levels below 0.02 ppm) and lower overall PU input to obtain a 5 or 6 log kill.

- The use of sanitizers, such as stabilized chlorine dioxide (ClO_2) or hydrogen peroxide (H_2O_2), in conjunction with the correct CIP and sanitizing regimes can provide a microbially stable environment for cans, glass, and PET bottled products.

- With flash pasteurization, a product shelf life of more than 9 months is a practical possibility.

ACKNOWLEDGMENTS

My thanks and appreciation to Spoetzl Brewery, Sprecher Brewing Company, and my colleagues at IDD Process & Packaging, Inc.

REFERENCES

Bunker, H. J. (1955). The survival of pathogenic bacteria in beer. Proc. Congr. Eur. Brew. Conv. 5:330-341.

Campbell, I. (2003). Microbiological aspects of brewing. In: Brewing Microbiology, 3rd ed., pp. 1-2. F. G. Priest and I. Campbell, eds. Kluwer Academic Publishers, New York.

Coulson, J. M., and Richardson, J. F. (1965). Chemical Engineering, Vol. 1. Pergamon Press, Oxford, U.K.

Del Vecchio, H. W., Dayharsh, C. A., and Baselt, F. C. (1951). Thermal death time studies on beer spoilage organisms. I. Am. Soc. Brew. Chem. Proc. 1951:45-50.

IDD Process & Packaging, Inc. (2012). Flash Pasteurization (FP & UFP Systems) Operation Manual. IDD Process & Packaging, Inc., Moorpark, CA. www.iddeas.com/documents/CompleteFPGenericManual5_24_12_000.pdf

Owades, J. L., Jakovac, J., and Vigilante, C. (1960). Analyses simplified: I. Chlorides. II. Pasteurization. III. Diacetyl. Am. Soc. Brew. Chem. Proc. 1960:63-67.

Pasteur, L. (1876). Études sur la Bière (Studies on Beer): Ses Maladies, Causes qui les Provoquent, Procédé pour la Rendre Inaltérable; Avec une Théorie Nouvelle de la Fermentation. Gauthier-Villars, Paris. (In French.)

FURTHER READING

Anderson, R. G. (1955). Louis Pasteur (1822–1895): An assessment of his impact on the brewing industry. Proc. Congr. Eur. Brew. Conv. 25:13-23.

Goff, H. D. (2002). Dairy Science and Technology: Dairy Processing: Pasteurization: Introduction: Thermal destruction of microorganisms. In: Dairy Education Series, University of Guelph, ON, Canada. www.foodsci.uoguelph.ca/dairyedu/TDT.html

CHAPTER 16

Tunnel Pasteurization

C. ALARCON
Barry-Wehmiller Companies

J. R. WILSON
Adolph Coors Company (retired)

The art of brewing has been a part of man's heritage for thousands of years. For most of that time, beer was brewed and consumed without the benefit of the microbiological stabilization processes used today. As late as the end of the nineteenth century, brewing was predominantly a local enterprise, and since the beer was not shipped long distances or stored for any appreciable period of time, its lack of stability was not a problem. It has only been since the late 1800s that there has been the need and the technology available for brewers to produce a packaged beer that remains stable even after extended storage at room temperature.

The beginning of modern microbiological stabilization processes can be traced to French chemist Louis Pasteur's work. He began his work on fermentation in 1857 when requested by a distillery to study yeasts. His early studies in fermentation led him to investigate beer and brewing in the 1870s. Pasteur's experiments, based on the German brewing practice of cleaning equipment with boiling water, demonstrated that heating finished products to sufficiently high temperatures destroys undesirable microorganisms and prevents subsequent quality impairment.

Pasteur's studies of fermentation began in Lille, France, when he was approached by an industrialist who was concerned about undesirable products that often appeared during the fermentation of sugar into alcohol by yeast. Pasteur postulated that these products came from microorganisms, called germs at that time. He soon illustrated this revolutionary theory with brilliant studies on the conversion of sugar.

Pasteur claimed that by using proper techniques, types of microbes could be separated from one another and shown to differ in nutritional requirements and in their susceptibility to antiseptics. He also suggested that, just as each type of fermentation was caused by a particular type of germ, so it was with many types of diseases. Pasteur became preoccupied with the origins of microorganisms and demonstrated that each microbe is derived from a pre-existing microbe and that spontaneous generation does not occur. Spoilage of perishable products could be prevented by destroying the microbes already present in these products and by protecting the sterilized material against subsequent recontamination. Pasteur applied this theory to the preservation of beverages and foodstuffs, introducing the technique of heat treatment now known as pasteurization. His findings were published in 1876 in his *Études sur la Bière* (*Studies on Beer*) (Pasteur, 1876).

Several other discoveries and developments were taking place about this same time, which fostered the development and demand for microbiologically stable products. Most notable was the discovery of a solution to the nonmicrobiological haze problem that plagued the brewer who endeavored to store or ship bottled product. Also important were the increasing consumer acceptance of bottled beer, the introduction of the modern crown top in 1892, and the growth of transcontinental railroads in the United States, which opened new remote markets.

The objective of all modern microbiological stabilization processes is to prevent microbial impairment of product quality while minimizing any adverse effect on product flavor and its physical stability, and thereby achieving extended shelf life. Fortunately for the brewer, the task is made easier because beer is not a good microbial growth medium. Support shows growth of only a relatively small group of microorganisms, namely certain yeasts and a few bacteria. Of equal importance to the brewer is the fact that even though beer supports the growth of a few organisms that impair quality, it does not support the growth of pathogens. Therefore, the objective of the microbiological stabilization process for the brewer remains strictly a matter of product protection and not consumer protection. The growth of so few organisms in beer can be attributed to its low levels of nutrients, low oxygen levels, and low pH, as well as to the presence of alcohols, esters, and hop bittering substances.

This chapter reviews the different commercial processes developed for achieving microbiological stabilization, and it touches upon theory and principles, equipment, operating parameters, advantages and disadvantages, and operational pitfalls of these processes. The sterile filling process bears a close relationship with two of the stabilization processes and will be covered in Chapter 26.

● PASTEURIZATION IN THE PACKAGE

Theory and Principles

Since its inception in the late nineteenth century, the practice of pasteurizing beer in the package has continued to gain acceptance and widespread application. Today in both North and South America, it is by far the most widely preferred and practiced method of achieving microbiological stabilization of beer. Well over 90% of the packaged beer sold in this hemisphere is pasteurized in the package. In the European Union, on the other hand, brewers and packagers have been slower to accept this method, and its application there is not nearly as widespread. The situation is changing, however, as more European Union brewers develop export beers. The current trend is to pasteurize in the package, with its greater assurance of effective microbiological stabilization for these beers.

The pasteurizer is a device for pasteurizing product. Pasteurization is performed to extend the shelf life of the beer while having a minimal impact on flavor. This operation is carried out by heating the beer or beverage, holding it for a prescribed time within a temperature range, and then cooling it to a level applicable to the next part of the process. The basic principle of beer pasteurization is the use of heat to destroy undesirable organisms. The aim, however, is not sterilization of the product. Those yeasts and bacteria capable of impairing beer quality are completely destroyed in the process of pasteurization. Certain harmless spore-forming molds and bacteria, however, may survive, but they present no problem to the brewer since they cannot propagate in beer.

Prior to the 1950s, the degree to which beer was to be pasteurized was determined empirically. This led to a wide variation of treatments. Early pasteurization treatment utilized 140°F (60°C) temperatures and holding times of 20–30 minutes as a rule of thumb. In 1950, it was shown that the same mathematical formulas applied to determining the proper thermal processing of canned foods could also be used in determining the appropriate level of pasteurization for beer. For the first time, it was possible for the brewer to define treatment requirements and to control the pasteurization process more precisely.

To evaluate any pasteurization cycle, two components are required: a lethal rate curve (also referred to as the thermal death time curve) of organisms that can gain entrance to and grow in a particular beer and a time–temperature curve of the beer as it is pasteurized. Lethal rate curves (Fig. 16.1) indicate the time required for the destruction of a known concentration of specific organisms when heated to a given temperature. Lethal rate data are plotted semilogarithmically: time in minutes is noted on the logarithmic scale (ordinate), and temperature in degrees Fahrenheit appears on the linear scale (abscissa). The curves are practically straight lines and can be defined by a point and a slope. The point is the intercept at a reference temperature. The slope is commonly called the Z value.

The reference temperature furnishes a standard of comparison. In the canned food industry, 250°F (121°C) is the reference temperature for the pasteurization of low-acid foods, and 1 minute at 250°F (121°C) is a unit of lethality. For acidic foods, 180°F (82°C) is the reference temperature, and 1 minute at 82°C is a unit of lethality.

As proposed in 1936 by H. A. Benjamin in an unpublished report drawn from research at the American Can Company's laboratory, the suggested reference temperature for beer is 140°F (60°C) (*unpublished data*). One minute at this temperature is termed one pasteurization unit (PU), or a unit of lethality. A PU is a nonlinear measurement of time and temperature, which reflects the kill rate of the bacteria within the product as follows.

1 minute at 115°F (46°C) = 0.01 PU
1 minute at 127°F (53°C) = 0.10 PU
1 minute at 140°F (60°C) = 1.00 PU
1 minute at 153°F (67°C) = 10.0 PUs
1 minute at 165°F (74°C) = 100.0 PUs

The time–temperature curve can be described in terms of PU accumulation. Lethal rate data were determined for a group of organisms commonly found in beer, including abnormal yeast cells, acetic acid bacteria, lactic acid bacteria, and thermo bacteria. This work was reported by Del Vecchio et al. in 1951 (Del Vecchio et al., 1951). The thermal death time for this suspension was determined at various temperatures and the results plotted on semi-log paper to obtain a lethal rate curve. The point at which the curve crosses the 140°F (60°C) line gives the thermal resistance of the particular suspension of organisms at the reference temperature. For Del Vecchio et al., the intercept point turned out to be 5.6 minutes, or 5.6 PUs, with a slope or Z value of 12.5. (When using Celsius temperatures, the slope has a Z value of 6.94.) This means that to ensure effective pasteurization at 140°F (60°C), it is necessary for the holding time to exceed 5.6 minutes. Other time–temperature combinations can be used as long as they fall directly on or to the right of the lethal rate curve depicted in Figure 16.1.

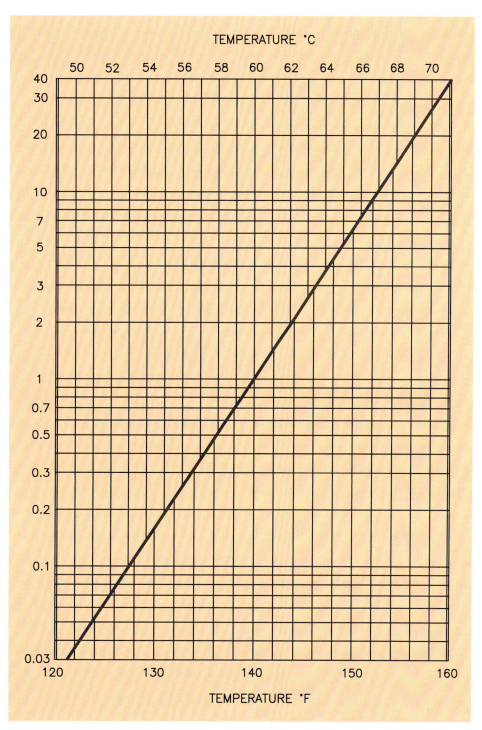

FIGURE 16.1. Pasteurization unit (PU) per minute curve, also known as a lethal rate curve. (Courtesy Barry-Wehmiller Companies)

The effectiveness of any tunnel pasteurization process can be evaluated from information derived from the lethal rate curve for organisms in the particular beer in question and the time–temperature curve of the coolest part of the package during the pasteurization process. These two components can be applied to a mathematical formula to calculate the lethal rate at any given temperature. Lethal effect (or PU) is simply the lethal rate (L) multiplied by duration (time at a given temperature, or t). This can be expressed mathematically as follows.

Lethal effect = PU = Lt

Since the lethal effect at the various temperatures in a process are additive, the sum of the lethal effect is the quality of sterilization achieved. If the sum exceeds the resistance of the organisms, microbiological stabilization has been accomplished. The lethal rate (L) can be expressed as below.

In English units:

$$L = \frac{1}{\log^{-1}\left(\frac{140°F - T}{Z}\right)} = \frac{1}{\log^{-1}\left(\frac{140°F - T}{12.5}\right)}$$

t = time held at temperature T
T = temperature °F
Z = slope of lethal rate curve

In metric units:

$$L = \frac{1}{\log^{-1}\left(\frac{60°C - T}{Z}\right)} = \frac{1}{\log^{-1}\left(\frac{60°C - T}{6.94}\right)}$$

t = time held at temperature T
T = temperature °C
Z = slope of lethal rate curve

Early work to quantify pasteurization treatment led to the adoption of 12.5 as the Z value to be used in these calculations. Additional work shows that this value is not as easily, nor as well, defined as might be expected and that it can vary depending on the particular organism and the conditions under which it is tested, as reported in 1978 by King et al. (King et al., 1978).

The amount of heat treatment (or PUs) necessary for microbiological stabilization of the product depends on a number of variables. The final number of PUs that the individual brewer decides is necessary represents a compromise between a minimal theoretical figure and a higher empirical figure, a determination that incorporates a safe range to cover beer and process variables. Under ideal conditions, beer with low microbial populations can be treated effectively with as few as 5 PUs and still be stable. However, most brewers feel uncomfortable with pasteurization treatments at that level, and they use 10–16 PUs. Treatment levels higher than these are generally avoided in order to avoid undesirable effects on the character of the beer.

Some of the variables considered when deciding on the level of treatment are the style of the beer, the physical condition of the beer (e.g., pH; carbon dioxide tension; and levels of nutrients, hop resins, oxygen, and alcohol), and the type and number of organisms present in the beer, including the possibility of sporadic high-count conditions. Also important is the presence of suspended matter, including colloids, which might shield or otherwise protect the organisms from the treatment.

Equipment

The equipment used in pasteurizing beer in the package has changed dramatically since it was first practiced. Early methods involved submerging the packages in a tank of water raised to the desired temperature and held for a period of time before cooling. This practice resulted in a batch-type operation and one that was very slow and labor intensive.

These early methods quickly gave way to a number of varied approaches aimed at making pasteurization in the package a continuous and labor-saving operation. One technique involved using a basket-type machine that required the hand loading and unloading of bottles. In this method, the baskets, driven by chain drive, were carried through a series of tanks or hot-water sprays. The bottles were gradually heated, held at pasteurizing temperature, and then cooled. Adjusting temperatures and times in each portion of the process varied the treatment.

Attempts were made to use a pocket approach similar to that used in bottle cleaners. Machines of this type carried bottles up and down through various tanks. Brewers, however, felt that the agitation and mixing of the beer with headspace air caused by this process was detrimental to beer quality, and the design never gained wide acceptance. Additionally, while the speed of production lines rapidly increased, there was a limit to the speed of the pocket pasteurizer.

These earlier designs led to the development of the current, horizontal spray-type machine. In this approach, packages are conveyed in an upright position on a horizontal conveyor through a long tunnel—hence the name tunnel pasteurizer (Fig. 16.2). Overhead water sprayers heat and then cool the packages as they pass through the machine. Water running off the packages is collected in reservoirs under the conveyor and pumped back to the overhead sprayers.

The packages pass through several zones and are showered with sprays of water heated to increasing and then decreasing temperatures. In the case of glass packages, zone temperatures are carefully graduated to avoid thermal shock and subsequent bottle breakage. Multiple preheat zones in newer machines allow brewers to easily control zone temperature gradients. During heating, gradients in excess of 40°F (22°C) are common on both bottles and cans. However, because glass is more sensitive during cooling, brewers should adhere to an upper limit of 40°F (22°C) of the gradient between cooling zones.

Cans may be pasteurized using greater temperature gradients during heating and cooling, thereby requiring shorter process times. Cans require 30 minutes for pasteurization compared with 45 minutes for bottles. Using superheat temperatures in the heating zone can further reduce the process time for cans.

For tunnel pasteurization, a package headspace of approximately 4–7% has to be provided to permit the beer to expand without breaking, rupturing, buckling, or otherwise damaging the package. Doubling the headspace results in approximately one-half the usual internal pressure buildup. Excessive headspace, however, should be avoided because it yields higher package-air values and greater material costs for the containers.

Today's tunnel pasteurizers are capable of handling line speeds of up to 180,000 bottles or cans per hour. In order to double capacity and/or reduce space requirements, tunnel pasteurizers are offered in double-deck as well as single-deck configurations.

In the past, packages were conveyed through the machine by means of "walking beams". This method provided good results since the walking beam only moved forward a matter of inches on each stroke and each section remained at the same temperature as the zone in which it operated. Stainless-steel strips standing on edge and running longitudinally through the machine were an integral part of the bed of the walking beam. The strips were alternately supported and attached to two separate transverse grate beams.

The smaller end sizes of cans (necking in) made it very difficult for pasteurizer manufacturers to carry the containers through the line using grate strips. The physical spacing between the three grate strips that is required to keep the container upright has been reduced significantly in recent times, and there are still many walking beam pasteurizers in use.

Currently, the preferred configuration for pasteurizers employs a continuous polypropylene belt driven by electric motors that are controlled using variable frequency drives (VFDs) and high-ratio gearboxes. This "belt" pasteurizer has reduced maintenance requirements almost to zero. The polypropylene belt is built in modular sections to allow a small section to be replaced if a break occurs. Recent advances in controlling pasteurizers through the use of programmable logic controllers (PLCs) or computers allow the use of a continuous belt.

PLCs have allowed brewers to precisely track a container as it moves through the pasteurizer, a capability not available until the early 1990s. A signal from the PLC controls the VFD. The VFD output drives the electric motor whose output shaft is direct coupled to a high-ratio gearbox. The gearbox directly drives the discharge end shaft. Multiple sprockets on the discharge end shaft pull the continuous belt through the pasteurizer. A timing disk and proximity switch provide feedback to the controller. This feedback signal feeds a counter that keeps track of specifically where the belt is at all times. This is very important information if brewers want to know whether the product has stopped while it is in the pasteurizer.

Two different types of walking beam pasteurizers are used currently: one that has two moving beams and another with one moving beam. These beams can be lifted under the packages, moved forward a few inches, and lowered again, depositing the containers on the other grate. The grate beam then returns to its initial position, ready for another stroke. The system with two moving beams is controlled with either a single hydraulic unit operating both decks of a double-deck pasteurizer or with two hydraulic units, each one operating a single deck of a double-deck pasteurizer. The single moving beam is controlled using an electrohydraulic power unit. The two decks of a double-deck pasteurizer are controlled

FIGURE 16.2. Double-deck tunnel pasteurizer. (Courtesy Barry-Wehmiller Companies)

individually with electronic controls that operate hydraulic components. Controlling the decks individually allows two different products to be run through the same pasteurizer on different decks. In hydraulic power units, cycle times and speeds are controlled with the use of flow control valves. In electrohydraulic power units, cycle times and speeds are controlled electronically.

A typical tunnel pasteurizer system is depicted in Figure 16.3. It includes the usual preheat, heating, holding, and precool zones. All of the preheat and precool zones are paired together as regenerative pairs of zones.

Pasteurizers use regenerative circuits in order to minimize water consumption, maximize energy conservation, and cut operational costs. Recovery rates of 100% on water and 71% on steam are possible in these machines during balanced running conditions. In addition to regenerative circuits, pasteurizers also utilize recirculatory circuits. These two types of water flows can be brought together in various combinations and arrangements to maximize water and energy savings. In a regeneration circuit, water is chilled in the preheat compartments as it flows over the cold packages entering the pasteurizer. This chilled water is pumped to the precool zones, where it is utilized to cool the packages leaving the holding zone. Water flowing over the hot packages in the precool zone is heated and pumped back to the preheat zone, where the cycle is repeated. The process shown in Figure 16.3 has three preheat and three precool zones, all coupled together in regeneration circuits to yield the highest level of energy conservation.

Water circulates through the heating and holding zones, and in this sense, they represent self-contained (or closed-loop) circuits. Water from the reservoir tank below the respective heating or holding zone is pumped to the spray headers. From there, it cascades over the packages and returns to the reservoir tank for recirculation. Steam coils, injectors, or heat exchangers make up any lost heat.

The very latest pasteurizer design, having only one heating source, is called a single heat exchanger. This heating source has a supply of 190°F (87°C) water available when heating is required. This hot water is injected directly into the piping that supplies the spray headers. This provides very quick heating. All water in the system is recovered, and the entire pasteurizer is a closed-loop system. The only time water is lost is when a gap is introduced into the pasteurizer. When this happens, cool water is injected into the preheat reservoirs to make up for the loss of cold product entering the pasteurizer.

Operating Parameters

Each pasteurizer's operating parameters depend upon the brewery's process requirements. The design specifications of a pasteurizer are based on the following criteria.

- Type and size of containers
- Desired capacity or rate of production
- Degree of treatment—number of PUs
- Maximum spray temperature to which beer can be subjected
- Beer-in temperature and beer-out temperature
- Summer and winter water service temperature

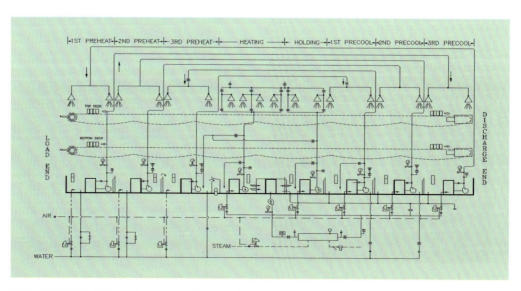

FIGURE 16.3. Schematic of a tunnel pasteurizer system. (Courtesy Barry-Wehmiller Companies)

From these specifications, a computer program determines the operating parameters for a particular container, such as those below.

- Process time in minutes
- Spray temperatures for each zone
- Gallons per minute of service water
- Steam requirements

Table 16.1 shows the temperatures and times required for a pasteurization process using a modern tunnel pasteurizer having three preheat zones and three precool zones. This particular tunnel pasteurization process was designed for 12-oz. returnable bottles processed at a speed of 2,000 bottles per minute (bpm) achieving 10.0 PUs of effective treatment.

Advantages and Disadvantages

The pasteurization of beer in the package presents a number of advantages. Of all the current methods for achieving microbiological stability, it offers the greatest assurance of a totally stable product. It has proven to be a reliable and effective method throughout the world under an almost infinite variety of brewery conditions. Because it takes place after the filling and closing operation, it is effective against organisms introduced during these operations as well as those occurring in the beer itself; thus, only normal sanitation and cleanup efforts in the filling and closing operation are required. Further, because it is a variable process and the degree of treatment can be optimized depending on a particular brewery's needs, pasteurization in the package allows brewers to avoid any adverse effects caused by overtreatment.

Nevertheless, pasteurization in the package has some disadvantages, which should be given consideration. Perhaps the most important is the adverse effect of heating on the flavor of beer. Heating beer to pasteurizing temperatures, particularly in the presence of oxygen, accelerates the formation of unwanted off-flavors. This problem has been minimized in recent years by holding pasteurization times and temperatures as low as possible and by reducing total package oxygen (TPO) levels. It can never be totally eliminated, however, since heating is basic to the process.

As a second major disadvantage, the process requires the use of heavier, stronger packages that can withstand

TABLE 16.1. Operating Parameters for a Tunnel Pasteurizer Running 12-oz. Returnable Bottles at 2,000 bpm and 10.0 PUs

Zone	Spray Temperature °F	Spray Temperature °C	Spray Time (min)	Process Time (min)	Infeed	Beer Temperature[a] °F	Beer Temperature[a] °C
First preheat	73.5	23.1	3.78	3.78	In	34.0	1.1
					Out	38.0	3.3
Second preheat	94.5	34.7	3.30	7.08	In	38.0	3.3
					Out	62.6	17.0
Third preheat	111.5	44.2	2.83	9.91	In	62.6	17.0
					Out	83.3	28.5
Heating	149.0	65.0	8.50	18.41	In	83.3	28.5
					Out	140.0	60.0
Holding	140.0	60.0	5.60	24.01	In	140.0	60.0
					Out	140.0	60.0
First precool	110.0	43.3	2.83	26.84	In	140.0	60.0
					Out	119.6	48.7
Second precool	93.0	33.9	3.30	30.14	In	119.6	48.7
					Out	99.2	37.3
Third precool	72.0	22.2	3.78	33.92	In	99.2	37.3
					Out	77.0	25.0

[a] Coldspot temperature on the central axis, 0.25 inch up from the inside bottom of the container.

the higher internal-package pressures occurring during pasteurization. With the price of packaging materials steadily increasing, this requirement becomes an important factor and significantly adds to product cost. Additional costs are also incurred when shipping these heavier containers to remote markets. Efforts to optimize the pasteurization process and container design in order to minimize package weight and related costs are taking place, but these factors remain a concern.

Increasing energy costs are also adding to the already higher operating costs of tunnel pasteurizers. Even when they are equipped with heat regeneration, tunnel pasteurizers have the highest energy requirements of any of the methods of pasteurization. The package materials as well as the beer itself are heated and cooled. Water usage is also higher and can be a significant cost factor, particularly in those areas where water is scarce. It is necessary to provide for extensive treatment of the process water in order to protect against biological fouling, corrosion, and scale formulation.

Initial costs are higher for tunnel pasteurizing because of the size and complexity of the equipment. The tunnel pasteurizer is many times larger than a filter or flash pasteurizer of equal capacity and much more complex because of its conveyors, drives, pumps, and controls. Initial costs can be further increased because of the equipment's larger footprint and greater requirements for floor space.

Operational Pitfalls

As with most automated processes, certain operational and equipment difficulties in tunnel pasteurization warrant attention. Few problems are likely to occur in the process during steady-run conditions, in which the packages are being constantly fed into and removed from the pasteurizer. Under steady-run conditions, the main concerns are plugged spray nozzles, improper cycle times, improper zone temperatures, loosely packed or downed bottles, and bottle breakage. If uncorrected, plugged spray nozzles can cause over- or underpasteurization of the beer. Bottle breakage can reach unreasonable levels if not given proper attention. However, the number of damaged bottles can be reduced to practically zero if the following conditions are avoided.

- Poor glass and/or rough handling of bottles
- Overfilling
- Abrupt temperature changes and/or overheating
- Jams and fallen bottles

With the exception of poor glass in the bottles, the brewer can directly control all of these factors, and they should be given constant surveillance. As discussed earlier, additional process problems can occur during the intermittent feeding of packages and can result in process temperature imbalance in the various zones.

Production stops downstream of the pasteurizer are a common occurrence in all bottle shops. Those of short duration (1 or 2 minutes) can be ignored, but longer stops adversely affect the pasteurization process and should be compensated for. Most modern pasteurizers have some method of limiting the maximum number of PUs accumulated in a product during long stops. This method is called PU control. The methods used to control overpasteurization monitor the amount of time and the specific intervals at which the product has been stopped. When using PLC control, brewers can track the progress of the product inside of the machine. As a result, brewers can ensure that, despite production stops, the product can get sprayed with hot water and cooling water for the same period of time as when moving through the sprays in the heating, holding, and first precool zones.

Proper temperature control in each of the zones is also critical to the process, especially during intermittent or imbalanced running. Improvements have been made in this area by utilizing properly sized reservoirs and faster responding control systems. The temperature controls and associated diaphragm valves are designed for a particular pressure and quality of steam. If the steam pressure or steam quality is variable, zone temperatures will not be within the process specification and under- or overpasteurization will occur. Single heat source pasteurizers provide one way for current pasteurizers to eliminate these problems. These pasteurizers employ direct heating by injecting hot water at 185°F (85°C) directly into the spray header piping. This eliminates the need to heat the water in each reservoir, which reduces the time to recover the temperature and maintains a more constant spray temperature.

Measuring Process Performance

The performance of the tunnel pasteurizer must be monitored on a regular schedule to determine whether the process conforms to design specifications. Its performance is usually monitored with the use of a traveling recorder, a device sent through the pasteurizer to check the time–temperature curve. The device consists of a temperature probe inserted in a bottle/can, a probe to record ambient temperature, and a recording device that stores temperature data against time through the machine. Operators can retrieve recorder data while in process, downloading the data to their computers via radio transmission. More commonly, operators use a hard connection to download the data at the completion of the recorder's passage through the pasteurizer.

These devices are also referred to as travelers, PU monitors, or clocks. The old units were just like clocks with a circular chart. These units could be sent traveling through the pasteurizer with a freshly filled cold can or bottle of beer attached to a thermocouple. The temperature change was picked up by an ink pen recording onto a circular chart. The chart had to be analyzed manually and the PUs calculated using the minutes above 140°F (60°C).

These served the purpose for many years, and in fact, many are still in use today. Several types of traveling recorders are currently available. The more modern travelers are electronic and use an internal program to calculate PUs. All of the data is then stored and analyzed in the quality assurance department's computer files.

Operational performance must be monitored as well and on a much more frequent basis. Floor personnel can carry out this monitoring with the aid of checklists and record sheets. Part of the monitoring involves simply being observant and catching problems such as jams, fallen bottles, broken glass, and pressure-damaged containers. Another important part of monitoring is observing and recording pertinent data such as zone temperatures and process time, reviewing control charts, and checking for plugged sprayers. A detailed checklist is particularly important if more than one package is run and the parameters are reset between runs. Each pasteurizer should have a checklist based on the manufacturer's data sheet (or better yet—one developed from plant experience) for each package to be run so that the variables can be set to yield the desired PU value.

Equipment problems associated with tunnel pasteurizers are most likely to occur in three areas: the walking beam conveying mechanisms in the older units, the temperature controls and automatic valves, and process water treatment.

While belt conveyors in newer pasteurizers seldom fail, problems relating to the walking beam conveying mechanisms in older pasteurizers include leaking hydraulic seals and fittings, malfunctioning valves, and binding or jamming conveyor parts. These problems can result in slowing or stopping the conveyor and affect a change in the process time–temperature relationship.

An effective preventive maintenance program can best handle problems of this sort and should include scheduled, routine inspections of the hydraulic drive components, the conveying mechanism, and timing of the conveying cycle.

Problems can occur at any time in the temperature controls and valves. It is extremely important that the air supply to the temperature controllers be clean, dry, and at a constant pressure. Dirty, wet compressed air adversely affects the controller operation and results in pasteurizer shutdown and improperly pasteurized beer. Regular monitoring of the temperature controls during operation of the pasteurizer is a must. The temperatures in the superheat and pasteurizer zones must be recorded continuously on a 24-hour chart or in the computer program. Operators can add high- and/or low-temperature safeguards to the control system, especially in the superheat and pasteurizer zones. These safeguards can provide warning and stop the process when necessary. In addition to regular monitoring, it is also important to have an effective preventive maintenance program for both the controllers and the valves in order to keep them functioning properly.

Water Treatment

Certainly the most critical factor affecting pasteurizer equipment is proper treatment of process water. Failure to adequately treat the water leads very quickly to problems with biological fouling, scale buildup, and corrosion. These result in plugged spray systems, inadequate heat transfer, and metal corrosion. Consequently, tunnel pasteurizers cannot be operated without proper water treatment. Maintaining the system under control requires constant monitoring, and the attention of a specialist in the field of water treatment is required.

● TROUBLESHOOTING

Water Pump Cleaning

If the spray headers and the box screen are clean but a full spray is not obtained, the pump suction head should be removed and the interior of the pump should be cleaned out (a slime condition sometimes occurs, necessitating cleaning the pump). While the suction head is removed, the impeller should be checked to see whether it has deteriorated to the point of replacing and also whether it is solidly mounted to the shaft.

Heat Exchanger Water Treatment

Each owner should secure a chemical analysis of the water that is being processed through each heat exchanger to determine the volume of calcium salts and iron oxides that may be present in the water. A water treatment program should then be established to prevent the deposit of minerals on the interior of the heat exchanger tube walls. The complexities of administering a good water treatment program usually require the services of a specialist in that field to monitor the program.

Pump Prestart Checks

Before initial start of the pump, the following inspections should be made.

- Check the rotation. Be sure that the pump operates in the direction indicated by the arrow on the pump casing since serious damage can result if the pump is operated with incorrect rotation. Check the rotation each time the motor leads are disconnected.
- Check all connections to the motor and starting device with a wiring diagram. Check the voltage, phase, and frequency of the line circuit with a motor nameplate.
- Check the stuffing box adjustment, if applicable.
- Ensure that the motor bearings are properly lubricated.
- Ensure that the pump is full of liquid (primed).

Pump Troubleshooting

Between regular maintenance inspections, brewers should be alert for signs of pump trouble. Common symptoms are listed in Table 16.2. Any trouble should immediately be corrected to avoid costly repair and shutdown.

Heat Exchanger Water Flow Impediments

A pressure differential of more than 8 pounds per square inch gauge (psig) across the input/output lines is an indication of a restriction of water flow through the exchanger. Possible causes include blockage by glass particles or by scale buildup on the tube wall. In either instance, corrective action must be taken immediately to prevent heat exchanger failure. If the tubes are blocked with glass particles, the heat exchanger tube bundle must be removed for cleaning (if the heat exchanger is of the U-tube design). If the heat exchanger is of the straight-tube design, the end cover of the exchanger can be removed and the tubes brush cleaned. Whenever a scale deposit does occur on the interior tube wall, this is an indication that the water treatment program has failed and corrective action must be taken. The scale deposit can be removed by subjecting the heat exchanger to an acid cleaning procedure as recommended by a reputable chemical company.

Acid Cleaning of Heat Exchangers

With a properly designed and controlled chemical treatment program, acid cleaning frequency should be minimal, if not eliminated. Whenever acid cleaning is required, it is normally the external heat exchanger tube bundles that require cleaning. A typical procedure is described below.

Preparation

It is extremely important to incorporate the following steps before acid cleaning is initiated.

- Drain and inspect the heat exchanger to determine the type of scale that is present and to estimate the total quantity of scale that must be removed.
- Select the strength and type of acid cleaning solution as well as the temperature and contact time for the cleaning solution. Most deposits that form in heat exchangers are calcium salts and/or iron oxides, which are readily dissolved in muriatic (hydrochloric) acid.
- Select the proper inhibitor for the muriatic acid and determine the percentage of inhibitor that will be needed. Uninhibited muriatic acid is highly corrosive to steel, copper, and copper alloys. <u>Never</u> attempt to acid clean heat exchangers without inhibiting the acid properly.
- Select the neutralizing solution and determine the volume of alkaline solution needed for neutralization.
- Determine what arrangements (if any) will be needed for disposal of the spent acid cleaning solution as well as for the alkaline rinse water. If those solutions cannot be discharged into normal disposal facilities (city sewer or plant waste treatment facility), arrangements must be made to haul off these waste solutions.

TABLE 16.2. Pump Troubleshooting

Problem	Probable Cause	Corrective Action
1. No liquid delivered	1. Lack of prime	1. Fill pump and suction pipe completely with liquid.
	2. Loss of prime	2. Check for leaks in suction pipe joints and fittings; vent casing to remove accumulated air.
	3. Suction lift too high	3. Check for obstruction at inlet; check for pipe friction losses. Static lift may be too great. Measure with mercury column or vacuum gauge while pump operates. If static lift is too high, liquid to be pumped must be raised or pump lowered.
	4. Discharge head too high	4. Check pipe friction losses. Larger piping may correct condition. Check that valves are wide open.
	5. Speed too low	5. Check that motor voltage is correct and receiving full voltage. Check for low frequency. Check for open motor phase.
	6. Wrong direction of rotation	6. Check motor rotation with directional arrow on pump casing.
	7. Impeller completely plugged	7. Dismantle pump and clean impeller.
2. Not enough liquid delivered	1. Air leaks in suction piping	1. Suction line can be tested by shutting off or plugging inlet and putting line under pressure. A gauge will indicate a leak by a drop of pressure.
	2. Speed too low	2. Check that motor voltage is correct and receiving full voltage. Check for low frequency. Check for open motor phase.
	3. Air leaks in stuffing box	3. Increase seal liquid pressure to above atmosphere.
	4. Discharge head too high	4. Check pipe friction losses. Larger piping may correct condition. Check that valves are wide open.
	5. Suction lift to high	5. Check for obstruction at inlet; check for pipe friction losses. Static lift may be too great. Measure with mercury column or vacuum gauge while pump operates. If static lift is too high, liquid to be pumped must be raised or pump lowered.
	6. Impeller partially plugged	6. Dismantle pump and clean impeller.
	7. Cavitation; insufficient net positive suction head (depending on installation pressure)	7a. Increase positive suction head on pump by lowering pump. 7b. Subcool suction piping air inlet to lower entering liquid temperature. 7c. Pressurize suction vessel.
	8. Defective impeller	8. Inspect impeller and shaft. Replace if damaged or vane sections badly eroded.
	9. Defective packing or mechanical seal	9. Replace packing and sleeve if badly worn; replace mechanical seal.
	10. Wrong direction of rotation	10. Symptoms show a flow rate of approximately one-half rated capacity. Compare rotation of motor with directional arrow on pump casing.
	11. Incorrect impeller	11. "Left hand" impeller in "Right hand" pump. Ensure that impeller type is correct.
	12. Suction inlet not immersed deep enough	12. If inlet cannot be lowered, or if vortex eddies persist when it is lowered, chain a board to suction pipe. It will be drawn into eddies, smothering the vortex.
	13. Foot valve too small or partially obstructed	13. Area through valve ports should be at least as large as area of suction pipe, preferable 1.5 times. If strainer is used, net clear area should be 3–4 times area of suction pipe.
	14. Too small of impeller diameter (probable cause if none of above apply)	14. Check with factory to see if a larger impeller can be used; otherwise, cut pipe losses or increase speed or both, as needed. But be careful not to seriously overload drive.

(continued on next page)

TABLE 16.2. Pump Troubleshooting *(continued from previous page)*

Problem	Probable Cause	Corrective Action
3. Not enough pressure	1. Pump speed too low	1. Check that motor voltage is correct and receiving full voltage. Check for low frequency. Check for open motor phase.
	2. Air leaks in suction piping	2. Check for leaks in suction pipe joints and fittings; vent casing to remove accumulated air.
	3. Mechanical defects	3. Check impeller, casing ring, shaft sleeve, and packing or mechanical seal. Replace if damaged or badly worn.
	4. Obstruction in liquid passages	4. Dismantle pump and inspect passages of impeller and casing. Remove obstruction.
	5. Incorrect impeller	5. "Left hand" impeller in "Right hand" pump. Ensure that impeller type is correct.
	6. Wrong direction of rotation	6. Symptoms show a flow rate of approximately one-half rated capacity. Compare rotation of motor with directional arrow on pump casing.
	7. Too small of impeller diameter (probable cause if none of above apply)	7. Check with factory to see if a larger impeller can be used; otherwise, cut pipe losses or increase speed or both, as needed. But be careful not to seriously overload drive.
4. Pump operates for short time, and then stops	1. Incomplete priming	1. Free pump, piping, and valves of all air. If high points in suction line prevent this, they need correcting.
	2. Air leaks in suction piping	2. Check for leaks in suction pipe joints and fittings; vent casing to remove accumulated air.
	3. Suction lift too high	3. Check for obstruction at inlet; check for pipe friction losses. Static lift may be too great. Measure with mercury column or vacuum gauge while pump operates. If static lift is too high, liquid to be pumped must be raised or pump lowered.
	4. Air leaks in stuffing box	4. Increase seal liquid pressure to above atmosphere.
	5. Air or gases in liquid	5. May be possible to overrate pump to point where it will provide adequate pressure despite condition. Better to provide gas separation chamber on suction line near pump and periodically exhaust accumulated gas. See item 7 in problem 2.
5. Pump takes too much power	1. Head lower than rating; thereby pumping too much liquid	1. Impeller's outside diameter may be incorrect; refer to factory for correct size.
	2. Mechanical defects	2. Check impeller, casing ring, shaft sleeve, and packing or mechanical seal. Replace if damaged or badly worn.
	3. Stuffing boxes too tight	3. Release gland pressure. Tighten reassembly. If sealing liquid does not flow while pump operates, replace packing. If packing is wearing too quickly, replace scored shaft sleeves and keep liquid seeping for lubrication.
	4. Shaft bent due to damage; improper shipment, operation, or overhaul	4. Check deflection of rotor; total indicator runout should not exceed 0.004 inch on shaft and 0.008 inch on impeller wearing surface. Check for friction between impeller and casing. Replace damaged parts.
	5. Mechanical failure of critical pump parts	5. Check bearings and impeller for damage. Any irregularity in these parts will cause a drag on shaft.

(continued on next page)

TABLE 16.2. Pump Troubleshooting *(continued from previous page)*

Problem	Probable Cause	Corrective Action
	6. Electrical defects	6. The electrical voltage amplitude and frequency may be lower than the original motor specifications or there may be defects in the motor. The motor may not be ventilated properly.
	7. Cavitation	7a. Increase positive suction head on pump by lowering pump. 7b. Subcool suction piping air inlet to lower entering liquid temperature. 7c. Pressurize suction vessel.
	8. Suction inlet not immersed deep enough	8. If inlet cannot be lowered, or if vortex eddies persist when it is lowered, chain a board to suction pipe. It will be drawn into eddies, smothering the vortex.
	9. Liquid heavier (in either viscosity or specific gravity) than allowed for	9. Use larger driver. Consult factory for recommended size. Test liquid for viscosity and specific gravity.
	10. Wrong direction of rotation	10. Check motor rotation with directional arrow on pump casing.
	11. Casing distorted by excessive strains from suction or discharge piping	11. Check piping alignment. Examine pump for friction between impeller and casing. Replace damaged parts.
	12. Speed may be too high (brake horsepower of pump varies as the cube of the speed; therefore, any increase in speed means considerable increase in power demand)	12. Check voltage on motor.

Recommended Equipment

Once proper acid cleaning preparations have been made, the following equipment should be available to ensure that the cleaning is performed quickly and safely.

- Operators must wear safety goggles, rubber gloves and shoes, and protective rubber aprons and/or suits whenever acid and caustic solutions are being added and/or recirculated. Respirators should be readily available since muriatic acid fumes present a serious breathing hazard.
- Small volumes of defoaming solution should be on site whenever carbonate scale is being removed. Dissolving calcium carbonate scale with muriatic acid will produce carbon monoxide gas, and these gas bubbles can produce severe foam that must be controlled with chemical defoamer. One to five gallons of a standard strength emulsified silicone defoamer will suffice for most heat exchanger cleaning needs.
- To facilitate cleaning, the acid solution should be added into a separate cleaning-in-place (CIP) solution tank and circulated through the heat exchanger with a large volume pump (Fig. 16.4). With this procedure, acid strength, temperature, inhibitor concentration, and defoamer levels can all be checked. Additional acid and inhibitor can be readily and safely added to the tank and recirculated through the heat exchanger as needed. The solution tank should be made of epoxy-lined carbon steel or stainless steel.
- Gear pumps are normally used to add acid from the carboy to the solution tank. Manual addition of muriatic acid is unsafe and should be avoided. Gear pumps should be plastic with either Teflon and/or stainless-steel gears and heads. Suction and discharge piping or lines should also be plastic or rubber. Hose and tubing can be used if they are properly secured. A 1- to 5-gallons per minute (gpm) capacity gear pump will be adequate for this application.

- The recirculating pump used to circulate the acid cleaning solution through the heat exchanger must be a centrifugal pump capable of moving several hundred gallons per minute of cleaning solution against low head pressures. The impeller and head should be made of a good grade of stainless steel, and all recirculation lines and fittings must also be made of corrosion-resistant materials. Often the acid cleaning solution is circulated through the heat exchanger using the pumps and lines provided by the pasteurizer manufacturer for normal water service. In this case, the acid solution must be well inhibited in the solution tank before it is pumped through the pasteurizer heat exchanger supply and return lines.

Recommended Procedures

While exact cleaning recommendations are determined by the thickness, density, and chemical composition of the scale being removed, the following guidelines for chemical cleaning of heat exchangers should apply in most cases.

- Maintain the acid strength between 5 and 10% by test.
- Maintain the inhibitor strength between 0.4 and 0.6% by test.
- Maintain the solution temperature between 120 and 150°F (48.9 and 65.6°C). Use steam to maintain these temperatures; 180°F (82°C) maximum.
- Circulate the cleaning solution for 2 hours. Add defoamer as needed to prevent foam overflow in the surge tank.
- When cleaning is completed, cool the solution to below 100°F (37.8°C). The entire system should be rapidly drained and immediately rinsed with fresh water.
- Drain the system and immediately refill with fresh water. Add alkaline neutralizing solution. Circulate this solution for 30 minutes. Test the pH and then drain and inspect the heat exchangers.
- Following inspection, refill the exchanger system with fresh water and recirculate using normal chemical inhibitors. The heat exchanger is ready for service.
- Warning! Do not attempt to neutralize the acid cleaning solution with any alkaline material until the acid solution is drained and completely rinsed. Acid cleaning solution and caustic solutions will react to produce large volumes of sludge, which will plug the heat exchangers and create more deposits than were originally present before cleaning.

Conveying Belt Alignment

The conveying belt needs to be aligned on both sides with a clearance of 0.25 inch per side. The belt needs to be aligned for better performance. There is an adjustment on the idler shaft for final adjustment (Fig. 16.5).

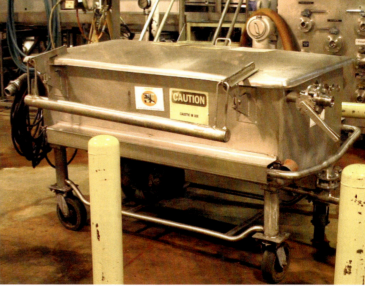

FIGURE 16.4. Examples of cleaning-in-place (CIP) tanks. (Courtesy Barry-Wehmiller Companies)

Conveying Belt Installation

The conveying belt comes in rolls. It needs to be placed on the deck, the roll pulled inside of the machine, and the pins inserted to connect the belt modules, ensuring the pins are secure on both sides (Fig. 16.6).

Conveying Belt Adjustment

The conveying belt needs to be checked and adjusted every year for elongation. If the catenary elongate more than 1 inch at the discharge end of the machine, the excess modules should be cut out.

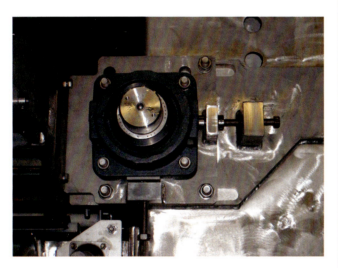

FIGURE 16.5. Idler shaft adjustment for belt alignment. (Courtesy Barry-Wehmiller Companies)

FLASH PASTEURIZATION

A second type of pasteurization, called flash pasteurization, involves pasteurizing the product prior to filling. In this process, the beer is handled in bulk and subjected to high temperatures, normally 160°F (71°C) for short periods, usually 18–20 seconds. Flash pasteurization requires a sterile filling operation.

The holding time and temperature required for pasteurization when using this system is determined from the desired PU value. The flash pasteurizer is based on a section-plate heat exchanger that has heating regeneration and cooling sections (Fig. 16.7). The incoming cold beer enters the inlet regeneration section, which provides 95% heat recovery. The beer is heated to the final pasteurization temperature using hot water generated from steam in one section of the heat exchanger. The steam is controlled to adjust the temperature. The beer then enters the holding tube. The pressure in the holding tube is controlled to ensure that the dissolved gas stays in solution.

After returning via the outlet regeneration section, the beer is cooled to the final discharge temperature using the available cooling medium. A variable-speed, high-pressure pump feeds beer into the inlet regeneration section. A booster pump then ensures that the pressure on the sterile side of the regeneration section is greater than that on the nonsterile side. A hygienic flow meter and control valve constantly adjust the flow rate to produce the required holding time.

FIGURE 16.6. Belt installation on a tunnel pasteurizer. The belt is green and in the center. (Courtesy Barry-Wehmiller Companies)

FIGURE 16.7. Flash pasteurizer. (Courtesy Barry-Wehmiller Companies)

The pasteurizer feeds beer into a sterile buffer tank (SBT). As the level increases in the tank, the flow rate of the pasteurizer is reduced, and as the level in the tank drops, the flow rate increases. In this way, a balancing point between the level in the tank, the filler production speed, and the pasteurizer flow rate is achieved.

When the SBT is full, the beer from the pasteurizer is replaced by water in order to maintain the temperature and pressure balance to allow for a quick restart when the SBT level drops to the restart level.

Flash pasteurizer features include

- a stainless-steel skid,
- automatic PU regulation,
- low temperature differential (ΔT) for gentle product handling,
- automatic recycling of beer or water,
- a capacity to hold pasteurized beer at a higher pressure than that for unpasteurized beer,
- hygienic centrifugal pumps,
- CIP programs,
- pasteurization at 10–40 PUs,
- a standby program,
- constant parameter monitoring and control, and
- full automation of the control system.

The flash pasteurizer calls for the highest quality components with an emphasis on clean design, ease of maintenance, and low operating and maintenance costs.

Troubleshooting

The flash pasteurizer components are easier to troubleshoot since the main component is a heat exchanger along with pumps, of which the maintenance and troubleshooting procedures are described in the tunnel pasteurizer section. The other components are valves, tanks, and electrical components, which mainly need to be replaced.

SUMMARY

Predicting the future course of any activity is a risky endeavor but not totally without merit. When making predictions, it is often beneficial to look first at the past. The process of microbiological stabilization has changed little since the 1960s. From 1880 through 1960, it was exclusively a heat pasteurization process in the package. The changes that occurred were mostly equipment refinements and they did nothing to alter the basic principle. The process then started to take place in the product (flash pasteurization) as an alternative option. In recent years, subtle changes have taken place in the existing methods, but nothing new or revolutionary.

The second step in making predictions should be to look at the factors of change. Those factors controlling change within the microbiological stabilization methods include intense competition within the brewing industry, technological advances, and governmental regulations. The competition factor include both quality and cost considerations. Recent major increases in the cost of basic energy are causing breweries to review the entire operation for ways of saving energy.

Heat pasteurization in the package will continue to be the most widely practiced in the Western Hemisphere and it will continue to gain popularity in the rest of the world.

Flash pasteurization with sterile filling will gain some converts, mainly in microbreweries, since it offers quality for the product at a lower cost for a small market. Since it virtually guarantees a biologically stable beer at the filler, the brewer needs only to contend with the problems of the sterile filling operation.

REFERENCES

Del Vecchio, H. W., Dayharsh, C. A., and Baselt, F. C. (1951). Thermal death time studies on beer spoilage organisms. I. Am. Soc. Brew. Chem. Proc. 1951:45-50.

King, L. M., Egan, L., Schisler, D., and Hahn, C. W. (1978). Development of required time temperature relationships for effective flash pasteurization. J. Am. Soc. Brew. Chem. 36:144-149.

Pasteur, L. (1876). Études sur la Bière (Studies on Beer): Ses Maladies, Causes qui les Provoquent, Procédé pour la Rendre Inaltérable: Avec une Théorie Nouvelle de la Fermentation. Gauthier-Villars, Paris. Chapter 1, page 1. (In French.)

CHAPTER 17

Pasteurizer Water Treatment

JACK L. BLAND
THOMAS J. SOUKUP
RICK BRUNDAGE
ChemTreat, Inc.

Pasteurizer water treatment has evolved significantly since the early 2000s, especially in more recent years due primarily to enhanced materials of pasteurizer construction as well as to improved technology and advances in chemical feed automation and control systems. Brewery managers now readily acknowledge that effective water treatment not only extends equipment life but also helps ensure the quality of the product when the treatment program is properly administered. In addition, most modern breweries now employ various types of water reclaim/recycle systems with the goal of saving both water and energy. Global water savings/reuse initiatives target a ratio of 3.5:1 units of water to unit of produced beer. While these ambitious water savings projects are commendable, there are new pitfalls to be avoided in order to realize these targets as sustainable initiatives.

The primary goals of pasteurizer water treatment programs are to prevent/minimize the following.

- Pasteurizer and heat exchanger corrosion
- Slime and other biological growth and accumulation in pasteurizers and heat exchangers
- Mineral scale and organic deposits in pasteurizers and heat exchangers
- Aluminum can dome staining and container spotting
- Musty and other off-spec odors on the packaging floor to ensure finished product quality
- Mat-top conveyor degradation and premature failure

The treatment program must address all of these areas simultaneously, since all of the above goals are interrelated.

For example, if biological growth is manifesting itself in a pasteurizer, underdeposit corrosion and subsequent metal attack will soon follow (Fig. 17.1). This corrosion will result in dissolved metallic oxides (rust) deposits elsewhere in the system. This example magnifies the importance of maintaining a comprehensive approach to the water treatment program.

● CORROSION CONTROL

Corrosion in pasteurizers and water reclaim systems can be pervasive and expensive. Nearly all pasteurizers manufactured today are constructed of 304 or 316 stainless steel. These units are much more durable and easier to keep clean than are the older types made of carbon steel, but they do pose some potential problems. Even in the newer 304 and 316 stainless-steel pasteurizers, corrosion can dramatically shorten service life of the equipment.

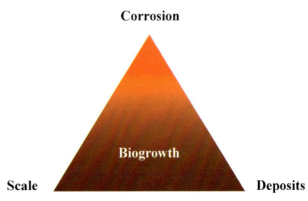

FIGURE 17.1. Relationship between corrosion, metal attack (scale), and dissolved oxide (rust) deposits in contributing to biological growth in a pasteurizer environment. (Courtesy ChemTreat, Inc.)

Pasteurizers are somewhat unique in that corrosion can occur in either the water phase or the vapor phase areas. Below the water line (water phase), corrosion can be mitigated by the use of various corrosion inhibitors, which are selected based upon system metallurgy and water quality. In the vapor phase areas, no inhibitor contacts the metal surfaces. So the focus must be based on maintaining a clean, deposit-free environment. In addition, the biocide combination used in pasteurizers are halogen-based and exhibit various degrees of volatility, which may increase corrosion potential. Thus, control of halogen feed to the pasteurizers, and choosing the best chlorine/bromine feed ratios is critical for minimizing corrosion rates. In addition to high halogen levels, other factors can increase the tendency for corrosion of system metallurgy.

- Bottle breakage, resulting in low pH in the pasteurizer water.
- Corrosion underneath existing deposits, especially in pasteurizer sumps and underneath welded seams where rapid localized attack (pitting) may occur, resulting in pin-hole leaks onto the packaging floor.
- Excessive exposure to alkaline or acidic cleaning compounds. Not only do these products increase corrosion, they also have a dramatic negative effect on polypropylene mat-top belt life.

When designing a corrosion inhibitor program, water quality is the most important factor. Various inorganic and organic compounds are employed to minimize corrosion on the metal surfaces. Phosphates, zinc, azoles, polymers, and organic phosphorous compounds are generally used as primary ingredients of a combination corrosion-deposit inhibitor program.

Program Monitoring

It is important to determine the effectiveness of the chemistries applied to the pasteurizer water. One or all of the following techniques are normally used to monitor pasteurizer metal loss.

- Weight-loss coupons are used in both the water and vapor phases. Coupons are pieces of metal made of the same composition as the equipment being monitored. They are placed into areas of actual use to measure the rate of corrosion being experienced by the equipment in service. Coupons are normally replaced on a quarterly schedule to monitor both general corrosion and pitting tendencies. Best practice standards for pasteurizers are shown in Table 17.1.

TABLE 17.1. Corrosion Goals for Metals in Pasteurizers

Metal	Water	Vapor
Mild steel	<5.0 mpy[a]	<10 mpy
Stainless steel	<0.2 mpy	<0.2 mpy
Copper	<0.2 mpy	<0.2 mpy

[a] mpy = Mils per year (1 mil is 0.001 inch or 0.0254 mm).

- Linear polarization measurement devices (corrosion-monitoring probes) provide an immediate readout of general corrosion and pitting rates.
- Measurement of dissolved iron and copper in the system provides an indication of corrosion rates on mild steel and copper alloy components.
- Periodic visual inspection and ultrasonic metal thickness determination.

Scale and Deposit Prevention

The most detrimental item to compromise the integrity of the stainless steel is deposition. Scale, biological slime, porous iron oxides, and organic deposits serve to disrupt the chrome-nickel oxide film that protects stainless steel and lead to pitting and metal loss. Potentially disastrous is the proliferation of anaerobic bacteria that grow in the oxygen-depleted environment beneath deposits. The organisms produce hydrogen sulfide, which is particularly aggressive toward the metallurgy.

In packaging departments operating with reclaim systems, the deposition of corrosion products from older pasteurizers onto new stainless-steel pasteurizers can be problematic. It is important to clean the unit if this iron staining is absorbed to prevent pitting underneath.

Inorganic Mineral Scale

In addition to biogrowth control and corrosion minimization, mineral scale deposits can be as troublesome as corrosion in both the pasteurizers and associated reclaim systems.

The potential for inorganic mineral scale deposition is directly related to the makeup (i.e., supply) water quality. Before specifying a treatment program for pasteurizers, the following makeup water characteristics should be considered: pH, alkalinity, calcium, magnesium, dissolved iron, total dissolved solids, chlorides, and silica.

Another useful tool for predicting the corrosive or scaling tendency of a specific makeup water source is the Langelier Saturation Index. This index is computed using system water temperature and the parameters mentioned previously. The index ranges from –3 to +3, progressing from very corrosive to very scale forming, with a midvalue of 0, predicting a "neutral" water quality that is neither corrosive nor scale forming. This calculation is particularly important with respect to newer-model pasteurizer heat exchangers because of the extremely high outlet temperatures of the effluent from the newer heat exchangers, where water temperatures can reach 180°F (82°C). The high heat flux occurring in these heat exchangers may promote the formation of mineral scale on the heat exchange surfaces. Components of the chemical treatment program, such as acrylic polymers and organic phosphorous compounds, minimize or prevent the deposition tendency. Warning signs of potential mineral scale problems are cloudy (milky) water and/or loss of efficiency of the heat exchangers.

Organic Deposits

Equally important to mineral scale prevention is the ability to prevent organic deposits in the pasteurizer. Organic contaminants have the potential to contribute to deposition, and a brewery should minimize their intrusion into pasteurizer water systems.

Conveyor lubricant can be especially problematic. Usually, these compounds are fatty acid esters, quaternary amine, or amine acetate–based combinations. Though useful to promote container mobility on the infeed conveyor, fatty acid–based products may cause deposition, provide a nutrient source for bacteria, and drastically increase the halogen demand in the pasteurizer water. Quaternary amine and amine acetate–based lubricants provide good biocidal efficacy on conveyors; however, it is necessary to minimize carryover of these products into the pasteurizer water since they may precipitate deposit-control inhibitor anionic polymer components, leading to program performance problems.

The fouling of suction box screens and pasteurizer sprays or distribution pans (Fig. 17.2) is the most common indicator of organic contamination. Excessive foam in pasteurizer compartments (Fig. 17.3) is an initial indicator of organic contamination reactions with halogen-based biocides.

FIGURE 17.3. Foaming in a pasteurizer pump suction box is an indicator of organic contamination. (Courtesy ChemTreat, Inc.)

FIGURE 17.2. Fouling of pump suction box screens. (Courtesy ChemTreat, Inc.)

BIOLOGICAL CONTROL

A primary goal in pasteurizer water treatment is the prevention of biological growth in both the water and vapor areas of the pasteurizer and the associated reclaim system (if present). The pasteurizer environment offers ideal conditions for microbiological growth because most compartment temperatures fall in the 70–130°F (21–55°C) temperature range. In addition, beer that enters the pasteurizer through container leaks, e.g., can leaks and bottle breakage, provides an excellent nutrient source for yeast, mold, and aerobic bacteria, which are naturally occurring in the packaging area due to the very nature of the brewing process. Conveyor lubricants used on the conveyor's early side (infeed) of a pasteurizer will be entrained on cans/bottles and enter the pasteurizer water to provide an additional source of nutrients for bacterial growth. These organic contaminants also react with the halogen biocides (bromine and chlorine) that are most often used for microbiological control, resulting in an increase in the dosage to ensure proper control.

Bacteriological deposition can result in severe pitting of metal surfaces. Corrosion cells are promoted because of an oxygen concentration differential between the pasteurizer water and the metal surface underneath the deposit. This corrosion can result in the need to replace a pasteurizer well before its expected life span. In addition, deposition in the bottom of the units can result in the proliferation of particularly troublesome anaerobic bacteria. These organisms produce corrosive hydrogen sulfide in their metabolic processes, resulting in the characteristic malodorous conditions and severe pitting of the pasteurizer metallurgy.

Visual evidence of slime growth can be seen in both the water and vapor areas of the pasteurizers if the treatment program is not performing. Foul odors emanating from the pasteurizer are almost always the result of bacteria present in slime deposits in pasteurizer sump compartments. These odors are most frequently observed during pasteurizer system startup, after weekend shutdown or other extended off-line periods in which extended layup procedures do not adequately address biogrowth prevention.

Halogen Biocides

The primary biocide chemistry in virtually all major and modern breweries is a combination of chlorine and bromine halogen compounds. This combination has numerous benefits over chlorine alone in that

- bromine is approximately 2.5 times less volatile than chlorine alone. This is beneficial in reducing chlorine odors on the packaging area, as well as minimizing vapor area corrosion in the pasteurizer.
- bromine and chlorine combinations are more effective at the higher pH values (7.5–8.5) normally found in the recirculating pasteurizer water and associated water reclaim systems.
- bromine/chlorine combinations are much less aggressive to pasteurizer metallurgy, especially copper and copper alloys found in heat exchangers, spray nozzles, and pump impellers.

Initially, solid bromine pellets were the product of choice. Disadvantages, such as higher cost and feed and control difficulties, necessitated a change to liquid sodium bromide, which is activated when fed in conjunction with sodium hypochlorite (bleach).

There are several advantages of this technology.

- It is approximately one-third the cost of solid bromine or chlorine pellets.
- It has a positive buffering effect on the recirculating water pH.
- It has the ability to vary the ratio of chlorine to bromine to optimize water phase and vapor phase cleanliness while minimizing vapor space corrosion potential.
- It is easier to feed a liquid combination. No manual labor is required to fill dry feeders (brominators).
- It has the ability to be fed and controlled at a central location in most systems.

The control of halogen levels in pasteurizer systems is one of the most difficult yet critical aspects of a successful water treatment program. If halogen levels are not controlled adequately, heterotrophic bacteria will proliferate and exceed the control limits for these organisms, which is less than 10^4 colony forming units per milliliter (CFU/mL) in the pasteurizer water. Left unchecked, heterotrophic counts can quickly reach 10^6–10^7 CFU/mL, at which point many serious problems will occur.

Lack of control utilizing any halogen source for biogrowth control will severely impact corrosion rates of the pasteurizers, resulting in the need for premature replacement of expensive equipment. Of particular concern are the vapor areas where no corrosion inhibitor is present. Chlorine and, to a lesser degree, bromine are volatile and will gas-off into these unprotected vapor areas of the pasteurizer. The warmer water increases the volatility of these compounds. Support structures, spray nozzles, and headers are severely impacted by excess halogen feed.

Breweries have always run tests on the water in the pasteurizers for biological activity. Listed below are the biological goals that have been promulgated by water treatment companies and several major breweries for both water and vapor phase cleanliness best practices.

- No visible slime in either water or vapor areas
- Pasteurizer recirculating water: total aerobic bacteria counts of less than 10^4 CFU/mL of sample
- Vapor phase standards: total bacteria (infeed-discharge of pasteurizer) counts of less than 400 CFU/m^3 of air
- Fungus and mold counts of less than 200 CFU/m^3 of air

Among the most common organic contaminants that may enter the pasteurizer are

- Can necker lubricants
- Conveyer lubricants
- Can lacquer overcoat varnishes
- Hydraulic oils or bearing grease
- Cleaning-in-place (CIP) chemicals, cleaners, and organic acids

Prerinse Stations

Perhaps the best method for removing residual traces of line lubricants and beer entrained on cans and bottles entering the pasteurizer is the use of prerinse stations located in the immediate area of the pasteurizer infeed conveyor. The stations should be positioned as close to the pasteurizer inlet as possible and have sufficient flow to rinse most of the contaminants away. The prerinse station water may come from a variety of sources. Some of the most frequently used sources include empty can/bottle rinse water, water from zone 2 or 3 of the pasteurizer, pasteurizer reclaim water, reclaimed carbon filter backwash water, and utilities cooling tower blow-down water. Any of these potential sources of prerinse water, with the exception of already treated water from the pasteurizer, should include some provision for chlorinating the prerinse water to minimize biogrowth problems associated with using unchlorinated water for prerinse.

Deposit/Fouling Control

Early detection of problems is critical. The pasteurizer water and vapor phases should be checked on a regular basis. If any deposits are detected, the material should be analyzed to any extent necessary to determine the origin since any deposition will negatively impact all facets of the water treatment program. Underdeposit corrosion, due to the oxygen differential concentrations above and below the deposits, will create a corrosion cell. This localized phenomenon will result in rapid metal loss and manifest itself as pitting-type corrosion. Biologically induced pitting is especially problematic in 300 series stainless-steel components.

Rouging

Rouging or halogen-induced corrosion in vapor spaces is another serious problem due to overfeed of chlorine/bromine-based biocides. Rouging can also occur on the exterior of stainless-steel pasteurizers. Rouging usually occurs in the warmer zones where the halogen is least soluble and manifests itself as a reddish brown thin stain and/or deposit. It occurs when a halogen destroys the chromic oxide protective layer and leaves the ferrous portion behind. If this is evidenced, the area should be cleaned and repassivated immediately with either citric or dilute nitric acid.

In addition, deposits prevent the corrosion inhibitor from functioning properly, in that protective inhibitor films cannot be formed except on clean metal surfaces. Deposit-fouled heat exchangers (Fig. 17.4) impact the efficiency of the equipment and promote corrosion.

FIGURE 17.4. Heat exchanger fouling. (Courtesy ChemTreat, Inc.)

BOIL-OUTS

It is necessary to maintain pasteurizers in a relatively "clean" state. An out-of-control pasteurizer can result in product problems and sanitation issues and can greatly increase the corrosion rate of the pasteurizer.

The life span of both carbon-steel and stainless-steel units are negatively impacted by dirty conditions. To clean biological growth, oily deposits, and process contaminants, boil-outs can be performed (Fig. 17.5). Two types of boil-outs have been routinely utilized. These procedures are defined as alkaline high-temperature boil-out and ambient-temperature boil-out/cleanout.

The alkaline boil-out involves the high-temperature application of cleaning compounds designed for older-type pasteurizers that have metallic "walking beam" conveyors or machines using stainless-steel mat-top belts. These boil-out compounds are generally alkaline and contain surfactants and dispersants in conjunction with boil-out temperatures of 130–170°F (54–77°C). As mentioned previously, the high-temperature boil-out is not recommended for use where polypropylene mat-top belts are installed.

The ambient-temperature boil-out effectively oxidizes organic material on contact, cleaning the deposit without the use of elevated temperatures. This cleaning procedure has been deemed safe for use in pasteurizers with polypropylene mat-top belts.

Boil-Out Schedule

As a minimum, each pasteurizer should be boiled out quarterly. The type of boil-out will be determined by the nature of the deposit and its reactivity to the boil-out chemical. A simple bench test can help determine which procedure will be most effective.

Other conditions, such as excessive breakage, high turbidity, or high biocounts, could also trigger the need for a boil-out procedure. It is imperative that during the boil-out procedure the sumps be thoroughly cleaned, as well as the vapor areas. Deck covers should be removed and cleaned along with the infeed and discharge areas of the pasteurizer.

A good working relationship between the chemical vendor and brewery personnel needs to be developed. Both parties should work closely together to police the packaging environment for any potential sources of microbiological growth. Drains, ceiling, floors, and overhead lines should all be treated as sources of contamination.

Safety

Certain species of bacteria can impact the health of people working in and around the pasteurizer if left uncontrolled. Of particular concern are personnel performing boil-outs when physical entry into the pasteurizer occurs. A pasteurizer with poor biological control can have a health problem associated with entry. Also, halogen overfeed can result in high vapor area oxidant levels. Personnel working on the packaging floor can experience eye and throat irritation due to these vapors.

MUSTY FLAVOR (OFF-SPEC TASTE) ISSUES

Recently, more emphasis has been directed toward vapor area cleanliness, while continuing to maintain clean metal surfaces below the water line. Breweries have discovered that airborne odors emanating from the

FIGURE 17.5. Zone 10 headers before boil-out (top) and after boil-out (bottom). (Courtesy ChemTreat, Inc.)

pasteurizer may produce compounds that can be detected by the human olfactory system at very low levels. These volatile amine and organic compounds present in the packaging area may be adsorbed onto inner can liners and can lacquer overcoat varnishes, resulting in consumer complaints related to medicinal taste/smell.

In the early 1990s, periodic "musty" tastes were detected in 12- and 16-oz. cans in a variety of beers produced in a large U.S. brewery. Approximately one million dollars in losses occurred because of rejected product in one medium-sized brewery alone. An intensive quality assurance audit of all brewing, packaging, and utilities areas identified several culprits as the possible cause of the problem.

The water treatment supplier was contacted to assist the brewery's quality assurance department with laboratory and in-plant studies to pinpoint the exact source(s) of musty tastes/odors and to develop long-term solutions to prevent future recurrences.

After extensive research, analysis, and process review, the offending compounds were identified as trichloroanisole and methyl-isoborneol. These compounds are produced by molds and associated microflora in the packaging environment. In most cases, they are absorbed in the empty, epoxy-based can liners prior to filling.

In some cases, the musty occurrence emanates from the outside of the can lacquer overcoat when the can is exposed to hot pasteurization temperatures. This exposure opens up the pores, and if the pasteurizer water is contaminated, a musty flavor problem can result.

Most brewers would probably react with a considerable degree of skepticism to the statement that "control of the packaging area environment is as important as the brewing process for producing a high-quality beer." In addition, the following statements would be viewed as equally unbelievable but do have a basis in fact.

- Pasteurizer microbial growth may result in millions of dollars of annual product loss because of off-spec flavor in beer, even in the presence of low bacterial counts and a significant free halogen residual in the pasteurizer system.
- Packaging floor layout (e.g., conveyor, pasteurizer, and filler locations) may contribute to off-spec tastes in the packaged beer.
- Airborne microbial contamination is rapidly adsorbed on the interior surfaces of cans and causes product rejection because of one compound that is detectable by the human nose at concentrations as low as four parts per trillion.
- The slightest foul odor in any area of the packaging floor is capable of contaminating the entire floor.
- In the absence of excellent ventilation and air circulation, can manufacturing materials and processes have a significant effect on the speed of odor adsorption on the interior linings of empty cans.

Minimize Aerosolization

In an effort to reduce the potential for aerosolization at the infeed and discharge of pasteurizers, stainless-steel covers should be installed to reduce the amount of water vapor emanating from these areas. In addition, stainless-steel shrouds may be placed around can rinsers and can conveyors directly above the pasteurizers to prevent or minimize aerosol adsorption onto can liner interiors.

Reduce Microbiological Contamination

A number of steps should be taken to minimize the total microflora counts in all packaging area systems. The following is a summary of proven actions necessary to minimize or prevent off-flavors in canned product for any brewery during future operations.

- Do not allow empty cans to remain in overhead can conveyors for more than 5–10 minutes before filling.
- Run out all cans before scheduled off-line periods.
- Evaluate the resistance of various can linings to the adsorption of off-odors, and use this information in the selection and qualification of vendors.
- Employ a biocidal conveyor lubricant on all filler discharge/pasteurizer infeed conveyors.
- Install prerinse stations on each pasteurizer infeed conveyor, just before the pasteurizer inlet.
- Install barrier doors and covers on the pasteurizer inlet and exit to minimize aerosolization of water vapor in these areas.
- Install barrier shrouds on overhead empty can conveyors, especially in those locations where the conveyor passes over or near the pasteurizer and adjacent area.
- Maintain a continuous free halogen residual of 1.0–3.0 parts per million (ppm) in all non-heat/hold pasteurizer compartments at all times. Autocontrol may be necessary. Run at the upper end of these limits if using bromine instead of chlorine as the halogen source.
- Specific liquid biocide addition is necessary on a periodic basis (in the absence of continuous recirculation) to maintain biological control during extended off-line periods in the pasteurizers.

- Devote equal attention to periodic sterilization of areas surrounding the pasteurizer (e.g., floors and drains) because almost any septic area is capable of contaminating the plant air.
- Perform an air circulation/ventilation audit at each brewery packaging location to ensure the optimum removal and turnover of plant and outside air.
- Install static removal equipment (grounding system) on empty can conveyors before the can rinsers.
- Increase the frequency of pasteurizer boil-out/high-pressure water washing if a problem is suspected. Pay particular attention to vapor areas.
- Perform an audit of overall equipment layout, pasteurizers, fillers, conveyors, and other equipment parts with the goal of minimizing conveyor location above pasteurizers and soakers.
- Use a separate air handling–air conditioning system for flavor lab and taste rooms.
- Train all operators and personnel responsible for sanitation/water treatment on the importance of routine cleaning/sanitation.

CAN STAINING, CAN SPOTTING, AND BOTTLE SPOTTING

Since the early 2000s, several U.S. breweries have experienced quality issues not evidenced in previous operations related to the package appearance of a variety of aluminum cans and 12- and 16-oz. aluminum bottles. The efficiency of water conservation programs, changes in can coatings, and compliance with stringent environmental standards are but a few of the issues that have increased the potential for can spotting and staining and for crown rusting and spotting on bottles due to increased organic presence in pasteurizers.

Can Staining

Classic staining of aluminum cans may be described as the deposition of layers of magnesium silicate salts in the interstitial pores of the can. This usually occurs on the uncoated dome of the can where no protective overcoat varnishes are present. The stain appears as a yellow-brown discoloration and may be a darker black if enough refractive layers of magnesium salts are present. Figure 17.6 illustrates staining on a raw can.

The primary environmental causes of aluminum can staining are high pH in the recirculating water (above pH 8.5) coupled with high hardness (above 200 ppm) and low inhibitor levels. The aluminum used in the manufacturing of beer cans is amphoteric. By definition, an amphoteric metal is susceptible to corrosion under acidic or alkaline conditions. This phenomenon begins to develop as varying degrees of discoloration on the aluminum surface as the pH and total hardness of the pasteurizer approaches the conditions mentioned previously.

The elevation of pH usually manifests itself initially in the hot zones of the pasteurizer, where an increased retention time and a high temperature may cause a concentration of these mineral salts and alkalinity, further aggravating the corrosion mechanism.

Can Spotting

Can spotting is manifested as whitish or brownish spots on the can dome or other nonprotected surfaces caused by the deposition of calcium salts, iron, or

FIGURE 17.6. Example of classic can staining. (Courtesy ChemTreat, Inc.)

FIGURE 17.7. Example of classic can spotting. (Courtesy ChemTreat, Inc.)

organic contaminants in the pasteurizer water (Fig. 17.7). Spotting can be mitigated by utilizing air blowers on the pasteurizer discharge or postrinse stations or by employing a temperature-stable surfactant to decrease the surface tension of the water, thus minimizing spotting.

Bottle Spotting

Organic contaminants may also cause spotting on bottle surfaces. These organics may originate from necker, closure, or conveyor lubes. Water conservation initiatives being adopted have resulted in longer retention times and a higher propensity for the contaminants to form deposits. Sidestream filtration has proven very useful in minimizing contaminants that may cause organic deposit spotting on bottles and cans.

MAT-TOP CONVEYOR DEGRADATION AND PREMATURE FAILURE

Polypropylene mat-top belts are now the industry standard, having replaced various stainless-steel configurations as the conveyor of choice in brewery pasteurizers. Figure 17.8 shows an example of one type of belt.

As mentioned in the beginning of this chapter, water conservation and water reclaim initiatives have raised some previously unforeseen challenges related to equipment life. Polypropylene belt life expectancy has been one issue related to these efforts. Across the spectrum, breweries have experienced reduced belt life as well as catastrophic failure during in-service operation in selected pasteurizers. Upon detailed investigation, root cause failure analysis (RCFA) revealed several primary causative agents related to belt failure problems.

- Increased feed of halogen-based (chlorine/bromine-based) biocides. The increased organic presence associated with reduced water loss from these pasteurizers resulted in a huge increase in biocide feed to maintain specified program halogen levels. These oxidants caused belt degradation in selected pasteurizers, based on the degree of contamination and level of halogen addition.
- High-temperature boil-outs. For years the industry norm has been to routinely clean the pasteurizer via high-temperature boil-outs in conjunction with a variety of alkaline (caustic) or acidic chemical additives. Boil-out temperatures of 170–190°F (77–88°C) were commonly employed on a routine basis while alkaline or acidic chemical cleaners were simultaneously added to the pasteurizer. This combination of high temperature and aggressive chemical cleaning also contributed to premature polypropylene belt failures or reduced service life.

Other factors contribute to premature belt failures. Figure 17.9 represents a simplified diagram of the complexity of the belt failure issues as well as the ancillary factors that may contribute to belt failure.

Belt Life Extension/Failure Prevention

There are three primary steps that can easily be implemented to extend polypropylene belt life even under rigid water savings initiatives.

- Ambient-temperature boil-out/cleaning. Products are now available that will accomplish the same degree of pasteurizer cleaning without the need for high temperatures, which adversely affect belt life.
- Sidestream filtration. Sidestream filters, installed on the central water reclaim system, have proven very effective in removing many of the organic contaminants. These filters thus minimize the amount of halogen-based biocides that need to be fed to maintain specified chlorine/bromine residuals.
- Adherence to best practices in the water treatment program. Table 17.2 contains a description of these recommended program control parameters.

FIGURE 17.8. New mat installation on the upper and lower decks. (Courtesy ChemTreat, Inc.)

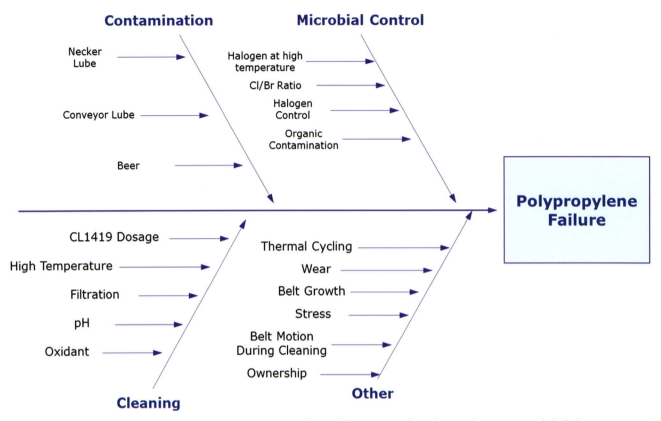

FIGURE 17.9. Fishbone diagram pointing to various causes from different areas for polypropylene conveyor belt failure in a tunnel pasteurizer. (Courtesy ChemTreat, Inc.)

TABLE 17.2. Best Practices Recommendations for Pasteurizer Water Quality

Parameter/Metric	Suggested Range/Target
pH (all compartments)	7.5–8.6 (±0.2 units)
Chlorides	<150 ppm as Cl_2[a]
Total hardness	<400 ppm as $CaCO_3$[b]
Total alkalinity	<300 ppm as $CaCO_3$
Total organic carbon (TOC)	<40 ppm as TOC (zone 1)
Turbidity	<40 NTU[c] (zones 1–6)
Conductivity/TDS[d]	<3.0 × makeup/reclaim μmho
Free residual halogen (non–H-H)	0.5–1.5 ppm as Cl_2
Free residual halogen (H-H)	<0.3 ppm as Cl*[e]
Cl_2 splits free radical and total Cl_2	<0.75 ppm of differential free vs. total
Biocounts (aerobic)	<10^3 CFU/mL
Biocounts (anaerobic)	Not detected in water samples
Active (filtered) polymer	Minimum 7–10 ppm via polymer test
Zinc	<0.5 ppm in all compartments and reclaim

[a] Chlorine (Cl_2).
[b] Calcium carbonate ($CaCO_3$).
[c] Nephelometric turbidity units (NTU).
[d] Total dissolved solids (TDS).
[e] * = Free radical.

● SUMMARY/BEST PRACTICES

In summary, adherence to the following recommendations will help ensure package quality optimization, extend useful service life of pasteurizer components and associated water reclaim systems, and minimize water and energy usage in the brewery.

- Install prerinse stations at the immediate pasteurizer inlet area.
- Provide adequate turnover of the water in the pasteurizer system.
- Perform regular, effective boil-outs and cleanings.
- Minimize organic intrusion into any pasteurizer compartment.
- Communicate with sanitation, can, and coating manufacturers on a regular basis to notify them of any unusual deposits seen on pump suction box screens or on pasteurizer sidewalls.
- Train brewery personnel to recognize upset conditions and follow proper testing procedures.

In addition, the following guidelines should always be followed to maintain pasteurizer water chemistry.

- Utilize the appropriate inhibitor, e.g., zinc, phosphate/polymer, and azole.
- Maintain an effective biological treatment program.
- Monitor the concentration of corrosion and deposit inhibitor components.
- Optimize the feed of halogen and inhibitor.
- Be certain an effective holdover biocide program is in place for those systems not practicing dry layup during weekends and other extended off-line periods.

The above recommendations are summarized in Table 17.2. While best practices must be developed for each brewery, these guidelines serve as a general template for universal adoption.

REFERENCE

Anderson, S. D., Hastings, D., Rossmore, K., and Bland, J. L. 1995. Solving the puzzle of an off-spec "musty" taste in canned beer . . . A partnership approach. Tech. Q. Master Brew. Assoc. Am. 32:95-101.

CHAPTER 18

Labels

MARK GLENDENNING
Inland Label

This chapter covers label type applications along with processes for designing and engineering beer labels that can ultimately save a great deal of time and money as well as yield better results. Most of the information about labels is universal to other printed packaging materials, e.g., carriers, cartons, and wraps, in that much of the process in label printing and its machinery is common to typical beer packaging. The last section of the chapter covers label finishing and common label defects.

● LABEL TYPES

Cut-and-Stack Labels

Cut-and-stack labels are the most common label application used by the beer industry and the second largest label segment in the world.

Pressure-Sensitive Labels

Pressure-sensitive labels have seen continued growth and popularity within the beer industry largely because of their ability to be used for small-volume applications up to high-volume product SKUs. The pressure-sensitive label market has overtaken the cut-and-stack label segment to become the largest label category in the world.

Roll-Fed Labels

Roll-fed labels are supplied on a roll and the labeling machine cuts them off one at a time with an eye mark that looks for the position to cut. The label is then applied to the container with hot-melt glue. Often times, roll-fed label market volume predictions are included with the cut-and-stack segment since they are similar applications.

Injection In-Mold Labels

Injection in-mold labels start with a polypropylene printed label. These are robotically placed into mold cavities and then molten polypropylene resin is fed into a die to create a plastic container, i.e., a beer crate. Essentially, the label becomes part of the container and there is no seam to the label edge. Although injection in-mold labels make up a small percentage of the market today, this is the fastest growing label segment in North America.

Blow-Mold Labels

Blow-mold labels are currently the most common form of in-mold labels in North America, but the injection in-mold label segment is growing significantly while the use of blow mold is declining steadily. The process starts with hot air being injected into a tube of plastic to heat the resin. With the label in the mold cavity, the resin begins taking the shape of the mold cavity, pressing into the label. A heat-activated adhesive assists in adhering the label to the container. Unlike injection in-mold labels, an edge can be felt and it is possible to peel the label away from the container. Common blow-mold applications are plastic detergent bottles, large juice jugs, and motor oil containers.

Shrink Labels

Shrink labels are one of the fastest growing label segments in North America because of the shelf impact they can offer. The shrink label market is the third largest label segment, behind pressure-sensitive and cut-and-stack labels, and the beverage industry is the largest user of shrink labels. There are new technologies being worked on for aluminum can applications geared toward smaller SKU efficiencies.

Certain label applications may be used more for specific product segments, but there are always opportunities to use different label decoration methods outside the norm.

Modular labeling equipment allows users to mix and vary label applications with one machine base. Because of the advancements in servo and other technologies, the modular labeling machine is essentially a big turntable that can then sync different labeling technologies. A modular base allows a bolt-on cold-glue unit, a hot-melt unit, a pressure-sensitive unit, etc. This provides tremendous flexibility for future use of different label types.

The glue-applied segment of labels includes both cut-and-stack and roll-fed labels and is the largest labeling technology used. In the early 2000s, they had a much bigger share but pressure-sensitive, shrink, and in-mold label applications are the three fastest growing segments, and all three are expected to grow steadily into the late 2010s.

A cost comparison is shown in Figure 18.1. The lowest cost option is the spot cut-and-stack label. In-mold labels are right around the midpoint in terms of cost, followed by pressure-sensitive labels. From the list of label types discussed in the beginning, shrink labels are the most costly.

Cut-and-stack labels (Fig. 18.2) get their name from how they are cut and packaged into stacks of labels. It is the most common label type used, especially in beer packaging; cold-glue–applied cut-and-stack labels have the overall majority.

Pressure-sensitive labels (Fig. 18.3) are very similar to stickers in that an adhesive is applied to the back of the label, which is then married to a silicone-treated liner that protects the adhesive. Similar to cut-and-stack labels, there are various substrate options: white paper or film, metalized paper or film, clear film, or specialty paper.

The common difference between cut-and-stack and pressure-sensitive labels is that the face stocks on pressure-sensitive labels need to be thicker simply because, in order to dispense a pressure-sensitive label, the liner is passed across a peel plate or a peel bar, which shoots the label off onto the container. Cut-and-stack cold-glue labels do not need stiffness. Typically, the face stock on a cut-and-stack label is going to be thinner, sometimes substantially thinner, than pressure-sensitive labels. Another major difference between the two is pressure-sensitive label's dependence on a liner.

Pressure-sensitive labeling is more expensive than cut-and-stack labeling. Typically, even with high-volume applications, the cost of pressure-sensitive labels is two to five times higher than that of cut-and-stack cold-glue labels. There is some savings in that they come with their own adhesive and, more importantly, there is no need to purchase glue adhesive. The cleanup is also much easier with a pressure-sensitive labeler than with a cut-and-stack cold-glue application.

At high speeds, pressure-sensitive labels require a film liner to handle the greater tension that a paper liner carrier could not support. The construction of pressure-sensitive labels is shown in Figure 18.4.

The substrate, ink, and coating or laminate are almost the same regardless of label type. The difference with

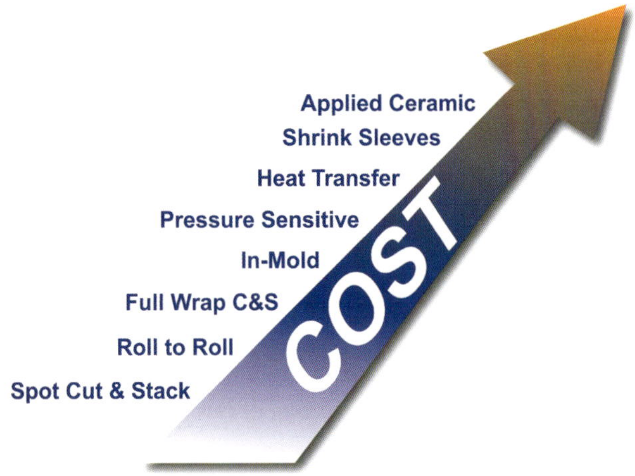

FIGURE 18.2. Cut-and-stack labels are applied with either cold glue or hot melt. There are various substrate options to choose from in terms of printing: white paper or film, metalized paper or film, clear film, or specialty paper. (Courtesy Inland Label)

FIGURE 18.3. Pressure-sensitive labels have an adhesive that is applied to the back of the label. The label is applied to a silicone-treated liner that protects the adhesive. (Courtesy Inland Label)

FIGURE 18.1. Cost comparison for label types. (Courtesy Inland Label)

Applied Ceramic
Shrink Sleeves
Heat Transfer
Pressure Sensitive
In-Mold
Full Wrap C&S
Roll to Roll
Spot Cut & Stack

pressure-sensitive labels is the liner that carries the label. The liner has to be silicone treated, which allows the adhesive applied to the face stock to release. This is the primary reason why pressure-sensitive labels are more expensive than cut-and-stack cold-glue labels.

Shrink labels (Fig. 18.5) have also grown in popularity. The label film has shrink characteristics, so when it goes through a heat tunnel, the label takes the shape of the container. Heat tunnels typically use hot steam because it is a very efficient heat carrier. Unlike the electric heat tunnels formerly used, steam provides a consistent heat all the way around the container, yielding better shrink characteristics.

The shrink process distorts the label to conform to the shape of the container, so the artwork has to be developed in a distorted appearance. Once the label shrinks around the container, it looks correct.

Shrink labels can come presleeved on a roll, where the labels are cut and dropped over a mandrel that applies them over the container, which then goes through the heat tunnel (Fig. 18.6). The other method is to feed the roll onto a vacuum drum that applies a flat label to the container, seams the label with either a solvent or laser technology, and then passes the container through a heat tunnel to shrink the label around the container (Fig. 18.7).

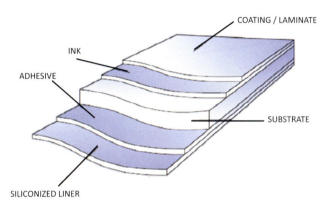

FIGURE 18.4. Pressure-sensitive label construction. (Courtesy Inland Label)

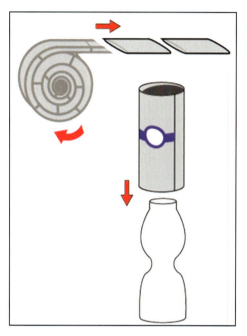

FIGURE 18.6. Sleeved shrink label process. (Courtesy Inland Label)

FIGURE 18.5. Examples of shrink labels on a glass bottle and an aluminum can. (Courtesy Inland Label)

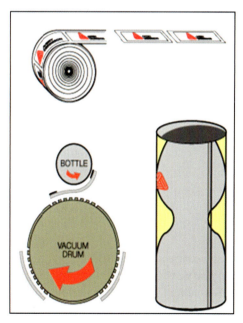

FIGURE 18.7. Roll-fed shrink label process. (Courtesy Inland Label)

One note of caution with heat shrink labels and glass bottles is that, when the label is heat shrunk around a bottle, it has the potential of hiding a breakage. It is important to be cognizant that there could actually be breakage and the shrink label is literally holding that bottle together.

● LABEL DESIGN

Seventy percent of the environmental impact of packaging is determined at the design stage. The reality is that about 99% of the label cost and runnability is also determined at the design phase. This is an area people all too often neglect, which can lead to increased costs later.

Label design is the area in which breweries can really improve the cost, shelf appeal, and runnability—the label efficiency on the bottling line—all at the same time. It starts with communication. When designing a new label, it is important to know who the glue supplier is, what labeling equipment manufacturer is being used (can it run on the labeler machine in the bottling line?), and of course, information about the container.

Marketing always plays a role in label design. Branding is very important to the brewery, as is point-of-purchase shelf appeal. Label design is what draws consumers in and plays the important role of portraying the brand image. It is also important for there to be open communication between marketing and operations so that the ideas being brainstormed are feasible and available.

Art specifications are an instrumental part to kick-start label design. To be proactive, it is important that the label company talk with the brand managers, graphic designers, or whoever is doing the design at the beginning of the label design process. This initial communication can save everyone a great deal of time and energy. Incorrect bar code placement, coloring that does not work on store scanners, or die cuts that cannot be run on the labeler machine are avoidable art specification issues. The label company will cover the basic artwork issues, e.g., minimum/maximum sizes, colors, what colors to stay away from on a unit price code (UPC), etc. However, it is best to start with clear communication up front with the designers.

Building sustainability into the label design adds value to the branding and typically increases throughput in the labeler. Sustainability also usually reduces the label-per-unit cost. Sustainability includes things such as reducing waste and lowering the carbon footprint. Figure 18.8 shows how label design can affect wastage and cost.

The labels at the top of Figure 18.8 represent the most wasteful, most costly, and least sustainable designs. These include die cutting instead of square cutting and label orientations that produce a lot of scrap material. At the bottom of Figure 18.8 is a chop-cut label—a label that has no border trim waste, which is the lowest cost, lowest waste, and most sustainable option.

Figure 18.8 (top right) shows an example of a label that is oriented on the neck at an angle. When run that way on the printing equipment, it will produce a large amount of waste. By changing the orientation through the production process, it is possible to at least minimize most of the waste and cost.

All too often, people designing the label are not designing to the container. If a designer has not been involved in packaging before, he/she may be used to designing flat layouts where everything is laid out on a computer screen, which makes all the graphics equal. Quite often, the designer does not have experience with a labeling machine and the constraints it may pose. It is very important when designing to the container that the designer realizes that once the label is wrapped around the container there is one place, the front and center, that really shows the prime visual. And other effects, as cool as they may be, may not be readily seen on the shelf.

Figure 18.9 is an example of a well-designed cut-and-stack beer label. This is a chop-cut label in which there is no additional waste as the label is processed. All the mandatory information is on the outside panels, and once the label is adhered to the bottle, this information does not stand out. The main visual showcases the brand with a nice red border.

Once the artwork is completed and approved, it goes to the label manufacturer. First, the file goes through a "preflight" procedure. This is to make sure that it fits all the specifications and standards to be processed during production. If it fails here, the label company will contact either the marketing personnel at the brewery or the designer directly to resolve the issue(s).

Once the details are worked out, the label is sent to the prepress department, where the proofs and color standards are developed. For simple art approval, a "soft" proof is done, meaning the proof is a PDF file sent via e-mail for approval. If the art is on a unique substrate or if it has unique colors, then typically a hard proof is produced and sent out. If the label uses custom colors, then drawdowns are provided. Drawdowns are a sample of the actual ink laid down on the actual substrate that the labels will be printed on to give an accurate representation of what the color will look like once printed. Densitometers and spectrophotometers are used on all label printing equipment today, but they still do not replicate the accuracy of a drawdown.

Once the proofs are sent for approval, it is very important that every detail is studied to make sure the wording and mandatory information is accurate. Having multiple people inspect the proof multiple times is recommended since this is the best time to catch a mistake or make a correction.

Once the proofs are approved and returned to the label manufacturer, the artwork is finalized and ready for production. The first phase is production planning. The production path is finalized and the press layout is done. Substrates, inks, and coatings are selected and finalized, if they have not been already. Tooling is created and ordered, which includes things such as the dies. The label converter also creates and adds the UPC to the label. Finally, a production schedule is put together.

Flexography (flexo) and offset (litho) plates are both typically created in-house at the label converter. Both types are computer to plate (CTP) and very efficient systems. An offset plate is constructed of aluminum and a low-cost

FIGURE 18.9. Example of a label with good sustainability traits. (Courtesy Inland Label)

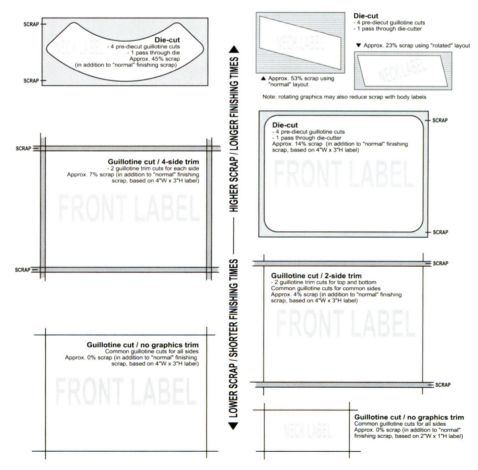

FIGURE 18.8. Sustainability of label designs is illustrated for various formats and treatments. (Courtesy Inland Label)

image carrier (Fig. 18.10). Flexo plates may be five to ten times the cost, depending on the material and size. Offset plates are used for one print run and recycled after use.

Gravure cylinders (Fig. 18.11) have to be engraved. This is typically not done in-house at the label converter and it is a longer process. It takes more time and planning to create gravure cylinders compared with flexo or offset plates.

If the label has a die-cut shape, it will have a die developed to cut it (Fig. 18.12). If it is a cut-and-stack label, then a high die will have to be machined. Dies are not manufactured in-house and will add expense as well as development time.

LABEL PRODUCTION

Label production includes label printing, finishing, and shipping. Once all of the up-front work from the prepress department and from production planning is finished, the actual production of the labels occurs. More time is spent in the up-front label design and file preparation stage than in the actual printing stage.

Printing is simply converting an image into something that is economically reproduced and mass distributed. Historically, before Gutenberg invented the printing press, print copying in the 1450s was a tedious and very manual process, typically completed by monks who did everything by hand, including color and type. Modern printing processes allow the art, four-color photography, four-color artwork, etc. to be broken down into dots, which allows printing on a mass scale using high-speed machines.

Printers talk about color loupes and small color dots, and almost every printing process uses these dots. Anyone who has been up close to a big four-color process billboard can see they are made from big color dots. Standing back, it looks like a continuous image but it is actually composed of large dots. Figure 18.13 shows the effect of dots in color and print composition.

FIGURE 18.10. Offset printing plate. (Courtesy Inland Label)

FIGURE 18.11. Gravure printing cylinder. (Courtesy Inland Label)

FIGURE 18.12. Cutting die. (Courtesy Inland Label)

FIGURE 18.13. Color in a printed image is actually composed of tiny dots. (Courtesy Inland Label)

An image is composed of a continuous tone color. A printer takes the color space and separates it into things that can actually be printed. Four-color process printing is also called CMYK (cyan, magenta, yellow, and black [K]). By combining those colors and putting them on top of one another, the printer ends up with many different colors (Fig. 18.14).

Four-color process printing does not cover the full color gamut however. Extended gamut printing, either six- or seven-color process printing, can provide the printer with a wider range of achievable colors.

By going to a six- or seven-color process, the color range is expanded. Color is actually three dimensional (3-D). A four-color process can only replicate about 85% of the 3-D color space. It looks good, but it still uses only 85% of the space. By going to an extended gamut, a six- or seven-color process can use 92–95% of the color space. Metallic colors and certain blues, certain reds, creams, and browns are colors that are hard to create with a four-color process, but the six- and seven-color processes produce a richer color using more of the color gamut and have become routine.

For any color process, the colors are applied one at a time. In a four-color process, the printing may start by laying down the black ink. Then the machine lays down the cyan, with the magenta over the top of that. Finally, the yellow is laid down and the label is complete.

If such a wide range of colors can be achieved using process printing, why are custom colors still used? Pure and simple, it is for branding purposes. A great deal of money is spent on brand building and many organizations want custom colors, especially if they have a difficult color to replicate. Sometimes a combination of custom colors with a custom substrate gives a brand a unique identity.

Flexo Printing

One of the most common print technologies is flexography (flexo). Flexo printing uses a plate that is like a rubber stamp. Flexo plates read "wrong". The anilox roll picks up the ink and the extra ink is docked or bladed off. The ink is transferred to the raised edges or the raised component of the flexo plate, and then it is transferred directly to the substrate. Just like a mirror, when it is transferred to the substrate, it now reads "right". Figure 18.15 shows the flexo components.

As in all printing processes, one color is laid down at a time; for instance, black is laid down first, then cyan, magenta, and yellow. The operator puts ink into the inkwell. The anilox roller then picks up the ink and transfers it to the plate. The plate then transfers the ink to the substrate and it prints on the label. By the time it gets to the end of the press, there is a four-color picture. The combination of all the colors going down on top of each other is what creates the final printed image.

Ink carryover from one plate to the next is avoided by drying the ink from one print station to the next. Small dryers are located on the machines between each printing plate. The process is literally printing and drying so that the next color is going down over a dry ink. The printing is typically done in one pass through the machine, which may have eight or nine stations if there are more color processes being used.

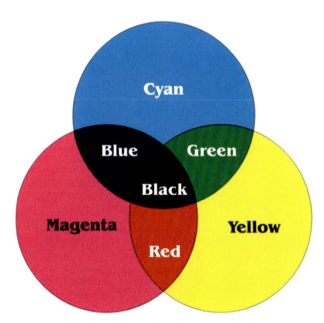

FIGURE 18.14. CMYK color interactions. (Courtesy Inland Label)

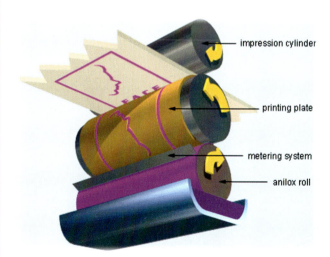

FIGURE 18.15. Flexo print process. (Courtesy Inland Label)

Gravure Printing

With gravure, the ink film can be varied in each station. That is because the size, depth, and shape of every one of those cells that are engraved can be changed. The patterns seen are millions of very small cells. This allows for greater flexibility. Heavier amounts of ink and deep, rich pigments can be used that could not be used in any other print process. This gives gravure printing a deep, rich color. It is an excellent process for coating and printing on specialty-type materials.

Although expensive to create, gravure cylinders last for millions of impressions and, therefore, provide superior consistency. The same set of cylinders can be used for several print runs and the print quality will not diminish. Figure 18.16 shows the gravure process.

In the gravure process, the cylinder is both the print surface and the pickup surface since the cylinder is rolling in a bath of ink, with the excess ink being removed with a doctor blade, and then the ink is transferred directly to the substrate. Similar to flexo printing, reverse or negative imaging is engraved into the cylinder, and then when printed it becomes a "right" reading image.

Another characteristic that flexo and gravure share besides the way the ink is applied is the viscosity of the ink. Both print processes use a thin, liquid ink that can be either water or solvent based.

Offset Printing

Offset lithography (litho) uses a thicker, higher-viscosity ink that is almost like a paste. This thick ink is oil based and typically incorporates vegetable or other renewable oils. Offset printing is based upon the principle that oil and water do not mix. Inside an offset press are a series of small rollers that carry ink and water down to the printing plate. Each series of rollers, typically 20–40, ensures that the proper amount of ink and water is applied to the printing plate.

Offset is a "right" reading process in which the process itself is really lithography. To actually take the image and get it to print "right" reading, it has to be offset. The image is transferred from the printing plate to a blanket, and then the blanket transfers the image to the substrate. Offset printing plates have chemistry that allows them to have oil-loving areas that will attract the ink and water-loving areas that will attract the water and keep the ink in the correct places on the plate. It picks up a thicker layer of ink and a very thin layer of water so that, when it hits the blanket, the ink transfers and the water does not. If water transfers a little bit, there can be color variation. The chemistry and the preciseness of all of the rollers are critical to produce consistent color. Figure 18.17 shows the offset litho process.

Unlike flexo and gravure printing, offset printing does not require as much drying between each of the colors being printed on the substrate. There are very small drying units between each unit on the press and then a larger drying unit at the very end of the press. Some offset presses use an ultraviolet unit at the end to help cure or dry the inks.

Printed sheets are coated with a layer of spray powder, which allows air to get to the printed surface of each press sheet so the inks can cure. While printed sheets may be

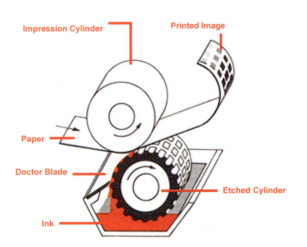

FIGURE 18.16. Gravure printing process. (Courtesy Inland Label)

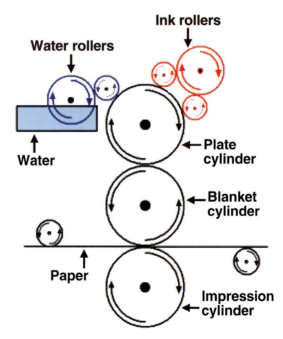

FIGURE 18.17. Offset (litho) printing process. (Courtesy Inland Label)

dry to the touch at the end of the press, the inks take time to cure. Unlike flexo and gravure printing where the label sheets are coming off the press equipment dry, the sheet-fed offset process requires curing time. The cure time depends on the substrate. It could be ready to cut in 6 hours on paper or it may take days before it is ready to cut on polypropylenes, styrenes, etc.

Heatset Offset Printing

Heatset offset printing is a bridge between gravure and sheet-fed offset printing. With heatset offset printing, the substrate is cured by running it through an oven. This process can be used on papers, metalized papers, etc. but is not used for films.

Digital Printing

Digital technology has come a long way and today can produce beautiful print. It is great for making samples and printing small quantities but cannot produce large quantities economically.

Where are these printing processes used? Why do they all still exist? High-volume cut-and-stack labels is a great example of why gravure printing is used to make large volumes of labels fast. It is all about total meters of substrate through the press, and that is where gravure printing is useful. In-line flexo printing is the predominant flexography technology and is used for about 90% of the flexo labels produced in the world. A small volume of shrink labels are also produced using flexo printing.

In-line flexo printing is predominantly used for pressure-sensitive labels, shrink labels, and small-volume roll-fed and cut-and-stack labels. Offset printing is great for small- to medium-quantity cut-and-stack labels. Some of the latest offset technology is running at higher speeds and rivaling gravure printing. The label converter is the ultimate source for helping the brand owner decide what is the most effective printing process. Table 18.1 summarizes the different printing processes.

LABEL FINISHING

Once the labels are off the press, they are in roll or sheet form. For cut-and-stack labels, the paper has to be put into the quantities ordered so they can be loaded into the label magazine on the labeler machine. Typically, 550–1,500 labels are in one bundle.

Jogging is the first step in the finishing process. An operator takes stacks of sheets and places them onto a jogging machine. This machine basically shakes the stack of press sheets to remove all of the air from between the sheets, which allows the stack to be squared up so that precise cuts can be made later (Fig. 18.18). Even with the quality assurance vision inspection systems, jogging provides a chance to visually inspect the sheets. If the press workers have a doubt about something, they can put a flag into the pile indicating they ran into something and requesting it to be checked; jogging is where that check is done.

Typically, if it is a high-quantity or die-cut label, a strip cut is done. With strip cutting, the waste is taken off the

TABLE 18.1. Summary of Process Uses for Printing Types

Gravure:	Flexography:
High-volume cut-and-stack labels	Pressure-sensitive labels
High-volume pressure-sensitive labels	Small-volume shrink labels
Medium- to high-volume shrink labels	Small-volume roll-fed (in-line) labels
Medium- to high-volume roll-fed labels	High-volume roll-fed labels (central impression)
Offset (Lithography):	**Digital:**
Small- to medium-volume cut-and-stack labels	Very low volumes of all label types
In-mold labels	

FIGURE 18.18. Jogging the labels into manageable stacks. (Courtesy Inland Label)

edges, and then the labels are put into strips that are going to be fed into automated finishing equipment, i.e., die cutters (Fig. 18.19). After cutting, the strips are fed into an automated die cutter (Fig. 18.20).

The die cutter may have a very small guillotine cutter. It cuts one strip at a time and then feeds it into a slot, where the label is literally rammed through the die. The dies are very heavy and they are made of different types of steel, depending on the type of substrate being run and the different cutting angles. Through experience and experimentation, a process has been developed to maintain the dies, sharpening the edges and/or pulling them out of operation at the end of their useful life.

All pressure-sensitive labels are die cut. The shape is cut out of just the top layer, not through the liner, and the waste is removed. Once the larger roll from the press is die cut, which is usually right in line at the end of the press, the large roll must be cut down into roll sizes that will fit the labeling equipment. The slitter-rewinder slits or cuts the large role into its final roll size. Rewind direction is important so there is an initial determination of what unwind is needed so that the label roll feeds in the correct orientation on the labeler.

To produce labels that will perform properly on labeling equipment, label manufacturing plants are fully air conditioned, heated, and humidity controlled. Typically, they are kept, on average, at 50% relative humidity and around 72°F (22°C).

After the cutting process, the labels are banded into bundles and shrink-wrapped, or they are banded into bundles and put into plastic bags. For a hot and humid environment, both the plastic bags and shrink-wrap are used. This is to maintain the controlled environment until they are opened and used.

The labels are packed into cartons and a carton tag is applied. Carton tags have production information that can be referred to if there is a problem at the brewery. The carton tag allows traceability from production, back through the subsuppliers, e.g., paper and ink suppliers.

Recommendations for Label Storage

- Do not double stack skids.
  - If they must be double stacked, make sure there is a thick layer of material to spread the load evenly on the top layer of label cartons.
- Provide the correct storage and labeling conditions.
  - Conditions should be climate controlled if possible, ideally 72°F (22°C) and 50% humidity.
- Only open those labels intended to run.
  - Ensure labels are at ambient temperature.
  - Check labels before loading.
    – Fan each bundle as it is loaded (for cut-and-stack labels).
- Open, unused labels must be protected.

LABEL PAPER

Typically, papers are designed with certain characteristics based upon the mill, the type of paper, and other specifications. The label company will lock in those characteristics and then receive very consistent paper from the mill. The labeler machine wants a paper that was designed for a specific purpose and, in turn, consistent. There are no two labelers that are exactly the same, or two totes of glue that are exactly the same, or two rolls of

FIGURE 18.19. Strips of labels after strip cutting. (Courtesy Inland Label)

FIGURE 18.20. Die cutter. (Courtesy Inland Label)

paper that are exactly the same. Likewise, working with the substrate manufacturers to get the right properties and specifications locked in at the very beginning is key. Rarely will changing those specifications and characteristics be the solution to solving a label problem.

The Cobb value of paper is its ability to take in moisture. There is a 1-minute and a 2-minute Cobb test. To do a Cobb test, take a specified machined cylinder and lock in a specified, preweighed amount of paper or label into this frame. Add a very precise amount of distilled water and then time it for either 60 or 120 seconds. Quickly dump the water, unclamp the material, run it with a very precise roller, and then reweigh it. The results will indicate how much moisture the label has absorbed in that 1- or 2-minute period. The Cobb value is expressed as the percentage of moisture gained during either test.

The problem with a Cobb test is that a labeling process does not wait 1 or 2 minutes before providing some feedback on whether the label works. An instantaneous Cobb test would work best, but there is no such thing. Instead, it is better to work with the label manufacturers to do experimentation on how the paper works in certain atmospheric conditions.

This is why questions are asked at the beginning of the design phase regarding the conditions the label will be in, e.g., will it be labeled on a cold, wet bottle directly off the filler or on a hot, dry bottle from a tunnel pasteurizer? For bottling in cold and wet conditions, air knives can greatly help the performance of the labeling process by removing bottle condensation and moisture.

Cobb values are fairly consistent (±5%), unless the paper is one of the natural grades, such as 100% recycled fiber. Label substrate is typically 100% virgin for a reason. It is to ensure that those characteristics expected from the label paper are consistent. Recycled fibers create a more open substrate and show more variation; this might require higher tack in the glue and more care during the labeling process to be used successfully.

● LABEL DEFECTS

Curl

Upcurl in paper is created when it is exposed to too much moisture (Fig. 18.21). An example would be a label pack opened in a very humid atmosphere, where it will take in water from the air. The uncoated back side of that label will expand, causing upcurl. Conversely, if the paper label is exposed to low humidity, it will give off moisture and curl down. By controlling the condition of the incoming paper and the plant temperature and humidity, the label converter can control the curl and produce flat labels. However, it is important in a brewery environment to control those same factors when possible, to only open the label packs that are to be used, and to protect unused open labels by sealing them in plastic.

Blocking

Blocking most typically happens because of a defect in the cutting blade used to cut the label sheets (Fig. 18.22). If the cutting blade or die becomes dull or if the wrong steel was used in the making of the cutting tool, then more of a tearing action can occur instead of a clean cut. This ends up tearing the sheets, and the fibers stick together.

FIGURE 18.21. Curling caused by exposure to high humidity. (Courtesy Inland Label)

FIGURE 18.22. Blocking caused by dull knives or dies. (Courtesy Inland Label)

Often, the label bundle can be fanned and given a couple of taps and a couple of waves before it is put into the magazine. This is no different than fanning a ream of paper before adding it to most modern copiers or printers to help the paper feed.

Fanning will not work if the blocking is on a coated paper. With coatings, the amount of pressure put on the labels when they are finished can actually weld the stack together. This is a defect that cannot be solved in the brewery, and the labels will have to be sent back to the label manufacturer.

Size Variation

Size variation is typically caused by improper pressure on the clamps when cutting the strips (Fig. 18.23) or an improper quality of contact point with the die or knife. These will cause size defects. A dull knife alone or a very spongy material could also be the culprit. To address this, the label converter can turn up the pressure during jogging so that more air is taken out between the press sheets, or it can use a counterpressure die cutter, where a ram comes through the die and preholds the paper before it is jammed up through the die. Using a counterpressure die cutter is a much slower process and the dies costs more because it has to have a mate.

Telescoping

Telescoping is seen occasionally on pressure-sensitive or roll-fed labels (Fig. 18.24). Telescoping is typically caused by poor tension on the rewinder during the printing process. Sometimes, this is unavoidable, especially when using more tactile types of labels, e.g., labels with raised edges, which may also be a design issue.

Poor Slit Edge

A poor slit edge looks like a wavy edge (Fig. 18.25). This condition comes about in two ways. It may come from the paper manufacturer if they have a gauge banding problem on their machine. This could be a difference in two rollers trying to mete out some material and creating a low spot, which creates a buckle. The other cause is at the label converter during the slitting process. If the slitter has a poor edge or a poor knife or if a poor choice was made

FIGURE 18.24. Telescoping caused by poor tension on the rewinder. (Courtesy Inland Label)

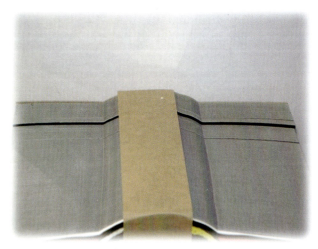

FIGURE 18.23. Size variation caused by improper cutting clamp pressure. (Courtesy Inland Label)

FIGURE 18.25. Poor slit edge. (Courtesy Inland Label)

on the slitting wheel or plow, it creates heat. The heat will actually distort the edge. Instead of cutting, there can be a tearing action, causing uneven, wavy edges.

SUMMARY

Successful labeling operations start with the design phase. Educated decisions made with the initial designs will set the stage for efficient throughput in the bottling line. Spending more time at the design phase and having the right people involved early on will lower the risk of issues down the road.

Make use of the label converter's technical field services. These people know the label production process and they have been through formal training with major labeler manufacturers. Call them and invite them into your plant so they can see your operations up close and personal. Let the technical representatives know who your glue and machine technicians are as well. Open communication is essential for issues to be solved quickly and efficiently.

CHAPTER 19

Labeler Operations

FRANK KACZMARSKI
Krones USA

When brewery engineers are looking for a labeling machine, there are several pieces of information that first need to be determined. What is to be labeled? What is the desired operating speed in bottles per minute (bpm)? What kinds of labels are to be used? Is the application labeling glass, plastic, or both? What will be utilized for the label materials; are they paper-based laminates, which are typical for most breweries? These are all major factors in determining the size of the labeling machine.

Figure 19.1 shows some of the basic label dimensions and placements. While most breweries seal with a crown, many others use a foil over the crown or even a foil over a cork and bale finish.

After distinguishing the brewer's needs, attention shifts to look at the minimum spacing required for the labels. The bottom label placement is about 12 mm (0.5 inch) from the bottom of the bottle.

A wraparound neck label requires 1–2 mm (0.04–0.08 inch) under the lip of the bottle finish area. Many breweries use bottles with recessed panels to create a small gap between bottles as they travel on conveyor lines and to protect the label from being scuffed by bottle-to-bottle contact or conveyor guides. When the bottles touch each other, they will contact the top and the bottom of the raised panel but the label area is protected.

The neck label overlap requires about 11 mm (0.4 inch) of lacquer-free paper without any sheen or varnish so the glue bonds and dries quickly. If there is any lacquer on the overlap area, the label may open up and will not seal properly on the overlap of the neck label, causing flagging.

Production speeds and machine speed are determined by the number of stations and pitch distance. Pitch distance is the distance between the bottles while they are

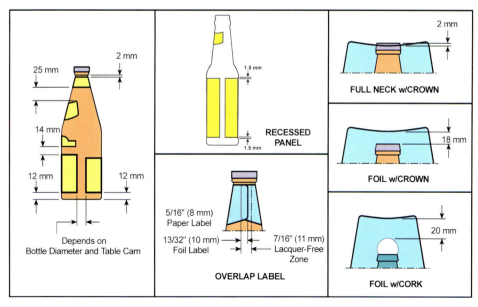

FIGURE 19.1. Label placement (minimum dimensions). (Courtesy Krones USA)

TABLE 19.1. Factors Influencing Machine Speed and Bottle Dressing

Factor	Limiting Condition	Increasing Condition
Machine size • number of stations • pitch distance	Fewer stations = longer pitch distance = longer label lengths = lower bottle output	More stations = shorter pitch distance = shorter label lengths = higher bottle output
Label length	Limits container output Longer label length = larger pitch distance = fewer label transfer stations = more wipe-down time	Increases dressing capability • multiple labels • wraparound labels
Bottle dressing complexity • number of labels	Limits container output More labels per container/more complex labels = more wipe-down time = more complex bottle turns for wipe down	Increases graphic appearance of package

transferred through the labeler. The fewer the stations, the longer the pitch and the longer the available wipe-down or brush-down time, but also the lower the bottle output speed.

Label length limits the bottle output. A longer label length requires a larger pitch distance, fewer label transfer stations, and more wipe-down time. The more wipe-down time available, the better the label bonds to the bottle. The less time available produces an increased chance of the label failing to bond to the bottle properly, resulting in flagging.

Labeling is one of the primary areas in packaging where production meets marketing. The bottle dressing, its complexity, number of labels, etc. are all affected by the desired graphic appearance of the package. Many times those efforts limit the output of the machine. When consumers are shopping for beer, they are looking for flavor, but they are also looking for a good appearance, i.e., a good-looking bottle. Table 19.1 lists some factors of bottle dressing and how they affect machine speed.

Other factors affecting machine speed include the number of label pallets and the configuration of the line. The label pallet receives adhesive from the glue roller, peels a label out of a label magazine, and transfers the label to the gripper cylinder, which transfers the label to the bottle, which then travels through the wipe-down area.

The configuration of a production line itself is affected mainly by accumulation areas on both the bottle supply and the discharge end. If the labeler has a jam or short-term shutdown, an accumulation area is needed to keep the filler from shutting down. Likewise, if the case packer goes down, then some accumulation is needed to keep the labeler from shutting down.

Cold-glue labeler designs are the most commonly used labelers in breweries. Machine speeds range from 35 to about 1,200 bpm in very large breweries. Speeds of fewer than 100 bpm can usually be handled with manual hand-on/hand-off packing. As speeds increase, the line will require automated uncasers and case packers. The diameter of the bottle itself ranges anywhere from 50 to 125 mm (2 to 5 inches) across and heights range from 50 to 480 mm (2 to 19 inches). The actual label length ranges from 40 to 180 mm (1.6 to 7 inches). Normally, these machines use precut paper labels either guillotine straight cut or cut with curves by being pushed through a die.

● MACHINE ORIENTATION

When ordering a machine, there are considerations of space, existing conveyors, and perhaps what works best with the existing system. The standard rotary labeler is either a left- or a right-hand orientation. This is determined by facing the front of the machine. If the bottle is coming in from the left and exiting out to the right, it is a right-hand orientation. If the bottles feed in from the right and discharge from the left, it is a left-hand orientation. This is not only a concern when ordering the machine

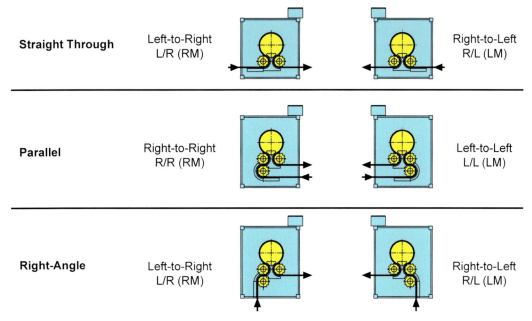

FIGURE 19.2. Typical machine directions (orientations) for rotary labelers. RM = right machine. LM = left machine. (Courtesy Krones USA)

but also when ordering parts. Figure 19.2 shows some examples of machine orientation.

There are also parallel machines, which have two infeed stars instead of one. In the parallel orientation, the bottle is entering from the right and discharging from the right, so it is a right-hand machine. This orientation is meant for tight areas, perhaps against a wall or in a corner. There is also the right-angle configuration, with bottles entering from the left and exiting on the right. For both of these two configurations, there are opposite options available as well.

There are many components that are directional on a machine, even the tension spool on a label basket is directional, and these parts cannot be exchanged from one direction to the other direction. The correct machine direction must be determined and specified when ordering to ensure that the right parts are received.

● LABELER MACHINE OPERATION

Figure 19.3 provides an overhead view of the typical rotary cold-glue labeler machine layout. This is a basic layout and the principle is common to all these types of machines on the market.

Number three on Figure 19.3 is the feed screw, which drives and indexes the bottle into the machine, giving it the proper pitch. The infeed screw spaces the bottles so they feed properly to each pocket of the infeed star. The infeed star transfers the bottles across dead plates to bottle pads. The bottle pads are controlled by a cam track and segment and spur gears, allowing rotation. This is part of the bottle table on newer models. The bottle pad can be servo driven on the modular labeler models.

A centering head applies approximately 25 pounds per square inch gauge (psig) spring pressure down on the bottle to hold it. Polyethylene terephthalate (PET) requires a different spring with a little less pressure. When running both glass and plastic on the same machine, sometimes a little less head pressure is used with the same spring. Springs are not changed out during a bottle changeover.

The bottle table rotates in a clockwise direction. The label station, or aggregate, is the complete system for applying the label and includes the label pallets, glue roller, label magazine, and gripper cylinder. The glue pump sends the label adhesive to the top of the glue roller. The scraper maintains a thin film of glue on the roller, enough to get the label to adhere but not too much, so as to avoid glue slinging and label swimming, or movement, on the bottle.

The label pallets rotate in, clockwise, to pick the adhesive off the glue roller. The label basket kicks in pneumatically, placing the label onto the pallet. The pallet then transfers the glued label to the gripper cylinder. The bottle comes in contact with the label and the sponge area at the gripper. Body labels are applied at the first station or aggregate. If there is a neck label, it will also be applied at this first station. If it is a neck application, the gripper sponge will push out via an internal cam track to meet the neck of the bottle.

When setting up the body gripper, there is no push-out, but the aggregate is moved toward the bottle plate to make sure there is an adequate amount of sponge pressure against the bottle. Then the neck gripper is set up so that the push-out is moving all the way out at the right time to meet the design of the bottle.

After all the labels are applied, e.g., body, neck, and shoulder, the bottle will go through a number of turns as it goes through a wipe-down stage, usually with a series of brushes. Brushes come in different degrees of stiffness. There are coarse and soft grades of brushes, and selection has to do with the actual label and its composition.

For a metalized label, especially if it is a wraparound on the contour of the bottle, the brushes may move the label and, especially if there is too much glue, the label may move around or "swim". This can also happen when the bottles are too wet at the time the label is applied. Rollers are also used to wipe down the label, they have less surface friction, and they roll with the bottle instead of dragging against it. This movement is sometimes too much action and will misalign the label.

Figure 19.3 includes a back aggregate. Back aggregates are used to apply back labels. While the front aggregate can apply a body, shoulder, and neck label, it cannot apply a back label. Most machines are fitted with bottle table cams designed for a future back aggregate possibility. Back label application requires the bottle pads to turn 180° from the front label. The back aggregate uses the same principles as the front aggregate and requires rollers or brushes to finish applying the label.

The centering head lifts off the bottle after the final wipe-down. The bottle is transferred to the discharge star and then to the conveyor/packer. Sometimes there is a jam table downstream of the labeler in case the bottles back up. In this event, the machine shuts down and stops production to decrease the chance of breakage.

● LABEL MACHINE GLUE STATION (AGGREGATE)

Figure 19.4A shows a typical cold-glue station. It shows a steel roller and rubberized glue pallets fitted for a body and neck application with corresponding body and neck label magazines and the brush-down stations.

The brewery could be running a 12-oz. beer bottle or a 40-, 60-plus-, or 10-oz. bottle. Figure 19.4B shows an example of a dial setup where quick adjustments can be made for different bottle sizes.

What is making the pallet move at different times, and what is making the bottle plate pad move at different times? Figure 19.5 shows a cutaway view of a label station.

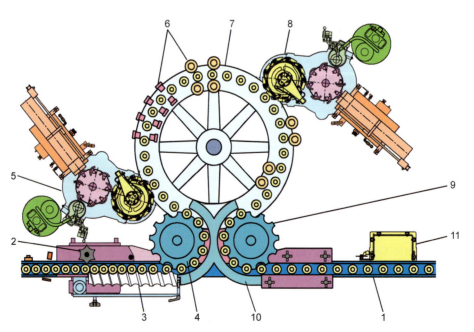

FIGURE 19.3. Typical rotary machine layout. 1 = Conveyor and bottle guides; 2 = bottle stop; 3 = feed screw; 4 = infeed star wheel; 5 = front labeling station; 6 = wipe-down station; 7 = bottle table; 8 = back labeling station (optional); 9 = discharge star wheel; 10 = center guide; and 11 = jam table. (Courtesy Krones USA)

The centering heads place pressure down on the bottle with the cam track operating. The cam track in the bottle table makes the spur and segment gears in the bottle table turn the bottle plate pads at different times. On newer models, the bottle pads can be servo driven.

Figure 19.6 shows a layout of the label pallet motion. It is showing an eight-pallet aggregate. After the pallets come in and pick up the adhesive, the glue roller rotates counterclockwise. The pallets move clockwise. The pallet picks the label out of the label basket. At this point, the gripper cylinder's fingers pull the label off the glue pallet at the recessed cutouts on the pallets. The gripper then transfers the label to the bottle, which travels through the wipe-down area.

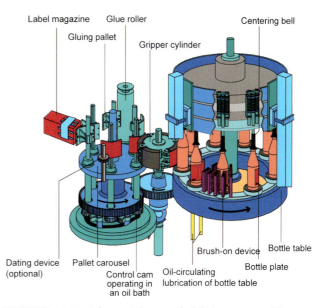

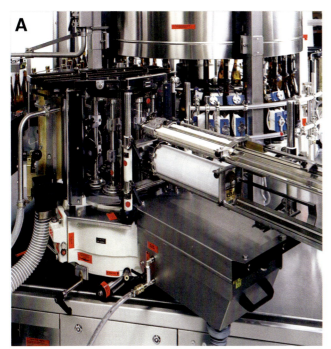

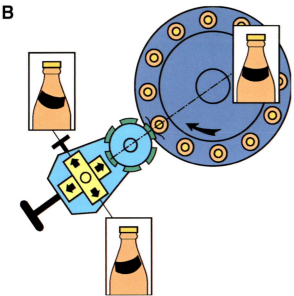

FIGURE 19.4. A, Cold-glue labeling station. The cast-iron labeling station housing (lower left white section) is mounted on a cross-slide for precise radial and tangential adjustment. B, Quick adjustment via adjustable indexed stops for different bottle types. (Courtesy Krones USA)

FIGURE 19.5. Schematic layout of a labeling station. The glue roller transfers glue onto the pallet. The pallet picks up a label from the label magazine and then transfers it to the gripper cylinder. The label is date coded (optional). The gripper cylinder picks up the label from the pallet via cam-controlled fingers. The gripper sponge presses the label onto the bottle. The bottle is rotated typically 90° for proper brush-down. The bottle turns to continue the label brush-down. (Courtesy Krones USA)

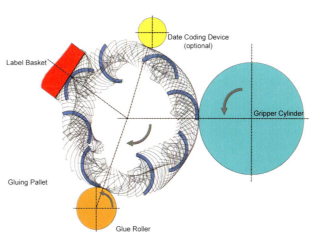

FIGURE 19.6. Schematic layout of label pallet motion in an eight-pallet aggregate. (Courtesy Krones USA)

Figure 19.7 shows the interior drives of a front aggregate. The main drive shaft is in the bottom left corner. The drive shaft powers everything on the aggregate and the gearing is bathed in oil. It is very important to keep the oil changed so it is clean and free of water and glue.

Glue can seep into the oil bath through faulty seals. With the machine rotation, faulty seals, high-pressure wash water, and an abundance of glue, both moisture and glue drive up underneath, through the seals, and into the oil compartment. Dirty oil significantly reduces the life of the aggregate. Many machines have sight glasses to check the oil level, as well as oil monitoring systems.

● GLUE ROLLERS AND LABEL PALLETS

Figure 19.8 shows the glue scraper and the adjustment knob used to fine tune the film level of the glue on the glue roller. Enough glue should be applied so that the label is completely covered but not so heavily that glue slings from the pallet onto the gripper or the label swims on the bottle.

Aluminum pallets are used with rubber glue rollers, and vulcanized rubber glue pallets are used with stainless-steel glue rollers. Figure 19.8A shows a glue station with a stainless-steel glue roller and rubber label pallets. This setup is typically used for higher speeds (>400 bpm). Setting the glue roller to the pressure of the rubberized pallets creates a very close tolerance and a tight firm top and bottom pull when utilizing a 0.05-mm (0.002-inch) shim stock. For correct setup, the pallets and the glue roller should line up parallel, left to right, in and out.

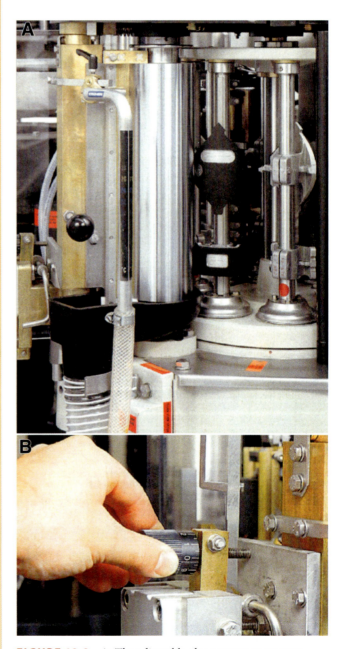

FIGURE 19.7. The drive and control cam are in a closed oil bath with oil-circulating lubrication. (Courtesy Krones USA)

FIGURE 19.8. **A,** The adjustable glue scraper guarantees constant, optimal glue application. **B,** The glue film thickness adjustments are precisely made with a scaled dial indicator. (Courtesy Krones USA)

The glue is applied to the recessed area of the rubberized pallet, not to the raised surface. These setups can be run at high speed, and with the correct amount of glue film, do not have slinging or webbing problems, producing a glue savings of up to 20%. With the reduced glue usage, there is also reduced cleanup time. In addition, rubber glue rollers cannot be left to rest on their sides since this will flatten the surface and create problems. A rubber roller, when laid on its side, may have to be replaced or resurfaced to be usable. Stainless-steel rollers do not have this issue.

Both rubber and aluminum pallets eventually show wear and should be replaced. Pallets should be replaced as a set rather than individually because they must be set up to the glue roller uniformly for best performance.

The rubber glue roller with aluminum label pallets is the standard in the industry (Fig. 19.9). The glue adhesive is applied to the aluminum surface of the pallet. Aluminum pallets have horizontal lines etched across their surface. The glue is transferred onto the etched lines and the label rests on the edges of the lines. Whether aluminum or rubber construction, the label pallets are slightly smaller than the label by about 1 mm (0.04 inch) in length and height. This allows for glue to squeeze out.

There is a proper tolerance for the space between the pallet and the glue roller. The tolerance is set to a center line. When the pallet is perfectly in line with the glue roller, either a plastic shim gauge or stainless-steel shim can be used to check for the right amount of pressure. If there is too much pressure of the glue roller against the pallet, the glue will squeeze out and there will not be an adequate amount of glue on the pallet. Commonly, the operator will balance this by increasing the glue pump volume and sending in more glue. This will complicate the situation and cause excess glue on the station without addressing the real problem. This scenario can occur when changing rubber glue rollers, whether resurfaced or new. This is obviously not an issue with stainless-steel glue rollers but can be a problem with new rubberized label pallets. Care must be taken with the rubberized pallets, which are more expensive to replace than the aluminum pallets.

Rubberized pallets will last longer than those made of aluminum if properly cared for. They should be cleaned using light detergent soap and a soft bristle brush; keep the putty knives away. A putty knife can cause damage to both rubber and aluminum pallets, as well as to rubber glue rollers. During shutdown, aluminum pallets should not be left positioned against the rubber glue roller because they will leave an impression or memory in the rubber, producing flat spots. Flat spots on a rubber glue roller will end up transferring too much glue to the pallet at times and not enough at other times.

Aluminum wears down twice as fast if highly caustic cleaners are used. If the aluminum pallets are turning gray-black and pitted, typically the chemicals being used are too harsh or too strong in concentration for cleaning. This will distort them, actually causing pinholes and corrosion.

Figure 19.10 shows a typical glue pump configuration pumping from a bucket of label glue. Sometimes a temperature strip is put onto the glue tube to monitor the temperature of the glue as it travels to the roller.

FIGURE 19.9. Rubber glue roller with aluminum pallets. (Courtesy Krones USA)

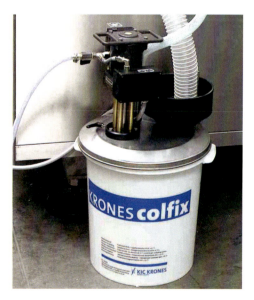

FIGURE 19.10. Pneumatic glue pump that has an adjustable pumping speed for accurate glue supply and an optional thermostat-controlled heating system for optimum processing temperatures. (Courtesy Krones USA)

Some glue pumps have integrated heaters for colder environments. If the glue becomes too hot, it will have a tendency to walk away from the scraper; if it is too cold, it webs and slings, making a mess and wasting glue.

● MACHINE FLOW CONTROL

Figure 19.11 shows a generic automatic flow control system. It would be considered a two-speed system with low and high running speeds. (Systems can also have variable speeds.) The bottles enter from the left. There are two inventory backup switches, 1 and 2, sensing the amount of stock available to feed the machine. There is some line accumulation entering, and an infeed gap sensor to ensure no broken glass or fallen bottles enter the machine. If that sensor is tripped, the machine shuts down. The optional cap sensor can detect crown presence.

The bottle stop can stop bottles from entering the machine. The bottle stop is used by the operator if the bottle flow must be stopped or when making a label change while keeping the same bottle size. The flow is stopped, the last of the product is run out, and the changeover is performed. Inventory switches 1 and 2 detect the bottle supply feeding the machine. When backup switch 1 detects an accumulation of bottles building up, it is going to run at the higher speed. If there is a shutdown upstream and the accumulation depletes, inventory switch 1 will not trip and the machine will go into low speed until the inventory replenishes.

The discharge includes a jam table in the event the flow suddenly stops, to avoid immediate machine shutdown. If bottle accumulation continues, it will trip backup switch 2 and the machine will drop into a lower speed. If an accumulation backs up to backup switch 1, the bottle stop will stop incoming bottles and run out the product in the machine. Once downstream processing resumes, the accumulation will dissipate and the backup switches will clear to allow low-speed and then high-speed production.

This is a very basic overview of the flow control system. There are other methods of controlling flow to the labeler machine.

● BOTTLE TABLE ROTATIONS

Figure 19.12 shows wipe-down stations on a front-label station running a single aggregate with a body, shoulder, and neck application. After leaving the aggregate, the bottle optimally receives wipe-down through 100% of the available wipe-down area. However, some applications include a back label, and the space taken up by the additional aggregate leaves only 50% of the wipe-down area for the bottle front labels. It is important to get the most out of the reduced wipe-down area.

The cam tracks have different turns (Fig. 19.13): a typical layout for a body front, neck, and body back application. There are seven turns in the layout in Figure 19.13, which are all machined into the cam track. The cam track turns the spur and segment gears through various wipe-down positions, thus turning the bottle plate and the bottle itself. The bottle table is rotating, while the cam track is stationary. After the body front and full-neck label application, the bottle first has a +90° turn. Each turn is a good place to troubleshoot neck label placement problems. The center of the neck label must be checked to ensure it aligns with the center of the body label prior to the first turn. If the body label positioning looks correct but the neck label is off, then the problem is the release timing on the gripper. If the labels are to one side or the other, the gripper is releasing too early or too late. It is important that labels receive an adequate amount of wipe-down in the first turn. The first 90° turn is followed by turn 2, which is +15°; turn 3, which is −30°; turn 4, which is −75°; and finally

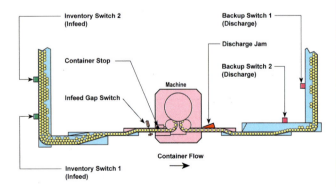

FIGURE 19.11. Overview of an automatic flow control system. (Courtesy Krones USA)

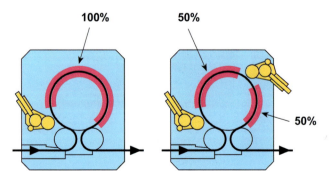

FIGURE 19.12. Wipe-down station layouts: body front-label station (left) and body front/body back-label station (right). (Courtesy Krones USA)

turn 5, which is +195°. At this point, the bottle is 180° from its position at initial label application. This places the bottle in position to receive a back label, if there is a back application. This last application would be followed by two more turns to brush down the back label prior to discharge.

Even if the brewery does not currently use a back label, marketing requirements may someday change, so machines are typically manufactured with the cam track machined to allow for a back label.

Bottles may be positioned so that the label is applied to a certain area, using an orientation system on the front end of the machine. Some bottles are made with an indexing lug that positions the bottle prior to entering the labeler. The lug receiver can be located inside the infeed conveyor after it leaves the infeed screw and before it enters the infeed star wheel before it arrives on the bottle pads. This is more common with wine and distilled spirits, especially those using embossed bottles, to ensure that the label is placed in a smooth area and not on the embossed sections, but it is also seen on some high-end beer packaging.

● MACHINE OIL SYSTEM

The bottle table oil system is shown in Figure 19.14. The system is composed of an oil tank with a filter system, a pump, an oil-injecting nozzle, and a return line. The bottle table, with the bottle plates and the bottles, rotates on the cam track. If the return hose or injecting nozzle becomes plugged and the oil pressure drops too low, the oil pressure switch will stop the machine. A warning light will illuminate and the machine will stop.

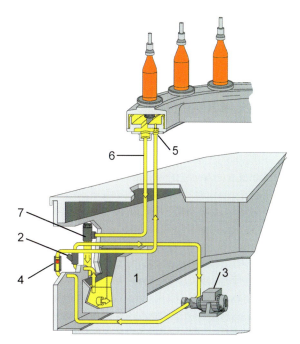

FIGURE 19.14. Bottle table oil system. 1 = Oil tank; 2 = oil filter; 3 = pump; 4 = flow indicator; 5 = oil jetting nozzle; 6 = oil return channel; and 7 = oil reservoir sight glass. (Courtesy Krones USA)

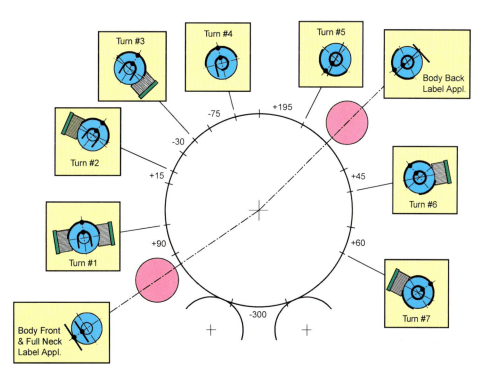

FIGURE 19.13. Typical bottle table turns (i.e., body front, neck, and body back). (Courtesy Krones USA)

The importance of regular oil changes cannot be overemphasized. Water ingress into the oil can be a major problem. High-pressure clean-up hoses can force water underneath the bottle plate pads and past the seals, so only low-pressure water, i.e., wash hose with no nozzle, must be used to clean the machine. If the oil turns yellow or has a milky appearance, the oil must promptly be drained and replaced.

● LABEL BASKET

The label basket or magazine supplies and transfers the labels to the glued label pallets. The label basket must not be tilted and must be straight and level on the brackets. The dimensions must be within specifications. Figure 19.15 shows a generic label basket design and dimensions. The generic dimension in Figure 19.15 is about 30.5 mm (1.25 inches).

There are different types of label baskets. They are available with stainless-steel, brass, or chrome-plated fingers. To adjust the fingers, the specific hold-down bolts should be loosened and the fingers should be adjusted for the length specified for the basket type. It is important that all fingers are adjusted to the same length. If they are not the same length, the label will not dispense properly and will not position correctly at the finger tips. The fingers will collect glue, especially if the pallets are too heavily coated with adhesive. The fingers should be cleaned using water and a cloth when needed. If the fingers have been nicked, they should be smoothed using an emery cloth to remove roughness. Do not use a file to remove excess material from the fingers. To reduce label drag on the fingers, the fingers should periodically be burnished using a light abrasive pad. On stainless-steel or brass fingers, the labels will actually ride upon the ridges of the fine scratches caused by the pad, thus lowering the drag. The harder surface of chrome fingers only requires being kept clean. Lubricants should not be used on the fingers.

Each side of the basket has linear bearings on which the back pusher plate slides. Light oil works well to lubricate the track. Silicone spray should not be used. Silicone builds up a thick waxy coating, picks up label dust, and works only for a short time.

The back pusher plate maintains pressure on the labels as the stack is depleted. The plate pressure comes from the tension spool. The tension spools operate in different directions, and the second to last number on the back of it will confirm the "left" or "right" direction. When replacing the tension spool, operators must make sure to replace the correct number *and* direction. The basket should be set up so that there is adequate pressure when it is one-half to three-quarters full of labels; that is the normal working range. When label supply is below one-half full, the plate pressure will slacken. If filled completely with labels, there will be too much tension. If there is too much or too little tension, the labels will not transfer properly.

The pallet penetration into the label stack should be checked and adjusted. The manufacturer specifications of 1.5–2 mm (0.06–0.08 inch) should be followed and basket travel should be adjust as necessary.

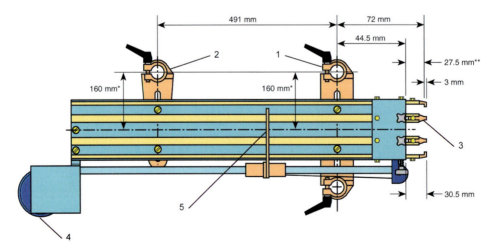

FIGURE 19.15. Label basket design. 1 = Front bracket; 2 = rear bracket; 3 = label prongs; 4 = tension roller; and 5 = pusher plate. * = For offset pallets, align the labels with the edge of the pallets; for label walking, move the label basket 2–4 mm (0.08–0.16 inch) closer to the rear support post. ** = Dimension is measured to the inside edge of the label basket finger. (Courtesy Krones USA)

An automatic magazine is shown in Figure 19.16. These are meant for high-speed machines in larger breweries, usually in a climate-controlled environment. Because of the large amount of labels and the additional time they are exposed to environmental conditions, without climate control, the labels can absorb moisture and curling can be a problem. The automatic feeders have an estimated capacity of 50,000 labels, depending on the thickness of the label.

GRIPPER CYLINDER

The gripper cylinder is shown in Figure 19.17. The gripper cylinder includes different sets of cams and cam followers, which require timing adjustments. The gripper's function is to transfer the glued label gently off the label pallet to the bottle. Note an imaginary center line from the shaft center point to the leading edges of the pallet and the anvil. The inside edge of the finger will close on an anvil and hold the label. Some machines have stainless-steel anvils and some have rubber anvils; this depends on the machine make and speeds. The finger taking the label off the pallet should have tension on the anvil of 1–1.5 mm (0.04–0.06 inch). As can be seen in the figure, as the finger closes on the anvil and takes the label, the cam (in yellow) is coming to its crown. The cam follower is spring loaded and, as it travels to the bottle transfer, the cam enters the lower lobe and the spring opens the finger to release the label. One timing area is at the top cam. Shoulder and neck applications use a push-out via an internal cam. The internal second cam for the push-out is set for the moment the sponge has control of that label against the bottle.

Cams are adjusted, depending on the size of the gripper, from the bottom or top. Typically, they are adjusted on the top. Small recessed Allen-head screws are loosened to gain movement of all the cams. It is very important, especially if only one cam is being adjusted, to mark the cam position, as well as that of other closing and opening cams, before loosening the screws.

The closing cam is the first cam. If a neck or shoulder label is used, or push-out is required, that is controlled by the second cam. The third cam underneath is the release cam. When the sponge has control of the label against the bottle, this is the point at which the finger will start releasing. As the cam follower is starting to move on the low lobe, the finger opens.

As soon as the label can pass from the gripper finger as the finger is opened, an air blast may be used to assist in the transfer. The air blast will be 4–5 psig, depending on the size of the label. Machines running at slow speed, such as 100 bpm or under, and that are clean and free of glue buildup, may not need an air blast.

There are different types of gripper sponge materials. Sponges come in different colors and different densities. The black sponge is standard and is a very dense material. There are also lighter materials available, depending upon the application. Sponge type is typically designed when the machine is made. A thin layer of flowable silicone, specific for the particular sponge type, applied to new sponges helps keep the sponges pliable and helps preserve them. An even, thin coating, essentially filling the sponge pores at the surface, will suffice. The silicone should be

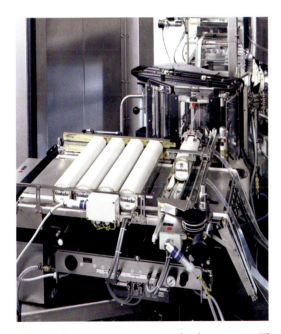

FIGURE 19.16. Automatic magazine loading system. This unit ensures handling up to 50,000 labels without a refill. All processes within the loading system are automatically controlled. Special advantages include the following: it is an important step toward line automation; only one operator is needed for several machines; and there is a reduced workload for the operator of the machine. (Courtesy Krones USA)

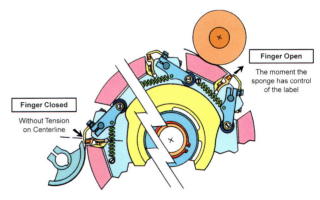

FIGURE 19.17. Gripper cylinder timing (finger-closing and -opening cams). (Courtesy Krones USA)

applied to a fresh set of sponges but not to used sponges that are already worn. When the gripper sponges age, they need to be replaced. When ordering sponges, this silicone application can also be ordered.

● WIPE-DOWN

Once the label is applied to the bottle, the next step is to wipe or brush the label down (Fig. 19.18). Regardless of whether the machine is running sponge rollers or brushes, there are a number of different adjustments to ensure maximum efficiency.

For a wide brush, a penetration of 3–6 mm (0.125 to 0.25 inch) is required; for a narrow brush, 6–10 mm (0.25 to 0.375 inch) is used. Penetration should be kept equal on both sides. Using the brackets, bristles should be aligned to the label and bottle shape at an angle, top and bottom. As the brushes wear and age, they will develop a curvature, like old broom bristles. When the brush bristles start losing consistency and break down, there is commonly a desire to compensate by adjusting the penetration deeper. Quite often, this will start moving the label around, especially if the machine is already running too much glue, or it may mar the label.

The brush should not be flipped over for extended life. Brush functionality is in the tip of the bristle. There are only so many hours of production that the brushes will provide, and flipping or setting them deeper will only create more problems and a lot more aggravation than would replacing them. In general, that is true with most worn-out parts. As a rule of thumb, when parts are replaced, go back to square one on the whole setup, because there are other parts for which compensation adjustments have been made due to wear. When one component is replaced, there are probably a number of other worn-out components to be dealt with.

● CHANGEOVERS

What needs to be done to change over from either label size or bottle size changes? For label size changes, changeover will be done with the gripper cylinder, pallets, label basket, and spacers. Operators should ensure the same pallet shaft is put back into the same cup (marked with a corresponding number) because they wear differently. When new shafts are received, they should be stamped to correspond with the cup to which they are to be fitted.

Certainly, when it comes to a different shape of label, it will require a different pallet and a different label basket. Figure 19.19 shows the key changeover parts to consider.

Gripper cylinders may tolerate a diverse label size difference when it comes to a body-neck application, and sometimes it is possible to avoid changing them. Bottle size differences require at least a change to the infeed and

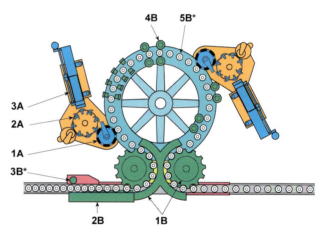

FIGURE 19.19. Changeover parts. Label parts: 1A = gripper cylinder(s); 2A = pallets; and 3A = label basket(s). Bottle parts: 1B = star wheels and guides; 2B = feed screw; 3B = bottle stop*; 4B = wipe-down station; and 5B = bottle plates*. * = Changeover part only if needed due to the bottle size or shape. (Courtesy Krones USA)

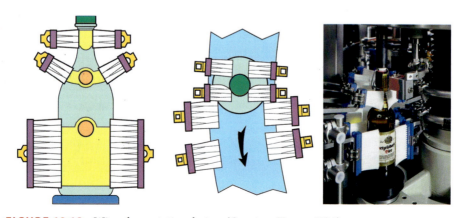

FIGURE 19.18. Wipe-down station design. (Courtesy Krones USA)

discharge stars and the infeed screw. It is rare to change the bottle stop. The wipe-down brushes are assembled on racks and changeover can be made by swapping out the racks, not the brushes. The bottle plate pads typically do not need to be changed unless there is a significant size difference. Many bottling operations group and label the changeover parts together to speed the changeover process. Some suppliers offer movable racks that hold changeover components per bottle type.

Other changeover adjustments include the bottle guide and the conveyor rails, opening or closing the spacing, depending upon the bottle size difference. The cross-slide may need to be adjusted. For a taller or shorter bottle, the head height will have to be adjusted. Some machines can be adjusted electronically, and others are adjusted manually.

The correct amount of pressure of the spring-loaded centering bell on top of the bottle is 25 psig. To adjust, the machine head height should be set so that a bottle on the bottle plate just past the entrance point raises the centering bell a distance of 10–12 mm (0.375 to 0.5 inch), equaling approximately 25 psig (Fig. 19.20).

● OTHER LABELERS

An in-line, cold-glue labeler is used for body label application only (Fig. 19.21). The in-line machines have a feed screw and fully functional cold-glue aggregate. The bottle is retained inside the feed screw as it is labeled.

Instead of a brushed wipe-down, there is an on-roll station. This is a stationary rubber pad or sponge and a rotating belt that captures the bottle and rotates it across the pad/sponge. The in-line machines can run up to 300 bpm.

Pressure-sensitive labelers (Fig. 19.22) come in a number of different models and many machine speeds. The speeds can be up to 700 bpm from one aggregate. To label faster, a second aggregate can be added. Pressure-sensitive labelers can be used for glass or plastic bottles. The label width can range between 70 and 200 mm (2.75 and 7.9 inches).

Pressure-sensitive labels are wiped down using customized brushes and/or pads (Fig. 19.23), which are shorter and softer than typical bottle wipe-down brushes. They also may use a rubber squeegee. A squeegee wipes air bubbles out from between the pressure-sensitive label and the bottle surface to compensate for bottle imperfections.

Pressure-sensitive labels are loaded on reels. Typically, the reels are 40–45 cm (16–18 inches) in diameter and many are autoloads, in which they splice the two reels. When one reel is running down, the other is automatically spliced. There is an unwind label discharge reel and a rewind empty web take-up reel to collect the web liner. The only place there is any adhesive buildup under pressure-sensitive applications is typically on the feeder plate and pressure-drive rollers.

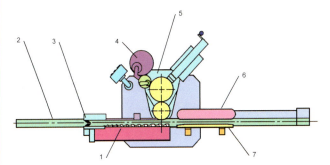

FIGURE 19.21. Typical in-line, cold-glue machine layout. 1 = Feed screw; 2 = conveyor; 3 = bottle stop; 4 = glue pump (glue supply); 5 = label station; 6 = on-roll station; and 7 = sponge pad. (Courtesy Krones USA)

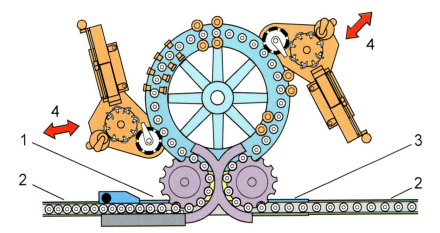

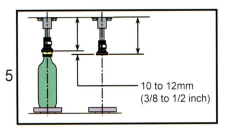

FIGURE 19.20. Changeover adjustments. 1 = Bottle guide (infeed); 2 = conveyor rails; 3 = guides (discharge); 4 = cross-slide (label station); and 5 = upper head height. (Courtesy Krones USA)

FIGURE 19.22. Pressure-sensitive, self-adhesive labeling station. (Courtesy Krones USA)

FIGURE 19.23. Wipe-down brush station for pressure-sensitive, self-adhesive labels. (Courtesy Krones USA)

Pressure-sensitive labels adhere best to dry bottles; if there is any dampness, the bottles will have to go through a blower tunnel to remove the moisture or risk poor adhesion.

TRENDS IN LABELING MACHINES

The modular labeler is the newest innovation in the marketplace. Pressure-sensitive labeling has also become more and more common in breweries, mainly because the operation is cleaner (no glue slinging) and the material cost of the labels is actually decreasing. Sleever machines are typically used more in the European market. One-way packaging trends, technologies for complete packaging solutions, and new developments in packaging lines include multifunctional labelers, modular, high-speed, flexible machines that are highly automated, utilize quick changeovers, and use cold-glue or pressure-sensitive labels.

Figure 19.24 shows one of the newest modular types of labeler. In the past, breweries primarily used traditional cold-glue or pressure-sensitive labels. However, breweries have been changing to modular labelers, saving floor space as well as increasing line speeds and reducing downtime. Modular labelers can affect quick changeovers between these applications. These machines utilize stand-alone label stations that disconnect and can be rolled away for setups and changeovers. Maintenance personnel can set up a cold-glue package by rolling the aggregate right into the machine shop or maintenance department. Attaching an optional docking station allows the aggregate to be powered up away from the labeler for fine-tuning adjustment procedures.

The modular machine base does not include aggregate stations. Whatever aggregate style is needed can simply be rolled up and attached (Fig. 19.25). The styles vary and it is possible to include a redundant setup, meaning that, if one station fails, the other aggregate is available to continue labeling.

Technical advancements in labelers include the following.

- Zero-backlash aggregates eliminate the backlash normally experienced between the spur gear and segment gears and even in between where the pallet cups are positioned, reducing wear.
- Fine-pitched thread regulators provide reproducible glue thickness.
- Sensor systems detect oil consumption, level, and viscosity.
- Covered aggregates have ergonomic locking systems. It is no longer necessary to remove the covers to change the pallets at changeovers.
- Optional cleaning-in-place (CIP) systems clean the pallets and gripper cylinder on the aggregate. When not running production, the machine can go into an idle mode and the CIP switch can be turned on to clean the adhesive and buildup automatically; although at the end of the shift, it should be taken apart and cleaned manually.

Figure 19.26 and Tables 19.2 to 19.10 are provided to help with various aspects of labels, adhesives, and labeling troubleshooting.

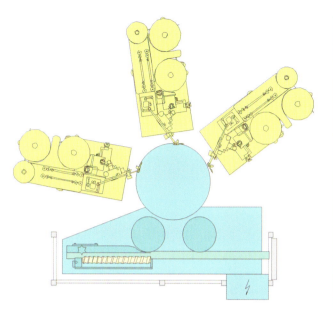

FIGURE 19.24. Modular labeler. Specific advantages include smaller machine size, better accessibility, shorter changeover times, lower maintenance cost, lower retrofitting cost, and higher flexibility. (Courtesy Krones USA)

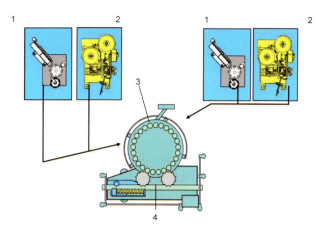

FIGURE 19.25. Modular machine with different bolt-on aggregate styles (cold-glue and pressure-sensitive). 1 = Cold-glue labeling station; 2 = pressure-sensitive label applicator; 3 = bottle table; and 4 = front table. The plug-and-label concept allows flexibility in handling different kinds of bottle decoration. It is designed along modular lines, allowing assembly from blocks of individual units. The label stations lock to the substructure of the machine. Utility supplies are attached with quick-disconnect fittings. (Courtesy Krones USA)

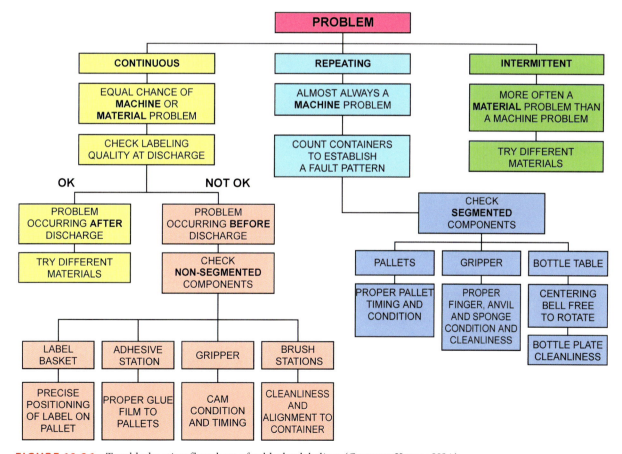

FIGURE 19.26. Troubleshooting flowchart of cold-glue labeling. (Courtesy Krones USA)

TABLE 19.2. Flagging Labels

Continuous

Labels or debris caught between the glue scraper and glue roller

Glue film thickness not correct

Temperature or humidity affecting adhesive tack and consistency

Label basket finger adjustment not correct

Glue buildup on label basket fingers

Pusher plate tension not correct

Basket penetration to pallet not correct

Label basket not aligned to pallets

Wipe-down devices not clean or not aligned/adjusted to label

Label stock problem: vendor, Cobb value, stiffness, age

Conveyor lubricant excessive

Centering bell pressure too light; adjust upper head height

Air pressure to label basket too low or not present

Repeating

Pallet to glue roller timing

Centering bell not rotating

Bottle plate worn; conveyor lubricant excessive

Pockets of discharge star wheel not clean

Intermittent

Temperature or humidity affecting adhesive tack and consistency

Label stock problem: vendor, Cobb value, stiffness, age

Bottle condensation excessive

Label release adjustment not correct

Glue roller out of round (rubber glue roller); glue roller surface damaged

TABLE 19.3. Missing Labels

Continuous

Labels or debris caught between glue scraper and glue roller

Glue film thickness not correct

Temperature or humidity affecting adhesive tack or consistency

Basket fingers not adjusted correctly

Glue buildup on label basket fingers

Pusher plate tension not correct

Basket penetration to pallet not correct

Label basket not aligned to pallets

Label transfer from gripper cylinder to pallets not correct

Gripper cylinder sponge contact and penetration to container not correct

Air pressure to label basket not correct or not present

Repeating

Pallet out of position

Gripper fingers not clean or worn, bent, or damaged

Glue buildup on gripper cylinder sponges

Gripper cylinder fingers, on one section, do not have good pressure on anvil to hold label

Intermittent

Labels not worked good before installation

Labels moving (walking) in label basket

Label release not adjusted correctly

Gripper fingers do not have good spring tension on anvil

TABLE 19.4. Crooked/Nonregistered Labels

Continuous

Glue film thickness not correct

Label basket not aligned to pallets

Cross-slide adjustments not correct; gripper cylinder not aligned to apply label on center line

Opposite wipe-down devices not adjusted with equal pressure to container

Repeating

Gripper fingers not clean or worn, bent, or damaged

Pockets of infeed star wheel not clean

Bottle plates not clean or worn or damaged

Intermittent

Wipe-down devices not clean

Containers bad, not within specification

TABLE 19.5. Cold-Glue Troubleshooting Guide

Problem	Cause	Solution
Labels curling away from bottles	1. Excessive adhesive	1. Adjust glue film to operating minimum
	2. Poor wiping (compression) of label	2. Adjust compression
	3. Label stock not good	3. Stiff, dry labels; wrong grain direction
	4. Not enough adhesive tack	4. Use adhesive with more tack
	5. Containers wet	5. Dry containers or use proper adhesive
Labels blistering or wrinkling	1. Containers surface not symmetrical	1. Adjust label placement or change container design
	2. Excessive adhesive	2. Adjust glue film to operating minimum
	3. Poor label stock	3. Check labels for proper humidity content
	4. Adhesive drying too fast	4. Use slower drying adhesive
	5. Poor wiping (compression) of label	5. Adjust compression
	6. Glue at wrong temperature	6. Adjust temperature of glue
Labels not being picked up from label basket	1. Pallets not properly contacting labels	1. Adjust machine
	2. Excessive adhesive	2. Adjust glue film to operating minimum
	3. Not enough adhesive tack	3. Use adhesive with more tack
	4. Magazine prongs/fingers too tight	4. Adjust machine
	5. Adhesive drying too fast	5. Use slower drying adhesive
	6. Back pressure low in magazine	6. Adjust machine
Adhesion only in spot areas	1. Adhesive has poor filming characteristics	1. Select another adhesive
	2. Bottle surface contaminated	2. Clean bottle
	3. Adhesive not correct for surface treatment on container	3. Select another adhesive
	4. Poor surface treatment on bottle	4. Check or change bottle supply
	5. Bottle coating excessive	5. Check or change bottle supply
	6. Pallets/glue roller have bad contact	6. Adjust machine
Labels tearing in machine	1. Adhesive setting too fast	1. Use slower drying adhesive
	2. Pallets out of alignment	2. Adjust machine
	3. Label basket not adjusted correctly	3. Adjust label basket
	4. Wipers/rollers dirty	4. Clean parts
	5. Labels too thin; bad label stock	5. Change label supply
Labels falling off containers	1. Excessive adhesive	1. Adjust glue film to operating minimum
	2. Adhesive not correct for surface treatment on container	2. Select proper adhesive
	3. Labels coated or glue resistant	3. Change labels or adhesive
	4. Insufficient adhesive	4. Adjust glue film thickness
	5. Container surface condition not correct for adhesive at time of labeling	5. Condition containers or select proper adhesive
	6. Container surface poorly treated or overcoated	6. Change bottle supply or adhesive

(continued on next page)

TABLE 19.5. Cold-Glue Troubleshooting Guide *(continued from previous page)*

Problem	Cause	Solution
Labels being stained or discolored	1. Label ink or metalizing is water or alkali sensitive	1. Select proper adhesive
	2. Label stock too thin	2. Use thinner glue film or change label stock
	3. Label stock highly absorbent	3. Use "cohesive" type glue, with low penetration
	4. Oil or grease from machinery	4. Check and clean equipment
	5. Glue contamination	5. Use fresh adhesive
	6. Excessive adhesive	6. Adjust glue film to operating minimum
Adhesive smearing on bottle	1. Excessive adhesive	1. Adjust glue film to operating minimum
	2. Wiper compression too tight	2. Adjust compression of wipers
	3. Adhesive buildup on wipers	3. Clean equipment
	4. Glue viscosity too low	4. Use higher viscosity adhesive
Labels not aligned	1. Uneven glue application	1. Adjust machine
	2. Excessive adhesive	2. Adjust glue film to operating minimum
	3. Gripper fingers loose	3. Adjust parts
	4. Wiper compression not even	4. Adjust parts
	5. Label magazine crooked	5. Adjust parts

TABLE 19.6. Bottle Characteristics

Condition	Definition	Desired Effect
Dimensions	The physical dimensions of the container: • Diameter: ±0.79 mm (±0.03125 inch) • Height: ±1.59 mm (±0.0625 inch)	Minimal tolerance variation to: • Provide good transfer and feeding of the container through the container handling parts • Allow good label application with minimal tolerance changes in the overlap of the label
Concentricity	The variation of the outer surface of the container, relative to the true vertical center of the container; rotate container 180° to measure tolerance: • Body spot label: 2.38 mm (0.09375 inch) • Wraparound label: 0.79 mm (0.03125 inch)	Minimal tolerance variation to: • Allow labels to be aligned after application and wipe-down • Reduce tolerance changes in the overlap of the label • Allow good transfer of the container between the bottle table and the centering head
Coatings	The substance applied to the container surface to prevent damage during production	The coating should not prevent the label from adhering to the container surface
Material	The composition of the container: plastic, glass, or metal	Determines the type of adhesive for good adhesion of the label to the container

TABLE 19.7. Label Characteristics

Condition	Definition	Desired Effect
Size	The physical dimensions in height, width, or shape of the label: • All labels: ±0.4 mm (0.015625 inch) • Tolerance within same pack: 0.4 mm (0.015625 inch)	Minimal tolerance variation to: • Reduce constant adjustment of label basket fingers • Allow good feeding of the labels from the label basket • Have good adhesive film applied to the edges of the label
Grain direction	The direction of the label fibers in relation to the graphics, shape, or application of the label	The label fibers should run horizontal
Weight	The density or weight of the label, including graphics	The label should have good stability during transfer and good wipe-down properties without curling of edges
Tensile strength	The resistance to tear the label, relative to applied stress, in the label's direction of transfer during production	Good transfer of glued labels without tearing
Coating	The layers of ink, laminates, or metallizing to create the desired graphic effect	Coatings should be on front side of the label only Coatings on the back side of the label are not desirable; sealing the back side of the label prevents good adhesive absorption or bonding
Water absorption	The moisture or glue absorption capability of the label; back side of label should absorb one pencil-tip drop of water within 1–2 minutes	Good glue penetration into the label fibers for a strong bond to the container; good fiber tear
Flatness	The capability of the label to remain flat in normal atmospheric humidity	Ideal storage conditions: 55–65% relative humidity; curled labels cannot be reworked

TABLE 19.8. Label Troubleshooting Guide

Cause	Adjustment
Tip curl and flagging	
Water sprays on label hitting top of crown	Adjust aim; reduce or shut off water
Excessive low wet tack glue applied	Reduce amount of glue
Dry labels or not embossed deep enough	Use more aggressive glue or change labels
Improper wipe-down by wipe-down station	Adjust wipe-down devices
Skewing	
Too much glue applied to low Cobb[a] label	Reduce amount of glue film
Excessive water sprays on label	Reduce or shut off water sprays
Excessive water on bottles	Adjust pressure of air blow-off
Wipe-down devices not aligned	Adjust wipe-down devices
Tearing	
Glue too aggressive	Increase amount of glue film or change glue type
Labels too dry or overembossed	Increase glue film; use less aggressive glue; change label
Perforation too deep	Increase glue film; change label stock

[a] Cobb is the numerical reference indicating the ability of a label to absorb water/adhesive. General rules: The lower the Cobb value, the less adhesive need be applied. The higher the Cobb value, the more adhesive that can be applied.

TABLE 19.9. Adhesive Characteristics

Condition	Definition	Desired Effect
Wet tack	The strength of the adhesive between two surfaces when the adhesive is wet	Good holding strength of the adhesive for: • Label pickup by the pallet • Label application to the container by the gripper cylinder
Ability for machining	The flow property of the adhesive as related to the manufacture's recommended application temperature	Transfer of adhesive without having it break apart, sling, or web
Fiber tear time	The amount of time for the glue to start bonding label fibers to the container surface	The minimum amount of time for label fiber tear after label application: 30 seconds to 2 minutes
Viscosity	The resistance to flow, or thickness, of the adhesive at a given temperature range	Stable adhesive application at the recommended application temperature; there should be an even adhesive film on the glue roller, pallet, label, and container

TABLE 19.10. Adhesive Types and Characteristics

Property	Jelly Gum[a]	Noncasein[b]	Casein[c]	Synthetic Resin[d]	Hot-Melt[e]
Speed of set	Moderate	Moderately fast	Fast	Fast	Very fast
Tack	Very high	Moderately high	Moderately high	Low/Moderate	Excellent
Water resistance	Poor	Very good	Excellent	Excellent	Excellent
Cleanup	Excellent	Good	Good	Poor	Poor
Label wet bottle	Fair	Good	Excellent	Fair	Fair
Label different surface	Fair	Good	Good	Excellent	Excellent
Temperature sensitivity	Moderate	Moderate	High	Moderate	High
Foaming	Low	Moderate	High	Moderate	Not available
Mileage	Fair	Excellent	Excellent	Good	Excellent
Stability	Good	Very good	Fair	Very good	Good
Cohesiveness	Excellent	Fair/Good	Good	Fair/Good	Not available
Adhesion to plastic	No	Possible	No	Excellent	Excellent

[a] Jelly gum: Starch-based product that has a high degree of tack and good humidity resistance.
[b] Noncasein: Modified starch resin product that has good water resistance (ice proof) and a high degree of tack and speed. Can be used on high-speed equipment. Second most common adhesive used in the brewery industry for nonreturnable bottles.
[c] Casein: Protein-based adhesive that has fast set speed, good wet tack, and water resistance (ice proof). Works well on cold, wet containers. Most common adhesive used in brewery industry for returnable bottles.
[d] Synthetic resin: Resin-based product used to adhere plastic. Very good water resistance with good set speed.
[e] Hot-melt: Adhesive initially used for can labeling and now being used for new label material types and increased speeds. Effective for labeling plastics and more difficult applications.

CHAPTER 20

Modern Package Coding Technologies

BRIAN BURKE

Videojet Technologies Inc.

The two primary coding technologies used in breweries are continuous ink jet (CIJ) printing and laser coding. This chapter describes these two technologies—how the technologies work, the technical considerations associated with the printers using these technologies, and how to apply production codes successfully in a brewing environment.

Why is product coding important? A situation involving a major brewer occurred years ago. It is a graphic example of why companies code and is called the "Mouse in the Can Caper". The story goes as follows. In the late 1980s, a disgruntled consumer of this brewer's beer brought forward a lawsuit against the brewery claiming that, when he went to consume his can of beer, he found a deceased rodent inside the can. The brewer's defense performed an autopsy on the mouse and established its time of death. They concurrently determined the production date and time of the beverage by inspecting the lot code that had been printed on the bottom of the can.

By comparing the time of death to the manufacturing date included in the lot code, it was proven that there was no way the mouse could have been encapsulated in the can at the time of production. The brewer's reputation was preserved, and the perpetrator was punished. Although this is a graphic example of why brewers code and why coding companies exist, product coding is used to protect the producer—the more information that is put on the product, the more the manufacturer can limit the volume of affected beer (and thus their liability) if something goes wrong and product needs to be recalled from the market. In this case, the use of marking and coding also indirectly protects the consumer.

OTHER CODING TECHNOLOGIES

There are other industrial coding technologies in addition to CIJ printing and laser coding. A third common technology is thermal transfer. The goal is the same: to apply a variable data code to a product. Thermal transfer technology is used to apply a code to a film-type substrate, e.g., the packaging used for snack foods. The thermal transfer coder uses heat to transfer ink from a ribbon to the film. Unlike CIJ printing or laser coding, thermal transfer technology is a method of contact coding, because the printhead actually comes into physical contact with the ribbon and film as coding occurs.

A fourth industrial coding technology is thermal ink jet (TIJ) printing. The technology is similar to that used by a desktop ink jet printer, but it is modified for use in an industrial environment. Typically, the ink is aqueous (water-based) and thus is suitable for porous substrates but not ideal for nonporous surfaces, such as glass, plastic, and metal.

A fifth industrial coding technology is large character marking (LCM). LCM coders are most commonly used for case coding. All LCM coders are designed to print LARGE and legible objects, e.g., text, bar codes, and/or logos, onto the sides of cases, and the ink is formulated specifically for porous surfaces, such as cardboard. Because these cases typically contain the producer's primary products, most manufacturers combine LCM with one of the first four coding technologies in their production environments.

COMPARING CIJ PRINTING AND LASER CODING

Table 20.1 shows the advantages and disadvantages of CIJ printers and gas laser coders.

The main advantages of CIJ printing are that the ink can be used to code just about anything and the integrity of the packaging is not affected by the ink jet printing process. Users of laser coders avoid mess and consumables and experience a lot less of the unplanned downtime that may be encountered with ink jet coders. However, the CO_2 lasers used in coding applications cannot effectively mark reflective surfaces, e.g., an aluminum can. Laser coders typically require a higher initial capital investment. The maximum speed that a laser coder can attain is determined by the substrate, since laser coding involves the transfer of energy.

CIJ PRINTING

Fundamentals

Five requirements must be satisfied in order for a CIJ printer to work.

1. A pressurized stream of ink must be broken into droplets.
2. The ink must be conductive.
3. Sources of pressure and vacuum must be available.
4. The printer electronics must be capable of selectively charging individual droplets at high speeds.
5. Ink viscosity must be monitored and controlled.

Two methods are used to create the ink pressure in a CIJ printer. One way of pressurizing the ink is to use externally supplied air (plant air). The air must be instrument quality—filtered, dry, and oil-free—in order to keep the ink free from contaminants. In an air-driven CIJ printer, use of low-quality air results in reduced uptime and poor print quality.

The other method used to pressurize the ink is through the use of an electrically powered, gear-type pump. A pump-driven printer requires only electricity in order to operate. Although the problems associated with plant air are avoided in a pump-driven printer, the ink pump generates heat, and this must be accounted for in the design of the printer cabinet. Some cabinets using pump-driven printers are fitted with vent ducting and forced-air circulation systems to help dissipate this heat. Other pump-driven printer cabinets are designed to be leak tight and dissipate the pump-generated heat through the use of externally supplied air and/or built-in heat sinks.

If ink jet coding is to be utilized, it is important to select a printer/cabinet model suitable for the printing environment. The printer's ingress protection (IP) rating indicates the ability of the equipment to withstand a harsh environment. The IP rating consists of two digits. The first digit is a measure of dust resistance, and the second digit is a measure of wash-down resistance. Typically, a rating of IP65 is desirable if the coder is to be employed in a brewing environment.

TABLE 20.1. Ink Jet Versus Laser Coding Systems

Continuous Ink Jet (CIJ)	Carbon Dioxide Lasers
Advantages	**Advantages**
Removable code (returnable bottles)	Permanent code
Invisible option	Low maintenance
Colors	Better uptime
Some prefer dot matrix print quality	Easier startup/shutdown/storage
Does not alter integrity of packaging	Low total cost of operation (TCO) (no consumables)
Virtually unlimited substrates	No mess
Portable—fewer integration hassles	Steered beam print quality
Can code irregular shapes	Lacks ink jet's bad reputation
Disadvantages	**Disadvantages**
Code permanence presents challenges	Limited substrates (no metal or high-density polyethylene [HDPE])
Unexpected downtime	Does not print colors
Startup/shutdown/storage issues	More challenging to integrate
Mess	Larger initial capital expense
Consumables	Laser safety concerns
Low-resolution dot matrix code	Alters the integrity of the packaging
Success requires training and experience	Limited line speed

CIJ printers are two-fluid systems. Figures 20.1 and 20.2 show bottle- and cartridge-style printers, respectively.

The two fluids utilized in a CIJ printer are ink and make-up. The ink contains four main ingredients:

- dye, which gives the ink its color;
- resin, which makes the ink adhesive;
- salt, which makes the ink conductive; and
- solvent, which dissolves the other ingredients into a homogenous solution.

The solvents used in CIJ inks are typically volatile solvents, such as methyl ethyl ketone (MEK), acetone, or ethanol. As the ink circulates in the printer, it naturally thickens as the solvent evaporates. CIJ printers have sophisticated viscosity monitoring and control systems. As the ink gets thicker, the printer adds solvent from the make-up cartridge/bottle to counteract the evaporation effects.

Theory

Figure 20.3 shows a block diagram of a CIJ printer printhead. CIJ printheads utilize five basic components.

Valve

The valve may be a mechanical valve or an electrical valve. The valve controls the flow of pressurized ink to the downstream components.

Nozzle

The nozzle creates drops. The input to the nozzle is a solid stream of pressurized ink. The nozzle disrupts the surface tension of the ink stream, causing individual droplets to separate from the stream soon after the stream exits the nozzle.

The nozzle uses a piezoelectric crystal to generate the droplets. The piezoelectric crystal is supplied with a high-frequency AC signal, called modulation. The modulation

FIGURE 20.1. A two-bottle system with ink and make-up bottles. (Courtesy Videojet Technologies Inc.)

FIGURE 20.2. Ink and make-up cartridges. (Courtesy Videojet Technologies Inc.)

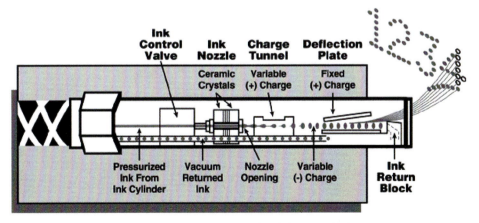

FIGURE 20.3. Diagram of a typical ink jet printhead showing the five major components (bold text). (Courtesy Videojet Technologies Inc.)

signal causes the piezoelectric crystal to mechanically vibrate. This mechanical energy is transferred to the ink stream, creating the disruptions in the surface tension of the stream. The frequency of the modulation signal is at least 60 kilohertz. Each cycle of the modulation signal creates one disruption in the surface tension of the stream, resulting in the formation of ONE droplet. Because the frequency of the modulation signal determines the number of droplets created per second, it also establishes the maximum speed of the printer.

The amplitude of the modulation signal is established so that the separation of the drop from the stream occurs in the geometric center of the charge tunnel. The amplitude of the modulation signal is an adjustable parameter. On older printer models, the adjustment is performed manually. On newer models, it is performed automatically by the operating software.

Charge Tunnel

The charge tunnel charges the drops. Printed drops are to be charged *negatively*. When the printing process is occurring, the charge tunnel is supplied with a short, *positive* voltage pulse for each drop that is to be printed. This pulse creates a temporary *positive* electric field within the charge tunnel. The ink is chemically formulated to be conductive. In the presence of a *positive* electric field within the charge tunnel, the *negative* charge carriers within the ink are attracted into the portion of the ink stream that protrudes from the nozzle into the tunnel. As the printed drop detaches from the stream, it carries with it an excess amount of *negative* charge.

Deflection Plate

The deflection plate is supplied with a fixed positive voltage, creating a permanent positive electric field. As a negative drop enters the vicinity of the deflection plate, it is deflected toward the positively charged plate. The amount of deflection is a function of the amount of negative charge on the drop, which was determined by the amount of negative charge supplied to the drop in the charge tunnel.

Ink Return Block

The ink return block collects the unprinted ink drops. CIJ printers create tens of thousands of drops every second. Even in high-speed applications, most of the drops enter the ink return block and are recycled.

The ink return block is supplied with a negative pressure (vacuum) to facilitate the collecting of the unprinted ink drops. The vacuum helps to return the unused ink to the printer cabinet via the interconnecting conduit (umbilical). Because the ink return block is normally under a negative pressure, it is important to refrain from cleaning the printhead until the vacuum is turned off. If printhead cleaning is performed while the ink return block is under a vacuum, then some cleaning fluid will be drawn into the ink system via the block. This may dilute the ink, resulting in poor print quality, poor print contrast, and poor ink adhesion.

In Figure 20.4, the negatively charged printed droplets are deflected toward the beveled deflection plate, while the unprinted drops travel in a straight line into the ink return block for recycling.

Figure 20.5 illustrates the letter "H" printed in a 5 × 7 print matrix. In this matrix, the printed characters are five drops wide and seven drops tall.

FIGURE 20.4. Ink jet printing in action. Note the stream of dots in the center of the photo. (Courtesy Videojet Technologies Inc.)

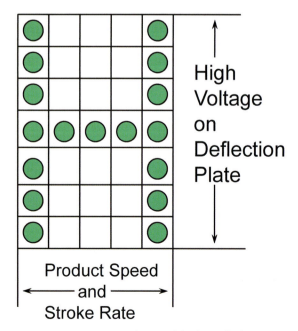

FIGURE 20.5. A 5 × 7 rendering of the letter "H". (Courtesy Videojet Technologies Inc.)

The negative charge on the ink drop determines its placement in the vertical direction. But the printer is able to print from left to right only through product motion. If the conveyor were to stop, then the "H" in Figure 20.5 would look like an "I".

CIJ printers utilize a standard set of print matrices: 5 × 5, 5 × 7, 7 × 9, 10 × 16, 16 × 24, and 20 × 34. The highest line speeds are achievable when the smaller print matrices are selected. Resolution improves when the larger matrices are utilized, but at the expense of speed.

Troubleshooting CIJ Printing Problems

Slanted Print

In Figure 20.6, a 5 × 5 single-line code has been printed at a line speed of 1,388 feet per minute. The slanted characters are the normal consequence of printing at extremely high speeds. To counteract the slant effect, the printhead may be physically rotated.

Stretched Print

Figure 20.7 shows the consequence of changing the line speed in the absence of a shaft encoder. As the speed increases, the code elongates. If a variable-speed conveyor is to be used, then a shaft encoder is recommended.

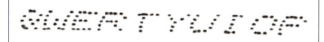

FIGURE 20.6. Italics effect from fast printing. (Courtesy Videojet Technologies Inc.)

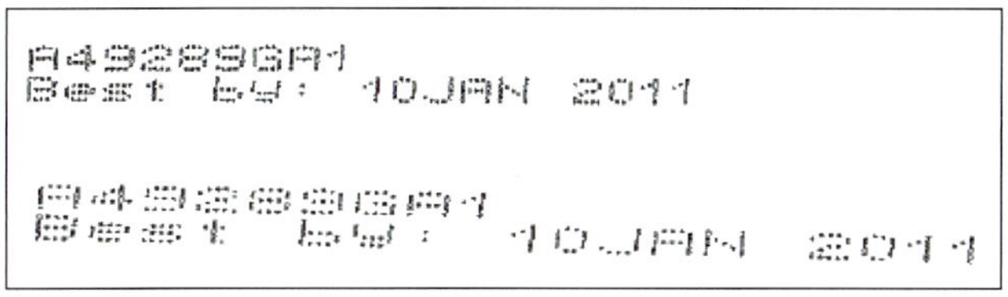

FIGURE 20.7. **Top,** Normal printing application. **Bottom,** Print caused by changes to the line speed, in this case, increasing the line speed. (Courtesy Videojet Technologies Inc.)

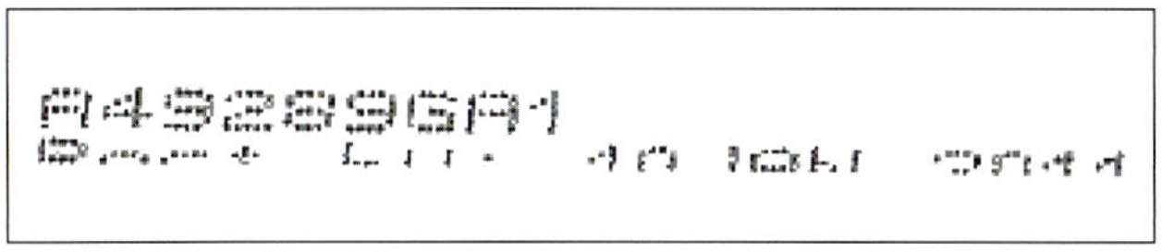

FIGURE 20.8. Print caused by clipping. (Courtesy Videojet Technologies Inc.)

Clipped Print

In Figure 20.8, the bottom of the code is missing. This phenomenon is called clipping. Clipping can be caused by a mechanical alignment issue or a printhead that needs cleaning.

The nozzle in a CIJ printhead is mechanically adjustable. Clipping may be caused by an incorrect alignment of the ink stream. If the ink stream is aligned too deep in the ink return block, then the lowest deflected drops are unable to clear the top of the ink return block. But clipping can also occur if the ink stream is aligned too high in the ink return block. Unprinted ink droplets will slowly build up atop the ink return block and eventually interfere with the trajectories of the printed drops.

Poor Vertical Resolution

In Figure 20.9, the code is stretched excessively in the vertical direction, resulting in poor vertical resolution. This is usually caused by excessive throw distance. The faceplate of the printhead is too far from the surface of the product. The typical recommended throw distance in an ink jet printer application from the faceplate to the product is 0.25–0.375 inch (6.35–9.5 mm).

Poor Drop Break-Off

In Figure 20.10, the quality of the top line of print has been compromised. Typically, this problem is caused by poor drop break-off. The amplitude of the modulation signal must be set so that the droplets separate from the ink stream at the geometric center of the charge tunnel. This is the precise location where the electric field created by the charge tunnel is the strongest. If the point of drop break-off is too far from the geometric center of the charge

FIGURE 20.9. Print caused by a throw distance problem. (Courtesy Videojet Technologies Inc.)

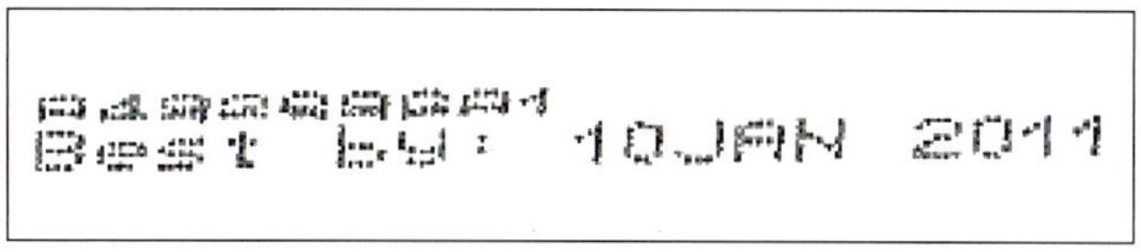

FIGURE 20.10. Print caused by poor drop break-off. (Courtesy Videojet Technologies Inc.)

tunnel, then some of the printed drops do not receive the correct amount of negative charge and the quality of print is degraded (Fig. 20.11).

Incorrect modulation amplitude can also result in the formation of satellites (Fig 20.12). Satellites are problematic because they strip away some of the negative charge from the printed droplets. This results in degraded print quality. Additionally, the negatively charged satellites are deflected by the deflection plate and slowly build up on the interior printhead surfaces. Eventually, the printhead will need to be cleaned.

CIJ Operation in a Harsh Environment

With respect to marking and coding, breweries qualify as harsh environments. Often the printing occurs after a cold fill, with condensation forming on the surface of the bottle prior to the printing event. The print band must be cleared of condensation prior to printing. Some inks are specially formulated to adhere better if condensation reforms after the code is applied.

In a cold-fill application in which condensation is a concern, the use of an air knife is highly recommended. The air knife should be positioned upstream of the printhead to create a dry area for printing (Fig. 20.13). The air knife must deliver enough air pressure to clear away the water, but not so much to cause the bottles to move. (Poor substrate control can cause print quality problems as well.) The air knife must be positioned so that the deflected water droplets do not interfere with the trajectories of the printed ink drops. If a multiline code is being applied, then it is important to ensure that the entire print band is blown dry.

A second system used to optimize the performance of a CIJ printer in a harsh environment is the positive air system. Positive air is a slight overpressure supplied by the printer to the printhead. When the printhead cover is fitted, the positive air may be felt exiting the printhead slot, helping to keep dust and debris out of the printhead. Without positive air, the dominant pressure inside the printhead cover is the vacuum inside the ink return block. Without positive air, contaminants in the atmosphere may be drawn into the ink system via the vacuum in the ink return block.

For an air-driven CIJ printer, positive air is generated via the plant air used to pressurize the ink system. For a pump-driven printer, an electric air pump is used to deliver positive air to the printhead. Note that the source of air for this electric air pump is the ambient environment. If the ambient environment is humid or wet, then the electric air pump is not suitable for positive air purposes. The electric air pump should be replaced by an external air filter/regulator assembly that converts plant air into the clean, dry, positive air required by the printhead.

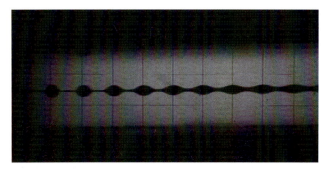

FIGURE 20.11. Late break-off. (Courtesy Videojet Technologies Inc.)

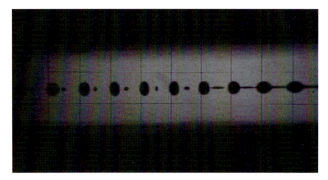

FIGURE 20.12. Satellites. (Courtesy Videojet Technologies Inc.)

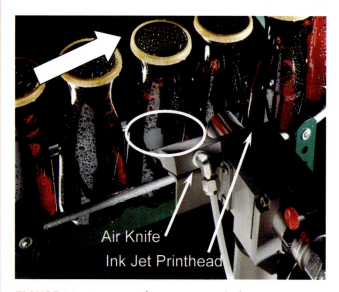

FIGURE 20.13. Wet surface preparation before printing: an air knife creates a condensation-free print area without moving the containers to be coded. (Courtesy Videojet Technologies Inc.)

Pigmented Inks

High-contrast printing onto a dark substrate necessitates the use of a special type of ink, known as a pigmented ink (Fig. 20.14).

In a pigmented ink, the color is provided not by a dye but rather by solid particulates (pigments) that are suspended in solution. Pigmented inks may be used only in printers specifically designed to accommodate the ink. The interior printer surfaces are deliberately tapered, curved, and angled to eliminate low-flow areas where the pigment would otherwise accumulate over time. The ink pump in a pigmented printer is also specially designed with hardened and corrosion-resistant gears.

The pigmented ink bottles/cartridges should be stored on their sides to prevent settling. Before the ink is added to the printer, it must be mechanically shaken to disburse the particulates. The printers themselves may also perform periodic, automated "mixing" whenever they are not running to prevent settling within the machine.

Product Detection

The product detector is a critical component within a coding and marking system. A product detector tells the printer when to print. Some method of external triggering is always needed to initiate the printing process. Different technologies (e.g., fiber optic, metallic proximity) may be used to detect the presence of moving products on the conveyor. The most common symptom of product detector malfunction or incorrect setup is the occasional missed print. It is always important to select the correct product detector for the application and to keep the product detector clean and properly aligned.

Safety Precautions with Inks

There are many different ink types available for use within CIJ printers. Refer to the material safety data sheet (MSDS) to learn the specific safety precautions and hazards associated with the ink type in use. Regardless of the ink type, the following precautions should always be observed when working with ink.

- Wear proper personal protective equipment (PPE), including safety glasses
- Dispose of ink and waste fluids as HAZMAT materials
- Establish adequate ventilation in the vicinity of the printer
- Store ink and cleaning fluids in flammable-liquid storage cabinets

● LASER CODING

LASER stands for light amplification by the stimulated emission of radiation. Industrial laser coders first became viable in the late 1990s. The most commonly used laser coders are CO_2 lasers. In these coders, the laser tube is filled with CO_2. The purpose of the laser tube is to create laser energy, which may then be utilized to create a code. The printing process begins when the CO_2 gas is subject to a high-voltage electrical discharge. The high voltage excites the CO_2 molecules in the tube to an elevated energy state. As the molecules return to a lower energy state, they emit excess energy in the form of photons (light energy). The light energy is internally reflected between two mirrors, one of which is partially reflective (output mirror). The reflected light stimulates the other CO_2 molecules to return to the lower energy state by emitting their photons. Because the output mirror is only partially reflective, some of the laser energy exits the tube via the output mirror in the form of a monochromatic laser beam. Figure 20.15 shows a diagram of a typical gas laser.

FIGURE 20.14. Yellow-pigmented ink printed onto an amber bottle. (Courtesy Videojet Technologies Inc.)

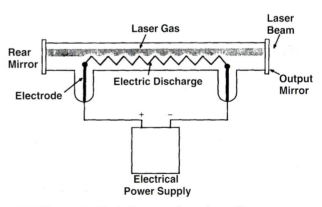

FIGURE 20.15. Block diagram of a gas laser. (Courtesy Videojet Technologies Inc.)

Once the laser energy has been created, it may be harnessed for marking and coding purposes. Early laser coders routed the laser energy through a stencil in order to create a legible mark on a substrate. Other legacy models employed frequency-controlled crystals in order to deflect short bursts of laser energy onto a moving product, creating a dot matrix code. Multitube lasers used a vertical stack of up to nine independently controlled laser tubes to create a high-speed dot matrix code.

Modern laser coders employ steered beam technology (Fig. 20.16). A beam of laser energy is directed through two rotating mirrors (called galvos) and then through an output lens to etch vectors onto the surface of a moving product.

Because the printed characters are formed by interconnecting lines, the print quality is superior to that obtained from dot matrix coders (laser or ink jet). Figures 20.17 and 20.18 show examples of dot matrix and steered beam laser coding, respectively.

Laser energy can be used to create a code in one of three ways, depending upon the type of substrate in use.

- The top layer of the substrate is burned off, exposing an underlying layer of a different color (Fig. 20.19). Lasers typically code on paper or cardboard by burning off the outer layer.
- The surface of the substrate is heated so that it undergoes a color change. This method is used to code materials, such as plastic or rubber (Fig. 20.20). Note that the color obtained is a function of the printed material and is not controllable.

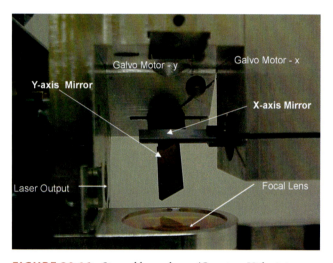

FIGURE 20.16. Steered beam laser. (Courtesy Videojet Technologies Inc.)

FIGURE 20.17. Dot matrix laser print. (Courtesy Videojet Technologies Inc.)

FIGURE 20.18. Steered beam laser print. (Courtesy Videojet Technologies Inc.)

FIGURE 20.19. Burn method on a paper substrate. (Courtesy Videojet Technologies Inc.)

FIGURE 20.20. Heat method used to mark a cable. (Courtesy Videojet Technologies Inc.)

- The surface of the substrate is molecularly altered (smashed) so that a change of reflectance occurs, making the printed characters visible. This method is used to code materials such as glass (Fig. 20.21).

The reaction of each type of substrate to the laser energy is unique. For this reason, a laser coder typically provides the user with a wide range of adjustable parameters to help manage the energy transfer at the surface of the substrate and thus optimize print quality.

Laser Safety

Like ink jet printers, laser coders pose a unique set of safety concerns. Both electrical hazards and beam hazards must be considered if a laser coder is to be utilized.

With respect to electrical safety, laser coders should be dealt with in the same manner as other electrical and electronic equipment in the plant. Laser coders are high-power, high-voltage devices, and therefore, all basic electrical safety precautions must be observed (e.g., lock-out/tag-out, use of grounding straps).

With respect to beam hazards, the specific safety guidelines to be followed are derived from local and national regulations. In the United States, the requirements for the safe use of lasers in an industrial environment originate in recommendations provided by the American National Standards Institute (ANSI). ANSI recommendations form the basis for laws enforced by the Occupational Safety and Health Administration (OSHA) and the Food and Drug Administration (FDA).

The laser beam used in CO_2 industrial coding equipment is categorized as a "Class Four" laser beam, which means that exposure to it can cause harm to the skin or eyes. ANSI and OSHA regulations both require that the laser coder be integrated into the production environment so that the system attains "Class One" status, which means that no hazard exists for personnel working in the vicinity of the laser. Typically, this is achieved through the use of interlocks and shielding.

In Figure 20.22, polycarbonate shielding integrated into the production line is used to contain the laser beam. The shielding is also fitted with interlocks—if the shielding is opened while the laser is in use, the coder is immediately de-energized. This protects personnel working in the vicinity of the laser from inadvertent exposure to the beam, helping the system to attain "Class One" status.

Fume extraction is not mandatory, but it is highly recommended. Laser marking generates by-products during the coding process—paper dust, glass dust, and/or hazardous vapors. The purpose of the fume extractor is to remove these by-products from the work area. Besides protecting people, the fume extractor helps to protect the laser itself. All laser coders are outfitted with expensive lenses—if not extracted, the coding by-products may build up on the lens over time, resulting in premature lens failure.

ANSI guidelines also outline PPE and personnel training requirements. Sites that use laser coders must have a designated laser safety officer responsible for implementing all of the OSHA and FDA requirements.

FIGURE 20.21. Smash method used to code a glass bottle. (Courtesy Videojet Technologies Inc.)

FIGURE 20.22. Laser coder with beam shields. (Courtesy Videojet Technologies Inc.)

Troubleshooting Laser Printing Problems

Incorrect Focal Length

Figure 20.23 shows a normal laser code print. In Figure 20.24, the laser is being operated at the incorrect focal length. Laser coders are optical devices, and the optimal distance between the coder and the substrate is dictated by the focal length of the output lens. Typically, this lens is available in different focal lengths. The lens helps to concentrate the laser energy at the distance specified by the focal length. If the coding surface is too close to or far from the lens, then the code appears blurry (Fig. 20.24).

Incorrect Font

In Figure 20.25, the vectors of the printed characters are overlapping, creating localized hot spots where too much energy has been concentrated. The integrity of the packaging may be compromised.

This problem may be corrected through font selection. A laser will typically allow the user to select a noncrossing font for character generation. Use of the noncrossing font prevents hot spots from being created. Note that the noncrossing font requires more complex movement of the galvos within the laser's marking head, and this reduces the maximum attainable line speed.

Incorrect Software Settings

Figure 20.26 shows a normal laser code print. In Figure 20.27, the print quality has been compromised by the presence of a tail at the end of most of the printed characters. This usually occurs when the laser beam remains on even as the mirrors begin to advance to the next character. This may be corrected through the use of an adjustable software parameter (off delay). The off delay synchronizes the turning off of the laser beam with the movement of the mirrors to the next character position.

The problem in Figure 20.28 is the opposite of the problem of Figure 20.27. In this example, there are gaps within most of the printed characters. This usually occurs when the laser beam turns on too long after the mirrors have begun the movements required to render the character. This may be corrected through the use of an adjustable software parameter (on delay). The on delay synchronizes the turning on of the laser beam with the movement of the mirrors.

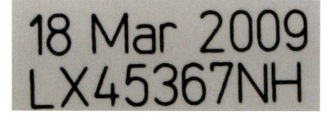

FIGURE 20.23. Normal laser printing. (Courtesy Videojet Technologies Inc.)

FIGURE 20.24. Print problem due to focal length. (Courtesy Videojet Technologies Inc.)

FIGURE 20.25. Overlapping areas cause hot spots. (Courtesy Videojet Technologies Inc.)

FIGURE 20.26. Normal laser coder printing. (Courtesy Videojet Technologies Inc.)

FIGURE 20.27. Tails on characters due to an off-delay adjustment issue. (Courtesy Videojet Technologies Inc.)

FIGURE 20.28. Example of an on-delay adjustment issue. (Courtesy Videojet Technologies Inc.)

In Figure 20.29, the curved portions of the printed characters are not smooth. A steered beam laser renders a curve by printing a series of interconnected, short lines. But a software parameter (mark delay) controls how long the mirrors pause in each position before advancing to the next vector. In this case, the mark delay is too long. Shortening the mark delay allows the laser to print smoother curves.

In Figure 20.30, the print quality is acceptable except for the beginning of the first printed character. In a steered beam laser, the mirrors move at different speeds when they are coding as opposed to moving to the next character. The mirrors move much faster between characters than when they are actually coding. A software parameter (jump delay) helps to manage the transition between coding and advancing. In this case, the jump delay is too short, and the mirrors are still decelerating at the precise instant that the laser beam turns on.

TRENDS IN PRODUCT CODING

Code Assurance

The majority of the mistakes made in product coding are not caused by the printer but rather by the programming. Mistakes made during message creation and editing may result in the wrong code appearing on the wrong product. Code Assurance is designed to prevent these kinds of errors. Coding companies are now producing machines offering a suite of software features to help eliminate data entry errors during message generation and selection.

Availability

A modern coder is capable of tracking its uptime. It can provide data, on demand, to allow supervisory personnel to analyze the root causes of downtime-causing events. Armed with this information, administrators may formulate and implement countermeasures to help optimize the performance of the coding equipment within the production environment.

FIGURE 20.29. Example of a mark-delay issue. Note that the curved portions of each number are not smooth. (Courtesy Videojet Technologies Inc.)

FIGURE 20.30. Example of a jump-delay problem. Note the distortion of the first letter. (Courtesy Videojet Technologies Inc.)

CHAPTER 21

Paperboard Manufacturing and Multipack Production

GRAHAM HAND
Graphic Packaging International, Inc.

Paperboard multipacks represent a rapidly growing segment of the global beer industry because of their increased use by beer marketers as a driver of sales volume. The high graphic impact, variety of styles, and range of configurations offered by paperboard multipacks result in increased opportunities for improved on-shelf branding, product differentiation, and consumer promotions, all of which can result in volume and margin growth.

The very opportunities offered to beer marketers by paperboard multipacks result in challenges to the beer packaging operation since the increased variety of package formats adds to the complexity of the packaging operation. Marketing decisions on the range of multipack formats needed to best target consumers dictate the range of finished package formats, but selection of multipackaging equipment must be based on production requirements and total economics.

The major factors influencing the choice of equipment include speed, flexibility, changeover time and repeatability, maintenance requirements, and overall production efficiency. An efficient multipackaging system requires both consistently high-quality packaging materials and a machine that is designed to efficiently handle the range of package formats demanded by marketing.

● PAPERBOARD MANUFACTURE

A paperboard multipack is the end result of a two-stage production process. First, the coated paperboard substrate is produced in the papermaking process. This paperboard substrate is then "converted" into multipacks, a production process that includes printing, die cutting, and gluing.

Paperboard is manufactured from a combination of softwood and hardwood on multilayer papermaking equipment (Fig. 21.1).

The combination of wood fibers used gives paperboard the required physical properties to make it suitable for packaging applications. The base layer of the sheet normally includes a high percentage of softwood, such as pine, which consists of long fibers. The length of these fibers results in good tear resistance and stiffness. The balance of the base sheet is made up of hardwood and recycled fibers. The top layer normally has a high proportion of hardwood, which has short fibers that provide a smooth surface.

For beverage-grade paperboard, a wet-strength additive is incorporated into the fiber to give the finished paperboard product an improved resistance to tear when exposed to damp conditions during packaging, distribution, storage, and refrigeration. Once the two-ply or three-ply sheet has been formed, a clay coating is applied to the top surface to provide a smooth, white surface for printing.

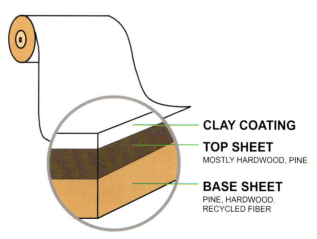

FIGURE 21.1. Wet-strength paperboard manufacture. (Courtesy Graphic Package International, Inc.)

309

CARTON-CONVERTING PROCESS

The paperboard multipack manufacturing process involves printing, die cutting, and gluing operations that "convert" paperboard into a finished carton ready for delivery to the brewery production line.

Printing

Three different print technologies are commonly used for the printing of beverage multipacks: rotogravure (gravure), lithographic (offset), and flexographic (flexo). These technologies are described briefly in the following paragraphs.

Rotogravure Printing

In the (roto)gravure printing process, ink is first applied to a cylinder that has been engraved with the desired image. Excess ink is then removed by a doctor blade (Fig. 21.2).

The ink remaining in the wells on the cylinder is transferred directly to the clay-coated surface of the paperboard. This process is repeated for each color required for the image on the appropriate number of print stations. Drying the ink for each color takes place between the stations. Gravure printing is particularly appropriate for long production runs of the same graphics, but the high cost of engraved cylinders makes the process less economically viable for shorter promotional print runs.

Offset Printing

The offset printing process (Fig. 21.3) uses a plate cylinder that is manufactured by chemically treating its surface so it repels water in the desired print areas. The treated plate cylinder is first dampened with water, which forms a film over the nonprint area, and then an oil-based ink is applied to the plate cylinder with an ink roller. The ink adheres only to the nonwetted areas of the plate cylinder, from which it is transferred first to an offset cylinder and then to the paperboard surface. The offset process can be either web fed or sheet fed. The high-speed web-fed process is the preferred process for long print runs, while the sheet-fed process is more suited for short runs because of reduced make-ready or changeover times and costs.

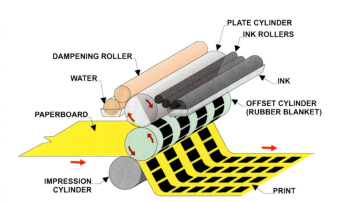

FIGURE 21.3. Offset printing process. (Courtesy Graphic Package International, Inc.)

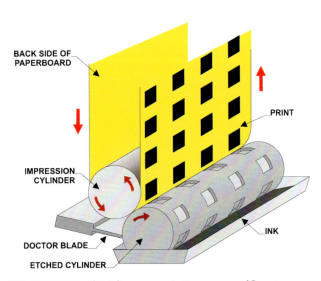

FIGURE 21.2. (Roto)gravure printing process. (Courtesy Graphic Package International, Inc.)

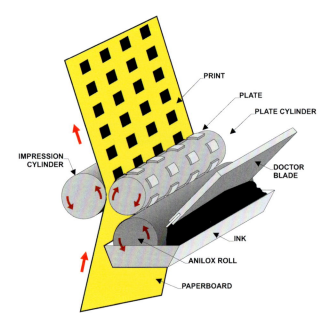

FIGURE 21.4. Flexographic printing process. (Courtesy Graphic Package International, Inc.)

Flexographic Printing

In the flexographic printing process (Fig. 21.4), ink is taken up by an anilox roll and regulated by a doctor blade. The plate cylinder includes the desired print area as a raised pattern, and ink is applied through contact with the anilox roll. The ink is transferred to the paperboard from the plate cylinder through pressure from an impression cylinder. Flexographic printing is growing in popularity for the printing of beverage multipacks, particularly for less-demanding graphics used by the soft drinks industry, because of the relatively low cost of plate production and the improving print-quality capabilities of the latest flexographic presses.

Die Cutting and Creasing

Once the carton graphics have been printed, the carton then needs to be die cut from the web or sheet of paperboard and creased to allow folding of the carton into the finished product. The die cutting and creasing may take place in-line with the printing press or off-line at a later time.

Two types of die-cutting equipment can be used: flat bed and rotary. With both types, the principles of cutting and creasing are the same, with a cutting form equipped with steel knives cutting against a counterplate. Following the die-cutting operation, the scrap material is stripped from the carton blank, and the blanks are palletized in stacks ready for the folding and gluing operation.

Folding and Gluing

With the exception of wraps and flat blank styles of multipacks (discussed in the following sections), the die-cut paperboard blanks must be folded and glued before shipment to the brewery production line. This process is achieved using high-speed folder–gluer equipment that employs a series of folding guides and glue systems to produce the finished multipack.

There are two distinct types of folder–gluers used in the production of beverage multipacks: straight-line and right-angle gluers. Straight-line gluers are used to produce relatively simple, end-load, fully enclosed packages at speeds of up to 60,000 packages per hour. Right-angle gluers are used for complex designs, such as basket carriers, which require glue joints in different orientations. Right-angle gluers are limited to lower speeds of between 15,000 and 20,000 packages per hour because of the complexity of the folding and gluing operations they perform.

MULTIPACK TYPES

Paperboard multipacks can be broadly categorized into one of four carton styles: fully enclosed packages, basket carriers, wraps, and clips. Each style has distinct manufacturing requirements, loading and sealing requirements in the brewery, and package features.

Fully Enclosed Packages

Fully enclosed packages are typically end-load designs that can be used for either cans or bottles. Traditionally used in 12- and 24-pack formats, they also offer the widest range of product configurations from 4-packs to 36-packs in both single and double layers. A wide range of configurations, shapes, and package features are used by various breweries to differentiate their brands and attract consumers (Fig. 21.5). The fully enclosed package is the only design that allows larger multiples and is, therefore, the most common style used in mature multipack markets, such as those in the United States.

Basket Carriers

Basket carriers are commonly used for bottled beer in the United States, but they are not widely used in international markets. This style of package is limited to smaller multiples, typically ranging from four-packs

FIGURE 21.5. Fully enclosed multipacks. (Courtesy Graphic Package International, Inc.)

FIGURE 21.6. Basket carriers. (Courtesy Graphic Package International, Inc.)

FIGURE 21.7. Wraps. (Courtesy Graphic Package International, Inc.)

to eight-packs, with six-packs being the predominant configuration (Fig. 21.6). The features of the basket carrier that make it the preferred bottle package in the United States are its convenient handle and the integral partitions that offer protection against bottle breakage.

Wraps

Wraps (Fig. 21.7) are used for both canned and bottled beer in certain markets, but they are restricted to smaller configurations, typically between 4 and 10 primary containers. Because this open-ended style of package uses a reduced amount of paperboard and is not preglued before shipment to the brewery, it offers an economical option. This lower cost is offset by the reduced print area available for graphics and by the limited options for handles and opening features.

Clips

Paperboard clips (Fig. 21.8) are not widely used in more mature markets, but they may be used as a first entry into multipackaging in developing markets or for limited retail promotions. Clip designs are available for cans and for glass and polyethylene terephthalate (PET) bottles, and they vary widely in design. Most designs are hand applied off-line either by contract packers or by retailers (consumers) at the point of purchase.

FIGURE 21.8. Paperboard clip. (Courtesy Graphic Package International, Inc.)

Automated clip application systems have been developed for unique market situations, such as the returnable glass bottle market in Europe, but these tend to be custom applications.

● MULTIPACKAGING MACHINERY FUNCTIONS

Multipackaging machinery is designed to load cans or bottles into multipacks on the packaging lines in breweries and soft drink bottlers. A key feature of the design of modern multipackaging equipment is its flexibility to handle a range of different primary container sizes and designs and to produce a range of package styles and configurations. This flexibility is demanded by sales and marketing trends, which tailor package types, sizes, and price points to meet different consumer and retail channel requirements. This demand for flexibility has resulted in great emphasis on the ease and repeatability of machinery changeovers to maximize packaging line efficiency and minimize production costs. The design of modern multipackers, such as the fully enclosed machine (Fig. 21.9), also takes into account the demand for improved ergonomics and ease of operation and maintenance. Low-level carton magazines meet ergonomic needs, and electronic control panels and full-height walk-in guard doors allow easy and safe operation and access to all machinery functions for both operators and maintenance personnel.

Multipackaging machinery systems have, in some cases, been developed to package more than one of the four major package styles defined earlier, but this flexibility tends to be at the expense of speed, efficiency, or range of package configurations that can be produced economically. Machinery is therefore predominantly dedicated to a particular multipack style and can be categorized into the same four carton design families: fully enclosed, basket, wrap, and clip packaging machinery systems. All these packaging machines are designed in such a way so that they can handle inherent variation in specifications resulting from the carton converting process and also the variation in dimensions of primary containers, particularly glass and PET bottles.

Although the demands on each of the four styles of packaging machine are different because of the differences in package style, four fundamental operations are common to all multipackaging machines. These are product infeed and selection, carton infeed, product loading, and carton sealing. Since different machinery manufacturers use a variety of combinations of technology for each of the four fundamental operations, it is useful to consider them individually before looking at machinery designs as a whole.

Product Infeed and Selection

The first function of the multipackaging equipment is to accept primary containers from the packaging line and collate them into the correct configuration for the finished package. This collation process is termed product selection and can be achieved by a number of different processes. The three most common methods—lug chains, selector screws, and selector wedges—are described in the following paragraphs.

Lug Chains

The principle of lug chain selection is illustrated in Figure 21.10 (top). This method of product selection employs chain-mounted lugs that enter between product groups and relies on the higher speed of the selector chain to accelerate product groups away from the infeed conveyor. Changeover between different package configurations is achieved by adjusting the phasing of the chain or by adjusting the placement of removable lugs.

Selector Screws

Selector screws are geometrically molded worms that gradually separate and accelerate product into the correct configuration. In Figure 21.10 (middle), the set of two selector screws is shown selecting a six-pack configuration on a two-lane infeed conveyor. Changeover between different configurations requires replacement of the screws, which are normally designed with quick-release fastenings.

FIGURE 21.9. Fully enclosed multipacker machine. (Courtesy Graphic Package International, Inc.)

Selector Wedges

The use of selector wedges is becoming more common for fully enclosed packaging systems because of their ability to efficiently select larger multiples of product. The principle of wedge selection is illustrated in Figure 21.10 (bottom). The wedges are fixed to a slat conveyor running parallel to the product infeed conveyor. Angled lane guides direct the product into the path of the geometrically designed wedges, which in turn separate the product into the correct configuration. Changeovers between product configurations are achieved by using different sets of wedges designed for quick release and replacement.

Carton Infeed

Multipacks are loaded onto a magazine from which they are fed into a transport system. Various types of carton infeeders are illustrated in Figure 21.11. On older and slower multipackers, reciprocating carton feeders are found. On modern, high-speed equipment, a variety of designs of rotary carton feeders are used to achieve the necessary speed and flexibility. A form of rotary feeder, the segment wheel feeder, is most commonly employed on the latest multipackers because of its speed, flexibility, and reliability.

Product Loading

Product loading is achieved in a variety of ways, depending on multipack type and equipment. Product may be drop packed, bottom loaded, or end loaded. Examples of different loading techniques are described in the Multipackaging Machinery Systems section below.

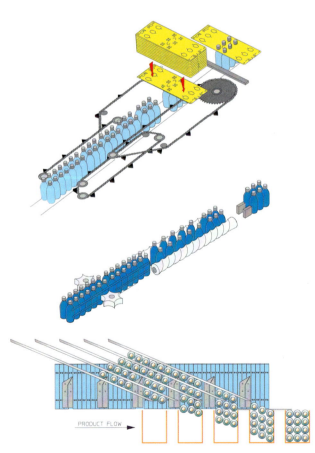

FIGURE 21.10. Lug chain (top), selector screw (middle), and selector wedge (bottom) product selection methods. (Courtesy Graphic Package International, Inc.)

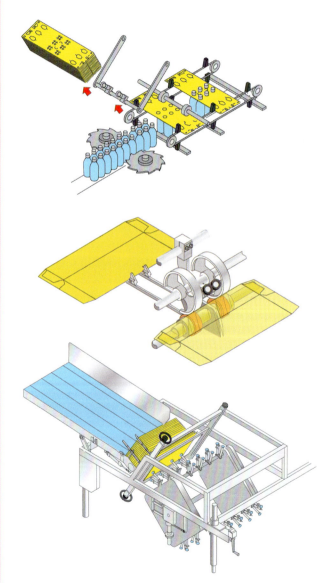

FIGURE 21.11. Reciprocating (top), segment wheel (middle), and rotary (bottom) multipacker carton infeeders. (Courtesy Graphic Package International, Inc.)

Carton Sealing

Once product has been loaded, carton sealing is generally achieved by either gluing or locking the multipack. Typically, wraps and baskets are bottom loaded, and the base of the package can then be sealed with a locking mechanism or by a glued closure, depending on the preference of the brewery customer. The locking mechanism is designed into the structure of the carton, and the applicable locking mechanism is designed into the multipacker. For a glued closure, hot-melt application is achieved through the use of a glue gun system, followed by compression to ensure that a glue bond is achieved before discharge of the completed multipack. End-loaded, fully enclosed packages are almost exclusively sealed using hot melt.

● MULTIPACKAGING MACHINERY SYSTEMS

The following section briefly describes the typical modern multipackers of each of the three major types discussed previously: fully enclosed, wrap, and basket. These demonstrate how the four elements of product infeed, carton infeed, product load, and carton sealing are integrated into a multipackaging machinery system design.

Fully Enclosed Multipacker

Figure 21.12 shows a schematic of a high-speed, highly flexible, fully enclosed multipacker capable of handling either cans or bottles. Typically, this design would be capable of handling a wide range of container heights and diameters and producing a wide range of pack formats, from 4-packs to 24-packs, at speeds of up to 300 packs per minute. The multipacker shown is designed with a low-level carton infeed magazine, for ease of carton loading, and a segment wheel carton feeder. Product selection is achieved with selector wedges, and the product is loaded from one side (the maintenance side) of the machine. Closure is achieved using banks of glue guns and a moving belt compression section that eliminates drag on the end flaps and ensures square gluing of the carton.

Another important feature of this latest design is the accessory rail, on which many of the mechanisms, such as guides, flap tuckers, glue guns, and compression belts, are mounted. This allows width changeovers for different pack sizes to be achieved with one simple and repeatable adjustment.

Basket Multipacker

Traditionally, the basket carrier multipack has been loaded either at the glass plant or the brewery, using drop-packing or pick-and-place equipment. This style of operation relies on separate basket erection, case stuffing, and basket-loading equipment and can lead to reduced efficiency and increased costs. Continuous-motion basket multipackers (Fig. 21.13) are a relatively recent development and achieve the basket erection and loading operations on a single piece of equipment.

The system in Figure 21.13 includes a rotary feeder and an elevated flight system that opens the baskets and brings them down over the product prior to either a gluing or a locking system to seal the base of the basket.

FIGURE 21.12. A high-speed, highly flexible, fully enclosed multipacker. (Courtesy Graphic Package International, Inc.)

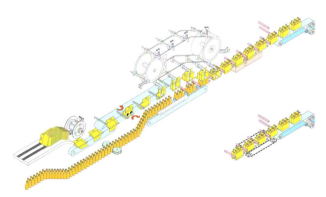

FIGURE 21.13. Basket carrier multipacker. (Courtesy Graphic Package International, Inc.)

Wrap Multipacker

A modern, high-speed, can wrap packaging machine is illustrated in Figure 21.14. This machine includes many of the features of similar bottle wrap machinery, but it has no diameter flexibility, since it is dedicated to cans, and there is no product selection system, since the cans and wraps flow through the machine in a continuous stream. This unique "pitchless" system results in maximum machine throughput and allows this type of multipacker to achieve speeds of up to 400 packs per minute, enabling it to produce six-packs at a rate matching a high-speed filler producing more than 2,000 cans per minute. In the example in Figure 21.14, a segment wheel feeder is included, and the machine uses a locking section in conjunction with a locked-base wrap design.

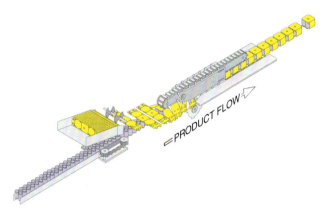

FIGURE 21.14. Modern, high-speed (unpitched), can wrap packaging machine. (Courtesy Graphic Package International, Inc.)

● CONCLUSION

The proliferation of paperboard multipacks in mature beer markets continues to offer increased variety and opportunities to marketers and consumers and results in increased complexity for brewery packaging operations. The manufacturers of paperboard multipackaging equipment continue to improve machinery speeds, flexibility, and efficiency, and the range of equipment available is extensive. The key to selection of a paperboard multipackaging system is the definition of the flexibility required of a particular packaging line and then matching the equipment to the required speed and flexibility.

Multipackaging machinery that is required to produce a wide range of package sizes and styles must be capable of fast and repeatable changeovers to minimize line efficiency losses. These multipackaging machines must also be designed to have a relatively high tolerance for the inherent variation in performance of paperboard that results from variation in the natural paper fibers and changes in temperature and humidity in packaging halls.

Because secondary packaging materials normally represent the largest component of total finished product cost and the multipackaging machine is one of the most complex pieces of equipment on the packaging line, the choice of multipackaging machinery, the structural design of the associated multipacks, and the physical properties of the paperboard substrate from which they are manufactured are all critical and interrelated elements of a successful brewery packaging operation.

CHAPTER 22

Container and Product Movement

CHUCK MCGRADY
Rexnord Industries LLC

A major factor in bottleshop and warehouse operations is product movement. This movement may be categorized by its direction (either horizontal or vertical). The methods to achieve this movement are varied, depending on the products being conveyed: empty or full containers, empty or full cases, kegs, and pallets. Conveyors link the individual bottleshop operations and the bottleshop with the warehouse. They also act as buffers between major pieces of equipment to enable the smooth flow of product and to provide space to handle minor line stoppages. It is a proven fact that line efficiency is much improved when line design allows for adequate buffering between individual machines.

Bottleshops need to move empty containers from the warehouse to the filler and full containers from the filler to and through the pasteurizer and from the pasteurizer through the labelers to the packing equipment. Warehouse operations require conveyor systems for the movement of empty cases to the packers, cased product from the packers to the palletizers, and finally palletized product from the palletizers to storage.

Conveyors perform a myriad of critically important jobs in the brewery. Many types of conveying equipment are available and their configuration and design need to match the requirements of each area. The choice of conveying method depends upon what has to be conveyed and where it is in the operation. Factors to consider are listed below.

- Package type
  - Containers: returnable or nonreturnable glass bottles; plastic or aluminum bottles; or aluminum or steel cans
  - Cases: corrugated cardboard, decorated paperboard, or shrink-wrapped or plastic cases
  - Kegs
- Area of the line
  - Empty or full (stable or unstable)
  - Machine—single file or mass conveying
  - Accumulation
  - Tunnel pasteurizer, warmer
  - Case packer infeeds
  - Empty or full cases
- Line speed
- Environment
  - Clean or dirty/abrasive
  - Wet side of the container filling line (up to the pasteurizer)
  - Dry side of the container filling line (after the pasteurizer)
  - Lubricated or dry lube or totally dry

● CONVEYOR TYPES

The main method for moving individual beer containers, either empty or full, are flat-top–style chains. They can be either tabletop (Fig. 22.1) or modular belt (Fig. 22.2) chains. Tabletop chains have narrow hinges with outer wings or "flights" (0.125–0.188 inch thick) in a range of specific widths. Tabletop chains have stainless-steel connecting pins, are guided on the sides of the hinges, and can be either straight running or sideflexing (able to flex around curves). Tabletop chains can be made of either metal (usually stainless steel) or plastic chain links. Metal tabletop chains, in general, are more durable and abrasion resistant, but they are also noisier, more difficult to install, require lubrication, and require larger horsepower drives. Plastic chains generally are not quite as durable, are lighter weight and quieter, are easier to install, require little or no lubrication, and require smaller drives. Both flat-top–style chains are driven by toothed sprockets.

Modular belt chains consist of thick plastic links (typically 0.34 or 0.50 inch thick) and plastic or stainless-steel connecting pins. The chain hinges are the full width of the chain and these chains are usually guided on the outer chain edges. They are available in a range of specific widths (like tabletop chains) or in wider widths made up of "bricked" modules. Sideflexing styles of modular belt chains are generally not suitable for individual container handling, so those conveyors are straight running only.

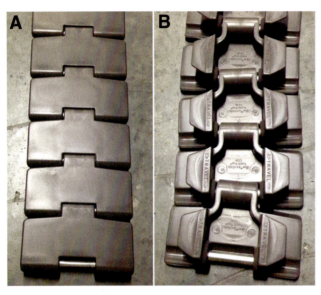

FIGURE 22.1. Tabletop chain. **A,** Top view and **B,** bottom view. (Courtesy K. Ockert)

FIGURE 22.2. Mat-top, or modular belt, chain. (Courtesy K. Ockert)

CONVEYOR SELECTION

Conveyors for Returnable Glass Bottles

Returnable glass bottles arrive at the brewery in either plastic or cardboard cases. The bottle mix is wide and bottle quality varies. There are dirt, broken glass, and glass debris present. Lubrication is usually needed to reduce conveyor friction and keep the conveyors clean. Stainless-steel chains are the most durable for this task, but plastic chains can also be used.

Conveyors for Nonreturnable Bottles

New nonreturnable glass or aluminum bottles arrive in bulk or in cases and have consistent bottle quality. Lubrication and cleaning are still required, but the empty side is not dirty as it is with returnable bottles. Stainless-steel chains (with lubrication) are widely used for this purpose. Plastic chains with water or no lubrication are also used, especially with aluminum bottles, but cleaning is still required.

Conveyors for Plastic Bottles

New nonreturnable plastic containers arrive in bulk on pallets. These are clean applications. These bottles are very lightweight and unstable. Once depalletized and single filed, empty plastic bottles are conveyed via air blowing on the necks of the bottles to propel them forward (discussed under Air Conveyors below).

Conveyors for Aluminum or Steel Cans

These containers arrive in bulk on pallets and are always clean applications. Plastic tabletop chains or modular belt chains are preferred. Lubrication may or may not be required. An alternative to flat-top chains are air conveyors. The air is blown up under the empty cans through angled louvers in the conveying surfaced (discussed under Air Conveyors below).

CHAIN MATERIALS: METAL VS. PLASTIC CHAINS

When designing the flat-top chain conveying system, the chain materials must be considered. The available chain materials fall into two broad categories: metal and plastic. Within these two categories, there are different subcategories. Each have certain characteristics that may work best for a particular application. In general, the differences can be summarized.

Metal Tabletop Chains

These are durable and abrasion resistant, are noisier, require lubrication, are more difficult to install, and require higher horsepower drives. They are usually only used with glass containers, especially returnable glass. There are two types of metal chains:

- ferritic stainless steel: less costly, not as corrosion resistant (must be used with magnetic corner tracks), and
- austenitic stainless steel: more expensive, more corrosion resistant, generally better wear life.

Plastic Tabletop Chains or Modular Belt Chains

These are generally less durable and abrasion resistant, are quieter, require little or no lubrication, are lighter weight, are less difficult to install, and require lower horsepower drives. They are usually used with cans, with plastic and aluminum bottles, and more recently, in certain areas of nonreturnable glass bottle and keg filling lines.

There are many different plastic chain materials, but the two most commonly used are below.

- Acetal (with or without special low friction and/or improved wear additives)
- Polybutylene terephthalate (PBT) polyester (with or without special low friction and/or improved wear additives)

Each group of materials has its pros and cons. The conveyor chain manufacturers can assist with the proper chain material selection for each application.

● TABLETOP VS. MODULAR BELT CHAINS

As previously mentioned, there are two basic types of flat-top chains: tabletop chain and modular belt chain. The differences between tabletop and modular belt chains can be summarized.

Tabletop Chains

Tabletop chains are the so-called "legacy" method of conveying individual beer containers. Single strands of narrow chains are used for single-file container conveyance, while multiple strands are used for mass flow. Metric conveyors typically use up to six lanes of 84-mm-wide tabletop chains, while imperial conveyors typically use two or three strands of wider chains. Sideflexing styles are used for going around corners. A recent trend is to use plastic sideflexing tabletop chains with more-durable, thick top plates in conjunction with straight-running modular belt chains.

Stainless-steel chains are still the preferred chain style for returnable glass conveyance and for single filing ("combining") and "decombining" containers on nonreturnable bottle lines.

Modular Belt Chains

Since plastic modular belt chains are thicker than most tabletop chains, they are more durable than plastic tabletop chains. In addition, they are available in a wider range of chain widths. For those reasons, plastic modular belt chains are becoming the standard for most straight-running container conveyors.

● SIDEFLEXING TABLETOP CHAIN STYLES

There are four styles of sideflexing tabletop chains, depending on the type of corner hold-down method. Each style has its pros and cons, so the style chosen is up to the end user and/or conveyor builder.

1. Tab-style chain provides a very positive hold-down, but the chain can tip up at its outer edges and it cannot be lifted anywhere (Fig. 22.3).

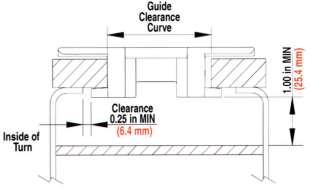

FIGURE 22.3. Tab-style conveyor chain. (Courtesy Rexnord Industries LLC)

2. Bevel-style chain has minimal hold-down and tips up on the outer edges, but it can be lifted anywhere, except in the corners, for cleaning or maintenance (Fig. 22.4).
3. Magnetic-style chain uses magnets embedded in the bottom of the curves. The ferritic stainless-steel chain links and/or pins are held down by these magnets. The chain stays flat in the curves. It has no tabs or bevels, so it can be lifted up anywhere (Fig. 22.5). However, the curve tracks are expensive.

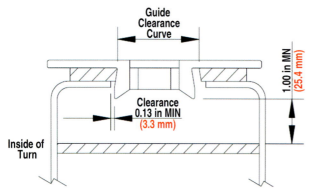

FIGURE 22.4. Bevel-style conveyor chain. (Courtesy Rexnord Industries LLC)

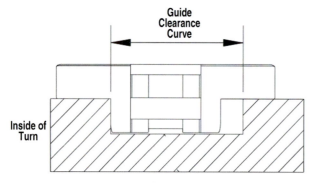

FIGURE 22.5. Magnetic-style conveyor chain. Note thick top plate chain. (Courtesy Rexnord Industries LLC)

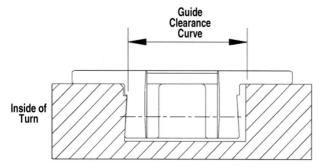

FIGURE 22.6. Low pin centerline–style conveyor chain. (Courtesy Rexnord Industries LLC)

4. Low pin centerline (LPC)–style chain uses moment forces to hold the chain down in the corners. The chains have no tabs or bevels and there are no corner magnets. The chain stays flat in the corners without expensive magnetic corner tracks. It can be lifted up anywhere (Fig. 22.6).

CONVEYOR STANDARDS

Flat-top chains have standard measurements, either metric or imperial. Tabletop chain will be available in either 84 mm or 3.25, 4.5, 6.0, 7.5, 10.0, or 12.0 inch widths. Mat-top chain, or modular belt chain, is available in similar metric and imperial widths, or it can be assembled in width increments of 85 mm or 2 or 3 inches.

Conveyor Lengths

Chains typically have more than enough strength capacity for the duties needed. Longer conveyors have more potential for elongation and pulsation. Length is usually limited by product accumulation that may damage the product. Typical container handling conveyor lengths are 25–30 feet (8–9 m).

Chain Pitch

Chain pitch is the relation of the chain teeth to the drive sprocket. The smaller the chain pitch, the smoother the operation due to sprocket "chordal" action. Chordal action has to do with the position in which the chain and sprocket engage with each other and which causes a fluctuation. This fluctuation causes the chain to vibrate, which can cause instability in the product transfer. Increasing the number of teeth in the sprocket reduces the vibration, while decreasing the number of teeth increases the vibration. The number of sprocket teeth has to do with the pitch length of the chain, which can only bend at the pitch point. The smaller the pitch, the better and smoother the transfers. To achieve this stability, smaller sprockets can be used and effect more stable transfers; however, the smaller the pitch, the weaker the chain.

CONVEYOR END TRANSFERS

The containers need to be transferred from one conveyor to another. The transfer methods vary depending on the type of container and the product flow, either in-line or when changing directions.

Conveyor In-Line Transfers

For empty cans, in-line transfers are generally directly in-line. Older conveyors typically used 1- or 1.5-inch-pitch tabletop chains or modular belt chains with dead plates in between (Fig. 22.7).

New styles of in-line transfers for empty cans use a small-pitch (0.5- to 0.75-inch) modular belt chain running over static or dynamic noseover bars (0.75–1.125 inches effective diameter). They are completely self-clearing but require bottom drives and have some application limitations (Fig. 22.8).

For other empty containers and full containers, the in-line transfers are usually offset (Fig. 22.9). These types of transfers are typically 3–6 feet (1–2 m) long (depending on chain widths). Figure 22.9 shows a diagram of a tabletop in-line side transfer. Figure 22.10 shows an actual tabletop in-line side transfer; mat-top side transfers are also possible.

CORNERS

There are two main methods used to change container direction.

Brush Transfers

For conveyor ends that are at 90° to each other, brush transfers are used. The product guide rails steer (or "brush") the containers around the corners. The

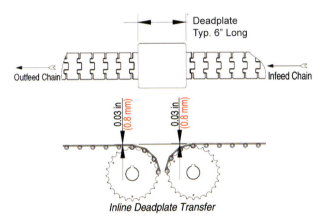

FIGURE 22.7. Conventional direct in-line transfer. Note that empty cans can be stranded on the dead plate. (Courtesy Rexnord Industries LLC)

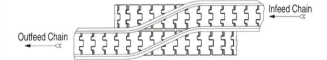

FIGURE 22.9. Tabletop in-line side transfer. Note that this is a self-clearing transfer and there is usually a slight gap between the hinge-guided chains. (Courtesy Rexnord Industries LLC)

FIGURE 22.8. Typical self-clearing empty can noseover transfer. (Courtesy Rexnord Industries LLC)

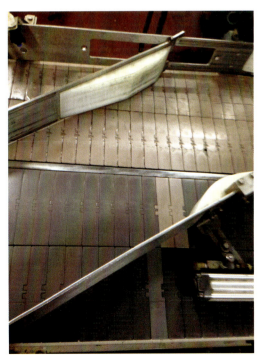

FIGURE 22.10. Tabletop in-line side transfer, also self-clearing with no gap between the chains. (Courtesy K. Ockert)

contour of the outer brush guide rail is critical to smoothly sweep containers around the corner. Between the infeed chain(s) and outfeed chain(s), there is either a dead plate (Fig. 22.11) or a special self-clearing live transfer chain (Fig. 22.12).

Sideflexing Tabletop Chains

Described previously, sideflexing chains can bend sideways, enabling them to travel around corners (Fig. 22.13). These curved conveyors can be anywhere from 0 to 180°, usually in 15° increments. They can also be S-shaped, typically used where there is a jog in the packaging line.

● PRESSURELESS "COMBINERS"

Transferring containers from a wide mass-flow conveyor to single file is frequently called a "combiner" (Fig. 22.14). Transferring from single file to a wide mass-flow conveyor uses a "decombiner". A decombiner is basically a mirror image of a combiner with its chains

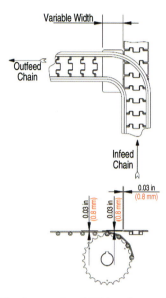

FIGURE 22.11. Conventional 90° brush transfer with a dead plate. Outer product guide rails "brush" the containers around the corner. Note that the stationary dead plate over the tail sprockets can strand containers. (Courtesy Rexnord Industries LLC)

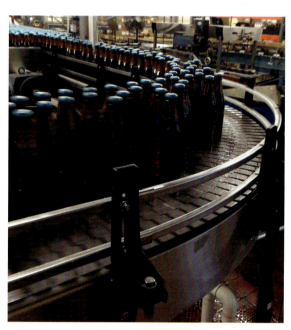

FIGURE 22.13. Sideflexing chains can turn corners without needing separate chains. (Courtesy K. Ockert)

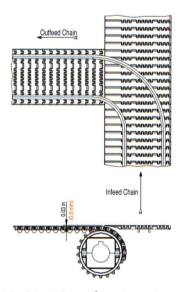

FIGURE 22.12. Live 90° transfer system using a special type of modular belt chain with thin wings or blades on one side of it. The moving blades replace the stationary dead plates, so these systems are self-clearing. (Courtesy Rexnord Industries LLC)

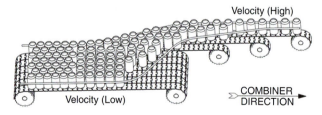

FIGURE 22.14. Tabletop-chain container combiner (single-filer) transferring from a wide mass flow at low speed on the left to a single file at high speed on the right. As the containers move to the right, each chain strand runs faster and faster. A container decombiner looks similar, but runs from right to left. (Courtesy Rexnord Industries LLC)

running in the opposite direction. Container size (diameter), stability, and line speed (cans or bottles per minute), as well as friction between the container and chain, dictate the length of the combiner or decombiner and the number of lanes utilized to make the transfers in combiners and decombiners. Glass bottle combiners and decombiners typically use stainless-steel tabletop chains, 84 mm or 3.25 or 4.5 inches wide. Combiners and decombiners for other containers typically use narrow plastic tabletop or modular belt chain.

Some plastic chains used on these conveyors have radiused edges for smoother side transfers. Modular belt chains can touch each other or are guided by tracking tabs. Some combiner and decombiner conveyors are tilted to assist product flow. Figure 22.15 shows a combiner using two sizes of tabletop plastic chain.

Modern combiners are pressureless. The main difference is that there are many more single-chain lanes with smaller speed differences between the lanes. These devices pull the individual containers away from the mass flow with little or no contact between them.

● CONTAINER ACCUMULATION

Efficient packaging lines allow for container accumulation between machines to accommodate the inevitable delays from equipment stoppages downstream. Container accumulation can be either off-line or in-line.

Off-Line Accumulation

This is where containers are transferred off of the main production line. The most common type is a bidirectional ("bi-di") accumulation table that fills up with containers as they accumulate and then feeds them back onto the line as the conveyors open up again (Fig. 22.16). Most bidirectional tables use plastic modular belt chains to protect the containers from damage.

Bidirectional tables are self-clearing but have the disadvantage of being first-in, last-out (i.e., the first containers in will be the last containers to be reinserted back into the line). Bidirectional tables move backwards and forwards using reversible motors and gearing (Fig. 22.17).

FIGURE 22.16. Typical bottle bidirectional accumulation table. Note the sweep arm in the foreground that clears the bottles off of the table when it empties. (Courtesy K. Ockert)

FIGURE 22.17. Bidirectional table motor and gear. (Courtesy K. Ockert)

FIGURE 22.15. Plastic tabletop chains are used to combine glass bottles into a single file. (Courtesy K. Ockert)

In-Line Accumulation

Most modern brewery packaging lines make more use of in-line accumulation. This process uses wider, slower-moving conveyors to accumulate containers. If those conveyors run at twice the required production speed, they are then only 50% populated. When a downstream machine stops, the open gaps on those conveyors can be filled with accumulated containers. That conveyor then stops until the machine restarts. The benefits of in-line accumulation are fewer controls; no 90° transfers, which can cause container tippage; and a first-in, first-out system in which packages flow to and from the equipment in order. Figure 22.18 shows an example of in-line accumulation on a bottling line.

OTHER CONTAINER CONVEYORS

Air Conveyors

Air conveyors are used to transport empty plastic bottles or empty cans. Air conveyors can gently handle these fragile empty containers. Plastic bottle air conveyors move the bottles by means of forced air applied onto the bottle necks or the bottle shoulders.

Empty can air conveyors force air up through angled louvers under the cans to propel them forward.

A clear plastic top keeps the cans from flying up off the conveyor and allows for easy visual inspection of the process.

Vacuum Conveyors

Another method of conveying empty plastic bottles uses vacuum in conjunction with a flat-top chain. The tabletop or modular belt chain has small holes through which air vacuum is drawn down into the enclosed conveyor frame. This keeps the unstable bottles upright on the flat-top chain.

TUNNEL PASTEURIZER CONVEYORS

Options for tunnel pasteurizer conveyors include walking beams, wire mesh belts, and plastic or metal hybrid modular belts.

Walking Beams

These conveyors use moving stainless-steel grate strips that move back and forth between stationary grate strips. This movement is operated by means of large cranks and levers on the outside of the tunnel. Walking beam machines are more complicated old technology and require more maintenance than other types. While they are not used much anymore in the United States, they can still be seen in other areas.

Wire Mesh Belts

Wire mesh belts are another old technology that is not used much in the United States any more. Changes in container configurations have contributed greatly to their demise.

Hybrid Modular Belts

Container changes, mainly lightweighting, have led to the use of plastic modular belts. The most common type is the raised-rib style. Container transfers onto and off of the modular belt are accomplished via transfer combs (Fig. 22.19). Most older walking beam and wire mesh tunnel pasteurizers have been converted to modular belt chain conveyors.

Plastic modular belt chains can expand with heat. The chain width and length "grow", which should be considered in initial designs and chain replacement. Sprockets must "float" on the shaft to accommodate the

FIGURE 22.18. In-line accumulation on a bottling line. (Courtesy K. Ockert)

heat expansions. Newer, stabilized, plastic chain materials are available to better handle the heat and chemicals that are present.

The newest innovation for conveyors in glass bottle pasteurizers is stainless-steel/plastic hybrids (Fig. 22.20).

● CASE CONVEYANCE

Both empty cases and full cases of finished containers are conveyed via several methods: gravity rollers and skate wheels, powered rollers, powered belts, and more recently, powered flat-top chains.

FIGURE 22.19. Plastic raised-rib modular belt chains in a double-deck pasteurizer. Note the transfer combs and how the water easily passes through the upper chain to the lower chain. (Courtesy Rexnord Industries LLC)

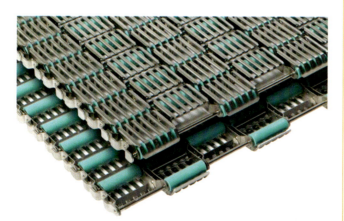

FIGURE 22.20. Metal/plastic hybrid chain includes stainless steel for abrasion, chemical, and temperature resistance and plastic for low friction and wear resistance. (Courtesy Rexnord Industries LLC)

Gravity (Nonpowered) Conveyors

These conveyors are obviously limited to areas where there is adequate elevation change and are normally only used in conjunction with other types of conveyors or on very small production lines. The simplest and lowest cost type is the gravity skate wheel conveyor. This design utilizes a series of small wheels with ball bearings mounted on shafts (1.9 inches in diameter on 3-inch centers or staggered so they overlap). The skate wheels can be plated steel or plastic. Both straight and curve skate wheel conveyors are available.

Gravity roller conveyors incorporate full-width steel or sometimes plastic rollers with ball bearings. On straight gravity conveyors, the rollers are straight cylinders. The rollers are usually 1.9 inches in diameter on 3-inch centers or 1.375 inches in diameter on 1.5-inch centers. On gravity roller curves, the rollers are tapered, which helps turn the cases as they negotiate the curve. The chief advantages of gravity conveyors are low cost and flexibility.

Powered Roller Conveyors

Powered roller conveyors are motorized applications of the roller conveyor design (Fig. 22.21). There are many different types of powered roller conveyors, but the two

FIGURE 22.21. Powered roller conveyor. (Courtesy K. Ockert)

most common types in brewery warehouses are driven by either belts or line shafts.

Belt-Driven Live Roller Conveyors

Belt-driven live roller conveyors typically use flat belts, V-belts, or round belts to drive the rollers. The high-friction belt is installed under the rollers and is held in contact with the drive rollers by pressure rollers. The belt is driven backwards under the rollers to rotate them in the forward direction. The drive belt is driven via a pulley, either from underneath the conveyor or at the infeed end of the conveyor.

Line-Shaft Powered Roller Conveyors

Line-shaft powered roller conveyors incorporate a drive shaft running the length of the conveyor underneath the rollers. Power is transmitted from the line shaft to the rollers via O-rings, which are wrapped around the rollers and spools on the shaft. For curves, short sections of line shaft are connected by U-joints. The motor and gearbox are mounted underneath the conveyor.

Another Type of Powered Roller Conveyor

One other type of powered roller conveyor is a system where each roller or a series of rollers is self-driven by internal motors.

With each of these powered roller conveyor types, various sensors, devices, and controls can be incorporated to provide for low-pressure or even zoned zero-pressure accumulation. In zoned accumulation, conveyor sections from 3 to 10 feet long can be completely stopped individually to prevent package damage.

Powered Belt Conveyors

Powered belt conveyors are mainly used to elevate cases (inclined belts), lower cases (declined belts), or control the flow of cases as brakes and metering belts. For example, when cases need to accumulate, a brake belt is stopped so it can hold back accumulated cases on the upstream conveyor. After a brake, a metering or speed-up belt conveyor spaces the cases out again. At each end of these conveyors, the belts are wrapped over end terminals consisting of pulleys (usually 4–6 inches in diameter). The belts can be driven either by the end terminal pulley on the discharge end or via a bottom drive underneath the conveyor where the belt wraps around a series of pulleys (Fig. 22.22). Between the two end pulleys, the belt is supported either by a steel slider bed (slider bed belt conveyor) or on a bed of rollers (belt-on-roller conveyor) to carry the load. Slider bed belts are less expensive but require more horsepower per length due to the higher-friction bed. Roller beds provide for increased capacity and longevity of the belt conveyor. Belt conveyors must have takeups on either just the infeed end or on both ends to keep the belt tight and to keep it centered (tracked or "trained") within the conveyor frame.

A hybrid type of belt conveyor is a belt-on-skate wheel conveyor. It uses a narrow 4-inch-wide belt running down the center of a skate wheel conveyor. Zones of mechanical sensors and linkages raise the belt to convey the beer cases and lower the belt to stop the cases when there is a downstream line stoppage. This conveyor system is an inexpensive style of zoned zero-pressure accumulation conveyor.

Most curve case conveyors in a brewery are powered tapered roller types, as described earlier. However, several conveyor manufacturers offer special slider bed turns with curved belts. The curved belt has a roller chain attached to its outer edge to propel the belt. The end pulleys are tapered.

Flat-Top Chain Case Conveyors

With the recent advent of a wide variety of thinner, more easily damaged packages, especially in North America, many of the legacy belt and roller conveyors are

FIGURE 22.22. Powered belt conveyor for cardboard boxes. (Courtesy K. Ockert)

being supplanted by flat-top chain conveyors. In general, roller and skate wheel conveyors have uneven conveying surfaces that can damage these newer cases. The bearings in the rollers and skate wheels wear out frequently, so the rollers must be replaced. They also tend to be noisy and belts require continual takeup adjustment to keep them tight or properly trained. Damaged belts can be difficult to repair or replace.

Although tabletop chains are sometimes used, most of these conveyors use straight-running and sideflexing modular belt chains. With their strong, low-friction chain materials and flat, smooth, supporting conveyor beds, they are far less likely to cause damage to these newer packages. For low-pressure accumulation, there are versions with small rollers on top. For zoned zero-pressure accumulation, narrow chains are used and are raised to convey the beer cases or lowered to stop the cases when there is a downstream line stoppage. To replace rubber belts, there are versions with rubber tops. For curves, sideflexing modular belt chains (Fig. 22.23) are available in a number of different hold-down styles for the curves: nontab, various bottom and side tabs, and even bearing style to withstand high conveyor speeds.

PLASTIC CASE CONVEYING

Plastic cases are used in many parts of the world for returnable bottles and full product. The returned cases may contain a lot of debris, so the conveyors must be heavy duty and lubrication is generally required. Stainless-steel chains are preferred, although plastic chain is used in certain applications and rollers, which do not require lubrication, are also used. Incline conveyors typically use a rubber belt or a chain with a rubber top. Figure 22.24 shows an example of plastic case conveying.

CASE MERGES AND DIVERTERS

Most brewery warehouses require flexibility whereby packages from one production line can be moved to another, i.e., to a different palletizer. This is accomplished via case merges or diverters.

The most common type of case merge simply uses a roller conveyor set at an angle to the main conveyor it is feeding onto. The angle between the two conveyors

FIGURE 22.23. Mat-top, or modular belt, conveyor is used for straight and curved parts of the line to convey cases. (Courtesy K. Ockert)

FIGURE 22.24. Plastic cases on an incline conveyor with a rubber-topped, stainless-steel tabletop chain. (Courtesy Rexnord Industries LLC)

is usually 30 or 45°. If necessary, controlled brake belts, controlled pop-up blades, or simple mechanic traffic cops are used to control the flow of cases from the two sources.

On the other hand, there are many types of case diverters that move cases off of one line onto another.

One type of case diverter is a swing-arm or gate diverter. The swing arm is essentially a section of hinged product guide rail operated by an air cylinder. When activated, it swings across the case infeed conveyor to sweep the cases onto a takeaway conveyor. The gate type of diverter consists of two sets of hinged product guides. It is mounted overhead above a wide belt or roller conveyor. It can be designed to steer cases from the infeed conveyor onto up to four different takeaway conveyors.

These diverters can be manually positioned or automatically actuated. To control the flow of cases, they usually require upstream brake belts or pop-up gates.

A second type of diverter consists of a series of pop-up wheels installed between the rollers in a section of roller conveyor. The wheels are set at an angle to the rest of the conveyor. When activated, they move up into the path of the product and divert the cases off the roller conveyor. The wheel-type diverter minimizes package damage, although it is dependent on friction to cause the directional change. A high-speed system can be designed to selectively divert packages. This feature, coupled with case sensors or bar code readers, allows the diverter to be used for a variety of different packages at the same time.

Some newer styles of diverters use special modular belt chains with internal angled rollers. Cases can be diverted in different ways by air-operated actuators from below the belt.

● VERTICAL PRODUCT MOVEMENT

Elevation changes are frequently necessary in any operation, especially in multiple-story facilities. The simplest and least expensive methods used to elevate and lower cases are inclined and declined belt conveyors (described previously), but they can take up a lot of floor space.

Conveyorized vertical lifts are sometimes utilized in the warehouse for vertical case transport. These are usually either continuous or indexing types.

Spiral case elevators and lowerators (Fig. 22.25) are a recent development being used by many breweries. Most use a special heavy-duty sideflexing roller chain with wide high-friction top plates. To lower the frictional drag,

FIGURE 22.25. Spiral conveyor to move packages up or down on the production line. (Courtesy K. Ockert)

bearings or cam followers are mounted to the sides of the chain links. Spiral conveyors have a small footprint and therefore provide substantial space savings and can move loads up or down in a continuous flow, thereby facilitating high throughput. A standard load capacity is 75 pounds per linear foot of conveyor for speeds up to 200 feet per minute. Spiral conveyors need only one drive motor, even for units several spiral layers tall. They are quite expensive.

A similar style of spiral conveyor, using wide sideflexing modular stainless-steel or plastic belting, is sometimes used to lower empty glass bottles in bulk to the bottle washer or rinser.

● KEG CONVEYING

Kegs returned back to the brewery can be very dirty. So, the initial conveyors up to the keg washer are subject to dirt and debris. Kegs are conveyed into and out of the keg washing and filling machines and to the keg stackers. The conveyors used must be particularly robust because the kegs can weigh as much as 45 pounds (20 kg) empty and 165 pounds (75 kg) full. These conveyors must also withstand hard impacts and strong chemicals. Traditionally, steel and stainless-steel tabletop chains have

FIGURE 22.26. Stainless-steel keg conveyor with dual strands of stainless-steel chain. (Courtesy K. Ockert)

been used (Fig. 22.26), but heavy-duty plastic chains can also be used. Lubrication is usually required to extend chain life.

● CONVEYOR CLEANING AND LUBRICATION

Wet Lubrication

Traditionally, conveyors on the wet side of container filling lines and on keg filling lines have used soap and water lubrication systems. This lubrication accomplishes several purposes.

- It reduces the friction between the conveyor chain and the conveyed product, thereby minimizing product jams and downed containers (less damaged or lost product).
- It reduces the friction between the chains and the wear strips and between the chain links and the hinge pins, thereby extending chain and wear strip life.
- The reduced friction reduces the horsepower necessary to drive the conveyor.
- The soap and water continually clean the entire conveyor.

There are disadvantages of soap and water lubrication.

- It uses a lot of soap and water and is therefore expensive.
- Most of it ends up in the sewer lines, adding to sewage disposal costs
- These chemicals can be harmful to the environment.

Dry Lubrication

Because of these disadvantages, since the 1990s, many breweries have opted for various types of dry lubes and/or have begun running larger portions of their lines completely dry. The dry lubes usually employ silicon, Teflon, or synthetic oil as the lubricating agent. The term "dry lube" is a bit of a misnomer since the lubricant is actually applied in liquid form, but the amounts are delivered only periodically and in very small microdoses. Various application methods are employed: spray nozzles, brushes, or nozzles built into the conveyor wear strips.

The advantages of dry lube over soap and water lubrication are excellent lubricity with much lower lubricant and water usage and no waste material to dispose of. So they are much less costly overall and there is no slippery mess on the packaging room floor. Disadvantages include more complicated controls for lubricant dosing and the need for more thorough, more frequent conveyor cleaning. Running completely dry is even more cost effective but has the disadvantage of possible shorter conveyor chain, sprocket, and wear strip life.

Without the continual cleaning advantage of soap and water lubrication, when running lines with dry lube or completely dry, spilled beer or other products can build up on chains and conveyor tracks and can result in increased wear and tear of chains, wear strips, and sprockets. Spilled product may also lead to increased product backline pressure and even damaged containers. In addition, wear debris from the containers, chain, and wear strips can accumulate in the conveyor, which can then lead to shorter conveyor component wear life. In some cases, the increased chain load can become so high that the conveyor drive motor overheats and trips out.

● GENERAL GUIDELINES FOR CONVEYOR CLEANING AND LUBRICATION

Cleaning Solutions

Many common cleaning chemicals can damage the chain materials. Therefore, when using chemicals, cleaning with chlorine (bleach), ammonia, and iodine should be avoided. Using phosphoric acid on plastic chains should be avoided. A pH of 4 to 10 is recommended for cleaning solutions. After each chemical cleaning, chain tops and undersides, wear strips, and tracks should be thoroughly rinsed with high-pressure water spray.

As indicated above, all cleaners and lubricants must be compatible with chain, wear strip, and sprocket materials. Your conveyor specialist should be consulted for advice on the compatibility of cleaners used on chain and other conveyor components.

Cleaning Frequency

A thorough and regular cleaning procedure is very important to the successful operation of any line, especially on dry lube or dry-running conveyor lines. Conveyors can harbor bacteria and molds (Fig. 22.27). Completely dry conveyor lines should be cleaned daily for maximum sanitation and performance. Minimally, these conveyors should be rinsed daily and thoroughly sanitized weekly. Partially lubricated or dry lube conveyor lines should be sanitized weekly.

PALLET LOAD MOVEMENT

Product movement within the warehouse, from the unloading docks, to and from the production lines, to and from storage racks, and to the loading docks must be flexible, fast, and reliable.

FIGURE 22.27. Molds and bacteria growing on the underside of a bottling line conveyor. (Courtesy Rexnord Industries LLC)

Powered Roller Pallet Conveyors

Powered roller conveyors use heavy-duty rollers, typically 2.5 inches in diameter on 3- or 6-inch centers. The rollers are usually driven on the side by roller chains, with the chain sprockets attached to the ends of the rollers. Many pallet-handling roller conveyors are in 5-foot lengths and handle only one pallet load at a time. They are started and stopped as needed to provide zero-pressure accumulations.

Chain Pallet Conveyors

Chain conveyors are also frequently used. The chain conveyors are of a rugged yet simple track design. They normally employ two or three strands of heavy-duty roller chain, steel tabletop chain, or modular heavy-duty plastic belt. The chains are driven by sprockets. The chains support and convey the heavy pallet loads. A variation of this is a hybrid whereby the pallets are supported on heavy-duty nonpowered rollers. One or two strands of chain are used to convey the pallets. The chain tracks can be moved up or down via air bags, thus providing zero-pressure accumulation between pallet loads.

Other Pallet Movement

Traditionally, pallet loads have been moved by manned forklift trucks. In larger brewery warehouses, automatic, wire-guided (or GPS-guided) vehicles (AGVs) are frequently utilized. These machines can be adapted to handle virtually any type of product assembled on pallets or slip sheets. The AGVs can be used to transfer product from point to point without any operator interface. Marrying the vehicle equipment with sonar technology results in vehicles capable of actually loading beer automatically.

The heart of this system is a computer. Information about product flow and availability, as well as destination and routing, is stored in the computer and relayed to the vehicles through cables embedded in the warehouse floor. These cables are easily installed in any concrete floor. A saw cut is made in the floor, the cable is installed, and the cut is then sealed with an epoxy.

The AGV can be adapted to many sorts of service, but perhaps the most attractive application for the brewery warehouse is the potential for replacing long conveyor runs or forklift trucks with AGVs. This approach can be made to be very flexible. A cable network can be designed that incorporates many modes of operation and can be installed in sections or as a complete system. It can be added to as new needs are identified. The usage of the network is then controlled by the programming of the computer.

Air flotation is an approach to produce transfer/vehicle loading that may represent considerable savings to the brewery. While this approach is not practical for replacing conveyor systems, it does present some attractive possibilities for the loading of vehicles. In application, the load is assembled on the dock or a plate nearly the size of the trailer. When the assembly is completed, the whole plate with its load is driven into a waiting trailer. Air is then applied to the bottom of the slip sheets or solid pallets, raising the product slightly. The assembly plate is then withdrawn, leaving the beer in the trailer. (It is necessary to provide a continuous surface under all of the assembled units of product so that enough surface area is provided to facilitate the elevation of the product with relatively low-pressure air.)

The advantages of this system include very high-speed loading. (The actual time that the trailer is required to be at the dock is only 5 minutes). The load can be assembled on the dock with a very low amount of product damage, and this assembly can be done very quickly outside of the trailer. This approach would also facilitate fully automatic loading since various existing conveying methods could be adapted to assemble the load on the plate according to some sort of programming.

VERTICAL PALLET MOVEMENT

Elevation changes are frequently necessary in any operation, especially in a multiple-story facility. Lifts, designed specifically for palletized products, are frequently utilized in the warehouse for vertical product transfers. These are usually either continuous or reciprocating types. Freight elevators are sometimes used, but these are unnecessarily expensive to install specifically for beer movement.

Continuous motion lifts offer a relatively high rate of operation and are, therefore, attractive but are fairly complex in design. This complexity results in slightly higher maintenance cost and downtime than those of a conventional hydraulic reciprocating beer lift, but the higher speed of operation offsets these drawbacks. The more commonly used telescoping hydraulic beer lift is normally an extremely reliable piece of equipment. It is, in reality, simply an elevator tailored to the size and shape of the pallet and stripped of all unnecessary walls, doors, etc. It should be designed so that its capacity encompasses the range of pallet sizes and weights that the brewery anticipates handling.

The hydraulic lift is relatively expensive to install and is normally slower in operation than the continuous lift. When properly installed, the hydraulic lift is very reliable. An appropriate maintenance program helps to ensure trouble-free operation of the lift.

A REVIEW OF CONTAINER HANDLING TRENDS

Conveyors are the arteries between the various machines in the packaging line and the operations in the warehouse. Proper selection of conveying method, construction, and materials will significantly improve the efficiency of the overall packaging line operation and upkeep. Lighter, thinner containers are driving a shift from metal to plastic chains or even to plastic/metal hybrids. Flat-top chains are moving toward modular belt chains and thicker-top-plate flat-top chains. Due to newer, more fragile secondary packaging, those conveyors are trending from rollers and belts to flat-top chain technology. Live, self-clearing transfers are replacing dead plates.

These trends are geared for larger high-speed lines that require less labor to operate and cannot tolerate downtime outages. To navigate the complicated world of conveyor design and equipment choices, it is advisable to seek the advice and experience of expert engineering consultants, conveyor manufacturers, and chain suppliers.

CHAPTER 23

Brewery Case Palletizing

FRANK PELLIGRINO
EARL WOHLRAB
Intelligrated

Palletizing prepares the finished cased product for shipment by stacking the product in a cubic form that can be handled easily by fork trucks. This cube of cases is generally called a load. Loads are usually built on wooden or plastic pallets.

Unitizing is basically the same process, but the loads are not placed on a pallet. Unitized loads can be built directly on a roller conveyor surface if the fork trucks are equipped with a side clamp, or the loads may be built on a slip sheet if the fork trucks are equipped with a slip-sheet gripper. For this chapter, the term "palletizing" is used to describe both processes.

A variety of technologies can be used for case palletizing in a brewery environment. This chapter defines these technologies and provides a guide toward selecting the appropriate technology for a given application.

CASE PALLETIZING METHODS

Three primary methods are used for palletizing cases: conventional palletizers, robotic palletizers, and hybrid machines, which combine both conventional and robotic technologies.

Conventional Palletizers

Conventional palletizers generally use a stripper plate or apron (Fig. 23.1), which is pulled from under a preformed layer of product to deposit the product on the pallet or the previous layer in the load. Conventional palletizers are capable of very high speeds, in excess of 200 cases per minute on 12-pack products. Layer deposit speeds can reach 20 layers per minute.

Robotic Palletizers

Robotic palletizers (Fig. 23.2) use a pick-and-place method. They generally pick a group of cases or a complete layer and place them on a pallet or the previous layer of the load. The end-of-arm tool on the robot typically uses vacuum or clamps to grip the cases.

Robots tend to be slower than conventional palletizers. Their rate is determined by multiplying the number of cycles the robot is capable of (generally between 5 and 12) by the number of cases that will be handled in each cycle. Higher rates can be achieved by using more than one robot per production line.

Robots are also sensitive to packaging materials because they have to grip the individual cases. For example, a robot with a vacuum end-of-arm tool may be well suited for palletizing sealed cases, but a change to shrink-wrapped trays or returnable crates would require new tooling.

People frequently say that they would like to purchase a robot instead of a conventional palletizer because robots are flexible. A robot is a flexible asset and can be retooled for a variety of applications, such as case packing or crate loading. Within the palletizing environment, however,

FIGURE 23.1. Case palletizer stripper plate. (Courtesy Intelligrated)

the conventional stripper-plate palletizer is more flexible because it can handle a broad range of stacking patterns without impacting speed and it can also handle a broad range of packaging materials without retooling.

The pick-and-place method is also used by conventional palletizers that are designed to handle returnable crates. Some conventional palletizers transfer a complete layer of crates by clamping the layer or inserting support fingers into the crate handles. Crates are usually designed to provide load stability by nesting into the previous layer. Picking and placing the layers can improve the accuracy of the nesting process.

Hybrid Machines

Hybrid machines use a combination of conventional and robotic technologies. In lower-speed applications, the layer-forming portion of a conventional palletizer can be used in conjunction with a robotic layer-transfer device. In higher-speed applications, one or more robots can be used to turn and position the cases in conjunction with the layer-transfer portion of a high-speed conventional palletizer.

Pattern Formation

A pattern is the arrangement of straight and turned cases that make up a layer or a tier. Patterns are generally formed in one of two ways: at a right angle or in-line.

With a right-angle pattern former (Fig. 23.3), cases are turned as needed and formed into rows. These rows are then transferred 90° to build the complete layer.

Right-angle row formers are very flexible but offer limited speed potential. A single infeed version can usually handle 50 to 60 24-pack cases per minute. Speeds can be increased by using more than one infeed, but flexibility decreases because higher speeds are only available if the number of infeeds divides evenly into the number of rows in the pattern being formed.

When higher speeds are needed, in-line pattern formation (Fig. 23.4) offers the greatest flexibility and gentlest product handling. With in-line pattern formation, a single infeed is divided into the number of rows that make up the stacking pattern. This dividing function takes place inside the machine, and the number of rows that are created can be different for each stacking pattern for which the machine has been programmed. Individual turners for each lane allow multiple cases to be turned at

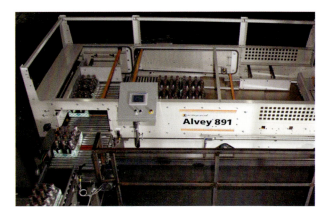

FIGURE 23.3. Right-angle pattern formation. (Courtesy Intelligrated)

FIGURE 23.2. Robotic palletizer. (Courtesy Intelligrated)

FIGURE 23.4. In-line pattern formation. (Courtesy Intelligrated)

the same time, increasing throughput and minimizing product damage by allowing the cases to be turned at very low speeds.

When the complete layer is formed, it is compacted and transferred to the apron. In-line pattern formation is a continuous-motion process that offers a potential for very high speeds.

A common hybrid concept uses one or more robots to turn and position cases in conjunction with the layer deposit components from a high-speed, in-line machine.

High or Low Infeed

Both conventional palletizers and robots can be fed at high or low elevations.

With a robotic palletizing system, the infeed elevation does not affect the primary movements of the machine. An elevation close to the center of the load being built minimizes cycle times, but a higher infeed elevation can be accommodated if the infeed must pass over fork truck or personnel aisles. Likewise, a low infeed elevation can be used to provide more convenient supervision and access to the pickup location.

With conventional palletizers, high and low infeed units place the layers in a completely different manner.

Low-level infeed conventional palletizers (Fig. 23.5) lift the preformed layer to the current height of the partially built load. The apron then moves into position over the top of the load so that it can deposit the layer. After depositing the layer, the layer-transfer carriage returns to its home position at floor level to receive the next layer. Floor-level infeed machines offer convenient access and supervision.

Unfortunately, they require more mechanical motions to place the layer and, therefore, tend to be slower. They also tend to take up more floor space because the layer is being formed to the side of the partially built load instead of over the top of it.

By comparison, high-level infeed machines (Fig. 23.6) form the layer at the height of the apron plates. After the apron plates open to deposit the layer, the partially built load is lowered into a position where it can receive the next layer. Because there are so few motions involved, the high-level infeed machine can be very fast. Unfortunately, platforms are required for access by operating and maintenance personnel.

In general, floor-level infeed machines are used where they can be close coupled to the production line. High-level infeed machines are generally used when the palletizers are located in the warehouse and when it is necessary to elevate the infeed conveyor system to cross fork truck or personnel aisles.

● DEFINING A PALLETIZING APPLICATION

The palletizer information form in Appendix I can be used as a guide to ensure that all relevant parameters have been given to potential suppliers.

Particular attention should be paid to defining the required palletizer speed. In the brewing industry, most customers want a palletizer speed that is 20–30% faster than the filler speed. This allows the palletizer to quickly drain the accumulation areas on the line after a shutdown.

FIGURE 23.5. Floor-level infeed palletizer. (Courtesy Intelligrated)

FIGURE 23.6. High-level infeed palletizer. (Courtesy Intelligrated)

BREWERY PALLETIZING SYSTEMS

Almost all brewery palletizing systems use a single-line concept, with one palletizer for each packaging line (Fig. 23.7). Large systems may use cross-overs in the infeed system to allow each line to be fed to an alternate palletizer in the event of equipment failure.

The single-line infeed concept offers simplicity, flexibility, and the ability to minimize the impact of a palletizer failure.

Infeed Conveyors

Infeed conveyors have changed significantly with the introduction of smaller pack sizes and lightweight packaging materials. These materials and their high-resolution graphics are easily damaged by traveling long distances on roller conveyors. Tabletop chains, modular plastic belts, and sleeved rollers can be used to reduce product damage.

Cases must be oriented correctly at the infeed of the palletizer. Most larger cases are presented with their length parallel to flow, and most smaller cases are presented with their length across the infeed conveyor.

The orientation of the case relative to the side guide of the infeed conveyor is also critical. Right-angle infeed palletizers generally require that cases be aligned to one side of the infeed belt for accurate turning.

Machines that use in-line pattern formation generally require that cases be presented on the center line of the infeed belt.

Cases must also be delivered back to back at the palletizer infeed for the machine to meet promised rates. Even small gaps can dramatically reduce throughput. For example, a 2-inch (52-mm) gap between 12-packs can reduce the machine speed by more than 20%.

Excessive line pressure from the accumulation conveyors upstream of the palletizer infeed belt is another potential problem area. This pressure can cause counting errors and jams inside the palletizer by decreasing the gap between cases. A good-quality low- or zero-pressure accumulation conveyor eliminates this problem.

The amount of accumulation conveyor required upstream of the palletizer infeed is dependent upon the speed of the machine. On low-speed production lines, a case accumulation conveyor can improve line efficiency by keeping the packaging line running while minor palletizer problems are resolved. On high-speed accumulation lines, it is difficult to buy enough time to resolve a simple problem with infeed accumulation conveyors. As a result, high-speed lines are generally diverted to a backup palletizer.

Discharge Conveyors

Palletizers can discharge completed loads at very high speeds. Frequently, the first section of discharge conveyor outside the palletizer is equipped with a variable frequency drive (VFD) so that loads can be accepted at the speed they exit the palletizer and be passed on at a much slower speed to the downstream system. The slower speeds help preserve load integrity. Soft starts or VFDs should also be used to control acceleration on the downstream conveyors to preserve the integrity of unwrapped loads.

The discharge conveyor system should provide enough accumulation between a palletizer and a stretch-wrapper to allow a film roll to be changed without shutting down the palletizer. The discharge system must also hold enough product to keep the normal response time of the fork truck drivers from shutting down the palletizer.

UNDERSTANDING PALLETIZER CAPACITY

The variables that impact palletizer capacity are as follows.

- Case size (i.e., length, width, height)
- Case stability
- Package material (e.g., corrugate, plastic, shrink)
- Product (e.g., powder, liquid, solid, brittle, fragile)
- Direction of case travel
- Pattern
- Pattern orientation
- Number of layers and load height
- Load stability
- Direction of load travel
- Slip-sheet and tier-sheet requirements
- Other products to be handled

FIGURE 23.7. A bank of single-line palletizers. (Courtesy Intelligrated)

Palletizer capacity (cases per minute [cpm]) if the infeed never stops is measured as follows:

$$\text{cpm} = \frac{\text{metering belt speed (feet/minute)}}{\text{case length (feet)}}$$

Palletizer capacity if the infeed stops during the machine cycle and lost time results is measured as follows:

$$\text{cpm} = \frac{\text{cases per load}}{\text{time to build load}}$$

time to build load = time to feed load + lost time

time to feed load = case length (feet) $\times \dfrac{\text{cases per load}}{\text{metering belt speed (feet/minute)}}$

Lost time can result from any of the following.

- Discharge cycle: Can a completed pallet load be discharged from the machine and an empty pallet be in position before the machine fills with product? If not, the infeed belt must stop.
- Apron/hoist cycle: Can the apron open to deposit a layer, the hoist lower to allow the apron to close, and the apron be back in position to accept more product before the next layer is formed? If not, the machine backs up and the infeed belt must stop.
- Row pusher cycle: Can a row, layer, and pattern be formed and advanced to the next stage before the next case enters the formation area? If not, the infeed belt must stop.
- Case orientation: Can a case be oriented (turned) before the next case arrives and collides with the turning case? If not, the infeed belt must stop.

Palletizer capacity can be improved by accumulating or buffering. Infeed lost time can be reduced or eliminated by the accumulation of cases, rows, and layers within the machine while downstream functions are being performed. This is the primary reason why the higher the capacity, the larger (longer) the palletizer.

IMPROVING PALLETIZER EFFICIENCY

The number one source of downtime on most palletizers is damaged pallets and misformed cases. Inspecting pallets prior to loading them into the palletizer and controlling the quality of incoming cases dramatically improves the efficiency of the machine.

Further increases in efficiency can be realized by keeping the machine clean and having a qualified maintenance person watch the machine run for a few minutes each week. This provides an opportunity to note and repair potential problems before they result in significant downtime.

Palletizing systems are becoming much more complex. Maintenance and operator training is critical, particularly with new machine installations.

PLANNING FOR THE FUTURE

The following packaging trends should be considered when defining an application.

- Small-case handling: The size of the shipping unit is shrinking. Six-packs are now being shipped loose in some markets. Handling these smaller products requires a different conveying surface inside the palletizer than that used for 24-packs and 12-packs. Larger case sizes are also being requested for warehouse sales.
- Speeds: Even if the filler rate remains constant, reducing the size of the shipping unit (fewer cans or bottles per package) dramatically increases the cpm speed required at the palletizer.
- Packaging: As corrugate and chipboard costs increase, palletizers need to handle packages with minimal corrugate and an increasing amount of shrink film.
- Tier sheets: Handling smaller packages with little secondary packaging and reduced corrugate content requires tier sheets or other stabilization techniques to enhance load stability and product protection. This is in addition to stretch-wrapping the loads.
- Pattern flexibility: Pattern flexibility is particularly important in competitive markets since market forces are driving package designs that include display packs, elaborate graphics, and an exploding variety of sizes and shapes.
- Diagnostics: As palletizers become more complex, advanced diagnostics are needed to increase line efficiency. Communication between machines and a central monitoring area is also a benefit.
- Infeed conveyors: Thin-wall packages with high-resolution graphics are easily damaged. Consider more transportation conveyor and less accumulation.

APPENDIX I

Request for Proposal: ☐
Order Entry: ☐

PALLETIZER INFORMATION FORM

The information contained in this package specifies design and operational parameters for supplier machinery. Engineering and fabrication will not proceed until this package is completed, in full, and signed by the supplier sales engineer. Revisions to this data after order entry may result in price increases and/or delays in delivery.

Supplier Sales Engineer: _____ Proposal No.: _____ Date: _____

Price Request:
Sales Requested Date: _____ Contract Date: _____ Ship Date: _____
Price: Firm: ☐   Budget: ☐   Turnkey: ☐

Estimating Response:
To: _____ Date Requested Received: _____
We Plan to Reply By: _____ Assigned To: _____

Customer Information:
Customer: _____ Location: _____
Ship to Address: _____

Customer Contract: _____ Phone: _____

Order Entry:
Proposal Number: _____ Date: _____ Addendum's: _____
Requested Ship Date: _____ Customer P.O. NO.: _____

Machine Specifications

Machine Type: Model and Description: _____
Note: Specify palletizer, unitizer, or combination

Layout Drawing: Number and Date: (Attach drawing or sketch) Plans: _____
Layout must show case infeed, dispenser feed, load discharge, and elevations for infeed and discharge direction of pallet loading and unloading and location of operator control stations.

Mechanical Specifications: ☐ Supplier   ☐ Customer
Electrical Specifications: ☐ Supplier   ☐ Customer
(Attach copy of customer specs for review)
*Controller Type: _____
*Operator Control Interface: _____
*Items required by Electrical Engineering.

Options:
Indicate with a **"B"** for Base Price or **"O"** for Extra Cost Option

☐ Operator Platform, Special Design: ☐
☐ Ladder ☐ Stairs   ☐ Red Stack Light for Diagnostics
☐ Piers, Height =: _____   ☐ Pusher Bar Jam Detection
☐ Ram Hoist   ☐ Low Pallet Warning with Stack Light
☐ Sanitary Preparation   ☐ Low Sheet Warning with Stack Light
☐ Special Paint: Specify Color: _____ ☐ Lower Control Station
☐ Automatic Load Centering Dams   ☐ Pattern Screens
☐ Air Operated Front Dam   ☐ UL Label
☐ Code Reader, Location: _____   ☐ Electrical Hoist Block Interlock

Special Features or Options: _____
_____

Sheet Dispenser: ☐   ☐

Location:
☐ Floor
☐ Top Over Front Dam
☐ Side Mounted (Under Apron)
☐ Slip Sheet (Under Load)   ☐ Tier Sheet (Between Layers)
How many Lips? _____   What Layers? _____
Lip Orientation: *Indicate Leading Edge On Discharge.*   How Many Lips? _____
Ref. Score Line? _____   Lip Orientation: _____
Magazine Capacity Required? _____   Ref. Score Line? _____
A= _____   B= _____   C= _____   Magazine Capacity Required? _____
                                                                                            A= _____   B= _____   C= _____

Machine Infeed: Infeed Belt: ☐ Standard   ☐ Extended   ☐ Length In Plan: _____
Conveyor Upstream of Machine Belt: ☐ Existing   ☐ New, by: _____
Conveyor Type: _____   Elevation: _____

Multi-line System: **Conveyors**   **Multi-Line Controls**   **Multi-Line Controls (By Supplier)**
Number of Lines: _____   ☐ Existing   ☐ By Supplier   ☐ In Machine
                             ☐ New By Supplier   ☐ By Others   ☐ With Conveyors
                             ☐ New By Others

Machine Discharge: Load Positions: _____   Discharge Elevation: _____
Conveyor Type: _____   Discharge Controls in Machine? _____
Side or End Unload of Full Pallets: _____
Other Equipment with Which Supplier Must Interface: _____

Plant Data:
Headroom at Machine Location: _____   Minimum Door Opening to Machine Location: _____ W × _____ H
NOTE: Be sure to check dock heights, door heights, R. R. sidings, ceilings, pipes, roof trusses, sprinkler headers, etc., to be sure equipment can be moved into place on arrival. Advise of any unusual conditions.

Plant Electrical: _____ Volts   **Ambient Temperature Range:**   _____ Low (Degree F)
                         _____ Phase   _____ High (Degree F)
                         _____ HZ

Shop Demonstration Required? ☐ Note: A maximum of 5 products will be demonstrated.
Start-Up CSE: _____   Bulletin #100   _____ Days in FOB   _____ Training

---

Sales Approver:
The information contained in this package accurately specifies design and operational parameters for equipment being purchased from _____. Revisions to this data may have an effect on price and/or delivery.

Approved by: _____   Date: _____

PROVIDE COMPLETE PRODUCT & PATTERN DATA

Indicate which parameters were used to select the rate (in cases per minute) listed (Please Check):

☐ (A) Filler ☐ (B) Filler + ____% ☐ (C) Packer ☐ (D) Packer + ____% ☐ (E) Desired Machine Capacity

Item Or Line	Product Name	Package Description	Package Dimensions (Direction of travel to P/L)				Prod. Rate CPM	Cases Per Layer	Layers Per Load	Patrn. No.
			L	W	H	Wgt.				

Indicate Pattern and Direction of Travel (Check Boxes):

3A ☐   4A ☐   4B ☐   5A ☐   6A ☐   7A ☐   8A ☐   8B ☐

8C ☐   9A ☐   9B ☐   9C ☐   10A ☐   10B ☐   10C ☐   11A ☐

12A ☐   12B ☐   12C ☐   13A ☐   13B ☐   14A ☐   15A ☐

Product Type: (Example: Steel or Aluminum Cans, Glass or Plastic Bottles, Powder Liquid, etc.): _____

Case Type: (ex.: Sealed Corrugated—give flap location; Trays—give tray height; Shrink Film—cap or full, etc.): _____

_____

☐ Sealed Corr. ☐ Corr. Tray ☐ Shrink Film ☐ Full Depth Open ☐ Plastic Tray ☐ Full Depth Plastic

---

DOUBLE FACE REVERSIBLE ☐ ☐

2WAY NON REVERSIBLE ☐ ☐

4WAY GMA ☐ ☐

4WAY BLOCK ☐ ☐

MULTI-STRINGER ☐ ☐

SINGLE FACE ☐ ☐

SOLID FACE 4WAY BLOCK ☐ ☐

4WAY DOUBLE SOLID FACE ☐ ☐

NON-REVERSIBLE ☐ ☐

DOUBLE WING REVERSIBLE ☐ ☐

4WAY CHEP MARK III ☐ ☐

4WAY CHEP MARK 55 ☐ ☐

Pallet Data: Pallet Type (See Above): _____
Check box for travel of pallet.
A= _____   B= _____   C= _____
Width of bottom boards: _____   How many? _____
On sketch, show direction of pallet travel. (As discharged out of machine).
If available, attach detail drawing of pallet: ☐

CHAPTER 24

Keg Line Operations

ANDY BREWER
Petainer, Inc.

This chapter focuses on single-valve keg packaging, including a discussion on keg washing and filling equipment and the best practices for the keg washing and filling process. The chapter also includes a discussion on the new technologies surfacing for one-way, single-use kegs.

● GENERAL INFORMATION ON THE SINGE-VALVE KEG

Starting in the 1970s, most breweries changed from side-bung styles of kegs, such as Hoff Stevens and Golden Gate, to the single-valve keg, often called the Sankey keg.

The valve on a single-valve keg, often referred to as the spear valve or keg valve, is spring loaded and seals out any outside contaminates when not opened for processing and dispensing. This reduces the possibility of contamination after washing and sterilizing, allowing the keg to be sanitary filled with the correct equipment.

Although, in North America, draft keg beer is generally unpasteurized, adding a flash pasteurizer onto the beer supply to a keg line with a sanitary filling capability allows beer to be stored in a single-valve keg for long periods of time without refrigeration.

Single-valve kegs come in many different sizes, ranging from 36 imperial gallons to 10 L. Over the years, with the decline of keg beer volumes worldwide, the trend has been to use smaller kegs. In North America, the general keg sizes used are one-half, one-quarter, and one-sixth U.S. barrels in the United States and 50-, 30-, and 20-L barrels in Canada and Mexico. The other trend is to go to slimmer kegs, which take up less floor space and allow bars to stock more brands. Figure 24.1 shows some of the different sizes of beer kegs available.

Figure 24.2 shows a diagram of the typical single-valve keg. The construction of the keg shell has four major components: the walls of the keg, the neck, and two sets of chimes. The top chime has handles for lifting the keg

FIGURE 24.1. Single-valve kegs are available in several volume and size configurations. (Courtesy Beverage Machinery)

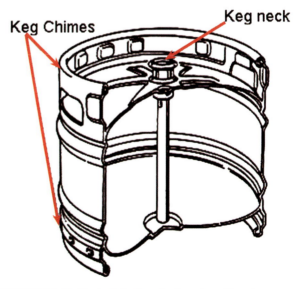

FIGURE 24.2. Typical single-valve beer keg. (Courtesy Beverage Machinery)

343

and may be embossed with the brewery's name. The bottom chime protects the bottom of the keg and provides a steady, level base. The keg's spear valve fits into the keg neck.

● TYPES OF SPEAR VALVES

There are many styles or designs of spear valves, but generally they come in two forms, well type and flat top, often called low-loss valves since there is less beer loss when filling a keg with this valve. Of course, it is important that the equipment used to wash and fill the keg is fitted with the right adapters to process the relevant spear valve. Most modern equipment is designed so these adapters can be easily changed out.

Although called a single-valve keg, all spear valves have two openings: the inner opening connects to the spear tube and the outer opening connects to the gas ports.

Figure 24.3 shows a Micro Matic D system well-type keg spear valve (Micro Matic USA, Northridge, CA) opened as it would be on keg processing equipment by a spear adapter and the flow of washing solution or purge gas in and out of the valve.

● IMPORTANT SAFETY ELEMENTS

Apart from the usual safety concerns and requirements for any packaging line, there are a few additional areas that need to be discussed when processing kegs.

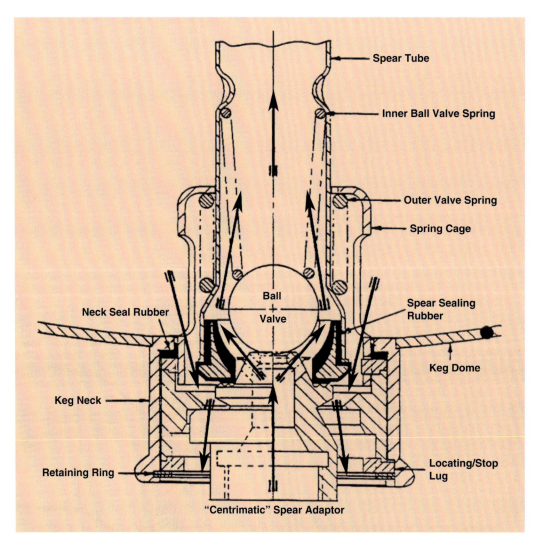

FIGURE 24.3. Typical well-type keg valve in the open position placed upside down on a cleaning head. The larger arrows indicate the flow when washing the keg. The flow is reversed when filling the keg with beer. (Courtesy Beverage Machinery)

The first is the need to ensure that any pressure supplied to the keg, whether during processing or dispensing, is below the safe operating pressure of the keg. Generally, kegs are constructed from steel, stainless steel, or aluminum; although there are now some plastic kegs available. The plastic kegs have lower pressure capacities than metal kegs and should be carefully observed.

It is important that all pressures supplied, from either gas or liquid, be regulated well below the manufacturer's recommended pressure and where possible, for safety, a pressure relief system should be fitted on the supply line.

Plastic kegs may have limits on the temperatures they can withstand. Therefore, it is important that the manufacturer's specifications on temperature be followed before subjecting these kegs to any steam sterilization, hot-chemical washing process, etc.

There are two basic methods for holding the spear valve in the keg. One method is with spears that are screwed into the neck. The other method, which is used for the vast majority of kegs in North America, uses a locking ring that fits into a groove in the keg's neck and stops the spear from twisting out of its bayonet fitting.

If a spear is not locked in place, it can come out of the keg when a great deal of force is generated, such as when being untapped at a bar or being inspected at the brewery, causing injury or even death.

It is of the highest importance that all kegs coming into the brewery, or at least leaving the brewery, are inspected to ensure that the spear is tight and, where locking rings are used, that the ring is present and installed correctly.

Also, before removing a spear valve for inspection or maintenance, the keg must be fully depressurized.

● KEG PROCESSING

There are a number of factors that go into designing a process to empty, wash, sterilize, and fill the kegs in the brewery. When the single-valve keg was first introduced into European breweries, especially in the United Kingdom, there was very tight control of keg floats, kegs were mostly shipped locally, and the beer sold was typically "regular" nonflavored or yeasty beers. Because of this, the kegs only required short washes and often only one chemical wash.

The North American market is much different, kegs are shipped long distances and the brewery has little or no control of the keg after it leaves. Often the keg remains for a long time under different climatic conditions before returning to the brewery. For instance, a keg may reach temperatures above 100°F (38°C) in Arizona in the summer and well below freezing in Minnesota in the winter. In addition, the kegs may take months or sometimes years to return to the brewery.

These differences, along with the shared keg float systems used by some breweries and the range of beers now run, from India pale ales dry hopped in the keg to heavily yeasted wheat beers to beers flavored with fruit, has meant that many breweries have had to greatly increase the amount of washing their kegs receive.

A brewery should look at all the above elements, along with factors such as the available utility services it can use and the required throughput desired, and then consult with its equipment suppliers to design a process that will be more than adequate to suit its needs.

Figure 24.4 shows the state of some kegs that have come back to a brewery and now have to be cleaned. When designing keg cleaning processes, it can be helpful to find or create badly soiled kegs and determine how well the process is able to clean them.

The more beer stone (calcium oxalate) in the keg, the bigger problem there is from a sterility point of view. It is worthwhile to perform a routine inspection on random kegs to check the ability of the current process to thoroughly clean the keg. Later in this chapter there is a discussion on what is considered current best practices for keg processing, but it is important that each brewery monitors the cleanliness of its keg float by random internal visual inspections and also consider whether any changes may be required when running new products.

The basics of keg line operations are as follows.

- Initial inspection of the incoming kegs. Regardless of whether it is a small brewery or a large brewery, there are important inspection steps that should be part of the overall keg cleaning and filling process. Inspection can be done automatically by automated equipment on high-capacity lines or manually by the keg line operator on smaller lines.

- External washing of the kegs. This is the cleaning of the external keg walls, chimes, and keg valve, as well as the removal of labels and previous production information.

- Current best practice for washing, sterilizing, and filling a keg. Although this is an ongoing development, there are current best practices for washing and filling kegs that are used in most major breweries.

- Final inspection of the kegs. This includes fill weights, leakers, and locking ring placement.

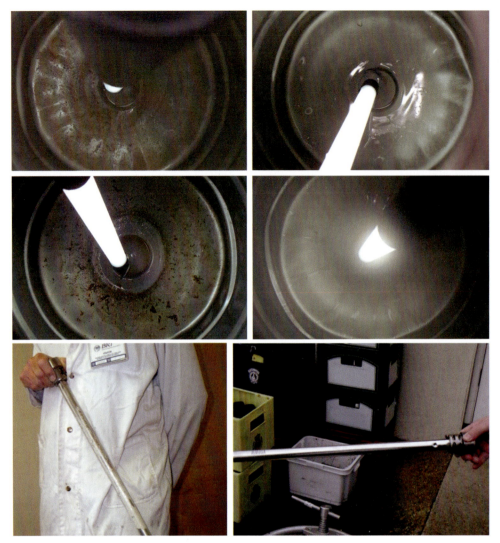

FIGURE 24.4. **Top and middle**, Before (left) and after (right) cleaning various kegs. **Bottom**, A badly stained keg spear (left) and the same spear after intensive cleaning (right). (Courtesy Briggs of Burton)

- Capping and labeling. After the keg is filled and inspected, it must be labeled and coded.
- Programming and controls. Keg lines must be tightly controlled to ensure that all the cleaning and filling operations are performed correctly and that no waste beer, chemicals, or other materials are included in the final package.

● INITIAL KEG INSPECTION, FIT-TO-FILL

When a keg comes back from the trade, the brewery does not know exactly how it has been treated, whether it has been damaged, or whether it has been tampered with. The term "fit-to-fill" is used to describe a process for checking the kegs and making sure they are acceptable to be placed on the keg line.

When kegs come back, they are loaded onto a conveyor line, whether manually or automatically. A certain amount of those kegs will fail because they are frozen, damaged, etc. The most efficient way to run a keg line is to only run the kegs on the line that will work perfectly. If there are 100 kegs put through the line but five of those kegs do not run, then the keg line efficiency drops to 95%. Fit-to-fill systems and procedures, whether it is someone looking and making manual inspections or some pieces of automatic inspection equipment, can intercept and cull out suspect kegs, taking the bad kegs off the line before they go to the main washing and filling equipment and enabling optimal performance from a brewery's keg line.

FIGURE 24.5. Examples of keg identification, including plastic label, painted sidewall, embossed top chime, readable number coding, and bar coding. (Courtesy Beverage Machinery)

Fit-to-fill incorporates several incoming inspections, including the following.

Foreign Kegs

A returned keg may not be the property of the receiving brewery, so the first inspection should be determining whether the keg belongs to the brewery or is a "foreign" keg. It is not legal or ethical to fill another brewer's keg with your beer. Each brewery should have their own keg float or use shared, leased kegs to fill with their beer. If a shared keg float system is used, then the brewery must purchase the rights to use that keg for that fill. Brewers should not, and must not, put their beer into another brewer's keg nor scrap it out, since this amounts to basically stealing that keg.

Keg Identification

There are a number of ways to identify a keg and to determine whether the keg belongs to the brewery. Permanent plastic or metallized labels with the brewery identification, painted colored striping, and embossed top keg chimes are commonly used to identify the keg's owner. Bar codes and transponders are sometimes used to not only identify the keg but track its use. These markings (Fig. 24.5) are meant for quick identification in the trade and also at the brewery to ensure that it is owned by the receiving brewery. There are issues and problems, of course, with all of these identifying methods. Plastic labels will surely be removed and damaged over time. Painting is very expensive and there are only so many colors and combinations available to use in a unique pattern. They will also inevitably be scuffed and discolored. But the idea is to ensure that the kegs, which are all mixed up in the trade, are identifiable in the market and make it back to the appropriate brewery.

When kegs are out in the trade, it can take weeks, months, or even years before returning to the brewery. During that time, they can be subject to very rough handling. The brewery does not know how they have been treated, where they have been, etc. One of the problems is that they can come back very dirty on the outside, so any form of vision system that is designed to automatically look at something such as chimes or number patterns will commonly have problems "seeing" through the dirt to the identifying pattern.

Keg Tracking

Bar codes are relatively easy to apply and work fairly well for keg identification, except that they also get dirty and damaged. Automatic keg lines working at fast speeds can have trouble reading a bar code. Even in the supermarket, where the packages are clean and have flat bar codes, they must sometimes be scanned two or three times before they read correctly. A bar code placed around the keg neck will last longer but is not a flat surface and a scanner will have difficulty reading it correctly.

Many brewers are now using radio frequency identification (RFID) chip transponders. These can be easily installed onto new kegs prior to purchase. Installing them on an existing keg float can be done, but it can be expensive. RFID is very good for tracking the keg all the way through the filling and distribution process. The system holds up well and can be read even through heavy soiling. Eventually, the keg will need some form of inspection and repair, and the RFID chip system is a good way of seeing how old the keg is, as well as evaluating the keg float in real time.

Damaged Kegs

A major item for inspection is damaged kegs returned from the trade. Damaged kegs do not run through equipment very well because they may be unstable or may not match up properly with the cleaning heads. Proper keg inspection procedures look for a number of kinds of damage to the kegs. If any of these things are seen, then the keg should be rejected and not allowed to go through the cleaning and filling systems.

Missing Locking Rings

The biggest problem, as mentioned previously, and a serious safety issue, is missing, damaged, or improperly installed keg valve locking rings. In North America, the spear is usually installed into the keg's neck using a bayonet type of fitting; tabs on the outside of the valve are twisted into grooves inside the neck. A locking ring, sometimes called a snap ring is then installed into another groove in the keg's neck to hold the valve in place.

If the locking ring is missing or improperly installed, it is likely that the valve will come out of the bayonet fitting when untapped and go flying upward with the force of the internal keg pressure. This is serious business and people have been badly hurt and even killed by this kind of problem. The liability to the brewery is huge because it is the brewery's responsibility to inspect and ensure that the locking ring is present at the time of shipment. Ideally, the locking ring should be inspected on the way into the keg line, but if not, then it must be inspected on the way out of the keg filling line, where the keg spear valve should now be clean, making it easier to detect. It is very important to note that locking rings must be used *only once*. They must not be reused since they will have lost the physical capacity to hold the keg valve in the neck properly.

Frozen Kegs

If the keg has been in a cold climate, it may come back to the brewery with frozen waste beer inside. Frozen beer cannot be easily removed during the initial cleaning processes, and it makes it impossible to process safely because cleaning chemicals will go into the keg and may not flow back out again, although the conductivity sensors or wet–dry probes will see them as empty. In the end, the filled keg may have a mixture of waste beer and cleaning chemicals along with the product.

Bent Necks

Bent keg necks can be a problem because the keg valve does not match up properly with the keg machine's cleaning and filling heads, causing washing solutions and beer to leak and/or spray out during processing. Bent necks can be caused by rough handling in the retail trade where, especially with the small-volume slimmer kegs, the keg may be tapped and then moved around by picking it up by the tapping head. Moving it and swinging it bends the keg neck.

Bent or Broken Tapping Lugs

The keg spear valve has lugs that the tapper uses to twist into when tapping the keg. If the lugs on the keg valve are damaged or missing, the keg can still be processed and filled, but it will not be able to be tapped and dispensed at the bar. This is less of a problem with the newer keg valves.

Damaged Chimes

Damaged, cracked, or bent keg chimes can cause problems on automatic equipment. Instead of going down the line in a level fashion, the keg may wobble along unsteadily or even fall off the walking beam transporting it from station to station. Also, hand injuries can occur if the keg handles on the chime are damaged.

Residual Beer

Some breweries actually weigh their kegs that are returned from the trade. The reason is that, if kegs come back with excessive beer in them, there may be a problem with the keg and its ability to be tapped. This may have been a keg returned by the retailer. A common reason for tapping problems is a worn out or damaged keg valve seal. This is the seal that meets the tapping head and, if damaged, allows carbon dioxide (CO_2) into the keg spear, resulting in foamy beer at the faucet. Damaged, chipped, or scarred keg valve seals must be changed out.

Also, since the keg has to be emptied as part of the keg processing and emptying, a full keg slows down production. In any event, it is best to either push that keg off to equipment that is dedicated to remove the beer or reject it for further inspection. Residual beer can be pushed out with compressed air or CO_2 gas that is safely regulated down below the keg manufacturer's recommended maximum safe operating pressure. A simple scale on the infeed is a good way of performing this initial fit-to-fill check.

Dust Caps

Dust caps present on kegs coming back are a real problem during processing. People in the bar think they are doing the brewery a favor when they put the cap back on the keg valve. However, when the keg goes through the cleaning and filling process, the machine does not know the cap is there. The machine cleaning or filling head is going to try to penetrate into the valve and pieces of plastic will get stuck in the pipe work, where they can cause all sorts of flow problems.

A variety of dust caps are available for breweries to use, and quite often they are used to identify the brewery or the brand of beer inside the keg. The simple dust caps that most breweries use are easily applied and also easily come off completely.

Tamper-proof caps are designed to be destroyed once they are opened. They are also designed to remain on the keg valve and serve as a tamper-evident seal. They come in various forms and are obviously more expensive. There are even some designs that are heat shrunk to hold in place. These kinds of caps may require more effort and time to remove and should only be present on kegs that have not been tapped.

There are various decapper equipment designs that can be used to remove caps left on kegs, but none is 100% effective and cap detectors should also be used to ensure that kegs with caps are removed prior to any external or internal keg washing.

Hydrocarbons

In Europe, hydrocarbon sniffers are sometimes used to detect gasoline or even oil that has been stored in the keg. Hydrocarbons in the keg will contaminate the entire keg wash system and cannot be completely removed from the contaminated kegs themselves.

EXTERNAL KEG WASHING

A keg is externally washed for a number of reasons. One reason is to remove any labeling put on the keg to indicate the brand of beer with which it was last filled, as well as any of the previous production information. Additionally, there may be required labels from the government for tax requirements that must be removed. (Some of these are plastic and may require a scraper to remove.)

The other reason to externally wash a keg is simply to make it more presentable. The customer may never see it, but a dirty keg makes the product look dirty, even though the inside may be sparkling clean and the beer is completely perfect. Beer is food, and food arriving in a dirty container does not inspire confidence on the part of the person handling and selling it.

External washers (Fig. 24.6) typically have three sections.

- The caustic section, where the keg is sprayed with a strong (2–3%) caustic solution.
- A draining section, where that caustic is allowed to drain off of the keg and back for reuse.
- A rinse section, which often uses reclaimed rinse water from the main keg line to rinse the outside of the keg and get rid of the caustic residue. If the caustic residue is not completely removed, then it will have a streaky white appearance that can come off on the hands of the people handling it.

There are a number of external washer designs. Most kegs are constructed of stainless steel and can be washed with caustic soda. If the keg is made out of aluminum, it should be cleaned with a noncaustic alkaline cleaner since the caustic attacks and corrodes the aluminum.

The amount of washing needed is dependent upon the type of labels used, how dirty the kegs come back, and the throughput required. Figure 24.7 shows a very small

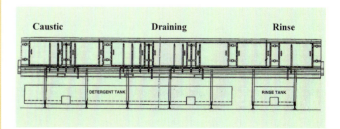

FIGURE 24.6. Typical external keg washer. (Courtesy Beverage Machinery)

external washer on a line producing 60–100 kegs per hour. Figure 24.8 shows another washer on a line capable of producing 1,000 kegs per hour. The key to external washing is good filtration. The more pressure the keg is pounded with to remove a label, the finer the particulate that is generated. And the finer the particulate, the finer the filtration has to be because, as it goes through the spray nozzles, the particulates start to build up and block the flow.

There is more to the design of an external washer than just a car-wash spray system. The drainage section is also very important. The keg goes through the washer upside down. The cleaning nozzles are spraying caustic all over the keg and the bottom chime (upside down now) retains a large amount of solution and has only a few small drain holes. If there is not sufficient time to drain off the keg, caustic is carried through to the rinse section, which wastes both caustic chemicals and energy.

To monitor and control the external keg washer, the keg line procedures should include the following.

- Checking the titration of the chemical wash manually and/or using an automatic dosing system that constantly monitors the conductivity of the solution for proper concentration.
- Checking the pump pressure automatically or manually to ensure they are delivering solutions to specification. Adding a pressure gauge on each pump allows for quick monitoring of the system. If the pressure starts to increase, this could indicate that the nozzles inside the external washer are blocked.
- Checking the temperature of the washes. This is extremely important for optimal chemical cleaning and rinsing but also because, if the external washer runs higher than 160°F (71°C), beer residues on the inside of the keg will "bake on" and be much more difficult to clean off later in the process. Overheating in the external washing can start to build up beer stain inside the kegs. Some lines have an initial internal keg prewashing step that removes the residual beer, provides an initial rinsing of the keg, and provides a spray of caustic wash prior to entering the external washer. But monitoring the temperature of an external washer is still very important to ensure no residues, beer, or chemicals are baked onto the interior keg surfaces. It is part of the whole cleaning process.
- Checking the ventilation fans on the washer to ensure they are working to reduce the amount of caustic fumes coming out of both ends of the external washer. This is very important for safety reasons.

It is also important that all spray nozzles are placed correctly so that, if labels are present, a majority of the washing takes place on those areas.

A simple external prerinse unit using reclaimed water from the rinse section of the external washer can be installed prior to the external washer to help remove heavy debris, e.g., dirt, sand, pizza, or whatever is left on the keg, and to also help keep the spray nozzles inside the external washer from blocking up.

FIGURE 24.7. Small external keg washer capable of washing 60–100 kegs per hour. (Courtesy Beverage Machinery)

FIGURE 24.8. Larger external keg washer capable of washing 1,000 kegs per hour. (Courtesy Beverage Machinery)

Turning the keg as it goes through the washer helps to ensure that the spray is applied correctly all the way around the keg's outer surface. This can be done simply by using two chains, working at different speeds, or using little bumps along the conveyor where the keg catches on one side and is dragged around. The external washer is more efficient if the kegs can be rotated as they travel through.

VARIOUS TYPES OF INTERNAL WASHING AND FILLING EQUIPMENT

There are various types of keg cleaning machines available. Figure 24.9 shows a small machine designed for brewpubs and small craft breweries. It has a programmable logic controller (PLC) and washes the kegs with modified keg tappers, which have larger bore sizes than regular tavern heads and no check valves. It washes the keg upside down and then fills it on a pallet right-way up.

Figure 24.10 shows a larger, but still manual, handling machine. The keg is manually placed on the machine, but it washes with a connection head instead of the keg tappers. The keg is clamped down onto the connection head, sealing it against the keg valve. The connection head then raises a spear adapter into the keg spear valve to open it, allowing the liquids into and out of the keg. The advantage of washing with a connection head is that the head can clean itself after each operation. On this particular machine, the first station removes the waste beer and washes and sterilizes the keg. The cleaned keg is then shifted over to the second station for counterpressure and filling.

It is good practice to keep the washing and filling heads completely separate from one another. A single-function head may contaminate the filling cycle. Any drains that come off the fill side must have at least an air space between the drain piping and the floor to ensure that there is no connection directly to the filling side and no chance of sucking drainage back into the cleaning or filling processes.

A higher-speed multihead machine is shown in Figure 24.11. It uses the same type of keg clamps and connection heads as the two-station manual machine (Fig. 24.12). The machine in Figure 24.11 is an automatic machine that

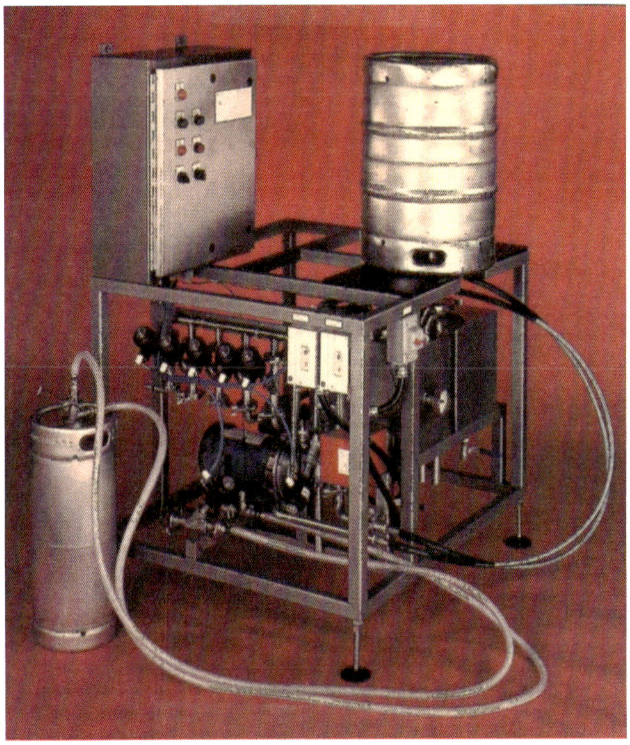

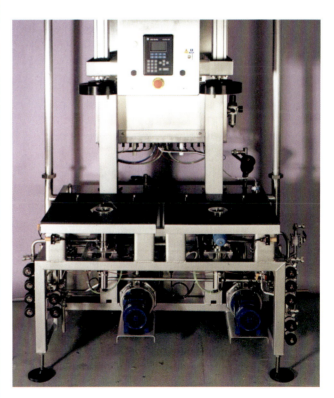

FIGURE 24.9. Small keg washing and filling machine that uses hoses and a modified keg tapper. The output of these types of machines is about 25–35 kegs per hour. (Courtesy Beverage Machinery)

FIGURE 24.10. Two-station manual keg washing and filling machine. The first station pushes out the beer residue and cleans and sterilizes the keg. The second station counterpressures and fills the keg with beer. (Courtesy Briggs of Burton)

uses a walking beam to move the keg through each of its cleaning and filling stations. By using various numbers of stations, every part of the operation, i.e., removing the beer and giving it a rinse, a caustic wash, and perhaps an acid wash, can be broken up onto separate heads so that increased production speeds can be achieved.

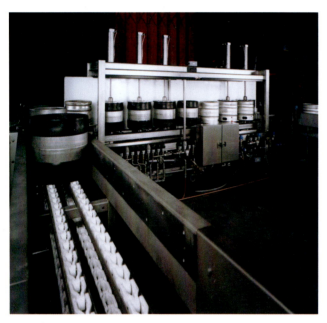

FIGURE 24.11. Automatic walking beam-style keg washing and filling machine capable of producing 50–80 kegs per hour, depending on the number of cleaning stations and cycle times. (Courtesy Briggs of Burton)

FIGURE 24.12. Example of a head and keg clamp used to clean or fill a keg. The keg is clamped down to the head and a spear adapter raises up into the positioned keg valve and seals it, allowing the passage of liquids or gases into and out of the keg. (Courtesy Briggs of Burton)

● BEST PRACTICES FOR CLEANING AND FILLING

For the purposes of this chapter, the definition of "best practice" for washing/sterilizing and filling a keg is as follows.

> Best practice is a safe and fully monitored process that gives the required line throughput and results in the kegs receiving more than an adequate amount of washing and sterilizing, then filling to the correct volume of beer while maintaining the required carbonation levels with low oxygen pickup and low beer loss while using the least amount of utilities.

Best practices for cleaning start with the particular keg float situation and product line for that particular brewery. What works for one brewer who is shipping a light lager beer relatively short distances with a quick turnaround may not work for a brewer shipping long distances and selling yeasty *Hefeweizen* or flavored beers. The first step is to talk to the machine manufacturer providing the equipment, explain where the keg float goes, explain what type of beer is used to fill the kegs, etc. Then have a program to inspect inside the kegs to ensure that the cleaning cycles used are working.

When a new product is formulated, the machine suppliers must be asked about any issues they might foresee with the cleaning; for instance, a cherry-flavored beer might leave a cherry stain inside the keg. And if that is not removed correctly, then the next product going in, say a light lager, might pick up a cherry flavor.

● VARIOUS TECHNIQUES FOR WASHING A KEG

A well-designed keg line should not use more than 3 gallons (11 L) of water for each keg processed. To conserve, water is reused for numerous types of rinsing steps.

A proper keg wash involves two types of washes in each cleaning (and rinse) cycle: a full-flow wall wash and a low-flow spear wash (Fig. 24.13).

A full-flow wall wash goes up the spear tube, hits the little dimple at the top of the inverted keg, and then showers the keg walls before leaving the keg at the bottom outlet. The dimple is extremely important because it helps spread the wash all the way around the keg walls. If this dimple is damaged in any way, some of the keg will never be washed correctly.

Low-flow spear washing, where the pressure and hence the flow are reduced, allows the liquid to go up the spear and then flow down around the outside of the spear tube. Generally, the washing pattern is pulsed to alternate these two wash patterns during the cycle, i.e., full flow, spear wash, full flow, spear wash, etc., as many times as necessary. This is called pulse washing and gives the best wash possible in the time available. With the pulse wash, every time the keg is depressurized to go into the spear wash, it then allows for a forceful increase of pressure for the full-flow wash, which helps to remove soiling on the keg walls.

The pressure of this wash is extremely important and the supply pump pressure should be set between 38 and 45 pounds per square inch gauge (psig) for proper full-flow washing. This is to create a certain amount of velocity to actually get around the walls of the keg. However, pressure that is too high is undesirable because the liquid could be added much faster than it can drain out. If the liquid starts to build up a level inside the keg, not only is that going to take longer to purge out but the cycle will lose its cleaning and stripping action all the way down the walls of the keg to the outlet at the bottom.

Spear washing does not involve high velocity. The cleaning solution simply cascades down the outside of the tube, relying principally on the action of the temperature and cleaning chemicals to dissolve soils on the spear surface. If a keg has not been washed on a machine equipped with a spear-washing cycle, it will probably develop beer stone deposits that cannot then be removed by using a machine with proper spear washing alone. Instead, the spear will have to be extracted, cleaned manually, and then kept on a cleaning program involving spear-washing cycles to be maintained.

Although pulse washing is generally considered the current best practice and the amount and length of the pulses depend on the amount of cleaning needed, there are other methods of inducing and cleaning a keg that are in use where extra cleaning is considered necessary.

Reverse Washing

To increase the velocity of the wash-through area where the valve's springs and seals are located, called the spring basket, the washing solution is forced up through the keg valve gas ports and then back out again (Fig. 24.14).

Rousing

To rouse a keg, the washing solution is put into the keg through the keg valve gas ports in a reverse wash until about one-half to three-quarters full and then air is pushed through the gas ports to rouse the solution. This has proved to give a good cleaning but uses a lot of solution, takes a long time, and should only be considered for the dirtiest kegs.

Scrubbing Bubbles

Some breweries inject air bubbles into their wash solution as it enters the keg, regardless of what type of washing system they use. The theory in this practice is to use the action of the bubbles to scour surfaces more effectively.

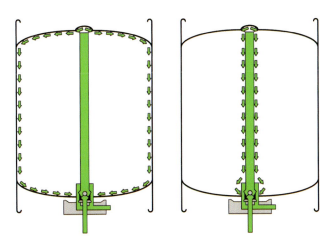

FIGURE 24.13. A full-flow wall wash allows the wash solution to travel up the spear against the top dimple of the keg and spread down the sidewall (left). A low-flow spear wash has a reduced flow that runs down the outside of the keg spear (right). (Courtesy Briggs of Burton)

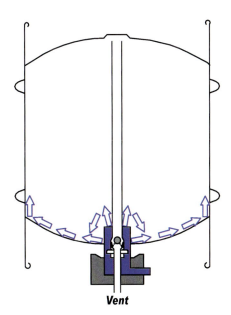

FIGURE 24.14. With reverse washing, the cleaning solution is forced up through the keg gas port and then drains back again. The wash solution pressure should be set between 38 and 45 psig. (Courtesy Briggs of Burton)

As mentioned earlier, designing a process that achieves what works for the brewery's particular situation may require more or less than what is mentioned in the rest of this chapter, However, what follows is considered the current best practice.

WASH AND FILL CYCLES

Pressure Check and Depressurization

The keg's first check is for residual pressure (Fig. 24.15). This is to check that the keg has some level of pressure in it, even just 2 or 3 psig, and helps determine whether the keg is a leaker or even whether somebody has tampered with it. If there is no initial pressure left in the keg, it should be pushed off to one side for a manual inspection. If there is residual pressure, then the next step is a long, initial depressurization.

When the keg comes back, there is going to be a little bit of beer residue inside. There also will be gas, most likely CO_2, which needs be removed as much as possible because CO_2 reacts and neutralizes caustic during the washing cycles, diluting and wasting the caustic cleaning chemicals.

De-ullaging

De-ullaging is a British term for removing the waste beer that is left in the keg (Fig. 24.16). Generally, waste beer is called ullage in the United Kingdom. So removing it is to de-ullage. Compressed air goes into the keg and pushes any remaining beer out of the keg away to a waste tank or the sewer and helps further remove CO_2 gas. Generally, there is some form of conductivity or wet–dry probe to sense that this step is completed. If it does not complete within a certain period of time, it is possible the valve is damaged, the keg is rejected, no further processing is done, and the keg should be inspected manually.

On a lot of equipment, the compressed air that is supplied for de-ullaging is sterile air, and it goes through a sterile filtration system. For this initial process, although it should be clean and oil free, sterile air is not required and may actually pose a contamination risk. If there is a blockage on the keg discharge, it is possible for the dirty gas from the keg to migrate back up into the air line and then every air application from that point forward will be contaminated. It is best practice to use a separate air line, with back-check valves, for the de-ullaging step until the keg has gone through the cleaning process later on.

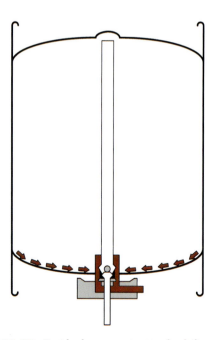

FIGURE 24.15. Residual pressure test to check for a leaker and initial depressurization to reduce the amount of carbon dioxide gas present in the returned keg. (Courtesy Briggs of Burton)

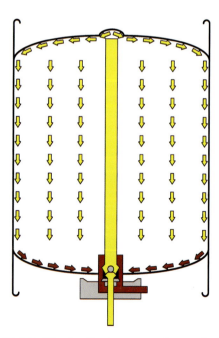

FIGURE 24.16. The de-ullaging step pushes residual beer out of the keg with compressed air and a conductivity probe senses the liquid leaving the keg. (Courtesy Briggs of Burton)

First Rinse

After a short depressurization time, the keg then receives a first rinse (Fig. 24.17) to get rid of most of the remnants of whatever beer remains after the de-ullaging step. This is often done with water that has been recovered from a rinse step later on. To save energy, water, and sewer costs, rinses are often recovered and reused. It is still fairly clean. There may be a caustic residue from the initial rinse but it can be reused for the first rinse step.

Second Air Purge

The residual water from the rinses is then purged out of the keg with compressed air for possible collection and reuse (Fig. 24.18).

Caustic Wash

At this point in the process, the waste beer has been removed, the keg has received a quick rinse and an air purge, and after a short depressurization, the keg is now ready for the chemical wash cycle.

Breweries use either a single chemical wash or two washes. Most machines then follow the air purge with a caustic wash.

Here again, for the caustic wash, the machine pulses full flow, low flow, full flow, low flow, etc. for at least 25 seconds but typically up to about 60 seconds in the fashion shown in Figure 24.13. Chemical concentrations and temperatures should follow the chemical supplier's recommendations.

Caustic Soak

Sometimes the cycle partially fills a keg with caustic to soak and clean the spring basket area of the keg valve.

The valve springs are areas that can trap bacteria, and the caustic soak helps to loosen soils and clean those areas (Fig. 24.19). The caustic soak step is normally a rest step in which the keg rests on the walking beam or transfer arm without any cleaning head attached.

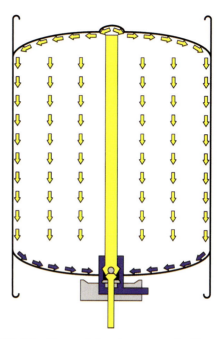

FIGURE 24.18. Clean, oil-free, but nonsterile filtered compressed air is used to push the remaining rinse water out of the keg. (Courtesy Briggs of Burton)

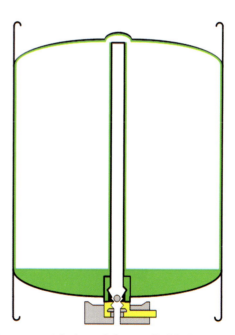

FIGURE 24.19. The keg is left partially filled with a caustic solution to help clean the spring basket area of the keg valve. (Courtesy Briggs of Burton)

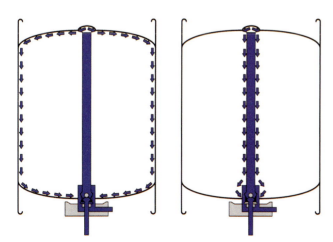

FIGURE 24.17. The de-ullaged keg is pulse rinsed with water on both its walls (left) and its spear (right). (Courtesy Briggs of Burton)

Sometimes all of the processes outlined so far occur on a prewash machine. The kegs then travel through an external washer and onto the main keg washing machine for additional washes and filling.

Third Air Purge

To remove the soak caustic, the keg is air purged again (Fig. 24.20). Generally, at this point, it is safe to start using sterile, filtered compressed air to push out the solutions. The chances of getting bacteria from the keg back into the air line at this point are negligible. The keg has now gone through a cleaning cycle and there is nothing mechanically wrong, e.g., no blockages. So now the system can use sterile air for all the rest of its push-outs. Some breweries, at this point, use steam for purging. Steam is acceptable but starts to degrade and dilute the caustic solution. Typically, a conductivity probe checks to ensure the solution is cleared out of the keg.

Second Rinse

The keg receives a second short rinse with recovered water, using the same full-flow and low-flow pattern to rinse both the keg walls and the outside of the spear, similar to the rinse pattern in Figure 24.17. The water rinse is used because the next step is an acid wash and there is going to be a little bit of caustic left in the keg. The water rinse removes the residual caustic so that it does not neutralize the acid cleaning solution. The rinse water can be collected and reused as a prerinse or in the external washer.

Fourth Air Purge

The second rinse is also air purged away, again with sterile air, similar to what is shown in Figure 24.20.

Acid Wash

The acid wash step is generally not as long as the caustic wash step, but it uses the same full-flow and low-flow pattern as the caustic wash (Fig. 24.21). Caustic removes organic materials, e.g., beer residue, yeast, or bacteria. The acid solution, generally a blend of nitric and phosphoric acids, primarily removes inorganic minerals, such as beer stone. Again, the chemical concentrations and temperatures used should follow the chemical supplier's recommendations. Many brewers in the world use only one chemical wash, whether it is caustic or acid, while most keg washing equipment and chemical suppliers recommend both types of washes for optimal washing performance. However, the more washing steps used, the slower the throughput and the more expensive the machinery is to purchase and run.

Some breweries do not figure they need as much acid washing as they do caustic washing, so they configure

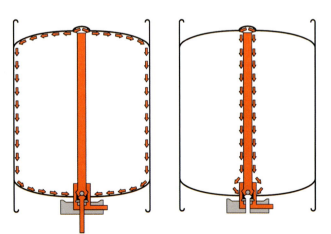

FIGURE 24.21. Acid washing with a blended solution of nitric and phosphoric acids is used to remove mineral deposits, such as beer stone. Pulse washing with full-flow washing through the spear to clean the walls (left) and low-flow washing to clean the outside of the spear tube (right) gives the most effective cleaning. (Courtesy Briggs of Burton)

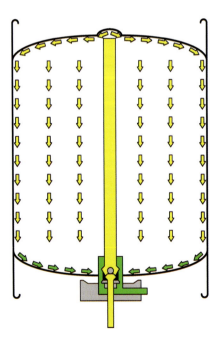

FIGURE 24.20. Air purge of the caustic cleaning solution back to the caustic tank for reuse. Sterile, filtered (0.2 µm) air can be used to push the solution out. (Courtesy Briggs of Burton)

their equipment for caustic washing for 3 weeks during the month and for 1 week during the month they wash with acid. The theory goes that kegs will come in and out within a year, probably receiving a caustic wash the majority of the time, but they might end up getting one or two acid washes annually along the way. Once again, this depends on the beer styles, water chemistry, and keg rotations specific to the brewery.

Fifth Air Purge

The keg is air purged again until it is empty of acid. Some systems may use steam for this purge but, generally, sterile compressed air is used.

Third (Final) Rinse

The air purge is followed by the final rinse, using the full-flow and low-flow pulse pattern. The final water rinse removes the last remnants of the chemical wash, in this case, acid. It is important that this water is clean because it is the last rinse on the cleaned keg and it is important not to contaminate the keg with microbes or particulates. The rinse water should be hot, at least 160°F (71°C), so that it does not carry live bacteria into the keg. This rinse is commonly collected and reused for earlier prerinse cycles.

Steam Purge and Sterilization

In most pieces of keg cleaning equipment, the next process is to steam purge the final rinse water out of the keg (Fig. 24.22). Steaming is going to accomplish three important final steps of the process. First of all, it is going to purge the final rinse water out. Second, it starts heating and sterilizing the keg. The beauty of steam, because it is a vapor, is that it gets into all the nooks and crannies to very effectively kill any microorganisms present. But the other advantage of steam is that it evacuates all of the oxygen out of the keg.

Generally, kegs are steamed until empty. The keg then is brought up to temperatures of about 217°F (103°C) using 40- to 45-psig (2.8- to 3.1-bar) steam. A temperature probe usually monitors the temperature exiting the keg, and if it is reading 217°F (103°C) on the exit, there is normally a bit of lag behind the actual keg interior temperature, which may be as high as 248°F (120°C). The drain valve is then closed and the keg is pressurized to about 20 psig (1.5 bar) so that the temperature inside the keg approaches 260°F (127°C) and sterilization is achieved. The key to successfully sterilizing the keg with steam during this process is to completely purge the air out so that there is close to 100% saturated steam in the keg.

The keg should rest with this volume of steam for at least 60 seconds to achieve sterility. Some systems boost the steam again during the rest cycle to maintain the high temperature during the rest period and then steam it one more time to sterilize the connection head prior to the filling cycle.

Alternative Sterilization Methods

Steam sterilizing is generally recommended for the most effective and reliable sterility performance. If steam is not available or the decision is made not to use it, then there are alternative methods to sterilize the keg.

- Hot water, about 190°F (88°C), can be pumped into the keg, holding it for at least 100 seconds. While hot water is an effective sterilizer, the hold time required is longer than that of steam and the results are not as reliable.
- Chemical sterilant solutions can also be used in a fashion similar to the chemical pulse-wash routines. Breweries generally prefer to use a no-rinse chemical sanitizer, such as peracetic acid or chlorine dioxide. Using chemical sanitizers does not remove the oxygen from the keg and relies on solution contact to penetrate and kill, whereas steam is a water vapor that gets into every possible orifice and surface of the keg, spear, and valve.

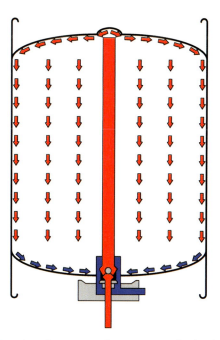

FIGURE 24.22. Steam is used to purge out the final rinse water, which can be reused, and then sterilize the keg. (Courtesy Briggs of Burton)

Gas Purge and Gassing

Once the keg has been sterilized, the sterilant must be pushed out of the keg, whether it is a chemical sterilant, hot water, or condensed steam, and then the keg is gassed to remove the oxygen. For carbonated beers, most breweries use CO_2 to gas the keg. For nitrogenated beer, the use of nitrogen or high-nitrogen mixed gas blend may be employed. The gas is introduced upward into the keg through the spear tube and is vented out through the gas port (Fig. 24.23).

Counterpressurization

The gassing step is typically done on a timed basis. After the purge time, the keg is then pressurized to the pressure setting needed to provide the specified backpressure to conserve the beer carbonation level. If the keg has been steam sterilized, the walls of the keg are still very hot. When cold beer is introduced, it is going to heat slightly, liberating some of the carbonation, which will produce some foam as well as lose a little bit of backpressure and carbonation saturation. To address this, a few breweries externally rinse the keg with chilled water during the gassing and pressurizing steps so that, when the beer goes in, the keg is as close as it can be to the same temperature as the beer.

Filling

Best practice is to resterilize the keg filling head prior to starting the fill process. The keg is then ready for beer to enter and fill. There are three-stage filling and multistage filling systems to fill a keg and reduce beer loss. Fill rates are very fast and must be accurate to within a few fluid ounces. The three-stage filling system starts with a slow fill, so there is initially low or no foaming, and then goes to a very fast fill rate and then slows down at the end so that the fill valve can be shut with acceptable accuracy. A multistage filling system ramps the beer fill up and then ramps it down again for acceptable accuracy.

The keg can be filled upside down or right-side up. It does not matter with a single-valve keg. Generally, when a keg goes through a keg line, because it has been washed and sterilized upside down, there is no point in turning it right-side up. When the keg is upside down, it is filled through the keg valve's gas ports and the beer is brought in slowly, forming a pool of beer at the bottom. Gas is vented through the spear via bleed-off venting valves, releasing the counterpressure gas against a backpressure control (Fig. 24.24). Forming the pool of beer initially avoids a lot of foam from being established in the hot, sterilized keg and also allows a cushion for a faster rate of beer to quickly fill most of the remaining volume.

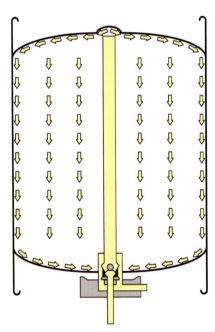

FIGURE 24.23. Purging the sterilant out of the keg with sterile gas, e.g., carbon dioxide, nitrogen, or mixed gas, depending on the product. Gas is introduced up through the spear and vented out through the gas port. (Courtesy Briggs of Burton)

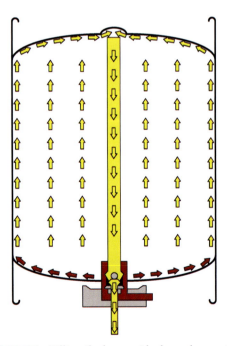

FIGURE 24.24. Filling the keg upside down, beer enters the keg valve's gas port at the bottom and counterpressure gas is vented out in a controlled fashion as it leaves through the keg's spear tube. (Courtesy Briggs of Burton)

On some of the smaller manual systems, the keg is filled right-way up (Fig. 24.25). In this method, beer enters using a modified tapper head through the spear tube and then the gas is vented out through the gas ports, which are fitted with a manual valve to control the backpressure venting.

With the D system well-style keg valve commonly found on kegs used in the United States and Canada, there is always a small amount of beer loss with each fill of about 3 fluid ounces (80 mL). European flat or low-loss keg valve heads lose almost no beer with each fill.

Tight control of the backpressure is important for a good, low-foam beer fill. Accurate fill levels depend on a good metering system as well as on constant beer pressure to the line. If the beer pressure fluctuates, then it does not matter how good the metering system is and the process will have issues with inconsistent fills.

A modulation filler system is shown in Figure 24.26. The connection head where the keg would sit is shown on the top. The beer goes through a three-stage beer valve and the cycle produces a 30-second fill. The fill starts with a low flow, goes to a full flow, and ends up on a low flow. This is to reduce beer loss and gain overall filling speed.

The filling valve should be placed as close to the head as possible to reduce beer loss. A blocking valve is used to steam and clean the head prior to filling. A head valve stops beer from going into the other valves.

Fill-by-weight systems can also be used. The system weighs the empty keg on the connection head and fills it by weight. The main problem with this method is that the head has to be floating to get an accurate weight, which is very difficult. These systems involve all sorts of calibration and moving conveyors, it is not recommended for anything but small manual systems that fill by hand.

Final Inspection

Final inspection for each keg going out to the trade is made after the keg has been processed. No rejected keg should be put out into the trade, and steps need to be in place to ensure this does not happen. Scales can be used to weigh the keg and ensure it has a proper fill so that

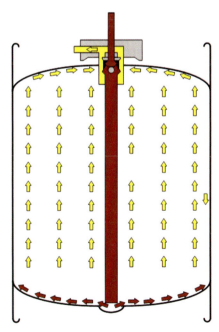

FIGURE 24.25. Filling the keg right-side up is done with a modified keg tapper head. Beer enters the keg through the spear tube into the bottom of the keg and counterpressure gas is bled off through a valve on the tapper and leaves through the gas port. (Courtesy Briggs of Burton)

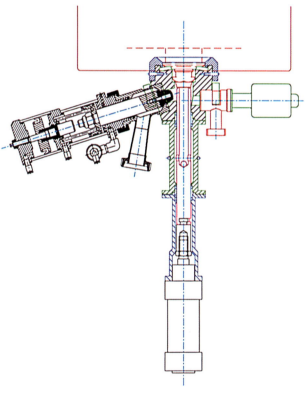

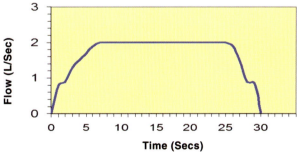

FIGURE 24.26. Modulation filler system, including a three-stage filling head (top) and a filling chart (bottom). (Courtesy Briggs of Burton)

partially filled kegs are not released. Other checks are made to ensure there are no leakers, this can be done with a vision or pressure monitoring system. Keep in mind that, if the keg is leaking, it may have gas coming out, which is difficult to detect visually, but when that keg gets out in the trade it is going to be flat. This is another reason to pull aside full kegs of beer returned from the trade.

Also, as mentioned previously, make sure the keg valve locking ring is in place!

Labeling and Capping

Before a keg leaves the brewery, it must be capped and labeled with the beer brand and production information if possible. In the United States, there is a required product warning label that must be put onto the keg. Although the dust caps can be placed on by hand with smaller-production machines, in higher-output machines, they are often applied with an automatic capping machine. The caps protect the keg valve from dirt and debris prior to tapping.

Product coding using continuous ink jet systems can provide valuable production information, including brand, packaging date and time, and lot codes. The product coding is normally placed on the keg prior to reaching the filling head.

● KEG MACHINE CONTROLS AND PROGRAMMING

The keg is the only package a brewery makes that has a valve. It is critical that the cleaning and filling processes are monitored and checked to ensure the wash and rinse cycles are doing absolutely everything correctly: putting the cleaning solutions in and then rinsing and purging them out. What is put in the keg, unless it is purged out correctly, remains in the keg, whether it be waste beer or cleaning chemicals. On a well-designed kegging machine, every part of the process is electronically monitored to ensure that it is performing to specification. The system checks to make sure nothing goes wrong, that the rinse water goes into the keg, that the water comes back out of the keg, etc. If it fails for any reason, the machine should reject the keg so that it is not filled with beer. This is a food safety and liability issue, no brewery wants to send chemically contaminated beer to its customers.

The program that checks the probes to make sure everything is carried out correctly must be protected from alterations by any but authorized personnel in the plant. In addition, procedures should be in place to check that any liquid, compressed air, or gas supplied to the machine is set to the proper pressures and that the temperatures and chemical concentrations are at their specified levels. These checks should be made prior to startup and at set times during each shift. Pressures and temperatures can be checked manually by looking at gauges or automatically with probes. Chemical concentrations can be checked with conductivity probes against actual titrations.

Chemical washes should be within the concentration and temperature ranges recommended by the chemical supplier. The final water rinse tank should be hot enough to sterilize the rinse water.

Test Kegs

Test kegs can help monitor the cycles for pressure and temperature. One method is to have a keg fitted with sight glasses as well as pressure and temperature gauges to visually see inside the keg during a cleaning audit and read off the pressures and temperatures as the keg goes through its different cycles. Obviously, the visuals can only be done with ambient-temperature water, while the temperature and pressure readings are made during actual process conditions. The information gathered must also be evaluated manually and can then be entered into a spreadsheet for analysis.

Automated test kegs can verify the process in real time. Automated test kegs are fitted with temperature and pressure probes that feed information into a recorder, which can then be downloaded to a computer. This type of test keg is especially useful when commissioning a new keg washing machine and fine tuning the cycle times, pressures, and temperatures or when making changes to the programming later on. Once set up, the PLC on board the machine should keep the settings intact.

PLC and Sensors

The PLC is the central collector of equipment information and executes a program based on the parameters that have been entered. The PLC relies on several types of probes and switches to send signals confirming that the cleaning, purging, and filling cycles have been performed correctly. These probes and switches include the following.

- Pressure transponders, or switches, ensure that the keg reaches the proper pressures.
- Flow switches check that the flow rates of liquids going into the keg meet specifications. This is important because, while the pressure gauge on a manifold could indicate the correct pump pressures, the flow switch signals a low-flow alarm and stops the process. There is probably a blockage in the line or cleaning head and the station is not getting the correct flow.

- Liquid conductivity detectors, or wet–dry probes, check that the liquid goes into the keg and comes out of the keg per the specifications of the program.
- Temperature probes may be used to indicate that the proper cleaning solution temperatures are met and also to ensure that the keg reaches the temperature needed for sterility.
- Proximity or read switches on the keg clamps tell the PLC whether a keg is present, and when clamped onto the cleaning or filling head, another proximity or read switch is used to check that the stroke is correct for the spear adapter and has opened the keg valve all the way.
- The beer flow meter helps ensure that the correct amount of beer is filled into the keg.

Likewise, the PLC programming in the machine is the product of the people who supplied that piece of equipment and a key part of their expertise is used to make sure that the entire process is done safely. Certain aspects of the program including settings for the chemical solution purges and other critical safety parameters, which may be adjusted only by the supplier. It is important that thought is put into making any program change and that a complete evaluation is done if program changes are made to ensure the process integrity remains intact. This does not mean that program fine tuning for wash times, steam holds, etc. cannot be made by the brewery, but the program should be password protected to ensure that an operator in a hurry cannot alter the integrity of the washing process. Only certain people should have access to the program.

Monitoring Washes

As mentioned before, it is important to monitor wash pressures, temperatures, and titrations where necessary. It is also of utmost importance to check the wash solutions as they enter and leave the kegs. A probe guard routine in the program can provide a double check on the cleaning cycles.

For instance, the flow switches can be used to check that the flow of a wash to a keg is correct and a conductivity probe at the exit of the keg can be used to check the flow out of it. As mentioned previously, when washing a keg, liquid enters the keg faster than it can exit, without any gas purging, so at the end of a wash there should still be some liquid present in the keg. If during the gas purge the keg is seen to empty too quickly, then not enough wash solution entered the keg and it should be rejected. Probe guard routines check that the wash did indeed enter the keg and not, as in the case of a keg with a bent neck or a faulty or leaking connection head, leak onto the floor.

● KEG LINE LAYOUTS

Figure 24.27 shows a simple keg line layout with two lanes capable of together producing about 100 kegs per hour. The operator puts the kegs on by hand, they run through the external washer and then into the lanes with two washing heads, one sterilizing station, and one filling head each. There is a three-tank, detergent-and-rinse-water reclaim system. The keg comes out and is turned from

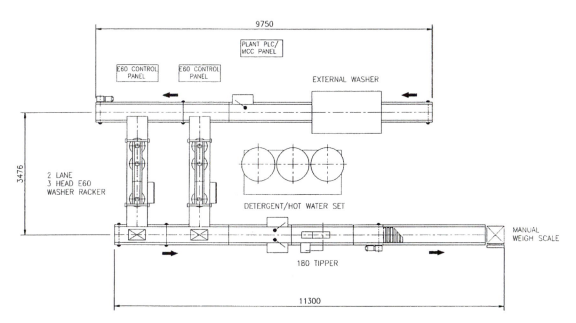

FIGURE 24.27. Keg line layout with two washing and filling lanes capable of together producing 100 kegs per hour. (Courtesy Briggs of Burton)

neck down to neck up and then weighed and palletized by hand, possibly using a hoist fitted with a load cell to check the weight and ensure it is full.

Figure 24.28 shows a more sophisticated line with six cleaning and filling lanes. Each lane cleans and fills 100 kegs per hour, so this is a 600-keg-per-hour plant. Unlike the line in Figure 24.27, this line features automatic depalletizing and palletizing. The keg turner on the infeed looks to see whether the keg needs to be turned upside down. Sometimes robotic arms are used to depalletize and turn the kegs onto the line and then turn and palletize them coming off the line.

● ONE-WAY KEGS

Because of the expanding marketplace, the increased cost of kegs, and the possibility of shipping kegs long distances and having no control over their return, there are new technologies surfacing for one-way or disposable kegs. They can come in various forms and have many advantages for certain applications.

One-way kegs are lighter than the standard stainless-steel kegs and are available on demand. One-way kegs do not normally require washing or sterilizing, so there is no need to spend the money, time, and utilities to clean the keg. Additionally, the kegs do not have to be returned, so the wait for kegs to come back from the trade is eliminated.

The energy required for the distributor to pick up the kegs and ship them back to the brewery is also eliminated. One of the most attractive points about the one-way keg concept is that there are no keg capital losses. A deposit collected on a keg from the distributor usually is about 25% or less than the actual cost to replace that keg. The one-way keg concept does not involve any deposits or any keg return. Additionally, there is no capital tied up with a large keg float dedicated to long-distance markets. While ready-to-use, one-way kegs can be brought in to order, for one type there are machines available that can blow-mold and fill these kegs as needed, saving a huge cost in keg capital and warehousing.

There are two types of one-way kegs. One is essentially a bag in a box. This type of keg is constructed of a steel or plastic keg shell with a valve and a spear, but attached to the spear is a plastic bag. To fill it, beer is introduced into the bag. When dispensing it, compressed air, instead of CO_2, can be used outside of the bag to push the beer out and through the draft system. The steel shell is then recycled.

The other system is constructed of polyethylene terephthalate (PET). The PET keg arrives at the brewery and is filled with CO_2 and then filled with beer. The PET material contains oxygen barriers and scavengers and also has CO_2 barriers to slow down carbonation loss. The working pressure is 42.5 psig (3 bar), the bursting pressure is about 101 psig (7 bar). The PET keg comes in two forms. It can be filled and then put into a box, or it comes in a

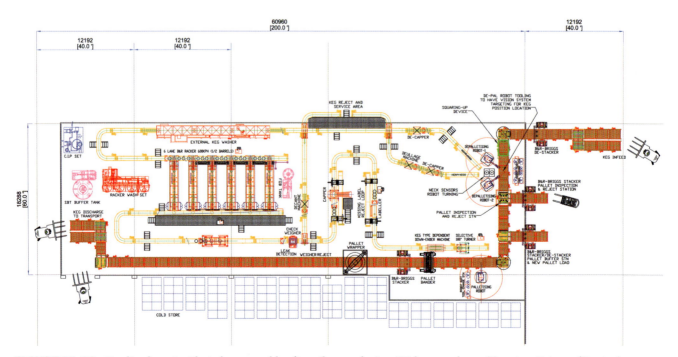

FIGURE 24.28. Keg line layout with six lanes capable of together producing 600 kegs per hour. (Courtesy Briggs of Burton)

shell that can be run through a regular keg line (without the washing and sterilizing steps) (Fig. 24.29).

These kegs can be filled manually with a modified keg tapper or by using a filling machine for higher production. The filling machines do not need to have cleaning equipment and they can come with a blow-molder to form the kegs from plugs prior to filling.

The keg valves are designed to be tapped twice, once during the fill and once during tapping in the trade. Once untapped, the keg depressurizes and it is then safe to dispose of or recycle it; it cannot be reused. If the keg is kept pressurized, then there might be a safety issue with its disposal.

FIGURE 24.29. PET one-way disposable kegs with box for manual filling (left) and a keg template for running through a keg filling line (right). (Courtesy Petainer, Inc.)

SUMMARY

Most kegs used worldwide are the single-valve keg, also called the Sankey keg. The single-valve keg allows for cleaning and dispensing through a single keg valve. Keg cleaning machines are designed to perform intensive washing cycles on returned kegs according to the needs of the brewery. The design of the keg washing program involves an analysis of the particular brewery's situation, including types of product run, keg float size, and return time for kegs from the trade. The keg rotation and product influences the type of washing program that should be used. A brewpub with in-house sales of filtered, nonflavored beers requires only a single, relatively short wash cycle. A brewer shipping very long distances and selling heavily yeasted or flavored beers requires a much more intensive wash program.

Regardless, attention must be paid to setting up the procedures for keg washing, from initial inspection through the cleaning and filling cycles to the final inspection, to ensure that the machine is performing correctly and that only properly cleaned and filled kegs are sold back into the trade. Periodic visual inspections should be built into any program to verify that the machine and the program are actually cleaning the keg.

New technologies are being developed to provide alternatives to the concept of a keg float and may one day replace kegs sent out to distant markets or indeed the concept of returnable kegs altogether.

CHAPTER 25

Brewery and Packaging Hall Cleaning and Sanitizing

GEORGE AGIUS
Diversey, Inc., part of Sealed Air—Food Group

Successful cleaning in brewing operations combines principles from various disciplines, including chemistry, microbiology, and mechanical, electrical, and software engineering. The same principles can be applied to operations of different sizes, ranging from brew-on-premises facilities to the very large manufacturing operations.

This chapter attempts to explain the interrelationship between the various physical and chemical principles in determining the mechanical design and operational steps to be taken in optimizing the cleaning of equipment surfaces, with specific reference to the conditions typically found in brewing operations.

What Is a Clean Surface?

A clean surface can be defined as one that is totally free from residual soils or films and any sort of harmful microorganisms, such as bacteria or yeast.

A strict application of these criteria means that a clean surface can never be achieved given the practical limitations of equipment coupled with economic and environmental considerations. Rather than define cleanliness in absolute terms, it is often useful to establish testable criteria that define clean surfaces. This enables an operator to monitor the success of a cleaning and sanitizing operation by means of tests that are based on measuring some chemical, physical, or microbiological parameter (Kulkarni et al., 1975).

The stage in the brewing process in which the equipment is cleaned determines the kind of test to be performed and the definition of satisfactory test criteria. For example, the microbiological criteria for defining a clean inside surface of a bright beer tank would be considerably more severe than that for the outside surface of a tank, because contamination in the former case can lead to spoilage of the beer (Plett, 1985).

The nature of the tests can be

- microbiological: less than 200 microorganisms per 100 cm^2 (15.5 square inches);
- physical: uniform sheeting occurs without breaks when distilled water is sprayed onto a surface; or
- chemical: tests for a specific class of compounds, such as proteins, fats, and minerals.

These types of tests can be done at periodic intervals to validate the success of a cleaning and sanitizing process and ensure the continued quality of the product produced.

Why Clean?

Cleaning is done to achieve a combination of different objectives. Which combination of cleaning objectives is more important at any particular processing stage would depend on what effect they might have on the quality of the beer being produced. Some of the objectives are

- eliminating microorganisms that can spoil beer;
- removing soils or films from surfaces that could harbor microorganisms;
- ensuring efficient plant and equipment operation, such as the removal of surface films or scales that could interfere with heat transfer efficiency;
- maintaining a visually appealing and safe working environment; and
- meeting existing regulatory mandates.

Cleaning surfaces usually involves a detergent step and a rinse to remove surface soils. This is followed by a sanitizing step designed to kill any residual microorganisms that have survived the previous steps. Sanitizing forms an integral part of the cleaning process.

Generally, sanitizing is not effective without the previous removal of soils that could shield microorganisms from the effect of sanitizers.

● FACTORS AFFECTING CLEANING

Several interrelated factors influence cleaning action. They are

- type of soil to be removed,
- water quality, and
- surface material and finish.

These first three factors are usually determined by the conditions of the plant.

The actual cleaning process can be controlled by these four critical variables.

- *Temperature* during the cleaning/detergent step
- Contact *time* during the detergent steps
- Mechanical *action*
- Detergent *concentration* or chemical activity

In a typical cleaning situation, the mode of cleaning can limit which of these variables can be controlled to maximize cleaning. For example, during manual cleaning, the temperature cannot exceed 105°F (40°C) and the detergent type and concentration are limited for safety reasons, but time and mechanical action can be quite high.

The following sections review these factors individually and discuss their interrelationship.

Types of Soil

The types of soil left over from processing can be characterized into two general types: surface adherent soils and loose soils.

Loose soils are usually easy to remove from surfaces, and this can be achieved by thorough water rinsing. Adherent soils are more difficult to remove and require the use of detergents. These soils are bonded to the surface and can be characterized as organic and inorganic soils. Organic soils include materials such as proteins, fats and oils, carbohydrates, and resins from polymerization reactions.

Inorganic soils include calcium carbonate or hard-water scales and beer stone soils. Most soils would normally consist of a combination of both organic and inorganic

TABLE 25.1. Detergent Choice Is Greatly Influenced by the Type of Soil to be Removed

Application	Soil Type	Frequency of Cleaning	Detergent	Temperature	Time
Milling to wort cooling	Proteins	Weekly to monthly	2–4% Blended caustic	175°F (80°C)	Hours
Brew/wort kettle	Proteins	Every two to six brews	2–4% Blended caustic	175°F (80°C)	1–2 hours
	Fats				
	Polyphenols				
	Resins				
Wort cooler	Proteins	After very brew	2–4% Blended caustic	175°F (80°C)	1 hour
	Fats		Sanitize		
	Polyphenols				
	Resins				
Fermenters	Yeast deposits	After each use	2–4% Blended caustic	Ambient to warm	30 minutes
	Polyphenol resins		Acid cleaning		
	Beer stone		Sanitize		
	Proteins				
Aging tanks/ bright beer tank/lines	Beer stone	Every 10 days	Caustic or acid cleaner under CO_2	Ambient	30 minutes
	Polyphenols		Sanitize		
	Yeast deposits				
Yeast area	Proteins	After every use	Blended Caustic/acid	Ambient	30 minutes
	Sugars		Sanitize		
	Fats				

components. The choice of detergent employed to clean a surface is necessarily greatly influenced by the type of soil being removed, as shown in Table 25.1.

Fats

Fats are long-chain fatty acid esters with glycerol. The removal of fats from surfaces requires that the detergent solution reaches a temperature greater than 120°F (50°C). This allows the soil fats to soften and liquefy, enabling the surfactant component to emulsify and suspend them in solution.

Alkali detergents are also used to hydrolyze the fats and break them down into glycerol and fatty acids, a process known as saponification.

Enzymes that break down fats, known as lipases, can also be used to help remove fat soils, although their use is very limited because of the fear that enzyme residuals will interact with beer and affect its properties.

Proteins

Proteins are made up of a large number of amino acids joined together via an amide link. Shorter sequences of amino acids are known as polypeptides.

Proteins can be removed by alkaline- and acid-based cleaners, both acting as catalysts to promote breakdown by water, a reaction known as hydrolysis.

The inclusion of oxidizing agents in the detergent helps to break down proteins, which are then easier to dissolve and suspend. Protease enzymes can also be used to aid in the breakdown of proteins; but again, fear of enzyme residuals on the cleaned surface and their possible effect on beer has limited their applications in the brewing industry.

Carbohydrates

Carbohydrates are made up of strings of sugar molecules. Starch and cellulose are carbohydrates and are also known as polysaccharides.

Starches and carbohydrates are also broken down by both alkaline and acidic cleaners, which promote the reaction with water (hydrolysis), to simple sugar units. The individual sugar molecules are much more soluble and therefore easier to remove in water solutions.

Amylase enzymes can also break down carbohydrates. The breakdown of carbohydrates to sugars by natural enzymes is used as part of the malting process.

Polymeric Resins

Resin deposits are formed through a reaction between sugars and amino acids and their subsequent rearrangement in the presence of heat. This reaction is collectively known as the Maillard reaction. This reaction usually starts during malting and continues during wort boiling. The same reaction is responsible for the browning of foods during cooking.

Mineral Deposits

Mineral deposits can be hardness scales—typically calcium and magnesium carbonates. Depending on the water quality, hardness scales are deposited on surfaces, especially heat-exchange surfaces where the higher temperature of a solution promotes the deposition of calcium carbonate. Calcium carbonate, unlike other salts, shows an inverse solubility—that is, it becomes less soluble with an increase in temperature.

Mineral deposits in brewing include beer stone, which is a mixed precipitate of a calcium phosphate and calcium oxalate.

Mineral deposits or scales are best removed by acids or by the use of sequestrants.

Water Quality

Water plays a large role in the cleaning and sanitizing process and is the liquid medium that carries, in dissolved form, the various specialized cleaning agents. In fact, water itself actually facilitates the breakdown reactions of various soils, where acids and alkalis act as catalysts to speed up this reaction.

Water is also the medium used to carry off nondissolved soil particles, especially during the first rinse steps of a cleaning process.

Water inherently has dissolved minerals. Which dissolved minerals are found in the water depends on the origin of the water source and the materials that have been in contact with the water, as well as any treatment the water may have been subjected to.

It is important to describe some of these materials and how they interact with other substances. Potable water usually has a number of positive metal ions (cations) dissolved in it, e.g., sodium, potassium, calcium, magnesium, and iron. Counterbalancing the cations are the anions, negatively charged ions such as chlorides, carbonates, bicarbonates, sulfates, and phosphates. The bicarbonates and carbonates dissolved in water play a large role in water chemistry.

Calcium and magnesium bicarbonates are soluble in water. However, when water is heated, the bicarbonates change to carbonates as carbon dioxide (CO_2) is driven off.

$$2HCO_3^- \rightarrow CO_3^{2-} + H_2O + CO_2$$

Carbonate salts of calcium and magnesium are insoluble and, therefore, precipitation of calcium and magnesium carbonate scales (hardness scale) occurs.

The hardness of water is expressed as parts per million (ppm) of calcium carbonate. Another measure used is grains per gallon, which converts to 17.1 ppm of calcium carbonate.

Rain and distilled water have no dissolved ions; however, on contact with air, CO_2 from the air immediately dissolves and reacts with the water to produce H^+ and bicarbonate ions.

$$CO_2 + H_2O \rightarrow H^+ + HCO_3^-$$

If rain water containing dissolved CO_2 comes into contact with limestone rock (calcium and magnesium carbonate), a reaction takes place in which the limestone dissolves to produce calcium bicarbonate.

$$CaCO_3 \text{ (limestone)} + CO_2 + H_2O \rightarrow Ca(HCO_3)_2$$

These dissolved calcium and magnesium ions in water cause the precipitation of anionic detergents (e.g., soap), rendering them ineffective.

To remove the dissolved calcium and magnesium hardness ions from water, the ions are exchanged with more soluble sodium ions in a process known as softening. This is done by passing water over an ion exchange resin bed, which is restored by periodic regeneration with a concentrated solution of sodium chloride.

Another way to neutralize the effect of hardness ions on anionic detergents is to include sequestrants or chelants with the detergent-formulated products. Sequestrants surround and tie up the hardness ions, thereby neutralizing their effects. Whether the water should be treated (softened) or it relies on the formulated detergent to control hardness depends on the economics of the application.

In addition to dissolved minerals, water can carry microorganisms. It is essential that the water used in brewing and cleaning be treated to remove any microorganisms. This is commonly achieved by injecting a low dose of chlorine. Other treatments include ultraviolet light, ozonation, or treatment with a low dose of chlorine dioxide.

Water and dissolved minerals also play a critical role in the corrosion of surfaces. Certain anions, such as chlorides, aggravate the corrosion process of stainless steels, especially if the water is acidic or has a low pH, such as an excess of H^+ ions.

In summary, water plays a critical role in many aspects of the cleaning process. Understanding the nature of the water being used is essential either to help with the selection of suitable detergents or the choice of the pretreatment used for the water that is used in making up cleaning solutions.

Surface Material and Finish

Stainless steel has become the material of choice for most processing equipment, although a variety of other materials may still be encountered in breweries. These include epoxy linings, plastics, synthetic rubber (hoses and gaskets), and a variety of metals that include aluminum, copper, brass, and mild steels. Stainless steel itself comes in a variety of grades, with some grades more corrosion resistant than others. Poor-quality welding can also present a corrosion-prone surface.

The adhesion of a particular type of soil to a surface varies with the chemical nature of the surface. For example, a scale deposit on stainless steel can be quite tenacious but can be much less adherent to a plastic surface. The finish on the surface can also affect the adhesion of soils. Recent work has shown that stainless steel should be purchased based more on surface defect parameters than on surface finish type (Frank and Chmielewski, 2000).

Noninhibited alkaline detergents can seriously corrode aluminum parts or other soft metals.

The choice of detergent needs to be carefully considered based on minimizing damage to the equipment surface material and maximizing the removal of any prevailing soil in the shortest time.

When considering a surface over which a cleaning solution is flowing (Fig. 25.1), three layers can be identified.

- Boundary or stationary layer
- Laminar transition layer
- Turbulent flow layer

Mechanical Action

The layers listed above may or may not all be present, depending on the mode of applications and flow conditions (Chapman et al., 1985; Paulsson and Tragardh, 1985).

To achieve effective cleaning, any detergent in the bulk of the solution turbulent layer must first reach the soil. These detergent components are carried to the edge of the laminar layer by the turbulence in the bulk flow. From

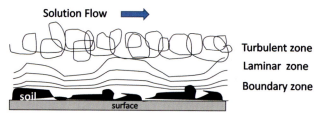

FIGURE 25.1. Solution flow layers. (Courtesy G. Agius)

here, the detergent has to cross (by diffusion) through the laminar layer to reach the soil and surface. Once the detergent reaches the soil, it then diffuses and reacts with the soil, dislodging it from the surface. The detached soils, soil breakdown products, and detergent diffuse out through the laminar layer, where the turbulent bulk flow layer carries them away (Hankinson and Carver, 1968).

From this brief explanation, some conclusions can be drawn about the best conditions to clean a surface.

- It is essential to minimize the thickness of the laminar layer, thereby reducing the detergent diffusion path to reach the soil. In fact, calculations have shown that the laminar layer achieves its lowest thickness when the mean flow velocity is 1.5 m/second (5 feet/second) in pipelines, and this value is the same for different pipe diameters (Timperley, 1981).
- The relative velocity between the turbulent layer and laminar layer should be as high as possible to create a shearing force that aids in the removal of soil.
- The concentration of the detergent should be as high as possible because diffusion processes increase if there is a concentration difference.
- An increase in solution temperature helps to speed up the diffusion rate across the laminar layer.

Temperature

As discussed in the previous section, temperature has an important effect on the action of detergents. Generally, as the temperature increases, the rate of reaction of the cleaner with soil increases, roughly doubling for every 50°F (10°C) rise. The increase in temperature also speeds up the transport of detergent components by diffusion through the laminar layer of the solution at the surface.

● CHEMICAL COMPONENTS OF CLEANING SOLUTIONS

This section explores the chemical components used to make up an industrial cleaner. It is the chemical component whose type and concentration provide the chemical activity needed to remove soils. As described in the earlier sections, different materials are used to react with, dislodge, and suspend breakdown products from a variety of soils. At the same time, materials are also used in an industrial cleaner to control hardness or create foam, depending on the desired application.

Alkalis

Strong alkaline materials or caustics, such as sodium hydroxide or potassium hydroxide, form the basis of many of the heavy-duty industrial cleaning products. Caustic materials provide hydroxyl ions (OH^-) that often speed up the reaction of water with soils (hydrolysis). Hydrolysis breaks up different complex soils into their simpler elements.

One of the most common and least costly alkali sources is sodium hydroxide, also known as caustic soda. Other alkali sources can be used, such as potassium hydroxide (caustic potash), whenever a formulator would like to overcome some solubility constraints with the design of a cleaning product.

The hydroxyl ions from these caustic materials react with CO_2 from the air or residual CO_2 present in the vessels to produce carbonates. Since carbonates do not clean as well as the hydroxides, this reaction severely degrades the cleaning performance of alkaline products, especially under reuse conditions (Fig. 25.2). In fact, the amount of carbonates formed in a cleaning solution needs to be continually monitored with suitable tests to ensure optimal performance. This is especially important because simple tests to determine the concentration of hydroxide ions do not distinguish these from carbonates, giving erroneous results.

The inevitable presence of carbonates in caustic solutions causes the precipitation of metal carbonates, particularly calcium and magnesium carbonates. Suitable chelants need to be present with the caustic to prevent this precipitation.

The high concentration of hydroxyl ions often also causes the precipitation of insoluble metal hydroxides. The most common of these are the calcium and magnesium

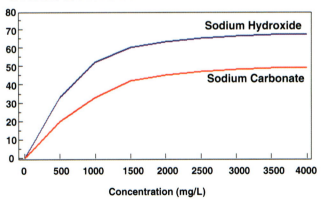

FIGURE 25.2. Protein removal with different concentrations of sodium hydroxide and sodium carbonate. (Courtesy Diversey, Inc.)

precipitates, brought in with the water used to make up solutions. Formulated detergents based on sodium hydroxide often include sequestrants to tie up the metal ions and prevent the formation of hydroxide or carbonate precipitates.

Caustics also react with and damage soft metals, e.g., zinc and aluminum. Alkaline cleaning products can incorporate suitable inhibitors to suppress this reaction. Notwithstanding this, great care needs to be exercised when selecting alkaline cleaners for use on soft metals.

Caustics, especially hot-caustic solutions, are unfortunately extremely dangerous because of their corrosivity to skin and eyes, and they require careful and safe handling procedures. Spent caustic solutions also contribute to high pH in the effluent and need to be neutralized before release. In spite of some disadvantages, caustics are widely used as the basis of every heavy-duty application cleaner.

Surfactants

Surfactants are organic molecules that have two distinct chemical groups on the same molecule (Fig. 25.3). One group tends to be soluble in water, or water loving (hydrophilic), and is typically a carboxylate, sulphonate, ether, amide, or ammonium. The other group tends to be oil loving, or water hating (hydrophobic), and is typically a long-carbon-chain paraffin. The most common and familiar natural surfactant is soap, which is made up of a long-carbon-chain paraffin attached to a carboxylate group.

Surfactants are able to lift and suspend soil materials that are normally incompatible with water, such as oil.

When a surfactant is added to water, the hydrophobic part of the molecule dissolves on the surface of the oil. The nature of the oil surface is changed since only the hydrophilic part of the surfactant now faces the water. This allows the otherwise insoluble oily soil to disperse in water when surrounded by the surfactant molecules. The oily soil breaks up into tiny droplets, each drop being surrounded by surfactant molecules, which can stay dispersed in the water.

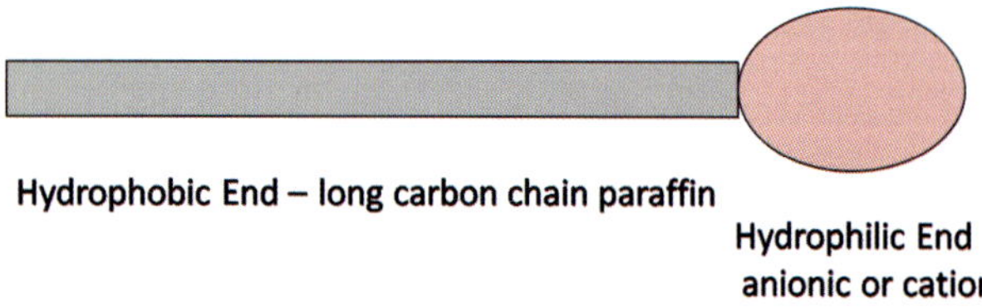

Surfactants therefore perform two essential functions. First, they allow the water to "wet" oily (hydrophobic) surfaces by reducing the surface tension between the water and the oil. Second, they allow the oil droplets to stay "dispersed", a process known as emulsification.

Natural soap, although a very useful surfactant, suffers from the fact that it forms insoluble precipitate with calcium and magnesium in the water. The precipitate is usually identified as a scum on the solution interface. To overcome this limitation, a number of synthetic surfactants have been produced that are better able to resist precipitation.

Generally, surfactants are classified according to the end water-loving group. If the end group is an acid, such as a negative carboxylate or a sulphonate group, the surfactant is classed as an anionic surfactant. Soap falls into this latter category.

If the end group carries a positive charge, such as ammonium, the surfactant is classed as cationic. When the end group is neutral, the surfactant is known as nonionic. Yet another class of surfactants, the amphoterics, have both cationic and anionic water-loving groups on the molecule. This results in a large number of surfactants in the marketplace with a variety of properties to cater to specific applications.

Surfactants are also used to perform other functions. It is beyond the scope of this chapter to discuss these in detail. However, depending on their structure, surfactants are selected for different applications based on their ability to create stable foam, act as defoamers, or mix with other cleaning ingredients to make stable formulations. Some are selected for their antimicrobiological or biodegradability properties.

The successful selection of surfactants to incorporate into a cleaning product to meet the need of a particular application requires a combination of great skill and knowledge together with lab and field experimentation.

Builders

Builders are substances that can aid in the cleaning process and can provide synergy with other cleaning components, improving the overall performance of a cleaning product. Builders can often perform more than one function.

Complex Phosphates

A class of compounds used as builders are the complex phosphates, the most common being sodium tripolyphosphate and sodium hexametaphosphate. Complex phosphates are used in alkaline cleaners, and they themselves contribute to the overall alkalinity of the

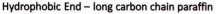

Hydrophobic End – long carbon chain paraffin

Hydrophilic End
anionic or cationic

FIGURE 25.3. Structure of a surfactant molecule. (Courtesy G. Agius)

product. In addition, the complex phosphates can sequester or chelate calcium and magnesium ions, preventing them from precipitating as carbonates, hydroxides, etc. They also act as "threshold inhibitors", in which a tiny nonstoichiometric amount of the material suppresses the formation of calcium/magnesium carbonate hard scales by suppressing crystal growth.

Complex phosphates also assist in the emulsification of organic soils. In many areas, phosphate levels in the effluent are restricted. While a brewery may have several other sources of phosphorous that can contribute to the effluent, the choice of cleaners that contain phosphates needs to be considered in relation to contribution from other sources.

Chelants/Sequestrants

Chelants are organic or inorganic compounds that have the ability to surround and lock up metal ions, such as calcium, magnesium, or iron, thereby preventing these metal ions from reacting to form precipitates such as carbonates.

Sequestrants, when included in cleaning products, can often help dissolve mineral deposits, which often bind complex soils. Sequestrants remove and tie up metal ions from the deposit, thereby assisting to loosen and remove a complex soil deposit.

The chelants do not exhibit some of the other useful detergent characteristics that the complex phosphates do. Some of the more commonly used chelants are ethylene diamine tetra acetic acid (EDTA) (Fig. 25.4), nitritotriacetic acid (NTA), gluconates, and organic phosphates. The latter two are widely used in heavy-duty alkaline detergent formulations. The organic phosphates also have threshold inhibition properties.

The choice of sequestrants in a cleaner is predicated on the type of soil being removed, cost, and effluent considerations.

Polymers

Several types of synthetic polymers are included in various cleaners. Some of the more common polymers used are the polyacrylates. Polymers exhibit properties similar to those of the complex phosphates and have, in many cases, replaced phosphates, especially in cleaning applications where phosphorus levels in the effluent are restricted. Polymers also prevent scale formation by threshold inhibition, such as interfering with the deposition of scale by interfering with crystal growth.

Acidic Cleaners

Acidic cleaners are gaining favor in recent years over alkaline cleaners for certain applications, especially for cleaning equipment following the fermentation stage. Their biggest advantage is that acid-based cleaners do not react with CO_2 and are excellent for protein deposit removal at low pH (Fig. 25.5). This simple fact results in great time savings in equipment turnaround and shorter cleaning-in-place (CIP) cycles since it eliminates the need to purge CO_2 before circulating the cleaner and to recharge with CO_2 after cleaning. It also eliminates the inherent risk of tank implosion that results when the reaction of alkaline cleaners with CO_2 creates a vacuum.

Modern acidic cleaners are formulated to include a number of ingredients that greatly enhance their soil removal performance. Acidic cleaners are excellent at

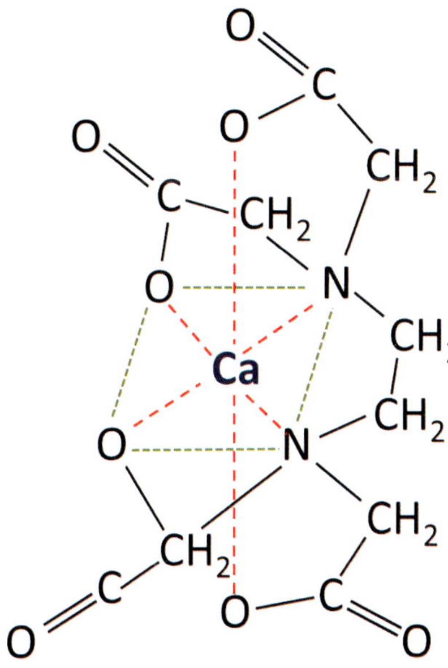

FIGURE 25.4. Calcium–ethylene diamine tetra acetic acid (EDTA) complex. (Courtesy G. Agius)

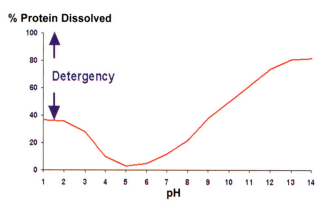

FIGURE 25.5. Protein solubility with pH. (Courtesy Diversey, Inc.)

removing mineral deposits. Typically, acidic cleaners are based on phosphoric acid, mostly because phosphoric acid is least corrosive to stainless steel. However, mixtures of phosphoric acid with other acids, such as nitric acid or complex organic acids, are also used in different situations.

Chemical Activity—Summary

Detergents play a key role in the overall process of plant hygiene.

The choice of raw materials in a modern industrial cleaner is governed to maximize performance during the cleaning steps and at the same time work within several other constraints, such as human safety, environmental impact, exiting plant materials, asset safety, and finally acceptable cost.

In a modern brewery environment, the cost of cleaning should not be based solely on the cost of the detergent or the detergent step only but rather should be based on considerations of the overall costs, which factor in all aspects of the cleaning process. This may include the costs of energy, water, labor, equipment turnaround, and effluent surcharges. Modern monitoring equipment and data logging provide the necessary tools to enable the relevant measurements of the parameters to determine overall costs relatively easily.

Finally, difficult cleaning situations demand expertise to identify the root cause of a problem and a structured analytical approach to arrive at a solution. Indiscriminate use of extra chemicals in a trial-and-error mode without consideration or understanding the mechanical configuration of the equipment can often lead only to costly operations or worse and to possible equipment damage.

● CHEMICAL SANITIZERS

The application of sanitizers usually follows a cleaning step, and it is designed to further reduce the number of any microorganisms that may survive the cleaning process. In North America, non-food-contact sanitizers are required to reduce target microorganisms by 3 log 10 after 5 minutes of contact time. A sanitizer that is applied to a previously cleaned surface should reduce the target microorganisms by 5 log 10 in 30 seconds. While ideally it is desirable to achieve total sterility, this may often be operationally difficult to achieve. Even so, the standard of sanitizing achieved can be remarkably high. Sanitizers should never be used to overcome the effects of poor cleaning. In fact, sanitizers are ineffective at reaching and killing microorganisms if soil residues have not been removed.

It is common practice in North America for a sanitizer rinse to be the last step when cleaning process surfaces. This implies that sanitizers are not rinsed off the surface of the process equipment but are only allowed to drain for sufficient time at the end of a cleaning cycle. The rationale for this mode of operation is that a water rinse could reintroduce microbial contamination. This approach is by no means universal around the world; there are places where rinse regulations may demand that a potable water rinse follow the application of a sanitizer. Sanitizers in North America are carefully scrutinized for human toxicity and product residuals. This necessarily limits the choice of sanitizers that are approved for use in brewing operations.

An ideal sanitizer should satisfy the following criteria.

- Have a wide range of antimicrobial activity
- Be nontoxic
- Leave residues that have no effect on beer taste, haze, or foam
- Act rapidly to kill microorganisms
- Be active over a wide pH range
- Be noncorrosive to surfaces
- Be cost effective

In practice, most chemical sanitizer categories fail one or more of these criteria and the choice of sanitizers for breweries can be limited considerably. In the sections that follow, different chemical types of sanitizers and their properties are described.

Quaternary Ammonium Compounds

Quaternary ammonium compounds (QACs) are a class of sanitizers made up of complex organic molecules. Their structure resembles that of a cationic surfactant, and consequently, they exhibit surface-active properties, such as wetting by lowering the surface tension of water, and foaming. QACs are fairly stable and noncorrosive to most surface materials. While generally effective against most microorganisms, some bacteria and yeasts are resistant to QACs.

QACs are not recommended for CIP applications because of their foaming characteristics. The surfactant properties of QACs are suspected to have an effect on the retention of beer foam. Therefore, QACs are not recommended for sanitizing the inside surfaces of beer process tanks, where QAC residuals can mix with beer.

However, QACs are effective for mold prevention on cellar walls or any outside surface cleaning. QACs are generally used and are allowed at up to 200 ppm of active quat.

QACs are believed to interfere with the structure of the microorganism cell wall, thereby disrupting the flow of metabolites and water across the cell wall. Because of their cationic nature, QACs are neutralized and rendered ineffective by anionic solutions.

Halogen Sanitizers

Halogen sanitizers include various molecular species or mixtures of species formed by the halogen family, which includes chlorine, bromine, and iodine.

Hypochlorite

The most common halogen sanitizer is chlorine. Chlorine gas reacts with water to produce hypochlorous acid (HOCl) at close-to-neutral pH. To avoid the dangers of handling chlorine gas, sodium hypochlorite solutions are conveniently used to make hypochlorous acid solutions. Sodium hypochlorite, sold at concentrations ranging from 6 to 12%, is the most commonly used product for this purpose. When sodium hypochlorite is added to water at close-to-neutral, pH 7, hypochlorous acid is formed. Sodium hypochlorite is used at up to 200 ppm of available chlorine to sanitize surfaces. The solution of hypochlorite is in contact with the surface to be sanitized for 30–60 seconds. Longer contact time is from 1 to 3 minutes.

Care must be exercised in controlling the concentration and contact time of hypochlorite solutions since excessive concentrations can attack and corrode stainless steel. Because of the corrosivity of hypochlorite solutions to most surfaces, including stainless steel, it is not recommended that hypochlorite solution stay in contact for extended periods. Often, a sterile water rinse follows the sanitizer. Alternatively, beer is processed immediately after the sanitizer solution has thoroughly drained from all equipment surfaces. Hypochlorite is readily deactivated by reaction with organic materials. Therefore, hypochlorite is not recommended as a sanitizing treatment in the presence of high soil loadings. Hypochlorite reacts with phenolic materials to produce chlorinated phenols, which can greatly affect beer taste at low levels. Therefore, beer that contains polyphenols should be prevented from coming into contact with substantial quantities of hypochlorite sanitizer residues.

Sodium hypochlorite stock solutions decompose over time when stored at elevated temperatures or when exposed to ultraviolet light.

Chlorinated Trisodium Phosphate

Chlorinated trisodium phosphate, a powder that readily dissolves in water, is also widely used as a convenient hypochlorite source in the brewing industry. Bromide is sometimes added to chlorinated trisodium phosphate. In solution, the bromide reacts with hypochlorite to produce hypobromous acid, which improves the sanitizer performance by increasing the speed of action and effectiveness over a wider pH range.

Iodine Sanitizers

Iodophors

Iodine has been long used as a disinfectant, particularly for the treatment of superficial skin infections. The main limitations in the past have been its poor water solubility and its powerful staining action on a number of surfaces.

A development that served to overcome these problems was the formulation of iodine complexed to nonionic surface active agents that carried the iodine. These complex iodine surfactant products are typically formulated in an acid medium and are known as iodophors. These products reduce the staining problems and provide a water-based solution of iodine upon dilution in water.

Iodophors have a very wide biocidal spectrum and react directly with the cell. Penetration is very rapid because of the presence of surfactants.

Because of the high content of surfactants, it is difficult to produce iodophors with very low foaming characteristics, which can cause problems in CIP applications. Care must always be exercised to ensure that the temperature of solution does not exceed 120°F (49°C); above that temperature, iodine vapor is released. Iodine solutions are typically used at concentrations of 12–25 ppm of iodine.

Iodine Inorganic Complex

A significant breakthrough in iodine chemistry was the development of a stable proprietary inorganic iodine complex (ICl_2^-). This unique blend of chlorine and iodine in an acid mixture releases iodine when diluted. Since no surfactants are involved, this blend is totally nonfoaming and therefore suitable for CIP application. Furthermore, the synergistic effect of this blend makes it extremely effective against a wide range of microorganisms, even in cold solutions (40°F [4°C]). The lower levels employed from this unique composition also reduce corrosion potential and use-solution residuals have no effect on beer. Concentrations of 6–25 ppm of available iodine are used for surface sanitation at temperatures between 32°F (0°C) to ambient and at contact times ranging from 15 to 60 seconds. The effectiveness, low foam, and acidic nature of this sanitizer make it an excellent complement to acidic cleaning programs under CO_2.

Chlorine Dioxide

Chlorine dioxide is an extremely effective surface sanitizer with some distinct advantages over hypochlorite or chlorine. The major disadvantage with chlorine dioxide is that it cannot be stored or transported; it needs to be produced at the site immediately before use. This requires reliable and safe equipment that reacts with suitable materials to produce chlorine dioxide at the highest yields possible.

Chlorine dioxide solutions can be generated by various methods. The more common methods all involve a solution of sodium chlorite. In one method, a solution of sodium chlorite is reacted with hydrochloric acid in a specially designed reactor. A second method involves the reaction of sodium hypochlorite, hydrochloric acid, and sodium chlorite solutions. These methods require specially designed reactors that can accurately blend solutions and react the components completely in order to safely generate chlorine dioxide (Environmental Protection Agency, 1999).

In a more recent development, the safety of generating chlorine dioxide has been greatly improved by reacting the hydrochloric acid and sodium chlorite reaction indirectly through the use of an acidified ion-exchange resin bed. The low concentration of acidified chlorite produced is then quickly converted to chlorine dioxide by passing the acidified chlorite over a special catalyst. This system has tremendously improved the safety of generating chlorine dioxide.

Another method of generating chlorine dioxide is an electrochemical membrane system that generates chlorine dioxide by electrolysis of a sodium chlorite solution. Electrolysis produces a stream of sodium hydroxide and hydrogen at the cathode, which requires care in handling when larger quantities of chlorine dioxide are being generated by this method.

Water solutions of chlorine dioxide have several advantages over chlorine and hypochlorites (Masschelein, 1979; Salisbury, 1983).

- They are effective at low concentrations (1–5 ppm) for sanitizing surfaces.
- They are not readily deactivated by organic soils.
- They are microbiologically effective over a wide pH range.
- They do not produce chlorophenols and trihalomethanes (THM).
- Chlorine dioxide can be used as a sanitizer with both caustic cleaners and acidic cleaners under CO_2 atmosphere.

Some of the disadvantages of chlorine dioxide are as follows.

- They can be more costly than chlorine.
- They require expensive generating equipment and some maintenance costs.
- They require care to ensure safe handling of the reactive chemicals.
- Tests for chlorine dioxide can give misleading results if interferences are not recognized.

When using chlorine dioxide, it is important that the concentration of chlorine dioxide in the air does not exceed safety limits. Modern chlorine dioxide-specific sensors can now easily determine the concentration of chlorine dioxide in the air. Chlorine dioxide is currently used in breweries in many applications, such as the treatment of process water and water in cooling towers and as a sanitizer during the CIP of fermenters and aging tanks (Agius et al., 2004).

Peracetic Acid

Peracetic acid (PAA) is sold as an equilibrium mixture formed by the reaction of hydrogen peroxide and acetic acid. PAA is an acidic sanitizer and is nonfoaming, making it suitable for CIP applications. It can also complement acid cleaning programs under CO_2 in brewing operations and be used in open-plant cleaning (OPC) applications. PAA breaks down into acetic acid and water. Solutions of PAA made with water containing chlorides can corrode stainless steel upon prolonged contact. PAA is used at 0.1–3.5% w/v and can be used cold. PAA possesses a wide antimicrobial action, but as with all sanitizers, some bacteria and yeasts can survive PAA at low temperatures.

Acid Anionics

Anionic sanitizers chemically resemble the anionic surfactants described earlier. They are formulated in an acid base. Acid anionics are used at 50–200 ppm and are thought to kill microorganisms by disrupting their cell wall permeability. Being acidic in nature, acid anionics can be used in conjunction with acid cleaning programs. Acid anionic sanitizers are specially formulated to suppress their tendency to foam and have been very successfully used in various CIP programs.

● MODES OF APPLICATION

Some of the general principles discussed in previous sections are used in different ways depending on the mode of application employed in cleaning an equipment surface.

Manual Cleaning

In the case of manual cleaning, or use of a bucket and brush, agitation of the solution reduces the thickness of the laminar layer. The mechanical scrubbing motion that is parallel to the surface produces a large shearing force that helps to dislodge the soil from the surface.

Manual cleaners tend to be milder and less concentrated for safety reasons. However, the increased mechanical action makes up for the lack of chemical action. This mode of cleaning is used for the occasional cleaning of some valves and removable small line pieces. Manual cleaning of equipment is necessarily labor intensive and requires suitable safety precautions. Its use tends to be limited to a minimum in any operation.

Soak Cleaning

In soak cleaning, the laminar layer is the thickest because of the lack of any form of agitation. Detergents have the greatest path to cross to reach soils. This mode of cleaning is, therefore, least efficient. It is often employed in the cleaning of small parts, which can be soaked for an extended period of time. This type of cleaning can be applied to hoses and connections that are not required immediately. Soak cleaning is also utilized for cleaning bottles.

Foaming and Gel Applications (Open-Plant Cleaning)

OPC is the cleaning of all surfaces not in direct contact with beer and consists mainly of foam cleaning but may include any other form of environmental cleaning, e.g., floor cleaning with a machine. Foaming and gel cleaning applications are often used for cleaning exterior surfaces, such as walls, ceiling, exteriors of vessels, and packaging equipment.

In the case of foaming, the detergent is applied by foaming it to the surface (air is allowed to mix with the cleaner solution during spraying to create foam).

The semirigid foam structure carries the detergent and provides some contact time as the foam breaks and runs down a vertical surface. There is very little agitation of the solution to provide any mechanical action on the soils. Mechanical action and soil removal are provided by spraying water under high pressure during the pre- and final rinses.

Gels can be used instead of foams. Gel products contain the necessary detergents and can also be sprayed. On touching the surface, the gel solution forms a semiviscous solution film that adheres to vertical surfaces. The same principles as those used with foam cleaning apply; however, gels can provide a more prolonged contact time during which the detergents can act on the soil. Gels can be rinsed quite readily with water.

Foam cleaners and gels often have to be formulated with safety in mind. Since foam and gel cleaners are applied to the outside surfaces, they are likely to encounter a variety of materials and the choice of cleaner needs to be taken into consideration.

Cleaning-in-Place

For most breweries, CIP is the only practical way to clean the interior surface of tanks, process equipment, valves, and interconnecting pipe work. In fact, CIP has become an integral part of brewery operations in terms of plant design, efficiency, and the way the cleaning process influences the microbiological quality of beer.

During CIP circulation, a high concentration of chemical detergents can be used since the process takes place in a closed environment with plant personnel having no contact with the cleaning solution. The temperature can also be high, up to 175°F (80°C). The time can also be long, but it practically has to be limited since the equipment needs to be returned to production as soon as possible.

During the cleaning step, the detergent solution is circulated through pipes, tanks, and valves to clean the inside surfaces. When the solution is circulated in pipes, the flow is ideally adjusted to reach 5 feet/second or 1.5 m/second. At these flows, the laminar layer is at its thinnest, and the relative velocity between solution bulk and surface is high to provide considerable mechanical shearing action on the soil (Timperley, 1981). This maximizes the mechanical action.

Inside the tanks, the detergent solution is sprayed via a spray ball or a rotating spraying head, and the solution cascades down along the vertical surface of the tank. This provides some mild mechanical action as the solution flows down along the vertical surface. With a rotary spray head, the detergent solution makes passes across the interior surface and is directed to a small area at high speed, and therefore, there is greater mechanical action to help remove soil.

When a puddle of cleaning solution forms at the bottom of the tank, the submerged surface is then essentially cleaned through soaking action and gets very little agitation.

CIP cleaners are formulated with no foaming characteristics since foaming creates cavitation at the circulation pumps.

This section explores in more detail how CIP integrates with plant design and discusses practical ways to maximize the cleaning efficiency while at the same time conserve water, detergents, energy, and time.

A typical general CIP cycle involves the following series of steps.

1. Prerinse step—Water is circulated to remove soluble residue and any loose soil.
2. Detergent step—A detergent solution is prepared to the right concentration, heated to temperature, and circulated for a period of time. In this step, any soil attached to the surface is softened or broken down and dislodged from the surface.
3. Postrinse step—The detergent solution from the previous step is removed along with any dislodged soil.
4. Second wash and rinse step—A second detergent cycle can sometimes be applied as in step 2, followed by a water rinse, depending on the soil being removed.
5. Sanitize step—A sanitizing solution is circulated to reach all the surfaces. This step is intended to kill any microorganisms not removed by any of the previous steps.

In many cases, the sanitizer solution is the last step in the cleaning process. Sometimes the sanitizer is followed by a rinse with sterile water to remove any sanitizer residual. It is important that the water used following the sanitizer be free from microorganisms so that it does not recontaminate the surface.

If the wash solutions are used once and allowed to go to the drain, the CIP is considered a single-use system. In reuse CIP systems, the wash solution and water rinses are recovered. The recovered wash solutions are adjusted for concentration in readiness for the next CIP.

Components of a CIP System

The various solutions are prepared, heated, circulated, and recovered using a dedicated CIP set shown in the schematic in Figure 25.6.

The generic components of a CIP unit are the following.

- A group of designated stainless-steel tanks where the detergent solutions and water rinses are prepared, stored, and recovered after circulation.
- Supply and return centrifugal pumps, usually with variable-speed capability to pump out and return solutions at different flows. This helps to select the best solution flow for the various equipment configurations, tanks sizes, and pipe diameters being cleaned.
- Detergent and sanitizer dosing pumps to add detergents to the preparation tanks when the solutions are being made.
- Heat exchangers to heat the solutions and bring them to required temperatures before starting circulation.
- Stainless-steel valves that can be automatically controlled by a logic controller. Automatic valves are usually activated by compressed air. The system usually includes manually operated valves with a plug or butterfly design.
- Sensors for temperature, flow, conductivity, pressure, and solution levels that send signals to the logic controller microprocessor to completely automate the cleaning cycle.
- Microprocessor programmable logic controllers (PLCs) that store the sequence of events or program to carry out a complete cleaning cycle. The PLCs receive signals from the sensors and, in turn, activate the valves and pumps. They are programmed to open or close valves to direct the flow of solution for completion of each stage in the CIP cycle. They also control solution temperature, concentration, and water levels.

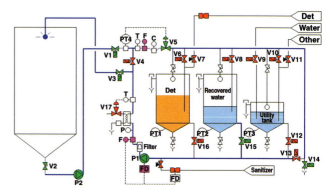

FIGURE 25.6. Schematic of a cleaning-in-place (CIP) system. V = valve, e.g., V2; P = pump; T = temperature sensor; PT = pressure sensor; F = flow sensor; C = conductivity probe; FD = frequency drive; and Det = detergent. (Courtesy Diversey, Inc.)

The detergent and sanitizer pumps used vary depending upon the application. One type of pump is the peristaltic pump. These are electrically driven, while the pumping action is achieved by squeezing a flexible hose in a circular housing. These pumps are used to pump detergents against zero head pressure. The flexible tubing can lose memory, causing a reduction of volume pumped, and must be replaced periodically. Peristaltic pumps are inexpensive.

Air-operated diaphragm pumps are driven by air pressure, which causes a piston attached to a diaphragm to oscillate back and forth and create a pumping action by alternately increasing and reducing the size of the pumping chamber. The pump is always pressurized with air and is activated when there is no backpressure, such as when a valve is opened. Therefore, the opening and closing of an in-line valve on the pump side can actually activate the pump. Air diaphragm pumps are economical and resistant to many chemicals.

Piston-type pumps can be electronically or mechanically driven. Mechanically driven pumps use the energy of the water flowing through a mechanical gear drive to move the piston back and forth. Piston-type pumps can pump product against a head pressure. The pump stroke length can be adjusted to increase or decrease the volume of detergent pumped. These pumps can be activated to proportion the amount of product pumped relative to the total water flow.

General CIP Design Considerations

It is normal for a single CIP unit to clean more than one tank and piping configuration. Connections to divert solutions to each CIP circuit being cleaned are usually done manually through a flow divert panel. It can also be automated and controlled by the PLC by using a valve-operated cluster.

Different CIP sets are used to clean different stages of the brewing process.

The design of the brewery and the way beer is moved between tanks should incorporate considerations for cleaning. Therefore, pipes should be installed and valves placed in such a way as to avoid dead ends that cannot be reached by cleaning solutions during CIP.

The CIP system, including pipes and tanks, should have no leaks. Air leaks on the suction side of pumps can introduce oxygen from the air, which causes undesirable oxidation of the beer at different process stages after fermentation.

To allow for different flows through various tank and interconnecting pipe configurations, variable-flow supply and return pumps are used. Solutions are introduced at the top of the tanks being cleaned by way of spray head devices. Spray heads can be spray balls or rotating spray heads. The flow through the spray heads should be such that the solution speed out of the head is not impinging or bouncing back off the vertical surface of the tank. If the solution bounces off the surface, it is prevented from cascading down the vertical tank surfaces and thereby missing large areas to be cleaned.

The spray heads should be positioned so that the entire tank surface is reached while ensuring that one spray head covers any shadowed areas not reached by another. The number and positioning of the spray heads also depend on the tank configuration being cleaned. Tanks can be tall and vertical or long and horizontal.

While the flow and pressure through the spray head must be adequate to avoid impingement, it must also be matched to the flow in the pipes to ensure that the cleaning solution is moving at the desired 5 feet/second (1.5 m/second) to maximize the cleaning action. This can be achieved by restricting the CIP supply pump's fixed flow to the spray head by inserting an orifice plate in the CIP line to the individual spray ball. It can also be achieved by carefully matching the spray head specifications to the minimum desired flow in the pipe.

The solution sprayed into a tank needs to be evacuated at the same rate with as small a puddle at the bottom of the tank as possible. Vertical areas of the tank below the level of puddle surface are limited to cleaning by action only. The cascading flow of the solution sweeping over these surfaces is absent.

The horizontal tank bottom should also be sloped 0.25 inch per foot and not less than 0.125 inch per foot for proper drainage. The drainpipe should come off the lowest point of the tank bottom and never from the side.

Water rinses should be administered as a series of bursts rather than as a continuous flow. There are two reasons for this. First, any undissolved soil that tends to float on the surface will be drawn out in the vortex created as the water rinse is pumped out to the drain. Second, a lot more of the dissolved detergents or soils can be removed for a given amount of rinse water by dividing it into a series of successive bursts, pumping each out, rather than by using the water to rinse in a continuous flow.

CIP Optimization

CIP Monitoring

There are several sensors on the return line to measure flow, conductivity, and temperature, and they are used to trigger events. The readings from these sensors, as well as signals from valves, can be data logged and displayed graphically against time on a computer monitor by special CIP management software. This enables the operator to verify that all the steps in the CIP have been performed as intended.

In addition, the actual readings can be displayed graphically alongside preset maximum and minimum preset limits, and an alarm alerts the operator when the readings fall outside preset limits. This enables the operator to take immediate corrective action during a CIP cycle, ensuring that all cleaning stages have been properly carried out. The software also archives a record of the full CIP sequence, noting any overrides, alarms, and corrective actions taken.

Interface Management

Breweries are often faced with stringent environmental restrictions, manifested as effluent surcharges and operational cost-control limitations. Therefore, they are prompted to look for ways to minimize the amount of both the water and detergents used. In most modern CIP systems, water and detergent solutions are recovered as much as possible, thereby reducing operational costs and limiting the load of undesirable materials in the effluent.

Interface management of the solutions between different stages of the CIP can further help to reduce water and detergent losses. In this technique, water rinses and detergent solutions are prevented from mixing with each other as changes occur from one step to the next. This helps to maximize the recovery of the detergent solution and avoids losses from mixing with water from pre- or postrinses to the detergent step. It also helps to reduce the amount of rinse water required to remove all traces of the detergent.

The following sequence of steps illustrates how this can work; refer to the schematic in Figure 25.6.

Imagine that the prerinse stage has just been completed and the detergent step is next. The CIP supply pump (P1) is switched on and valve V16 is opened. The pump is left on for a sufficient time so that the detergent solution pushes all water in the lines ahead of it and fills the lines up to the spray ball of the tank being cleaned. Pumping is then abruptly stopped.

In the meantime, the water at the bottom of the tank from the previous rinse continues to be pumped out by the CIP return pump (P2) and directed to the drain.

As soon as the water is completely pumped out and the flow meter (F) signals no flow, the CIP supply pump (P1) is again activated to push the detergent solution through the spray head and cascade down the tank.

As soon as a small puddle of detergent collects at the bottom of the tank being cleaned, the return CIP pump (P2) is activated to start removing the detergent solution, chasing the water in the return line.

As soon as the detergent solution in the return line is sensed by the conductivity meter (C), the programmable control activates a valve (V6) to ensure that the detergent is sent back to the detergent tank, hence preventing any detergent from going to the drain.

This procedure also limits the surface interface between water and detergent to the cross-sectional area of the return line and prevents mixing of the detergent with water over a large area in the tank. Such interface practices can reduce water and detergent losses by up to 20%.

Shortening the CIP Cycle

Shortening the overall cleaning time naturally improves efficiency by reducing the time to return the equipment back to production. The largest gains in this respect can be achieved in the brewing section from the fermenters to the bright beer tanks. Cleaning is traditionally done using alkaline detergents. Unfortunately, cleaning with alkaline solutions forces breweries to remove CO_2 gas before introducing the alkaline detergent since alkaline detergents react quickly upon contact with CO_2. This creates three effects: (1) the alkaline detergent cleaning effectiveness is markedly reduced by the reaction; (2) the sudden removal of CO_2 causes a drop in the pressure and creates the risk of a costly tank implosion; and (3) the CO_2 gas is irrecoverably lost.

Therefore, extra steps are necessary to vent the CO_2 before any alkaline cleaning takes place. It is then necessary to recharge the system lines and tanks with CO_2, purging out all air before the equipment is ready to receive beer. The presence of air in the tanks after fermentation is undesirable because of the risk of oxidation of the beer.

The extra steps necessary to handle CO_2 can be eliminated if acidic detergents are used (Table 25.2). Acidic detergents do not react with CO_2 (Salisbury, 1983). It is important to distinguish between acidic detergents and straight acids. Acidic detergents are specially formulated to help dissolve a variety of organic beer soils, which acids alone are poor at doing. While acids are normally better at removing beer stone organic deposits, acidic detergents are good at removing both organic and inorganic soils.

Cleaning under CO_2 pressure involves some minor mechanical modification to the CIP system. These modifications are designed to prevent the escape of CO_2 from the system as the water rinses and acidic cleaners are circulating. In the meantime, it is important to prevent the introduction of air or oxygen into the system as the water rinses and acidic cleaners are circulated through the system.

One modification is to have a pressure sensor (PT4) on the return line that can activate a return line valve (V5) (Fig. 25.6). The pressure sensor is set at a slightly higher pressure than the pressure of the CO_2 in the tank (D. Funnel, Diversey Inc., Oakville, ON, Canada, *personal communication*).

During normal flow, the PT4 senses pressure that is higher than its set pressure and signals valve V5 to stay open. If there is no solution circulating, PT4 senses a drop in pressure below its set point and signals valve V5 to close, thereby preventing a loss of CO_2 gas. Other precautions could include maintaining a CO_2 or nitrogen blanket over the solutions in the CIP tanks to prevent solutions from dissolving air and introducing it into the system. The water used for CIP should also be deaerated.

TABLE 25.2. Savings Possible when Replacing Caustic Cleaning with Acidic Cleaning[a,b]

Caustic Cleaning	Acidic Cleaning
5 hour 5 minute cleaning process	50 minute cleaning process
Wastes $31,000 of CO_2 per annum	No CO_2 wastage
Uses $42,000 of caustic per annum	Reduced water and energy usage
	Acidic detergent cost of $24,000
Inconsistent cleaning because of variation in detergent concentration and composition	Consistent cleaning result
Beer oxidation risk	Minimized beer oxidation risk
Inherent tank implosion risk	No tank implosion risk

[a] Saving 4 hours 15 minutes per clean and $49,000 per annum.
[b] J. Cornford, Diversey Inc., *personal communication*.

Regular examination of the seals on the suction side of the CIP pumps and valves ensures that no air leaks into the system.

PACKAGING HALL CLEANING

In the packaging hall, there are several different types of soils and surfaces. Table 25.3 shows these areas and the different soil types found in each. Some of the surfaces encountered in the packaging hall, such as the internal surfaces of fillers, bottles, and kegs, will come into contact with beer. Cleaning and sanitation procedures for these areas are more critical, need to be carried out regularly, and require verification.

Although the soils and the associated microorganisms found in the other areas around the packaging hall do not come into contact with beer, they provide a source of environmental contamination. It is important to remember that in the packaging hall there is a lot of movement by conveyors and bottles, and contamination can easily be transported from one area to the next.

Therefore, controlling the number of microorganisms in these nonbeer contact surfaces minimizes the overall risk of contamination to the more critical surfaces. The following sections discuss ways to clean, sanitize, and remove or control soils that could harbor microorganisms.

Returnable Glass Bottle Washing

There are still several breweries that recover and return their bottles to the brewery for washing. The packaging process starts by washing the bottles. The objective of the bottle washer is to remove all soils, including labels and adhesive, and to return the bottles to a commercially sterile state (Duncan, 1982). Typically, the dirty bottles

TABLE 25.3. Packaging Hall Soil Types and Cleaning Methods Employed

Packaging Hall Area	Soil Type	General Cleaning Method
Returnable glass bottles	Dried beer residue, molds, crown rust deposits	Soaking and spraying of hot caustic
Conveyors, under pans	Wear debris, dried lubricants, bearing grease, microorganisms	Spraying of gel or foam cleaners
Filler interior	Beer stone, resins	Cleaning-in-place (CIP)
Filler exterior	Dried beer, wear debris	Automated or manual spraying of gel or foam cleaners
Tunnel pasteurizer	Microbial slime, broken glass	Ongoing treatment to control, boil-outs
Keg interior	Scale, beer residue	CIP
Keg exterior	Dust, dried beer spills	Spraying of hot caustic

are returned from the trade containing beer residues, molds, rust stains, and possibly foreign objects. Bottle-washer machines are employed to wash the returnable bottles. The bottle washer consists of rows of pockets fixed to a moveable chain (Schildmann, 1998). The dirty bottles are placed on conveyors and automatically loaded into the pockets. They are then transported to a series of compartments containing heated caustic soda. In these compartments, the bottles are filled with hot-caustic soda solution, allowed to soak for some time, and then emptied. This emptying and filling with caustic may be repeated several times. Caustic soda concentrations range from 1 to 4%, and the temperatures range from 140 to 175°F (60 to 80°C). In some of the compartments, hot caustic is also sprayed to the inside of the bottles to provide extra mechanical action for cleaning. The action of the hot caustic cleans the internal and external surfaces of the bottle and removes labels and glue residues.

Following the hot-caustic treatment, the bottles are thoroughly rinsed with water using a series of water sprays. The water used for rinsing is treated with chlorine or chlorine dioxide to avoid recontaminating the disinfected internal surface of the bottle during rinsing.

Upon exiting the bottle washer, the clean bottles are placed on the conveyor from where they are transported to be checked for foreign objects on their way to be filled with beer. As a control, the brewery spot checks a few bottles by draining some bottles and testing the drained water with phenolphthalein to ensure that they do not carry any residual alkalinity.

While a full description of bottle washers are available in Chapter 9, it is important to note that a bottle washer, in addition to cleaning bottles, has to remove the labels and needs to have a system to clean and separate the fine particles from the caustic by settling (Agius and Tobia, 2005). Settling involves transferring the bottle-wash solution to a vertical tank and allowing the fine particles to fall to the bottom by gravity. This process can take up to 48 hours but can be speeded up by adding special flocculants.

Conveyors

The conveyors in a brewery, whether made of stainless steel or plastic, can generate considerable soil. This soil consists of wear debris generated by friction when two surfaces are not moving at the same speed. This condition exists when the conveyor rides over the fixed plastic wear strips or when the bottles or cans slip over the conveyor as they are being transported. Another area of constant friction is caused by the hinge pin that holds the conveyor track slats together (Fig. 25.7).

To reduce friction on all of these surfaces, water-based lubricants are sprayed on the conveyors. The combination of wear debris, water, chemical components of the conveyor lubricant, and sometimes grease used on the bearings can combine to form a complex soil. These soils can embed themselves on the underside of the conveyor and the hinge pins and can be carried and collected on the pans that are sometimes placed under the conveyor to channel away foam and lubricant solution to the drain. It is natural that these soils harbor all kinds of microorganisms, which by the very movement of the conveyor and packaging containers can quickly spread around the packaging hall. A clean empty bottle, or an open can riding on the conveyor on its way to be filled, can easily be contaminated.

To overcome these problems, modern conveyor lubricants need to have good detergent properties to keep the soils suspended and help prevent their accumulation. They must also suppress microorganisms from growing and flourishing on the conveyors. This is especially important on lines that run continuously and cannot be stopped for cleaning.

Even with the best of lubricants, conveyors need to be cleaned regularly. To clean the hard-to-reach parts of the conveyor, a gel and foaming method is used. On some large packaging lines, this procedure can be quite labor intensive. To overcome this, the conveyor lines are fitted with a PLC system and fixed spray nozzles. The PLC automatically directs the cleaning procedure of the conveyor tracks by spraying rinse water and foam detergent in the proper sequence.

More recently, in an effort to reduce the water used in breweries, dry or semidry lubricants that do not require dilution with water are being introduced. Since there is very little water to suspend and mobilize soils, it is important to supplement the use of these lubricants with a regular cleaning regime.

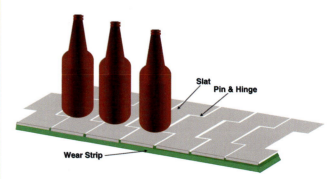

FIGURE 25.7. Conveyor chain made of slats held together by pins and hinges and the conveyor riding over the wear strip. (Courtesy G. Agius)

Filler Interior Cleaning

The filler is a key piece of equipment in the packaging hall. The internal surfaces of the filler come into direct contact with beer, and therefore, it is essential that they are free of any soils that could harbor microorganisms, which can contaminate or even damage the beer.

A typical rotary filler consists of several filling valves set in a circle. As the machine rotates, the empty clean containers feed into the machine, where each container is paired to a filling valve. Beer is pumped from the finished beer tank to an annular tank on the filler, which in turn feeds beer to each filler valve. In the time it takes for the filling valve to complete one rotation, the container is filled with beer to a set level. At the end of the rotation, the filled container is released to a conveyor that transports it to the capping machine (Kunze, 1999).

The filling valve is an intricate device with many ports and associated valves and seals that supply beer and CO_2 and allow venting of CO_2. During CIP, the cleaning solution and rinse water are directed to reach all possible internal surfaces (Fig. 25.8).

Fillers using downstream tunnel pasteurization and running continuously are typically cleaned in place once per week. Fillers used for sterile fills must be cleaned more frequently, normally in smaller operations at the end of each shift. Before starting the CIP procedure, caps are fitted under the filling valves, which are pressed firmly to seal against the filling valve. Once all the filling valves are capped, the CIP solution is circulated, reaching all the contamination sites in the filler tank and the filling valves, and then returned to the CIP tank. The cleaning procedure for the filler is very similar to a tank CIP procedure and involves the following steps.

- Rinsing with fresh water
- Circulating the detergent solution at 140°F (60°C) for about 20–30 minutes
   - The detergent solution could be caustic based, but sometimes chlorinated alkalis are used to remove persistent soils.
- Rinsing
- Running the sanitizing solution and allowing it to flow to the drain for 5 minutes

The sanitizer solution can be any of the ones recommended earlier in this chapter and should be made to the prescribed concentration. In some cases, the sanitizing step involves circulating hot water at 175°F (80°C) for 20 minutes. The advantage of hot sanitation is that the temperature can kill microorganisms that may have been shielded in areas where a chemical sanitizer could not reach them. On the other hand, hot sanitation is quite energy intensive and hard on gaskets and seals and can cause the filler bearing grease to melt, thereby requiring more frequent preventive maintenance. The expansion and contraction of the filler can also result in leaks and, again, more frequent maintenance.

To avoid these difficulties with hot sanitation, combination programs are employed in which one CIP uses hot sanitation, and this is interspersed with three or four CIPs using chemical sanitation (Agius and Burkeen, 2005). In this way, microorganisms in hard-to-reach places are kept in check but, at the same time, a reduction in energy and heat stress on the filler is achieved.

If there is a time delay of longer than 4 hours between the end of the CIP cycle and resumption of production, then a sanitizer is run through the filler immediately before resuming production. If the filler runs for a period of time in operations using a tunnel pasteurizer downstream, such as 8 hours in 1 day, and is stopped until the next day, then it is flushed with water and sanitized immediately before resuming operations. In smaller operations that rely on microfiltration or flash pasteurization or rely entirely on a sterile fill, then the filler should undergo CIP after each bottling operation or within 24 hours prior to the start of the next shift with a sanitizing step immediately prior to the start of filling.

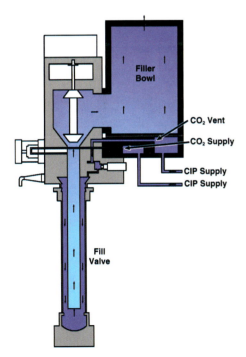

FIGURE 25.8. Arrows show the flow of cleaning-in-place (CIP) solution through the filler valve. (Courtesy Diversey, Inc.)

Filler Exterior Cleaning

Soils on the exterior of the filler can be a source of contamination to the containers entering or leaving the filler, especially considering the air movement caused by the rotation of the filler. Soils around the filler can be caused by dried beer spills or wear debris transferred in with the bottles. Such soils on the exterior of the filler can shelter microorganisms. It is therefore important to thoroughly clean the exterior of the filler. This is done once per week and employs a gel or foam spraying procedure.

A manual cleaning sequence involves rinsing the outside with water from a pressure water gun. This is followed by the application of the detergent to the surface in the form of a gel or foam. After about 30 minutes in the case of gel and about 10 minutes in the case of foam, the surface is rinsed with water again. The surface is finally sanitized by spraying a sanitizer solution.

The manual procedure is somewhat labor intensive and poses some safety issues to the personnel applying the cleaning solutions. It is also difficult to ensure that all the critical areas are cleaned.

To overcome these difficulties, automated filler cleaning is used. In this method, a series of fixed nozzles and a set of nozzles that swing in place are used. These are placed and designed to reach all the exterior areas of the filler. The cleaning sequence as described above is performed, but in this case, the steps are controlled automatically by a PLC (Figs. 25.9 and 25.10).

Automated filler cleaning becomes more critical when filling containers with beer that has been flash pasteurized or sterile filtered, where there is no safeguard afforded by the pasteurizer. If the filler is in an enclosure, automated cleaning can be extended to clean the walls and ceiling of the enclosure.

Tunnel Pasteurizers

The main purpose of a tunnel pasteurizer is to gradually heat the beer in the cans or bottles to 140°F (60°C). The beer is held at this temperature for a period of time until it reaches the desired pasteurizer units (PUs), which kill any harmful microorganisms that could damage the beer. One PU is defined as 1 minute at 140°F (60°C). Heating is achieved by spraying the containers that move along the tunnel with water held in compartments at increasing temperatures. After being held at 140°F (60°C) for the desired time, the containers are gradually cooled to near-ambient temperatures, and the containers are then released to the conveyer. Flash pasteurization and tunnel pasteurization are covered in-depth in Chapters 15 and 16, respectively.

From this description, it can be seen that there are compartments where the water temperature is between 50 and 130°F (10 and 55°C), which are ideal temperatures to allow microorganisms to thrive. Beer leaks or container breakage provide a food source for microorganisms. In fact, the growth of microorganisms can be quite vigorous, and if left unchecked, some bacteria produce copious amounts of slime that produce slime "hangers". The slime produces offensive odors and can block water spray nozzles and interfere with the heating or cooling of the containers. It is also possible that these conditions could sustain bacteria that can cause sickness to personnel around the pasteurizer. The air movement in and out of the pasteurizer can, of course, be a source of contamination for the rest of the packaging hall, including the empty conveyors traveling over the pasteurizers.

To overcome these difficulties, it is important that the pasteurizer water be treated on an ongoing basis

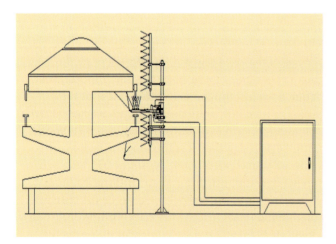

FIGURE 25.9. Fixed spray nozzles to spray cleaning solutions as the filler rotates. (Courtesy Diversey, Inc.)

FIGURE 25.10. A filler to which a foaming cleaning solution was applied. (Courtesy G. Agius)

to control the growth of microorganisms. This type of treatment involves dosing oxidizing substances, such as chlorine, to the water at regular intervals to maintain a residual concentration to kill or control the growth of microorganisms. Such treatment with oxidizing materials is most effective when the pasteurizer is running continuously. If the pasteurizer is not used for a period of time, such as 8 hours or more, it becomes important to add a nonoxidizing antimicrobial just before stopping the pasteurizer to keep the bacteria from growing during this inactive period.

It is also important that the water be treated to prevent corrosion of the pasteurizer. This is done by adjusting the water chemistry, i.e., pH, alkalinity, and total dissolved solids, to ensure that the water does not have corrosive tendencies. Using the pH, alkalinity, and total dissolved solids, the corrosive tendency of water can be determined for a given temperature by working out the Ryznar index (Ryznar, 1944). It is also important that the treatment does not cause aluminum can dome staining. Can dome staining can be prevented by maintaining the pH of the water, especially in the hotter zones, between 7.0 and 7.5. Special additives can also be added to further suppress the staining. Pasteurizer water treatment is covered in Chapter 17.

By monitoring the pasteurizer and adjusting the treatment, it is possible to go for extensive periods without requiring additional cleaning except for accumulated broken glass. If for some reason the pasteurizer gets out of control, it is essential to clean it thoroughly to kill and remove all microorganisms. This cleaning procedure, often referred to as a boil-out, involves manually spraying water to remove any loose slime and then circulating a chlorinated alkaline product at an elevated temperature of 175°F (80°C) for about 2 hours. When the treatment is complete, the solution is discarded and the pasteurizer is rinsed thoroughly before being returned to production.

Kegs

Kegs have to be cleaned on the outside and the inside. External cleaning is done by spraying high-pressure presoaking, cleaning, and rinsing solutions. The cleaning solution is circulated. This process is typically automated in a keg-filling machine. However, it could be done manually by employing handheld spray guns and brushes.

The interior of the keg is cleaned using a CIP method. In fact, the keg is fitted with a fixed spray head to spray the water rinses and cleaning solutions. The cleaning solutions used to clean the interior of the kegs are typically either caustic or acid. Kegs are usually sterilized by steam injection following the CIP cycle. Kegging is covered in Chapter 24.

CONCLUSION

Cleaning of process surfaces is a fundamental operation in a brewery because of its effect on the integrity and quality of the beer. In fact, in breweries that are adopting a hazardous analysis and critical control points (HACCP) or good manufacturing practices (GMP) program, the cleaning of process surfaces is often identified as a critical control point. A critical control point is defined as "a point in food processing where there is a high probability that improper control may cause, allow or contribute to a hazard or to filth in the final food or decomposition of the final food" (U.S. Code of Federal Regulations, 2012). This means that the brewer needs to ensure that the cleaning process has been done according to a set procedure. Furthermore, documenting that the various steps in a cleaning process have been properly carried out is essential. Records and operator verification must be kept for parameters such as cleaning time, solution flows, detergent concentration, and temperature. Equipment that logs this kind of data automatically can be extremely helpful and is fast becoming the industry standard. The results of a cleaning process and the state of a cleaned surface also need validating according to a standard. This creates the need for tests that can very quickly ascertain the soil level and the microbiological state of a cleaned process surface. It is likely that quicker surface tests will evolve in the future.

The need to turn production equipment around will become more pressing for brewers, necessitating the optimization of all cleaning processes. The move toward well-designed plants that not only process beer efficiently but are designed to totally automate the cleaning of tanks, filters, fillers, and lines will continue. Automating and optimizing these cleaning processes will also reduce the amount of chemicals, water, and heat energy needed to clean and sanitize. Therefore, a rise is expected in the use of acidic cleaning for cellars, optimization of the cleaning processes, instrumentation to verify the CIP process, automated exterior filler cleaning, and conveyor lubricants that do not require water dilution.

On the horizon is the evolution of new cleaners that reduce the cleaning time and minimize their impact on the effluent and the environment.

REFERENCES

Agius, G., and Burkeen, S. (2005). Partial substitution of hot filler sanitation by a cold chemical sanitizer. Tech. Q. Master Brew. Assoc. Am. 42:54-56.

Agius, G., and Tobia, A. (2005). Enhancing the performance of bottle-wash solutions. Tech. Q. Master Brew. Assoc. Am. 42:117-119.

Agius, G., Burkeen, S., and Mynatt, J. (2004). Benefits of using chlorine dioxide as an alternative to hot-water sanitation. Tech. Q. Master Brew. Assoc. Am. 41:42-44.

Chapman, T. W., Machado, R. M., Mathias, M. F., and Barton, K. P. (1985). Effects of mass transfer on surface reactions. In: Fouling and Cleaning in Food Processing, pp. 59-78. D. B. Lund, E. Plett, and C. Sandu, eds. University of Wisconsin, Madison.

Duncan, D. G. (1982). Basic principles of bottlewashing. Brew. Dig. 57(2):29-33.

Environmental Protection Agency. (April 1999). Chapter 4 Chlorine Dioxide. In: Alternative Disinfectants and Oxidants, Guidance Manual, EPA 815-R-99-014, p. 15.

Frank, J. F., and Chmielewski, R. (2000). Influence of surface finish on the cleanability of stainless steel. J. Food Prot. 64:1178-1182.

Hankinson, D. J., and Carver, C. E. (1968). Fluid relationships involved in circulation cleaning. J. Dairy Sci. 51:1761-1767.

Kulkarni, S. M., Maxcy, R. B., and Arnold, R. G. (1975). Evaluation of soil deposition & removal processes: An interpretive review. J. Dairy Sci. 58:1922-1936.

Kunze, W. (1999). Beer production. In: Technology Brewing and Malting, English translation 2nd ed., p. 403. Translated by T. Wainwright, p. 470. VLB Berlin, Berlin.

Masschelein, W. J. (1979). In: Chlorine Dioxide, pp. 162-163. R. P. Rice, ed. Ann Arbor Science, Ann Arbor, MI.

Paulsson, B.-O., and Tragardh, C. (1985). A method for measurement of hydrodynamic effects during cleaning of a solid surface. In: Fouling and Cleaning in Food Processing, pp. 358-371. D. B. Lund, E. Plett, and C. Sandu, eds. University of Wisconsin, Madison.

Plett, E. (1985). Cleaning of fouled surfaces. In: Fouling and Cleaning in Food Processing, pp. 286-311. D. B. Lund, E. Plett, and C. Sandu, eds. University of Wisconsin, Madison.

Ryznar, J. W. (1944). A new index for determining amount of calcium carbonate scale formed by a water. J. Am. Water Works Assoc. 36(4):472-486.

Salisbury, M. (1983). Cleaning storage vessels in CO_2 atmospheres. Brew. Dig. 58(6):34-36.

Schildmann, E., ed. (1998). In: Cleaning Returnable Glass Bottles: A Practical Manual, pp. 88-91. VLB Berlin, Berlin.

Timperley, D. (1981). The effect of Reynolds number and mean velocity of flow on the cleaning in-place of pipelines. In: Fundamentals and Applications of Surface Phenomena Associated with Fouling and Cleaning in Food Processing—Proceedings, p. 402. B. Hallstrom, B. D. Lund, and Ch. Tragardh eds. Lund University, Lund Sweden, and University of Wisconsin, Madison.

U.S. Code of Federal Regulations. (Last revised April 1, 2012). U.S. Good Manufacturing Practices, Title 21, part 110.3.

CHAPTER 26

Final Beer Filtration for Microbiological Stability

RON JOHNSON

DAVID SCHLEEF

Pall Corporation

Final filtration is a method of cold stabilizing beer by reducing yeast and beer-spoilage bacteria to an acceptable concentration in the finished product. Also referred to as microbial (or cold) stabilization, this filtration step is the last physical treatment of the beer prior to filling. Thus, it serves as brand insurance for packaging breweries.

A final filter assembly in breweries is utilized for fine clarification and microorganism removal, normally applying filters with a microbial rating of 0.45 to 0.65 µm to prefiltered bright beer just prior to filling and packaging. The most economical designs of microfiltration systems include traditional sheet filters, module lenticular housings, and membrane cartridge assemblies. Filter media may be conventional depth-type or membrane filters, in sheet or cartridge form, but should have published removal ratings for beer-spoilage organisms as well as proven operating experience in a brewery.

Optimum performance of a final filter system, in terms of both microbiological removal and economy, depends on the entire production process and particularly on prefiltration and cleaning regimes. Prefiltration of beer should be designed to remove yeast and other particulates commonly found in freshly matured beer. Final filter assemblies generally cost more to operate, so they should be employed for the designed bacterial removal work. A system consisting of three stages (i.e., particle or trap, prefilter, and final filter) of postdiatomaceous earth filtration provides the highest operational efficiency and best economy.

● MICROFILTRATION

Filtration is the physical removal of contaminants from a fluid stream. While filters are generally thought of as a screen or sieve, most media applied for beer filtration have depth, which creates a tortuous path for retaining contaminants. This mechanism enhances filter efficiency through a higher loading capacity and absorptive effects.

Target microorganisms for pre- and final filtration are yeast and common beer-spoilage bacteria, such as *Pediococcus damnosus*, *Lactobacillus brevis*, and *Lactobacillus lindneri*. Filters employed to retain these organisms from beer are not considered to be sterilizing grade. Sterilizing grade specifically refers to a membrane filter cartridge that removes more than 10^7 *Brevundimonas diminuta* cells per square centimeter of filter medium. If used for beer, this fine level of filtration could result in the loss of bitterness units and beer character. Instead, brewers balance filtration needs for organism removal with preservation of beer quality, utilizing 0.45- to 0.65-µm microbially rated filters. Therefore, final beer membrane filters provide a reduction of microorganisms (Table 26.1) and not necessarily a sterile product.

Filter Ratings

Filter particulate removal efficiency is the measure of a filter's ability to remove particles of a specific size from a known fluid. The filter ratings for the removal of

TABLE 26.1. Beer Microbes and Approximate Sizes

Microbe	Approximate Dimensions
Bacteria	
Pediococcus damnosus	>0.6-µm short rods, clumping
Lactobacillus brevis	0.5 × 2-µm rods, clumping
Lactobacillus lindneri	0.5 × 2-µm rods, mostly single cells
Yeast	
Saccharomyces sp.	~3 µm

hard particles and microorganisms are different because of the level of single particle or microbe resolution. When selecting a final filter for bioreduction/removal, a microbially challenged filter is preferred.

Filter manufacturers rate filters with either a nominal or absolute efficiency rating. Nominally rated filters remove some percentage (10–99%) of the given particle size. These filters are generally best suited for coarse, or prefiltration, stages. Absolute-rated filters are normally tested against an International Organization for Standardization (ISO) standard by the manufacturer. These ratings ensure that the filter will remove more than 99.9% (β-1000) or more than 99.98% (β-5000) of all nondeformable particles of the given size under well-defined, specific test conditions. Because of limits in particulate rating methodology, the highest beta ratio is 5000. A single element may have multiple beta ratios at different particle sizes. For example, a filter may have a 1-μm beta ratio of 10 (90% removal efficiency) and a 10-μm beta ratio of 1000 (99.9% removal efficiency).

Traditional depth filters, such as filter sheets, have a nominal particulate removal rating. While their efficiency is measured by the ability to remove particles of a specific size from a known fluid, this measure does not necessarily correlate with a microbiological removal rating.

Microorganism-reducing grade filters often express microbial removal efficiency in the removal of a number of microbes per square centimeter of filter area or per 10-inch cartridge. The microbial challenge level is a critical factor to establishing the log reduction value (LRV) or titer reduction. The LRV may also have a reported statistical confidence level. This titer reduction should be correlated to a filter integrity test if using a polymeric membrane filter with a microbial rating less than 1 μm. A microbial rating is not an indication of the largest opening or pore in the filter. Because the microbes multiply to produce colonies, this improves the possible resolution of the organism far beyond the limitations of particulate detection. For example, a microbial rating could be expressed in >12 LRV per 10-inch cartridge. A particulate-rated filter with a beta ratio of 5000 could be expressed in an LRV for particulates. Based on the limits of particulate detection, the best particulate-rated filter has an LRV of 3.7.

- The 0.65-μm microbially rated filters are typically challenged with yeast, *Saccharomyces cerevisiae*.
- The 0.45-μm microbially rated filters are typically challenged with bacteria, *Serratia marcescens*, which are similar in size to *Escherichia coli* and *Lactobacillus* sp.

Titer reduction is the number of organisms in an unfiltered test divided by the number of organisms in the filtrate. A filter with 10^6 microbial removal rating that is challenged with 1,000,000 microorganisms may have 1 colony forming unit (CFU) on the filter outlet.

Beer Filterability

To ensure the best operational efficiency and microbial security of a final filter system, brewers should target the incoming beer yeast load to be less than 5 cells per 100 mL of beer and the bacterial load to be less than 100 cells per 100 mL of beer. Similarly, haze readings below 0.3 EBC (with 90° measurement angle) and 0.2 EBC (with 25° measurement angle) indicate adequate upstream prefiltration.

Simple bench scale testing with membrane discs can indicate beer filterability. Beer at 32–36°F (0–2°C) is filtered through a 50-mm-diameter membrane disc until complete blockage of the membrane occurs. As a guideline, the following yields should be achieved:

0.45-μm membranes = more than 1,200 mL of beer

0.65-μm membranes = more than 2,500 mL of beer

Yields substantially below these figures suggest inadequate prefiltration or high levels of beta-glucans and/or protein complexes that will prematurely block final membranes. To determine upstream filter needs, similar tests with more open media can be used. These test results will indicate the best combination of media to maximize filter throughput.

Best Filtration Practices

Pressure differential across the filter system is the primary measure of filter operation and life. For dead-end (one-way) filtration, pressure drop is simply determined by subtracting housing outlet pressure from the inlet reading. Where solid loads and/or microbe counts are the most significant factors affecting filter life, management of flow rate and media regeneration schemes has the biggest impact on performance. Final filters that are run to maximum differential pressure tend to be less able to regenerate than those with more frequent cleaning. Filter systems that are sized properly and operate with proper prefiltration and thorough cleaning provide the most operational flexibility to meet packaging requirements.

The duration between prefiltration and final filtration may affect beer filterability. Certain beer components, such as polyphenols and proteins, are subject to chemical modification as a function of time. These highly reactive substances form new structures within a few hours by polymerization and condensation. The agglomerates thus formed have a negative effect on filter output and on service life of the final filter assembly.

Determined by beer filterability, a staged filter system should be employed for cost-efficient final beer treatment. The function of the first two stages is to remove the bulk particulate. With this removed from the process stream, the final filter load is limited to fewer particles and microbes. Each process stage should perform optimal work, allowing the lowest operating cost and maximizing equipment availability for larger batches and maximum throughput before filters must be regenerated.

Final filter performance (and resulting beer quality) can also be negatively impacted by high biological loads in the brewery. Strict cleaning procedures should be employed to reduce microbial load from the upstream processes; in particular, hygienic conditions should be observed in operating final filtration and packaging equipment. Storage and working tanks should have sterile air vents to reduce the risk of contamination by spoilage organisms. The water supply used for flushing or cleaning filters should be free of particulates (1-µm particulate rated) and preferably filtered with a 0.2-µm microbial membrane to reduce the contamination risk further. Carbon dioxide (CO_2) and compressed air supplied to these systems should be sterile filtered to reduce the risk of contamination with microbes or microbial spores.

● MICROFILTRATION SYSTEMS AND OPERATION

Although a range of separation technologies are commercially available, the filter configurations most utilized by breweries for microorganism removal are based on depth filters or membrane cartridges. The most common system platforms to house these filters in breweries are sheet filter presses, sheet module lenticular housings, and cartridge housings.

In selecting any microfilter system platform, the following factors should be considered.

System Capacity Requirements

Desired flow rate and expected volume throughput will dictate the filter system sizing and performance required. An optimal final filter system operates at the speed and volume needed for packaging operations without excess buffering tanks or stoppage for filter regeneration during the batch.

Cost and Operational Efficiency

While capacity required for packaging operations is the initial sizing basis, functionality of various filter types should be considered. Sheet filters have low capital and media cost but require a high level of labor to operate and change filters. Membrane cartridges have the highest filter purchase price but require less labor to operate and provide consistent security and beer quality. Change-out frequency (labor), product hold-up volume and loss, and level of microbial stability are all factors to consider. With any system, oversizing for the operation may offer more capacity and even allow for future production increase; however, utility consumption, volume beer losses, and other aspects can offset these benefits with a higher operating cost.

Microbiological Security

Fine and final depth filters with nominal removal ratings and membrane cartridges that are not integrity testable tend to be less expensive than those that may be validated. Depending on shelf-life requirements of individual brands, final filter cost needs to be balanced with the level of microbiological removal required by the brewery.

Microbreweries with limited (local or regional) distribution tend to find that the most suitable systems are sheet and lenticular filters. These configurations serve smaller craft brewers with low capital investment, flexibility in filter grades (for various brands), and relative low costs to expand capacity as the brewery grows. As product distribution increases, so does the need for longer shelf life and brand protection. Therefore, breweries with larger volume operations and multistate or national distribution may prefer cartridge-based systems to achieve a higher level of automation and the security of membrane filters.

Sheet Filtration

Fine/Final Filtration with Sheet Filters

While decades have passed since the development of modern depth filter sheets, they continue to be widely employed in beer filtration. Filter sheets provide excellent beer quality and flexibility but lack the security of a cartridge filter with a fixed pore structure. Therefore, constant attention to operating conditions is necessary to prevent system pressure shocks and potential microorganism unloading from a final sheet filter.

The most common filter sheets for beer applications are made of cellulose, kieselguhr (diatomaceous earth [DE]), and perlite, bound together by a food-quality resin. Filter sheets that are appropriately formulated for beer filtration should have high wet strength to withstand multiple sanitizations. When utilized as final filters, the product should also have a typical removal efficiency with yeast and beer-spoilage bacteria under operating conditions that model those at the brewery.

Equipment used to hold the sheets is generally known as a plate-and-frame filter, filter press, or sheet filter. A range of sizes and types is available, from small, portable units to large presses holding 150 frames or more. Single flat sheets are inserted between filter plates, or fold-over types may be inserted into two filter positions to reduce the number of sheets that operators handle. In either case, a plate separates the inlet and outlet sides of each sheet, with incoming flow to the rough sheet side and beer exiting the smooth side. Once sheets are loaded to the equipment, the frames are tightened against each other by means of a hand crank or hydraulic ram. Special attention should be given to inlet/outlet frame O-rings to obtain a good seal and prevent leakage.

Sizing and Operating Recommendations for Sheet Filters

Recommended flow of filter sheets is 250 L per square meter of filtration area per hour for microbial-reducing applications. The most commonly utilized filter sizes are 40 × 40 cm and 60 × 60 cm, which can offer a range of approximately 1- to 95-m^2 filtration area in the filter press. Larger capacity systems are available but tend to be replaced with cartridge filters at brewery production volumes greater than 25,000 hL per year. The functionality of sheet filters is advantageous for craft brewers, considering the various number of sheets that may be used for batch volumes and flow requirements and the possibility to combine two filter grades (polish or prefilter and final filter) into one system.

In preparation of filtration, the filter sheets must be thoroughly rinsed in a forward flow. Optimum rinsing temperature is 68°F (20°C) at a capacity of 7.1–9.5 gallons/square foot/minute (1.5–2.0 hL/m^2/hour) with particle-free, soft brewing water. Following rinsing, the unit should be sterilized for filtration. The first volume of beer filtered may need to be recirculated or sent to drain if there is no buffer tank or blending prior to packaging. Throughout filtration, differential pressure of the sheet filter should not exceed 22 pounds per square inch gauge (psig) (1.5 bar) and flow should remain at or below 250 L per square meter of filtration area per hour to attain the specified level of microbe retention.

Sheet Filter Sterilization

All hot rinsing and cleaning procedures should be performed with compression released from the filter. Hot water or steam may be used to sterilize sheets, although water in the forward flow direction is the most common approach. Once the equipment has reached a temperature of 194°F (90°C), a water flow rate of 6.2–9.5 gallons/square foot/minute (1.3–2.0 hL/m^2/hour) is recommended for 30 minutes.

The filter can also be sterilized with low-pressure steam (wet steam at approximately 230°F [110°C]). The steam should be fed via the filter inlet side, with condensation cocks open. When steam escapes from vents and drains, a sterilization time of 20 minutes should be observed.

Filter Sheet Regeneration

Loss of flow and increased differential pressure dictates the need to regenerate the filter sheets. While filtration time between regeneration may be up to 20 hours, upstream filtration plays the greatest role in batch length. For regenerating, the filter should be backflushed as soon as possible following filtration. For this procedure, the water temperature should start at room temperature and be brought up to 158–176°F (70–80°C) at a flow capacity of 14.2 gallons/square foot/minute (3 hL/m^2/hour). The backflush should last about 10 minutes. If backflushing is performed, it should take place prior to sterilization to maximize filter sheet life.

Lenticular Module Filtration

Fine/Final Filtration with Lenticular Filter Sheet Modules

Lenticular filters evolved from flat sheet filters to an enclosed, modular design. Early types had a disc-in-housing format that has developed into modules and, more recently, into a cartridge-style filter. All formats of disc filters are based on depth filter sheets in lenticular cell form. Therefore, these modules offer filtration characteristics similar to those of sheet filters, with the advantages of a closed housing. Oxygen pickup in the beer and product loss are reduced, and labor to operate and change filters is lower than that of a sheet filter. Use of lenticular cartridges continues to increase among craft breweries due to relative low capital investment and ease of use. Lenticular modules have a higher media cost than filter sheets, although overall operating cost tends to be lower than that of a filter press. As with traditional sheet filters, modular sheet filters offer a flexible range of sheet grades and certain types may be regenerated by backflushing.

Sizing and Operating Recommendations for Lenticular Modules

The recommended flow of lenticular sheet modules is based on the same specification as the filter sheet grade utilized (250 L per square meter of filtration area per hour for microbial-reducing applications). Lenticular filter modules are available with 12-inch (287-mm) and 16-inch (410-mm) diameters in housings that can accommodate from one to four cartridges. A 16-inch module has a filter area of up to 5 m^2, the equivalent of thirty-one 40 × 40-cm filter sheets. The largest housing (four modules) has a capacity of 50 hL per hour (22 gallons per minute). Throughout filtration, differential pressure of the housing should not exceed 15 psig (1.03 bar). Following filtration, the housing may be blown down with nitrogen or CO_2 to push out the remaining beer.

Lenticular Module Sterilization

Lenticular modules are operated in much the same way as filter sheets. In preparation for filtration, the filters should be thoroughly rinsed with ambient water in a forward direction at a maximum of 1.5 times the operating flow rate for 5–10 minutes. Following rinsing, the unit should be sterilized for filtration. A stepped temperature increase to 180°F (82°C) and water flow for 20 minutes is recommended.

Lenticular Module Regeneration

Once the maximum differential pressure is reached, or the filtration batch is completed, the housing may be flushed with particle-free, ambient or warm water. If a backflushable cartridge is used, reverse flow should be limited to half the operating flow rate and no more than 7 psig (0.5 bar). The water temperature may be gradually increased to 120°F (50°C) and the flushing cycle should last 15–20 minutes.

Cartridge Filtration

Final Filtration with Membrane Cartridges

Cartridge-style filters are more modern formats than are flat or lenticular sheets. Most large brewery operations use cartridges, since this filter type can handle much greater flow rates and volume throughput in a compact design. Depth filter media in a cartridge format is most often a graded density polypropylene, which can have a stable media matrix and absolute rating. Depth filter cartridges have a high solids holding capacity and are ideal for particle- and yeast-reducing applications (prefilter to membrane); however, unlike membranes, depth filters are not integrity testable so users must be aware that, while the filter may meet a manufacturer's standard of an absolute removal rating, they cannot be reasonably verified for microbial removal once in service. For this reason, membrane cartridges are preferred over depth cartridge filters for microbiological stabilization.

The standard final beer cartridge is a 30-inch (762-mm), single, open-ended filter with double 226 O-rings and locating fin. Various filter manufactures label their end-cap codes differently, but the configuration and dimensions are industry standard. Double, open-ended filters are available, but they are not as secure and, therefore, not recommended for final filter applications.

Polymeric membranes in cartridge form have become one of the most commonly used materials for the final filtration of beer. These membranes are characterized by a very stable and consistent pore structure, excellent cleaning and sterilization characteristics, and most importantly, their verifiable ability to remove beer-spoilage microorganisms.

Membrane cartridge filter systems installed directly prior to the packaging equipment, e.g., if a buffer tank is not incorporated, must account for the feed pattern to packaging. This particularly applies to keg plants where the intermittent feed rate can be two or three times higher than the effective hourly output of the plant. Up to 30% higher flow rates should be allowed if the beer is directly routed from the filter station to the bottle or can filler.

Cartridge Housings

For final beer filtration, housings are designed for cartridges with a 226-style, double O-ring, bayonet lock. Housings may have conventional upright mounting of the cartridges, but an inverted configuration offers the following advantages:

- rapid and complete venting of the system, resulting in minimum oxygen pickup during the startup phase; and
- even flow distribution, enhancing the regeneration effect during backflushing of the prefilter cartridges.

Automated Systems

For medium-sized to large breweries, fully automated cartridge filter systems are employed. With the exception of manual mounting and dismounting of the cartridges, all processing steps are performed via a programmable logic controller (PLC). Simple operation and supervision, process visualization, and individual programming requirements are standard.

Sizing and Operating Recommendations for Membrane Filters

The recommended flow rate for membrane filters typically is between 0.4 and 0.6 gallons per minute (1.5 and 2.3 L per minute) per 10-inch filter segment. While the filters can be run at a higher flow rate, differential pressure will increase significantly and filter life will be reduced. The standard flow rate for cleaning is 1.5 times the operational flow in the forward flow direction. In regard to differential pressure, membranes can generally withstand 50 psig or more of differential pressure; however, filter flow rates tend to drop off (the so called "knee" of the pressure/flow curve) around a differential pressure between 9 and 13 psig. Prefilters are normally installed just upstream in order to protect the final filters from premature blockage. Depth filters in the range of 0.5 to 1.5 μm with an absolute rating are typically selected for this application.

Membrane Filter Regeneration

Because most of the material held back by the filter membranes is proteinaceous in nature, caustic (normally NaOH) cleaning is the method of choice for extending the service life of membrane filters. Cleaning is typically performed at 1.5 times the normal flow rate at a temperature of approximately 120°F (50°C) to aid removal of soluble components trapped on the media. Temperatures up to 180–185°F (82–85°C) are routinely utilized for sanitization after element cleaning. As in other parts of the brewery, it is important to monitor the temperature, duration, and concentration of the cleaning process in order to ensure a consistent level of cleaning and to avoid thermal and chemical damage to the filters.

When filtering beer containing high levels of colloids, membrane cartridges may block rapidly. The colloids are to a large extent dissolved or detached and rinsed from the system by a multistage temperature rinse with water. For the purpose of regeneration, cold water is used first, followed by a short intermediate rinse with warm water up to 122°F (50°C) and finally a hot-water rinse at a maximum of 185°F (85°C) until the pressure differential has dropped to a stable figure of below 0.8 bar. Regeneration should be carried out daily in a forward flow direction.

Integrity Testing of Membrane Filters

One of the key advantages of membrane filters as opposed to using sheets or modules is the ability to test the integrity of the filter prior to use. Several tests have been developed for testing the integrity of filters. However, the test pressures/flows vary according to manufacturer and type of membrane used and are only valid if correlated to the retention of a specific microorganism, preferably a beer spoiler. The following tests are commonly used for this purpose.

Bubble Point Test

The bubble point of a membrane filter is the pressure at which a wetted filter membrane begins to allow mass gas passage through its pores. If the filter allows gas to pass through the membrane at any pressure lower than the bubble point, then the filter is not integral and therefore cannot be expected to retain microorganisms. Air or nitrogen pressure is applied to the previously wetted (but not submerged) membrane filter and slowly increased until a gas passage is observed downstream of the filter.

Pressure Hold Test

A pressure hold test is similar to a bubble point test in that a gas pressure is applied on the upstream side of a wetted filter element(s). Instead of raising the pressure slowly and waiting for the gas passage, a known pressure is applied upstream of the filter membranes, just below the bubble point of the filter. The upstream volume is isolated by closing the valve from the pressure source. The downstream side of the filter is then opened to atmospheric pressure and the rate of pressure drop is measured. The rate of pressure drop is proportional to the diffusional gas flow through the wetted pores. If the rate of pressure decay exceeds the specified pressure hold rate, then the filter is deemed to be nonintegral.

Forward Flow Test

The forward flow test is similar to the pressure hold test, except in this case, the set pressure is continuously applied upstream of the wetted filter membrane and then the diffusional gas flow through the wetted pores across the membrane is measured using instrumentation.

It should be noted that the bubble point test and the pressure hold test can be carried out manually without any special instrumentation or equipment other than a pressure gauge and stopwatch. However, the gauge may require 0.1-psig resolution for an operator to obtain a valid test result.

Operating Costs of Membrane Filtration

The typical operating cost range for membrane filtration can vary widely depending on which type of system is used and which type of beer is filtered. This cost can range from $0.30 per U.S. barrel (117 L) for a fully automated and cleanable system that runs light lagers up to $3.00 per U.S. barrel and higher for a fully manual system that filters primarily dark all-malt beers. In any case, the filterability and volumes of the individual beers to be membrane filtered should be tested when sizing and evaluating membrane filter equipment.

SUMMARY

Final filtration plays an important role in the brewery since it is the last process step where the quality, shelf life, and thus appearance of the beer can be decisively influenced. It is a modern, sustainable method to produce beer free of spoilage organisms without using thermal treatment.

Cold-stabilized beer filtration cannot be regarded as an individual step; it is an integral part of the entire production process, where efficiency is affected by upstream processes. When properly configured and sized for the application, final filters provide the quality and security required by packaging breweries.

REFERENCES FOR FURTHER READING

Duchek, P. (1992). Position and development of cold sterilization of beer. Brauindustrie 77(2):98-103.

Goldammer, T. (1999). The Brewers' Handbook. KVP Publishers, Clifton, VA.

Starbard, N. (2008). Beverage Industry Microfiltration. Wiley-Blackwell, Ames, IA.

CHAPTER 27

Packaging Quality Assurance

PETER TAKACS
Spoetzl Brewery

JEFF EDGERTON
BridgePort Brewing Company

Defining Quality

If 10 people were asked to define quality, 10 different definitions could be obtained. This indicates a lack of agreement about how quality is defined. Dictionaries define quality as "an essential characteristic or trait of any product or service" but do not offer any guidance as to what these characteristics or traits are, except that they can be used to grade these products and services. This implies that quality is a matter of perception. A consumer might say, "I know quality when I see it." While this is too vague to be of use to a manufacturer of consumer products, it does bring to light the importance of consumer perception. If it is accepted that quality is a matter of perception, then quality can be defined from the components that form the foundation of and influence this perception. For manufactured products, these three components are product design, consumer persuasion (marketing), and manufacturing execution.

The first component in creating a positive consumer perception (quality) is product design. Because product design is the foundation of the product, the necessity of good product design should be obvious. For example, well-constructed cars without engines might be attractive, but they hardly fulfill their intended function.

The second component is consumer persuasion. In a crowded marketplace, no matter how well a product is designed and manufactured, consumers will not purchase a product until they have been persuaded to have a positive quality impression of the product.

The third component is manufacturing execution. This is simply manufacturing or making the product as designed. It can be argued that this component does not matter if the product is poorly designed or poorly marketed because, without the other components, consumers will not buy a product no matter how well it is made. On the other hand, excellence in manufacturing execution is crucial, for no matter how exceptional the design or persuasive the product promotion, in the end, poor manufacturing negates positive quality perceptions. This is especially true for industries such as brewing, which rely upon repeat purchasing from the consumer. Packaging quality assurance is a quality program, and the purpose of any quality program is to minimize the risk of poor manufacturing execution ruining positive quality perceptions.

Formal quality programs are known as either quality control or quality assurance. For most people, the terms are synonymous and they share many common features, but there is an underlying difference. Since this chapter is about quality assurance, it is important to draw a distinction. First, the commonality in both programs is that they sample a product population, evaluate or test the sample, and act on the total population based on results from the sample. The difference is that control programs act on the population from which the sample originated, while assurance programs act to improve future populations. Both types of programs have certain drawbacks and benefits, but the very nature of packaging and methods of analysis available for package testing forces most quality programs into the assurance mold. For example, when evaluating labeling quality, no change can be made to the bottles already labeled, the present population sampled, if the labels are upside down. A change to correct label inversion only affects unlabeled bottles, a future product population.

Quality Philosophies

Quality programs can be categorized in several ways. One way is through quality philosophy. A commonly used philosophy is to inspect products and cull defective products. This can be referred to as "inspecting quality into the product". Another philosophy is to ensure that the product is made as designed. The two approaches seem identical, but they differ in emphasis. In the first method, the emphasis is on removing defective products, not on correcting the problem process. The emphasis in the second philosophy is on fixing the problem, rather than on removing defective products. The trouble with the first philosophy is that, the smaller the percentage of defective products, the greater the effort necessary to cull defective products. This translates to a much more-expensive and, in the end, less-effective quality program than that of the second philosophy.

Types of Quality Programs

Whether quality assurance or quality control, all quality programs must have some type of organizational structure, which can range from simple to complex, with many shades in between. At the most extreme, all quality-related tasks are integrated with production. This is the simple end of the spectrum. At the opposite end, all quality tasks are separated from production and assigned to a separate department. This is the complex end of the spectrum. Both ends have their advantages and disadvantages. The location of any specific quality program on this spectrum is often related to the size and resources of the organization. Smaller breweries with fewer resources likely favor the simple model, while larger breweries, with more resources, usually adopt the more complex models.

The main advantage of the simple model—integration of quality and production tasks—is the potential to lower costs through labor savings. That is, the costs of a separate quality department are eliminated when production personnel also conduct quality testing. A secondary advantage is the potential for a faster response to quality issues through a decrease in bureaucracy with the elimination of the "quality middleman"—the quality assurance department.

The systemic disadvantages of the simple model are the overburdening of production employees with nonproduction tasks, motivational confusion, inherent conflict of interest, lack of organization, and lack of expertise. The integration of quality tasks into production tasks is a reallocation of resources. In this integration is an implicit assumption that the operational departments have the labor resources to absorb these tasks. Complications arise when this assumption is not true, leading to overburdening those employees whose task it is to make the product.

The second disadvantage is motivational confusion. This arises when the production workers are unsure whether their primary task is to keep production moving or to do the quality tests.

Conflict of interest is a natural result from the policing nature of many quality tests and because verifying the quality of one's production is self-policing. By nature, production employees are reluctant to call attention to their own mistakes. For example, how many people have made a traffic error, escaped without notice, and then driven to a police station to turn themselves in?

Both motivational confusion and conflict of interest produce similar results in that both reinforce negative motivation to perform quality tasks.

The fourth disadvantage, lack of organization, occurs since quality tasks are distributed throughout operations during the process of integrating quality and production tasks. This creates confusion with respect to who is ultimately responsible for the administration of the quality program. Operators may be aware of the quality of their own production, but without a structured quality organization, overall awareness of final product quality is very difficult to realize.

The last systemic disadvantage is the lack of competence and expertise in the performance of quality tests and the interpretation of results. Both of these skills take some time to acquire, and the latter demands a greater understanding of the packaging process and of the product than just the operation of a single packaging machine. Even if the machine operator is trained to develop testing expertise, training is rarely given for interpreting results. Costly errors in product quality are often the result. Because of the systemic disadvantages of the simple model, a common result is that quality assurance testing is not taken seriously and ultimately becomes ineffective. Subsequently, the quality of the product suffers.

In the more complex organizational models, operational and quality functions are separated into their own departments. This permits both departments to become more focused and efficient in their specialties. It creates a division that allows for focused, nonconflicting attention to be given to production as well as to quality testing. However, it increases base operational costs because of extra personnel in the quality department, and it increases internal organizational bureaucracy, which can slow responses to quality issues. The quality department has a dual role in these complex models. It is a captive service department to the operations departments. As such, it provides expertise and resources to these departments to perform essential tasks. The second role is as the quality conscience of the organization. As such, the quality department has police powers to suspend operations and to isolate products, either alone or in combination, as necessary to protect quality.

Many programs, such as total quality management (TQM) and the International Organization for Standardization (ISO), have been developed in part to resolve and avoid seemingly opposing goals between production and quality departments. While the intent of these programs is to make quality a universal way of thinking, they may be very bureaucratic in nature and often structured to assign blame. Their strong emphasis on punishing those who make mistakes can easily destroy any cooperative spirit between production and quality departments. A better solution for many breweries is to foster a constructive atmosphere from within, aimed at solving problems.

A universal solution to achieve quality goals has not yet been invented. By and large, a constructive and cooperative atmosphere between quality and operational departments is dependent on trust. This in turn is more dependent on the personalities involved than on departmental structures. However, there is one universal axiom. Achieving quality goals begins at the top. Quality, as manufacturing excellence, will never be an important goal to any organization unless the principal manager of the organization believes in it.

The benefit of any quality program is minimizing the risk of inferior manufacturing quality. However, every effort has a cost, and quality programs are no exception. There are direct operational costs, such as for personnel and equipment, and indirect costs, such as lost time due to sampling or to halting production to prevent producing a substandard product. The calculations for the most favorable ratio between risk, benefit, and cost are complex. Each brewery must determine where this ratio lies; but too often costs are emphasized over the risks or the benefits. Cost is important, but the cost of quality programs can be equated to the cost of being vaccinated. It is much less painful and expensive than curing the disease.

PACKAGING MATERIAL QUALITY

Much of a product's final quality is dependent on the quality of its components. Logic, therefore, dictates a quality inspection of all these components before use. However, few endeavors in packaging quality assurance provide so little benefit for the cost. The reasons, as always, lie in the details, but they can be summed up as looking for a needle in a haystack.

There are two general procedures for inspecting packaging material: total inspection and auditing. Total inspection is preferable but is often impossible (Fig. 27.1). By default, this leaves auditing, which is inspecting a sample from a lot and then accepting or rejecting the lot based on the sample results. Regardless of the sampling rationale used, packaging component inspections utilize some form of visual inspection in which samples are evaluated for defects. These techniques are very subjective, and although inspection error varies with each individual inspector, it is always very significant. In addition, a number of other factors compound this error. First, the acceptable quality level, or percent defectives, of the packaging components must be very low; and second, packaging components come in very large lot sizes.

Defect levels of packaging components must be low because, as these components are combined, so are the defects. Small defect levels in each component are at the very least additive and more often can magnify the final package defect levels. For example, one delayed breakage bottle in 9,600 bottles represents just over 0.01% defective as far as bottles go. However, if the bottle is encased in a customary 24-bottle case, it ruins that case. The defect level in that situation has grown to one case per 400 cases, or 0.25%, a 25-fold increase.

Packaging components come in very large lot sizes, which necessitates large sample sizes. For example, a brewery wants to audit every truckload of glass, approximately 40,000–70,000 bottles, and have it pass an acceptable quality level of 0.1% prior to acceptance. Using general inspection levels of MIL-STD-105E, a frequently used method for determining sample size of attribute-type inspection, 800 bottles would have to be inspected for

FIGURE 27.1. Empty bottle inspector, an example of total inspection. (Courtesy Spoetzl Brewery)

such a lot size. No more than two defective bottles may be found in the sample to accept the lot at 0.1% acceptable quality level.

Combining the low acceptable defect levels with the massive sample sizes promotes testing fatigue and inspection error. It takes a well-trained technician approximately 2 hours to inspect 800 bottles. Ignoring the fact that this sample size represents a lot roughly equivalent to a 1-hour run on a modern filler, by the end of the 2-hour period, the inspector likely is experiencing a high level of fatigue and has lost a significant degree of accuracy.

Several methods have been employed to overcome the analytical limitations of these procedures. One is to improve analytical protocols by allotting more time to it. However, this does little in the long run to relieve the mental fatigue associated with this type of testing, and rarely does it improve inspection error. Another method, widely practiced when visual inspection points, known as light-out stations, were placed on every packaging line, is to frequently rotate inspectors. If the sample is distributed among many inspectors, the sample size each inspector is responsible for is decreased. This eliminates some of the fatigue and consequent error associated with this type of testing, but inspection costs rise dramatically.

Other, more complicated sampling schemes besides the MIL-STD types can be used to decrease the sample size and inspection error. Some of these schemes change the evaluation from attribute (i.e., good or bad, no shades between) to variable (i.e., measurements of specific features and grading the results). These sampling schemes have their own sets of complications with regard to sample size, the number of permissible defects, methods of analysis, and other variables. The bad news is that, no matter how the auditing scheme is structured, inspection is estimated to add 10–40% to the labor costs of operating a packaging line, with only a 50% decrease, at best, in outgoing defect levels.

Other factors can add additional problems and complications to these types of audits. One is the concept of lots and lot size. While brewers can usually look at the side of a box of crowns or labels and get information regarding production dates and lot numbers, they frequently mix lots during the course of a production run. A brewer may discover that defective materials have made the product unsalable and may have to destroy an entire run of product, even though, by the vendor's definition, the brewery used numerous lots within the run. A second complication to incoming material inspections is modern inventory systems. Warehousing packaging material is expensive. To decrease these costs, most modern industries have gone to some form of just-in-time inventory systems. Under these schemes, there is a good possibility that, if a lot is rejected, there may not be sufficient material available to keep production operating. Lost production is an indirect cost that very often equals or surpasses labor costs.

A philosophical approach to the quality control of packaging materials may be stated as follows. A brewery purchases materials from a vendor with the understanding that the materials are of high quality and that the vendor has its own quality assurance program. By spending large amounts of time and money on massive sampling plans and extra labor, the brewery is, in effect, letting the vendor off the hook for quality assurance of its product. This is not to say that breweries should not carry out materials quality assurance programs to some degree but that the ultimate responsibility for the quality of any product lies with the manufacturer and seller. This is true whether a brewery is selling beer to a consumer or a vendor is selling crowns to a brewery.

The previous paragraphs make it seem that any efforts to control the quality of packaging materials are futile at best. However, there are alternative methods that provide equal or better quality assurance and control. First, modern technology has come to the rescue for some packaging material and has made 100% inspection feasible and relatively inexpensive. This has been realized for bottles in the form of empty bottle inspectors. The key to success with this technology is the equipment, which must be properly designed, installed, calibrated, and maintained. The mechanical parts must unfailingly position the bottle correctly under the sensor. The optics must be able to accurately focus and resolve the inspected portions. The programming, or software, must contain the necessary algorithms to evaluate the picture that the sensor gives it, and the electronic or computer part must be fast enough to run the software at reasonable speeds. The brewery must be diligent in challenge testing the empty bottle inspector, in calibrating the unit both when out of adjustment and at specified intervals, and in arranging service for the unit at appropriate intervals. Failure to perform these tasks can result in a completely ineffective and expensive empty bottle inspector and a false sense of security about the integrity of the bottles being used.

A second and more traditional method is to document material performance for every supplier and to use this documentation to make relevant supplier decisions. These programs are better known by their acronyms DPMR (defective packaging material report) or SCR (supplier complaint report), and their primary purpose is to document defective material on the production floor. After a period of time, the documentation can be reviewed and summarized. Logical decisions regarding vendor relations can then be made based on these summaries.

Needless to say, a number of criteria must be established for such a program to be effective. Policy regarding these programs must be developed. This policy should be clear about what is to be expected from a vendor, what is to be documented, what the review periods are, and what weighting is to be given for defects. The weighting is very important because defects have various levels of severity. For example, can lids with insufficient compound that cause leakers at a 3% rate are usually considered a more serious problem than 10 crushed cans in every fifteenth pallet of incoming cans. The latter is a nuisance but can be culled rather easily before reaching the filler; the former cannot.

The DPMR policy should also designate what documentation is to be used, who is to manage the documentation, and how, who, and what information is to be documented. In addition, documentation on total packaging supplies by vendor and component must also be maintained. This can originate from either the packaging or warehousing department, but it must be data rich; that is, dates, times, and other pertinent information must be supplied along with quantities of material used. Often, these policies and programs are coupled with vendor or supplier qualification programs. If this is so, then qualification steps, methods, and policies should also be spelled out. Finally, vendors must be made aware of these policies, and the policies must be adhered to in order for these programs to have a motivating effect on vendors to provide better quality material.

● PACKAGING OPERATIONS AND TESTS BEFORE FILLING

Rinsing

Breweries, like any food establishment, need to clean their utensils before use. This includes containers, both disposable and nondisposable. Disposable containers, nonreturnable bottles or cans, are generally cleaned by rinsing the bottle or can to remove any large debris. This debris can consist of cardboard dust, bits of plastic wrap used to wrap pallets, and more. In most cases, rinsing should not be relied on to sanitize or sterilize a package before filling.

While some breweries use domestic water as the rinsing agent, others include a sanitizer, such as chlorine dioxide, in the rinse water. The effectiveness of using such a sanitizing agent is arguable. From a microbiological standpoint, most microorganisms that are indigenous to cans or bottles are not beer spoilers. Most are gram-negative bacteria or molds. Gram-negative bacteria do not, as a rule, grow or survive in beer. Molds may survive as spores but definitely do not grow or multiply in the anaerobic environment of a sealed beer package. Therefore, even if the rinsing agent kills microorganisms, it likely does little to prevent beer spoilage.

Breweries that pasteurize their beer use rinsing solely to remove particles, while breweries that do not pasteurize use rinsing to remove particles and as a possible safeguard against microorganisms.

Generally, containers are rinsed just before arriving at the filler. Contact time is therefore very short, and the sanitizing effect is not very effective. An important point to keep in mind about rinsing is that introducing a rinse agent into a package may actually increase the number of microorganisms present in that package if the rinse agent itself is not sterile.

Two tests for rinser effectiveness are commonly used. The first is to analyze for particles. Before and after rinsing, sample packages are taken from the line and examined. The simplest way to do this is to rinse the package thoroughly with filtered water, vacuum filter the water through a 0.45-μm-membrane filter, and examine the debris collected on the filter. A dissecting scope is very useful for the examination. The second common test is to take a microbiological analysis of the inside of the package. This can be done by swabbing the package with sterile swabs and plating on appropriate media. This method is qualitative at best. Another way is to rinse the packages with sterile water blanks and then plate this water blank using the membrane filter technique with appropriate media. This can be quantitative as well as qualitative for making comparisons. Again, the rinsing process is not typically effective at killing microorganisms, and it is important to look carefully at the types of microbes that are found.

The most frequent cause of poor rinsing is malfunction of the rinser. The best way to avoid this and control the quality is to use interlocks. Interlocks are sensors and control logic built into the machine that prevent it from functioning unless all of its parameters are met. In other words, if the water flow to the rinser is inadequate, a flow sensor senses it and shuts the line down until it is fixed. However, even with interlocks, the rinser should be visually checked for function, especially at startup and frequently throughout the day. Once correct function has been verified, checks can be made for particles, and microbiological testing can be done on a routine or a random basis. If a problem with the rinser is suspected, the quality assurance department in cooperation with packaging personnel should do additional testing to diagnose and correct the problem.

Bottle Washing

Cleaning returnable bottles is a much more challenging and complicated problem than rinsing one-way (nonreturnable) packages. The machines that do these processes are called bottle washers, commonly referred to as soakers. In general, bottles are soaked in a strong, hot, alkali (caustic) solution to remove the soil and labels. After soaking, the bottles must be rinsed and then inspected.

The primary mode of action is saponification and hydrolysis reaction between the caustic and the soil and glue on the bottles. Caustic is destroyed in these reactions, and unless the concentration is replenished, cleaning efficacy diminishes. These reactions are affected by both caustic concentration and temperature. Therefore, the primary goal of any quality assurance program to monitor these machines is to make sure that the parameters of caustic concentration and temperature are maintained within the operating specification range. Another goal of any program for these machines is to ensure that the containers are completely rinsed. Caustic is detrimental both to beer and to the consumer, so care should be taken to ensure there is no carryover from the soaking machine.

As with rinsers, an interlock system to monitor the three primary soaker parameters of caustic concentration, temperature, and carryover would be ideal, but only an interlock for temperature is easily achievable. The reason caustic is not easily amenable to automated control is that the sensors that monitor caustic concentration are usually the conductivity type. As the caustic is destroyed in the cleaning reaction, conductivity diminishes, but it does not diminish linearly with respect to concentration. Therefore, it is possible to have conductivity within the specification range but a low caustic concentration. To ensure that the caustic concentration is at the appropriate strength, some sort of titration testing has to be performed on a routine basis. Most quality assurance programs specify a concentration titration at least twice per shift for each reservoir—once at startup and once midway through the shift. These frequencies should be adjusted up or down, depending on the capacity of the caustic reservoir. The larger the reservoir with respect to the number of bottles cleaned per unit of time, the less impact caustic degradation has on overall caustic concentration.

To ensure that the rinser section of the soaker is operating properly, routine testing for caustic carryover must be done. This is a simple test. A small amount of distilled water is poured into a bottle at the soaker discharge. The bottle is swirled so that the distilled water washes the interior surface. The water in the bottle is poured into a beaker or another test container and a drop or two of phenolphthalein indicator solution is added to the beaker. If the solution remains clear, there is no caustic carryover; if it turns pink, there is caustic carryover.

When there is caustic carryover, the machine should be stopped and all production since the previous test should be placed on hold. The extent of the problem should then be verified by sodium testing if possible; beer that contains caustic will have elevated sodium levels. The defect in the rinser must be repaired before starting the line to prevent the problem from recurring. This should be attended to immediately because there are still bottles in the caustic section of the soaker, and glass has limited resistance to caustic etching. If the downtime continues beyond this point, these glass bottles will be damaged and may have to be discarded.

Caustic soaking does not remove all soils. Also, large objects may be jammed into the bottle so firmly that they do not slip out when the bottle is inverted. To ensure that the bottles exiting the soaker are clean, an inspection should be done. This may be just a simple visual inspection station (light-out station); however, visual inspection alone is often ineffective. A much more effective method is an electronic/mechanical empty bottle inspector. The keys to effective inspection with this kind of machine are selecting a machine that has appropriate capabilities, proper maintenance, and frequent testing of the machine to verify proper function.

Keg Cleaning

There are numerous keg designs, but they all share two common features: they are designed to be used many times over, and unlike bottles, the keg and beer combination is never pasteurized. Consequently, kegs must be very clean before refilling. Many procedures and machines have been designed for this purpose. Usually, the process involves a draining of the residual liquid; an outer rinse, wash, or both with caustic; interior rinses and caustic washes; possibly an acid wash; and a final rinse. In addition, modern combination cleaning, sanitizing, and filling machines may provide a steam-sanitizing cycle just prior to a carbon dioxide (CO_2) purge. The final step, of course, is filling. Regardless of the details of the cleaning process or the type of keg, it is desirable to monitor and check the cleaning process. The same parameters as those for bottle soakers are important: temperature, caustic concentration, acid concentration, and chemical carryover. In addition, because the package and beer are not pasteurized as a unit, a more formal microbiological evaluation of the cleaning process should be done.

The methods employed to check temperature, caustic strength, and chemical carryover in a soaker can also be used for kegs. However, because the caustic reservoirs of these machines are smaller than those of soakers in relation to the amount of packaging surface each machine has to clean, more frequent testing may be desirable. With open-bunghole kegs, such as Golden Gate and Hoff Stevens, residual rinse water can be used to check for chemical carryover. A sample of the rinse water is collected from the keg and then titrated for chemicals or, if caustic soda is the chemical, checked for a reaction with phenolphthalein. For closed-system kegs, generically called Sankeys (straight-walled kegs), the keg stem must be removed to gain access to the interior of the keg. Special tools are available through keg manufacturers for doing this. As an alternative, if sample ports are available or can be installed, the samples can be collected from chemical or rinse drain lines.

The modern Sankey-type keg has only one entrance for both filling and emptying. These kegs are not amenable to interior inspection without disassembling the tapping mechanism. Older keg types have separate filling ports (bungholes) and tapping ports. These kegs are washed through the bunghole, and interior inspection is possible as the kegs exit the washing machine. A light is inserted through the bunghole to illuminate the interior of the keg. An operator then looks through the bunghole to visually inspect as much of the interior as possible. Any keg with soil still adhering to the interior walls is rejected and rewashed or otherwise remediated. Particular care must be taken to inspect the drawtube—especially of the Hoff Stevens variety of kegs. These tubes are plastic and are cleaned by attaching a gun to the Hoff Stevens tap and shooting cleaning solution through the drawtube. The gun and the keg can be misaligned, causing the tube to not be cleaned. Because the tubes are usually translucent plastic, soils and films are noticeable.

The same techniques for collecting rinse water samples for chemical carryover may be used for microbiological sampling; however, drain line sample ports should not be used for this purpose. In addition, aseptic sampling techniques must be used to collect rinse water. If the keg has insufficient residual rinse water, sterile water or microbiological buffer may be added to the keg to wash the interior walls of the keg. Caution is warranted here because the aseptic sampling of kegs is difficult. A keg is large and difficult to manipulate, and the rinse water may touch the outer surface of the keg as it is collected. This can easily compromise the aseptic nature of the sample. To overcome this difficulty, a portion of the outer surface should be sterilized with liberal amounts of alcohol or with flame prior to sampling. After collecting, the samples should be plated for beer-spoilage organisms. Keep in mind that microbiological plating, while traditional, is not useful for the run sampled because the plates need several days before results can be determined. The results can be used only to spot problem areas and track trends.

An instant technique rapidly gaining favor for checking the efficacy of cleaning is bioluminescence. Many companies are currently offering devices that combine swabbing with bioluminescence technology to provide an on-the-spot evaluation of cleaned surfaces or final rinse water. The technology exploits the fact that organic material on surfaces contains the energy molecule ATP. ATP reacts with luciferin and luciferase in the sampling units provided by the manufacturers of these devices and produces light in quantities that cannot be noticed by the human eye but can be read by the bioluminescent devices. The light reaction is quantified and displayed as a value on the device. Based on predetermined ranges, the person doing the test can then make a judgment about whether the surface is clean. This technology allows for nearly instantaneous feedback and may prevent the use of unclean equipment.

Another method to check keg cleaning at each step is to utilize a keg adapted with sensors to monitor the internal conditions throughout the cleaning process. Many breweries have a keg with a sight glass, an analog thermometer, and analog pressure gauges attached that they send through the line to confirm the keg cleaning program parameters. The problem with the traditional "sight keg" is that it requires someone to stand next to the keg and manually record the information (i.e., times, temperatures, and pressures) as it occurs. This is next to impossible, since activity happens very fast within the program, often in split seconds, and very few people can keep their eyes on three instruments at once while noting rapidly occurring values.

New versions of monitoring kegs are available. They are adapted with digital sensors and microprocessors to record information at frequent intervals (Fig. 27.2). These instruments ensure that accurate measurements are taken and recorded so the information may be evaluated in detail after the process has been completed. Additionally, temperatures and pressures of detergent washes and rinses can be monitored as they occur inside the keg, making it possible to optimize the cleaning process.

FIGURE 27.2. Modern electronic and digital sight keg for monitoring keg cleaning effectiveness. (Courtesy BridgePort Brewing Company)

These monitoring kegs are especially valuable for auditing steam disinfecting of the keg after cleaning has been completed. Steam is an excellent keg disinfectant for a number of reasons. Most breweries have a ready source of available steam, and steam is more effective than CO_2 at displacing air inside the keg. In addition, the sterilizing steam can be readily purged with CO_2 prior to filling. The quality of the steam must be closely monitored to ensure that it is saturated, because only saturated steam disinfects satisfactorily. If the steam is either supersaturated or mixed with air, it does not perform effectively in the time allowed. Without monitoring the internal conditions of the keg, the brewery may be operating under the belief that their disinfecting is adequate, when in fact it is not.

● FILLER CHECKS

The old brewmaster complained that it took the packaging department only an hour to ruin the beer that took a month to make. As much as packaging managers may see this as an unfair assessment, it contains a germ of truth. The preservation of the delicate flavors of beer in cans, bottles, or kegs through the filling process is not an easy task. Beer is a fragile creation and its flavor molecules react negatively to contact with oxygen, light, and reactive surfaces. Furthermore, beer is carbonated to levels that have to be maintained within narrow ranges. Therefore, filling containers with beer is tricky at best, with many conflicting forces and parameters that must be balanced and met for filling to be successful. It is not surprising that filling is the central focus of most packaging quality assurance programs.

Like bottles and cans, beer is a packaging component, and like other components, it is supplied by a vendor. In this case, the vendor is the brewing department, and like other packaging components, the beer must meet defined quality levels. The three primary quality parameters of interest to the packaging department are temperature, carbonation, and dissolved oxygen (DO) levels of the beer in the package release tank. If these parameters are not within operating or product specification, there is nothing the packaging department can do to remedy or rectify them. The use of beer that is out of specification only results in a packaged product that is out of specification.

Reasons for Testing Air, Fill, and CO_2

The main reason for checking carbonation levels (CO_2 concentration) is that beer is a carbonated beverage and its consumers expect a certain fizz. To maintain consistent fizz, carbonation has to be maintained within a narrow range, because a difference of 0.20 volume of CO_2 produces perceptible taste differences to many consumers.

Another reason for monitoring carbonation is that it is a flavor suppressant. The higher the carbonation, the more flavor is suppressed. To maintain uniform flavor, carbonation must be maintained within a narrow range.

Yet another reason for maintaining carbonation levels within a specified range is to avoid overpressuring a container during pasteurization. The higher the initial carbonation, the greater the internal pressure of the container at the maximum temperature during the pasteurization cycle. A danger exists if the initial carbonation is too high; the pressure limit of the container could be exceeded. This could result in a pasteurizer full of bulging can ends or broken bottles.

The reason for monitoring the air content of a package is that air is approximately 20% oxygen. Oxygen is very destructive to the flavor stability of beer, and flavor stability is equivalent to beer shelf life. Air is entrapped in the headspace of the container, which is the volume of a container not filled with liquid. This air must be expelled in some fashion before closure to prevent the entrapment of oxygen in the container. Multiple methods are employed to expel this air. For cans, the headspace is typically flooded with CO_2 to expel air. For bottles, the product is agitated to cause foaming and expel the air. However, no matter how well air is removed from the package headspace, if the DO content of the beer is high, the oxygen content of the beer in the container is high.

The main reason for monitoring fills is honesty. Fill volumes are declared on the package. It is only ethical that brewers deliver the volume of beer they say they will.

Another motivation to check fills is to comply with regulations that affect this parameter. United States federal regulations are quite loose in that they allow a maximum variation of ±0.5% of stated fill based on plant average fills over three consecutive calendar months. State and local regulations, however, may be much more stringent.

Still another reason to check fills is to meet target fill values with a minimum of variation. Once a beer filler has been adjusted, the fills should be monitored for drift, with respect to both target and variation. This drift can be caused by normal wear and tear of the filler, minute changes in container volume, or a myriad of other factors.

Analytic Methods for Measuring Fill

Before discussing appropriate sample sizes and frequencies to achieve these goals, a short description of how these tests are performed is offered. Fills can be done either gravimetrically or volumetrically. In the volumetric method, the beer from a container is poured into a volumetric flask designed for this task. Usually, some type of antifoam agent, such as octanol or hexanol, is added to suppress foaming and loss of liquid. Once the foam has settled, the fill is obtained from the alignment of the meniscus with the graduation lines etched in the neck of the flask. In the gravimetric method, the full container is weighed and then emptied. The empty container and closure is then weighed to obtain a tare weight. The tare is subtracted from the full weight, and the difference is divided by the specific gravity of the beer to obtain a volume measure. Of these two methods, the latter is generally more accurate.

Analytic Methods for Measuring Air and CO_2

The brewing industry in general uses Zahm-Nagel piercing devices (Zahm & Nagel Company, Holland, NY) to measure package air and CO_2 (Fig. 27.3). Using this device, the package is clamped and pierced. The clamped package and piercing equipment are then shaken. For CO_2, the maximum internal pressure and the temperature of the package are measured. These two readings are then correlated using a table (Table 27.1) to obtain the CO_2 concentration. This concentration can be percent

TABLE 27.1. Beer Carbonation, Expressed as Volumes of CO_2, at Various Temperatures and Pressures[a]

Temp.		Pressure in Pounds per Square Inch Gauge (psig)																				
°C	°F	5	6	7	8	9	10	11	12	13	14	15	16	17	18	19	20	21	22	23	24	25
−1	30	2.25	2.37	2.48	2.60	2.71	2.83	2.94	3.05	3.17												
−1	31	2.20	2.31	2.43	2.54	2.65	2.76	2.87	2.98	3.10	3.21											
0	32	2.15	2.26	2.37	2.48	2.59	2.70	2.81	2.92	3.03	3.14	3.24										
1	33	2.10	2.21	2.32	2.43	2.53	2.64	2.75	2.85	2.96	3.07	3.17										
1	34	2.06	2.16	2.27	2.37	2.48	2.58	2.69	2.79	2.90	3.00	3.10	3.21									
2	35	2.02	2.12	2.22	2.32	2.43	2.53	2.63	2.73	2.83	2.94	3.04	3.14	3.24								
2	36	1.97	2.07	2.17	2.27	2.37	2.48	2.58	2.68	2.78	2.88	2.98	3.08	3.18								
3	37	1.93	2.03	2.13	2.23	2.33	2.43	2.52	2.62	2.72	2.82	2.92	3.01	3.11	3.21							
3	38	1.90	1.99	2.09	2.18	2.28	2.38	2.47	2.57	2.67	2.76	2.86	2.95	3.05	3.15	3.24						
4	39	1.86	1.95	2.05	2.14	2.24	2.33	2.43	2.52	2.61	2.71	2.80	2.90	2.99	3.09	3.18						
4	40	1.82	1.92	2.01	2.10	2.19	2.29	2.38	2.47	2.56	2.66	2.75	2.84	2.93	3.03	3.12	3.21					
5	41	1.79	1.88	1.97	2.06	2.15	2.24	2.33	2.43	2.52	2.61	2.70	2.79	2.88	2.97	3.06	3.15	3.24				
6	42	1.76	1.85	1.93	2.02	2.11	2.20	2.29	2.38	2.47	2.56	2.65	2.74	2.83	2.92	3.00	3.09	3.18				
6	43	1.72	1.81	1.90	1.99	2.07	2.16	2.25	2.34	2.43	2.51	2.60	2.69	2.78	2.86	2.95	3.04	3.13	3.21			
7	44	1.69	1.78	1.87	1.95	2.04	2.12	2.21	2.30	2.38	2.47	2.55	2.64	2.73	2.81	2.90	2.98	3.07	3.16	3.24		
7	45	1.66	1.75	1.83	1.92	2.00	2.09	2.17	2.26	2.34	2.43	2.51	2.59	2.68	2.76	2.85	2.93	3.02	3.10	3.19		
8	46	1.64	1.72	1.80	1.89	1.97	2.05	2.13	2.22	2.30	2.38	2.47	2.55	2.63	2.72	2.80	2.88	2.96	3.05	3.13	3.21	
8	47	1.61	1.69	1.77	1.85	1.94	2.02	2.10	2.18	2.26	2.34	2.43	2.51	2.59	2.67	2.75	2.83	2.91	3.00	3.08	3.16	3.24
9	48	1.58	1.66	1.74	1.82	1.90	1.98	2.06	2.14	2.22	2.30	2.38	2.47	2.55	2.63	2.71	2.79	2.87	2.95	3.03	3.11	3.19
9	49	1.56	1.64	1.71	1.79	1.87	1.95	2.03	2.11	2.19	2.27	2.35	2.43	2.50	2.58	2.66	2.74	2.82	2.90	2.98	3.06	3.14
10	50	1.53	1.61	1.69	1.76	1.84	1.92	2.00	2.08	2.15	2.23	2.31	2.39	2.46	2.54	2.62	2.70	2.77	2.85	2.93	3.01	3.09
11	51	1.51	1.58	1.66	1.74	1.81	1.89	1.97	2.04	2.12	2.20	2.27	2.35	2.43	2.50	2.58	2.65	2.73	2.81	2.88	2.96	3.04
11	52		1.56	1.63	1.71	1.78	1.86	1.94	2.01	2.09	2.16	2.24	2.31	2.39	2.46	2.54	2.61	2.69	2.76	2.84	2.91	2.99
12	53		1.54	1.61	1.68	1.76	1.83	1.91	1.98	2.05	2.13	2.20	2.28	2.35	2.43	2.50	2.57	2.65	2.72	2.80	2.87	2.94
12	54		1.51	1.59	1.66	1.73	1.80	1.88	1.95	2.02	2.10	2.17	2.24	2.32	2.39	2.46	2.53	2.61	2.68	2.75	2.83	2.90
13	55			1.56	1.63	1.71	1.78	1.85	1.92	1.99	2.07	2.14	2.21	2.28	2.35	2.43	2.50	2.57	2.64	2.71	2.78	2.86
13	56			1.54	1.61	1.68	1.75	1.82	1.89	1.96	2.04	2.11	2.18	2.25	2.32	2.39	2.46	2.53	2.60	2.67	2.74	2.81
14	57			1.52	1.59	1.66	1.73	1.80	1.87	1.94	2.01	2.08	2.15	2.22	2.29	2.36	2.43	2.49	2.56	2.63	2.70	2.77
14	58				1.56	1.63	1.70	1.77	1.84	1.91	1.98	2.05	2.11	2.18	2.25	2.32	2.39	2.46	2.53	2.60	2.67	2.74

[a] To find the volume of carbon dioxide (CO_2), locate the temperature reading in the left-hand column and then find the pressure reading across the top. Where the two intersect is the volume of CO_2.

FIGURE 27.3. Package carbon dioxide and package air testing devices. (Courtesy BridgePort Brewing Company)

volume/volume (in the United States) or percent weight/weight (in other parts of the world). For package air, a valve at the top of the piercing device is opened after shaking and the CO_2 gas is allowed to exit the package into a Schwartz burette. This is a closed, inverted burette with a large reservoir at the base. The reservoir and the burette are completely filled with a hydroxide (caustic) solution. As the CO_2 bubbles through this solution, it is destroyed, but the hydroxide does not react with air (oxygen and nitrogen). The unreacted gas is permitted to float to the top of the burette, where its volume is measured against the graduations of the burette. This procedure is repeated several times to ensure that all the air in the package is expelled and measured.

These devices are frequently combined. Their combination produces an inherent error in either the air or the CO_2 reading. If the piercing needle is not purged before piercing, the entrapped air in the needle elevates the air reading. If the needle is purged (usually with caustic) before piercing, some of the CO_2 in the container is destroyed and a lower CO_2 value is obtained. Therefore, it is recommended that piercing devices be dedicated to one function or the other.

Package Dissolved Oxygen

An alternative method for evaluating the air elimination efficacy of fillers is to measure the DO of the package. This method is sometimes used in place of and sometimes in conjunction with the headspace air method. The advantage of this method, over the headspace air method, is that the oxygen concentration is in the same units as those of the package release tanks. This permits evaluation of the efficacy of the filler air elimination device by directly comparing the package oxygen and package release tank oxygen.

For the DO value to accurately reflect the amount of oxygen in the package, all the oxygen in the package must be in equilibrium between the headspace and the liquid. To achieve this equilibrium, the package needs to be shaken or agitated before piercing. The type, amount, and length of agitation and the temperature of the beer during agitation are important in order to achieve a uniform and accurate equilibrium. If the agitation is too little, or the agitation time is too short, there is a possibility that equilibrium will not be achieved before testing. If the agitation is too vigorous or too long, there is a potential for the oxygen in the package to react with the beer components. Both of these circumstances might give artificially low DO values. Since higher temperatures increase the reaction rates for both the equilibrium reaction and the oxidation reaction, temperature is also a factor affecting the DO equilibrium.

The piercing device used in this method is connected to a DO meter. This piercing device clamps and pierces the package of beer, after which the long piercing needle is pushed deep into the container. To obtain a DO value, the beer in the package is pushed by CO_2 gas through the piercing needle into the DO tester.

In addition to chemical factors, three equipment factors affect this test. First, in some piercing devices, the drawtube and the piercing needle are combined. Because the drawtube is a relatively long, thin tube, the piercing edge tends to become dull. The duller it becomes, the more pressure is needed to pierce the container. This increases the possibility of bending the drawtube. Second, the seal around the drawtube can leak and permit the gas in the package to escape. This might affect the oxygen equilibrium in the package. Generally, bent needles and ruined seals go hand in hand. The third equipment factor is the DO meter. Most DO meters used in this type of test are of the Clark electrode design. As a rule, these testers process approximately 150 mL of beer per minute and, at the end of each minute, are 95% closer to the true DO value than at the start of the minute. If the starting DO value in the tester is very high, the beer in the package might be used up before a stable and true reading is obtained. For example, the true DO value of a package of beer was 0.010 parts per million (ppm). The tester was at 12.7 ppm at the start of the test. Within 1 minute, the tester should read 0.635 ppm. After 2 minutes, the tester should read 0.032 ppm. At this point, the package might be empty and the test cannot be continued, but the declared DO value is still three times greater than the actual DO value. This is a substantial error.

Some of these equipment drawbacks can be overcome by having a piercing device that separates the piercing and drawtube functions. By always maintaining positive counterpressure during the piercing process, any leaks around the drawtube seal are minimized. Flushing the DO meter with extra samples before running actual test samples season the sensor to the appropriate range and eliminate error caused by slow sensor response time. Running samples at the same temperature as the DO meter sensor also decreases response time and increases testing accuracy. Finally, adhering to rigid sample preparation protocols with respect to temperature and agitation provides more repeatable and reliable results.

A very useful aspect of this method is that the contribution of the filling process to the total dissolved oxygen content load of the individual package can be determine directly. This is accomplished by performing the test without agitating the package. From the total package DO, the packaging release tank DO, and the headspace air DO contribution, the actual DO pickup while filling the container can be calculated.

Sample Sizes

At this point, a discussion of sample sizes for these tests is warranted. The discrepancy between what is statistically valid and what can be accomplished in the packaging laboratory is quite large. Yet, a wealth of evidence shows that the statistically illogical sample sizes work. Therefore, some other criteria, besides statistical validity, must be used to determine sample size.

Sample Sizes for CO_2

The sample size rationale used for testing carbonation is based on the fact that carbonation levels are not changed from the level the beer had in the packaging tank during filling except by the deaeration device. This device should work consistently for all valves or stations on the filler. If one of these stations malfunctions, it is clearly apparent by the low fill result as opposed to a difference in carbonation. Therefore, the only justification for running multiple samples for carbonation is to verify the initial result. If variation exists between multiple samples, it has more to do with gauge repeatability than with actual differences between packages.

Sample Sizes for Air

For the package air test, two rationales can be used as logic to determine sample sizes. Both are based on the assumption that the quantity of headspace air is determined by the performance of the filler and of the air elimination device on the filler.

The first rationale is based on the assumption that a possibility exists for the filler or the air elimination device to malfunction. The air elimination device can malfunction if it is set at a very marginal level or is acting erratically. If there are multiple devices, such as undercover gassers for cans, the malfunction only needs to be with one of the devices. In this rationale, sample size is either set at a fixed number large enough to ensure all air elimination devices are sampled or at the number of air elimination devices. For cans, this would be the number of stations on the seamer.

With this rationale, there is an implication that each sample can be traced back to a specific air elimination device. To meet this traceability requirement, provisions must be made on the filler to enable sampling at operational speeds and maintain registration to the air elimination device. While this would be a wonderfully accurate process, anyone who has ever tried to match individual containers with a seamer or crowner head of a modern high-speed filler can testify that this is a daunting task.

The second rationale for determining air test sample sizes is founded on the fact that this type of testing falls in both assurance and control categories. That is to say, because the operating parameters of the sampled lot cannot be modified, the test falls in the quality assurance category. However, the information from this test allows adjustments to be made to the filling equipment, which will affect future lots or the packages to be filled. This is a control aspect. The more rapidly this information is obtained and acted upon, the greater is the control aspect. To enhance this control aspect, the sample size should be small enough to enable results to be generated within a reasonable time frame.

Sample Sizes for Fills

The first rationale for setting the sample size for fills is to view each filling station on a beer filler as a fill control device. According to statistical process control protocols, five samples should be taken from each filling device at each sampling interval. For a typical 72-spout filler, this would be 360 samples. The sheer volume of samples is so large that analytic and destroyed-product costs are very high, but the main disadvantage is that analytic time is so long that any control aspect to this test is lost.

The second rationale for setting the sample size for fills is based on the assumption that, if catastrophic failure were to occur to one or more of the filling heads, it should be readily apparent to the filler operator. Therefore, routine quality assurance fill tests should not be considered protection against catastrophic failure. Once a filler has been set up and each filling head has been determined to provide repeatable, on-target results with low variability, the filler can be considered as one filling device. In this case, using standard statistical process control protocols, the sample size should be five samples at each sampling interval.

An alternative apparatus that can be used as a substitute or in conjunction with fill tests is a check weigher. Check weighers are machines that weigh each individual package after the filler discharge. Better models also maintain registration with filling heads. These machines can provide a tremendous wealth of information that can be used to modify and improve filler performance. As a practical measure, check weighers are more useful with cans than with bottles because can tare weights are more uniform than those of bottles. Again, the key to proper function for these machines is, as with any other packaging machine, periodic maintenance and calibration.

Sampling Frequency

The basic rationale of sampling frequencies is risk tolerance. If a brewery's tolerance for risk is low, sampling frequency can be increased. If a brewery's tolerance is high, sampling frequency can be decreased. Risk tolerance is very much affected by the reliability of and trust in the packaging equipment.

The advantage to high-frequency sampling is decreasing the quantity of defective material if defective packaging were to occur. The disadvantage is higher quality assurance costs for sampling and analysis. These advantages/disadvantages are reversed for low-frequency sampling.

Another rationale of sampling frequency is to sample at every lot change. This is based on the assumption that most problems, if they were to occur, would occur here. Most breweries define a lot, for this purpose, as change of packaging release beer. Therefore, sampling should occur at startup and whenever a tank change occurs.

● OTHER TESTS AT THE FILLER

Beer

The correct identity of all packaging components has to be verified to ensure that the completed combination is as specified. The beer is no exception. This verification can be realized in a number of ways, depending upon the complexity of the brewery operations. For small breweries with minimal complexity, i.e., relatively few brands that are easily differentiated visually, verification can be made by visual tracing of line hookup or by the appearance of the product alone. For larger, more complex brewery operations, in addition to visual verification, chemical analysis should be done to match product at the filler with the chemical analysis of the packaging release tank. The sample for this verification should be taken either at a sample port at the filler base or from a first-round bottle or can. Whether the filler should be started and run while this verification is taking place is dependent on the risk tolerance of the brewery.

Closures—Crowns

One of the oldest closures still used for beer packaging is crowns. These are circular, stamped pieces of metal with a gasketing material on the inner surface. Crowns are applied to the sealing surface or opening of the bottle. During application, their outer edges, called skirts, are pushed down over the side of the opening.

The primary quality check of crown application is the crimp or diameter of the applied crown. The acceptable range for this parameter is very limited. Too tight and the crown may damage the finish of the bottle, too loose and the sealing integrity may not be ensured. A second quality check is whether the gasket material, on the inside surface of the crown, makes a seal.

At the filler, the operator should take a set of samples that is representative of the number of heads on the crowner. The crowns should be checked for proper crimp using a crimp gauge. The sealing gasket of these crowns, often a vinyl liner, should be checked for an impression from the finish of the bottle. This indicates that a seal has been achieved.

If the crown crimp is too loose or too tight, the crowner should be adjusted accordingly. If the crown crimp cannot be adjusted to the specified range, the crowner should be checked first for broken springs or other mechanical faults. If the crowner is working properly, the crown metal should be checked for temper.

With the advent of twist-off crowns, a new complexity was added to the testing of these closures. Twist-off crowns need a certain amount of torque or rotational force to remove them. If the torque is too loose, the package seal integrity may be too easily compromised; if it is too tight, the consumer may not be able to twist off the crown.

The primary check for twist-off crowns, as well as for pry-off crowns, is appropriate crimp. The gas release and removal torques of these samples should be checked next. Finally, a visual examination of the sealing surface is needed to check for an impression of the bottle finish.

The three factors affecting the torque of the crowns are liner material, glass sealing-surface roughness, and in a minor way, crowner adjustment. If either of the first two reasons are the cause for the out-of-specification torques, the packaging department can do little except switch to different crown lots, glass lots, or both and complain to the vendors. Any attempt to cure torque defects with crowner adjustments is acceptable as long as crimp tolerances are not exceeded.

Closures—Caps

Another type of twist-off closure is the aluminum cap. The primary test is to visually examine the applied caps from each closure head for complete threads and for a properly crimped pilfer ring. A secondary test is for gas release and removal torques.

The factors that affect the removable torque for caps are similar to the ones for crowns. The cap liner and glass sealing finish are important factors. Since considerably more of a cap is in contact with the glass than it is with a crown, glass smoothness in the threaded area has more bearing than does the liner. Another important factor is the amount of metal holding the pilfer ring to the cap. This ring has to separate from the cap when it is twisted off. Too much metal or inadequate scoring raises the removal torque.

Cappers have greater roles in determining the removal torque for caps than the crowners do for crowns. If threads are not well formed, the removal torque may be too low. If the rollers on the capper are maladjusted; if the springs controlling these rollers are improperly sized, weak, or broken; or if the rollers are not sufficiently lubricated, there is a danger that the caps will be cut. Depending on the location of the cut, the cap may not maintain sealing integrity.

Torque

For packages with twist-off–type closures, it is important to evaluate the torque required to remove the closure. There are two torque values for crowns and caps. The first is for pressure release and the second is for closure removal.

At each sampling, one package from each closure head should be evaluated. This is done using a simple torque testing device that employs a clamp at the base of the bottle that is mounted on a maximum-reading strain gauge. The crown or cap is twisted off—mimicking a normal removal—while allowing the clamp to support the bottle. The maximum torque required to remove the closure registers on the strain gauge and can then be read as the closure's torque. It should be noted that torque values obtained at the filler are not representative of torque values obtained after pasteurization and should be done primarily as a quality control analysis. For quality assurance purposes, samples should be taken from the pasteurizer, refrigerated for 24 hours, and tested. These readings are more representative of the torques the customer experiences.

Crowns are a more robust than caps as a closure. The frequency of sampling and evaluation for crowns should be at startup and at least every time the samples are routinely measured for air fills or CO_2. A more frequent sampling and evaluation regime should be maintained for caps.

Closures—Lids

The most commonly used closures for beer containers are can lids. The evaluation of the application of this type of closure is much more complicated than that for either crowns or caps.

A can lid is applied to the can in the can seamer, which is a rotating machine affixed to the can filler and operating synchronously with the filler. Each seamer comes with a certain number of stations, and each station has to be considered an independent machine.

Seaming is a critical process. If incorrectly performed, the seam leaks, making the product unsalable. Often, a can with a leaking seam can be caught (usually by fill-height devices) before encasing or palletization, but just as often, it is not observed until palletized and warehoused. In these instances, the telltale sign are numerous flying insect pests around the affected pallet. When this occurs, not only the seamed can, but the whole pallet, is unsalable.

Sample Sizes for Can Seams

Because each station on the seamer is an independent machine, and because this operation is so critical, at least one sample per station must be taken at each sampling. In addition, the sampling must be performed so that registration or traceability of the seamed can to a particular station is maintained.

The seamer should be checked at startup and at predefined intervals, usually midshift or every 4 hours.

Testing Methods for Can Seams

The primary parameters of interest are countersink, seam width, seam height, pressure ridge, cover hook, body hook, overlap, and wrinkle rating. These parameters can be examined a number of ways.

The oldest technique for evaluating can seams is with a micrometer. The exterior of the seam is evaluated first visually for smoothness, pressure ridge, and appearance. After measuring the countersink, seam height, and seam width with a micrometer, the seam between the lid and the can is cut so it separates from the can without damaging either the cover hook or the body hook. Both the body hook and the cover hook are measured with a micrometer and the cover hook is examined visually for wrinkling.

A more modern technique is to cut two slots in the seam using a specialized seam saw. The metal between these cuts is removed, and the cut seam is placed on the inspection section of a seam scope, where it is illuminated. In older scopes, the illuminated picture was projected on a screen. The picture was rather dim, and lighting around the scope had to be dimmed to view the picture. In newer scopes, the reflected picture of the seam is captured digitally. The picture is then shown on a monitor with knobs to control dimensioning lines on the screen. The seam parameters of height, width, cover hook, body hook, and overlap can then be measured with these dimensioning lines. No matter which technique is used for evaluation, adjustments to the seamer are based on these measurements.

As a rule, seamer adjustment responsibility is assigned to the packaging maintenance department. Sometimes, for the sake of efficiency, seam checks are also assigned to the packaging maintenance department. This may present a quandary to the quality department for a couple reasons. One, unless the test is routinely performed, testing expertise is lost and expertise regarding the seaming operation is lost. Two, seamer monitoring by the quality department becomes more difficult, yet ultimate quality responsibility for can integrity often remains with the quality department.

Can Liners

One quality check that more properly belongs to Chapter 29, Packaging Materials and Beer Quality, than to this chapter is can liner evaluation. However, because sampling for these tests is frequently made at the filler, it is included here.

Beverage cans are made from aluminum or, more rarely, steel. Beer is corrosive to both. To prevent corrosion, cans are lined with a lacquer or enamel. This coating, called a liner, must be uniform and completely cover the interior of the can. The test for this coverage is called enamel rating, and the apparatus used is called an enamel rater.

The technique for the test is to place a can on a conducting surface. This is considered an electrode. The can is filled with a conducting solution, such as copper sulfate. Another electrode is immersed into the can filled with conducting solution, making sure the can walls or can bottom are not touched by this second electrode. The electrodes are connected to a meter to measure current, and current is induced through the electrodes. The greater the amount of current passed and recorded by the meter, the poorer the liner coverage, either in thickness or in voids in the liner.

The frequency of sampling and the sample size for this test is very rarely, if ever, performed to attribute acceptance sampling standards. One reason is that the test is even more time-consuming than are the visual inspection tests for other packaging material. Another reason is that sample sizes are every bit as large as for other packaging material. A third reason is that, by treating the results as a characteristic instead of an attribute, smaller and less frequent samples are needed.

Online Inspection—Fills

If the fill of a single container is sufficiently below the specification range, it is a gross underfill. It can occur for a multitude of reasons. As a rule, it is not a common occurrence; however, since it occurs at random, it is a problem. This randomness makes quality auditing as a monitoring tool quite worthless. To prevent these defective packages from reaching the consumer, online, automatic fill-height inspectors have been invented.

Online fill-height inspectors work by shooting a weak beam of low-level radiation through every container that is conveyed in front of it, at a specific height, unique to every package type and design (Fig. 27.4). The machines sense the amount of radiation passing through the container. If the radiation density is too high, insufficient radiation was absorbed by the package, and the package is underfilled.

Most fill-height detectors are set up to trigger an air-actuated ejector mechanism that removes defective packages

FIGURE 27.4. Fill-height inspector. (Courtesy Spoetzl Brewery)

from those conveyed in a single file in front of the inspector. The fill-height detector can also be set up to detect high or cocked crowns, as well as missing crowns, on bottles.

These fill-height detectors are quite robust instruments but are built into lines that experience significant vibration, moisture, and frequent stops and starts. This stress, as well as other factors, can cause them to malfunction. To monitor their function, the inspectors need to be challenged with known defective "blanks" on a routine basis throughout the operating shift. Recommended testing frequency for these testers is at startup and at least twice a shift.

Online Inspection—Sealed Package Integrity

Another type of inspection becoming more common is to inspect for sealed package integrity after filling by projecting sound waves at the package and then listening to the echo (Fig. 27.5). If the echo is outside an appropriate range for frequency or decibels, it is rejected. The reject mechanism is usually the same type as that used for fill-height inspectors.

The frequency and decibel results of every package inspected are added to a histogram, which is maintained for these parameters by the instrument. As new values are added to the histograms, older values are purged. In this manner, the operating range for the package type and operating condition is constantly updated. Acceptability ranges can be set and altered based on these results.

However, these instruments need to be challenged with a known defective at the same frequency or more as that for fill-height inspectors.

In addition to inspecting individual sealed package integrity, full-case inspectors are also becoming more common (Fig. 27.6). The purpose of these inspectors is to inspect sealed cases and reject any that do not have a full complement of individual packages or has a broken container in it, either alone or in combination. These inspectors function in a manner similar to that of individual package fill-height inspectors with a similar, albeit generally less violent, reject mechanism. Recommended challenge sampling and frequency are the same as those for individual fill-height inspectors. The challenge sample is either a case with one of the bottles or cans removed or a case that has a known underfilled container within it.

● BOTTLE CONDITIONING

For most breweries, the presence of any living organism in the packaged product is undesirable. However, breweries that perform a secondary fermentation, known as bottle or keg conditioning, actually add live yeast, along with a fermentable sugar source, back to the beer to be packaged. This accomplishes several things. First, it creates natural carbonation. The amount of carbonation created can and should be controlled by carefully controlling the amount of fermentable sugar added back to the beer. Second, the conditioning process uses up a certain amount of the DO and headspace air in the beer, adding a degree of protection from oxidation. And third, the yeast successfully competes for and uses up available food sources for spoilage bacteria. Of course, this beer cannot

FIGURE 27.5. Package seal integrity inspector. (Courtesy Spoetzl Brewery)

FIGURE 27.6. Full-case inspector. (Courtesy BridgePort Brewing Company)

be pasteurized or filtered in any way on route to the filler or racker because the yeast would be removed or killed. When bottle conditioning is done in a strictly controlled and measured fashion, the result is bottled beer with a predictable and repeatable amount of natural carbonation. The amount of sugar and yeast added back to the beer is calculated to slowly increase the carbonation of the beer naturally to a predetermined endpoint. The beer is bottled at a lower tank CO_2 level and, after bottling, is held at an optimal conditioning temperature to referment the product in the bottle over a set time period. This process must be calculated and carried out very carefully or the result may be unpredictable carbonation levels.

Since bottle conditioning is a somewhat tricky process, it is important to evaluate the beer at each step very carefully. As with non-bottle-conditioned products, tank carbonation levels should be checked before bottling to determine the exact starting point. Bottle carbonation levels should be checked not only during the run but also after the warm conditioning period. Bottles can be forced to a final endpoint by agitating them on a wrist shaker for 24–36 hours at room temperature and checking carbonation. Following the conditioning period, the bottles should be checked for endpoint carbonation levels.

Since these products cannot be microbiologically stabilized using traditional methods, it is especially important to run thorough microbiological analyses on the bottled product. Generally, sampling frequency should be at least as frequent as sampling for routine packaging analysis throughout the run and one or more bottles should be plated from each sampling. Since the product contains yeast, it must be plated using either the pour plate or the spread plate method. Membrane filtration cannot be utilized because the membrane becomes plugged with yeast almost immediately. While bottle conditioning is a process that can produce excellent final products, it is also a process that is fraught with possible problems and should be approached very carefully.

MICROBIOLOGY AND MICROBIOLOGICAL STABILIZATION

Stabilization

While current brewing microbiological dogma makes the reasonable assumption that pathogenic microorganisms are not a danger in beer, it is still a food product that supports the growth of nontoxic spoilage organisms. More than a century and a half ago, on trading ships bound for India, it was discovered that highly hopped beers were less likely to spoil during the voyage. This was because of the natural bacteriostatic effect of the hops. Many beers still have this natural effect from hops in addition to a natural preservative quality from fermentation. Fermentation lowers pH, creates ethanol, and uses up readily available food sources for microorganisms. This natural tendency of beer is still utilized to a large degree by small brewers and by some very noteworthy large brewers. While it is commonly relied upon to impart some degree of microbial stability to beer, the results of fermentation alone do not guarantee microbial stability. To impart long-term stability, active stabilization techniques have been devised.

Many brewers and breweries believe that pasteurization and sterile filtration are severe and strip the beers of many of their subtle flavors. It is indeed still very common practice to use the "passive stabilization" (natural preservative effect) method with kegged beer. The kegs are filled and kept cold until the keg is emptied, thereby delaying spoilage by retarding the growth of spoilage microorganisms. This is effective when it is understood that the package is to be kept cold until consumed, but it cannot be relied upon to completely stabilize beer in packages that will be sold or stored at room temperatures. Techniques had to be devised to stabilize beer in packages for the long term. Chemical stabilization of beer has not curried favor because of consumer resistance. Only three methods—sterile filtration, bulk (flash) pasteurization, and tunnel pasteurization—are currently in widespread use. Each method boasts advantages and disadvantages, but because of their more complex methodology, flash pasteurization and sterile filtration require a higher level of maintenance and monitoring than does tunnel pasteurization.

Flash pasteurization is a method that utilizes heat exchanger technology to heat the beer to a specified temperature for a specified residence time and then to cool the beer back to the desired filling temperature (Fig. 27.7).

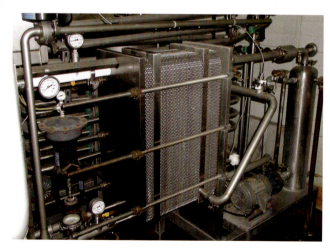

FIGURE 27.7. Flash pasteurizer. (Courtesy Spoetzl Brewery)

This process is frequently used for kegged beer and is finding favor with some bottled and canned products as a cost-saving measure. Current technology for plastic beer packaging prohibits the practice of pasteurizing the product in the package, so flash pasteurization may be an attractive alternative.

One frequent mistake used with these pieces of equipment is to use the same lethality factors as the ones employed in tunnel pasteurizers. This works only if time, temperature, and pressure are identical to what would be achieved in the container in tunnel pasteurizers. Variance in any of the factors could lead to an inadequately pasteurized product.

As with traditional tunnel pasteurizers, it is important to remember that the process is only as reliable as the machinery used to achieve the process. And since this process is in-line, the quality assurance process does not have the luxury of running a pasteurization unit clock as it does with tunnel pasteurizers. The only parameter that can be measured and used for quality control of this process is to monitor and adjust the flow rate (time), pressure, and temperature. These factors determine the final effectiveness of the flash pasteurization treatment and the condition of the beer when it reaches the filler. Modern technology allows for continuous monitoring of these parameters with alarms for any major deviations from set parameters. If a unit is not so equipped, periodic checks and documentation of the parameters are warranted at intervals based on the concept previously discussed, risk tolerance.

FIGURE 27.8. Sterile filtration apparatus. (Courtesy BridgePort Brewing Company)

Another method that is used for microbiological stabilization is sterile filtration (Fig. 27.8). This method has become popular in recent years because of the public's demand for freshness and a perception by some that pasteurization is damaging to beer flavor. In this method, beer is filtered through one or more filters designed to remove residual particulate matter and, most importantly, microorganisms. It is important to note that the removal of particulate matter is generally done as a separate filtration step to protect against plugging the very-fine-pore (usually 0.45 µm) microorganism filter. Quality control of these setups is essentially preventive. The filters generally have a specified lifespan and should be changed when indicated. The filters have an optimal operating pressure range that should not be exceeded. Sometimes these parameters are measured automatically and sometimes they are not. No matter how they are measured, maintaining these parameters is critical to the performance of this form of microbiological stabilization.

Flash pasteurization and sterile filtration have one important characteristic in common. Both of these methods treat the beer before reaching the filler, so the filling process and the equipment between the sterile filter or flash pasteurizer and the filler must be aseptic to maintain the effect of the treatment. For quality assurance of these methods, samples must be taken at various intervals for plating. Again, this is quality assurance because microbiological results are not available for several days after the product is packaged. The quality control of each of these methods is different and should be discussed separately.

Tunnel pasteurization is simply conveying a package of beer through a tunnel equipped with hot-water spray nozzles preset at a temperature calculated to microbiologically stabilize beer. It is important to remember that pasteurization is not sterilization. The process has been designed and refined as a method to keep food products from spoiling. Spoilage is defined, in this case, as making food unpalatable.

The process, in practice, is not as simple as its definition, but that is a lengthy subject covered in Chapter 16. Pasteurization is measured in pasteurization units (PUs). One PU is defined as 1 minute at 140°F (60°C). The algebraic equation used to derive PUs over a curve of increasing and decreasing temperatures is as follows.

$$PU = t \times \log^{-1}\left(\frac{T - 140}{z}\right)$$

In this equation, the t is time in minutes, T is temperature, z is the constant 12.5, and $\log^{-1}$ is the antilog.

PUs are generally measured using PU clocks, or traveling thermographs, that are loaded into a pasteurizer and allowed to travel through the pasteurizer the same as a package of beer would. When the PU clock reaches pasteurizer discharge, it is removed and evaluated. Most PU clocks have a temperature probe that is adapted to fit through the opening of a bottle with the end of the probe in the center of the package, which is typically the coldest part. Older traveling thermographs used waterproof versions of circular chart recorders affixed to the temperature probe to obtain a time vs. temperature profile of the pasteurization cycle. Another of the older types had a power cord, instead of a circular chart, that had to be attached while the unit went through the pasteurizer. The big disadvantage to this was that the pasteurizer had to be empty during this process, thereby giving a skewed picture of the performance of the pasteurizer when full. To determine the PU value, the curve on the paper chart is read and the PU conversion charts are used to calculate a final value. Newer versions employ a small computer that records the temperature profile, calculates the PUs over the total cycle, gives key temperatures achieved during the cycle, and finally provides a detailed printout for future reference. The frequency that these units should be run is the subject of some debate, but it is an important point that they should be used only for monitoring, not for control. A guideline is to run PU clocks once per shift, after any major adjustment or utility problem, and after any change of package size or type.

Tunnel pasteurizing technology has reached the point in which many of the functions of the traveling thermograph and the outside controllers have been integrated. These pasteurizers not only monitor temperatures and water flows but also keep track of the containers and the amount of pasteurization they have received. From this information, the belt speed and spray temperatures can be calculated and adjusted to ensure that all containers receive the same amount of pasteurization. Not only are these pasteurizers able to sound an alarm in cases of under- or overpasteurization conditions, but they can also modify operating parameters to correct these situations.

On older pasteurizers, accurate thermometers and water level indicators should be used to set and adjust the pasteurizer. The PU computer should only be used to validate performance. To use the PU computer to adjust the pasteurizer would likely result in large amounts of product being over- or underpasteurized during the experimentation runs. This would, of course, be repeated with every change of package type. Setting the pasteurizer by using historically determined levels is much more effective and preferred.

A second, but less useful, method for verifying pasteurization is using the invertase test. Invertase is an enzyme that breaks sucrose into its component sugars, glucose and fructose, and is destroyed during pasteurization. This test is simple to perform. Several milliliters of beer are poured into a test tube and a small amount (1–2 g) of sucrose is added. The sample is allowed to incubate at room temperature for approximately 30 minutes. After incubating, a piece of glucose test tape (the same type used by diabetics) is dipped in the tube and allowed a minute or so to react. If the tape changes color, glucose is present. Therefore, invertase is still present in the beer and the beer has not been properly pasteurized. Several factors can interfere with the results of this test. First, invertase is present on skin, so care must be taken to not touch the beer, sugar, or test tape. Second, this test is not a measure of pasteurization, only an indicator. Invertase can be denatured very easily by just a couple of PUs; so the test does not guarantee adequate pasteurization, only that the beer has had some pasteurization. And last, this test cannot be used if glycosidic enzymes were added to the beer at any previous point in the processing. These enzymes are not denatured completely during pasteurization and can give false negatives with the invertase test.

Theoretically, if temperatures and water levels in the pasteurizer could be maintained without fail, the routine measurement of PUs would never be necessary. However, brewery steam sources do not always reliably maintain temperatures in pasteurizers and devices to maintain water levels can fail. Spray nozzles inside the pasteurizer can plug. Any of these conditions can result in uneven pasteurizer performance or, at worst, failed pasteurization. Temperatures and water levels on pasteurizers can be monitored to help ensure proper pasteurization, but this is not fail-safe. The risk tolerance of an individual brewery and the condition of its pasteurizers determine the monitoring frequency of its pasteurization process.

Packaging Microbiology

To restate a key principle from the beginning of this section, the current school of thought is that brewery microbiologists need not be concerned with pathogenic microorganisms growing in beer. While no text will ever completely rule out the possibility, beer is generally a very inhospitable environment for human pathogens and toxic food-poisoning organisms. It is usually cold; the pH is quite low; it contains ethanol, hops, and CO_2; and it is—or should be—always nearly oxygen free. All of these conditions serve to generally exclude known pathogens. So the purpose of running a microbiological analysis on packaged beer is essentially to ensure that the beer is microbiologically stable from nontoxic spoilage organisms.

While many species of microorganisms have been isolated from beer, very few of these actually cause beer to spoil. This makes the brewing microbiologist's job very straightforward in that he or she will constantly be plating and looking for only four principle types of organisms. The organisms that the microbiologist finds are dependent on the brewery and the processes used in that brewery. As a rule, the lactic acid bacteria group, which includes the genera *Lactobacillus* and *Pediococcus*, is nearly always unwelcome in beer and can result in serious spoilage. This is, of course, especially important to nonpasteurizing breweries. The second group is yeast and molds. While molds are aerobic and do not grow vegetatively in beer, wild yeast can contaminate a packaged product and cause enormous flavor and haze problems. The third group is gram-negative bacteria. For the most part, these organisms do not survive or grow well in beer. However, the presence of this type of bacteria is an important indicator of the potability of local water sources that may be used for bottle rinsing. The fourth group a brewing microbiologist may run across is gram-positive spore formers. These bacteria are survivors, frequently making it through kettle boil and into the final product as spores. Fortunately for brewers and brewery microbiologists, these bacteria are virtually all strict aerobes and the spores do not germinate or grow in beer.

In spite of the many different philosophies that exist for making beer, the basic tenets of brewing microbiology remain essentially the same. These basic tenets are outlined here in relatively general terms. The reasons for doing bacteria counts on beer in nonpasteurizing breweries are clear. Beer spoils easily and the methods for stabilizing products in these situations may not be as effective or as reliable as pasteurization. But many ask why a pasteurizing brewery needs to do bacteria counts on packaged beer. The answer is simple. It is not to discover cases of inadequate pasteurization. It is to confirm that the level of pasteurization is adequate to impart microbial stability. In a sense, it is reconfirming the z factor (the factor for microbiological load) in the pasteurization equation. To discover cases of inadequate pasteurization, it is best to rely upon the alarm capabilities of the pasteurizer controls.

Basic absence–presence testing can be performed on bright-filtered, but not on package-conditioned, beer, even without microbiological testing tools or knowledge. The test is performed by holding packaged beer at room temperature for 10–30 days and then examining the beer for turbidity and sediment. The results of this test, an increase in turbidity or sediment, unambiguously indicates whether the beer is microbiologically stabilized; increased turbidity indicates microbiological growth. Of course, this method works only as a go/no-go type of test and does not indicate how badly the beer is contaminated or what it is contaminated with.

If a brewery has a relatively well-equipped microbiology lab and a competent microbiologist on staff, more sophisticated methods of analysis can be used. The advantage to these more-sophisticated techniques is more and much better quality information with which to control brewing and packaging processes. The three basic methods of these more-sophisticated techniques are pour plating, spread plating, and membrane filtration.

Pour plating and spread plating are traditional methods of examining liquids for bacteria. The idea is that a known quantity of a sample is added to bacterial growth media in a petri dish or plate. The dish is then incubated in a controlled environment for a specified length of time and examined for the growth of organisms, which appear as small clusters, known as colonies. Each colony is assumed to have risen from one original viable organism, so the number of colonies is then reported as the number of organisms per the plated quantity of sample. Growth media is usually agar based, which solidifies at room temperature to form a semisolid. To use the pour plate technique, the sterile media is first heated in a suitable container to liquefy and then tempered to just above gelatinization temperature (approximately 113°F [45°C]). Known quantities of the samples are then aseptically dispensed (without contamination) into the petri plates, usually with sterile pipettes, and the tempered media is poured over and mixed with the samples. The plates are then allowed to cool before incubating. Incubation is typically done by placing the plates in an incubator and leaving them for a period of time that allows for any bacteria to grow. Beer-spoilage bacteria are either anaerobic (can grow only in the absence of oxygen) or facultative anaerobic (can grow with or without oxygen). Therefore, plates should always be made in duplicate so that one can be incubated aerobically (with oxygen) and the other can be incubated anaerobically (without oxygen). This ensures the most complete recovery of contaminating organisms. Spread plates are done by dispensing the liquid sample onto to the surface of a prepoured and cooled media plate and incubating. Both of these methods have the advantage of being relatively rapid and easy to set up, but both share the disadvantage of working only with small sample sizes, generally between 1 and 5 mL.

To evaluate larger sample sizes, membrane filtration is the most common and effective method. With this method, the sample size is only limited by the size of the funnel on the membrane filtration apparatus and by the particulate load of the sample. The basic idea is that a known sample size is filtered through a sterile membrane filter designed to trap bacteria. The membrane filter is then aseptically transferred to growth media in a dish and incubated. The nutrients soak through the membrane and allow microorganisms to grow on the surface of the membrane. The organisms are then quantified using the same theory and technique as those for pour plates or spread plates. The apparatus used is specialized for this purpose and usually consists of a funnel, a filter support, a clamp to hold the funnel and the filter support together, and some type of vacuum source to pull the sample through the membrane filter. The filters generally have a pore size of 0.45 μm or less to trap very small bacteria as well as the larger yeast. The media for membrane filtration can be either prepoured plates of various types of growth agar or broth media dispensed onto sterile pads in petri-type dishes sized for membrane filters.

The media that should be used for plating brewery bacteria is the subject of much discussion and debate. The most common is universal beer agar and variations of it. Universal beer agar is designed to enhance the growth of the most common beer-spoilage bacteria quite well and is easily modified for the various requirements of brewing microbiology. Universal beer agar with a yeast suppressant added (usually cycloheximide) is frequently used for plating beer that contains live yeast. Additives such as bromocresol green may be added to differentiate the bacteria growing on a plate. Other media, such as Schwartz differential agar, NBB (Nachweismedium fuer Bierschadliche Bacteriem), and Barney-Miller media, are being used very effectively for growing brewery bacteria. Again, several media are available for elucidating wild yeast, including Lin's, lysine, and MYPG (Malt extract and maltose Yeast extract Peptone Glucose media) (multiple variations). No single media is considered by all to be perfect for brewing microbiology.

The determination of a sample size is relative to the type of sample and to the location that the sample is taken from. As a rule of thumb, a brewery microbiologist will look at beer that has been filtered and is ready to package as being biologically the cleanest beer in the brewery. This means that extraneous matter, such as trub, yeast, or any other type of solid, is not expected to found in beer at this stage of the process. Therefore, the microbiologist should expect to not only find fewer microorganisms but be able to hold this beer to the highest standard because it is considered ready for packaging and consumption. Using this line of reasoning, the microbiologist would take larger samples, possibly as much as 100 mL, and use the membrane filtration technique to look for contaminating microorganisms. The microbiologist is then 100 times more likely to recover bacteria from this sample size than from a 1-mL sample. At this stage, even brewer's yeast is usually considered a contaminant. Therefore, the microbiologist would plate the larger sample using the membrane filter technique on a media that did not contain a yeast suppressant so that the yeast would grow and be detected. Of course, if a brewery is bottling or racking unfiltered beer or beer that is bottle conditioned with yeast, these principles do not apply. This beer may be too heavy with solids to be membrane filtered and may need to be plated using one of the other techniques. To select for bacteria and avoid confusion with the yeast, a yeast suppressant must be used in the media. The process at the sample point for each brewery must be looked at individually to determine the best plating protocol.

Sampling schemes for packaging microbiology need to be tailored to fit each brewery. With respect to acceptable quality level, statistically correct sampling frequencies of packaged product for microbiological analysis is usually not feasible in a brewery setting. The sampling scheme is also a matter of risk tolerance. Those in charge of each brewery have to decide how comfortable they are with its microbiological condition and sanitation procedures. As with chemical analysis, the beer from one packaging tank should be considered to be one lot. The microbiologist should sample this lot at as many points as is reasonable from the tank to the package, e.g., at the packaging tank, at the distribution tree, before and after any in-line filters, at the filler base, an unpasteurized package, and a pasteurized package. Using this kind of continuity-of-flow series accomplishes two goals. First, it allows the microbiologist to pinpoint contamination sites and trends; and second, it generates multiple samples and multiple results from the same lot of beer.

In addition to sampling the beer, rinse water and jetter water should be sampled and plated on a regular basis to ensure that they do not become microbiological inoculation points for the packages. Specialized media for recovering waterborne organisms should be used instead of the brewer's-type media for this. While the organisms found in water are not usually beer-spoilage organisms, they are important indicators of the cleanliness of the source water. If coliform bacteria are recovered from a brewery's water source, this indicates that the water source has been contaminated with sewage and is not suitable for use in food processing. Water quality standards are very clear that water must be free from coliform bacteria to be considered potable. Water used for rinsing and jetting comes into direct contact with the product and must be potable. This type of sampling is typically done once a week to ensure that the source has not become contaminated.

Racking

Racking systems present special aseptic sampling problems. As with bottled and canned beer, setting up a series for each tank, or lot, to be racked is the best way to get a complete picture of the process. However, aseptic sampling of kegs is a difficult process at best and usually requires some specially adapted equipment to take a proper sample. It is desirable to check the efficacy of the cleaning process of the kegs by plating a sample of rinse water from a cleaned keg. This can be accomplished with old-style Golden Gate– and Hoff Stevens–type kegs by either aseptically collecting some of the residual rinse water in the keg after cleaning or aseptically adding sterile buffer to the keg, swirling the solution inside the keg, and collecting aseptically. This is more difficult with modern single-entry Sankey-type kegs since these kegs are normally a closed system. However, there are tools for removing the keg stem, which would allow a rinse water sample to be collected. The above procedures are generally fairly difficult to do without compromising the samples and should be looked at as only a part of the necessary microbiology for kegged beer.

Collecting the beer represents the second big problem with racking microbiology. The common sense way that a microbiologist samples a keg is to sterilize a tapping device, sterilize the surface that the tap touches on the keg, and take the sample through a sterile tube or port attached to the tap. The problem with this is that most taps are not built to withstand the temperatures of sterilization and are not equipped with microbiological sampling ports. Therefore, the tapping device must be modified to allow for some type of sterile sampling. This may be as easy as attaching a barbed fitting and a piece of plastic tubing or as complicated as buying and welding on a sanitary septum port. Regardless of the collection method used, extra care must be taken to keep from contaminating the sample.

Microbiological Summary

It is said that all breweries fall into one of two categories, breweries that have microbiological problems and breweries that will have microbiological problems. While whoever first made this observation may have based it on years of experience, it does not have to be true. Modern engineering makes it possible to design and build a sanitary brewery. While this makes keeping breweries clean much easier, it also tempts breweries into using less-severe methods of stabilization to meet the consumer demand for the freshest-tasting product possible. More than ever, this means that the presence of a competent microbiologist running a well-designed microbiology program needs to be an integral part of all modern brewing concerns. The microbiological testing of stabilized packaged beer is seen by some breweries as a last line of defense and is used as release criteria. While this may provide comfort to the management of the breweries, microbiological stabilization should not be used as a substitute for sanitary brewing and packaging practices. A solid microbiology program and a well-trained microbiologist can make this an achievable goal.

● LABELING AND CODING

Labels

Label appearance has two aspects: application and graphic design. Of these, the latter is a measure of graphic composition and is a very subjective parameter that does not lend itself to quantification, and because of this, many feel it should not be a quality function. When graphic design evaluation is demanded of a quality assurance program, the following approach might be helpful. One, there must be an authorized master or standard label available for comparison. Two, label examinations should be done only under authorized lighting and conditions. This is because color, sheen, and other characteristics appear different in incandescent light, fluorescent light, and natural light. Three, such evaluations should be done only by authorized personnel. Four, and most important, all authorization must come from the person authorized to approve label design, not from quality management.

In addition to graphic design, label appearance is affected by application. Certain application faults, such as upside-down labels, are obviously defective. They can be considered critical defects. Other labeling defects, such as scratches, tears, flagging, excess glue, and poor registrations, are assigned to either major or minor categories, depending on severity. There are no hard-and-fast rules on the weighting to be given to these defects. In essence, it is quantifying a rather subjective evaluation. Each brewery must assign its own values for these defects.

Label application evaluation can be done at any point after the labeler. Most breweries prefer the audit site to be after the labeled bottles have passed through all handling processes. This is usually after the packer. At this site, the influence of all machinery, such as packers and conveyors, is included within the audit. Unfortunately, the farther the audit site is from the labeler, whether in distance or time, the less control this audit has. However, these audits should not be used for control purposes at all unless those at a brewery are willing to double the labor and cost devoted to labeling by stationing an auditor at the label discharge in addition to the label operator. A much more efficient use of labor is to empower the label operator to ensure label quality and then hold that person responsible for it.

A complete package audit plan is practiced in many breweries for the purposes of determining average outgoing quality levels. Label inspection is a large component of this audit, and often the label quality audit is coupled with it.

Coding

It is good manufacturing practice to mark packaged product, be it kegs, cans, or bottles, so that the package can be traced back to the date packaged. Of the many ways to encode packaged product, one of the older methods is to notch the side of the labels. There are two notching methods: single and multiple notches.

In the single-notch method, the area of the label notched is part of the code. No special appliance is needed to read the code. In the multiple-notch method, the spacing between notches contains the code. This type of coding needs to align a special decoding device with the notches to read the code. Notch coding has gone out of favor for many reasons, but the primary reason is that the notch on the side of the label promoted tearing on modern, high-speed labelers. A second reason is that labels have to be notched before application. Excess notched labels have to be discarded if not used for the day they were notched for, resulting in considerable label wastage. More modern methods all involve affixing some sort of alphanumeric code via ink jet printers, label piercing, or lasers. These types of codes permit more-enriched data and can be deciphered easily.

Because codes can change frequently and coders can malfunction, it is important to verify that the code being affixed is correct. For the sake of efficiency, this verification is often assigned to the person responsible for changing the code; but often the primary verification is by quality assurance personnel. In addition, reverification by someone else, besides the primary verifier, is desirable.

Verification can be as simple as a glance at the code, but errors in the code can be overlooked very easily. It is therefore best if written verification is made. This verification should not be a checkoff on a form indicating that someone looked at the code. The code on the package should be rewritten in a grid just below an example of the code. Comparison of characters between the example and the code determine whether the code is correct.

In addition to can, bottle, and keg codes, cases are also frequently coded. The main purposes of these codes are to differentiate beer types that may use the same mother carton or wrap and to be an aid to warehouse stock rotation. These codes are applied primarily with ink jet–type printers or coders and rotary-wheel stampers. All of the reasons and methods for verifying code for packages should be used for full cases.

Codes should always be reverified whenever a code is changed. The frequency that codes should be reverified between changes is dependent on the reliability of the coder. Rotary-wheel stampers tend to break down frequently, and audit frequency should be increased for these coders.

● WAREHOUSE AND STORAGE QUALITY MONITORING

Palletizing

After a case of beer is sealed and coded, it usually becomes the responsibility of the warehouse. The job of packaging quality assurance personnel would seem to be complete. But this is not the case. The handling, palletizing, and storage of the product influence the perceived and actual quality of the product in the marketplace. As stated earlier, beer is a relatively fragile product that does not respond well to rough treatment. This is equally true for the package. Brewers work hard to make a product they are proud of and do not want to see torn cases, dented cans, or scuffed labels. Quality assurance personnel must be certain that guidelines for handling the cased product are followed.

The final step after sealing cartons is palletizing, which can be done by hand or machine. A palletizing pattern specific to the size of the cases and the pallets is used, and typically the pattern is alternated with each layer. When hand palletizing, that pattern should be spot checked to ensure that the correct number of cases is stacked on the pallet. The main quality check is to visually inspect pallets for uniformity (no protruding cases). If the pattern is loose and has protruding cases, those cases can snag on other pallets, damage the cases, and on occasion, cause pallets to topple. In this case, the palletizing operation should be stopped and adjusted. While the pallets are inspected for pattern and tightness, the cases on the pallets should be inspected for excessive dirt, oil, water, or other debris picked up during conveying and palletizing. If the cases show evidence of oil or water, the problem must be rectified as soon as possible to prevent excessive rework. If the cases are oily, the most probable cause is hydraulic fluid from the palletizer mechanism. Water can be dangerous not only because it may ruin the decorative quality of the cases but also because it can weaken the structure of the cardboard and cause pallets to topple.

One common method used today to bond cases together on a pallet is the use of adhesive or nonskid material on the cases. The idea of this is to apply a slightly sticky substance to the tops of cases to keep the cases from sliding on top of one another. The treated pallets can then be easily moved without concern for the cases separating during transport. In some cases, this is so effective that shrink-wrapping the pallets is not needed. Quality assurance personnel should monitor the application of palletizer adhesives and nonskid materials to ensure they are applied properly. Overly heavy application can look very messy and cause cases to tear when separated. Weak application does not provide sufficient adhesion of the cases, which permits cases to shift. This can cause pallets to topple.

When palletizer adhesives or nonskid materials are not used, or when extra support is still desired, shrink-wrapping the pallets with plastic film is the method of choice. Shrink-wrapping can be done by hand or machine, but either method can cause damage to cases. The main quality concerns with shrink-wrapping are excessively tight or excessively loose wrapping. If wrapping is excessively tight, cases are damaged, especially in the corners of the pallet. These damaged cases do not have a quality image. They most likely will need to be reworked to be made presentable. In addition, light-gauge film can tear very easily if stretched too tightly, leading to a loss of pallet integrity. If pallets are wrapped too loosely, the cases may slide on top of one another and sustain damage during transport. Quality assurance personnel should frequently monitor the appearance of outgoing pallets of product to ensure that the wrapping is properly tensioned and that cartons are not being damaged.

Warehouse Storage

Flavor compounds in beer react slowly as the product ages. As with any reaction, the rate increases with temperature. This holds true for the oxidation reactions that create stale flavors in beer. Warehousing beer at 85°F (29°C) rather than at 65 or 45°F (18 or 7°C) negatively affects the flavor shelf life of the product. Along with excessively high temperatures, in some climates there is a danger of excessively low warehouse temperatures. If beer freezes, the beer may throw a sediment and destroy its salability. At extremely low temperatures, the packages may burst in the cartons, again ruining its salability. Quality assurance personnel should monitor warehousing operations carefully to ensure that temperatures do not reach extreme highs or lows.

Breweries have given considerably greater emphasis to beer flavor shelf life in recent years. To achieve uniformly fresh product, breweries practice a "first-in, first-out" stock rotation system. This emphasis has been, and should be, extended to distribution channels as well as to retail outlets and draft accounts. Quality assurance personnel should monitor these practices to make certain they are being adhered to.

● PACKAGE HOLD

An unpleasant situation that inevitably occurs, even in the tightest controlled breweries, is held product. At some point, quality assurance personnel place packaged product on hold for some quality-related problem. During these occurrences, it is the responsibility of the quality assurance department to make certain that the appropriate amount of product is held and isolated. A good rule of thumb is to try to isolate 15 minutes of production at both ends of the suspect portion.

Product isolated for quality problems should be tagged as "HOLD" in the warehouse. The hold tag should include the date held, product description, quantity held, reason held, and location the product is being held to ensure that it does not become mixed with released production. When problem product is discovered, the problem should be brought to the attention of all concerned parties. The problem should be discussed by this group and a group decision made on the course of action that should be taken to resolve the problem.

Often the held product must be audited to ascertain the severity and extent of the problem. Audits are generally done by the quality department, but production personnel are often deputized for these investigations. Product disposition becomes the responsibility of the operational departments after quality disposition has been made.

In many instances, held product is released because the defect was not confirmed in the audit, the defect severity was not as bad as envisioned, or the remediation would create more problems than it would cure. If the disposition is to salvage the product through some form of remediation, then it might be desirable to retag the pallets as "REWORK" for organizational purposes. Rework is a term for manually culling defective product to repair a problem. It is an expensive process and can cause more problems than it cures. The extreme solution would be to destroy the product. In that case, "HOLD" tags should be replaced with "DESTROY" tags to avoid comingling distressed with acceptable product.

It is desirable to keep a log of product holds to organize the product hold program. This type of documentation can be used to discern what packaging process is causing quality problems.

Along with maintaining product hold logs, it is the responsibility of the quality department to remove or alter product disposition tags. This authority and responsibility should not be delegated by the quality department, so the integrity of the hold program can be maintained. In the event this authority is delegated, the quality department should retain supervision of this process.

DOCUMENTATION AND ANALYSIS

It has been said that those who do not remember the past are condemned to repeat it. It has also been said that the best way to remember the past is to document the present, because the present will be the past before long! This is the basic justification for documentation. However, documentation is a tedious chore. It interferes with other tasks, and the more frequently it interferes, the more aggravating it becomes. This aggravation drains mental and emotional energy and increases the desire to abandon documentation. Unless this tendency is countered, documentation will fall to the wayside, mistakes will be repeated, quality assurance will decline, and ultimately the quality of the product will suffer.

Motivation and Cardinal Rules

There are two ways to counteract this tendency: the stick and the carrot. The stick method is simple. Those responsible for documenting are threatened with punishment unless they complete their assigned documentation. This works well to a certain point but has a down side. Threats of punishment garner little goodwill toward the organization and, if sufficiently severe, can foster very negative attitudes.

The carrot method is more desirable but also more difficult. It falls on the shoulders of management to design documentation methods and protocols that can both encourage documentation and relieve its tedious aspects as much as possible. Properly designed documentation has several features. First, forms should be kept as simple as possible to eliminate confusion on the part of the user. Second, forms should be provided so that the same type of information is recorded in the same place each time. Third, forms should be designed so that information may be recorded in as logical a sequence as possible. If, for example, during routine filler checks, carbonation levels are obtained first, they should be recorded in the first data column—not in some other column. Fourth, forms should be designed to be cueing. That is, in addition to storing data, they should prompt the user concerning what, if anything, should be done next. Fifth, the information on a form should be organized so that it is presented in a meaningful manner to the end user, the person evaluating that information.

Methods

At one time, the only method for documentation was pencil and paper. This time-honored method is still very useful. With the advent of the computer age, a second method has been created. Computers offer advantages in documentation that would have required an army of clerks to reproduce. The first advantage is to reconcile the third and fifth rules of good documentation. These two rules are often at odds with each other; that is, the logical progression of data acquisition may not be compatible with the requirements of the end user. Computers can accept data in one type of logical progression and regurgitate it in a different, and hopefully more meaningful, format. This is especially true for statistical process control (SPC).

SPC is very helpful in controlling product quality, and it can be practiced with pencil and paper. The routine calculations necessary for its practice are not difficult, although quite time-consuming when done by hand. Computers and statistical software ease these tasks considerably.

Computers and modern office software can also help with the first rule of documentation—keeping forms and documents simple. As processes change, the documentation forms should also change. If they do not, confusion slowly creeps in. Changing a paper form used to be a difficult process. It could take months to go from a change of design, to printer setup, to final approval. Now, the form can merely be changed on a computer, the old form can be discarded, and new forms can be printed.

A novel aspect of computerization is the ability of some machines to talk directly with computers. This permits automatic documentation and relieves the operator of many documentary burdens. In addition, the increased frequency possible with such documentation is an improvement in process (and subsequently, quality) control over the occasional sampling.

Common Problems with Computers

Along with benefits, computerization has brought opportunities to compound documentary burden. The two most frequent misuses of computerized documentation are to treat the computer as a typewriter and to fail to provide simple and uniform thematic rules for the users. An indication of the first mistake is to record data in a spreadsheet or word processor program. Usually, the recording sheet is designed to be the reporting sheet. The only benefit to this is to make the recording document look pretty, but it does nothing to alleviate data discontinuity. Data discontinuity occurs when there is a break between rows of data, such as keeping data grouped by date on separate spreadsheets. This prevents statistical and other types of computer programs from evaluating and sharing the full range of information collected, unless the data is reentered. In practice, using spreadsheets or word processing programs increases documentary burden because it promotes double entry and because the computer document format is set up for reporting rather than for producing a logical data-gathering sequence.

The second error of computerized documentation occurs when gathered data resides in a multitude of computer files. This places an extra burden on the user because it is necessary to remember which file is used for what. If, in addition to multiple files, a multitude of software is used, then thematic rules of software usage are no longer simple. The user not only has to remember what goes where but also must be familiar with the idiosyncrasies of each software maker.

Another misapplication of software is using evaluative statistical programs for primary data gathering and storage. Some of these programs are designed to hold only one data type. So to enter any other data type collected during a normal filler check, the user has to climb out a menu tree and descend another to input the other values. Aside from increasing the time needed to enter data, it does not take a user long to become aggravated with the whole situation.

To make data meaningful, identification information, such as date, time, brand, package, and label, has to be affixed to observational information, such as air or fills. Some evaluative types of software have limited ability to store this type of data. The customary solution, creating record tags and storing identification information in a second table, again forces the user to climb and descend menu trees and slows down data entry.

Like production software and hardware, some software is amenable to direct input of values from measuring tools with limited user intervention. This type of programming and hardware has been created for seam inspection with great success. Nevertheless, other applications for such systems may be more of a curse than a blessing. It can be more time-consuming for a user to access and focus the appropriate record to place the data input in the correct spot than it is to enter it manually. The threshold compromise for cost/benefit of this type of automation is different for each user, but a rule of thumb, 10 analyses per hour, is a good starting point.

Almost all commercially available software, whether off-the-shelf or written for a specific client, is designed on the narrow table model. A narrow table model has a multitude of tables with only a few fields per table. Only one of these fields contains actual data; the others contain relational information used by the program that allows the tables to link to each other. The advantage of these programs is that they are open ended in that new parameters can be added without altering program design. The major fault is that the tables are very long (contain very many records). Very long tables degrade system performance. Modern, high-speed computers, faster data storage systems, and improved software have overcome some of this drawback, but not all of it. To keep these systems performing at an optimum, record keepers must resort to archiving, and archiving by its very nature causes data discontinuity.

No matter how much it is desired, no information system is perfect. Errors creep in that, if not eliminated, cause the information system to fail in part or totally. Considering the various software options available, the best course is usually to hire a competent programmer who has some experience with packaging quality assurance. This person should not only be able to custom design a system that is optimized for the facility it serves but also be able to maintain this system. In the end, the cost is about equal to an outside vendor's software, but the system integrity is better maintained with a much stronger potential for all to utilize the documentation system.

Basic Data Analysis

The flip side of documentation is analysis. As with most things, this can be done in a number of ways. At the basic level, observations can be compared with specifications. If the observation is within specs, life can continue as usual. If it is not, the problem must be fixed.

Superior Data Analysis

The next level in data analysis sophistication is the exception report. An exception report is a tabular report or a report that presents data as rows and columns and highlights any value not within the specification range. Often, specifications for the values and a section to summarize the results are added to provide the user with more information. The data span of a report—that is, the range of data included in the report—along with starting and ending dates, can vary from a single record to thousands of records. If the data span is analyzed correctly, experienced users of these reports can gain a fair sense of process quality by the amount of highlighting on the report.

Sometimes only summary information is presented on these reports. The statistical data usually presented are the average, standard deviation, minimum and maximum values, number of samples, and how many samples were out of specification for various parameters. This type of report can give a user insight into how well a process has performed over the data span summarized, but it does not give a historical perspective. Using other statistical techniques, additional useful information can be mined from documented observations.

Sophisticated Data Analysis

The primary tool for mining more information from documentation is SPC. Fortunately, of all the process areas in a brewery, none lends itself better to SPC analysis than packaging quality assurance. This is because sampling frequency is so much greater in packaging than in other process areas of the brewery. The main advantage of using SPC in packaging is that it can change the emphasis from assurance testing to control testing. It does this by delineating trends faster than any other method of analysis. This promotes process correction before trends get to the failure stage. The following example illustrates this technique; however, this example is not comprehensive. A more thorough explanation can be found in the many excellent texts available on this subject.

Assume that a process is sampled every hour. At every appointed sample time, five random samples are measured for a quality parameter, such as package fills. The observations are assumed to be normally distributed; that is, a frequency graph of their values should resemble a bell-shaped curve. Each sample average (indicated by $\bar{x}$) is plotted on a trend chart, or X-bar chart, where the x axis is the sample number and the y axis is in units used for measuring the parameter (Fig. 27.9). After sufficient samplings (usually at least 60), the standard deviation and the average of all observations are calculated. This standard deviation is multiplied by 3 and is often called 3-sigma, since the Greek letter sigma is used to denote the standard deviation of a set of numbers. To obtain the upper control limit, the 3-sigma value is added to the average of all observations. To obtain the lower control limit, the 3-sigma value is subtracted from the average. The chart is then redrawn with the control limits included (Fig. 27.10). The reason for using 3-sigma in setting the control limits is that, in normal distribution, more than 99% of a set of numbers will be within 3 standard deviations above and below the average (or mean) of the numbers. Since

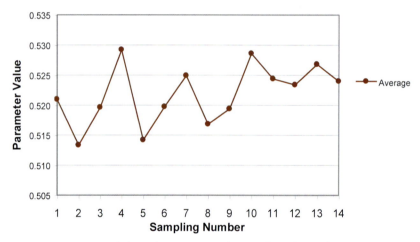

FIGURE 27.9. Trend chart. (Courtesy P. Takacs and J. Edgerton)

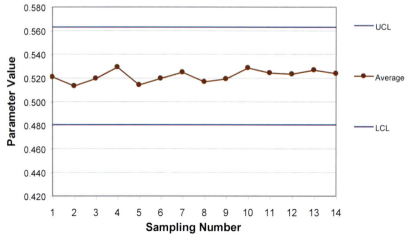

FIGURE 27.10. Trend chart with control limits. UCL = upper control limit. LCL = lower control limit. (Courtesy P. Takacs and J. Edgerton)

each individual average $\bar{x}$ fell within the 3-sigma limit, it is assumed that all the variation encountered so far is variation without assignable causes. Unless there is change in the process, it is expected that, in future samplings, about 99 out of every 100 (99%) would be within the range defined by the upper and lower control limits, and perhaps 1 out of every 100 (1%) would be outside the limits. The probability that 2 out of 100 samplings will be outside the control range is so low, especially if consecutive, that, if it occurs, it signals that the process is out of control.

In this type of charting, there are other signals that describe process performance. Each successive point on the chart can be higher, the same as, or lower than the previous point. The probability of six or more points all higher (or lower) than the previous point is quite remote. Therefore, six or more successive points going in the same direction is a signal that the process is changing. A partial list of the more common out-of-control signals is in Table 27.2.

Even if the process average for a parameter is in control, there is the possibility that variability is changing. To analyze for this, a chart similar to the X-bar chart is created, usually called an R or range chart, but the value plotted is the range of values at each sampling (Fig. 27.11).

TABLE 27.2. The More Frequent Control Chart Signals Indicating Out-of-Control Situations

One or more points outside the control limit
Two of three consecutive points outside the 2-sigma warning limits but still inside the control limits
Four of five consecutive points beyond the 1-sigma limit
A run of eight consecutive points on one side of the center line
Six points in a row steadily increasing or decreasing

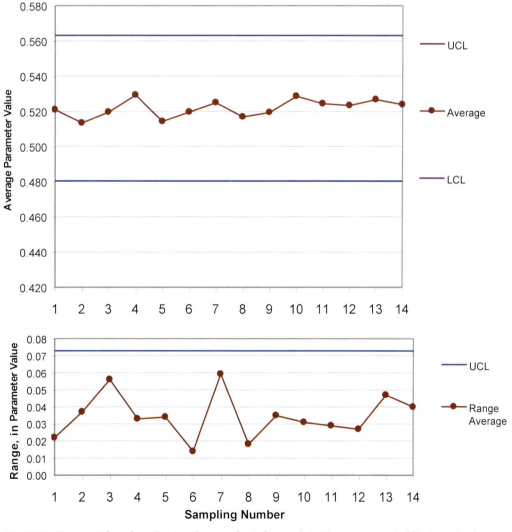

FIGURE 27.11. X-bar chart (top) and range chart (bottom). UCL = upper control limit. LCL = lower control limit. (Courtesy P. Takacs and J. Edgerton)

The range of values is obtained by subtracting the lowest value in a sample group from the highest value. These range values are summarized in a manner similar to that of X-bar charts to calculate means (averages) and control limits. The logic behind X-bar chart signals is applied in a similar way for range chart signals. The difference is that the signal represents a change in variability rather than in sample group average.

Statistical Decision Assistance

In conjunction with SPC, another widely used statistical tool is Pareto analysis, named after the man who devised the technique. This method organizes attribute data into categories and sorts these categories by frequency of occurrence. Attribute data is information that has only two values, such as true or false, yes or no. Many occurrences in processing have this nature. For example, the filler did or did not stop, labels were or were not put on, pallets did or did not topple in the warehouse, and so on. The categories would be the causes for these occurrences. The filler could have stopped because it ran out of cans, because of seamer jams, because of a power outage, or because of a hundred other reasons. If, within a given time span, each occurrence were recorded and assigned to a category (cause of occurrence), and the sum of these categories was inversely sorted, from the highest to the lowest, a Pareto histogram could be created. In this histogram, the first bar would represent the most frequent occurrence, the second bar the next, and so forth. Such a graph can then help an organization focus its decision-making and assign scarce resources to correct the most urgent problems.

Common Mistakes

In doing SPC-type statistical analysis, there are a few common mistakes. The first is misperception. Many believe that, since statistical analysis of a process can signal out-of-control situations, it also shows how to correct the problem. This is very rarely true. To correct the cause in the process creating the problem requires an engineering understanding of the process. Without this, effective action is not possible.

A second common mistake is not recognizing that the observed variation in a sample group is more often the result of gauge variation than of a true sample variation. For example, during a sampling period, five observations of package CO_2 varied from 2.72 to 2.76. During the next sampling period, when the beer came from a different source tank, the variation was from 2.62 to 2.66. During the third sampling, from a third source tank, the variation was from 2.82 to 2.86. After many observations, X-bar chart values were calculated for this parameter. The centerline turned out to be 2.74, but because the variation within samplings was so small, the control range was minute. This caused practically every sampling to signal an out-of-control process.

A third common mistake is not recognizing that the resolutions of the analytical instruments with which observations are obtained during packaging quality assurance testing are limited. For example, a Schwartz burette used to measure package airs is graduated in 0.10-mL units and the control range for package airs is 0.20 mL. This gives only two increments in the control range. Instrument variability is ±1 increment of graduation. A 0.18-mL air value can be just as easily 0.10 mL, within the control range; 0.20 mL, at the upper control limit; or 0.30 mL, above the control limit. In this situation, the probability of false signals are very high.

A guideline is that there should be 10 increments of resolution between control limits. Both of the previous two examples violated this rule in some fashion. If this condition cannot be met, the recourse is to use either instrument to better discern the actual value or to use different and more-sophisticated types of statistical analysis. A number of SPC variations exist, such as moving range analysis and attribute control charting, to handle these situations.

Specifications, Control, and Process Capability

A fourth common mistake is confusing specification ranges with control ranges. Specifications are quantified characteristics and attributes of product design. Because of variability, they must be defined as a range. Control ranges are also quantified characteristics and attributes of product design. They too are defined as a range because of variability. Specifications define a range within which product is acceptable. Controls define a range in which product can be produced reliably.

Process capability is the ratio of the control range to the specification range. For example, a brewery has a control range for crown torques of 4 to 8 inch-pounds but the specification range is 5 to 7 inch-pounds. Assuming crown torques are randomly distributed within the control range, 50% of the crowns would be out of specification for torques. Either the process or the specification range would have to be changed to correct this.

The larger the process capability ratio, the more capable the process. This must be kept in mind when defining the specifications. As a motivational tool in the desire to provide ever better quality, specification ranges are too often set too close to the target. Frequently, the effect of this is to make the specification range smaller than the control range. This is self-defeating because the process or equipment would never be able to reliably make product.

Other Methods

There are many other methods for analyzing collected data, from scatter diagrams to analysis of variance (ANOVA). Each has its uses. Some are to monitor quality, some are for process improvement, and some are to elicit novel information about processes. Modern computers and software programs have automated many of the odious computational tasks of statistical techniques. Most modern statistical software programs have gone a step beyond this. Not only do they automate computations, but they guide the user into selecting the appropriate statistical technique to use. Many of these analytic software programs also accept input directly from other computer programs. The parting thought on data analysis is that time spent on acquiring the skills and knowledge to use statistical techniques is well spent because the techniques provide a lot of return on investment.

Validating Quality and ISO

Most of this chapter has been devoted to a quality program, generally in the mold of a quality assurance department, checking to ensure the other departments are doing their jobs. This gives rise to the question, Who is checking the checkers? A number of answers have been devised.

One common solution is to remove the quality department from the operational hierarchy by having it report to a corporate manager instead of to the facility's operational manager. A variant of this approach, used by some larger breweries, is to divide the quality department into quality assurance and quality control. Quality control is made a local or plant department reporting to the local operational manager, while quality assurance is made a corporate department and assigned the task, among others, of monitoring the quality control department.

The logical assumptions in these approaches are that quality and operational concerns can be antagonistic and a conflict of interest is created by making one department responsible for both concerns. This conflict of interest is the primary cause for the quality department not adequately executing its assigned tasks. If this conflict of interest is eliminated by making both departments independent, policing of the quality department will be unnecessary.

The most logical way to make the quality department independent is to not have it report to the operational department. However, because all departments belong to the parent organization, conflict of interest cannot be eliminated, only minimized. In addition, the divisions of departments that these approaches espouse create innate antagonism between these departments. This antagonism can be more debilitating to the parent organization than can an unmonitored quality department.

A third approach to validating the quality program is to hire an outside firm or institution to audit the quality department. It is assumed in this outsourcing that conflict of interest is eliminated, interdepartmental antagonism diminished, and adequate monitoring of the quality department obtained. The current industry practice to doing this is to become ISO certified.

ISO

ISO is an international organization that creates standards, principles, and protocols, the purpose of which is to provide standardized definitions of product characteristics that are accepted and used by all companies in that industry. An industry obtains these standards and protocols by becoming ISO certified, which is obtained through an agency specializing in this. In general, the steps are to contact a certifying agency to come and audit the facility and define what modifications to, for example, procedures the facility would need to obtain ISO certification. The facility would then have to implement these modifications, and afterward, the certifying agency would reaudit the facility. If the facility passed the audit, the certifying agency would bestow the appropriate ISO certification to that facility. To maintain ISO certification, and to ensure that ISO guidelines are being complied with, the facility would have to be routinely audited and recertified by the verifying agency.

It should be noted that ISO is not a governmental agency nor is it affiliated with any governmental agency. Second, ISO does not stand for International Standard Organization although the name of the organization is the International Organization for Standardization. The name comes from the ancient Greek word for "equal", as in isotherm or isobar. Third, the standards, principles, and protocols promulgated by ISO are created by experts within industry, academia, and government. These standards have considerable wisdom and rationality behind them. Fourth, the central theme of conducting business in an ISO fashion is to say what you do and do what you say. And fifth, this service is not free.

ISO certification has numerous advantages. The primary advantage is as a marketing tool, because it signals to customers that attention is being paid to producing quality product. A second advantage is to reassure clients that they will not have to provide oversight to their production facility because an outside agency specializing in this is already doing it. The third advantage is to reorganize an industry into a potentially more effective model. Fourth, while it is possible to have just a portion of the facility, such as the laboratory, certified (under ISO 17025), in general, the whole facility, not just the quality department, would and should be certified.

Along with the advantages, there are a number of disadvantages to the ISO system. One, there is an implication in adopting the ISO system that no quality system is currently in place and that whatever rationale for business practices currently being used is defective. Two, the philosophical and operational reorganization provided by the ISO concept may or may not be compatible with the current corporate culture, and as a replacement, it may or may not be an improvement. Third and most important, in practice, ISO tends to be quite bureaucratic, not only during the initial certification but for as long as it is used. This increased bureaucracy elevates documentation costs and, in so doing, raises routine operational costs. However, the most potentially damaging consequence to increased bureaucracy is to move the corporate focus away from producing quality product to producing quality paperwork.

SUMMARY

In today's competitive world, customers can choose from a staggering variety of beers. With such a wide array of choices, it is difficult to maintain customer loyalty with poor quality. Therefore, it can be argued that quality makes the difference between success and failure.

To prevent poor manufacturing quality from reaching the customer, breweries create packaging quality programs. These quality programs range in organizational structure from very simple to very complex. They are a combination of traditional methods and new technologies. In this discipline, continual progress is being made in procedures, methods, instrumentation, documentation, and data analysis. Although this discipline is constantly changing and improving, its main objective has not changed—to ensure manufacturing excellence.

With today's consumer demanding ever higher quality products, the need for a well-designed packaging quality program is more important than ever. A crucial component of a successful quality program is that it is staffed with qualified people. Communication and cooperation between departments is another crucial component. But the hallmark of a successful quality program is that the attitude of quality must filter down from the highest positions within the organization. Without this, no quality program can be successful.

ACKNOWLEDGMENTS

Lars Larson and Charles Benedict extended the benefit of their experience by providing information on computerized test kegs and dissolved oxygen testing. The authors express their gratitude to Jaime Jurado for his encouragement in the preparation of this chapter and to Carlos Alvarez, president of the Gambrinus Company, for his support and permission to publish this chapter.

REFERENCES FOR FURTHER READING

American Public Health Association. (1995). Standard Methods for the Examination of Water and Wastewater, 19th ed. American Public Health Association, American Water Works Association, Water Environment Federation, Washington, DC.

American Society of Brewing Chemists. ASBC Methods of Analysis, online. The Society, St. Paul, MN.

Broderick, H. M., ed. (1982). Beer Packaging. Master Brewers Association of the Americas, St. Paul, MN.

Garfield, F. M., Klesta, E., and Hirsch, J. (2000). Quality Assurance Principles for Analytical Laboratories, 3rd ed. AOAC International Press, Gaithersburg, MD.

Gray, P. P. (1951). Some advances in microbiological control for beer quality. Wallerstein Lab. Com. 14:169-183.

Green, S. R., and Gray, P. P. (1950). A differential procedure applicable to bacteriological investigation in brewing. Am. Soc. Brew. Chem. Proc. 1950:19-32.

Hardwick, W. A., ed. (1995). Handbook of Brewing. Marcel Dekker, New York.

Levin, R. I. (1978). Statistics for Management. Prentice-Hall, Englewood Cliffs, NJ.

Montgomery, D. C. (1996). Introduction to Statistical Quality Control, 3rd ed. John Wiley & Sons, New York.

Priest, F. G., and Campbell, I., eds. (1996). Brewing Microbiology, 2nd ed. Chapman & Hall, London.

CHAPTER 28

Inspection Equipment in the Brewing Industry

JEFF DEVOY
Heuft USA, Inc.

Inspection equipment has evolved over the years, much like other types of packaging and processing equipment. The capabilities of today's inspection devices are much greater than even those of a few years ago, and they are able to combine numerous inspection technologies into a single platform. The increasing power and lower costs of microprocessor-based devices have enabled inspection equipment to perform more difficult inspections, at higher speeds, and with greater reliability than ever before. Typical systems in the past have been outfitted with the technology to perform, for example, only underfill inspection or only can pressure/vacuum inspection. The packaging line may have had one manufacturer provide empty glass inspection for returnable bottles, one manufacturer provide equipment for fill-level inspection, another manufacturer provide equipment for crown integrity, and so on.

Common platforms for the various types of inspection equipment found on beverage lines still may not be the norm, but a few in the industry have embraced this as the way of the future. There are several advantages to this, among them, commonality of spare parts (inventory and cost reduction), similar operator interface screens (reduced training costs), and the ability to network different machines on the line together. It is now possible to network machines around the globe, reducing downtime by providing a means for a technician in one plant to access machines in another plant. The benefit of this is that it is possible to provide a fast response without the high costs of travel and without the typical waiting period while the technician travels to the plant site.

The combining of several different types of inspections into one platform reduces the amount of space required for installations, reducing overall line footprint size, and also reduces the amount of conveyor that needs to be provided for the packaging line. Manufacturers can either reduce the amount of square footage required for the installation or provide for additional accumulation that could result in more efficient production line operation. Reducing the total number of devices on the packaging line also provides for faster installation and, in general, results in startup and commissioning times that are shorter than those of traditional systems that perform only one or two inspections per device. Inspection devices can be used throughout the bottle or can filling process (Fig. 28.1).

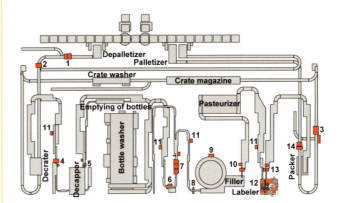

FIGURE 28.1. Typical process flow in a returnable bottling house. 1 = Returned crate check; 2 = crate color sorting; 3 = empty crate check; 4 = empty bottle sorting; 5 = residual liquid detection; 6 = presorting for empty bottle inspector; 7 = empty bottle inspector; 8 = detection of residual alkaline cleaning solution; 9 = filler and closer inspection and management; 10 = postfiller full-bottle inspection; 11 = conveyor speed control; 12 = labeler; 13 = postlabeler full-bottle inspection; and 14 = full-case check. (Courtesy Heuft USA, Inc.)

The inspection systems typically function in the following manner.

- The container, traveling on the conveyor, passes by or through a sensor that signals the control system that a container is present and ready to enter an inspection area.
- The control system attaches a data sheet (often thought of as an electronic checklist) to the container and begins to track the container through the inspection zone.
- Tracking is typically performed using an encoder that is attached to the drive shaft of the conveyor. All container movement and tracking is based on the movement of the conveyor, so it is critical that the container's position on the conveyor not change through the inspection and rejection area.
- Tracking can be tracked through a filler and closer by treating the filler as a positive displacement conveyor.
- The inspection module checks the container as it passes through the inspection zone and places the pass or fail values into the data sheet for that container.
  - It is preferred to start with the assumption that the container has not passed any of the inspections and can only pass once the electronic checklist has been cleared of faults. This is a fail-safe mode in the event there is a malfunction of a sensor.
- If the container has passed all inspections, then the control system allows the container to pass by the reject device and into the production stream.
- If the container has not passed any individual inspection, then the control system typically will
  - issue a stop-pulse for the line to halt production, and
  - provide the appropriate reject signal(s) so that the container is moved off-line and into a bin, pushed onto a table, guided onto an accumulation conveyor, etc.
- The style of rejector is an important part of the inspection system. The customer needs to determine what to do with the defective container.
- Another means of ensuring that the defective container does not enter the production stream is to verify that the container has actually been taken off line. It is preferable to accomplish this with a sensor mounted on the "good container" conveyor and not the reject conveyor. This avoids the situation in which bottles may back up on the reject conveyor and falsely trigger the sensor that the container has been moved onto the reject conveyor.
  - For example, a sensor is mounted downstream of the reject device on the "good container" conveyor. The control system still tracks the container, even after it has passed the rejector, and expects NOT to see a container at a certain position on the conveyor. If the control system senses a container in the position on the conveyor that should be empty, then a stop-pulse may be initiated, since there now is a faulty container in the production stream.
- It is important to work with the inspection system supplier's engineering group to determine what an actual defect is and what is commercially acceptable to let pass through.

Defect Evaluation Should Not Be an Afterthought

It is important to note that the handling of defects that are rejected plays an important role using the inspection system as a production tool. It is particularly important to handle the rejects properly during the initial qualification of the equipment.

Here are some things to consider for reject handling.

- Will the rejects be evaluated to determine whether they are false rejects?
  - This can be accomplished as simply as putting them back on line ahead of the inspection device. If they fail again, they are most likely actual defects. If they pass, they were most likely false rejects. The decision to pass these through again depends on your company's corporate quality philosophy and your level of risk tolerance.
  - For example, underfill rejects can usually be visually identified as false rejects and placed back on line. Defects from contaminant inspection, such as detecting glass in glass containers, may be discarded anyway to reduce the risk of these types of defects getting into the market.
- It is important to note that if your company is tracking defect rate as a percentage of production, then each time a defect is passed back through to determine whether it passes a second time, the data set is skewed for overall line performance. For example, if 100 containers are run through with one reject, the defect rate is 1.0%. If the rejected container is run back through to see whether it is an actual defect, and it is rejected again, the system now totals two rejects in 101 containers, or double (approximately) the reject rate of actual production.

- It is important to consider the reject bin, reject table, and reject conveyor, etc. before the project scope is defined. These items need to be large enough to accommodate the expected number of rejects. Reject tables and conveyors need to be easily accessible for operators and technicians. Reject bins need to be able to be removed from the production area. So the ability to get pallet jacks, forklifts, etc. into the area to remove the bin or container is important.
- When considering the reject table or conveyor, it is important to know whether the rejector that is used for defects will be the same rejector that is used for sampling. If it is to perform double duty and be used for sampling also, then it is important to be able to separate the sample set from the defect containers. A foolproof method is to use multiple rejectors, one for defects and one for sampling. Multiple rejectors can be used to separate, for instance, underfill rejects, bottles with no crowns, bottles with no labels, etc. Some of these may be reworked easily, reducing process losses.

Equipment Qualification

Qualification of inspection equipment needs to be carried out using a statistical approach. This removes the ambiguity in determining whether the system has met the requirements in the original contract.

Here are some items to consider during this phase of the project.

- Containers to be run on the line for qualification
- Definition of defect types to be rejected
- Definition of defect reject limits
- Acceptable false reject percent
- Acceptable false accept percent
- Qualification protocol:
  - Number of containers to be run for the qualification procedure
  - Will the qualification of one container type suffice as representative for all container types, or will each container need to be qualified individually?
    – In the case of label inspection, it may be necessary to qualify numerous (sometimes upward of 100) different labels, which can be extremely costly and must be figured into the overall project budget.
  - Who will be designated to work with the equipment technician during the qualification phase?
  - Who will gather the data on containers run/rejected?
  - Who will evaluate the rejected container to determine whether it is a false reject (customer's personnel, manufacturer's personnel, or a combination of both)?
  - How to randomly sample the containers downstream to assess the false accept rate
- If the equipment manufacturer's technician is to be on site during the qualification phase (recommended), then schedule changes can be costly. For example, if the plant schedules a technician for equipment qualification on Monday morning and the production schedule has been delayed and the product to be qualified cannot run until Tuesday morning, then the company will be responsible for the technician's cost for Monday as well. This is particularly important for service technicians that travel to the site from distant cities. If not enough notice is given to the service technician, then extra costs will be incurred.
- During the qualification process, it is also important to accurately determine the difference between the actual reject rate and the false reject rate.
  - It is imperative that the people performing the evaluation of the rejects be well trained regarding what they are looking for. The rejects must be individually inspected, and the condition of the reject must be documented. If the rejects are not evaluated correctly, the plant runs the risk of accepting the equipment based on false information. Consequently, the plant may judge the qualification as failed even if it is not the case.

Equipment Training

Equipment training is extremely important and often overlooked. In some cases, training can be accomplished by having the plant operators and technicians stay with the service technician during the installation and commissioning phase. For more complex pieces of inspection equipment, formal training classes might be required. Many times what is needed depends on the technical aptitude of the plant personnel, which can vary from plant to plant within the same company.

Equipment ownership is important not only for inspection equipment but for all equipment that is installed in the plant. You may designate a plant point-person who is responsible for training all in-plant people. Another approach is to designate a "superuser" who is the in-house expert on the equipment. Yet another approach is to designate a team of plant people to be responsible for initial training and keeping the in-plant people updated on the system(s) in the plant. Be cautious, however, since having multiple people responsible may result in having no one responsible.

Some other items to consider when evaluating inspection equipment include the following.

- Multiple user access levels
  - The system should be able to be configured to provide multiple user access levels.
  - Access by plant personnel should be logged at each occurrence.
  - When accessing a machine, it is helpful if the system is able to track the changes that each user has made over a period of time, giving others the benefit of seeing what was tried by technicians before them when troubleshooting a problem.
  - A feature such as a "go back" choice is helpful in returning to a previous state in the event a parameter change is not helpful.
- Saleable and expandable
  - Additional inspection modules should be able to be easily added to the base system. Hardware and/or software changes that are made once the equipment is installed and running may be complicated to perform. Getting line time to perform a complicated upgrade may be difficult to do.
- Messages logged to hard disk or flash drive
  - It is important to have the capability to store inspection data.
  - Systems that have the operating system and the data storage files are better off using flash drives rather than typical computer hard drives, which are guaranteed to fail after a certain period of time.
- Networking capabilities, structured query language (SQL) for automatic data collection
  - The inspection system should function as an extension of the plant's data collection process. Modern systems have the capability to communicate with plant data systems, enhancing their function within the plant as production tools rather than as simple pass/fail devices.
  - The machine operating conditions should be able to be shown on designated computers throughout the company.
- Remote access to multiple machines
  - The capabilities of inspection devices to communicate with each other are important to reducing line downtime.
  - The ability of inspection devices to communicate with other similar devices in other plants can reduce the cost of ownership. For example, if the devices can communicate to similar devices in other plants, the user can take advantage of the technical expertise that may not exist in a particular plant.
- Historical data storage and reporting
  - This is important to track the production line performance over time.
- E-mail and/or text message production reports at the end of the production period
  - Today's systems can compile data and send concise reports via e-mail regarding the performance of the line for a particular period of time.
  - It is possible for alarms, both critical and noncritical, to be sent via text message to the appropriate person's cell phone, greatly reducing downtime.
- On-line operator and maintenance manuals, on-line parts lists
  - The ability to access operator and technical manuals at the machine's operator interface helps reduce the amount of time that the machine is down for repairs. Intuitive help screens and help bubbles associated with various components in the inspection system also help to speed up the troubleshooting process.
  - An on-line parts list can help the technician troubleshoot and identify the correct part that needs to be replaced. Actual stored photographs of the various machine parts speed up the troubleshooting process as well.
- Self-diagnostic capabilities
  - Systems should have self-diagnostic capabilities to warn the plant before failure occurs. For example, a power supply that monitors its own current draw can send an alarm to the operator well in advance of failure, avoiding unnecessary downtime. In vision-based inspection systems, the ability to send a noncritical alarm as the light source degrades is important to maintain the integrity of the inspection.
- Capability for remote service through the Internet
  - Despite the efforts of information technology departments everywhere, the ability of the manufacturer to access the machines through the Internet, in real time, can be critical to the overall performance of the line.
  - Technical service departments can work with the plant personnel to diagnose and troubleshoot performance issues without the need to travel to the plant site, saving maintenance costs.

- On-line prompting of maintenance tasks
  - The system should have the capability to alert the plant personnel when regular maintenance tasks are to be performed. These can be messages on the operator interface of the device or messages sent as an e-mail or text message to the appropriate person.
  - These tasks should be displayed in order of priority and should provide a means of logging and resetting each once it is completed.

● INSPECTION EQUIPMENT PRIOR TO THE EMPTY BOTTLE INSPECTOR

Inspecting Empty Cases/Crates

Inspecting returned crates with empty bottles is the first step toward high line efficiency. The inspection system (Fig. 28.2) must examine the suitability of the crates for unpacking, as well as examine the bottle mix and other criteria, and must distribute the bottles accordingly. The inspection system must be able to reliably inspect and sort returnable cases that contain glass (or returnable polyethylene terephthalate [PET]) bottles.

Inspecting and sorting returnable cases typically involves a combination of transmitted light and incident light. For example, base inspection uses transmitted light, or light that passes through the base of the container and into the camera that is mounted above. Foreign objects lying on top of the bottles in the crate rely on incident light, or light that shines from above.

Here are some of the functions of the empty case/crate inspection system.

- Detect bottles that sit too high or too low
- Detect bottles with caps or crowns still attached
- Detect neck rings on PET bottles
- Differentiate between glass and PET bottles
- Detect bottles on their side
- Detect bottles that are jammed or upside down in the crate
- Detect foreign objects in the case
- Detect glass bottles in crates designated for PET
- Detect bottle color
- Detect case/crate brand
- Detect and verify case/crate color

Sorting Bottles

The efficiency of a production line for returnable containers is determined to a large extent by the way in which the empties are sorted. The bottle inspector must evaluate a large number of criteria to ensure that only the correct bottles arrive at the washer.

Here are some of the functions of the bottle sorting inspection device (Fig. 28.3).

- Detect bottle shape
- Detect bottle color
- Detect finish shape
- Detect closure
- Measure height
- Detect labels
- Distribute different types of bottles onto separate lanes
- Detect and reject off line broken bottles and foreign objects

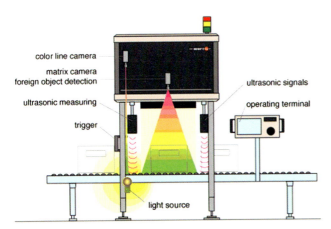

FIGURE 28.2. Empty crate inspection system. (Courtesy Heuft USA, Inc.)

FIGURE 28.3. Bottle sorting inspector. (Courtesy Heuft USA, Inc.)

Detecting Bottles that Are Too High or Too Low

Returned containers are inspected and identified by height. Ultrasonic sensors (Fig. 28.4) may be used to determine the height of all containers in the crate. Multiple sensors are used in the inspection since the correct bottle height is critical. Once the crate passes through the inspection device, a processed "picture" of the absolute bottle heights is created and evaluated (Fig. 28.5). The system may also measure the height of the case. If the measured container height is outside the preset limits, the system considers this result as a foreign container (too big or too small) (Fig. 28.6). The system must also differentiate between a bottle that is too short and an empty crate cell.

Ultrasonic sensors display the height of the case and contents by assigning various colors to height measurements.

Detecting Foreign Objects in Crates

The detection of foreign objects in the returned crate is important from quality and safety standpoints. It is important to detect and reject cases with foreign material in them to reduce the chances of problems at the unpacker. Foreign objects typically fall in between the rows of bottles and are generally detected using incident light (Fig. 28.7) and a camera-based system. This system is also used for detecting upside-down bottles in the crate or bottles that are lying on top of the case walls.

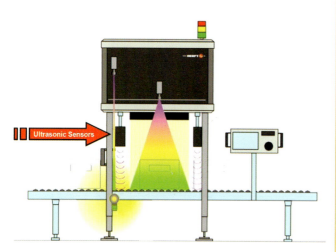

FIGURE 28.4. Ultrasonic sensor placement on a returned container system. (Courtesy Heuft USA, Inc.)

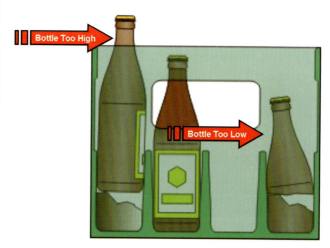

FIGURE 28.6. Different bottle heights in a returned crate. (Courtesy Heuft USA, Inc.)

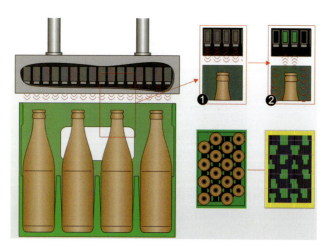

FIGURE 28.5. Process of generating a "picture" of bottle heights within a returned crate. (Courtesy Heuft USA, Inc.)

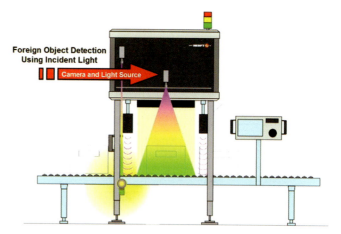

FIGURE 28.7. Detecting foreign objects in returned bottles. (Courtesy Heuft USA, Inc.)

A camera takes a picture of a passing case from above (Fig. 28.8). The evaluation routines examine the case wall structures. The system first checks the corners of the case walls. If a corner is identified, the system continues to check each sidewall of the case. The sidewall identification is important in that the more precise the system can identify the sidewall, the lower the probability of foreign objects being missed. Also, the more precisely the case walls and dividers are identified, the lower the probability that the case will be falsely rejected.

The quantity and quality of the lighting has a large impact on the accuracy of the inspection. Lighting must be configured so that the direct and indirect reflections are consistent for all areas of the crate.

Detecting closures in returned crates (Fig. 28.9) also involves incident light and a camera-based inspection. This inspection detects closures on bottles by using a sophisticated software routine. The system evaluates the picture for reflecting light in areas (individual case cells) where the closures would typically be present. Caps that provide strong reflections are more easily detected. Caps that do not provide strong reflections may be more difficult to reliably detect and may contribute to false rejects if the system parameters are not optimized for the particular type of closure.

Detecting Bottles with Different Colors

Identifying the correct color bottles involves transmitted light (Fig. 28.10). The crate is illuminated from below (Fig. 28.11) as the case passes above through a break in the conveyor.

The camera records the images of the passing containers in the case. The software takes the images and evaluates them based on a reference value for the color(s) to be detected.

FIGURE 28.8. A case with a foreign object. (Courtesy Heuft USA, Inc.)

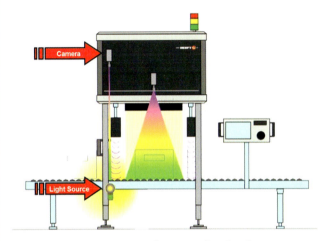

FIGURE 28.10. Detecting the correct bottle color in crates. (Courtesy Heuft USA, Inc.)

FIGURE 28.9. Bottles returned with closures. (Courtesy Heuft USA, Inc.)

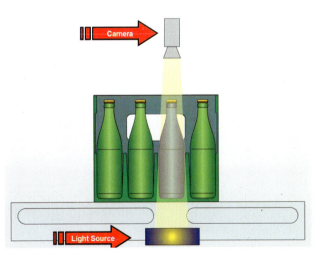

FIGURE 28.11. Detecting the color of bottles in crates by illumination. (Courtesy Heuft USA, Inc.)

If the software cannot reliably determine a correct match with the reference value (Fig. 28.12), the container is marked as a defect, or foreign container. The case may be rejected, depending on the parameters set by the bottling floor personnel. The system reliability may be hindered if the containers have liquid remaining in the bottom of the bottle.

Detecting PET Bottles with Different Neck Rings

The neck ring inspection distinguishes between neck ring types that differ in shape and size.

The containers within the crates are evaluated based on neck ring shape, and the neck ring contours and shapes are compared with the preset values. Containers that are not part of the fleet to be processed are rejected.

Detecting Case Colors and Brands

A light (transmitter) illuminates the sidewall of a case and a color camera (receiver) divides the arriving light in its excitation purity (Fig. 28.13). The color detection process is carried out via three sampling distances, of which the position on the sidewall of a case can be programmed. This permits price tags and symbols with a color that is not coincident with that of the case to be exempt from the detection process. Two "good colors" can be set for every program. The colors for programming can be primary colors or secondary colors.

A charge-coupled device (CCD) camera takes a picture of the logo during the passage of a case. The evaluation electronics compares the photo taken with the different case logos previously learned. The system generates a fault signal when a logo cannot be identified, and the corresponding case is rejected as a foreign case. Cases with detected logos can be distributed to different lanes.

FIGURE 28.12. Detecting color in a crate of mixed glass. (Courtesy Heuft USA, Inc.)

Detecting Case Handle Holes

Detecting cardboard inserts in the area of the handle holes is important in order to avoid disturbance at the unpacker or the case packer. This check is carried out laterally to the moving direction by means of a laser photocell. Different sampling distances can be programmed within the area of a handle hole. A case is evaluated as faulty when the programmed minimum number of pulses is not achieved within one of these programmed distances.

Detecting Case Shape—Case Dimensions

The case is evaluated for proper size (i.e., length, height, and width) and also inspected for squareness (Fig. 28.14), and cases that do not meet the specification are rejected off line.

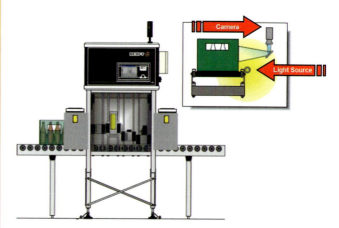

FIGURE 28.13. Case color detection system. (Courtesy Heuft USA, Inc.)

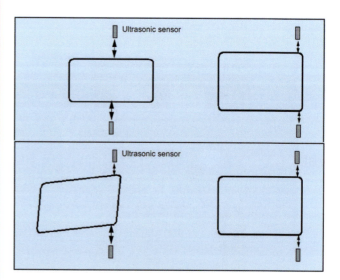

FIGURE 28.14. Detecting proper case size (top) and squareness (bottom). (Courtesy Heuft USA, Inc.)

Detecting Case Shape—Swing-Top Bottles

Detecting swing-top bottles in a returnable crate is important so that the production line is supplied with bottles of the same type and brand and also so that the downstream packaging machinery is protected. Bottles that are outfitted with swing tops must never be allowed to enter into the production stream and into an unpacker that is set up for conventional bottles. The ability to reliably detect different swing-top bottles involves software that cannot only detect the presence of a swing top but also the presence and color of the gasket material that is part of the top (Fig. 28.15).

It is critical to inspect swing-top bottles because it is difficult without special software to determine whether the swing top is actually a closure and not a foreign object. The swing top must be detected even if it is in the open position. The software must be able to determine the difference between a closure and, for example, a normal crown. Items that fall into (or get stuffed into) the container opening need to be reliably detected to ensure efficient production.

The inspection system must reliably detect swing tops from other bottles (Fig. 28.16), and these must be kept out of the production stream. To accomplish this, other bottle characteristics must be taken into consideration. Among these are bottle height, finish type, closure logo, and color of the rubber seal (Fig. 28.17). These features must be processed within the control system's software and a reliable determination be made whether the container is allowed to pass through or should be rejected. Typical inspection systems may find it extremely difficult to make a reliable determination when inspecting crates with swing-top bottles.

Checking Empty Cases

Once the case is emptied of the returnable bottles, the crate itself can be inspected. This inspection typically is performed to detect damaged crates. The crates are inspected for damage to the case sidewall, case dividers, and case bottom. It is also possible to detect foreign objects remaining in the case bottom once the bottles are unpacked. This inspection uses transmitted light, similar to what is used when inspecting full crates for foreign objects. The light is transmitted from below the case, and a picture is assembled from this to indicate defects in the crate (Fig. 28.18).

FIGURE 28.15. Swing-top bottles in a returned crate. (Courtesy Heuft USA, Inc.)

FIGURE 28.16. Swing-top bottles. (Courtesy Heuft USA, Inc.)

FIGURE 28.17. Color and height differences in swing-top bottles. (Courtesy Heuft USA, Inc.)

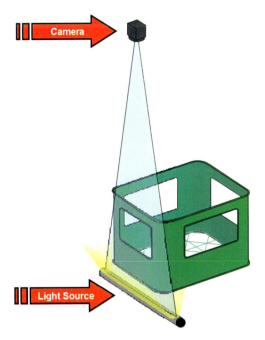

FIGURE 28.18. Light pattern for inspecting an empty crate. (Courtesy Heuft USA, Inc.)

The software determines the ratio between dark and bright pixels per compartment (Fig. 28.19). The case is evaluated as faulty if the ratio falls short of or exceeds the programmed limit value.

● EMPTY BOTTLE INSPECTION (EBI)

In this section, empty bottle inspection (EBI) refers to the receiving and processing of the empty containers, primarily in the returnable glass markets. EBI is more recently being used to perform the inspection of new glass in one-way markets, such as the United States. Since the new glass displays variabilities, end users must use technology to ensure that the glass suited for their particular product is of the highest quality. On returnable bottles, the appearance of the bottles slowly degrades over a period of time due to handling (i.e., scuffing). This reduces the optical appeal for consumers and may have a negative impact on sales. For scuffing defects, it is possible to prolong the number of cycles for the bottle by applying a coating during the filling process, but a good inspection system is critical to providing the customer with bottles that are visually appealing.

There are three generally known types of EBIs in use today, each with its advantages and disadvantages. The three general types are turret machines, star wheel machines, and in-line (belt) machines.

There may be close to 100 defects that have been identified by the glass industry as requiring inspection. These can be categorized by the area of the bottle in which these defects occur. In the brewing industry, with returnable bottles, inspection equipment typically relies on inspection of the finish area, body (or sidewall) area, and base area. Finish inspection typically refers to the inspection of the sealing surface for chips or other irregularities. Some of the defect types that are critical to new glass inspection may not be as important in the returnable market. For example, it might be assumed that an overpress finish would be detected in the manufacturing process and, once removed from the bottle fleet, has almost no chance of occurring in bottles that are returned to the bottling plant for reuse.

The bottling plant typically inspects for defects in the bottle that are caused by normal wear in the bottle's life cycle. Typical finish defects that are checked are for chips in the finish of the container. These can occur in the normal transportation and handling of the bottle. A bent finish, for example, once it has been detected in the manufacturing process, has little chance of presenting itself in the returned bottle fleet.

A similar statement can be made for sidewall defects. Stones in the sidewall have little chance of appearing once the bottle is produced and should be eliminated at the bottle manufacturing facility. Body dimension faults, once checked during manufacturing, are not likely to occur as part of the typical process of filling and refilling. Still, these defects are inspected for at the bottling house to be sure that the new glass being used is acceptable.

This section focuses on inspecting for the types of defects that typically occur in the returnable markets. The typical problem areas arising with nonrefillable glass bottles involve damage incurred during the bottle manufacturing process and damage sustained during shipment, e.g., bottles containing glass threads and damaged bottle mouths. It is noted where it is important to take these into consideration.

Checking the Infeed

The infeed check is used to identify containers before they can cause damage to the downstream inspector. This check is also used to prevent unnecessary stoppages in the production line due to improper containers being fed into the EBI. This check is typically performed using photocells and ultrasonic and inductive sensors.

The infeed check can be used to generate a stop signal to shut down the line before the bottle enters the EBI. At this point, the bottle must be manually removed, and typically the operator is required to acknowledge the removal before the line will start again. A more acceptable solution is to provide a reject device downstream of the infeed check module to remove the container from the production stream without stopping the line. The infeed check provides a level of security at the infeed of the EBI but should not be considered a substitute for an effective bottle-sorting unit.

The infeed check module for an EBI is a low-cost method of adding additional safeguards for the line. The

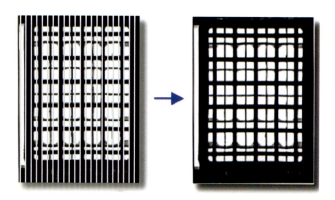

FIGURE 28.19. Image of an empty crate bottom. (Courtesy Heuft USA, Inc.)

infeed can usually be installed at the infeed of the EBI, and typically takes up little conveyor space and requires little maintenance.

Here are some typical examples of faults that can be detected at the infeed check.

- Containers that are too short or too tall
- Containers lying on the conveyor
- Containers that are tilted
- Containers that are too wide or too narrow
- Containers with metal closures

When using a ram-style rejector at the infeed check, it may be more reasonable to provide a stop-pulse in the event a bottle lying on its side is detected. Bottles that are lying on the conveyor are difficult to remove using a simple ram-style rejector. Once the stop-pulse is generated, the operator is prompted to remove the container and only then can the conveyor be restarted.

Inspecting the Sidewalls

The sidewall inspection system checks the outer sidewalls of the container for the following.

- Visible contamination on the sidewall
- Presence of visible foreign objects within the container
- Damages to the container sidewall itself

The operating principle is such that the container is illuminated using a light source. A picture of the container sidewall is taken using a CCD camera and various filtering methods (Fig. 28.20). The image processing unit analyzes the picture and evaluates the container as good or faulty according to the programmed limits. It is important that the optics hardware be designed so that the container can be fairly evaluated whether it is round, rectangular, square, triangular, etc.

The system should have the capability to process containers that have various transparency values without requiring a technician to change the machine settings. This is accomplished using sophisticated electronics and image processing software, and these capabilities (or lack of) should be identified prior to machine purchase. It is important that the field of view for sidewall inspection be appropriate for all container sizes, including containers with the smallest diameter and containers with the largest diameter. Also, detection accuracy may be improved by using digital zooming, but the quality of the digital zooming function is important and should be discussed with the equipment supplier.

In most cases, a gap of some degree must exist between the containers to allow for proper evaluation. This gap must be taken into consideration when designing the line controls and is an important part of the overall conveyor design. This gap is required to ensure the all-around inspection of a container. Speed control of the individual conveyors ensures that the proper gap is achieved. In general, the speed of the outfeed conveyor is designed to be higher than the speed of the infeed conveyor. The control of the conveyors downstream of the EBI is critical to the ability of the system to catch up once a gap in the bottles is realized. It is also important that there be no backup into the discharge of any EBI, and conveyor controls must take this into consideration.

First Sidewall and Second Sidewall Inspections

A single sidewall inspection system takes one picture of the container as it passes in front of the camera (Fig. 28.21). This image is evaluated for visible faults such as contamination on the sidewall, damages to the container sidewall, or the presence of visible foreign objects on the sidewall. This is the most basic sidewall inspection, and it relies on the probability of objects on the back side, or objects not directly in the field of view of the camera, to show up in the camera image of the front side.

As shown in Figure 28.21, one sidewall inspection module alone cannot check the marginal areas of the individual sidewall views and the surfaces not visible on these views. Therefore, an alternate solution is to rotate the containers using the transport belts so that, at the discharge of the machine, a second photograph can be taken of the bottle that is 90° from the original photo.

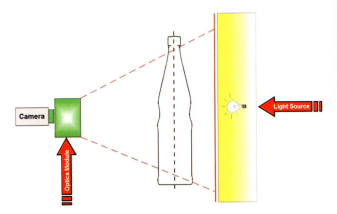

FIGURE 28.20. Sidewall image projection. (Courtesy Heuft USA, Inc.)

The second sidewall inspection module in the outfeed area (Fig. 28.22) checks the surfaces not yet inspected for the presence of faults. The drive for the belts must be precisely controlled so that each container presents itself to the cameras at exactly the same position at the outfeed.

Third Sidewall (Inner Sidewall) Inspections

The third sidewall inspection module checks the inner sidewall of containers that may have the defect blocked from the camera. This inspection is especially important for checking behind applied ceramic labeling (ACL) labels (Fig. 28.23) since this area cannot be adequately inspected by the standard (exterior) inspection methods as described above.

This type of inspection is also effective in containers that may have excessive scuffing or structures in the side or neck area that make it difficult to detect defects on the inside of the container when looking through the structured area. The inspection company's engineering group should be consulted to get a performance guarantee of the percentage of area that can effectively inspected using this type of module.

Stand-Alone Supplemental Sidewall Inspections

For containers that have heavy structures on the surface of the glass, it is possible to add an additional set of sidewall inspection modules. This allows faults that are opposite to the camera side to be detected. This system is typically installed at the infeed of the EBI, with the camera mounted on the opposite side of the conveyor (Fig. 28.24). This additional camera system allows the container to be inspected with a higher resolution than that with the standard single sidewall systems.

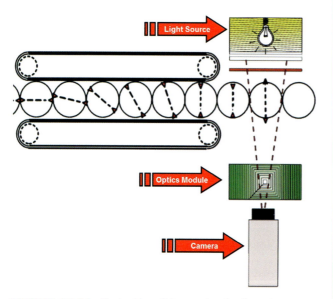

FIGURE 28.21. Basic sidewall inspection for detecting inclusions and damage. (Courtesy Heuft USA, Inc.)

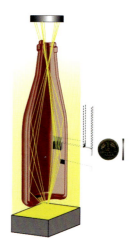

FIGURE 28.23. Inner sidewall detection for any fault covered by labels. (Courtesy Heuft USA, Inc.)

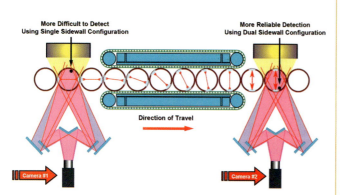

FIGURE 28.22. Sidewall detection using rotations on belts. (Courtesy Heuft USA, Inc.)

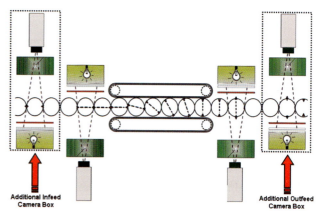

FIGURE 28.24. Additional sensors used for sidewall inspections at the infeed and outfeed. (Courtesy Heuft USA, Inc.)

Inspecting the Finish

The finish inspection is used to check the bottle finish, or sealing surface, for defects. It is important that the bottle have a smooth and defect-free surface for the cap or crown to be properly sealed. The bottle finish works in conjunction with the closure to provide a seal to maintain the integrity and quality of the product inside. The finish inspection is a valuable tool when inspecting finishes for crowns, screw caps, and other closures. In PET bottles, it is possible to monitor the carrier ring, and the inspection automatically detects out-of-round bottle openings. Bent necks can also be detected using this method.

There are many types of defects that impact the finish inspection, and the customer must be aware that some of the finish "defects" as identified by the inspection may be commercially acceptable. It is important to work with the inspection system supplier's engineering group to determine what an actual defect is and what is commercially acceptable to let pass through. In some cases, due to the inspection method, the finish inspection may be required to reject defects that the customer might deem acceptable.

There are many different types of finish defects, including the following.

- Chipped finishes
- Missing finishes
- Tears on the sealing surface—grooves in the sealing surface (the larger ones can be felt, smaller ones cannot)
- Split finish—large cracks on the sealing surface that reflect light
- Crizzled sealing surface—very small cracks on the sealing surface that reflect light
- Overpress finish—a vertical upstanding pipe around the bore of the bottle
- Skin blister—bubbles on the sealing surface (or close to the sealing surface) of the glass
- Finish not blown up—wrong finish geometry due to insufficient filling of the mold
- Seam flange—glass fins over the sealing surface caused by worn out or damaged mold pair
- Orange peel—sealing surface not smooth, rough when felt
- Offset finish—mold pair of the finish is offset in a horizontal and/or vertical direction
- Sealing surface not horizontal
- Displaced finish—finish is offset horizontally in relation to the bottle centerline
- Edged sealing surface—sealing surface has no defined radius

The finish inspection unit (Fig. 28.25) uses reflected light to determine the quality of the finish. The finish is illuminated from above by a light source. The light that is reflected back into the camera is evaluated by special software to determine the type and magnitude of any defects.

The image software processes the reflected image and evaluates the container as good or faulty according to the programmed tolerances. Once the container is identified as faulty, the reject device is activated and the container is rejected off line. It is important to note that different lighting is required for the proper evaluation of different types of finishes. It is important to consult with the supplier's engineering group when choosing a finish inspection system.

Moistening the Finish

In some cases, the finish may be scuffed but still provides an acceptable sealing surface for the bottle. Finishes with scuffing absorb light in those areas where the reflection ring is located and reflect light from areas that normally do not reflect light. In this case, it is possible to get better results by moistening the finish slightly (coating the finish with a thin film of water) just before the bottle enters the inspection device. The film of water stabilizes the reflection characteristics of the finish.

Blowing Off the Finish

In general, a blow-off can be provided when PET containers are processed. This air blow-off may be necessary in order to minimize the number of false rejections due to drops of water on the finish or on the neck ring. The air blow is installed in the area prior to the inspector, where the containers are generally close

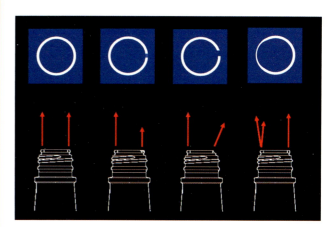

FIGURE 28.25. Inspection pattern for bottle finishes. (Courtesy Heuft USA, Inc.)

together. Since empty PET containers have a tendency to tip over, the system is programmed to not activate the blow-off when an individual container passes through. It is also recommended that the system be programmed to not activate the blow-off for the first or last in a group of containers to prevent them from falling over.

Inspecting the Base

The base inspection is used to check the container bottoms for defects. These can be either defects in the glass container or objects lying in the bottom of the bottle. The base inspection uses transmitted light to inspect the container. A light source is energized below the bottle, and this light passes through the base of the container and into the CCD camera through a specially designed optics module (Fig. 28.26). The light that passes through the container base and into the camera is evaluated by special software to determine the type and magnitude of any defects. Once the container is identified as faulty, the reject device is activated and the container is rejected off line.

The image software processes the image and evaluates the container as good or faulty according to the programmed tolerances. The software must be able to detect faults in the base of the container while ignoring things such as structures in the glass, e.g., knurling. On PET containers, for example, the injection point appears to the camera similar to an object on the bottom of the container. The software must be able to filter out these types of structures while still rejecting containers with actual defects. Software enhancements, such as base centering, are critical to the performance of the inspection system, and a thorough discussion with the system's engineering department is crucial to getting a system that meets expectations. An example of a base inspection system is shown in Figure 28.27.

There are several types of defects that can be detected using a base inspection system, including the following.

- Contamination
- Foreign objects
- Damaged base
- Clogging in the container neck

Some features that should be considered when investigating the purchase of a base inspection system include the following.

- There should be automatic cleaning of the light source. In the event that there are consecutive faults, the base lighting fixture is cleaned using compressed air.
- The software should be able to compensate for varying bottle quality within the same container type. The quality of glass from the manufacturer can vary, even within the same lot. If the software cannot compensate for these naturally occurring variations, the false reject rate will be excessive.
- There should be provisions for special procedures for processing containers with variable transparency values without having to change the setting of the optical components.

Inspecting the Base for Transparent Faults

The inspection of container bases is different when detecting opaque faults and transparent faults. For transparent defect detection (such as cellophanes), the

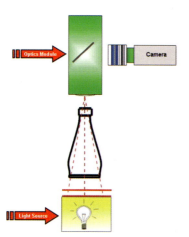

FIGURE 28.26. Base inspection pattern. (Courtesy Heuft USA, Inc.)

FIGURE 28.27. Bottle base inspection system. (Courtesy Heuft USA, Inc.)

design of the optics modules installed above the passing containers is different. The transparent base inspection, when combined with a system for detecting opaque faults, together represents a double base inspection.

This inspection for transparent faults may rely on the same light source as that of the standard base inspection. To reliably perform this inspection, the optics module must present the exposed picture to two different cameras (Fig. 28.28). The cameras are connected to separate image processor cards and function independently. The second base inspection module should be designed to be extremely sensitive for transparent faults so that the two inspection modules supplement each other.

Inspecting the Bottle Finish Thread

Thread inspection systems are primarily used to check screw closure threads for damages of the thread turns. The thread inspection may be limited to certain thread geometries, and consultation with the supplier's engineering group is mandatory when considering this type of inspection system.

A thread inspection system relies on an image processing system typically consisting of multiple cameras and optics modules (Fig. 28.29). This type of system uses reflected light to determine whether the threads are defective. The optics module(s) must be specially designed to evaluate the complete thread and provide a 360° image to the processing software for evaluation.

At the point of inspection, the threads must be clear of water droplets. This may be achieved by a thread blowing device. Clip-lock bottles may be inspected reliably, but consultation with the supplier's engineering group is necessary to determine the reliability. For bottles with crowns, this module may be able to detect chips under the finish (underchip), but engineering consultation is once again required.

Thus, the interruption lengths of damages can be measured or coarseness can be accurately detected and evaluated.

Detecting Residual Liquid

There are two prevalent means of detecting the presence of residual liquid in the base of the container after cleaning. One uses high-frequency technology, the other uses infrared technology. It is possible to use a high-frequency system for checking nonmetal containers for even the smallest amounts of liquid in the base. In this case, two measuring heads (emitter and receiver) are mounted to both sides of the conveyor at the height of the container base (Fig. 28.30).

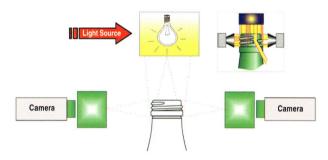

FIGURE 28.29. Twist-off thread inspection. (Courtesy Heuft USA, Inc.)

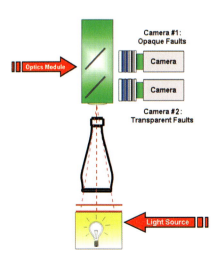

FIGURE 28.28. Double bottle base inspection pattern. (Courtesy Heuft USA, Inc.)

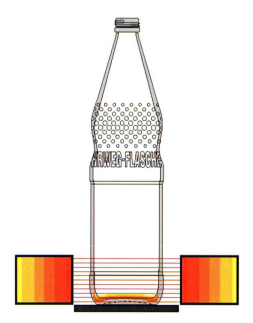

FIGURE 28.30. Residual liquid inspection pattern. (Courtesy Heuft USA, Inc.)

When a container with residual liquid in the base passes between these measuring heads, it changes the field between the emitter and the receiver. The magnitude of the change is measured and compared with the preset values. The system then determines whether the container is passable or is faulty and needs to be rejected off line. This type of system is impacted by the conductivity of the liquid to be detected. The container diameter also needs to be considered when deciding whether to use this type of system.

It is possible on some systems to use a second detection module. The use of two modules improves the reliability, further reducing the risk of containers passing through to the filler with small amounts of caustic still in the container.

Another method of detecting whether there are undesirable liquids in the base of the container prior to filling uses infrared light technology. The use of infrared light is most appropriate for the detection of liquids that absorb infrared light (e.g., oil and many solvents and lacquers).

An infrared residual liquid detection system requires a light source and may use the same light source from the base inspection (Fig. 28.31). A special sensor measures the absorption behavior of the container. A reference sensor compensates for influences caused by container tolerances, such as glass thickness and color. The standard device compares the result with the entered values and evaluates whether a container should be rejected as faulty. This system is not adversely impacted by small amounts of water that may remain in the base of the container. This inspection method is acceptable for both glass and PET, but in the case of PET, the reliability may be less and/or the amount that the system can detect (e.g., oil) may be larger than with glass bottles.

Inspecting for Scuffing

On returnable bottles, the appearance of the bottles slowly degrades over time due to handling (i.e., scuffing). This reduces the visual appeal for consumers (Fig. 28.32) and may have a negative impact on sales. The scuffing inspection examines the glass or PET containers for glass wear due to bottle-to-bottle contact during the handling process.

The scuffing inspection is performed using the sidewall inspection cameras and utilizes special software to evaluate the container sidewall. The customer is required to determine the degree of scuffing permissible in the bottle fleet.

PET bottle scuffing is a particularly difficult inspection to manage. The body of the container may require inspection utilizing up to four separate views. The inspection is impacted negatively by the tendency of the bottles to mist on the inside or outside. It is important that the customer work closely with the inspection company's engineering group to determine the effectiveness of this inspection based on the customer's layout.

Inspecting the PET Vent Slot

The inspection of the vent slot in PET containers typically uses two cameras (Fig. 28.33). The thread area is illuminated by a light source from above, and the

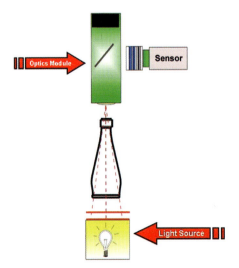

FIGURE 28.31. Base inspection equipment used for infrared residual liquid detection. (Courtesy Heuft USA, Inc.)

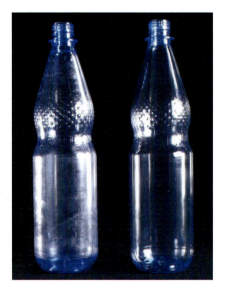

FIGURE 28.32. A scuffed bottle (left) compared with a new bottle (right). (Courtesy Heuft USA, Inc.)

CCD cameras record the images for the vision software to evaluate. Special optics and filtering methods may be used to detect nontransparent contamination within the vent slots, as well as in the inner and outer areas of the thread.

The image processing software determines whether the container is passable based on preprogrammed limits. If PET containers have differing colors, it is important to discuss this with the inspection company's engineering department to determine the effectiveness of this inspection.

Removing Old Containers from the Bottle Fleet

Sometimes it is desirable to remove old, unattractive containers from the bottle fleet. For example, the brewer may wish to present an upscale image, and containers that appear "old" may not be desirable. The brewer may wish to reject bottles that have not actual defects but are undesirable for the particular bottle fleet. Older containers can be recognized by outer characteristics such as scuffing. There are several other attributes that can be evaluated to determine whether the bottle should be kept in the fleet or removed. The following inspection technologies are typically used to evaluate the wear and aging process of the containers.

- Scuffing of the exterior of the container
- Thread damage, such as chewed threads
- Finish damage
- Stress cracks in the base of PET containers

Software is available in today's inspection systems to automatically provide for the removal of old containers based on several criteria. This is configurable and can be adapted to each customer's needs.

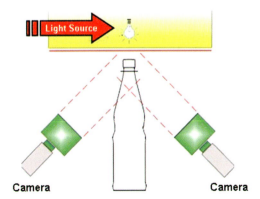

FIGURE 28.33. PET vent slot detection pattern. (Courtesy Heuft USA, Inc.)

A system for bottle inspection may incorporate reject rate control to ensure that there are certain minimum reject rates that are maintained, even if the containers that are rejected by the inspection system do not achieve these quotas. Typically, these modified inspections include finish, thread, and scuffing inspection. This is another way to control and remove old containers from the bottle fleet. The customer may wish to remove, for example, containers that may be considered old after one or two more circuits.

Special software is used for this purpose. It is not desirable to simply increase the sensitivity of the various inspections to achieve this result, since actual defects may very well be allowed to pass through. A reject rate control system makes it possible to keep to the prescribed minimum reject rates, even if the containers rejected by the inspector as faulty do not achieve these quotas. The customer must first establish the quota, or desired reject rate, that the inspection software should target. Systems used to control reject rate can either control the total reject rate or the old container reject rate to achieve the desired mix of old and new containers in the bottle fleet.

For example, if the desired reject rate is 5%, and 1.2% of this has already been rejected due to faulty containers, then the remaining 3.8% will be composed of old containers that will be rejected afterwards in order to achieve this reject rate. The control system calculates the degree of wear above which old containers are rejected so that only the most worn old containers are rejected. If 2% is composed of faulty containers, then an additional 3% would be composed of old containers to be rejected. Faulty containers are always rejected, even if the desired reject rate for an interval is exceeded as a result.

The result is that old containers are rejected long before the container pool includes unsightly containers. This has the side benefit in that extremely worn old containers are rejected. The system software must be written so that, as soon as new glass is identified, the reject rate control system becomes inactive. Once this happens, the low reject rates due to new glass are not made up.

Analyzing Test Bottles and System Challenge Samples

It is important that the proper test bottle protocol be adhered to so that the equipment is guaranteed to perform at optimum levels. All inspection systems should be challenged on a regular basis to make sure they are performing at their highest capability. Test bottles are typically set aside specifically for this purpose, to make sure the inspection equipment is in proper working order. To accomplish this, the test containers are allowed to pass through the inspection machine, and it is noted whether all faults are detected. If all faults are not detected, then the inspection equipment must be adjusted so that the system passes the test. If all faults are detected, then it can be assumed that the inspection equipment is functioning properly. The test bottle protocol can be run, for example, at the beginning of each shift, each day, or each week. It really depends on the risk tolerance of the plant personnel.

It is recommended that the inspection equipment incorporate the appropriate software to prompt for the test to be performed and that the software be configured so the test bottle performance can be documented and stored for future reference if need be.

Developing the Project Scope for the EBI

Other things to consider when developing the project scope for the EBI include the following.

- Is it a new project or an integration into an existing line?
- What budget is considered for this project?
- How many different bottles (e.g., diameter and height) are to be inspected?
- Might there be different sizes and/or shapes in the future?
- How is the overall average quality of the bottle fleet?
- What inspection criteria are requested (EBI)?
- Is easy future expansion capability an advantage?
- What capacity (e.g., bottles per hour) is required and what is the filler speed?
- What is the qualification of the operators and what degree of technology and engineering can they handle?
- Are the costs of operation (e.g., spares and service) considered?
- Which supplier offers additional (future) benefits (e.g., line flow control)?
- Does the potential supplier offer close and reliable service?

● FILL-LEVEL INSPECTION

There are several technologies that are available for determining the fill level in a container. A general comparison of technologies is included later in the section. Some of the technologies can be used for both underfill and overfill detection; however, the limits for underfill and overfill may require the use of dual sensors. The supplier's engineering department should be consulted if it is desired to perform both underfill and overfill with the same device.

Some common methods of performing fill-level inspection include the following.

- X-ray
- Radioactive isotope (gamma)
- High frequency (HF)
- Vision
- Infrared

The features available in fill-level devices may provide cost savings, yield savings, etc. depending on the particular installation. Here are some items to look for when researching fill-level devices for breweries.

- For postfiller fill-level inspection, perhaps the most reliable technology that is used is the high-frequency (HF) principle. This technique provides for the compensation of foam typical of beer filling and is able to account for the product that is present in the foam collar when inspecting the container immediately after the filler.
- It is important that the customer discuss the product foaming potential with the supplier's engineering group, since the software that specifically addresses this heavy foam collar may vary from manufacturer to manufacturer, and caution must be taken when evaluating the expected performance.
- In the case of burst bottles, detecting and rejecting bottles that could contain glass splinters is important. A burst bottle system might have the capability to send a signal to force the underfilling of bottles to be rejected, reducing the chances of these containers being placed back on the conveyor. The burst bottle system should be easily customized, and the customer is advised to perform their own risk analysis so that a balance between product safety and product yields is achieved.
- A filler valve monitoring package can be a valuable tool in reducing operating and maintenance costs and, at the same time, in increasing yields. Detecting intermittently badly filling valves is just one of the benefits of this type of system, while another benefit is the ability to view production data in real time. In this manner, corrections can be made to the equipment promptly.

Tables 28.1 through 28.3 provide the comparisons between the available technologies.

X-Ray Technology vs. Gamma Technology

- Both use a similar means of detecting fill level and are generally considered to be interchangeable (but not always). Gamma rays occur as the isotope naturally degrades, X-rays are electrically generated. The wavelengths of the two are similar.
- In some cases, it is preferable to use X-ray in lieu of gamma technology, and the manufacturer's engineering department should be consulted when making the final determination.
- In either case, they are good alternatives in that neither are affected by bottle color or bottle/ product transparency, and neither are affected by water drops on the container or fogged containers. Either can be used to detect the fill level behind the labels, and both are a good choice if the fill level is behind the cap or tamper band.
- The americium source that is the basis for this type of fill-level inspection equipment requires no maintenance, and these sources will last many years.

TABLE 28.1. General Comparisons Between Technologies

	Gamma	X-Ray	High Frequency	Vision
Measuring method	Horizontal	Horizontal	Horizontal	Horizontal
Approval requirements	Yes	Yes	No	No
Waste disposal	High	Low	Low	Low
Maintenance	Very low	Very low	Dependent on product	Dependent on product
Quantifying	Possible	Possible	Possible	Possible
Can inspection	Possible	Possible	Not possible	Not possible

TABLE 28.2. More Detailed Comparisons Between Technologies

	Gamma	X-Ray	High Frequency (HF)	Vision
Measuring method	The gamma and X-ray methods are pure height measurements that relate to a fill level from the upper edge of the conveyor belt.		The HF method measures the change in the electrical field between the measuring heads caused by the filled product in relation to the upper edge of the conveyor belt.	With the vision method, the measuring reference point is user determined, e.g., relative measurement from the upper edge of the finish to the fill level.
Approval requirements	Customers contact local authorities to obtain approval for installation of a gamma/X-ray device in accordance with the regulations of that particular region.		None	None
Waste disposal	Disposal of radioactive gamma devices subject to strict regulations.	Disposal of X-ray devices subject to local regulations. Components classified as electronic waste.	None	None
Maintenance	Generally maintenance free. Trigger photocells require regular cleaning.		Must to be regularly cleared of moisture, e.g., water splashes.	
Wear and tear	In accordance with radiation protection laws, gamma sources have to be checked regularly for possible leakages.	Should be designed for task in hand. Is additional cooling required?	HF device is nonwearing. Provided there are no signs of mechanical damage, operating time is not restricted.	Strobe life average life of 50–100 million flashes.

TABLE 28.3. General Comparisons Between Technologies of What Influences the Fill-Level Detection

	Gamma	X-Ray	High Frequency (HF)	Vision
Sloshing fill level	Low	Low	Hardly at all	Slightly
Label presence (nonmetallic)	Not at all	Not at all	Not at all	Dependent on position and/or size
Foil (metallic)	Not at all	Not at all	Measurement not possible	Measurement not possible
Bottle color	Not at all	Not at all	Not at all	Dependent on color or shade
Product transparency	Not at all	Not at all	Not at all	Low
Bottle geometry tolerances	Low	Low	High	Low
Bottle contour in measuring range	Low	Low	Low	High
Foam formation	Medium—Gamma and X-ray systems can produce good results with foaming (not creamy foam) if a clear transition is visible. Usually a transition occurs again several feet behind a filler. The development of foam back into liquid cannot be taken into consideration here as with HF technology.		Very low—The software must be written specifically to compensate for inspection of fill levels behind a beer filler.	High—The lack of a clear liquid level that cannot be identified makes this generally unsuitable.
Formation of drops or fogging	No influence—Drops of water on the bottle to be examined do not affect the gamma or X-ray detection.		Low—Very wet surface can lead to slight deviations in the result with HF if the wetness is not even on all bottles.	High—Results with the vision systems can be negatively impacted by a wet or strongly fogged up surface.
Contents of the product (e.g., oil, pure alcohol)	Low	Low	High	No
Guide rails	Medium	Medium	High	Medium
Glass thickness	Glass absorbs gamma and X-rays 1.6 times as much as water does. Varying glass thickness in the measuring area has a relative strong effect on the detection of properties for gamma and X-ray. Special attention must be made to checking the detection in a narrow bottle neck using gamma or X-rays if the glass wall is relatively large in relation to the diameter at the liquid level.		Minimal	By comparison, the optical methods are hardly influenced by the thickness of the glass. Faults in the glass are more likely to play a part.
Bottle tolerances	Gamma and X-ray are not influenced by this as long as the glass thickness is constant.		HF strongly influenced by off-centering positioning. Large bottle deviations from the desired bottle shape can also alter the measuring result.	Minimal for optical detection systems, as long as the optical path through the bottle geometry is not altered.
Contents	Salts absorb gamma and X-rays more than normal liquids. A high salt concentration can have a slight effect on the result.		The HF measuring bridge reacts to the electrolytic properties of the liquids to be measured.	Not affected by product composition.
Temperature	No effect		Products that are hot filled can cause a condensation effect on the measuring heads due to the heat radiation. This can lead to variable measuring results with the HF and vision systems if the conditions are not kept constant.	

- X-ray devices require the replacement of the X-ray generator after a period of time. Depending on use, the life expectancy of this type of equipment may be 3–10 years.
- X-ray can be switched off; the gamma source is permanently active.
- It is always a good idea to check with the local agencies regarding the regulatory and filing requirements and to be aware of the exact procedures to be followed when installing gamma-based fill-level inspection equipment.
- In either case, a radiation safety officer (RSO) is required, and the plant must understand the duties the RSO will be required to perform. It is important to fully understand the training that is required for the RSO. In the case of gamma fill-level inspection devices, the RSO must follow certain guidelines that are more time consuming than are those with X-ray devices.
- Disposal costs for americium-based fill-level inspection devices should be considered before the time of purchase, since these may change from year to year.

A typical gamma installation checklist consists of the following.

- File for reciprocity if not in the state of sale, and obtain approval from the local jurisdiction.
- Gather all required documents, manuals, and regulations.
- Wear badge and ring dosimeters.
- Test the survey meter function and battery and document the check.
- Unpack the device according to the written procedures.
- Fill out the question-and-answer form for each device.
- Perform a survey, shutter switch, and lamp tests and document the tests.
- Perform a leak test and fill out associated paperwork.
- Make certain that the customer's equipment manual contains copies of the required regulations.
- Provide training on radiation safety and use and document the training.
- RSO provides the survey and leak test results to the customer and reports the distribution to the required regulatory agencies.

There are certain requirements that must be met for each installation of gamma-based fill-level inspectors.

These requirements may change from time to time and may differ depending on the jurisdiction the installation is in. It is recommended that the designated RSO stay in close contact with the local governing agencies to make sure that the requirements are met.

Here are some general requirements for gamma gauges.

- Information labels must be maintained and legible and may not be removed.
- Leak tests must be performed and documented at specified intervals.
- On/off mechanism and indicator must be tested at specified intervals, and the results of these tests must be documented.
- Must be installed, serviced, relocated, and removed from service only by persons with a specific license to do so.
- Must report any failure of leak test, shielding, or on/off mechanism.
- May not abandon the device.
- May only dispose of the device by transfer to a specific licensee authorized to receive that device. A report is required to be filed.
- Typically may not store the device for more than 2 years.

The general principle of operation for either technology (Fig. 28.34) includes the following.

- Gamma rays (or X-rays) are sent across the container at the targeted fill level.
- A certain amount of this beam is absorbed by the product.
- The remaining portion is measured by a receiver on the other side of the container.
- The software makes a determination of the fill level based on the amount of the beam that has been absorbed.

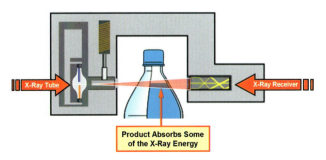

FIGURE 28.34. X-ray fill-level sensor pattern. (Courtesy Heuft USA, Inc.)

It is important to note that for either X-ray or gamma technology, the diameter of the neck and the thickness of the glass can have a huge impact on the accuracy and reliability of this type of inspection. For example, Table 28.4 shows the volume measurement difference between a 12-oz. bottle and a 12-oz. can.

Vision-Based Fill-Level Inspection Systems

Vision-based systems for fill level are camera based and are generally backlit to provide the proper lighting to show the difference between the product and the air space above. For this technology, it is best if the product is a darker liquid in a clear or lightly colored bottle, but proper lighting and software can accommodate even difficult applications such as red wine in dark bottles. Vision is the only relative measuring procedure that can measure the fill level from the upper edge as well as from the base or from any preset reference point on the container (Fig. 28.35).

Here are some important notes regarding vision inspection for fill-level evaluation.

- Can perform both underfill and overfill inspections.
- No wipe tests required.
- No RSO required.

TABLE 28.4. Container Volume Comparison

	12-oz. Long-Neck Bottle	12-oz. Can
Neck diameter	20 mm	66 mm
Volume in 1 mm	0.01 oz.	0.1 oz.

- Fill-level measurement can be made from container reference points rather than from the container base, removing the inaccuracies that various container heights might present.
- Very precise measurements where the liquid level is steady.
- Not affected by different product compositions.
- Can be combined with closure inspections.
- May be affected by bottle color or transparency.
- May be affected by label placement on the container or water drops or fogging on the container.
- May also be used on the same system for other inspections, such as cap presence, high/cocked cap, tamper band evaluation, etc.

High-Frequency (HF) Fill-Level Inspection Systems

This type of system checks for the presence of liquid between the sender and the receiver. The system might look similar to the one in Figure 28.36.

The operating principle is such that the change in the electrical field between the measuring heads caused by the filled product is proportional to the fill level. In general, if a voltage is applied between two electrodes, the current flow between them is a function of the area (and distance) between the electrodes, as well as the dielectric properties of the medium between them. The area (and distance) between the electrodes is fixed, so that leaves the product itself to affect the flow of current, which is quantifiable. There is no contact with the containers during the measuring process, and it is important that the container be exactly centered when passing through this inspection module.

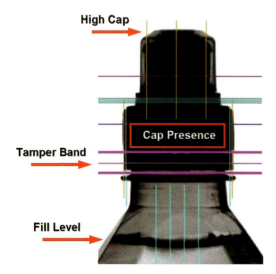

FIGURE 28.35. Vision-type detection. (Courtesy Heuft USA, Inc.)

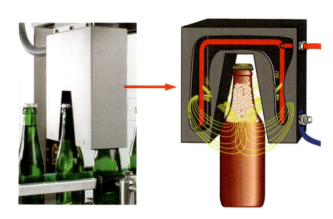

FIGURE 28.36. High-frequency fill-level detection. (Courtesy Heuft USA, Inc.)

The sensitivity of this type of system depends on the product within the container, and this technology is an excellent choice for water-based products in glass and PET. This technology is not suitable for cans or for products with an extremely high alcohol content, but it is an exceptional choice for the beer industry in bottling since it provides for the compensation of foam typical of beer filling and is able to account for the product that is present in the foam collar when inspecting the container immediately after the filler.

Here are some of the highlights of this type of measurement technology.

- No wipe tests required.
- No RSO required.
- Compensates for glass thickness differences.
- Product must be conductive, liquid, and not pastelike.
- Affected by different product compositions, e.g., diet vs. regular cola.
- Only for glass and PET bottles, not cans.
- Not affected by bottle color or bottle or product transparency.

Monitoring the Filler Valve

The filler valve monitoring systems available have transformed the postfiller inspection devices into production tools that can be used for optimizing yields and reducing downtime and maintenance costs. The filler valve monitoring system tracks the containers through the filler and closer (and corker, if required) and out to the inspection device. When a container enters into the filler area, a data sheet (or electronic checklist) is electronically attached to the container. Once the container is evaluated at the inspection device, the information that is gathered from the inspection system is transferred onto the data sheet for the individual container.

In simplest terms, the data sheet might look like the one in Figure 28.37 if it were to be written by hand.

The data from the filler valve monitor can be useful as a preventative maintenance tool for the filler and/or closer. Filling valves that perform erratically are identified based on actual statistical data rather than on opinions from lab technicians or plant personnel. This, in turn, makes the job of the quality assurance department much easier and fact based and removes the emotion from the decision-making process.

A typical summary screen might look like the one in Figure 28.38. In this summary, it is shown that the overall filler performance is acceptable, with a standard deviation within acceptable limits and an average fill that is also within acceptable limits. It is obvious that filler valve #22 is performing as expected, with the average fill right on target and the standard deviation acceptable. It can be assumed that this particular valve does not require any maintenance at this point. Filler valve #34, however, has an acceptable average fill, but the standard deviation may be outside the acceptable limits and this should be addressed. Valve #54 appears to have an acceptable standard deviation; however, the average fill from that particular valve is higher than acceptable. Valve #33 has a standard deviation that is unacceptable and an average fill that is

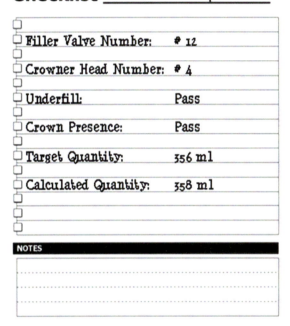

FIGURE 28.37. Filler valve checklist. (Courtesy Heuft USA, Inc.)

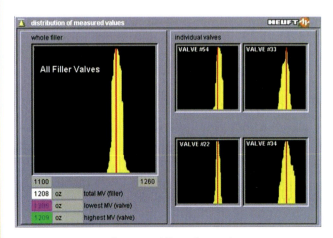

FIGURE 28.38. Electronic filler valve performance report. (Courtesy Heuft USA, Inc.)

also unacceptable and is frequently underfilling. The filler valve monitoring system can warn operators about trends that might result in shutdowns, allowing them to remedy the situation well ahead of time. Based on this data, the plant maintenance and engineering departments can prioritize the work to be performed on the filler.

The filler valve monitor can be used to indicate the line performance at the filler/closer. This information can be displayed in a written format (Fig. 28.39) or in a graphical format (Fig. 28.40), which is easier for plant personnel to interpret.

If the example illustrated in Figures 28.39 and 28.40 is taken further, the total reject rate for underfilled containers is shown to be 0.34%. If the breakdown of these underfills is investigated further by valve number, a significant percentage of the underfills may be found to come from filling valve #27. In this case, by addressing this one poorly performing valve, the overall reject rate can be reduced by a significant percentage.

The ability to provide statistical information regarding the line performance, and the ability to present this information in a variety of formats, makes the filler valve monitor package a useful production tool. The justification for this type of system is sometimes difficult to provide because the system may first need to be in place to realize the inefficiencies in the filler. Detecting the costly overfills, missing crowns, etc. can contribute to significant savings over the course of the year and also results in an increase in product quality.

```
total counters
-----------------------------------------=
Processed Containers         143275    100.00%
Produced Containers          142592     99.52%
Rejected Containers             683      0.48%
Without Closure                 156      0.11%
Underfilled Containers          481      0.34%
Overfilled Containers            82      0.06%
```

FIGURE 28.39. Filler report. (Courtesy Heuft USA, Inc.)

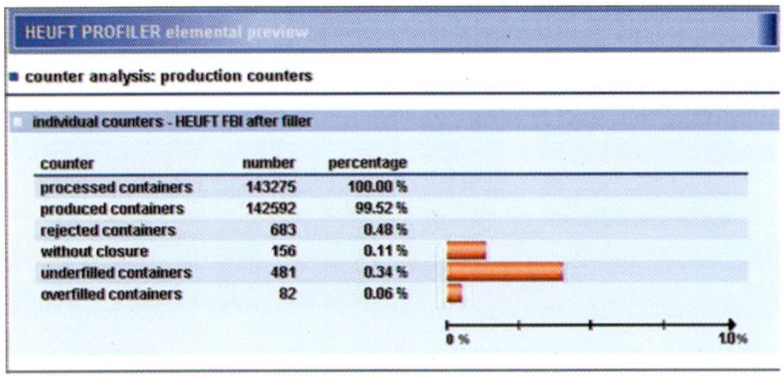

FIGURE 28.40. Graphical representation of filler performance. (Courtesy Heuft USA, Inc.)

Typical information that can be provided by a filler valve monitoring system includes the following.

- Average for individual stations
- Average for all stations
- Distribution curves for individual stations
- Distribution curve for all stations
- Standard deviation for individual stations
- Standard deviation for all stations
- Valve/closer performance over time
- Localization of defective positions
- Detection of intermittently defective filling valves and/or closer heads

It is important to note that, while the filler valve monitoring system focuses on the filler, the closer is also monitored during this process. For example, the system tracks faults on the part of the closer and issues reports based on individual closer head performance. Similar to the previous example for the filler, the system may show that the overall reject rate for misapplied closures is 5.0%, but a good percentage of these may have come from closer head #4. In this case, the operator would be kept informed in real time regarding the performance of this particular closer head and could alert maintenance that repairs need to be made. The production department can then make the decision to shut down at once or wait until an upcoming changeover to make the repairs. If a changeover is scheduled shortly, then the plant may choose to wait until then to perform the repairs. If a changeover is not scheduled for many hours, the most cost-effective approach may be to shut down the line and make the necessary repairs at once.

The data that is generated by the system allows the plant to make the most prudent decision regarding maintenance scheduling and may easily result in savings that are greater than first projected when the system was first installed. As the operators and maintenance personnel get accustomed to working with the system, they can find that their decisions can be made based on fact rather than on how they "feel" the line is performing.

Detecting Missing Fill Tubes

Detecting fill tubes made of steel in nonmetal containers is possible using two general technologies. The vent tubes can be detected on-line downstream of the filler using sensors that can detect a change in magnetic field brought about by the metal vent tube passing between them. The detection of fill tubes is performed using two metal detectors mounted on each side of the conveyor. If a container with a fill tube in it passes by the detection module, this change is registered by the sensor, amplified by the evaluation electronics, and read in by the control system. This analog signal is then analyzed by the software. If a container with a fill tube is detected, it is rejected. In addition, a stop signal can be generated so that the fill tube can be found immediately on the rejection table and mounted again in order to prevent containers with faulty fillings from the outset.

Vent tube detection can be accomplished at high speeds but requires that the vent tube be made out of metal (Fig. 28.41). Because the conveyors may be constructed of metal chain, or at the very least constructed of metal frames, the tube must rest in the container at a certain height above the bottom of the container. When chains made of synthetic material are used as conveyor belts, it is possible to reach considerably larger ranges for the detection because then the fill tube is the only metal object in motion. It is recommended that the inspection company's engineering group be consulted to determine the reliability of this on-conveyor detection.

Another type of vent tube detection uses sensors mounted within the filler. These sensors send an input to the control system whenever a filling station passes in front of the sensor. The control system monitors the rotation of the filler and expects an input at each filler valve position as the filler rotates. If a tube falls into the container, then the control system does not get an input as expected and a critical alarm is sent, possibly stopping the line until the container is found.

Managing Broken Bottles in the Filler

A beer filler can create high pressure during the filling cycle, causing some bottles to burst. It is important to manage the glass containers that burst within the filling zone. When a container bursts completely, this is fairly easily detected. The difficulty arises when the container partially bursts or a section of the container bursts out of the sidewall, for example. It is possible that the flying glass from these containers can contaminate other containers in the filling zone. If the detection is left for the fill-level inspector to pick up, then the glass splinters that could have adhered to the filler valve may have already gotten into other containers by the time the bottle position has reached the fill-level device.

Systems that use various sensors, including acoustic sensing devices, can reliably detect the burst bottle the instant it happens, reducing the risk of glass fragments entering other containers and reducing the risk of containers that may have fragments in them getting into the production stream. Systems that provide bottle burst detection are generally configurable, and each manufacturer can adapt the level of protection to their own quality philosophy. Bottle burst systems typically have an investment cost that is far lower than the cost of contaminated bottles getting into the marketplace.

Once the bottle burst is detected, it is necessary that all of the bottles that may potentially contain glass fragments be identified and rejected. The filling valve components must be washed to clean off any splinters that may remain on the valve assembly. At the same time, a preprogrammed routine is initiated to perform a variety of actions. These routines are determined at the time of installation by the customer.

Here is an example of bottle burst detection at filling valve #12 (Fig. 28.42).

1. A sensor at the infeed of the filler registers that a container has entered the filling zone.

FIGURE 28.41. Vent tube in a glass bottle coming off the filler outfeed. (Courtesy Heuft USA, Inc.)

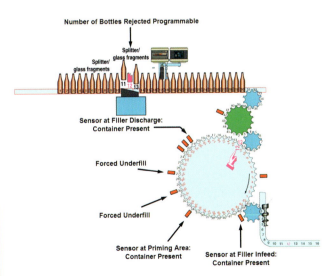

FIGURE 28.42. Bottle burst protection system showing mechanisms for a bottle burst at filler valve #12. (Courtesy Heuft USA, Inc.)

2. A sensor at the end of the priming area verifies the container presence.
   - If the container is present, then OK.
   - If the container is not present, this might mean a burst container.
3. If the container is considered burst, then the system will send a signal to the filler to underfill bottles (if applicable); in this example, underfill the bottles in positions #11, #12, and #13.
   - Forcing the filler to underfill serves two purposes:
     - If the container(s) are to be rejected anyway, then underfilling them reduces product losses.
     - Underfilling these containers helps prevent plant personnel from placing these back on the production conveyor. At first glance, if the operator does not know the reason the container has been rejected, they may look at it and think it is a false reject, since the fill level appears to be within range.
4. A fill station rinse out is initiated.
5. Once the bottle in position #11 reaches the reject area, this bottle is rejected, along with the bottle in position #12 (or what remains of the bottle) and the bottle in position #13.
   - It is possible to configure the system to reject many bottle positions on multiple revolutions of the filler to reduce the risk even further.
6. The valve shower is activated so that all valves are cleaned.

Inspecting the Cap/Crown

Closure inspection is normally performed in two places on the beer line. Postfiller inspection devices, in general, inspect for closure presence. For plastic caps, a tamper evidence inspection may be performed at this point, and the metal roll-on caps may be inspected for defects using vision-based inspection equipment.

There can be several reasons for misapplied closures.

- Defective closures delivered from the manufacturer
- Misalignment between bottle and closure
- Capper chucks in need of maintenance
- Container finishes and/or threads that are out of specification
- Foreign material on the bottle finish area or inside the closure
- Closures that are applied too tightly (or too loosely)

Detecting the presence of metal crowns can be accomplished using an inductive proximity sensor. This is an economical means of detecting the presence of metal crowns or caps. The sensor is mounted above or to the side of the area where the crown sits, and the change in magnetic field determines the presence of the metal closure. This same technology can be used for detecting the presence of metal lids on can lines.

In Figure 28.43, the passing of the metal closure through the inspection area is detected by the sensors.

The presence of closures other than metal can be detected using retro-reflective sensors that focus on the area where the closure would normally sit. This technology may work with metal crowns, but the engineering group of the equipment manufacturer should be consulted to determine the reliability of this inspection for each of the crown designs to be inspected. Figure 28.44 illustrates the principle that is used.

The detection of high caps is economically accomplished using a through-beam sensor. The sensor is placed just above the position of a normally closed container, and if the closure is high (or sometimes cocked),

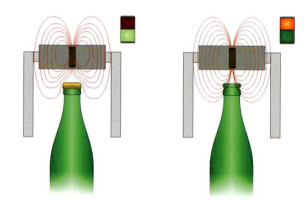

FIGURE 28.43. Inductive proximity sensor for detecting the presence of metal crowns. (Courtesy Heuft USA, Inc.)

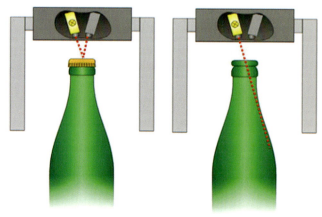

FIGURE 28.44. Retro-reflexive sensors for detecting nonmetallic crowns and caps. (Courtesy Heuft USA, Inc.)

then the beam is broken and the bottle is rejected. This configuration is shown in Figure 28.45.

Cap inspection on PET containers can also be accomplished using a camera-based system. This inspection is preferred when the absolute height of the container finish varies in relation to the conveyor top. In these cases, it may be more likely to get too many false rejects due to high cap. A camera system that references the cap height in relationship to the neck ring is a better alternative. As can be seen in Figure 28.46, the camera system is capable of inspecting other attributes of the container as well. In this example, the system is inspecting a number of variables, including the following.

- Cap presence
- High (or cocked) cap
- Tamper band integrity
- Fill level

Vision is not an appropriate technology for fill-level inspection for all containers. However, a system for bottles that can combine X-ray for fill-level inspection with vision for cap inspection is a good example of the capabilities of a manufacturer to incorporate different technologies into a single platform, thus benefiting the customer.

Detecting Residual Air

It is desirable to detect gas bubbles beneath correctly applied crowns and closures with a false deformation (e.g., bullnoses) when the filled product is normally foamed up to the closure at the detection position. The principle is such that the crown is hit with an electromagnetic pulse, and the acoustic response signal from the closure is analyzed.

Based on the response, the control system makes the determination of whether the containers are completely foamed up to the crown (Fig. 28.47). In case of containers that are not completely foamed up to the closure, the gas bubble between the foam and the closure has a measurable influence on the closure response. In the event that it is determined that the container has not foamed up all the way to the crown (indicating the presence of oxygen in the bottle), the container is rejected.

This inspection is also able to detect containers with misapplied closures, e.g., bullnoses, stacked closures, or closures damaged by the closure machine. It is possible to incorporate the crowner into a filler valve monitoring package to provide a statistical evaluation of each crowner head. This allows for efficient maintenance of individual crowner heads. It is important to note that closures of the same type, but manufactured by different producers, may cause variable results when using an inspection module such as this. Outside influences such as conveyor vibration and water on the crown may negatively impact the reliability of this type of inspection, and they should be eliminated or reduced. It is important to consult with the system's engineering group to determine the best approach in this case.

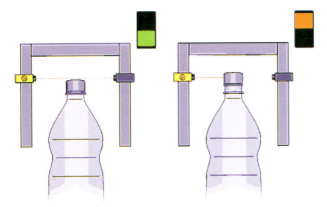

FIGURE 28.45. Detecting high or cocked caps. (Courtesy Heuft USA, Inc.)

FIGURE 28.46. Camera-based PET cap inspection. (Courtesy Heuft USA, Inc.)

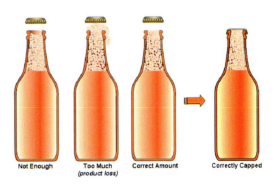

FIGURE 28.47. Gas bubble formation at crowning. (Courtesy Heuft USA, Inc.)

Automatic Sampling Systems

Automatic sampling systems are important in that they allow sample sets to be removed from the conveyor without stopping the line. When equipped with an accumulating conveyor, it is possible to remove many samples at one time. For the removal of many consecutive samples, it is best to have a multisegment style of rejector that can guarantee removal from the line and maintain the proper order of containers. On a typical manual sampling system, an operator or technician presses a button and the reject device removes containers from the production stream until the operator presses the button again, stopping the process. This type of system is much more beneficial than stopping the line to remove samples or trying to remove them while the line is running, but it is not as beneficial as a programmable system.

Automatic sampling offers many more advantages. For example, on a high-speed can line, it would be nearly impossible to reliably remove one sample from each of the seaming heads without stopping the line. Even taking individual random samples can be tricky. A programmable system that tracks cans through the filler and seamer is able to reject cans from specific head(s) on demand or at preprogrammed intervals. For example, if the plant technician would like to evaluate the next 10 cans from seamer head #4, the sampling system will reject each of the next 10 cans from that particular head. Sets of containers can be rejected as well, and a full round of cans from a filler or closer can be rejected if desired. The system can, for example, be programmed to reject filler valves #1 through #20 at 5 minutes past the hour, valves #21 through #40 at 10 minutes after the hour, etc. This is all accomplished without stopping the line and is even more useful if the control system can document this at each occurrence for reporting purposes later.

LABEL INSPECTION

Sensor-Based Label Inspection

Label inspection is generally performed in one of two ways on bottles. Sensor-based absence/presence inspection relies on the reflective properties of the label for detection. These types of systems can also provide a limited degree of detection for flagged labels, folded corners, etc. These systems can use sensors mounted within the labeler or sensors mounted on supports that are mounted to the conveyor downstream of the labeler.

Sensor-based label detection relies on using a diffuse reflective sensor that detects an object by the reflection of light from that object (Fig. 28.48). On smooth glass, the light reflects from the bottle at an angle that equals the angle of transmission. There is not enough light reflected back to the sensor and the inspection system registers the label as "not present". When a label is applied to the container, the light from that label is reflected in many directions, including back into the sensor. The inspection system evaluates the light reflecting back into the sensor and compares it with the programmed value to determines whether a label is present.

When using sensor-based systems, it is important to note that the color and surface texture of the label has an impact on the ability to reliably detect label presence. For example, lighter-colored labels are easier to detect than darker labels. The distance that the sensor is mounted from the label is critical, since lighter labels can be detected at greater distances than darker ones. The texture of the glass is also important and can trigger "false accepts" if not taken into consideration when choosing a mounting position for the sensor. These systems can be installed using sensors mounted within the labeler or on the conveyor. When mounting sensors within the labeler, it is best if one position can be found that accommodates all labels that are run. This may be difficult to do and is best left to the inspection system technician to determine during the installation and commissioning phase of the project. If one position cannot accommodate all of the face label designs, for example, then the customer will be required to relocate the sensor when performing a product changeover or to install additional sensors that can be switched in and out depending on the product to be run. It is generally not recommended to change the position of the sensors for different products since the alignment of the sensors is critical to reliable performance.

It is also possible to place the sensors on fixtures that are mounted to the conveyor downstream of the labeler. Advantages of this type of system are that the sensors generally stay cleaner than sensors mounted within the

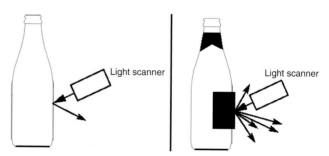

FIGURE 28.48. Detecting labels using a light scanner and reflection. (Courtesy Heuft USA, Inc.)

labeler, the sensors are easier to work on, and there is less chance of fouling due to airborne glue, paper dust, etc. A disadvantage is that this setup might require additional sensors and up-front capital costs not needed in an in-labeler system. It is difficult to catch flagging labels with this type of system if the label is not fully flagged. Characteristics such as folded corners, horizontal and vertical position, and label verification are not detected with much certainty.

Camera-Based Label Inspection

Camera-based systems rely on CCD cameras and image processing software. These types of systems can detect the following.

- Missing labels
- Labels upside down
- Flagging labels
- Folded corners
- Incorrect label size (height/width)
- Incorrect label position
- Incorrect label placement relative to other labels (e.g., front/back)
- Incorrect label placement relative to container features
- Torn label edges
- Label brand verification
- Incorrect bar code
- Product weight and/or volume verification

Similar to sensor-based systems, camera-based label inspection systems can be installed using cameras mounted within the labeler or on the conveyor. When mounting camera(s) within the labeler, it is best if one position can be found that accommodates all labels that are run. This may be difficult to do and is best left to the inspection system technician to determine during the installation and commissioning phase of the project. If one position cannot accommodate all of the face label designs, for example, then the customer will be required to relocate the camera(s) when performing a product changeover or to install additional camera(s) that can be switched in and out depending on the product to be run. It is generally not recommended to change the position of the cameras for different products since the alignment of the cameras is critical to reliable performance.

As with the light scanner technology, it is also possible to place the cameras in fixtures that are mounted around the conveyor downstream of the labeler. Similarly, advantages of this type of system are that the sensors generally stay cleaner than those mounted within the labeler, sensors are easier to work on, and there is less chance of fouling due to airborne glue, paper dust, etc. Also similarly, the disadvantage is that this setup might require additional cameras and up-front capital costs not needed in an in-labeler system. This type of system takes advantage of sophisticated software that can process individual images and perform many inspections with one system.

These systems can be equipped with as many cameras as the inspection requires. For example, to inspect a face label on a nonround container, only one camera may be required. To inspect a face and back label on a nonround container, two cameras might be required. The addition of a neck label may or may not require an additional camera, depending on the container size coupled with the capabilities of the optics and software.

With an on-conveyor inspection system, the orientation of the bottles is not guaranteed to be consistent as they travel past the cameras, thus it is necessary to take multiple images and utilize special software to link the pictures together for evaluation (Fig. 28.49).

The multiple images are first processed within the software, and a picture of the label is generated within the software. As shown in Figure 28.50, the software must orient the pictures so that the evaluation can be consistently performed. Masks (or areas of interest) are then outlined, and the inspection is performed by comparing these areas of interest with preprogrammed values.

These systems are ideal for inspecting labels of containers that are traveling on the conveyor at random orientation. It is important to note that containers that are square, rectangular, triangular, etc. are more difficult to inspect, and the engineering group of the system's manufacturer should be consulted so that accurate performance guarantees can be obtained.

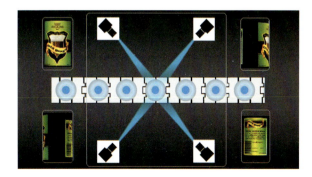

FIGURE 28.49. Multiple camera sensors for on-conveyor label detection. (Courtesy Heuft USA, Inc.)

Lighting is an important part of the inspection system, and different container shapes and sizes may require different lighting for optimum performance. Some systems rely on simple fluorescent lighting, others rely on high-intensity strobes, and systems today are rapidly adopting LED sources as the lighting of choice. These LED sources can be automatically turned on and off based on the product to be run and may result in more reliable performance. The use of LED lighting may reduce the need for antiglare shields, reducing the number of components to maintain in the system. It is important to discuss with the manufacturer the lighting types that are used and how the system compensates for this at changeover.

A performance guarantee should be very specific, with reliability, false reject, and false accept rates well defined for each label (Fig. 28.51).

Startup and commissioning costs can be high with these types of systems, depending on the number of containers and labels that are to be run on the line. It is generally recommended that the manufacturer's service technician be responsible for qualifying the system. Depending on the production schedule, this may take quite some time. If the service technician is traveling to the plant from another city, then the ability of the plant to stick to the production schedule will have a great impact on the project costs for this phase. If, for example, the service technician travels to the plant site for the qualification run of a particular label, and the plant production schedule changes due to downtime or demand change, then the unbudgeted costs for the technician to wait until the product run begins will be absorbed by the project. Also, label qualification may take quite a bit of run time to fine-tune the equipment. The line efficiency will play an important part in how long the

FIGURE 28.50. Label composite from four different camera positions. (Courtesy Heuft USA, Inc.)

	\multicolumn{8}{c	}{Face (Front)}	\multicolumn{8}{c	}{Back (Rear)}
	Presence	Reversed	Flagging (mm)	Label Size (Height, mm)	Skew	Y-Position	X-Position	Verification	Presence	Reversed	Flagging (mm)	Label Size (Height, mm)	Skew	Y-Position	X-Position	Verification
Vodka #1	Y	Y	10×10	±3 mm	±3 mm	±3 mm	±5 mm	Y	Y	Y	10×10	±3 mm	±3 mm	±3 mm	±5 mm	Y
Vodka #2	Y	Y	10×10	±3 mm	±3 mm	±3 mm	±5 mm	Y	Y	Y	10×10	±3 mm	±3 mm	±3 mm	±5 mm	Y
Vodka #3	Y	Y	10×10	±3 mm	±3 mm	±3 mm	±5 mm	Y	Y	Y	10×10	±3 mm	±3 mm	±3 mm	±5 mm	Y
Gin #1	Y	Y	10×10	±3 mm	±3 mm	±3 mm	±5 mm	Y	Y	Y	10×10	±3 mm	±3 mm	±3 mm	±5 mm	Y
Gin #2	Y	Y	10×10	±3 mm	±3 mm	±3 mm	±5 mm	Y	Y	Y	10×10	±3 mm	±3 mm	±3 mm	±5 mm	Y
Rum #1	Y	Y	10×10	±3 mm	±3 mm	±3 mm	±5 mm	Y	—	—	—	—	—	—	—	—
Rum #2	Y	Y	10×10	±3 mm	±3 mm	±3 mm	±5 mm	Y	—	—	—	—	—	—	—	—

FIGURE 28.51. Performance guarantee specifications for detection sensors by product label. (Courtesy Heuft USA, Inc.)

technician will be required to remain on site. Scheduling back-to-back runs for products to be qualified will also reduce project costs and result in fewer trips and lower travel costs for the technician.

The plant may determine that the qualifications can be accomplished using plant personnel to reduce costs. In this case, it is important that the plant select the right person to be a point-person for the qualifications and training of the plant people. Vision-based equipment for label inspection requires quite a bit of training, and these costs should not be overlooked in the project budgeting phase. Ongoing training is important to the reliable performance of the system and should not be overlooked.

Checking Pressure

For bottle lines, the principle for checking the pressure of bottles with metal crowns is similar to that described above. The principle is such that the crown is subjected to an electromagnetic pulse, and the acoustic response signal from the closure is analyzed (Fig. 28.52). The pitch of the closure is an indication of the internal pressure of the container. Much like a drum head changes pitch when it is tightened or loosened, the crown is analyzed for "tightness". The systems that perform this inspection may use different methods of analysis, but the intent is the same.

In the brewing industry, this inspection is typically left for postlabeler inspection since it requires the contents to build pressure in order to detect any significant tightness in the crown. It is important to note that crowns from different manufacturers may have different baseline readings. If the mixing of crowns from different manufacturers is an issue, it is possible to provide a comparative measurement between the filler discharge and the labeler discharge. Once the bottle leaves the filler/crowner, a magnetic code is written on the crown and this information contains the baseline reading for the crown with minimal pressure inside. The crown is then inspected downstream, after pressure has built up in the container. The inspection device reads the magnetic code, indicating the initial reading, and then performs another test of the crown tightness and compares the two to determine whether it is passable. In this manner, it is possible to reliably mix crowns of different suppliers and still get a reliable reading.

For can lines, the principle for checking the pressure in cans utilizes an analog proximity sensor to measure the lid deflection (Fig. 28.53). As the can passes below the sensing device, the lid is measured to determine whether it is convex (internal pressure) or concave (internal vacuum). The system is used in the beer industry to measure internal pressure, which in turn is an indication of a good lid seam. For food products such as vegetables, the same system is used to measure vacuum in cans, also an indicator of a good lid seam.

FULL-CASE INSPECTION

New Box Quality Inspector

The cardboard box inspection system checks to see whether the box has been correctly unpacked and whether it is damaged. The inspection system also checks to determine whether a box that has been erected is of the proper shape and size. The inspection device is typically located at the infeed to the case packer. The system can also be installed immediately after the box-folding machine.

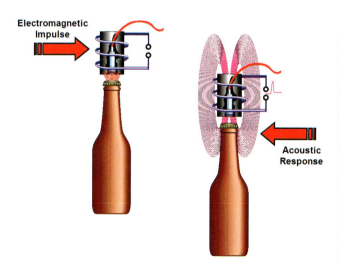

FIGURE 28.52. Checking pressure using an electromagnetic pulse and its response on the crown. (Courtesy Heuft USA, Inc.)

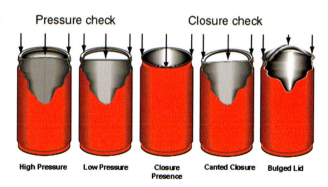

FIGURE 28.53. Detecting can pressure using a proximity sensor to detect lid presence and pressure deflection. (Courtesy Heuft USA, Inc.)

The system illuminates the box from above, and the camera system takes a picture of the box, dividers, etc. (Fig. 28.54). The camera picture is then evaluated by an image processing system. Incorrectly produced cardboard boxes, defective cardboard boxes, and cardboard boxes with bottles are detected and rejected as faulty.

The following fault characteristics are checked.

- Position check of the cardboard box flaps.
  - It is distinguished whether the cardboard box flaps of a good case have to be folded up or down.
- The cardboard box flaps must be approximately vertical. A cardboard box flap that is open too wide can obstruct the transport of the cardboard box. If a cardboard box is closed by a flap, it cannot be filled correctly with containers.
- The cardboard box flaps have to be folded down vertically. The cardboard box flaps are held in this position by cardboard strips.
- Divider and compartment check.
  - All dividers must be located at their defined position. This also applies to used six-packs. A missing divider can make containers topple over. If a divider is located at an incorrect position, the case cannot be filled correctly with containers.
- Geometry check.
  - A case with incorrect geometry can get jammed during transport or cause malfunctions in the packer since it cannot be filled correctly with containers.
  - The length and width of the case must be within specified limits.
  - All sides of the case must be parallel to each other.

Full-Case Inspection

A full-case inspection system typically uses X-ray technology to check that all containers are present within the case. This is the final inspection prior to shipping, and it is important to be sure that there are no missing containers. The systems that use the X-ray principle are also able to detect even an individual container that is underfilled (Fig. 28.55).

As shown in Figure 28.55, the operating principle is similar to that of a system designed for single bottle inspection. An X-ray beam passes through a row of containers. Part of the X-ray beam is absorbed by the product within the containers. If a container is missing, or if the fill level has leaked down below the target fill level, then the system detects this due to the higher level of X-ray energy passing through to the receiver. Systems such as these can use a gamma ray that is either electrically generated or emitted by a radioactive source. This type of system is capable of inspecting full cases, trays, cases with dividers, etc. This system is appropriate for inspection of cans, PET containers, and glass containers.

Systems that are less costly than an X-ray–based inspection device can use proximity or inductive sensors to simply "count" container closures as they pass beneath the detection module. A system such as this is shown in Figure 28.56.

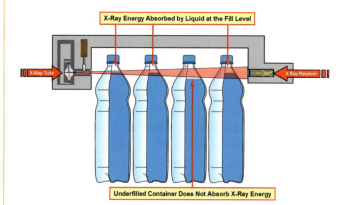

FIGURE 28.55. Inspecting full cases for low fill levels and missing containers. (Courtesy Heuft USA, Inc.)

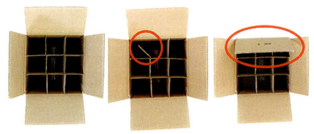

FIGURE 28.54. Case inspector looks at the sidewalls, partitions, and flaps. (Courtesy Heuft USA, Inc.)

FIGURE 28.56. Full-case inspection using proximity sensors to count metal closures. (Courtesy Heuft USA, Inc.)

This type of system may not be suitable for full-wrap cases, and an application test should be performed to determine whether the sensor(s) can detect the container closure with the flaps closed. These types of systems may be located just upstream of the case sealer, where the sensors get a good "look" at the containers below. Once again, an application test should be performed since sometimes the raised flaps make it necessary to locate the sensors too high to reliably detect the closures beneath.

Other systems for full-case inspection use weighing technology to determine whether a container is missing. These check-weighing systems typically have more mechanical parts to malfunction than do the X-ray systems and may result in higher maintenance costs. Also, the aggregate weight of the case may be within the acceptable range, even if there is one container that is underfilled.

Rejection Systems

The rejection system may be as critical a component as the inspection device. Rejection systems typically fall into two categories. The first type consists of a simple pneumatic or mechanical ram that pushes the container off-line (Fig. 28.57).

This system uses an air cylinder to push the container from the conveyor. The container can be rejected into a bin or onto a table for evaluation. This system is very cost-effective but may not guarantee upright rejection. In the brewing industry, where glass is typically used, this system may cause the glass bottles to shatter after they are rejected and crash into each other.

In very-high-speed operations, this type of rejector may not be suitable for multiple rejects or sampling in which a series of containers needs to be rejected off-line for quality evaluation.

A more suitable type of reject device for upright rejection in the brewing industry uses multiple segments to guide the container off-line and onto a table or reject conveyor (Fig. 28.58).

This style of rejector is suitable for sampling systems, in which large numbers of consecutive containers need

FIGURE 28.57. Pneumatic ram-type rejector. (Courtesy K. Ockert)

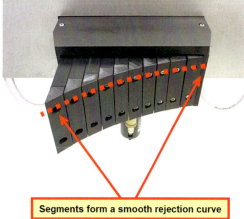

FIGURE 28.58. Curve-style rejection device for upright bottle rejection and sample collection. (Courtesy Heuft USA, Inc.)

to be rejected off-line. It is also a good choice for moving full containers off-line without spilling the contents in the event they do not have closures applied.

● SUMMARY

As packaging lines increase speed and complexity, the necessity for inspection systems becomes more critical. Inspection systems have to keep up with the kinds of machinery advances being made, the types of packaging materials that are used, and the plant quality assurance and regulatory functions demanded. Proper inspection and rejection will save the company in terms of line efficiencies, possible market embarrassments, and even lawsuits, so a thorough understanding of what is available and how the equipment works is an important aspect of packaging line planning and operations.

CHAPTER 29

Packaging Materials and Beer Quality

PHILLIP D. ISRAEL
Anheuser-Busch Companies (retired)

The brewer, having selected the choicest raw materials, next directs all efforts toward ensuring that the subsequent processes of brewing, fermentation, and storage result in a finished beer that meets all expectations. Brewers use all of the quality assessment procedures available to them at each stage of the process so that the beer meets all analytical, flavor, and physical specifications.

Unfortunately, however, it is possible that carefully nurtured and controlled product may be subsequently negatively influenced by the packaging materials used. It then becomes apparent that these materials must also be carefully selected and that everyone in the brewery must be equally concerned that the packaging materials are being processed so as to ensure their quality. To accomplish this, the people in charge of product quality in a brewery must be completely familiar with the materials and processes used to manufacture the packaging materials.

Ideally, brewery packaging and quality assurance personnel visit the packaging material supplier's plant and assess the supplier's procedures. They ensure that good housekeeping and good manufacturing practices are in place and that the supplier is evaluating the packaging materials production at each stage of the process. They establish that appropriate quality control procedures and statistical process control (SPC) practices are being followed.

The most insidious and most likely negative influence on beer by a packaging material is on its flavor. As is well known and documented, infinitesimal amounts of certain compounds associated with some packaging materials can have a major impact on the flavor of the beer housed in that container. It is, of course, possible to manufacture these packaging materials so that no detectable product flavor or stability problems occur. To prevent the manufacture of these materials from contributing negative influences on the beer, it is necessary to be aware of the potential problems that may occur. As has been stated, knowledge of the manufacturing process, materials used, and quality control measures being utilized are all of great importance. Tight control of the quality of these packaging materials can be ensured by having an active program to evaluate incoming packaging materials and having procedures in place to assess changes made by the manufactures before approval of said changes. This chapter is devoted to reviewing the potential problems that may occur with the various packaging materials that are in general use by brewers.

● CANS AND LIDS

Cans

Of all the packaging materials used for beer, the one that has the most potential for negatively affecting beer quality is the can. The very process of manufacturing cans is fraught with many possible areas of contamination, and brewery personnel charged with ensuring can quality must be aware of this so they can ensure that their suppliers are controlling these materials and processes effectively. To begin with, the brewery packaging materials analyst must be aware of the materials the can maker uses as well as the particular process as part of the overall process in which these materials are utilized. These materials are

- lubricants,
- can washer solutions/mobility enhancers,
- inks and coatings, and
- storage and shipping materials (e.g., pallets, separator sheets, and covers).

Lubricants

Lubricants are usually made with unsaturated fatty acid bases and are used on the incoming body of stock coil during the process of rolling the aluminum. The rolling process effectively reduces the gauge of the metal through various stages from ingot to coil. The lubricant is heavily imbedded into the aluminum. Subsequently, another lubricant, designated as a prelube or postlube, is sometimes used to coat the coil prior to shipment to the can plant. The prelube is intended to protect the aluminum body stock en route to the can plant and to aid the can maker during the process of drawing and ironing the metal into the shape of a can. Although there is a relatively heavy amount of lubricant on the metal surface of the coil as received by the can maker, the processes of pressing the metal into a cup and drawing the cup into a cylinder in the body maker requires additional lubrication. Therefore, the can maker covers the coil with a lubricant before the press, which is designated a cupper lube. The body maker also uses a lubricant during the forming of the cylinder, and this lube is referred to as a body-maker lube. Collectively, these lubricants, as applied at the aluminum plant and at the can plant, are on the unflanged cylinder as they exit the body makers on the way to the can washers.

Can Washer Solutions/Mobility Enhancers

The purpose of the can washers is to remove the lubricant from the external and internal surfaces of the cylinder. The cylinders move through the six-compartment washers on a mat as solutions of sulfuric acid of various concentrations are sprayed over the cylinder surfaces, followed by water rinses. It is of the utmost importance that all the lubricant be removed from these surfaces. If any lubricant remains, the subsequent applications of coatings and varnishes will not adhere properly to the can, and the oven bakes to cure those coatings will also result in another problem—one that may affect the flavor of the beer that will be filled into that can. The flavor problem results from auto-oxidation of the unsaturated fatty acid lubricant remaining on the can if it was not effectively removed during the washing process. Unsaturated fatty aldehydes are formed, which can give the beer a cardboardy, greenwood, and slightly oily off-flavor. This off-flavor is akin to beer oxidation and was referred to by one brewer as "labox". Lubricants have been developed that have a reduced amount of unsaturated fatty acids and are less susceptible to form these aldehydes if left on the can after washing. The packaging quality assurance person should visit the can supplier to ascertain that proper lubricants (i.e., low in unsaturated fatty acids, particularly linoleic acid) are being used and that the washers are removing these lubricants completely. The latter can be established by examining the last compartment of the washer, which is a deionized (DI) water rinse, to determine whether any oily residue is present in the reservoir tank. Another method to establish this is to take a can off the washer conveyer belt at that stage and dip it in the DI water reservoir to determine whether any "water break" or globules of water remain on the surfaces of the can. The process of measuring the water break does not work as effectively if a mobility enhancer is added to the DI water.

The concentration of the acid solutions and the resulting pH have a direct bearing on the effectiveness of the washer's ability to remove the lubricant. The packaging quality assurance person should be aware of the can maker's targets for acid concentration and lubricant buildup in the washer solutions so that they can occasionally monitor their effectiveness. Since the products of fatty acid lubes (the polyunsaturated aldehydes, such as 2-nonenal and others) are present at very low levels and are the perpetrators of very deleterious off-flavors, it is important to establish through monitoring whether the cans are free of these products. *Trans*-2-nonenal, it should be remembered, can be detected as an off-flavor in beer at levels below 1 parts per billion. Therefore, anything that can be done to prevent its formation and migration, either alone or in combination, is key to good can manufacturing. Mobility enhancers can be used to promote better movement of the cans from the washer oven through the conveyers to the decorators. These enhancers are applied to the surface of the cylinders in the washer's last stage, the DI water rinse. This addition of mobility enhancer, while beneficial to the can maker, eliminates one stage of the washer process (one of the rinses). Because all stages of the washer are required to ensure complete lubricant removal, this may present a problem. The extension of the system to apply the enhancer after the DI water rinse is preferred.

Inks and Coatings

Inks used in the decoration of the cans, as well as exterior and interior coatings, can also negatively affect the quality of the cans both aesthetically and with respect to their potential influence on beer flavor and stability. These materials should, of course, be Food and Drug Administration (FDA) approved and should be screened to ensure that they will not negatively affect beer quality. The decorating inks, which are partially cured in the ovens following their applications, are finally fully cured in the oven used to cure the interior coating after that application. The materials used to manufacture those inks may include fairly substantial amounts of linoleic acid or their esters and can be absorbed by the interior coating and migrate subsequently through the cured interior coating into the beer.

Obviously, the other coatings used in the process, such as base coats, varnishes, and in particular, interior spray coats, should be evaluated to ensure their quality. It is a requirement that should be placed on the can maker by the brewer, and the brewer must insist that these wishes in that regard are being met.

The complete coating of the interior surface of the can is obviously very important. Exposure of the beer to bare aluminum, even if only a very small portion of the can is left uncoated, can result in flavor as well as beer clarity problems. A method to determine the extent to which the interior of a can is uncoated is made with an instrument called an enamel rater, and the limits of exposure are determined by a numeric measurement. Can makers perform these measurements several times each operating shift and may have standards that are even more stringent than industry standards. The brewer must be satisfied that the can maker is meeting the required standards in this respect.

Last, it should be remembered that an additional line of defense against off-flavor compounds that can migrate into the beer are the interior can-coating materials. These coatings, which are usually epoxy acrylates, have limited barrier properties, but some are better than others. These coatings must be carefully selected to ensure that they are beer compatible as well as capable of obstructing the ready migration of undesirable metal surface impurities.

Storage and Shipping Materials

In the mid-1990s, the brewing industry found out the hard way that the materials used for storing and shipping finished empty cans can result in very serious and extensive product flavor problems. Specifically, these materials are the pallets used for storing and shipping empty cans to the brewery and, more importantly, the separator or divider sheets upon which each layer of cans are placed on a pallet. Each of these materials may contain compounds that are sufficiently volatile and offensive to cause major flavor problems. Owing to the absorptive nature of can interior coatings, as well as their shortcomings as barriers, these compounds are absorbed by the coatings and are subsequently transmitted to the beer in contact with those coatings. In the case of wooden pallets, which are usually made from pine, the compound α-pinene can be absorbed by the interior coating, migrate to the beer, and impart a musty, pinelike odor and flavor. Coatings used to preserve the wood pallets can also have a negative effect on can quality and should be selected discriminately.

The separator or divider sheets are made from chipboard. Chipboard, in turn, is made from recycled materials, which can include cartons, newspaper, carbon paper, and other forms of discarded paper waste. The chipboard sheets, owing to their origin and the addition of materials such as inks, coatings, oil, glue, and other debris, can therefore be a source, in whole or in part, of unsaturated fatty aldehydes of the type described above when discussing can-making lubricants. Unlike lubricants, however, there is no opportunity to eliminate these aldehydes before they negatively affect the odor and flavor of the beer. Owing to the proximity of the divider sheets to the empty cans and their highly absorptive linings, the opportunity for contamination is quite high. Not all divider sheets nor the entire surface of a given sheet are problematic. Depending on the nature of the recycled materials used to produce the chipboard sheets, some may be innocuous while others may be extremely deleterious. New sheets, for obvious reasons, are a greater threat than are sheets that have been used four to five times. The length of time between palletization and the filling of the cans also can be a factor.

Since "virgin kraft" board (made from nonrecycled paper sources) is no longer available, only separator/divider sheets made from plastic, such as polypropylene, will eliminate this potential flavor problem. Most major brewers have recognized that the use of chipboard sheets can result in the problems described and are using plastic sheets for all cans supplied to their breweries worldwide.

Lids

Lids, as compared with cans, have a more limited exposure to beer and are less likely to result in a flavor, odor, or stability problem. That is not to say that lids cannot or do not negatively influence beer quality. The lubricant on the lid stock that is used to ensure the appropriate formation of the lid, the sealing compound, and the tab lube (used in the formation of the opening device on the lid top) can all have an effect on beer quality. In the case of the sealing compound, the likelihood of a flavor-affecting problem is minimal, since that material is contained within the double seam and is unlikely to contact the beer. Nevertheless, proper curing of even waterborne or high-solid versions of these compounds is necessary to ensure that the solvent portion has been adequately dissipated and that the lids do not have any solvent aroma prior to use. It is also recommended that these sealing compounds, which appear to be ever changing because of ever more stringent volatile organic compound (VOC) regulations, be evaluated to ensure their acceptability. The supplier can prepare glass rods, which are coated with a suitable amount of the compound for immersion in bottled beer. The bottles of beer with the compound can then be pasteurized, cooled, and tasted against a suitable control and a beer control.

The material used in the can lid manufacturing process that has the greatest potential for compromising beer quality is the tab lube. As indicated, this lube aids in the operation that converts the lid into one that has an easy opening—that is, a tab and tear drop-shaped orifice. The application of the lube (usually butyl stearate) to the tab stock must provide sufficient lubrication to form the opening device without being excessively applied. Excessive lubricant transfers to other lids as they nest in the bags of lids that are delivered to the brewery, and that lube can affect the clarity and foam stability of the canned beer sealed with lids of that ilk. The brewer must be assured that this process is sufficiently controlled so as to avoid this problem.

The bags that contain the lids and the inks used for stenciling the identification of the lids therein can be problematic. New sources of these materials, as used by the lid manufacturer, should be evaluated to ensure that they will not have a deleterious effect on beer. The preferred way to do that is to use the new source of bags and/or inks and to store the lids in them for a period of time. The lids from that test condition are then used to seal cans, which are evaluated against appropriate controls.

● GLASS BOTTLES

Bottle quality has improved dramatically since the 1990s but was never the threat to beer quality that cans have been and still are. Glass is basically an inert material, and flavor, odor, and stability problems from that source per se are not significant. The problems that can arise from bottles are largely caused by the coatings used, the glass color, the distribution of the glass thickness around the entire bottle surface, and the finish at the neck of the bottle where the seal with the crown is made.

The development of the press-and-blow process in the mold, which shapes the bottle, was a significant advance. This process ensures improved glass distribution so that thin walls on one side of the bottle versus a thick wall on the other side are no longer as problematic. Lightweight, nonreturnable bottles were approved as appropriate containers subsequent to the implementation of the press-and-blow process. Improved glass distribution, along with the elimination (by breakage) of defective bottles undergoing pasteurization and the accompanying advanced internal pressures to which they are subjected, has greatly assisted in eliminating glass bottle safety concerns. In addition, hot and cold end coatings aid in reducing abrasion and enhance bottle mobility on the packaging line.

The application of the cold end coating, which is now almost exclusively a water mixture of polyethylene, can be a problem source. The polyethylene is sprayed between the rows of bottles exiting the lehr in the glass plant. The sprays are intentionally directed to strike the bottles below the shoulder, where it is needed for bottle mobility and protection. Misdirection of the spray can result in globules of the spray entering the bottle at the orifice. Subsequently, bottles with internal spray upon filling have flakes of this lube floating in the beer. In addition to being unsightly, there is also the possibility that such a condition will affect beer stability and flavor.

The amber color of the bottles protects the beer from sunlight and fluorescent light exposure by significantly reducing their transmission. Otherwise, exposure to this light promotes the development of sulfury compounds that affect the beer flavor and aroma in a most deleterious and unacceptable manner. The beer develops aroma and flavor generally referred to as skunky or light-struck. The extent to which color is added to the glass depends on several factors, primarily on the glass thickness. Lightweight bottles are thinner, so more coloring is needed to protect against excessive light transmission. While redness ratio is used mostly for aesthetics and uniformity, it is a combination of reduced transmission and a redness that affords light protection. The amber color should have a range of light transmission from 15 to 22%, inclusive, at a wavelength of 550 nm for a glass thickness of 0.125 inch. There are charts that can be used to establish whether the redness ratio of the bottle produced meets specification. The redness ratio, defined as the ratio of light transmission (%T) at 650 nm divided by the %T at 550 nm, is part of the quality specifications for most of the brewing industry. Glass bottle manufacturers monitor the redness ratio on a day-to-day basis, and the calculated redness ratio value for a given %T at 550 nm should be kept above an established lower limit. It has been shown that amber glass is effective in absorbing light at wavelengths of 400 to 520 nm (the visible light range that causes light-struck flavor in beer).

When visiting the glass plant and when evaluating incoming bottles, the brewery representative must be assured that bottle color specifications are being met and that potential bottle defects are also being eliminated through the following appropriate quality control measures.

- Resistance to internal pressures of 175 pounds per square inch for returnable bottles and 150 pounds per square inch for nonreturnable bottles.
- Adherence of finish surfaces to specifications to ensure adequate seal and twist crown removal requirements.
- Thermal shock resistance that meets American Standard Testing Methods (ASTM) requirements.

CROWNS AND CLOSURES

Since the 1990s, it has become readily apparent that crowns and closures can present many more problems to beer than were previously realized. It used to be that the main areas of concern were that the crowns/closures adequately sealed the bottle and, in the case of twist-off crowns and closures, that the torque requirements were within easy-removal specifications. We are now faced with the following additional concerns.

- The effect of the plastic liners on beer flavor.
- The toxicity of phthalates when used as plasticizers in the liner compound.
- The environmental concerns resulting from the incineration of polyvinyl chloride (PVC).
- The ready migration of oxygen through a PVC liner.

It has been established that PVC plastic liners can affect beer flavor. The liner material is composed of a variety of compounds—the polymer, a plasticizer, stabilizers, a lubricant, and in the case of foamed liners, a blowing agent. The selection of these compounds, as well as the blending and processing of them in the lining material manufacturing operation, is key to ensuring that no problems with them occur in the crown manufacturing operation. Of course, the handling of the lining material in pellet form by the crown manufacturer is equally important in preventing flavor as well as sealing problems. The brewer would do well to monitor these operations to ensure that the problems described do not occur. While it is difficult to imagine that the exposure of the small surface of the liner can affect beer flavor, it has been established that this, indeed, may occur. To further ensure that the liner quality does not affect beer flavor, incoming crowns can be evaluated in the following manner. The liner should be removed from the crown shell by gently heating the decorated crown surface with a Bunsen burner and then pulling the liner away from the internal coating. The liner, which now has two exposed surfaces, should be placed in a cold, fresh, unpasteurized bottle of beer. The bottle should be tapped to remove the air and then recrowned using the crown being tested. A control should be prepared by handling a bottle of beer in a similar manner but without inserting the liner. The test and control packages should be pasteurized, cooled, and then tasted.

Diethylhexyl phthalate (DEHP) and dioctyl phthalate (DOP) have been investigated for years to establish carcinogenicity. More recently, it has been shown that phthalates cause cancer in mice and other animals. It is certainly in the realm of possibility that this type of plasticizer will lose FDA approval status and that a substitute for it or the PVC that requires a plasticizer will be required.

In addition to the questions raised above, another concern for the continued use of PVC is the allegation that the incineration of PVC is environmentally unacceptable. There is a belief by environmental conservation groups that PVC incineration produces dioxin, which contributes to acid rain. In Europe, several countries have banned the use of PVC, and less-acceptable and -forgiving substitute materials are required. As an environmental accommodation, in the United States, at least one major soft drink maker is no longer using PVC-lined crowns.

Perhaps the greatest concern for the continued use of PVC in its current form as a crown or closure liner is its lack of barrier properties. It has been established that as much as 0.002 mL of oxygen migrates through the crown liner and into the bottled beer daily. Since beer oxidation is of primary concern to the brewery, this finding is of great significance.

It is, however, difficult to find a material as suitable as PVC for a crown liner because of its physical properties. The properties that make PVC ideal as a liner are its durability, viscosity, and relatively low cost. It lends itself well to bottle-sealing requirements, and it can accommodate the need for an added lubricant (for twist needs) because the lube can readily blush to the surface. It will be difficult to find a replacement for PVC that has its virtues for sealing bottles without its inherent problems (e.g., lack of barrier properties and environmentally questionable). The search for such material nevertheless goes on.

Closures for use with wide-mouth as well as standard-size bottle finishes are available in both plastic and metal (aluminum). While PVC is also used for closures, ethylene vinyl acetate (EVA) and polyethylene are used as well.

EVA has slightly better barrier properties than does PVC, but it is more expensive and has the additional problem of scalping more beer flavor. With the use of PVC, the problem of oxygen migration is also prevalent with closures. However, aluminum closures are dramatically superior to plastic closures in barring oxygen from entering the bottle.

The oxygen migration deficiency that accompanies the use of PVC liners for crowns and closures can be accommodated to some degree by the use of oxygen scavengers. The scavengers, which are incorporated into the liner material, are known beer stabilizers. These oxygen scavengers, sodium sulfite and sodium ascorbate, have been used historically as stabilizers in bulk beer. These compounds are currently in very limited use for bulk beer treatment because of the negative consumer reaction to the use of preservatives. It has, however, been demonstrated that, when incorporated into the PVC liner, these scavengers react with the oxygen in the filling operation as well as with that migrating through the liner and do not allow it to leach into the beer. The use of oxygen-scavenging crown liners has been gaining acceptance even though they cost more than conventional crowns. Prolonged testing of oxygen-scavenging crowns has demonstrated that beer freshness can be extended by their use, and some brewers have embraced the technology for some of their products.

● PLASTIC PACKAGING

The use of plastic bottles in the soft drink industry is widespread, and the material of choice is polyethylene terephthalate (PET). From the soft drink bottler's point of view, PET is preferred because it is relatively less likely to remove product flavor. The problem of gas migration out of the bottle and oxygen permeation into the bottle is accommodated by carbonating to a higher degree. Oxygen is much less of a problem with soft drinks than it is with beer, so that problem is considered less significant. It is true, however, that as soft drinks in PET bottles age, some loss of flavor occurs despite that industry's protestation to the contrary. Since the early 2000s, there has been increased interest by the brewing industry in using plastic bottles for packaging beer. While this has been tried before in Europe and in the Far East, American brewers have, until now, resisted putting significant amounts of beer in plastic containers. The obvious reason for the resistance by brewers to plastic is its lack of gas barrier properties—that is, the loss of carbonation and the ingress of air, as well as the cost and concern for consumer acceptance. Development to overcome these major problems and that of some loss in flavor are described as follows.

- Polyethylene naphthalate (PEN)—It has slightly better barrier properties than PET, is more expensive, has improved thermal stability, and can be pasteurized.

- Scavenger/barrier plastic bottles—In an effort to overcome the lack of gas barrier properties of plastic, multilayer plastic bottles that incorporate scavengers and/or barriers in one or more of the layers have been developed. In the case of active scavengers, several types have shown sufficient gas control properties and have been tested by major brewers. One example is a type that uses a metal-catalyzed, nylon scavenger combination in two of the five layers, but it is not yet in widespread use because of questions regarding its marketability (cost being a very important factor). Another variable is a three-layer bottle that incorporates a patented scavenger/barrier method.

- Barriers—Multilayer bottles with either ethylene vinyl alcohol (EVOH) or nylon in the middle layers are being developed and used to improve the barrier properties. These barriers can provide the needed carbonation retention but usually require the addition of oxygen scavengers to fully protect the beer from oxygen ingress.

- Coatings—Coatings that have been developed incorporate such barriers as an epoxy amine or amorphous carbon to be applied to either the inside or the outside of the bottle. The passive barrier types, such as the coatings mentioned herein, have not yet been shown to be as effective as the scavenger/barrier types, but they are significantly less expensive. A major concern with the coatings is their ability to adhere and stretch with the bottle. Coated bottles must be evaluated under the expected carbonation and temperature levels they are expected to encounter in commerce. If coatings fracture under the stress of carbonation and pressure, a significant amount of their oxygen barrier properties can be lost.

Brewers interested in using plastic bottles should thoroughly evaluate the various technologies available. It will be important to establish how the shelf life of the beer is affected by the plastic bottle, whether the product flavor is compromised, and to what extent the beer stability is affected. Another consideration is the recyclability of the bottles since, unlike the soft drink industry which uses virgin PET exclusively, the beer bottles will incorporate other materials. PET bottles are currently recycled for use as carpet fiber, but there is some concern that the volume of recycled PET, owing to its use in beer, may exceed the demand for that use.

● SUMMARY

Packaging materials of the various types used by the brewing industry have been shown to be capable of compromising the flavor and stability of beer. The brewer needs to monitor the materials both in the supplier's manufacturing facility as well as at the brewery. The brewer should also be knowledgeable of the materials and processes used by the manufacturer of these packages and the controls used to ensure their quality. A brewery program to monitor proposed changes by the manufacturer, whether they are process or material related, is strongly advocated. It is through such a program that potential flavor or stability problems can be prevented.

REFERENCES FOR FURTHER READING

Israel, P. D., and White, S. A. C. (1998). Preserving beer quality via oxygen scavenging packaging. (Abstr.) Am. Soc. Brew. Chem. Newsl. 58(2):16.

Kuroiwa, Y., and Hashimoto, N. (1961). Composition of sunstuck flavor substance and mechanism of its evolution. Am. Soc. Brew. Chem. Proc. 1961:28-36.

Lea, C. H., and Swoboda, P. A. T. (1958). The flavor of aliphatic aldehydes. Chem. Ind. 4:1289-1290.

Office of the Federal Register. (1998). Code of Federal Regulations. U.S. Government Printing Office, Washington, DC.

Wisk, T. J., and Siebert, K. J. (1987). Air ingress in packages sealed with crowns lined with polyvinyl chloride. J. Am. Soc. Brew. Chem. 45:14-18.

INDEX

absolute pressure, 64
accumulation. *See under* packaging lines
actuators, 58, 65
air, package testing, 401–402, 403
air pickup, 163, 164–165, 171, 177, 178
aluminum hydroxide, 135
aluminum roll-on closures. *See* caps
American Can Company, 84, 225, 236
American Glass Research, 217
American National Standards Institute, 305
American Society of Brewing Chemists, 232–233
americium, 441, 443
analog level control, 65
analytical measurements, 67–68
ancillary equipment, 5–6, 8, 10
Anheuser-Busch, 13
anticipate and command control, 48
antifoam agents, 401
Armstrong Cork Company, 210
asset management, 13, 18, 39
automation, 2, 7, 13, 51–52

Barry-Wehmiller Companies, 131
Bayern Brewing Company, 11
Becker, K., 143
beer conditioning, 164–165, 171
beer contaminants, 201–202
beer flavor. *See also* beer quality
    acetaldehyde and, 151–152
    cans, 80, 458–459
    carbonation and, 400
    chipboard divider sheets and, 459
    factors affecting, 151
    glass bottles, 117
    lubricants and, 458
    oxygen and, 152, 153, 163, 400, 461
    packaging material quality and, 457
    PET containers, 151–152
    plastic crown liners and, 461
    scalping, 212, 462
    trans-2-nonenal, 458
    unsaturated fatty aldehydes and, 458, 459
    warehouse storage and, 415
    wooden pallets and, 459
beer loss, 201, 359
beer quality, 457–463. *See also* beer flavor
    air pickup and CO_2 levels, 164–165
    cans and, 457–459
        can washer solutions/mobility enhancers, 458
        inks and coatings, 458–459
        lubricants, 458
        storage and shipping materials, 459
    crowns and closures and, 461–462
    beer stabilizers, 462
    EVA liners, 461–462
        oxygen scavengers, 462
        phthalates, 461
        PVC plastic liners, 461–462
    glass bottles and, 460–461
        bottle coloring, 460
        bottle defects, 461
        cold end coatings, 460
        press-and-blow process, 460
    lids and, 459–460
        bags and inks, 460
        sealing compounds, 459–460
        tab lube, 460
    packaging area environment and, 257
    packaging department primary parameters, 400
    plastic packaging and, 462–463
        coatings, 462

gas migration, 462
    PEN, 462
    PET, 462
    scavengers/barriers, 462
beer stone deposits, 345, 353, 356, 367
Benjamin, H. A., 225, 236
bioluminescence, 399
blanks and blanking, 72, 73, 78
Bond, Samuel C., 209
bottle conditioning, 164, 407–408
bottle fillers, 201–202. *See also* fillers
    annular ring-type chambers, 190
    bottle knockers, 198
    bottle stop star, 190, 193
    bottle supply to, 193
    burst bottle detection, 201–202
    cleaning and sanitizing, 164, 168–169, 171, 201
    cooling, 169
    crowners, 163, 170, 200–201
        crown chute, 200, 223
        crown crimp gauge, 170, 215
        crown feed hoppers, 8, 10, 200, 223
        crown platforms, 200–201
        crown sorter and guides, 170
        crowner dial, 200
        crowner heads, 171, 200, 223
        rectifier chute or tube, 200
    electric drives, 199
    filler bowls, 190, 192, 194–195
        center, 194–195
        torus or ring, 194, 195
    filler tubes, 195
    flow meters, 191, 192, 195
    gas tube spreaders, 88
    guides, 10
    half-pocket transfer chains, 189, 201
    hydraulic drives, 199
    importance of, 189, 191
    infeed worms (timing screws), 10, 189, 193
    jetters, 89, 199
    jockey pumps, 192
    long-tube fillers, 163, 195
    maintenance, 202
    manifolds, 164, 168, 169
    metering chambers, 191, 195, 196
    modern fillers and filling sequence, 196–198
    older fillers and filling sequence, 198
    pneumatic infeed gate, 190
    precautions, 201–202
    pressure bowls, 163, 164, 168, 169
    product distributor, 195
    short-tube fillers, 163, 195–196, 198
    speed, 191
    star wheels, 9, 10, 193, 201
    synchronous drives, 199
    ultrasonic foamers, 198
    vacuum system, 88
    wormgears, 10
bottle filling, 168–171, 189–207. *See also* crowns and crowning
    beer supply and delivery, 191–193, 194–195
    bottle conditioning, 164, 407–408
    bottle supply and bottle indexing, 193
    crowning, 170, 200–201
    displacement filling, 191, 195
    filling sequence, 196–198
    filling step, 196, 197, 198
    filling to a level, 190–191, 195–196
    foaming, 163–164, 170, 198–199
    headspace air evacuation, 198–199
    jetting, 190, 199
    long vent tube system, 195
    maintaining smooth operation, 171

pre-evacuation, 163, 170, 190, 196, 197
    pressurization, 196, 197
    reducing oxygen content, 164, 190
    scope and importance of operations, 191
    short vent tube system, 195–196
    on small bottling lines, 168–171
    snifting, 170, 197, 198
    starting procedures, 169
    troubleshooting guide, 202–206
        bottle breakage, 204–206
        incorrect bottle fill, 202–204
        incorrect liquid level in bowl, 204
        missing crowns and uncrowned bottles, 206
    turbulence, 163
    typical small-scale arrangement, 171
    vent tube testing, 195
    volumetric filling, 191, 195, 196
bottle manufacturing, 117–127
    annealing process and lehr, 123–124, 217–218
    batch house, 117, 118
    birdswings, 125
    cavity identification, 126
    cold end, 117, 124–127
    dipped finish, 125
    forces affecting glass bottles, 126–127
    forehearth, 119, 120–121
    furnaces, 118–120
        melters, 118–119
        operation, 120
        oxygen-fueled furnace, 119
        refiners, 119, 120
        regenerators, 118, 119
        sideport furnace, 118–119
    glass container factory, 117–118
    glass flow, 120
    gob formation and delivery, 120–121, 122
    hot end, 117, 118–124
    inspection for defects, 3, 125–127
    narrow-neck press-and-blow process, 122–123, 460
    palletizing, 127
    parison (blank) formation, 121, 122
    polariscope, 124
    polyethylene spraying, 124–125
    scabby bottoms, 125
    split finish, 125
    stones, 118, 125
    transfer to cooling plate and conveyor, 122, 123
bottle washers (soakers), 129–146
    blush or caustic bloom, 131
    bottle handling prior to, 136–137
    caustic carryover, 133, 143, 398
    caustic concentration, 67, 133, 138, 142, 143, 398
    challenges, 11
    cleaning, 142
    components, 138–141
        bottle transport (carrier chain), 138–139, 145
        chain drive or cardanic system, 140
        heating system, 140
        label removal, 140–141
        synchronized sprays, 139–140
        tank, 138
    discharge position, 139
    Dupre's effect, 131
    final rinse, 132
    health and safety, 145
    high-volume label removal system, 140–141
    inspection for cleanliness, 398
    loaders and loading, 136–137, 139
    loading position and report form, 137, 139
    main cleaning, 132

466 • INDEX

bottle washers (soakers) (*continued*)
   maintenance, 145
   multitank, modular, 137, 138, 140
   operating procedures, 129, 141–142
   performance, 145
   prejetting, 132
   presoaking, 132
   process, 379–380
   quality assurance parameters, 397–398
   rinse section performance inspection, 143–145
   single- and double-ended machines, 132, 137
   single-tank, 137
   soak and rinse compartment draining, 144–145
   startup and shutdown, 141–142
   submersion or contact time, 131
   temperature, 398
   types, 137–138
   washing solutions
      composition and makeup, 130–131, 133, 134
      differential titration, 143
      electrical conductivity, 143
      formulated premixes, 135
      germicidal-equivalent required concentrations, 133
      management procedures, 142–143
      properties of, 132–134
      temperature, 131, 133
   water hardness, 131
   water softeners, 131–132
bottles. *See also* crowns and crowning; glass; polyethylene terephthalate (PET) containers
   aluminum bottles, 223
   aluminum roll-on closures, 220–222
   Codd bottle stopper, 209
   conveying system, 136–137
   cork stoppers, 209
   crown closure history, 209–210
   Hutchinson stopper, 209
   hydrodynamic load, 126, 127
   impact, 126
   inspection of. *See under* inspection equipment
   internal pressure, 126
   Lightning stopper, 209
   lightweight nonreusable (one-trip), 12, 233
   loop seal closure, 209
   nonreturnable, 129, 147, 223
   normal trade returns, 129
   one-trip, 12
   recycling of, 12, 117
   returnable, 11–12, 129–130, 135, 145, 147–148, 223
   RingCrown closures, 223
   rinsing, 169, 170, 171
   storage bottles, 130
   surge, 127
   swing-top, 431
   thermal shock, 126, 131
   transfer of, 9, 10
   uncasing, 136
   uncleanable, 130
   vertical load, 126
   washing of, 379–380. *See also* bottle washers (soakers)
bottling lines. *See also* bottle fillers; bottle filling; bottle washers (soakers)
   bottle rinse tray, 169
   bottling downtime report, 14
   bright tanks, 164, 167, 168, 171
   bulk glass lines, 6
   centrifugal pumps, 164, 192
   conveyors, 318
   crowners, 9, 10, 170, 198, 200–201
   gravity systems, 192
   hoses, 171

   in-line meters, 192
   line speed and efficiency, 191
   loop or manifold systems, 192–193
   manual rinsers, 169
   optimum efficiency, 189
   positive-displacement pumps, 192
   release tanks and beer supply systems, 191, 192
   small-scale, 6, 9, 10, 161–171
   twist rinsers, 169
Bourdon tube pressure gauges, 64, 69
breakdowns, 13, 15, 16
Brewing Industry Recommended Closure Purchase Specifications, 214–215
bromate, 36
bromide, 373
bromine, 252, 254, 255, 257, 259, 373
Brouwerij Martens, 148
budgeting, 28–29, 32
bulk glass systems, 5–6

calcium carbonate, 367, 368, 369, 371
can fillers, 91–94. *See also* fillers
   can handling infeed, 89–91, 92, 93–94
   center column, 92, 93
   charging needles, 94
   check ball gas tubes, 88
   CIP, 93, 94, 179–180
   closing cams, 99
   electronic, 12
   fill sensors, 177, 178
   fill tubes and foam tubes, 177
   filler bowl supply piping, 93
   five-head automatic, 174, 175, 176, 177
   fluid director and umbrella, 88, 96, 97, 98
   lid dispensers, 178–179
   pressure and temperature control, 177
   purge and snift cam setup, 99
   semiautomated, 174
   tulips and tulip actuators, 92, 94, 96, 98
   two-head manual, 173
   valve actuating levers, 95
   valve assembly, 94
   volumetric, 12
can filling, 87–100, 176–178
   can capture, 90, 91, 92, 93, 94, 95
   can handling, 90–91
   equipment, 87
   fill stop and snift, 98–99
   filling step, 96–98
   foam formation, 88, 99, 177, 178
   fundamentals, 87–90
   machine setup, 99–100
   pre-evacuation, 177
   pressurization, 96, 97
   purge step, 88, 94, 95–96, 99
   on small canning lines, 176–178
   troubleshooting, 100
can liners, 257, 406
can packers, 44
can pallet packs, 82–83
can seaming. *See* double seams and double seaming
can washers, 76
canning lines
   bright tanks, 173
   caliper micrometers, 181, 182–184
   can seam micrometers, 181–182
   conveyors, 318
   depalletizing, 174–176
   digital seam inspection workstation, 180
   dry end packing, 179
   filling, 176–178
   fully automatic lines, 174
   infeed table, 175
   large-scale, 7
   lid application, 174, 178–179
   lid quality assurance, 405

   maintenance checks, 188
   manual seam teardown, 180–181, 182–184
   manual two-head lines, 173
   plastic ring application, 174, 179
   seam-cutting workstation, 180
   seamer bearings, 187–188
   seamer lift table, 179
   seamers, 12, 173, 174, 179, 184–188
   semiautomatic three-head lines, 174
   shaker motor, 175
   small-scale, 173–188
canning operations, 71–86
   bodymakers, 71, 73–76
   can and end specifications, 80–82
   can end manufacture, 78–79
   can manufacture, 71–77
   glossary of terms, 84
   lubricants, 458
   major developments in manufacturing, 84
   shipping and storage of empty cans and ends, 82–84
   two-piece aluminum manufacturing line, 71
   wall ironing machines, 71, 73–76
cans. *See also* double seams and double seaming
   aluminum advantages, 173
   aluminum vs. steel, 71, 77
   axial load, 80, 85
   bearing surface, 85
   bottom profile, 74, 80, 85
   buckle resistance, 73, 78, 80, 85
   bulge resistance, 85
   can body, 115
   can lid opening, 90
   coatings, 77, 85
   curls and curling, 78, 81, 86, 102–103, 115
   easy-open ends, 80, 84
   end unit, 115
   finished height, 85, 102
   flanges and flanging, 77, 81, 85, 96, 102, 115
   inspection, 4, 77–78
   interchangeability dimensions, 80, 81
   large opening end (LOE), 86
   lightweighting, 80, 90
   liners, 257, 406
   lithography, 76–77, 83, 85
   neck-plug diameter, 81, 85, 102, 115
   neck profile, 73, 85
   necking and necking-in cans, 77, 80, 82
   palletized, 82
   reduced-gauge, 80, 82
   rinsing, 173, 179
   sizes and capacities, 80, 85
   specifications and performance, 80–82
   starting gauge, 72, 73, 80, 82, 85
   stay-on-tab (SOT) ends, 71, 78, 79, 80, 84, 86
   tabs and tab formation, 78, 79, 84, 86
   thick and thin walls, 73, 85
   third-stage wall-ironed can, 75
   three-piece cans, 71, 84
   tolerances, 91, 102
   two-piece manufacturing progression, 75
   ultra-lightweight ends, 80, 82
   wall thickness, 73
   washing of, 76
capacitance level probes and control, 12, 59–60, 65–66
capacity, 80, 85
capital investment, 39–40, 155, 156, 157, 158
capital projects, 29
caps
   cap removal torque, 222, 405
   closure application, 221–222
   in-shell manufacture, 221
   liner-inserted manufacture, 221
   quality assurance, 405
   roll-on pilfer-proof closures, 220–221
   shipping and storage, 221
   top-seal, pilfer-proof closures, 220

carbon dioxide (CO_2)
    can filling and, 92–93, 94, 95–96, 97
    carbonation and, 87–88
    detergent reactions, 378–379
    equilibrium, 165, 166–167
    flow rate, 66, 67
    gas leaks, 166
    levels and beer quality, 164–165, 169
    lid application and, 178–179
    package testing, 400, 401–402, 403
    pre-evacuation, 163, 170, 177
    undercover gassing, 99
    volume displacement, 165
    volumes of gas, 87–88, 165–167, 171
carbonation
    adjustable CO_2 regulators, 168
    beer freshness and, 151, 152
    bottle conditioning and, 407–408
    carbonating stones, 167–168
    CO_2 and, 87–88
    pressure and, 165–168
    procedure, 164
    retention of, 152–153
    stability, 171
    tank carbonation, 165–168
    testing for, 400, 401–402, 403
    traditional method, 167
    at various temperatures and pressures, 401
case packers, 10
cases
    coding, 414
    erecting and stuffing equipment, 6
    inspection of. See under inspection equipment
    prepacked or "shipper", 5, 6
    retrippers, 136
    single-trip cartons, 136
    wrap-around–style cartons, 7
catch-up speed, 47
caustic carryover, 133, 143, 398
caustic soda. See sodium hydroxide
caustics, 369–370, 398–399, 402
center panel formation, 78
changeover time, 13, 16
chelants. See sequestrants or chelants
chemical oxygen demand, 11
chloramines, 36
chlorides, 368, 374
chlorinated trisodium phosphate, 373
chlorine, 36, 144, 254, 368, 373, 380
chlorine dioxide, 36, 233, 357, 368, 374, 380
chlorite, 36
CIP. See cleaning in place
circular chart recorder, 63
cleaning and sanitizing in brewery operations, 365–383
    amylases, 367
    bottle fillers, 164, 168–169, 171, 201
    bottle washers (soakers), 142
    CIP. See cleaning in place
    cleaning objectives, 365
    cleaning solution components, 369–372
        acidic cleaners, 371–372, 378, 379
        alkalis (caustics), 369–370, 378, 379
        chelants/sequestrants, 371
        chemical activity summary, 372
        complex phosphates, 370–371
        polymers, 371
        surfactants, 370
    conveyors, 329–330
    detergents, 366–367
    foaming and gel applications, 375, 380, 382
    keg line operations, 349–358, 383
    label pallets, 283
    laminar layer reduction, 368–369, 375
    lipases, 367
    manual cleaning, 375
    mechanical action, 368–369, 375
    open-plant cleaning, 374
    oxidizing agents, 367
    packaging hall cleaning, 379–383
        conveyors, 380
        filler exterior automated cleaning, 382
        filler exterior manual cleaning, 382
        filler interior cleaning, 381
        returnable glass bottle washing, 379–380
        soil types and cleaning methods, 379
    proteases, 367
    protein removal and solubility, 369, 372
    sanitizers. See sanitizers
    sanitizing, 365–366, 372–375, 381
    saponification, 367
    soak cleaning, 375
    soil types, 366–367
        carbohydrates, 367
        and detergent choice, 366, 367
        fats, 367
        loose vs. adherent, 366
        mineral deposits, 367, 371
        organic and inorganic, 366–367
        polymeric resins, 367
        proteins, 367
    solution flow layers, 368–369
    surface material and finish, 368
    temperature, 369
    testable criteria, 365
    water quality, 367–368
cleaning in place (CIP), 375–379
    air-operated diaphragm pumps, 377
    bottle fillers, 164, 168, 197, 201
    Bourdon tubes, 69
    can fillers, 93, 94, 179–180
    CIP ports, 96
    components of system, 376–377
    defined, 68
    design considerations, 377
    filler interior cleaning, 381
    flash pasteurization systems, 228–229
    kegs, 383
    labelers, 290
    open-loop control and, 57
    optimization, 377–379
        CIP monitoring, 377–378
        interface management, 378
        replacing caustic cleaning with acidic cleaning, 378, 379
        shortening CIP cycle, 378–379
    peristaltic pumps, 377
    piston-type pumps, 377
    sanitary differential pressure cell, 69
    sanitizers for, 372, 373, 374, 375
    single-use or reuse systems, 376
    thermowells, 69
    touchscreen, 179–180
    tunnel pasteurization systems, 247, 248
    typical cycle, 376
    water management, 38, 39
cleaning out of place, 68
closed-loop process control, 57–58, 59
closing machines, 82, 86, 116
coatings
    Actis, 148, 155, 159
    beer quality and, 458–459
    on cans and ends, 76, 77, 78, 80, 84, 85
    on glass bottles, 460
    on PET containers, 155–156
    Plasmax, 155, 159
Coca-Cola Company, 1
coding. See also coding technologies
    of bottles, 298, 302, 303, 305
    of cans and pallets, 83
    of cases, 414
    of kegs, 347, 360
    notch coding, 414
    quality assurance, 414
coding technologies, 297–307. See also inks
    continuous ink jet printing, 297, 298–303
        air knife, 302
        bottle-style printers, 299
        cartridge-style printers, 299
        charge tunnel, 300
        clipped print, 301
        deflection plate, 300
        in harsh environment, 302
        ingress protection (IP) rating, 298
        ink pressure, 298
        ink return block, 300–301
        late break-off, 302
        modulation signal, 299–300
        nozzle, 299–300
        piezoelectric crystal, 299–300
        pigmented inks, 303
        poor drop break-off, 301–302
        poor vertical resolution, 301
        positive air system, 302
        print matrices, 300–301
        printer requirements, 298
        printheads and components, 299–301
        product detection, 303
        satellites, 302
        slanted print, 301
        stream of ink dots, 300
        stretched print, 301
        troubleshooting, 301–302
        valve, 299
    importance of, 297
    ink jet vs. laser coding systems, 297–298
    large character marking, 297
    laser coding, 297, 303–307
        availability of equipment, 307
        beam shields, 305
        burn method, 304
        CO_2 lasers, 298, 303
        code assurance, 307
        dot matrix laser print, 304
        fume extraction, 305
        gas laser block diagram, 303
        heat method, 304
        hot spots, 306
        incorrect focal length, 306
        incorrect font, 306
        incorrect software settings, 306–307
        jump-delay issues, 307
        legacy models, 304
        mark-delay issues, 307
        off-delay adjustment issues, 306
        safety guidelines, 305
        smash method, 305
        steered beam technology, 304
        tails on characters, 306
        troubleshooting, 306–307
    thermal ink jet printing, 297
    thermal transfer, 297
coil car/upender, 71–72
coining, 78, 79, 85
cold and hot junctions, 63
cold filtration, 153, 156, 157. See also final beer filtration; sterile filtration of beer
coliforms, 36, 386
complex phosphates, 370–371
compound liners, 78
computer-aided design, 8, 45
computer simulations, 56–57
computerized maintenance management systems, 13, 18
conductivity measurements, 67, 398
conductivity probes, 195, 356, 361
container and product movement. See conveyors; pallet movement
container friction coefficient, 45
container stability, 45
Continental Can Company, 84, 210
contingency plans, 31
contracts, 31–32

control logic, 54–57. *See also* programmable logic controllers
control loop applications, 59–61
control units or domains, 47–48, 50, 51
controlled variable, 57, 58
controllers
    line flow control, 52–54
    process control, 58, 59, 61
conversion presses, 78
converted unit depth, 85
conveyors, 317–331
    accumulation and, 42–43, 323–324
    accumulation conveyors, 8, 43, 324, 336
    air conveyors, 318, 324
    biogrowth on, 330, 380
    case conveyors, 325–327
        belt-driven live roller conveyors, 326
        belt-on-roller conveyors, 326
        belt-on-skate wheel conveyors, 326
        flat-top chain case conveyors, 326–327
        gravity roller conveyors, 325
        gravity skate wheel conveyors, 325
        line-shaft powered roller conveyors, 326
        for plastic cases, 327
        powered belt conveyors, 326
        powered roller conveyors, 325–326
        slider bed belt conveyors, 326
    case merges and diverters, 327–328
    chain pallet conveyors, 330
    chain pitch standards, 320
    changing directions, 321–322
        conventional brush transfers, 322
        live transfers, 322
        sideflexing tabletop chains, 322
    chordal action, 320
    cleaning and lubrication guidelines, 329–330, 380
    combiners and decombiners, 322–323
    dry lubrication, 329, 380
    flat-top–style chains, 317–320
        acetal plastic chains, 319
        austenitic stainless-steel chains, 319
        bevel-style chains, 320
        ferritic stainless-steel chains, 319
        low pin centerline–style chains, 320
        magnetic-style chains, 320
        modular belt chains, 317–318, 319, 327
        polybutylene terephthalate polyester chains, 319
        sideflexing modular belt chains, 327
        sideflexing tabletop chains, 319–320, 322
        tab-style conveyor chains, 319
        tabletop chains, 317, 319–320, 322–323
    hinge pins, 380
    in-line transfers, 321
        conventional direct in-line transfer, 321
        self-clearing empty can noseover transfer, 321
        tabletop in-line side transfers, 321
    keg conveyors, 328–329
    length standards, 320
    line design and, 42
    machine availability and, 48
    in palletizing systems, 336
    powered roller pallet conveyors, 330
    safety and, 21
    selection, 317, 318
    speeds, 45, 47, 52
    spiral case elevators and lowerators, 328
    tunnel pasteurizer conveyors, 324–325
        metal/plastic hybrid chains, 325
        plastic raised-rib modular belts, 324–325
        walking beams, 324
        wire mesh belts, 324
    vacuum conveyors, 324
    vertical product movement, 328
    wet lubrication, 329, 380
coolant for can manufacture, 76

corrosion
    bottle-washing solutions, 133
    can staining, 258
    pasteurizers, 67–68, 242, 243, 251–252, 254, 255–256
    stainless steel, 368
    stress corrosion fatigue, 229
    tab openings, 179
Coulson, J. M., 228
countersink formation, 78
craft (artisan-scale) breweries, 2–3, 12, 161, 173, 176
critical control point, 383
critical path, 28
crowns and crowning, 209–223. *See also* caps
    chromium/chromium oxide coatings, 211
    coatings and inks, 212
    crimp diameter, 215–216
    crown back-off, 217
    crown crimp, 215–216
    crown liner patterns, 213
    crown liner specifications, 214
    crown metal, 210–211
    crown production, 212
    crown sealing ring impression, 219
    crown shell dimensions, 214
    crown testing, 214–215
    foamed liners, 213
    gas bubble formation, 449
    high foam collar, 217
    history, 209–210
    inspection and counting, 213
    metal thickness and hardness, 210, 211
    molded lined crowns, 213
    offset lithography, 212
    oxygen-scavenging and barrier liners, 164, 213–214, 462
    package testing, 218–219, 222
    packaging problem analysis, 219–220
    process, 170, 200–201
    pry-off crown caps, 213–214, 215, 220
    punch presses, 212, 221
    PVC and non-PVC plastic liners, 210, 212, 213–214
    quality assurance, 404–405
    removal torque, 216–218, 220, 222
        cold-end coating and, 217–218
        dried beer solids and, 217
        excessive hot-end coating and, 217
        glass extrusions and, 216–217
        motorized cap torque testers, 216
        spring torque tester, 216
        testing, 405
    residual air detection, 449
    RingCrown closure, 223
    Rockwell hardness tester, 210, 211
    sealing rings, 213
    secure seal tester, 218–219, 222
    shipping, 213
    spin-lined crowns, 213
    tempers of tin mill products, 210–211
    tin-free steel, 211, 212, 213
    tinplate, 211, 212, 213
    troubleshooting issues, 220
    twist-off crowns
        crimping, 215
        invention of, 210
        lubricant, 212–213
        metal used for, 211
        removal torque, 216, 219, 405
        thread inspection, 437
Cryptosporidium, 36
cup, 72, 73, 74
cupping press, 71, 72–73, 74
customer contacts, 51

damage caused by conveyor, 45
data analysis. *See* documentation and data analysis

Database of State Incentives for Renewables & Efficiency, 40
dead bands, 61, 65
dead time, 59
Del Vecchio, H. W., 225, 226, 236–237
depalletizers
    automatic, 175–176
    empty can unloading, 83, 174–175
    on keg lines, 362
    lift-off, 6
    location, 8
    on-demand, 44
    operator responsibilities, 19
    semiautomated, 175
    speed, 42
    sweeper, 6
description of operation, 29
dial thermometers, 63
diethylhexyl phthalate, 461
differential pressure, 65, 66, 67, 69, 195
differential pressure flow transmitters, 67
differential pressure transmitters, 66
dioctyl phthalate, 461
discharge controls, 51
dissolved oxygen (DO), 89, 93, 95, 96, 227, 400, 402–403
dissolved oxygen meters, 402–403
distribution, 161, 162
documentation and data analysis, 416–421
    3-sigma, 418–419
    basic data analysis, 417
    common mistakes, 420
    computerized documentation errors, 416–417
    control limits, 418–419
    control ranges, 420
    custom design, 417
    data discontinuity, 416, 417
    exception reports, 417
    methods, 416
    motivation, 416
    narrow table model, 417
    out-of-control situation signals, 419, 420
    Pareto analysis, 420
    process capability, 420–421
    range charts, 419–420
    specification ranges, 420
    statistical process control, 416, 418–420
    trend charts (X-bar charts), 418, 419
dome, 73, 85
doming progression, 74, 75
double action shell die, 78
double seams and double seaming, 101–116
    axial load and, 80
    base plates and adjustment points, 184, 187
    body hook and end hook length, 111, 182, 183, 184
    body hook and overlap, 102–103, 108, 116, 179
    body hook R-ring/hairpinning, 113
    body wall fracture/penetration, 107, 112, 113
    body wall thinning, 113, 114
    can end manufacture and, 78
    can ends reformed in, 82
    chuck spindle parts, 187
    closing machine components and operation, 103–104, 116
    conventional vs. new technology ends, 103
    countersink depth, 106, 108
    critical can and end components, 102–103
    defects and causes, 111–115
    defined, 3–4, 86
    double seam evaluation, 4, 106–111, 180–184, 405–406
    double seam formation, 104–106, 179
    double-seaming chuck, 103, 104, 113, 114, 116, 179
    end countersink radius, 103
    end hook (cover hook), 116, 179, 183, 184

excessive body wall compression, 109
external and internal components, 101–102
false seam/knocked down flange, 114
first-operation double seams, 105, 106–107, 113, 179
fractured seaming panel/clam shell, 112
glossary of terms, 116
hairing or wooling, 115, 116
looseness wrinkles, 110, 111
micrometer, 405–406
misassembly, 114
pressure ridge, 110, 116
primary seal, 105
quality assurance, 405–406
sealing compounds, 85, 105–106, 115, 179, 459–460
seam distortion, 109
seam gap, 111, 116
seam height, 108, 112, 116, 181–182, 184, 188
seam overlap, 184
seam scope, 406
seam thickness, 106, 108, 110, 116, 181, 184
seam tightness or looseness, 107, 108–111
seam troubleshooting, 186
seaming rolls and adjustment, 179, 184–186
second-operation double seams, 105, 108–111, 179
in small-scale canning operations, 179, 184
thick can wall and, 73
typical bearing, 187
undercover gassing, 89, 99, 102, 104, 106, 116
Vees or pleats, 107, 110, 111, 116
down-gauging cans, 80
downtime analyses, 14, 15, 16
draw punch, 72
drop packers, 15, 16, 44
dynamic accumulation, 43

economic value added (EVA), 29
EDTA. *See* ethylene diamine tetra acetic acid
efficiency-improvement tool display, 56
electrochemical measurements, 67–68
electromotive force, 63
electronic bottle inspectors, 3, 11, 19
electronic control systems, 59, 68
emergency stops, 19
employees
    labor, 2, 17, 20, 162
    management structure, 17–18
    operators, 18–20
    safety of, 2, 18, 21
    training of, 2–3, 20, 21, 39, 68, 425–426
empty bottle inspectors, 395, 396, 398. *See also under* inspection equipment
end opening forces, 80
end pallet packs, 82, 83
enteric viruses, 36
environmental management. *See also* recycling
    anaerobic wastewater treatment, 39
    biogas production, 39, 40
    brewer implemented systems, 37–39
    capital investment, 39–40
    CIP interface management, 378
    governmental regulation, 22, 35–37
    greenhouse gas contributions, 22
    incentives, 40
    ISO 14001 certification, 37–38
    label design, 266, 267
    operations environmental aspects examples, 38
    PET bottles, 147, 153–154
    publicly owned treatment works, 36
    PVC-lined crowns, 461
    reduced use of aluminum, 82
    regulated air pollutants, 36–37
    returnable bottles, 11–12
    short-interval control of environmental impacts, 39
    solid and hazardous waste disposal, 37

volatile organic carbons, 36, 37, 460
wastewater discharges and treatment, 36, 37, 38, 39–40
water contaminants and treatment, 36, 38, 243, 368
water sources and usage, 35–36, 38, 39, 251, 412
well-head protection plans, 36
equipment selection, 42, 162, 163–164
ergonomics, 21
Escherichia coli, 386
ethylene diamine tetra acetic acid (EDTA), 134, 371
ethylene vinyl alcohol, 159, 462
Études sur la Bière (Pasteur), 225, 235
EVA. *See* economic value added

fill-height detectors, 19
fillers. *See also* bottle fillers; can fillers
    aseptic, 12
    choosing, 163–164
    CO_2 pressure, 87–88
    electronic-controlled fillers, 11
    exterior cleaning, 382
    filler application on human–machine interface, 53
    filler-bowl counterpressure control, 65, 93
    filler-bowl level control, 59–60, 65–66, 93, 96, 195
    filler-bowl supply piping, 93
    filler checks, 400–401, 403–404, 406–407
    filler valves, 381
    fixed spray nozzles, 382
    gas tubes, 88, 94, 98–99
    gravity and, 87, 192, 401
    interior cleaning, 381
    legacy fillers, 87, 91–94
    and line flow, 45–47, 48
    monoblocs, 9, 10, 12
    mean time between failures, 49
    in packaging line examples, 6, 7
    speed, 5, 42, 44, 45, 46
    valve screen, 89
    volumetric fillers, 87, 400–401
filling. *See also* bottle filling; can filling
    contribution to dissolved oxygen, 403
    fill-level inspection. *See under* inspection equipment
    kegs, 8
    pressurization, 96, 97, 126
    sterile and near-sterile, 6, 12, 153
    wastewater, 38
filter aid management, 38
filters and filtration, 12, 153, 156, 157, 259
final beer filtration, 385–391. *See also* cold filtration; sterile filtration of beer
    beer filterability and filtration practices, 386–387
    bench scale testing, 386
    biological loads and performance, 387
    pressure differential, 386
    staged filter system, 387
    cartridge filtration, 389–390
        automated systems, 389
        bubble point test, 390
        cartridge housings, 389
        depth filter cartridges, 389
        forward flow test, 390
        membrane cartridges, 389
        operating costs, 390
        pressure hold test, 390
    cost and operational efficiency, 387
    filter ratings, 385–386
        absolute rated filters, 386
        nominally rated filters, 386
    fine/final filtration, 387–388, 389
    lenticular module filtration, 388–389
    log reduction value, 386
    microbiological security, 387

microorganism-reducing grade filters, 386
regeneration, 388, 389, 390
sheet filtration, 387–388
size and operating recommendations, 388–389, 389–390
sterilization of filters, 388, 389
system capacity requirements, 387
target microorganisms, 385
titer reduction, 386
traditional depth filters, 386
final control element, 58, 59
finished goods dispatch, 17
Finn-Korkki Oy, 223
first-in, first-out movement, 8, 136, 323, 324, 415
flash pasteurization, 225–234, 249–250. *See also* pasteurization
    advantages and disadvantages, 233
    back-pressure control, 231
    boost pumps, 229
    BTU load chart, 232
    CIP system, 227, 228–229
    CO_2 equilibrium chart, 231
    control console, 232
    cracked plates, 229
    description, 227–230
    equipment, 227–229, 408
    flow control, 231
    flow diversion, 231
    flow rate, 228–229
    formulas used for designing systems, 232
    heating system, 228
    holding tube, 227, 228
    invertase test, 232–233
    kegs, 7, 226–227, 343
    minimal recirculation of beer, 228
    in North America, 226–227
    operating outline, 229–230
    PET bottle packaging and, 153, 156, 157
    plate heat exchanger (PHE), 227, 228, 229, 230, 231, 249
    pressure and pressure drop, 229, 231
    quality assurance, 408–409
    sanitizing, 229
    schematic of, 230
    skid-mounted system, 228
    steady-state flow, 227, 230
    sterile beer tank (SBT), 227, 228, 230, 231, 250
    temperature control, 229, 230–231
    troubleshooting, 250
    vs. tunnel pasteurization, 12, 227, 233
    variable flow, 227, 230, 249
float items in project, 28
floats, 59–60, 65, 66, 195, 196
flow control, 66–67
flow meters, 45, 66–67, 191, 192, 195, 361
flow switches, 67, 360, 361
Food and Drug Administration, 305, 458
forklift trucks, 330

G. Krueger Brewing Company, 71, 84
Gantt chart, 28
Giardia lamblia, 36
glass, 117, 118, 126
Glass Packaging Institute, 214
gluconates, 371
good manufacturing practices, 383
Graham Packaging Company, 148, 157, 159
grain handling, 38
gram-negative bacteria, 397, 411
gram-positive bacteria, 411
growth of cans, 85
A Guide to the Project Management Body of Knowledge (PMBOK Guide), 23, 24, 25, 26

HACCP. *See* hazard analysis and critical control points
haloacetic acids, 36

halogen biocides/sanitizers
    pasteurizer water treatment, 252, 253, 254–255, 259
    for surface sanitization, 373
Hawaiian Brewing Company, 84
hazard analysis and critical control points (HACCP), 21–22, 68, 83, 383
hazardous wastes, 37. *See also* environmental management
head foam potential, 164, 165
headspace
    beer freshness and, 2
    cans, 80, 81, 98–99
    defined, 85, 115
    tunnel pasteurization, 239
headspace air
    defined, 89
    expelling, 198–199, 400
    foaming and, 88
    oxygen levels, 89, 152
    shelf life and, 163–164
    undercover gasser, 99
hearing loss and protection, 21
heat-exchanger water pump, 60
Heineken, 15, 16
HEPA/ULPA filtration, 12
high-cone machines, 7
high speed and high-speed sensor, 44, 45, 51
hop aromas, 164, 165
hot and cold junctions, 63
human–machine interface, 51, 53
humidity, 15, 273
hydrochloric acid, 37, 244, 374
hydrogen gas production, 135, 145
hydrogen peroxide, 233, 374
hypochlorite solutions, 144. *See also* chlorinated trisodium phosphate; sodium hypochlorite

idle time, 13
incoming materials delivery, 17
inks
    beer quality and, 458–459
    can decorating, 76–77
    for continuous ink jet printing, 298, 299, 300, 303
    crown decorating, 212
    on foil labels, 135
    as hazardous waste, 37
    ignitability, 37
    label printing, 269–271
    for large character marking, 297
    lead-free, 212
    multiple pen recorders, 64
    for paperboard carton printing, 310–311
    pigmented, 303
    pressurizing ink, 298
    safety precautions, 303
    for thermal ink jet printing, 297
    volatile organic compounds, 37
inorganic contaminants in water, 36
inspection equipment, 423–456
    automatic sampling systems, 450, 455–456
    bottle color detection, 429–430
    bottle heights determination, 428
    bottle sorting inspector, 427
    cap/crown inspection, 448–449
        camera-based PET cap inspection, 449
        high (or cocked) cap detection, 448–449
        inductive proximity sensors, 448
        retro-reflexive sensors, 448
        through-beam sensors, 448–449
    cardboard box inspection system, 453–454
    case color detection system, 430
    case handle hole detection, 430
    case size and shape detection, 430
    charge-coupled device (CCD) cameras, 430, 433, 436, 439, 451

closure detection, 429
common platforms, 423
defect evaluation, 424–425
empty bottle crate inspection system, 427
empty bottle inspection, 432–440
    base inspections, 436–437
    blowing off finish, 435–436
    defect types, 432
    double bottle base inspection pattern, 437
    finish inspections, 435
    infeed checks, 432–433
    infrared residual liquid detection, 438
    inspector types, 432
    moistening finish, 435
    old bottle removal, 439
    PET bottles, 435–436, 438–439
    PET vent slot inspection, 438–439
    project scope development, 440
    reject rate control system, 439
    residual liquid detection systems, 437–438
    scuffing inspection, 438
    sidewall image projection, 433
    sidewall inspections, 433–434
    test bottle protocol, 439–440
    thread inspection systems, 437
    transparent fault detection, 436–437
    twist-off thread inspection, 437
empty crate inspection, 431–432
equipment qualification, 425
equipment training, 425–426
features to consider, 426–427
fill-level inspection, 440–448
    bottle burst protection system, 440, 447–448
    container volume comparison, 444
    filler/closer line reports, 446
    filler valve checklist and report, 445–446
    filler valve monitoring systems, 440, 445–446, 449
    foaming considerations, 440
    in full cases, 454
    gamma gauge requirements, 443
    gamma installation checklist, 443
    high-frequency systems, 440, 441, 442, 444–445
    missing fill tube detection, 446–447
    online fill-height inspectors, 406–407
    technology comparisons, 441–442
    vent tube detection, 447
    vision-based systems, 444, 449
    X-ray fill-level sensor pattern, 443
    X-ray technology vs. gamma technology, 441, 443–444
foreign object detection, 428–429
full case inspection, 407, 454–455
    using proximity or inductive sensors, 454–455
    using weighing technology, 455
    X-ray–based inspection, 454
label inspection, 450–453
    camera-based, 451–453
    label composite from multiple images, 451, 452
    light scanner and reflection, 450
    lighting sources, 452
    on-conveyor label detection, 451
    performance guarantee specifications, 452
    sensor-based, 450–451
    system qualifications, 452–453
neck ring inspection, 430
pressure detection, 453
    bottles with crowns, 453
    cans, 453
process flow in returnable bottling house, 423
reject tables and conveyors, 425
rejection systems, 455–456
    curve-style rejection device, 455
    pneumatic ram-type rejectors, 455
    upright bottle rejection, 455–456

residual air detection, 449
swing-top bottle detection, 431
typical process flow, 424
ultrasonic sensors, 428, 430
Institute and Guild of Brewing, 20
instrument calibration, 70
internal machine faults, 48, 49
internal rate of return, 29
International Organization for Standardization (ISO), 386, 395, 421–422
inventory levels, 18
invertase test, 232–233, 410
iodine inorganic complex, 373–374
iodophors, 373
Iron City Brewing, 84

Jennings, W. G., 131

keg line operations, 343–363
    best practices for cleaning and filling, 352, 354–359
        acid wash, 356–357
        caustic soak, 355–356
        caustic wash, 355
        chemical sterilization, 357
        counterpressurization, 358
        de-ullaging, 354
        fifth air purge, 357
        filling, 358–359
        first rinse, 355
        fourth air purge, 356
        gas purge and gassing, 358
        hot water sterilization, 357
        pressure check and depressurization, 354
        second air purge, 355
        second rinse, 356
        steam purge, 356, 357
        steam sterilization, 357
        third air purge, 356
        third (final) rinse, 357
    caustic soda concentrations, 67, 398–399
    chemical carryover, 398–399
    dirty returned kegs, 345, 346
    easy-read gauges, 8
    external keg washers, 7–8, 349–351, 383
        external prerinse unit, 350
        filtration, 350
        monitoring and controlling, 350
        rotating kegs in, 351
        sections, 349–350
    fill-by-weight systems, 359
    filling right-side up, 359
    filling upside down, 358
    final keg inspection, 359–360
    initial keg inspection (fit-to-fill), 346–349
        bent keg necks, 348
        bent or broken tapping lugs, 348
        damaged chimes, 348
        damaged keg valve seal, 348–349
        dust caps, 349
        foreign kegs, 347
        frozen kegs, 348
        hydrocarbons, 349
        keg identification, 347
        keg tracking, 348
        missing locking rings, 348
        radio frequency identification, 348
        residual beer, 348–349
    internal washing and filling equipment, 383
        automatic walking beam-style machine, 351–352
        connection heads and keg clamps, 351, 352
        small machines, 351
        two-head manual machines, 351
    keg cleaning quality assurance, 398–400, 413
    keg floats, 345, 347, 348, 352, 362, 363

keg machine controls and programming, 360–361
    monitoring washes, 361
    PLC and sensors, 360–361
    test kegs, 360
keg processing, 345–346
    labeling and capping, 360
    layouts, 361–362
    microbiological sampling, 399
    modulation filler system, 359
    monitoring or sight kegs, 399–400
    multistage filling system, 358
    planning, 7–8
    prewash machine, 356
    rackers, 8
    safety, 344–345
    steam disinfection, 357, 398, 400
    three-stage filling system, 358
    washing techniques, 352–354
        full-flow wall wash, 352, 353
        low-flow spear wash, 352–353
        pressure control, 353
        pulse washing, 353, 356
        reverse washing, 353
        rousing, 353
        scrubbing bubbles, 353
kegs
    beer stone deposits, 345, 353, 356
    conveyors for, 328–329
    flash pasteurization, 226–227, 343
    flat-top spear valves, 344, 359
    Golden Gate, 343, 398, 413
    Hoff Stevens, 343, 398, 413
    keg chimes, 343–344
    keg neck, 343, 344
    one-way, 362–363
        bag in a box, 362
        PET, 362–363
    open-bunghole kegs, 398, 399
    PET, 150
    pressure supplied to, 345
    shell construction, 343–344
    side-bunge styles, 343
    single-valve (Sankey), 7, 226, 227, 343–344, 399, 413
    single-walled, 7
    spear valve attachment, 345
    spear valve openings, 344
    tamper-proof caps, 349
    temperature limits, 345
    well-type spear valves, 344, 359
Kerzner, Harold, 24
key performance indicators, 3, 4, 13–14, 22, 38, 39
Kortec, 148

labelers and labeler operations, 277–296
    adhesive types and characteristics, 296
    automatic flow control system, 284
    automatic magazine, 287
    back aggregates, 280
    back pusher plate, 286
    bottle characteristics, 294
    bottle dressing, 278
    bottle pads and table, 279, 280, 289
    bottle stop, 284, 289
    bottle table oil system, 285–286
    bottle table rotations, 284–285
    changeovers, 288–289
    CIP systems, 290
    cold-glue labelers, 278
    covered aggregates, 290
    crooked/nonregistered labels, 292
    discharge star, 280, 288–289
    feed screw, 279, 280, 288–289
    fine-pitched thread regulators, 290
    flagging labels, 292
    glue film thickness, 282, 283
    glue pumps, 283–284
    glue rollers, 279, 282–283
        rubber, 282, 283
        stainless-steel, 282, 283
    glue scraper, 279, 282
    gripper cylinder, 287–288
        anvil, 287
        cams, 287
        changeovers, 288
        labeler machine operation and, 279, 280, 281
        sponges, 287–288
        timing, 287
    in-line cold-glue machine layout, 289
    infeed star, 279, 280, 288–289
    label basket (magazine), 279, 286–287
    label characteristics, 295
    label pallets, 278, 279, 281, 282–283
        aluminum, 282, 283
        cleaning of, 283
        rubber, 282, 283
    label troubleshooting guide, 295
    labeler set up for body and neck labels, 11
    labeling stations, 278, 279, 280–282
        bolt-on, 290, 291
        interior drives of front aggregate, 282
        schematic layout of label pallet motion, 281
        schematic layout of labeling station, 281
        typical cold-glue labeling station, 281
    line flow and, 46–47
    machine operation, 279–280
    machine orientation, 278–279
    missing labels, 292
    modular labelers, 11, 290–291
    operator responsibilities, 19
    pitch distance, 277–278
    pressure-sensitive labelers, 289–290
    production and machine speeds, 277–278
    production line configuration, 278
    quality assurance, 413–414
    sensor systems, 290
    speed, 42, 45
    troubleshooting flowchart, 291
    troubleshooting guides, 293–294, 295
    typical rotary machine layout, 280
    wet glue labeler, 11
    wipe-downs and wipe-down stations, 278, 280, 284, 288, 290
    zero-backlash aggregates, 290
labels, 263–275
    aluminum foil, 132, 133, 135, 144
    application of, 2, 15, 413–414
    applied ceramic labeling labels, 434
    blow mold labels, 263
    chop-cut labels, 266, 267
    Cobb value of paper, 273
    cost comparison, 264
    cut-and-stack labels, 263, 264, 268, 271
    cut-and-stack vs. pressure-sensitive, 264–265
    defects, 273–275
        blocking, 273–274
        curl, 273
        poor slit edge, 274–275
        size variation, 274
        telescoping, 274
    design, 266–268
        cutting dies, 268
        drawdowns, 266–267
        flexography (flexo) plates, 267–268, 269
        gravure cylinders, 268, 270
        offset (litho) plates, 267–268, 270
        preflight procedure, 267
        production planning, 267
        proofs, 266–267
        quality assurance, 413
        sustainability, 266, 267
        UPC, 267
    finishing, 271–272
        bundling and wrapping, 272
        carton tags, 272
        die cutters, 272
        jogging, 271
        slitter-rewinders, 272
        strip cutting, 271–272
    injection in-mold labels, 263, 264
    inspection of. *See under* inspection equipment
    label converters, 271, 275
    metallized, 280
    paper labels, 131, 132, 133, 144, 272–273, 278
    placement and dimensions, 277
    pressure-sensitive labels, 11, 263, 264–265, 271, 272, 289–290
    printing, 268–271
        CMYK color interactions, 269
        digital printing, 271
        flexography (flexo) printing, 269, 270, 271
        four-color process (CMYK), 268–269
        gravure printing, 270, 271
        heatset offset printing, 271
        offset (litho) printing, 270–271
        six- or seven-color process, 269
        small color dots, 268
        summary of processes, 271
    removal of, 129, 132, 135, 140–141
    roll-fed labels, 263, 264, 271
    shrink labels, 263, 264, 265–266, 271
    storage, 272
    types, 263–266
Lactobacillus, 233, 386, 411
    brevis, 385
    lindneri, 385
ladder logic, 55
lag time, 59
laminar flow of beer, 88, 95, 96, 98
Legionella, 36
Leipner, W., 144
light and beer freshness, 151, 153
line flow control, 45–57
    control logic, 54–57
    controllers, 52–54
    line flow, 45–50
    machine control components, 50–52
line rating or speed, 5, 42, 50
lost time studies, 15, 16
low speed and low-speed sensor, 44, 45, 51

machine availability, 43, 48–49
machine controls. *See* line flow control; packaging process control
machine damage protection, 50, 51
machine faults, 48, 49
machine interfaces, 55
machine logic, 51
machine maintenance, 39, 145
machine speeds, 42, 43–45, 50, 52
macrostops, 49
magnesium carbonate, 367, 368, 369, 371
magnetic flow meters, 12, 66–67, 69, 192
Maillard reaction, 367
management, 17–20
manipulated variable, 57, 58
Manning, H., 16
manufacturing execution systems, 13
market evaluation, 161–162
mass flow meters, 12, 67, 69
Master Brewers Association of the Americas, 20, 21–22
maximum line production, 43
mean time between failures, 49
mean time to repair, 49
measured variable, 57
measurement recorders, 63–64
mechanical controllers, 58
mercury, 36, 37, 212

metal exposure specifications, 80
methane biogas, 39, 40
method of control, 58
Methods of Analysis, 218
microbial growth in beer, 151, 153
microbiological stabilization, 408–410. *See also* final beer filtration; flash pasteurization; tunnel pasteurization
    chemical stabilization, 408
    flash pasteurization, 408–409
    passive stabilization, 408
    sterile filtration, 408, 409
    tunnel pasteurization, 409–410
microbiology, 410–413
microstops, 49
minimum efficiency reporting value (MERV), 12
modulating control valve, 58
modulating machines, 44–45
molds, 397, 411
monoblocs, 9, 10, 12, 19
motion control encoders, 55
motor starters, 45, 52
multiple-pen recorders, 64, 231

near-sterile and sterile filling, 12
Nernst equation, 68
nitritotriacetic acid, 371
nylon-MXD6, 148, 153, 154, 157, 158, 159

Occupational Safety and Health Administration (OSHA), 305
offset, 59
OMAC Packaging Workgroup (PWG), 13
OMAC PWG PackSoft Committee, 13
on-demand machines, 44
open-loop process control, 57
open-plant cleaning, 374, 375
opening disc, 80, 86
opening force, 80, 86
operating expenses, 29
operator inputs, 55, 59
organic phosphates, 372
Organization for Machine Automation and Control (OMAC), 13
original equipment manufacturer vendors, 13
overall equipment effectiveness, 13–14
overspeed, 46–47
overvarnish, 77, 85
Owens, Michael J., 209
oxidation catalysts, 154
oxidation of beer, 88, 151, 163, 461
oxygen barriers, 152, 164, 213–214, 461, 462

package holds, 415–416
package release tanks, 17
packages
    alternative, 2
    options for cans, 179
    testing, 218–219, 407
packaging
    costs, 162
    crown problem analysis, 219–220
    essential functions, 1
    global beverage packaging (2012), 147
    history of, 1–2
    levels of, 1
    materials and beer quality, 457–463
    in PET, 151–154
    quality, 2
    technological advances, 3
packaging charges, 22
packaging hall cleaning, 379–383
packaging line performance-monitoring software, 55–56
packaging line theory, 4–5, 45
packaging lines. *See also* bottling lines; canning lines; keg line operations; project management
    accessibility, 8, 9
    accumulation, 323–324
        accumulation tables, 8, 42–43, 323
        conveyors, 8, 43, 324, 336
        dynamic accumulation, 8, 43
        in-line accumulation, 324
        line design and, 42–43, 45
        line flow and, 46–47
        time to go back to normal state, 49
    anticipate and demand control, 48
    catch-up speed, 47
    control units or domains, 47–48, 50, 51
    delays, 45
    design, 42–45
    efficiencies, 14–21
    engineering, 8–14
    examples, 5–7
    increasing complexity, 9, 11
    instrumentation, 62–70
    layouts, 4, 5, 8, 176
    line flow, 45–50. *See also* line flow control
    line rating or speed, 5, 42, 50
    machine speed control elements, 45
    management of, 2
    overspeed, 46–47
    physical constraints, 5
    planning, 4–8
    simulated lines, 56–57
    waste, 13, 14
packaging microbiology, 410–412. *See also* microbiological stabilization
    absence-presence testing, 411
    beer spoilage, 411
    membrane filtration, 411–412
    plating media, 412
    pour plating, 411
    rinser and jetter water testing, 412
    sampling sizes and frequency, 412
    spread plating, 411
    universal beer agar, 412
    yeast suppressants, 412
packaging planning strategies, 20
packaging process control, 57–61
packers and packer stations, 19–20, 42, 44, 47–48
Painter, William, 209
pallet movement, 330–331
    air flotation loading, 331
    automatic wire-guided vehicles, 330–331
    continuous motion lifts, 331
    conveyors, 330
    hydraulic lifts, 331
    vertical, 331
palletizers and palletizing, 333–341
    adhesives, 414–415
    capacity, 336–337
    conventional stripper plate palletizers, 333, 334, 335
    defining an application, 335, 337
    diagnostics, 337
    discharge conveyors, 336
    efficiency improvement, 337
    floor-level infeed palletizer, 335
    high-level infeed palletizer, 335
    hybrid palletizers, 334
    infeed conveyors, 336, 337
    on keg lines, 362
    location, 8, 9
    nonskid materials, 414–415
    on-demand, 44
    operator responsibilities, 19
    packaging trends and, 337
    pallet of packaged ends, 83
    palletized cans, 82
    palletizer information form, 335, 338–341
    palletizing systems, 336
    pattern flexibility, 337
    pattern formation, 334–335
        hybrid concept, 335
        in-line pattern formation, 334–335, 336
        right-angle pattern formation, 334, 336
    pick-and-place method, 333, 334
    process, 82–83
    quality assurance, 414–415
    robotic palletizers, 11, 333–334, 335
    shrink-wrapping, 415
    single-line palletizers, 336
    small-case handling, 337
    speeds, 335, 337
    tier sheets, 337
    typical can and end pallet packs, 82
paperboard multipack production
    carton-converting process, 310–311
        die cutting and creasing, 311
        flexographic (flexo) printing, 310, 311
        folding and gluing, 311
        lithographic (offset) printing, 310
        right-angle gluers, 311
        rotogravure printing, 310
        straight-line gluers, 311
    multipack types, 311–313
        basket carriers, 311–312
        clips, 312–313
        fully enclosed packages, 311
        wraps, 312
    multipacking machinery, 313–316
        accessory rail, 315
        basket multipacker, 315
        carton infeed, 314
        carton sealing, 315
        continuous-motion basket multipackers, 315
        flexibility required, 316
        four machine styles, 313, 315–316
        fully enclosed multipacker machine, 313, 315
        lug chains, 313, 314
        pitchless systems, 316
        product infeed and selection, 313–314, 315
        product loading, 314
        reciprocating carton infeeders, 314
        rotary carton infeeders, 314
        segment wheel carton infeeders, 314, 316
        selector screws, 313, 314
        selector wedges, 314, 315
        wrap multipackers, 316
    paperboard manufacturing, 309
    wet-strength additive, 309
Pareto analysis, 420
Pasteur, Louis, 225, 235
pasteurization. *See also* flash pasteurization; pasteurizer water treatment; tunnel pasteurization
    avoiding overpressured containers, 400
    and filling, 6
    forces affecting bottles during, 126
    history of, 225–227, 235, 236
    invertase test, 232–233, 410
    pH control of water systems, 67–68
    pressure switches for pumps, 65
    temperature control, 60, 61
    thermal death time (lethal rate) curve, 225, 226, 236–238
    time–temperature curve, 236–238
    water usage, 38
pasteurization units (PUs), 69–70, 225, 230, 232, 236–238, 409–410
pasteurizer water treatment, 243, 244, 251–261, 382–383
    aerosolization minimization, 257
    best practices, 259, 260, 261
    biogrowth, corrosion, and metal attack, 251, 254
    biological growth control, 254–255, 382–383
    boil-outs, 256, 259, 383
    bottle spotting, 259
    can staining and spotting, 258–259, 383
    conveyor lubricants, 253, 254
    corrosion goals for metals, 252
    corrosion inhibitors, 252, 254, 255

corrosion prevention, 383
deposit/fouling control, 255
foaming in pasteurizer compartments, 253
fouling of heat exchanger, 255
fouling of suction box screens, 253
goals, 251
halogen biocides, 252, 253, 254–255, 259
inorganic mineral scale, 252–253
Langelier Saturation Index, 252–253
microbiological contamination reduction, 257–258
monitoring, 252
musty flavor issues, 256–258
organic deposits, 253
polypropylene mat-top belt failure, 259–260
prerinse stations, 255
rouging, 255
sidestream filtration, 259
tunnel pasteurizers, 382–383
Pediococcus, 233, 411
   damnosus, 385
PEN containers. *See* polyethylene naphthalate (PEN) containers
peracetic acid, 180, 357, 374
PET containers. *See* polyethylene terephthalate (PET) containers
PET Resin Association, 147
pH monitor or controller, 67–68
phase-gate process, 29
phenolphthalein, 143, 380, 398, 399
photoelectric eye sensors, 54
phthalates, 461
piece variance, 13
pin ovens, 77
Plat, Sir Hugh, 1
plate lubricator, 71, 72
PLCs. *See* programmable logic controllers
pneumatic control systems, 58, 59, 60
point level control, 65
Poland, 22
polyesters, 149, 154
polyethylene naphthalate (PEN) containers, 149, 154, 223
polyethylene terephthalate (PET) containers, 147–160
  advantages of, 147, 148
  barrier technologies and materials
    active oxygen scavengers, 152, 154–155, 157, 158
    examples in commercial applications, 159
    external coating technology, 156
    internal coating technology, 148, 155–156, 159
    monolayer barrier blends, 148–149, 153, 157–158, 159
    multilayer containers, 148, 156–157, 159
    passive permeation barriers, 154, 156, 157, 158
  beer packaging in, 151–154
    carbonation retention, 152–153, 154, 155, 156, 157, 158
    oxygen protection, 152, 154–155, 157, 158
    pasteurization, 151, 153, 155, 156, 157, 158
    safety, 147, 148, 153
    sustainability, 153–154
    visible and UV light protection, 153
  blowing containers, 151
  bottle expansion, 152–153, 155, 156, 157
  bottle storage, 155
  closed-loop recycling, 21
  container design and manufacture, 150–151
  crystallinity, 149–150
  extrusion blow molding, 150
  filling containers, 151
  flash pasteurization, 227, 233
  glass transition temperature, 149, 150
  injection-molding preforms, 150–151, 156–157, 158
  labeling, 279
  microcracks, 155, 156
  one-way kegs, 362–363
  oriented PET, 150
  output, 21
  RingCrown closures, 223
  volumetric filling, 195, 196
polyphenols, 373, 386
PolyShield resin, 148, 153, 154, 158, 159
position measurement, 55
potassium hydroxide, 369
predecessors, 27–28
prefiltration, 385, 386
pressure
  carbonation and, 165–168
  and CO_2 solubility, 165–166, 169, 171, 191
  in flash pasteurization, 229
  tank headspace pressure, 167, 168
  wetting pressure, 167, 168
pressure measurements, 64–65, 69
pressure on packaged product, 8, 9
pressure switches, 45, 65, 360
pressure tanks, 165–168
pressure transmitters, 64–65
pricing, 162
prime sensor, 44, 50–51
The Principles of Project Management, 24
printing. *See* coding technologies; inks
process sanitation, 67
product age control standards, 18
production efficiencies, 14
production planning function, 16, 17
profit calculation, 162
programmable logic controllers (PLCs)
  bottle fillers, 191
  can fillers, 90
  CIP systems, 376
  control logic, 54–55
  on conveyor lines, 380
  defined, 52
  filler-bowl level control, 60
  keg machines, 360–361
  packaging line control systems, 45, 50, 52
  pasteurization, 61, 231, 239, 242
project management, 23–33
  communication management, 30–31
  cost management, 28–29
  defined, 24
  fundamentals, 24–25
  history of, 23
  human resource management, 29–30
  implementation strategy, 32–33
  innovation, 32
  integration management, 32–33
  procurement management, 31–32
  program vs. project, 25
  project closeout, 25, 33
  project definition, 23–24
  project implementation, 25, 26
  project initiation, 25
  project life cycle, 24–25
  project manager definition, 24
  project organization chart, 30
  project planning, 25
  quality management, 29
  risk management, 31
  scope management and statement, 26, 32
  stakeholder management, 32
  strategic plan, 24
  team meetings, 30, 31, 32
  time management, 26–28
Project Management Institute, 23
proportional band and control, 59, 231
proportional–integral–derivative instruction, 60, 65
propylene glycol, 69
proteins, 367, 369, 372, 386
proximity sensors, 45, 54, 361, 448, 453, 454–455
PU clocks, 410
punches, 73, 74

quality, beer. *See* beer quality
quality, packaging
  inspection, 3–4
  materials, 457–463
  sampling plans, 2
quality assurance, 29, 257, 393–422, 415–416
  beer verification, 404
  bottle conditioning, 407–408
  bottle washing effectiveness, 397–398
  can lid and seam checks, 405–406
  can liner checks, 406
  check weighers, 404
  closure checks, 404–405
  complex organizational models, 394–395
  consumer perception, 393
  documentation and analysis, 416–422
  filler checks, 400–404, 406–407
  flash pasteurization effectiveness, 408–409
  ISO and certification, 395, 421–422
  keg cleaning effectiveness, 398–400
  labeling and coding, 413–414
  lubricant removal, 458
  manufacturing execution, 393
  online inspections, 406–407
  package hold, 415–416
  packaging material quality, 395–397
    auditing, 395–396
    defective packaging material reports (DPMR), 396–397
    empty bottle inspectors, 395, 396, 398
    MIL-STD-105E, 395–396
    supplier complaint reports (SCR), 396–397
    total inspection, 395, 396
    weighting of defects, 397
  palletizing, 414–415
  product design, 393
  quality control vs. quality assurance, 393, 421
  quality philosophies, 394
  quality programs, 393, 394–395
  rinsing effectiveness, 397
  sampling sizes and frequency, 403–404
  sealed package integrity, 407
  simple organizational models, 394
  sterile filtration effectiveness, 409
  total quality management, 395
  tunnel pasteurization effectiveness, 409–410
  validating quality, 421
  warehouse storage, 415
quaternary ammonium compounds, 373

racking microbiology, 413
radiation safety officer, 443
radionuclides, 36
real-time performance management, 15
recycling
  of empty cartons, 136
  of glass bottles, 12, 117
  one-way keg shells, 362, 363
  of packaging materials, 21
  of PET bottles
    barrier technologies and, 155, 156, 157, 158
    for beverage packaging, 147, 154
    for secondary applications, 147, 154, 463
    volume vs. demand, 463
  of plastic packaging, 462–463
redraw progression, 74
redraw ring, 73, 74
reformable end, 81, 86
refurbished equipment, 8, 9
reset, 59
resistance temperature detectors (RTDs), 52, 60, 61, 62–63, 70
responsibilities and roles in project, 30, 32
responsibility matrix, 30
rest diameter, 85
retroreflective photoelectric eyes, 54
return on investment, 29
Reynolds Metal Company, 84
Reynold's number, 228

Richardson, J. F., 228
rinser/filler/crowners. See monoblocs
rinsers
    interlocks, 397
    quality assurance, 397
    rinser in monobloc system, 9, 10
    rinser types, 169
    speed, 42, 45–46, 47
risk avoidance equipment, 3–4
risk chart, 31
risk-response plans, 31, 32
risk tolerance, 404, 409, 410, 424
robots, palletizing, 11, 333–334
root cause failure analysis, 259
rotameters, 66
RTD. See resistance temperature detectors
Ruff, D. G., 143
run speed and run-speed sensor, 44, 45, 51
Ryznar index, 383

SABMiller, 13
Saccharomyces, 385
    cerevisiae, 386
safety
    beer carbonation and, 166
    biogrowth and, 256
    bottle soakers and, 11, 135, 145
    cleaning solutions, 370, 375
    floor, 21
    inks, 303
    interlock systems, 50
    kegs, 344–345
    laser coders, 305
    management's responsibility for, 2, 18, 21, 50
    PET bottles, 147, 148, 153
    training and education, 21, 50
sampling plans, 2
sanitary differential pressure cell, 69
sanitary flow measurement, 69
sanitary pressure measurement, 69
sanitary requirements of sensors, 68–69
sanitary temperature measurement, 69
sanitizers, 372–375. See also cleaning and sanitizing in brewery operations
    acid anionics, 374–375
    bottle-washer cleaning, 142
    chlorine dioxide, 374, 397
    CIP, 168, 169, 180, 229
    for filler interior cleaning, 381
    flash pasteurization and, 233
    halogen sanitizers, 373
    ideal criteria, 372
    iodine sanitizers, 373–374
    peracetic acid, 374
    quaternary ammonium compounds, 372–373
scheduling, 27–28, 32
Schwartz burette, 402, 420
score and score residual, 80, 86
seaming. See double seams and double seaming
Seebeck, Thomas Johann, 63
separator sheets, 82, 83
sequestrants or chelants
    bottle-washing solutions, 133, 134
    in detergents, 368, 369, 370
    EDTA, 134, 371
    gluconates, 371
    mineral deposit removal, 367
    nitritotriacetic acid, 371
    organic phosphates, 371
    polyphosphates, 131
Serratia marcescens, 386
servo technology, 12, 199, 264, 279, 281
set point, 57, 58, 59, 60
shell press, 78
shrouded enclosures, 12

simulation software, 14–15, 16–17
single controllers, 61
single-set-point, dual-actuator controllers, 61
sloping conveyors, 45
smooth die neck process, 77
snake wrap, 83
snifting, 94, 99
soakers. See bottle washers (soakers)
soap, 370
sodium aluminate, 135, 143
sodium–aluminum–silicate compound, 135
sodium ascorbate, 462
sodium hexametaphosphate, 370
sodium hydroxide (caustic soda). See also caustic carryover; caustics
    bottle-washing solutions, 130–131, 134, 380
    concentration management, 67, 143
    corrosiveness, 37
    label removal, 135
    sequestrants and, 134
sodium hypochlorite, 229, 254, 373
sodium sulfite, 462
sodium testing, 398
sodium tripolyphosphate, 370
solar panels, 40
solenoid valves, 45
solicitation and solicitation planning, 31
solid-state PU computer, 69–70
sonar technology, 330
source selection, 31
Spire, C. L., 17, 18
spray header pump, 60
Stage-Gate process, 29
stakeholders, 25, 30–31, 32
standard cost structure, 17
standardization, 31–32
start-and-stop loss, 17
statistical process control (SPC), 416, 418–420, 457
sterile and near-sterile filling, 6, 12, 153
sterile filtration of beer, 12, 408, 409. See also cold filtration; final beer filtration
Stolle Step, 78, 79, 86
strapping stations, 83
strategic packaging planning, 20
strip charts, 63–64
sulfuric acid, 36, 37, 143, 458
surface tension, 89, 98
surfactants
    boil-out compounds, 256
    in bottle-washing solutions, 132, 133, 134
    can spotting prevention, 259
    classification of, 370
    emulsification, 367, 370
    structure of molecule, 370
    surface wetting, 133, 370
surge speed, 44, 45, 51

tank carbonation, 165–168
task force, 24
task leaders, 30
temperature
    and beer conditioning, 164, 171, 191
    and CO_2 solubility, 165, 169, 171
    in warehouse storage, 415
temperature control systems, 45, 60, 61, 231
temperature measurement devices, 62–63, 69, 361
thermocouples, 63
thermowells, 69
threshold inhibitors, 371
throughput capacity, 5
time to go back to normal state, 49
torque testing, 405

total package oxygen (TPO), 88, 89, 93, 96, 190, 241
total productive management, 16
transition of can wall, 73, 85
traveling thermographs, 410
tray-making machines, 7
triblocs. See monoblocs
trihalomethanes, 36
trimmers, 71, 74, 75
tunnel pasteurization, 235–250. See also pasteurization; pasteurizer water treatment
    acid cleaning heat exchangers, 244, 247–248
    advantages and disadvantages, 241–242
    barrier technologies and, 153, 155, 156, 157
    beer freshness and taste, 151
    belt pasteurizers, 239, 243, 256
    CIP tanks, 247, 248
    conveying belt maintenance, 248–249
    conveyors, 324–325
    double-deck tunnel pasteurizer, 239
    equipment, 238–240
    vs. flash pasteurization, 12, 227
    heat exchange water flow impediments, 244
    measuring process performance, 242–243
    operating parameters, 240–241
    operational pitfalls, 242
    package headspace, 239
    PU measurement and control, 242, 410
    pump prestart checks, 244
    pump troubleshooting, 244, 245–247
    quality assurance, 409–410
    regenerative and recirculatory circuits, 240
    single heat exchangers, 240, 242
    slime growth, 382
    system schematic, 240
    theory and principles, 236–238
    traveling recorders, 242–243
    walking beam pasteurizers, 239–240, 243, 256
    water pump cleaning, 243

ultrasonic cleaning of tubes, 201
uncasing equipment, 9, 11, 42, 136
uncoilers, 71, 72, 78
unitizing, 333. See also palletizers and palletizing

valve actuating levers, 95
valve springs, 96
variable frequency drives, 45, 52–53, 140, 192, 239
volatile organic compounds, 36, 37, 460
volumetric control systems, 12

warehouse storage, 415
water and wastewater. See under environmental management
water hardness and softening, 367–368
Wheatstone bridge, 63
work breakdown structure (WBS), 26, 27, 28, 29–30, 31, 32
work order fulfillment report, 19
wort, 38, 366, 367

yeast
    beer conditioning, 164
    bottle conditioning, 407–408
    cleaning to remove, 356, 366, 372, 374
    filtration to remove, 385, 386, 388
    growth in beer, 235, 254
    handling and transfer, 38
    pasteurization, 233, 236
    wild yeast contamination, 411, 412
    yeasty beers, 345, 352, 363

Zahm-Nagel piercing devices, 401–402